1 MONTH OF
FREE
READING

at

www.ForgottenBooks.com

By purchasing this book you are eligible for one month membership to ForgottenBooks.com, giving you unlimited access to our entire collection of over 1,000,000 titles via our web site and mobile apps.

To claim your free month visit:

www.forgottenbooks.com/free785130

ISBN 978-0-483-50304-5
PIBN 10785130

THE JOURNAL OF EDUCATIONAL METHOD

OFFICIAL ORGAN OF
THE NATIONAL CONFERENCE ON
EDUCATIONAL METHOD

*An Association Devoted to the Improvement
of Teaching and Supervision*

JAMES F. HOSIC, EDITOR

ADVISORY COMMITTEE:

C. L. WRIGHT	MARGARET MADDEN
C. C. CERTAIN	MARY E. PENNELL

VOLUME I

September 1921—June 1922

Yonkers-on-Hudson, New York

WORLD BOOK COMPANY

1922

INDEX

Volume I: September 1921—June 1922

INDEX

INDEX

INDEX

The Journal of Educational Method is published by WORLD BOOK COMPANY, Yonkers-on-Hudson, New York, for the National Conference on Educational Method. Subscription $3.00 per year; single copies 35 cents.

The Journal of Educational Method

Volume I   SEPTEMBER, 1921   Number 1

CONTENTS

THE NATIONAL CONFERENCE ON EDUCATIONAL METHOD
506 West Sixty-ninth Street, CHICAGO, ILLINOIS

$3.00 a year   Monthly Except July and August   35 cents a copy

Application for entrance as second-class matter has been made at the post-office at Chicago, Illinois, under the Act of March 3, 1879

THE NATIONAL CONFERENCE ON EDUCATIONAL METHOD

An Association of Persons Interested in Supervision and Teaching

---

Address applications for membership to the Secretary of the Conference, 506 West Sixty-ninth Street, Chicago, Illinois. The fee for active members is $3.00, for associate members, $2.00; $2.00 in each case is applied to the support of the journal, for which each member receives a year's subscription. The editorial office is at 525 West One Hundred and Twentieth Street, New York City.

The Journal of Educational Method

VOLUME I   SEPTEMBER, 1921   NUMBER 1

EDITORIALLY SPEAKING

WHEREFORE

In founding a monthly journal, the National Conference on Educational Method seeks to provide a means of unification of effort in the field of supervision and teaching. Some of the existing periodicals do, it is true, give more or less space to the discussion of method, but they are so much concerned with other interests that they fail to accomplish for the active workers in the schools all that is possible. The new journal will devote itself whole-heartedly to the improvement of teaching.

This does not imply, however, a narrow concentration upon classroom methods as such. The term educational method will be interpreted to mean, not only the procedures of teachers, but also those of the pupils, on the one hand, and those of the supervisors and trainers of teachers on the other. The emphasis will fall upon principles that should be common to the activities of all of these. Thus it is

AS HE SEES HIMSELF

hoped that the best theory and practice may be brought together and a larger measure of educational economy be secured—more and better results with less waste of time and energy.

The new journal ranks as moderately progressive. Radical experimentation will be reported, but it will not be confused with those more limited changes which alone are possible when reforms are proceeding on a large scale. It will assume conditions as they are, not as they might be in Utopia, and will endeavor to point the way to the next possible steps in progress. With the stars as a goal, the good old wagon road, winding slowly up, will be depended upon as the way of transit.

Educational diagnosis is forging ahead of educational treatment. We have an elaborate technique of surveys but no organized follow-up. In general the hope seems to be to get teachers to do better the kinds of things they are already doing.

But what is needed, in many, many instances, is a new view of the task. Not greater skill in the old game but adequate skill in a game quite new must be attained. This requires a restatement of aims in the light of a new philosophy of education and a new psychology of human behavior. The *Journal of Educational Method* hopes to perform a useful service in these regards.

THE MENU

The contents of the first number of this *Journal* are typical of what is to follow. The various departments—(1) brief editorial comment on current issues, (2) serious discussions of principles, (3) concrete accounts of actual experience, (4) brief · exchange of opinion and experiment, (5) news of the activities of the National Conference and of similar societies, (6) discriminating reviews of important books and articles, and (7) concise, informing notes on new books and pamphlets—will be regularly maintained. The *Journal* will seek to become indispensable to all who pride themselves on keeping up with progress in the field of supervision and teaching.

No apology is needed for devoting much attention to the project method. In the first place there is growing confusion as to the significance of the term. As it becomes popular, the enterprising, naturally enough, more and more identify it with their own pet theories. One recent publication, on the other hand, applies the term loosely to a miscellaneous collection of lessons which may or may not have involved the psychological factors which alone distinguish a project from a cleverly organized topic.

One writer urges the possibility of a new subject of study to be called the project, and so it goes. What ought to be interpreted as a new and vital synthesis of modern educational ideas is in danger of becoming merely a passing shibboleth.

While making no claim to the only and final interpretation of the project method, the *Journal* will present it as a serious and consistent point of view, likely to have far-reaching effects in bringing about a reorganization of the curriculum, methods of teaching and supervision, and ultimately of equipment and testing of results. Two series of articles on this theme will run through the year, one by Professor Kilpatrick and one by Professor Hosic. The first will analyze the principles involved; the second will illustrate these principles at work in the process of improving the English teaching of a system of schools.

Other contributors from the classroom, the office, the laboratory, and the training college will deal with the choice and use of textbooks, the making and interpretation of courses of study, the grading and promotion of pupils, the administrative conditions necessary to good teaching, modern equipment, and the practical uses of tests and measurements, as well as with the specific problems that arise in actually organizing and directing the activities of children in the classroom and in the school as a whole. *Every number of the Journal will be planned with reference to its possible use by a supervisor in his meetings with his teachers or by an instructor in his classes in education.* It should besides prove a welcome addition to each teacher's own professional library.

THE FUTURE OF THE PRACTITIONER[1]

JAMES E. RUSSELL
Teachers College, Columbia University

The most significant advance in education within our generation has been in the invention of standards of measurement in school achievements. We owe a debt of gratitude to Professor Thorndike and to his students and the scientific workers in other institutions for their discoveries— discoveries as significant in our field as is the invention of the thermometer in physics or of logarithms in mathematics. They have supplied us with a footrule, a quart measure, and a pound weight.

In this connection, I am reminded of an experience I had a few years ago on a visit to the Island of Guernsey, one of the Channel Islands off the coast of France that claim to be the only part of the British Empire not won by conquest. They were originally part of Normandy, and are all that is left to Britain of the overseas holdings of William the Conqueror. Proud of their historic connections with the conquest of Anglo-Saxon domains, they are still Norman-French in language, customs, and laws. Twelfth-century traditions still remain. My interest, however, was not in history, but in cows. And when I asked what the Guernsey cow could do on her native heath, I was told that this one gave fourteen pots of milk a day, and that one two stone of butter. I wanted to know next what a "pot" was, and was told that it was neither a quart nor a liter. A "pot" was a jug of tin or brass or copper made by the local tinsmith. And I found that a "stone" was a weight selected from the pebbles on the beach of about the size of a man's fist—twelfth-century standards of measurement in a world teeming with the science of agriculture; a fit analogy to the situation in education a generation ago.

We shall soon have specialists in educational tests and measurements of every kind. They will tell us what normal performance is at different stages of educational progress; they will measure and weigh the extent of individual divergences; they will diagnose abnormal conditions; they will standardize the means and instruments of education. But the greater the degree of specialization in the understanding of fundamentals, and the more refined the means of treatment, the greater the need of experts in diagnosis and prescription. The development of the science of chemistry, the advance in pharmacology, the discoveries in physiology and anatomy, and the use of the X-ray have made a place for an army of experts in the field of medicine; but the service of these experts has not lessened the need for physicians and surgeons, nor lowered their prestige in the eyes of the world. On the contrary, the demands made upon physicians and surgeons have increased with every step in the advance of the sciences underlying medicine. Experts supply the tools, make the tests, and dig up the information needed for diagnosis, but it is the physician or surgeon who determines the method of procedure and applies the remedy. The practitioner is at his best when he can deal with facts.

Soon we shall have experts capable of supplying all the facts needed for the direction of normal procedure in education and for the diagnosis of special conditions. Indeed, there is danger that for a time the

[1] From an address at the annual banquet of Teachers College, Atlantic City, March 1, 1921.

output of such specialists may exceed the supply of skilled practitioners. One specialist in laboratory analysis or one X-ray operator may suffice to back up a hundred physicians. So a few specialists in education will determine the procedure of hundreds or thousands of teachers. I venture the prediction that in the near future—say, ten or twenty years—the place of the specialist in education will be comfortably filled and properly recognized. And, when that day comes, the skilled practitioner in education will be held at a premium. Our teachers' colleges may not give less attention than now to the training of such experts, but I am certain that we shall be far more interested than we are now in equipping teachers and leaders of teachers for expert service in educational practice. It will be taken for granted that our leaders should know the significance of the work of specialists, but it will also be recognized that the training of practitioners should not stop there. The practitioner works in the schoolroom, not in the laboratory; he needs all the facts that the laboratory can supply and the best of tools and all necessary equipment. Then give him the insight that comes from a sympathetic imagination, the wisdom gained from experience and the guidance of masters, and a little child shall lead him.

AN EXAMPLE OF A METHOD FOR PRODUCING DESIRABLE QUALITIES OF CITIZENSHIP

C. L. WRIGHT
Superintendent of Schools, Huntington, West Virginia

It is practically axiomatic that it is a chief function of our schools to produce a robust citizenship. And it is almost equally obvious that much of the subject-matter and a great deal of the method that has in the past been found in our schools is not calculated to produce such a citizenship. When we talk of citizenship or of the somewhat newer term, Americanism, we are talking of rather vague generalities unless we compel ourselves to analyze these terms and to hold pretty definitely in mind the qualities or traits or characteristics of this citizenship, or this Americanism. Then, when we have done this, it is our task to select such subject-matter and to direct our school procedure in such a way as will produce these traits or qualities or characteristics.

We should probably be able to agree most easily upon what these desirable quali-ties really are if we should select certain typical Americans and determine definitely the qualities which, in spite of their many differences, they have held in common and which have rendered them typical or admirable. Suppose we should take, for example, men like Washington, or Franklin, or Jefferson, or Lincoln, or Roosevelt. Or suppose we should take Clara Barton, or Dr. Anna Howard Shaw, or Frances E. Willard, to give the women their deserved recognition. We should find certain outstanding qualities which rendered them desirable types of citizens. Such qualities the limits of this discussion will not permit me to enlarge upon. It will be sufficient for our purposes, I am convinced, merely to enumerate them without much attempt at definition or discussion. Such a list would surely include such individualistic traits or qualities or characteristics as intelligence, initiative, self-reliance, self-respect, adaptability, industry. It would include others of a social bearing, such as sympathy, respect for majority rule, sense of responsibility, habit of co-operation, the ideal and spirit of service. There is the temptation to yield to the wish to enlarge upon a discussion of these qualities as desirable ends to be achieved by our school processes. But the mere enumeration of them here must suffice. It is pertinent to observe, however, that our classrooms as they have traditionally functioned have not particularly distinguished themselves by their product in these directions. Indeed, much of our classroom procedure has been such as to dwarf or repress these very qualities. What we have gained has been gained largely as a by-product of the schools and because of our playgrounds and student activities. But if these be really desirable ends, then it is certainly needful that we so modify our subject-matter and school procedure as to directly and consciously produce in our boys and girls a citizenship of this sort.

As an example of a school method which produces desirable qualities of citizenship, I desire to tell briefly the story of a junior high school project which began in some English and social science classes in the Enslow Junior High School in our city last spring. The credit for whatever success was realized belongs entirely to the boys and girls and to the teachers concerned. About all that the superintendent can claim is that he was sympathetic and that he did not interfere, at least not overmuch.

I walked into an English classroom in this junior high school one morning last spring. The room was in a condition that several years ago would have given me a case of nerves. The teacher was seated at her desk in one corner of the room, looking at some papers. The students had arranged, or disarranged, their movable seats and were collected in groups of three or four, each group with heads close together. They had not only disarranged the order of the rows of seats but they were actually "talking out loud" in time of school! Occasionally one voice would be raised slightly above the rest, as a member of one group would attract the attention of another group and converse with the members of that group. Interested, I walked to one side of the room. The presence of a visitor attracted but little attention—none, in fact, beyond a casual glance. In a short while, however, one little girl came over to where I was standing and asked, "Mr. Wright, does this topic belong under the commerce of the Ohio River or under locks and dams?" In order not to deprive the girl of her right to solve her own problem, and possibly in order to follow the teacher tradition, I answered by asking one or two other questions. But the questions evidently gave the girl the glimmer that she needed, for she shook her head in a satisfied way and went back to her group. And in a moment there was an impromptu and animated debate between her group and another near as to which was entitled to use the topic in question, a debate which was soon settled to the satisfaction of the groups.

Now what were these boys and girls doing? It developed that the teachers mentioned above had hit upon the plan of suggesting to their classes the possibility of their making a survey of their section of the city. They were mildly interested at first but soon realized that here was an opportunity actually to do something interesting to themselves and have it accepted as school work. And they had already in their community-civics classes felt the need of just such information as this would give them. So they voted to undertake the work. Now the section of the city in which this junior high school is located is a rather diversified one. The Ohio River flows by it on the north for about two miles. The district has one section of good residences; it has others of much humbler and less attractive homes, where some of the more poorly paid, unskilled workers live; it has factories and shops, churches and elementary schools, and in every way is typical of a city district of diversified interests. The first task, therefore, was to decide what should be looked for in such a survey, which is what I would have called in the good old times, "finding the main heads in the outline." Of course the teacher had good judgment enough not to use such terms. She merely asked, "What different things ought we to look for in making a survey of this district?" And with crayon in hand, she stood at the blackboard and wrote the topics suggested by members of the class. "Factories" was one immediate suggestion, and that was accordingly written on the board. "The Ohio River" was another; "churches," another; "schools," another; "parks and playgrounds," still another. Several others were suggested but were finally ruled out by students themselves as inconsequential or were considered by them to be included in one of the larger topics previously listed.

The next suggestion was that they determine the things they ought to look for under each of the selected topics. "Finding the sub-heads," I suppose we should have called it in one of my old classes. But still again this teacher was wise and did not allow terms of rhetoric and composition to interfere with live thought which she hoped

to have translated through interest into effective English. It was while this discussion was in progress that it developed that the "Ohio River" was too much for one topic for investigation and it was accordingly divided into "The History of the Ohio River", "The Commerce of the Ohio River," and "Ohio River Improvements"; and these subjects were then elaborated upon. It was in the course of the working out of these topics that the debate above referred to occurred.

When the field for investigation had been fairly satisfactorily worked out for each topic, the question was asked, "How shall we find out about these things and how report them?" After some discussion the students thought it best to divide themselves into committees to get first-hand information; and committees were accordingly formed, consisting of three to five, each student serving in the committee for the subject in which he was most interested. In some instances the class helped some particular boy or girl to decide upon the subject of his choice because of some special ability or advantage he might have in securing the information upon that subject. The committees then organized themselves and set to work. Library, field trips, text-books, other classes, interviews, and many persons and things else were to be sources of information.

The committee on shops and factories, with notebooks in hand, visited the offices of the Chesapeake and Ohio Railroad shops, the American Car and Foundry Works, and other industrial plants. They not only interviewed the superintendents in their offices but also inspected the work in the shops. They were received everywhere with uniform courtesy, and had demonstrated to them the fact that every man is a born teacher if only the questioners themselves evince an intelligent interest. The interviews proceeded quickly in accordance with the outlines which had first been suggested by the class and which later the committee itself had extended and elaborated. They learned the size of the plant, the number of employees, the hours of labor and wages of the workers, the amount of the weekly pay-roll, the source of the raw material used and its value; the type of finished product, its value, and how and where it is marketed. They learned to see in these places not merely buildings surmounted by huge smokestacks and surrounded by high fences within whose inclosures engines roared and whistles sounded, but the places in which their own fathers and brothers or friends performed their daily work. As they studied the sources from which the raw materials came, the routes over which they were brought in, the distribution of the finished product, and the uses to which it was put, they came upon a first-hand and, to them, novel view of the complexity of modern industry and the interdependence of section on section and community on community. Let it be granted that they did not view it nor understand it nor report it as you and I as adults would have done. The fact still remains that they themselves and their classmates through them were gaining a clearer and better understanding of it all than they could have had in any other way. •

The committee which had selected the Ohio River topic as the field of their inquiry read every available historical reference to the Ohio; they talked with old rivermen to get the stories and traditions not in the books; they eagerly consulted more geographies and books of reference than under other circumstances they could have been induced or driven to consult.

Of course this work required time, and a considerable amount of time' was devoted to it. And very naturally, too, the plans grew and expanded as the survey progressed. A number of teachers joined in the project. It was recognized that here was something that was easily and naturally related to many subjects and departments—was, in fact, a part of these many subjects. Here was history, and geography, and community civics, and general science, and written composition, and the livest material for public speaking. The readily apparent value of much of the material suggested a plan which was early adopted: the preservation of the reports for future reference. So it was decided that each committee should write a book—write it in longhand with pen and ink—and place the finished book in the school library for the use of other classes. To every member of the committee was delegated, by committee action, the preparation of a certain definite part of the report. Someone suggested one day that bindings for the books be made and decorated in the drawing classes, and accordingly the ripple of correlation widened and took in another department of the school.

The necessary limitations of a discussion of this sort will not permit me to describe the activities of all these committees nor the methods by which they worked. I cannot forbear, however, to mention briefly the work of that committee which chose as its subject the parks and playgrounds. Their section of the city is one of the newest parts of the city which itself is only about one generation old. They consequently found that the rapid growth of population had caught the city unawares and that adequate provision had not been made for parks and playgrounds. School playgrounds were almost the only ones that had been provided and they were not extensive. So the committee undertook to find where the children of that section of the city actually were playing. Systematically they began to cover on foot that whole section of the city. This took time after school hours and on Saturdays for a considerable period. And they found the actual though unofficial playgrounds of their community. They found, for example, that at the corner of such-and-such a street and avenue there were two vacant lots where twelve boys ordinarily played, and they named the boys and described the type of play. At another place they found fourteen vacant lots where thirty-nine boys spent their leisure time, playing baseball and football and other games in season. And so they covered the whole territory. Before they had finished their survey, however, they were confronted with a problem which gave them no little concern. A real estate company had bought the fourteen vacant lots where the thirty-nine boys were playing and had begun to build some houses on the playground! What was to become of these boys? What was to become of other boys and girls as other vacant lots were filled with houses? After consulting among themselves, they decided that some action ought to be taken, or at least some action recommended. So they set to work to devise a playground scheme for their district. One member of the committee, a boy, was a member of a mechanical drawing class. Working from an engineer's map of the city, he drew an enlarged map of the district, indicating streets, avenues, blocks, and squares. On this map were marked in color the locations of the vacant-lot playgrounds. In other color were marked the locations of what seemed to them desirable spots for real playgrounds. Of course the work was possibly not such as adults would · have done. But it is worth mentioning that this little group of junior high school boys and girls reached about the same conclusions that the playground authorities have reached as to the distance young children can be expected to go from their homes to a playground.

When they took their ideal locations on the map and actually went to see them, they found some of these locations already filled with permanent and valuable buildings. So they formed the sound business judgment that it would be better to suggest another nearby location where lots were vacant or property not so valuable. They learned who owned this property and what it could be bought for. In other words, they not only prepared a playground scheme but they drew up a playground budget. The amounts of money that were suggested seemed so large to them that they feared they were suggesting too much of a provision for the play of boys and girls. So one day a member of the committee called my office on the telephone and asked how much provision other cities made for parks and playgrounds. I asked the questioner why they did not themselves find the answer by writing to the mayors of certain cities and asking what those cities did. It was decided to write to such cities as Gary, Indiana; Lexington, Kentucky; Dayton, Ohio; Rochester, New York; and others. Here was real work in the writing of real business letters for certain real and definite purposes. And you may be sure that the letters which were written were subjected to the critical examination of the whole committee. And replies came, too, illuminating and encouraging replies. It was a natural matter then to prepare charts with graphs showing the relative size of Huntington and the other cities and the relative amount of park and playground space in them, a comparison which immediately demonstrated to the committee that their proposals were indeed very conservative rather than extravagant.

I wish you might have heard, as I did, the little girl of twelve or thirteen who gave as a public-speaking project the report of this committee. Her report was full of information, and argument, and appeal. And she presented it with the fervor of an apostle. I was so impressed by it that I invited her and the teacher and the boys of the committee to a meeting of the Rotary Club, in order that, for the good of their own souls and to help the boys and girls, this group of representative business men might hear the girl's story. With the boys to hold the map and the charts for her, this little girlish advocate told these men of the inadequate provision that had been made for playgrounds and plead for favorable action. In concluding her report she shook her little finger at the group of interested men and said, "Just recently a group of you business men along with others purchased a large tract of land up on the Guyandotte River (the new Country Club golf links) where grownups may go to play. Don't you think it is just as important that children have some place to play?" The cheers and applause which greeted this effective closing of her appeal indicated what these men felt: a new and keener

interest in proper provision for the play of their boys and girls.

Much more was done, of course, by other committees of these boys and girls in this survey of the varied interests of their community. It must remain untold in this paper, for space and time forbid an attempt to include it. What has been told must suffice to tell, if it may, of an example of school method which produces desirable qualities of citizenship. These boys and girls were assuredly securing and compiling facts and information. But were they not at the same time even more developing *intelligence* in the use of information? Were they not developing *initiative* and *self-reliance?* Were they not *adapting* themselves to circumstances? Did not the things they accomplished minister to their *self-respect?* The decisions of the classes and of the committees assuredly helped them to understand the wisdom of *majority rule*, and their discussions and work together just as certainly gave them a keener and more *sympathetic understanding* of each other. Can the traditional memory-testing recitation of our schools show comparable results in the formation of *habits of co-operation?* In the action of these junior high school students in assuming *responsibility* for some provision for playgrounds for the younger children of their neighborhoods, is there not discernible a likeness to the feeling of personal *responsibility* for the welfare of the group which animated Washington or Lincoln or Roosevelt or Clara Barton? And is it too much to see in it also the gleam of the high ideal of *service?*

SOME PROBLEMS OF METHOD IN SUPERVISION

MARGARET MADDEN
Principal of the Doolittle Elementary School, Chicago, Illinois

It is a significant fact that the card index of a public library in a very large city shows one card only on the subject of school supervision. It bears the legend, "See School Administration." The "School Administration" card is evidently unwilling to bear the entire responsibility, for on it is the further direction, "See School Management." This does not mean that the library is ill equipped or that it is badly catalogued; it simply indicates that there is not a clear conception of the nature of supervision, and that, to date, no book on the subject has reached the library. School supervision is not school administration; it is not school management. It is a field in itself, or should be, directly concerned with questions of classroom instruction.

It is not difficult to understand why so important a phase of school work has, until very recently, been slighted by writers on education in favor of questions of management and administration. These problems loom large. They are so pressing that the individual school fails definitely if they are not efficiently met. The failure, moreover, is evident, one might almost say, to the passer-by. But the problem of supervision is not so insistent, perhaps because teachers, with varying degrees of skill, live up to their responsibilities and save the day. Yet it is the most vital problem of all, if our schools are to be regarded as educational institutions and not merely well-ordered business houses.

The problem of supervision, however, is the most difficult for the school principal to meet. Setting aside for the moment all questions of method, there is the very great difficulty of finding the necessary time for actual classroom contact, especially in schools of considerable size. It is not necessary for me to enumerate the increasing demands made on the principal who conceives the school as a vital force in the community and himself as a community leader in the highest sense. All are familiar with the everyday questions of organization, promotion, discipline, truancy, parent-teacher associations, interviews with parents, relief of needy children, etc.—in short, all those things which the principal *must* attend to in order to make it possible for instruction to go on in any kind of fashion. When you realize, too, that to all this are added hours of clerical work and a feeling on the part of the principal that whatever he is doing he ought to be doing something else, you must be reminded of the colored man's story of the chameleon. He had been told that the little animal would assume the color of the piece of cloth on which it rested. He put it on a piece of plaid and said that it "done busted itself trying to make good."

But there is not much gain to the principal in emphasizing his difficulties. The situation is there; he must meet it. He cannot dismiss the problem with the statement: "I simply haven't the time for adequate supervision." When I find myself making that statement, I recall how I was corrected by a former teacher when I offered the "time" excuse for not having prepared some home work. "Oh, yes," she said, "you had the time. You had all the time there was, you know. You simply mean that there was something else that you chose to do." That seemed to me very unreasonable at the time, but it has come to mean more and more every year. However, the time element is undoubtedly a very big one, and no doubt committees on economy of time in education will try to determine how supervision can be done most economically and effectively, in other words, they will try to develop *method* in supervision.

And what are some of the problems of method in supervision as applied to the individual school? It seems to me they are all bound up with or grow out of one main problem: how to secure within the school the feeling that the entire group—all the teachers, including the principal—are united by a common purpose; that each has something to contribute; that the contribution is welcome, nay, ardently desired; that classroom experience is the most vital foundation for advance in method; that the whole question of classroom procedure is a *project* which the school must launch as a group; that each teacher will investigate and report what the problems are; and that the group will come to some sort of agreement on their solution.

The skill of the supervisor will appear in his ability to stimulate each teacher to survey her own methods and results in the light of modern educational principles; to discover her own problems in the light of her own experience; and to define for herself her aims. It is the supervisor's business to be ready to suggest to her where she can find professional help bearing on her problems and to provide means for organizing the results of each teacher's findings, thereby enabling the whole group to share in the benefits, criticize the aims, and define specific ideals and objectives.

All this means co-operative supervision, getting everybody in, developing initiative, an attitude of experimentation and self-criticism—a wide departure, surely, from that type of inspection which puts the teacher on one side, the principal on the other—he sitting in as a visitor, sometimes a silent, perhaps hostile observer, sometimes a meddling nuisance; the teacher, ill at ease all the while because she and the principal have established no common denominator by which her work can be evaluated. I do not mean to imply that classroom visitation is not desirable; on the contrary, it is indispensable, but it has value only as one phase of the group activity. It is the means which the principal must take to inform himself of the problems of the schoolroom and the way in which they are being met, in order that he may the more intelligently and efficiently play his part in guiding the teachers who are working with him.

And he *must guide*. It is assumed that he has been selected because he is professionally well equipped and because he has qualities of leadership. Besides, he is in a position to develop a wider vision than the teacher who is concentrating on her smaller problems. He should not allow himself to be effaced any more than the teacher should in the conduct of her class. Such elimination of the principal might be labeled "democracy," but it is not; it is democracy gone to seed and is quite as bad as the autocratic type of domination which seems to have for its motto, "Government *of* the teachers, *to* the teachers, and *at* the teachers."

But it is not my intention to give a general talk on supervision. It seems to me more worth while to state as definitely as possible in the time allotted how I have tried to supervise, on the co-operative plan, the work in my own school. I will confine what I have to say to the subject of English for three reasons:

1. The subjects coming under the head of English are so fundamental and so far-reaching that they touch every other subject.

2. Because I believe that *method* established in the teaching of English will carry over to the other subjects and render their supervision comparatively easy.

3. Because I have the good fortune to be in charge of a school in Chicago known as an English Center. That is to say, the school is one of thirteen, selected by the superintendent of schools in different parts of the city, each representing some typical problem—varying nationalities, home conditions, advantages or handicaps—and all working under the active supervision of the head of the English department of the Chicago Normal College, to bring about an essential harmony between the English work in the schools and the instruction given to the students at the Normal College.

When the English problem was put before the teachers at the Doolittle School, they agreed that one very great need was an improvement in oral composition. They reported their difficulties, such as rambling, aimless talk, indistinct and incorrect speech, etc., and decided that much of the trouble lay in the fact that they, themselves, did not have clearly defined ideals of oral composition and hence had failed to develop them in the pupils. This represented a beginning of an attitude of self-investigation and criticism, a questioning of purposes and objectives which has grown until it has tended to become a habit.

Once the problem was determined, the plan and its execution were obviously the next step. A committee was appointed to gather samples of oral compositions which the teachers considered Superior, Excellent, Good, Fair, and Poor. These were gone over by the committee, regraded when necessary; the findings were discussed, and it was not long before each teacher had ·a reasonably clear conception of what constituted these varying degrees of excellence in composition for the school. The committee formulated its conclusions in the shape of grade standards, a copy of which became the property of each teacher, with the understanding that these standards were local and tentative and would be the guide until it was seen that new standards should be made.

In order that the work of each might be available to all, a card index of composition topics was called for, each teacher contributing a list of topics which she considered suitable for her grade. These were all based on children's experience, and were organized under various interests, such as "Pets," "Visits," "Play," "Feelings," etc.

As a contribution to a theory of teaching the subject, but primarily as means of setting her to thinking about it, each teacher was asked to list five points which she considered important in the teaching of English composition. These were gone over in grade meetings and referred to a committee for formulation.

So far we have the teachers' activities. While these things were being done, it was the part of the principal to know what teachers were doing the most intelligent, purposeful work; to commend them; to find those who were floundering; to help them by suggestions, and constructive criticism and by arranging for their visiting the more skilful teachers. .

All this implies, of course, a thoroughly socialized school. It is part of the principal's duty to secure this feeling of unity and professional fellowship. When that is done, his visits will not be feared; on the contrary, the only complaint will be that they are not more frequent.

The instances I have given will serve, perhaps, as typical of the way in which each phase of English study was attacked. The report of the committee on spelling, for example, was the result of the combined recommendations of the teachers, plus such an authority as Tidyman. General principles were laid down, a clean-cut method of teaching spelling was agreed upon, minimum word lists, gathered from the actual written work of the pupils, were arranged by grades and put into the hands of the teachers as part of the report. In the same democratic way a committee worked out an agreement on minimum requirements in the mechanics of written composition and in the study of grammar. Other committees are at work at present—one on the teaching of silent reading.

It is not necessary to point out that all this involves supervision, stimulation, interpretation, follow-up by means of various devices; bulletins, suggestive questions, slogans perhaps, surveys, standardized tests, personal visits, and all the means commonly used to keep a school at its highest efficiency.

A typical example of a certain kind of follow-up is the use I was able to make of the cards which the teachers contributed to a reading repertoire for the school. Each teacher was asked to make ten cards, each containing the name of a selection which she had found suitable for her grade. . She was requested to state the name of the author, the book in which the selection could be found, and the reasons for her choice. I was interested particularly in the reasons for her choice. These fell under rather clearly defined heads: ideals (of conduct, beauty, patriotism, etc.); information; story interest; nature interest; dramatization; humor; biography; power (skill in recognition of words, etc.).

Examination of the cards showed that the teaching of some ideal was by far the predominant motive except in first grade. Here the dramatic interest came first and the desire to develop ability in the recognition of words second.

Such a survey made it possible to raise the following questions: Where do the interests lie for the various grades? Where do they lie for the school as a whole? Should a wider range of interests be represented? Is there enough fun? Is there enough reading for the sake of the story? Is there enough on the informational side?

These questions are important for the school as a whole, especially as a guide in ordering and distributing supplementary reading material. A discussion of these questions with the teachers showed plainly that the making of the index was of great value to the teachers individually as well. One, for example, in first grade saw that almost all her emphasis had been put on the developing of ability in the recognition of words. It is natural that a first-grade teacher should be especially interested in this motive in the reading lesson, but it is interesting to note that all of that teacher's work was rather barren; it lacked that vision and imagination which keeps first grade from being a place for mere word-getting. The teachers whose work is the richest and most varied showed the keenest sense of values in selecting reading material.

Moreover, some realized that they had not expressed themselves clearly because they had not thought clearly, and that the lesson would have value for the child only in so far as the teacher's purpose was clear. For example, one teacher said that she chose a certain selection because the content was good. After the discussion she realized that she was merely saying that she chose it because it was there.

But the questions naturally arise: "What has all this to do with the children? How is it going to affect their reading, their power to get the thought? Profoundly, I believe, for the teacher's interest and grasp register unmistakably in the work of the children.

I will not attempt to touch upon other phases of English study that are going on in the school and in all of the English Centers in Chicago. Dr. Hosic will describe in this *Journal* the entire experiment which he has conducted. Perhaps I have said enough to emphasize the fact that the essential of supervision is co-operation, that the essential of co-operation is purpose, that there is a possibility of establishing a technique of supervision, and that the supervisory function is the highest and most worth-while function of the school principal.

THE MEANING OF METHOD

WILLIAM H. KILPATRICK
Professor of Education, Teachers College, Columbia University

"I don't understand the speaker. Did he say there is no such thing as a problem of method, that we cannot study method by itself? That the only real problem is one of curriculum? Is that what he said? And what did he mean?"

Some teachers discuss an educational address

"It sounded as if he said that, but surely he didn't mean that a first-grade teacher need only study reading, that anyone who can read can teach reading. I well remember when I was a child of about ten—more years ago than I care to tell—what a furor there was when a new teacher said she didn't teach the alphabet first, that she taught the words first, and letters and spelling later. My head went round. It sounded like building a chimney from the top down. My uncle said it was foolishness; that it couldn't possibly work; that the school board ought to turn off such a teacher. He certainly was surprised, however, to find his little Mary actually reading in less than half the time his older children had taken."

"Yes, and then we had the sentence method, which some claimed was better than the word method; and later we had all kinds of method, the phonic method, the phonetic method, the Aldine method, and I don't know how many others. The Grube method in arithmetic came and went; and then we had the Spear method, I believe. In those days our institute lecturers had a great deal to say about methods. They spoke bravely about the 'new methods' as something great; but I think of late years I have noticed a superior sort of smile sometimes as 'methods and devices' are mentioned. Am I right?"

Various "methods" are recalled

"You are right, I am sure; but I got a new idea last summer at the university.

The psychological study of methods is mentioned I took a course in educational psychology. Our professor said that some day we'd have a science of method, or rather that the scientific psychologist would tell us which of two ways of learning anything is more economical and would give us definite rules. He made us read Whipple's *How to Study Effectively*, and talked besides a great deal about the laws of learning, about set, readiness, exercise, and satisfaction. It was awfully hard at first, because I had never heard of such things; but after a while I got into it, and now I believe he is right. I have been watching myself and how I learn, and my class, too. And those laws of learning certainly work —it's all a matter of exercise with satisfaction or annoyance.

"Well, suppose your psychologist is right as you think. I don't see much difference

The old and new are compared between method when we talk about the 'word method' of reading and the study of method by your psychologist. It seems to me that the psychologist is just doing more carefully what we all did when we decided that children learned quicker and better by the word method than they did by the old alphabetic method. I was myself at summer school last year, and in one course I took it was brought out that science and common sense don't differ much except in

A definition of method is proposed degree; science is more exact. Whether you proceed by common sense or by science, method seems to me to be a matter of the most economic way of teaching or of learning anything."

"You don't agree then with our speaker of today. You think method can be studied?"

"Certainly method can be studied. Anybody who thinks is bound to admit that. I can't say as yet whether I disagree with the speaker, because I don't know what he meant."

"I don't believe the speaker would object to what you have said about psychology, because he is obliged to know that educational psychology has established itself. I believe he is more interested in curriculum than anything else—he talks a great deal about minimum essentials—and he just forgets that curriculum isn't everything. But I think he had also in mind another kind of method, a broader kind. I believe it was this he meant to deny. At any rate, whether he did or not, I want to raise a question that has been troubling me. There are more reasons why I should prefer the word method to the old alphabet method than simply because the child sooner

A wider notion of method is suggested learns to read. That's good, but there's more to it than that. That old dry humdrum alphabet and spelling method made the children hate the school and hate the teacher. The word method of teaching reading somehow encourages the children. They seem more alive. If I wanted to make the children just docile, like the old serfs you know, and always 'keep them under' and 'break their spirit,' and run the world on the principle 'that children should be seen and not heard,' then I'd favor such spirit-killing methods as the old alphabet method or nowadays, if I believed some, the newer Aldine method. But if I believed in all that old slavish docility, I'd be consistent and give up democracy and accept Prussianism outright."

"Yes, I know, I have heard you on this before. I am not going to dispute now whether your way of treating children is better or not. I know you'd begin by telling me that children are less outbreaking in school than they used to be; I remember what you said before about child suicides in Germany because of the harsh school treatment. But I am interested in your idea of method. You mean, if I understand you, that the problem of method includes more than the best way of learning the lesson immediately at hand, that method is more than a matter of the most economical way of teaching a child how to read or how to learn a long poem. This sounds reasonable, but I don't quite understand. I wish you'd discuss it more fully."

"Well, it is just this. There is, as I see it, a narrow way of looking at method and **The two views** a broader way of looking at **of method are** it. It might be better to **contrasted** employ different words for the two uses, but so far no one has proposed the different terms. The narrow way is all right as far as it goes. It asks what is the best way of learning to read. What is the best way of learning a French vocabulary? And such like. This is what the older generation had in mind when they made so much of 'methods.' Only they had little or no scientific procedure for testing whether one method was better than another. If the difference between two rival methods was great, the better would likely win out in the end. In this way the old alphabet method, as was said before, has gone entirely. Scientific psychology and the tests and measurement movement will undoubtedly place method considered narrowly on an increasingly scientific basis, to the great advantage of all concerned if only we know how to make it work together for the best education of the children. But right there comes the rub. I have seen children, after they had passed the history

examination, slam their books down and say, 'Never again! I hope I may never look into another history as long as I live!' Now it seems to me that our pupils ought not only to learn what was in the history course, but learn also to love history. I have seen older children study their civics and government and come out not caring a rap whether their city was well governed or not. There is something to learn besides what is written in the books and a child may learn the one without learning the other. Then I know too that some of the pupils who make the highest marks—at any rate under some teachers—are afraid to call their souls their own. They can't think independently, they don't know how. They are afraid to trust their own judgment—they hardly have any judgment. If it is in the book or if the teacher says it, then it's true and that ends it. But surely that isn't the kind of citizens we need in a democratic country."

"Do you mean that whether pupils come to like history or to wish good govern- **Is it method** ment or be able to think **or subject-** independently is a matter of **matter?** method? It seems to me that each of these is something to learn just as truly as is the subject-matter of history or government. How about it?"

"It is something to learn. You are exactly right. Learning the subject-matter of history is one thing. Learning to love history is another thing, related but different. Learning how to reach independent but dependable judgments in history is still another thing. Each learning is valuable and needs consideration. We should not trust to luck in the last two any more than in the first."

"But you have not answered my question. You admit that all these things are something to learn, but you say nothing of the method. A while back you were making big claims about method, you said you were widening the reach of method. In the end it seems that everything alike is something to learn, everything merely some kind of subject-matter—different kinds of subject-matter to be sure, but all subject-matter. Why not agree with the speaker today that after all curriculum is the one question? For curriculum seems to me to be nothing but a selection of desirable subject-matter, of desirable things to be learned. How do you answer that?"

"In one way it is all a question of things to be learned. But method comes in. To **A second defi-** each thing to be learned **nition of** belongs its own way of being **method** learned. To learn anything we must somehow practice that thing. To learn how to form judgments we must practice forming judgments—under conditions that tell success from failure and give satisfaction to success and annoyance to failure. To learn to think independently we must practice thinking independently. Now method is exactly a matter of arranging such conditions as give the right kind of practice for learning, a practice that will tell success from failure and attach satisfaction to success and annoyance to failure. To each thing you call subject-matter (the term is a slippery one) belongs its own style of method. Self-respect is a thing needful to be learned—you wish it called subject-matter. At any rate, to the learning of self-respect its own style of method, namely discriminative practice in exercising self-respect. Now, isn't it true: to each learning its own method? Do we see how method attaches to learning history, to learning to love history, to learning to think trustworthily in history?"

"Yes, I must admit it. I had not before seen how intimately—I might almost say how correlatively— **Is it not one** subject-matter and method **type of method** are related to each other. To **after all?** each thing to be learned belongs its own appropriate method. Perhaps I'll wish to ask you more about that later. But I have now another question. A while back you spoke of a wider sense of method and a narrower sense of method. I don't yet see any two senses of method. You have pointed out perhaps unusual fields in which to seek and find method, but all the instances you have given—once they are found—belong to the same kind. All reduce themselves to one formula: the most economical way of learning the thing at hand. There may be more things at hand, more things to be learned at one time and together than I had thought; but the same notion of method—your narrower sense of method—fits them all. What then becomes of your broader sense of method? I believe you have forgotten it or rather have been confused in your thinking."

"Don't be too hasty. Perhaps we shall yet locate the broader kind of method. You spoke a moment ago of several things at hand to be learned, many things to be learned at one and the same time. Can a child just learn several things at a time or must he learn just one at once?"

"I don't understand. I have always heard that we can do only one thing at a time, or at any rate can pay attention to only one thing. How then can we learn more than one thing at a time?"

"I'll tell you how several things may be learned at one time. Suppose a shy little girl enters the kindergarten. **Many learnings** She shrinks at first from the **go on at once** other children, but at length is coaxed into trying the slider. (You know our kindergarten has in it a children's toboggan slide.) This little girl learns how to mount the stairs, how to get herself ready, how to turn loose and slide down. She forgets her shyness and enjoys sliding tremendously. The next day she comes a different child. Why different? She has learned some things. What has she learned? Wherein is she different? She already has decided that she likes the kindergarten assistant who helped her yesterday. She likes Mary and Tommy who helped her on the slide. She likes the slide. She knows how to use it, how to take her turn. She is less shy. She told her mother that she likes the kindergarten. Each of these things represents a something learned. Each represents an exercise with satisfaction. Did she learn these several things, one at a time, in a set order? Clearly not. Nor did she learn them all exactly simultaneously or in one moment. But they are inextricably interwoven. Learning each was in some measure bound up with learning the others. It would have been impossible for her to practice with the slide without at the same time acquiring some sort of attitude toward the other children using it, some sort of attitude toward the kindergarten assistant who supervised, some sort of attitude toward herself in the total situation, some sort of attitude toward the kindergarten as a whole. And note how large a part method played. Suppose the assistant were an impossible sort of kindergartner who had greeted the shy stranger sternly and had gruffly ordered her at once to mount the slider stairs. Would the child's learning have been the same in any way? On the contrary, wouldn't it all have been different?

"The wider sense of method then takes into account the fact that the child inevitably responds to many different aspects of a situation at one and the same time. We **The wider** need not split hairs as to how **sense of method** many things a person can **defined** attend to at once. We know that during the half-hour a boy is facing his grammar lesson, he is not only learning or failing to learn that specific lesson, but he is also fixing or unfixing or failing to fix an attitude toward the subject of grammar, another attitude toward his teacher, another toward schools, another toward himself with reference to grammar and school and his ability and disposition generally. He may be getting interesting suggestions for further study into language when a favorable moment may occur or he may be hardening his heart on the whole matter. He may be saying, 'It's no use. I can't learn anything.' He may be deciding that school and parents and the whole tribe of governors are unfeeling tyrants, that wrong to them is right to him, that right to him is success in 'getting by' with his unbridled impulses. What he does think or does not think, what he feels or does not feel, what, in short, he brings with him out of the total situation depends in large measure upon the teacher, upon his way of handling the boys in and about the school. The narrow sense of method singles out for consideration one specific thing to be learned and pays for the time being exclusive attention to that *as if that alone* were going on at that time. The wider sense of method knows that in actual life one thing never goes on by itself. This wider method demands that we consider the actual facts, the real world. The narrow sense of method faces always an abstraction, an unreality—a part of a total situation, a part that can no more exist by itself than could a man's head continue to live apart from his body. We have to make such abstractions for the sake of economy in studying such things as method; but we should know what we are doing, we must never make the mistake of supposing the abstracted element is real life. The problem of method in the wider sense is thus **The problem of method in its wider sense** very general: How shall we treat children, seeing that whether we like it or no they are going to learn well or ill not only the thing we choose to set them at, but also at the same time a great many other things perhaps of far greater importance?"

"We now see the answer to the lecturer today. Method must be studied. I see now as I never saw before that there is a problem of method as wide as life itself. But it puts a great responsibility upon the teacher. I am almost sorry I see it. Why, I cannot teach stocks and bonds next week without wondering whether I am doing more harm than good! I cannot shut my eyes any more to what you call the wider problem of method. But what about this problem of method? Can we study it, and how is it related to the narrower problem of method?"

"We do have these two problems of method, one narrow, the other wide; one **Method in the wider sense is the problem of life** has to do with learning the details that go to make up education, the other concerns education as a whole, education considered as the correlative of the whole of life. We can and must study both. The psychologist and experimental educator will help most on the first problem, the problem of method in its narrow sense. The second problem is in a way the problem of life itself. The answer to the second problem, the wider problem of method, will depend on the answer we give to the problem of life. That is why the old Prussian type of method doesn't suit us

in America. They wanted their children, some to fill this station in life, others that, but all to be docile and obedient; some to be tradesmen and shopworkers, others of the upper classes to be officers in the army, government officials, but all to accept the rule of the Kaiser without question. So they hunted out a way of treating children that made them able each to do his own work, but did not make them independent in judgment. I once heard Dean Russell discuss this. He said the method was the same for all the Prussian children whether they went as the common people to the *Volksschule* or whether they went as the upper class to the *Gymnasium*. The curriculum was different to fit each for his place in their scheme; but the method was the same to make them all into the Prussian type of character."

"That's exceedingly interesting and very important for us. You know I wonder if we don't have some Prussians in this country, I mean people who are anxious to fit our immigrants into some sort of lower working class. I have heard certain persons talking a great deal about 'instinctive obedience,' as if they wanted some of our people to grow up especially strong in obedience while others perhaps should grow up especially strong in commanding those more obedient ones. It doesn't sound like democracy to me."

"Yes, it is a very important problem, and perhaps equally important that it **A democratic society should have a democratic method** should be recognized. If we are going to make a success of the democratic experiment begun about 1776, we must have a type of education that fits democracy. A democratic society should have a democratic school system, and in this system a democratic method will occupy a most important part."

AN EXPERIMENT IN CO-OPERATION

I. LAUNCHING THE PROJECT

JAMES F. HOSIC

Associate Professor of Education, Teachers College, Columbia University

Team-play marks the efficient school system. It is none too easy to bring about, however, as everyone knows, especially if the system is a big one. A certain mechanical or external uniformity comes easy. Peremptory orders will secure that. But real unanimity based upon preferred ideas is more rare. To secure it requires time, patience, and real leadership. But it is worth all it costs.

In the series of brief articles, of which this is the first, I shall try to give a true and circumstantial account of an attempt, continuing for a period of about three years, to improve the teaching of English in Chicago through better co-operation of all concerned with the problem, namely, the supervisory officers, the classroom teachers, and the training school. Emphasis will be given to the procedure followed, inasmuch as the by-products of the enterprise have proved nearly or quite as valuable as the results directly aimed at. I shall write, therefore, on the topic, How to improve the work of a school, while describing an experiment in the supervision of the teaching of English.

FIRST STEPS

The late superintendent of the Chicago schools, Mr. John D. Shoop, was always interested in English. He was a fluent speaker, occasionally wrote poetry, and was fond of literature, particularly writing of a moral and patriotic type. As president of the Department of Superintendence of the National Education Association he arranged a program in which one full session was devoted to addresses on the improvement of the teaching of the vernacular in school and college. It was to be expected that he would give special attention to the subject in his dealings with the schools in his own city.

He did. He called the writer into council in the spring of 1918 and proposed that I undertake to assist in the work of a number of selected schools in various parts of Chicago in order to bring the English work of those schools into harmony with the instruction given in the Normal College. "If," said he, "We can get the yeast to working in a few schools, we can perhaps leaven the whole lump." I replied that the college teachers could lay no claim to perfect wisdom in the matter but probably would profit as much as anyone from the closer contact which his plan promised. We would do our best to help the schools get together, however we might find it to be sound policy to depart from our own present practices. In a word, we were ready and willing to learn.

A meeting with the superintendents of the ten districts into which the Chicago schools are divided was then called. Mr. Shoop explained his plan, asked for advice and co-operation, and, when questioned as to the duration and probable outcome of the experiment, declared that this was the Alpha. He could not foretell the Omega.

I had prepared in advance a tentative list of schools to be chosen as English centers. This list was now sifted and amended in committee of the whole. Among the considerations involved were variety of nationality of the pupils, accessibility of location, probably willingness and ability of the principal to co-operate, and the representative character of the teachers. About half of the schools finally selected were on my original list—a fact typical of the spirit of give and take which was in evidence throughout the experiment.

The schools in the various districts with the prevailing nationality or race of the pupils were as follows:

District	School	Principal	Nationality or Race
I...	Knickerbocker	Mary G. Guthrie	German-American
II...	Hibbard	Chester C. Dodge	American
III...	Burr	Samuel R. Meck	Polish
IV...	Delano	G. A. Osinga	American
V...	Jefferson	Mrs. Catherine Delanty	Jewish and Italian
VI...	Hammond	John A. Long (afterward Adrian M. Doolin)	Bohemian
VII...	Goodrich	Mrs. Esther P. Hornbaker	Italian
VIII...	Lewis-Champlin	Henry Crane	American*
IX...	Oglesby	Daniel J. Beeby	American
X...	Doolittle	Margaret Madden	Negro

* At the beginning of the second year the Lewis-Champlin was replaced by the Farren, Principal, Isabella Dolton; Nationality or Race, Negro.

Shortly afterward Mr. Shoop invited the principals of the selected schools to a conference with the district superintendents. At that conference I submitted for discussion the following prospectus:

PROSPECTUS FOR ENGLISH CENTERS
Motto: Effective service to our city by means of intelligent co-operation.
Basis: Agreement on essential principles; individual variation in meeting actual conditions and in providing for initiative.
Procedure:
1. Ascertain the actual conditions.
2. Attack one subject at a time.
3. Three supervisors plan the launching of the project.
4. Enlist the co-operation of the teachers as a social group—lead all to enter heartily into the project, to contribute plans, to carry out experiments, etc. Proceed with the teachers as we wish them to proceed with the children.
5. Make use of the recognized instruments of effective supervision—syllabi, observation, conference, group meetings, committees, model lessons, visiting by teachers, reference reading, tests, etc.

Exhortation:
1. Let us define the social values and objects of the work.
2. Let us analyze the studies as types of reference, involving certain controls through the growth of certain specific abilities, that is, knowledges, habits, skills, interests, ideals.
3. Let us employ the inventory, the school standard, and objective measurements of results.
4. Let us seek to provide the best conditions for improvement and for transfer.
5. Let us confer together, placing the experience of each at the service of all.
6. Let us keep record of our experience in carrying on the work.

The consideration of this statement of principles tended to unify our thinking and prepared the way for definite planning of the campaign. This now followed—at a luncheon. Good eating undoubtedly makes for intellectual *rapport*. The talk first went round, each in turn saying frankly what he thought it best to do, until all had been heard from. On the issues thus raised the following decisions were made:

1. For the sake of massing our experience, all the centers would undertake the same tasks.

2. The work would proceed in the light of fundamental principles, believed by all to be applicable to school studies in general.

3. The aspects of English taken up would be those having most vital and far-reaching relations to the work of the school as a whole.

4. The case would be presented (without prejudice) to the teachers of each center as a group and their best collective judgment obtained as to what it were best to do and how it were best to do it.

Further discussions revealed the fact that the principles and superintendents present were virtually unanimous in the opinions, strongly expressed by two of their number, that the crying weaknesses of present-day instruction in English are, first, failure to teach children how to talk and, second, failure to teach them how to study. They said:

> The mechanics of primary reading seem to go pretty well, but when the time comes for the pupils to use books in the pursuit of their studies, they do not make good. Equally certain it is that their talk is scrappy, indistinct, and ineffective. They run their sentences together and mumble their words. Even the teacher fails to make out what is meant, let alone the pupils seated a few feet away. The speaker seems to have no notion of how to play the game.

With a perfect good understanding established among themselves, the leaders went their several ways.

ENLISTING THE TEACHERS

The next step required the planning of a series of conferences in the schools. The district superintendent, the principal, and the special supervisor first talked informally together and agreed upon a procedure. When the meeting had been called to order, the superintendent made a statement in which he explained the general purpose and plan of the enterprise and emphasized the value of the service which could be rendered, not only to the school itself, but to the district and to the city as a whole.

The special supervisor then called out frank expression from the teachers, writing on the blackboard the points made by each. When the question was pressed home, "What are the most far-reaching aspects of the English work?" the teachers answered in their turn, "Oral English and silent reading and study."

The principal closed the discussion, expressing his appreciation of the opportunity which had come to his school and expressing his feeling of confidence in the willingness of all to co-operate. He prom-

ised the fullest support possible to each one in trying out new ideas and urged that suggestions be freely made.

The first group which conferred chose to begin the experiment with silent reading, and hence this phase became the topic for the first semester. A single educational principle was proposed as the theoretical lode star for the opening weeks, namely, the principle that *learning proceeds most effectively in the light of a specific purpose.* The following quotation from John Dewey was made to serve as a sort of motto:

> Perhaps in no other way could so great an improvement be brought about in education as by teachers with one accord seeing to it that children should never set about studying any lesson without first having a clear notion as to just what it is they are undertaking to learn, and what they are to do in order to learn it.

Definite reinforcement of the idea was found in the article entitled "Reading as Reasoning," by Edward L. Thorndike, in the *Journal of Educational Psychology* for June, 1917. The subtitle, "A Study of Mistakes in Paragraph Reading," indicates the purpose of the article,

> To show that reading is a very elaborate procedure, involving a weighing of each of many elements in a sentence, their organization in the proper relations one to another, the selection of certain of their connotations and the rejection of others, and the co-operation of many forces to determine the final response.

The article tells how the following test was given to two hundred pupils in the sixth grade:

> Read this and then write the answers to 1, 2, 3, 4, 5, 6, and 7. Read it again as often as you need to.

> In Franklin, attendance upon school is required of every child between the ages of seven and fourteen on every day when school is in session unless the child is so ill as to be unable to go to school, or some person in his house is ill with a contagious disease, or the roads are impassable.

1. What is the general topic of the paragraph?
2. On what day would a ten-year-old girl not be expected to attend school?
3. Between what years is attendance upon school compulsory in Franklin?
4. How many causes are stated which make absence excusable?
5. What kind of illness may permit a boy to stay away from school, even though he is not sick himself?
6. What condition in a pupil would justify his non-attendance?
7. At what age may a boy leave school to go to work in Franklin?

The responses were most unintelligent, often ludicrous. For example, in answer to Question 1 the following were given: "Franklin"; "In Franklin"; "Franklin attending school"; "It was a great inventor"; "What the school did when the boy was ill"; "Oh diseases"; "The roads are impassable"; "Made of complete sentences"; "Subject and predicate"; "To begin with a capital"; "Leave half an inch space."

Professor Thorndike explains that

In correct reading (1) each word produces a correct meaning, (2) each such element of meaning is given a correct weight in comparison with the others, and (3) the resulting ideas are examined and validated to make sure that they satisfy the mental set or adjustment or purpose for whose sake the reading was done. Reading may be wrong or inadequate (1) because of wrong connection with words singly, (2) of over-potency or under-potency of elements, or (3) because of failure to treat the ideas produced by the reading as provisional, and so to inspect and welcome or reject them as they appear.

After analyzing the mistakes made by the pupils in answering each of the seven questions, Professor Thorndike continues:

Understanding a paragraph is like solving a problem in mathematics. It consists in selecting the right elements of the situation and putting them together in the right relations, and also with the right amount of weight or influence or force for each. The mind is assailed as it were by every word in the paragraph. It must select, repress, soften, emphasize, correlate and organize, all under the influence of the right mental set or purpose or demand. . . . .

In educational theory, then, we should not consider the reading of a textbook or reference as a mechanical, passive, undiscriminating task, on a totally different level from the task of evaluating or using what is read. While the work of judging and applying doubtless demands a more elaborate and inventive organization and control of mental connections, the demands of mere reading are also for the active selection which is typical of thought. It is not a small or unworthy task to learn "what the book says. . . . ."

In school practice it appears likely that exercises in silent reading to find the answers to given questions, or to give a summary of the matter read, or to list the questions which it answers, should in large measure replace oral reading. The vice of the poor reader is to say the words to himself without actively making judgments concerning what they reveal. Reading aloud or listening to one reading aloud may leave this vice unaltered or even encouraged. Perhaps it is in their outside reading of stories and in their study of geography, history, and the like, that many school children really learn to read.

It was the universal testimony of the teachers in the English centers that the test passage used by Professor Thorndike was no harder than many to be found in the books in use in the schools, and that they received with great frequency answers exhibiting weaknesses comparable to those which he reported. They were eager to apply his principles of diagnosis and attempt to teach their pupils to "reason" upon what they read in the light of "the *purpose* for which the reading was done."

In succeeding articles in this series an account will be given of how they went about the task, of the part played by the supervisors, of the topics of succeeding conferences, and of the work in oral composition which presently began.

RECLASSIFICATION OF CHILDREN ON BASIS OF TESTS IN PORT CLINTON SCHOOLS[1]

A. F. MYERS

Superintendent of Schools, Port Clinton, Ohio

One of the most serious weaknesses in school men, as in a measure with all professional men, is that they are long on theory and short on practice. As a result of this weakness a great many school men, while they understand quite well the theoretical aspects of retardation, the need for reclassification, etc., absolutely fail to make the application to their own school system; or, making the application, fail to provide the remedy.

It is a fact, as any school man may discover for himself, that the great majority of our school children are very poorly classified. Give a spelling test to your fourth, fifth, and sixth grades. Collect your results. If you have never attempted this before you will be amazed to learn how many fourth-grade children are superior in spelling ability to some sixth-grade children. The same is true of silent reading, fundamental operations of arithmetic, and intelligence.

In October, 1920, the teachers and superintendent of the Port Clinton schools, assisted by some outside educators, attempted a survey of certain conditions in the Port Clinton schools. One of the first things we did was to make an age-grade study. Briefly, the results of this study showed that 50 per cent of our children were retarded one year or more, that 48 per cent were normal, and that 2 per cent were accelerated. This was enough to convince us that somewhere we had a condition that was not right. One of two things was evidently true: either there was a very low rate of intelligence among the children of the Port Clinton schools, or our children were very poorly classified.

We determined first to test the intelligence. The results show one thing very clearly: Port Clinton school children are not below the normal in intelligence. Expressed by Grade iQ, our results were as follows:

First grade	iQ .963
Second grade	iQ 1.00
Third grade	iQ 1.00
Fourth grade	iQ .925
Fifth grade	iQ 1.055
Sixth grade	iQ 1.03
Seventh grade	iQ 1.017
Eighth grade	iQ 1.04
Ninth grade	iQ 1.03
Tenth grade	iQ 1.01
Eleventh grade	iQ .905
Twelfth grade	iQ 1.04

School iQ 1.01

The following achievement tests were then given: Monroe's Standardized Reasoning Test in Arithmetic, Courtis Research Test in Arithmetic, Monroe's Silent Reading Test, Trabue's Language Test, Holly's Sentence Vocabulary Test, Starch's Punctuation Test, Buckingham Extension of the Ayres Spelling Scale, Hahn-Lackey Geography Test, and Harlan's Test of Information in American History. The results of these tests showed the widest possible range of ability, both within the class and from one class to the next higher. It was not infrequently that we found a pupil in a class who was well above the median of the next higher class. The chief reason for the existence of this condition was the fact that, with annual promotions in effect, it was deemed too hazardous an

[1] Summary of a talk given at Northwestern Ohio Superintendents' Meeting, April 15, 1921.

undertaking to skip a child over an entire year of work. The result was that the exceptionally bright child had no opportunity to advance more rapidly than his fellows. The child who failed had to repeat an entire year of work, and in every subject, even though he may have had failing grades in only two subjects, and these may have been only a very little below the passing mark. It was only natural, then, in a school system of this kind that retardation and poor classification should prevail.

The Port Clinton teachers were unanimous in believing that the first step in remedying conditions should be to put in midyear promotions. It was determined that at the end of the first semester, January 17, 1921, the midyear promotion plan should be put into effect. Conditions here are probably about as nearly ideal for the successful working of midyear promotions as could be imagined. Our school plant is all on one campus. We have two teachers for each grade. Therefore midyear promotions do not in any way increase the teaching load of the teacher. In order to put the system into effect, we determined to select the upper 40 per cent of each grade and to advance them one-half year, to select the lowest 10 per cent and to have them repeat the last one-half year's work. The remaining 50 per cent would advance to the next semester's work. In this way we secured about the same number of children for the B section of each grade as for the A section. For example 40 per cent of the fourth grade advanced to Grade VB. Ten per cent of the children who had just covered the work of Grade VB repeated it with the 40 per cent who entered from IVB. The selection of children was made strictly on the basis of intelligence and achievement tests. Every child in each grade was given his rank in the class according to his grade in each test. For example, a child may have stood first in mental age, fifth in silent reading, third in spelling, etc. On the basis of these three his composite rank, or his class rank, would be third.

It is interesting to note that an age-grade study made after the midyear promotion had gone into effect showed 49 per cent normal, 36.5 per cent retarded, and 14.5 per cent accelerated. Thus we have reduced our retardation from 50 per cent to 36.5 per cent, and have increased our accelerance from 2 per cent to 14.5 per cent.

We expect the following advantages to result from the midyear promotions: (1) Exceptionally bright children will be moved along more rapidly. This will be taken care of through having a definite time at quarterly intervals at which those children who show by achievement tests that they can do advanced work will be placed in the next grade. (2) Children who fail will not be so greatly retarded as formerly, because they will have to repeat only the last half year of work.

We are taking two other steps in the interest of better classification. They are: (1) Promotion by subject. This will be introduced in the seventh and eighth grades next year where the work is already departmentalized. We also have under consideration the matter of departmentalization of grades five and six. When this is accomplished, we will promote by subject in these grades also. (2) Ungraded rooms. We have at the present time seventy children in our first six grades who are more than two years retarded. We hope to provide facilities in ungraded rooms for the majority of these children next year.

A PROJECT FOR THE ENTIRE TERM

MINETTA L. WARREN

Critic Teacher, Marr Practice School, Detroit, Mich.

The geography course in Grade IVA included the United States with the exception of the groups bordering upon the Atlantic, which had been studied the term before.

TEACHER'S AIMS

(1) To find a project big enough to motivate the work for the entire term, and from which many smaller projects might grow, in order that the big project might not lose its force. (2) To follow the course of study in working out aim (1).

HOW THE TEACHER'S NEED WAS MET

Geography, with its richness of content, seemed to offer the greatest possibilities, so, to "The Course," which was new to me at that time, I turned. Almost instantly these words caught my eye: "North Central States—one of the greatest food producing sections of the world!"

Here was certainly an opportunity for the much-desired *big* project. The subject of food and its production touched not only the life experience of every child in the room, but that of every human being. Numerous projects might grow out of it and thus interest in the original project be maintained.

The question now arose as to the possibility of getting this over to the children so that working upon the subject in the various lines which seemed to me to present themselves should be a "purposeful act" upon the part of the children. This came about in the following way.

LAUNCHING THE PROJECT

In connection with a letter received in return for a box of clothing which had been sent to a French orphan, the crying needs of the people across the sea at the close of the world-war were discussed, from which followed an animated conversation upon the four great needs of the human race. The pupils wished to study about them.

I suggested that we had not time to learn about all of them, but that they might vote for the one which seemed to have in it the greatest possibilities for interesting us, and we would find out all we could about it.

Ballots were prepared and the children voted. Thirty-two voted to study food, six little girls, true to the feminine instinct, voted for clothing, five for shelter, and one for fuel. The "foods" had it.

It was suggested that to study *food* sounded as if they were going to study hygiene. They then decided *it was not food*, but *certain things about food* which they wished to find out.. After some discussion they proposed the following as their undertaking for the term:

PUPILS' AIMS OR PURPOSES

To find out: (1) Where, in the United States, we get our food supply. (2) Of what it consists, chiefly. (3) How we get it and who helps us get it.

On the first page of our new geography notebook we wrote:"Our Problem-Project," and under this heading we wrote the three problems the solutions of which we had undertaken, *determining to keep these before us through the term*, and at the end *to look back and see if they had been solved to our satisfaction.*

Two of the children had been to California, another to Colorado, one to Portland, Oregon, and one, the summer before, had visited the Yellowstone.

They had seen snow-crowned mountains, giant redwood trees, great deserts and fertile river valleys, such as we, in the Middle West see only in imagination or when we travel far. Those who had been so privileged agreed that all of the children must see them, too, if only through pictures, their own reading, and our most vivid descriptions as spurs to the imagination. So "Imaginary Journeys" was added to our general plan, simply as a means of giving and getting enjoyment and so enriching experience.

HOW THE PUPILS HELPED WITH THE COURSE OF STUDY

We seemed ready now to begin work, but I said, "*You* have determined upon several things which you wish to accomplish this term, but there is one thing which *I* wish to do, if possible, and that is to follow our 'Course of Study' in geography; and I wonder if there are not many things included in it which our three problems and imaginary journeys will not cover. If so, what are we going to do about it?" Finally, the youngest boy in the room remarked, "Why don't you just skim through the Course of Study and let us decide about it now?"

I followed this advice and as we progressed said, "Now here is one thing: 'The Iron Mines of Michigan,' what are you going to do with such a subject?" They accepted the challenge and almost instantly the answer came from many members of the class: "Why, every machine the farmer uses in raising our food has iron or steel about it, the machinery in the mills and factories where much of our food is prepared has also, and so have the boats and trains that bring our food to us."

I then said, "Well, here is something which you can't get around, 'The oil wells of Texas and Oklahoma and the gold mines of the Plateau and Pacific States.'" Again the answer came instantly, "In the country, people cook their food on oil stoves and farmers and factorymen couldn't use their machinery without it; and gold is made into money with which we can buy our food."

There was just enough of the puzzle element as we continued our discussion to make it thoroughly enjoyable to the children, and it was found that everything of importance could be placed either under one of our three "things to be found out" or under "Imaginary Journeys." Finally we had worked out and written on the board the following outline:

OUR PROBLEM-PROJECT

To find:

A. Where, in the United States, we get our food supply

B. Of what it consists, chiefly

C. How we get it and who helps us get it (see below, C. 1., etc.)

We found our answers in studying the following groups of states, and in C. 1, 2, 3, and 4.

A.-B. 1. The North Central states
   Wheat, corn, oats, pork
2. The South Central states
   Cane sugar, rice, corn, fruits
3. The Plateau states
   Beef, mutton, apples and other fruits
4. The Pacific states
   Fruits, wheat, beet sugar, salmon

(The lines where the agricultural products are written were left blank and were filled in, in our notebooks, as we learned the contribution which each group makes to our food supply.)

C. 1. The farmer:

    a) What helps the farmer to help us get our food:

    Sufficient heat, rainfall, long growing time

    Deep, rich soil

    Level land

    Facilities for transportation

    b) What prevents the farmer from helping us:

    The reverse of *a*)

    Unseasonable frosts

    Severe summer storms of wind, hail, rain

    Drought (overcome in favorable locality by irrigation)

    Floods (levees and jetties of the Mississippi)

    Insects and disease

(The causal relation between natural controls and life-responses was given much attention through 1*a*) and *b*) and at all necessary points thereafter, and was entirely within the comprehension of the children, as it was *simply* treated.)

    2. The factory worker

    3. The men who work upon trucks, trains, boats, etc.[1]

    4. The wholesale and retail grocer.

The boys had been planning various constructive projects and felt that they were now ready to work out their ideas concretely; but the girls were sadly crushed by a sense of feminine inferiority. They finally formed two committees which met after school on two successive nights, and they planned to make bags to hold grain, prepare labels, collect appropriate postcards, pictures, and can labels, and to help in other ways that might arise later.

EXECUTION

We had now reached the interesting moment when we could put our plans to the test. It was surprising to see how those little fourth-graders settled down to real work. They searched newspapers, magazines, books at home and in the public libraries, collected pictures, old boxes to be used in constructive work, clay, modeling wax, beaver board, and cardboard. They used paints and crayons, utilized erector and mechano sets and brought letters and cards from friends in distant parts of the country.

Following is a list of projects worked out concretely, part of them at home (because of our lack of facilities), sometimes alone, in one or two instances with father and mother helping, but more often with two or three other children in the neighborhood.

PROJECTS GROWING OUT OF *MAIN* PROJECT

Type I. Projects

    1. Reaper and binder made of heavy pasteboard

    2. Threshing machine, with engine and connecting belt—pasteboard

    3. Numerous aeroplanes: monoplanes—wood and erector; biplanes—wood, erector, and mechano (one fine one, with material like a drum head, would fly, and sold for $12. Fifteen-year old uncle helped)

    4. Farm wagon—wood

    5. Trucks—erector, filled with foods

    6. One large wooden boat, supposed to be a Mississippi steamer, was loaded with produce from the South Central states

    7. Large train of cars and tracks brought, former loaded with wheat, corn, oats, and rye from the North Central states

    8. Large cross-section of a coal mine, showing shaft house, shaft, elevator, levels, oar cars, etc. (excellent)

    9. Oil derrick, with drill, worked from a kind of windlass

    10. Lower course of Mississippi, levees and jetties

---

[1] We named important railroad and boat lines in connection with 3 and traced their routes. We did the same with our imaginary journeys.

11. California orange grove

12. Many, small, farm tools

Type II. Projects. Will be given under "Language"

Type III. Project. Solving problem

Type III was used repeatedly as in the following: In studying the North Central states, for instance, from previous knowledge of surface, drainage, climate, etc., of the group, the children decided that agriculture must be the leading industry. This was accepted until proof either for or against could be given, and this problem was written on the board: "Why is agriculture the leading industry in the North Central States?" These reasons were given: (1) sufficient heat; (2) sufficient rainfall; (3) long enough growing time; (4) level land, easy to cultivate; (5) deep, rich soil; (6) ease of transportation both by water and rail; (7) ease with which railroads were built.

At the close of the lesson, the pupils *used their index*, looked up all the points in question and *verified them*. This *was always done* with lessons of this type.

HOW THE GEOGRAPHY PROJECT WORKED OUT IN LANGUAGE

Written.—1. When the pupils brought in their concrete projects they wished to tell me how they had made them. I told them I wished very much to hear about it, but not having time to listen to over forty children, I suggested that they tell me on paper, which they did.

2. A young niece, who was spending the summer in the mountains near Denver, sent me a collection of Rocky Mountain wild flowers. Among them were some fine specimens of the Indian kinnikinnik. With them she inclosed a beautiful legend concerning it, which had been told her on Long's Peak by Enos A. Mills, the well-known naturalist. The children wrote and thanked her for both legend and flowers.

3. A young college girl, without training in method, began teaching in a small town in Oregon and asked for suggestions. Without telling my pupils, I sent her a list of their names, requesting that her pupils write to mine, asking anything they cared to know about Detroit and Michigan and telling us about something of which we knew but little, such as the salmon fisheries, mountain scenery, and anything else which would be of interest.

My pupils were much surprised a few weeks later, when the postman left a letter for each one from some unknown boy or girl.

They answered, giving points of local interest and inclosing a colored postcard. I wrote to the teacher, giving some interesting facts in the early history of Detroit and Michigan, and inclosed two dozen postcards. From this quite a vigorous correspondence resulted.

4. The children all wrote, when we were studying the great wheat farms of the valley of the Red River of the North, to a Minneapolis publishing company asking for pictures of the wheat industry. From the number I selected about half a dozen of the best letters, which were examined by a committee which chose one from among these six.

5. A Detroit lady whom we did not know sent us some large, beautifully colored pictures of Yellowstone, for which we wrote and thanked her.

6. The legend of the kinnikinnik was quite short, so we wrote it and put it up so that visitors might learn it.

7. We planned to write to a friend in Hawaii for pictures and information.

Oral.—1. Reproduction of the legend of the kinnikinnik.

2. Keeping as closely as possible to the language of the Bible, I condensed the story of Ruth, which the pupils learned and dramatized.

3. We read and memorized Whittier's "Corn Song" and copied it in our note-books because we liked it.

HOW THE GEOGRAPHY PROJECT WORKED OUT IN READING

1. Pupils looked through their reading books to find lessons on foods, or those that had some bearing upon foods, made list, and gave me.

2. Books were brought from home containing stories or articles relating to our subject. These were looked over by a committee and if the story was deemed both appropriate and interesting, it was read to the class on Friday by the one who brought it.

3. Poems of harvest were interpreted and read.

HOW THE GEOGRAPHY PROJECT WORKED OUT IN SPELLING

1. When the children wrote to me telling me how they had constructed their concrete project as described under "Language," the misspelled words were listed and learned.

2. The same was done with all common words incorrectly spelled in the letters mentioned in written language work relating to the project.

3. Words which we needed to know in the written geography lessons were learned.

4. The children looked through the list of supplementary words in our spelling course and listed all those that in any way related to foods. Of course we learned others also.

HOW THE GEOGRAPHY PROJECT WORKED OUT IN ARITHMETIC

1. Pupils cut market reports from the papers and made their own written problems. They were asked to make sensible ones, difficult enough for a fourth-grade class, *not* something they could do mentally.

2. Problems were made from their own daily experiences in going to the store for their mothers.

3. This led to the making out of grocery bills and making change from five-, ten-, and twenty-dollar bills, in all of which they became quite proficient.

4. The exact cost of trips to interesting points was found out by the pupils and these facts were made into problems.

HOW THE GEOGRAPHY PROJECT WORKED OUT IN DRAWING

1. We planned for a vacant wall panel, a very large basket, which we filled with grains, fruits, and vegetables painted in the natural colors.

Over it, in large black letters, painted and cut out, were the words: "The United States, the Bread Basket of the World." This was well done and proved very decorative.

(The children knew that the North Central states had particularly earned this title, while some portions of the country made but little contribution.)

2. Individual baskets of various shapes were made, filled with fruits, and taken home.

JUDGING

At the close of the term's work the pupils turned back in their notebooks to the aims which they had set before themselves at the beginning of the semester, and determined that their purpose had been satisfactorily accomplished. Judging also continued through the entire term, as minor plans were changed for better ones.

In the consideration of values growing out of this particular problem-project, these, it seems to me, are some of the strong points:

1. It unquestionably aroused interest, increased the interest span, and held attention, on to the end.

2. It developed initiative and leadership.

3. It gave continual opportunity for genuine participation upon the part of both pupil and teacher.

4. It afforded an excellent opportunity for the teacher to know the pupil and the pupil to know the teacher.

5. It developed Yankee ingenuity in the utilization of all materials.

6. It developed thrift.

7. It developed mechanical skill in working out the various constructive projects which grew out of the main project.

8. It developed "a great capacity for taking pains," much needed in these days when speed is too often the only consideration.

9. It led to continued application in the face of difficulty,—ability to "carry on."

10. It offered an opportunity for interesting the pupil who is naturally poor in his work with books, and proved to him that he, too, can excel in something; that he has power of a different kind.

11. It gave opportunity for keeping boys occupied upon work that is worth while.

12. It was a means of interesting the family and so led to co-operation between the home and the school.

13. Finally—*everybody* liked it!

THE CLEARING HOUSE

A VISIT TO THE KINDERGARTEN

Situation.—A large, wooden spool on the work bench suggested to a boy the construction of an engine. During the conference period many helpful suggestions were given. Several other boys became interested and built engines, adding new parts and initiating new and clever ways of putting on the wheels. A coal car and passenger and freight cars were added. Then one morning during the conference period a little girl asked, "What are you going to do with your trains?" Immediately came the replies: "Take the dolls riding," "My train is a freight train and is to move things in." Where could the dolls go? They could go to the kindergarten to visit. What will we need?

Activities.—1. Building of the station. Since the first grade did not have large floor blocks, a request was made to the kindergarten for the use of their blocks in building the station. A visit was made to a nearby railway station to find out what we needed in our station. Signs were printed: "Penn. Station," "Ticket Office," "Baggage," "Information," "News Stand," "Restaurant," "Restroom," etc.

2. While in the kindergarten the children noticed the need of doll furniture. Since the kindergarten did not have a work bench, a group of boys decided to make a set of wooden furniture. One boy made a doll bed of new and clever design, for which the girls made a mattress, linens, and spread. They also dressed a celluloid doll to fit the bed and gave it to the kindergarten girls.

3. Benches and furniture for the station were made at the work bench.

4. Trunks, hand bags, and suit cases were made of cardboard and leatherette.

5. Girls prepared their dolls for the trip by making hats, coats, capes, etc.

Comments.—The social aspect which developed along with this project became more and more evident as the activities grew. The discussions during the conference period led to much representative and dramatic play in preparation for the trip, in deciding what the dolls needed, in buying and selling of tickets, checking of baggage, putting up signs and signals, etc. A close co-operation developed between the kindergarten and first grade. The kindergarten became interested in how the toys were made and enjoyed playing with them while the first-grade children were anxious to explain their work, and took great pleasure in being of service to the kindergarten children. They were given many opportunities to investigate, to test, tö arrange, and to judge values. They discovered the durability of their construction projects, as in real life, through use. It was found in pulling the trains some distance filled with passengers, baggage, or freight, that the wheels must be fastened more securely; that the station, to stand several days, must be built more carefully; and that the tracks, to be of service, must be laid very carefully. Many valuable language and reading lessons resulted from the experiences gained and excursions taken during the progress of this project. These records were made by the children and kept in a large class book. This project with its outgrowth lasted several weeks, all the children in the room taking some part in its development.　　　MABEL K. HOLLAND

JEFFERSON SCHOOL
FORT WAYNE, IND.

A PROJECT IN SECOND GRADE
THE EASTER SHOP

Situation.—Our class had completed a clothing store. As Easter time drew near the children began bringing Easter baskets and eggs and asked if we could use them in our store. Some of the children remarked that we couldn't do this because clothing stores didn't sell Easter toys.

After talking over the matter, we decided we could make another store and sell Easter things. We visited a downtown store to see what was sold in an Easter store and how they were arranged:

I. Language opportunities utilized by the pupils:
1. Writing a letter to their mothers to secure permission to go uptown
2. Planning what to look for on their excursion
3. Telling another group what they saw on their excursion
4. Writing about their trip and reading the best paper to another class
5. Discussing how to make duck carts and bunny wagons
6. Planning how to make marble bags, using a pattern which they themselves made
7. Planning a name for the store and how to arrange the counters
8. Writing to the manual training department for a board to be used as a counter
9. Planning and writing signs
10. Writing of posters advertising the opening of the store
11. Writing an advertisement for a delivery boy
12. Discussing which of the children who applied for the position seemed most capable
13. Discussing what kind of a storekeeper and cashier we must have
14. Planning what the buyers should say
15. Planning what the storekeeper and clerk should say to make people want to buy
16. Planning how to telephone an order
17. Playing store, putting into practice the standards previously developed
18. Writing letters to sick children, telling them about our store

II. Handwork and art opportunities:
1. Drawing things they saw at the store
2. Making and painting clay eggs
3. Modeling and coloring clay bunnies and chickens
4. Making duck carts and bunny wagons
5. Modeling and painting marbles
6. Painting calendar rolls to represent logs and placing clay chickens on the log
7. Measuring and cutting patterns for marble bags
8. Cutting and sewing marble bags out of tarlatan
9. Dyeing real egg shells
10. Weaving Easter baskets
11. Making a postcard rack
12. Making Easter postcards
13. Making clay flower pots, painting and shellacking them
14. Making paper windmills
15. Making paper bags

III. Writing opportunities utilized
See Language opportunities

IV. Minimum essentials in language covered in this project:
1. Proper pronunciation of "again," "get"
2. Use of "may" instead of "can"
3. Use of "It is I" (developed in phoning)
4. Elimination of "and"
5. Enlargement of vocabulary ("apply," "obliged," "splendid," "prefer")
6. Use of complete sentences
7. Use of good beginning and ending sentences
8. Use of proper forms of common verbs
9. Use of "I haven't any"
10. Use of comma in a series; in the heading, salutation, and ending of a letter
11. Use of the period at the end of statements; after the abbreviation of Mo., Mr., Mrs.
12. Paragraphing
13. Addressing an envelope
14. Use of margin

15. Use of capitals in titles and in the various parts of a letter

V. Minimum essentials in arithmetic covered in this project:
   1. Practice in the use of the fifth and tenth tables
   2. Review of the addition and subtraction combinations
   3. Column addition
   4. Writing of numbers and prices on articles
   5. Use of dollar and cent marks
   6. Solving problems
   7. Use of inch, foot, yard

VI. Spelling words reviewed in this project: Store, board, room, dollar, open, here, paid, price, cash, apply, delivery, between, bundle, wrap, wrapper, charge, change

VII. Spelling words taught for the first time: Easter, town, eggs, basket, rabbit, bunny, wagon, sign, glass, grass, pansy, marbles, purple, better, ducks, wrote, short, race, easy, painted, which, open, clerk

RUTH BLANTON
HUMBOLDT SCHOOL
KANSAS CITY, MO.

A PROJECT IN THIRD GRADE

Situation.—A teacher asked her children what they would like to do for Miss B's children who had entertained them at Easter with an egg hunt. Various suggestions were given, the most popular one being to give them a party.

Then came a discussion as to what they could do for entertainment. A program involving the regular school work was finally selected.

RECITATION PERIODS UTILIZED

A. In language:
Oral
   I. Planning for the party
      a) Subjects for discussion:
         1. What entertainment could be furnished?
         2. What must be done in preparation for the party?
      b) Technical points to be kept in during discussion:
         1. Variety of ways to begin sentences.
         2. Elimination of "and" in enumeration of things to be done.

   II. Discussions necessary at different times to check up the progress made in various lines.

   III. Teaching a poem to the entire class. One child is to be chosen to recite this on the day of the party. (A method of memorizing should be developed in these periods.)

   IV. Composing the invitation for the party:
      a) Decide what an invitation should tell.
      b) Getting variety in ways of expressing these points.

   V. Discussion of possible decorations for the room and program.

   VI. Discussion of results of handwork.

   VII. Making original stories based on pictures.
      a) Making an outline of points to cover.
      b) Deciding points to keep in mind in telling the stories.

   VIII. The telling of a story by the teacher.

   IX. Developing an organization of the foregoing story with the children to help them in retelling the story.

Written
   I. Writing the invitations to the party:
      a) The points to be covered should be recalled.
      b) Technical points to be observed should be called to mind.
      c) Original ways of expressing themselves should be encouraged.

B. In reading:

    I. Choosing those to take parts in the dramatization.

    II. Choosing those to read a story by parts.

C. In arithmetic:

    I. Deciding who will be responsible for finding out the cost of articles chosen for refreshments, for buying, and serving these.

    II. Reports from various committees on prices of articles.

    III. Estimating amounts necessary and probable cost of refreshments.

    IV. Solving original problems based on the party.

    V. Measuring for the programs.

D. In spelling:

    I. Selecting and teaching the words necessary for their invitation, program, and original stories.

E. In writing:

    I. Practicing the writing of the invitation, program, and original stories.

F. In handwork and art:

    I. Discussing possible decorations for the room, program, plates, and napkins.

    II. Developing standards for

        a) Color combinations used.

        b) Units of design.

        c) Placing of designs on the articles to be decorated.

    III. Discussing results of experimental periods and thus raising standards of work.

G. In music:

    I. Teaching and practicing songs to be used at the party. Old songs were reviewed and new ones taught, then selection of those best liked was allowed and further practice on these given.

II. Victrola favorites were suggested for the afternoon. Some of these the children were to interpret through dancing, some they were to play and have the visitors tell what familiar sounds they heard in the selection, or which of two pictures the music reminded them.

BETWEEN RECITATION PERIODS UTILIZED

A. In language:

Group work:

    I. Drilling on the poem. The one who says it best in each small group will say it before the class and from these one will be chosen to recite the poem at the party.

    II. Practicing the telling of original stories from pictures. (The outline developed in the class period and the technical points to be stressed should be kept in mind.)

    III. Retelling the story told by the teacher being careful to:

        a) Follow the organization made.

        b) Use good beginnings in their sentences.

        c) Select choice expressions.

Individual work:

    I. Writing invitations, programs, and original stories to be exhibited at the party.

B. In reading:

Group work:

    I. Discussion of stories selected for dramatization and reading by parts.

    II. Practicing the reading of selections chosen to see which children are best qualified to take the parts.

    III. Practicing by those finally chosen.

Individual work:

    I. Reading of review stories to choose the best for playing and reading by parts.

II. Practicing reading the above stories silently.

C. In arithmetic:

I. Practicing operations that will be involved in buying so as to be chosen on the purchasing committee.

II. Keeping individual scores on problems and examples based on the party, to see which ones can safely be chosen to purchase supplies.

III. To make up original problems based on the party.

D. In spelling:

I. Drilling on the words necessary for their invitations, programs, and original stories.

E. In writing:

I. Practicing the writing of the invitations, programs, and original stories.

F. In handwork and art:

I. Experimenting on the decoration of the invitations, programs, articles to be used for room decorations and for refreshments.

AS REPORTED

THE OPENING MEETING OF THE NATIONAL CONFERENCE

The first meeting of the National Conference on Educational Method was held at Atlantic City, March 1, 1921, in connection with the meeting of the Department of Superintendence of the National Education Association. The call sent out by the Program Committee included the following statement:

Among those directly concerned with the actual work of teaching there has been a growing desire for a means of unification of effort. Existing organizations are primarily concerned with other interests, and although much valuable experimentation in method is going on, there is no adequate provision for exchange of ideas and criticism in this field.

Encouraged by results obtained through conferences already held, a group of teachers and supervisors have ventured to invite others to join them in founding a permanent society for the study and promulgation of educational method. While avoiding the assumption that any particular concept of method now current may suffice for a complete synthesis, nevertheless they believe that on the laws of learning and the principles of democratic group life all educational procedure should be based, both in teaching and in the supervision of teaching.

All who are interested in the purposes of the conference are cordially invited to attend and participate in it.

When the time came for the opening of the program at the first session, the high-school auditorium, seating 600, was filled to overflowing and many were turned away. Professor William H. Kilpatrick, of Teachers College, who had been announced as chairman, was ill and sent a letter of regret and of expression of confidence in the purposes of the new organization. In his absence, the secretary, Professor James F. Hosic, then of the Chicago Normal College, presided. Before introducing the speakers he pointed out in a brief paper that educational method is an essential factor in economy. It determines the actual experience and therefore the possibilities of growth with which the pupils are provided. For this reason more attention should be devoted to the technique of learning and less to formal recitation. He thought that supervisors have a great responsibility in themselves exemplifying the methods which should be followed by pupils and teachers. With proper leadership the quality of teaching can be enormously improved. The principles of method are to be derived from modern educational psychology and from modern educational sociology. From the principles of these sciences a new synthesis of method must be made. The purpose of the new society he declared to be to give opportunity for greater participation in the discussion and report of experiments by supervisors and teachers in the field.

The program as announced was carried out except for the fact that Superintendent Fred M. Hunter, president of the National Education Association, was detained by business matters pertaining to the Department of Superintendence. This program was as follows:

FIRST SESSION

TUESDAY, MARCH 1, 9:30 A.M.

"The Scope and Significance of Educational Method"—J. F. HOSIC, Chicago Normal College.
"An Example of Method for Producing Desirable Qualities of Citizenship"—C. L. WRIGHT, superintendent of schools, Huntington, W.Va.
"A Supervisor's Experience in Directing a Tryout of the Project Method"—ROSE A. CARRIGAN, assistant director, Boston, Mass.
"Some Problems of Method in the Supervision of Teaching"—MARGARET MADDEN, principal of the Doolittle Elementary School, Chicago, Ill.
"The Possibilities of the Project Idea in the Ordinary Classroom"—FRED M. HUNTER, superintendent of schools, Oakland, Cal.

37

SECOND SESSION

TUESDAY, MARCH 1, 2 P.M.

"Administrative Conditions of Good Teaching Methods"—C. C. CERTAIN, assistant principal, Northwestern High School, Detroit, Mich.

"How We Are Evolving a New Course of Study"—EDA WILLARD, assistant superintendent of schools, Cleveland Heights, Ohio.

"How the Textbook May Aid the Teacher in Getting Projects to Going"—MARGARET NOONAN, professor of elementary education, Harris Teachers College, St. Louis, Mo.

"By Precept and Example"—ZENOS M. SCOTT, superintendent of schools, Louisville, Ky.

Since most of these papers will appear from time to time in this *Journal*, no attempt is here made to summarize them. The fact that a large audience remained until late in the afternoon to hear the last is sufficient evidence of their interest.

At the close of the morning session the following committee on organization was appointed: C. L. Wright, Huntington, West Virginia, chairman; Mary E. Pennell, Kansas City, Missouri; J. A. Starkweather, Duluth, Minnesota; W. F. Tidyman, Farmville, Virginia; Katharine Hamilton, St. Paul, Minnesota. This committee reported at the afternoon session the following constitution, which, after a brief discussion, was adopted:

CONSTITUTION OF THE NATIONAL CONFERENCE ON EDUCATIONAL METHOD

ARTICLE I

Name.—The name of this Society shall be "The National Conference on Educational Method."

ARTICLE II

Object.—The object of the Society is the improvement of supervision and teaching.

ARTICLE III

Membership.—SECTION 1. There shall be three classes of members—active, associate, and honorary.

SEC. 2. Any person who is desirous of promoting the interests of the Society is eligible to membership and may become a member by paying the annual dues, provided his application has been approved by the Executive Committee.

SEC. 3. Active members shall be entitled to vote, to hold office, to participate in discussion, and to receive the publications of the Society.

SEC. 4. Associate members shall receive the publications of the Society, and may attend its meetings, but shall not be entitled to hold office, to vote, or to take part in discussion.

SEC. 5. Honorary members shall be entitled to all the privileges of active members, with the exception of voting and holding office, but shall be exempt from the payment of dues.

A person may be elected to honorary membership by vote of the Society at the annual meeting on nomination by the Executive Committee.

SEC. 6. The annual dues of active members shall be three dollars and of associate members two dollars.

ARTICLE IV

Officers and Directors.—SECTION 1. The officers of this Society shall be a president, a vice-president, a secretary-treasurer, and an executive committee.

SEC. 2. The Executive Committee shall consist of the president, the secretary-treasurer, and three other members of the Society.

SEC. 3. The president and vice-president shall serve for a term of one year, the secretary-treasurer for three years, and the other members of the Executive Committee for three years, one to be elected each year.

SEC. 4. The Executive Committee shall have active charge of the affairs of the Society, subject to the approval of the Board of Directors.

SEC. 5. The Board of Directors shall constitute the governing body of the Society. It shall consist of fifteen members, whose term of office shall be three years, five to be elected each year at the annual meeting in such manner as the Society may determine.

The Board of Directors shall elect from their own number the officers of the Society, who shall serve also as the officers of the Board. The Board shall be the custodian of the property of the Society, shall have power to make contracts, and shall make an annual financial report to the Society.

ARTICLE V

Meetings.—The Society shall hold its annual meetings at the time and place of the Department of Superintendence of the National Education Association. Other meetings may be held when authorized by the Society or the Board of Directors.

ARTICLE VI

Publications.—The Society shall publish a journal and such supplements as the Executive Committee may provide for.

ARTICLE VII

Amendments.—This constitution may be amended at any annual meeting by a vote of two-thirds of the active members present.

On motion the Committee on Organization was nominated as members of the new Board of Directors and instructed to select ten other names. The new Board as finally constituted is as follows: C. C. Certain, assistant principal and head of Department of English, Northwestern High School, Detroit, Michigan; Bessie Bacon Goodrich, director of elementary education, Des Moines, Iowa; J. M. Gwinn, superintendent of schools, New Orleans, Louisiana; Katharine Hamilton, assistant superintendent of schools, St. Paul, Minnesota; James F. Hosic, associate professor of education in charge of extramural courses, Teachers College, Columbia University; Fred M. Hunter, superintendent of schools, Oakland, California; William H. Kilpatrick, professor of philosophy of education, Teachers College, Columbia University; Margaret Madden, principal, Doolittle Elementary School, Chicago, Illinois; F. M. McMurry, professor of elementary education, Teachers College, Columbia University; Margaret Noonan, professor of elementary education, Harris Teachers College, St. Louis, Missouri; Mary E. Pennell, supervisor of primary grades, Kansas City, Missouri; J. A. Starkweather, assistant superintendent of schools, Duluth, Minnesota; W. F. Tidyman, director of the training school, State Normal School, Farmville, Virginia; John W. Withers, dean of School of Education, New York University; C. L. Wright, superintendent of schools, Huntington, West Virginia.

The Board met the next day at the Traymore Hotel and in accordance with the constitution elected the officers and members of the Executive Committee as follows: officers— president, C. L. Wright, Huntington, West Virginia; vice-president, Margaret Noonan, St. Louis, Missouri; secretary-treasurer, James F. Hosic, New York City. Executive Committee — the president and the secretary ex officio: C. C. Certain, Detroit, Michigan; Margaret Madden, Chicago, Illinois; Mary E. Pennell, Kansas City, Missouri.

The main topic of discussion at the meeting of the Board was the advisability of establishing a periodical as the organ of the Conference. It was at length decided to undertake the publication of a magazine to be issued monthly during the school year under the editorship of Dr. Hosic, secretary-treasurer of the Conference. Two dollars for each membership will be set aside for the publishing fund.

The business office of the Conference and of the *Journal* will be at 506 W. 69th Street, Chicago, Illinois. Communications for the editor should be addressed to Teachers College, Columbia University, New York City. The *Journal* will be issued so as to reach subscribers on the first of each month from September to June, inclusive.

THE NATIONAL ASSOCIATION OF ELEMENTARY SCHOOL PRINCIPALS OUTLINES ITS PLANS AND PURPOSES

For many years progressive elementary-school principals have been working out advanced methods of instructions for their schools, but this professional group as a whole has been advancing very slowly because it did not have a central organization which could give to each principal the results of the studies of other principals. The National Association of Elementary-School Principals has been organized in order that progressive principals may have a means of communication; in order that the younger principals may have easy access to the work and studies of the older principals; and in order that the principals may meet once a year and discuss their problems.

For many years there have been programs at the National Education Association meeting and at the Department of Superintendence meeting which included talks and papers dealing with the problems of the elementary school. Very infrequently, however, did these papers deal with the problems of elementary-school principals. Therefore the principals have organized a separate society.

This organization is not going to strive for a large membership merely to exhibit a long list of names, but every principal in the United States who desires to learn what other principals are doing or who desires to tell other principals what he is doing, will find this organization ready to help him. Until the volume of contributions from principals is increased to a point where a separate journal or bulletin would be sure of sufficient materials, contributions will be sent to journals and professional periodicals now being published. The present plan is for the principals to send their contributions to the office of the president, Leonard Power, at the Franklin School, Port Arthur, Texas, or for the authors who have easy access to periodicals to inform the office of the president of the name of the journal and the issue in which their articles will appear.

The policies and purposes of the organization as tentatively outlined by President Power are as follows:

1. This Association shall put into the hands of all of its members a monthly bibliography of articles and books in which the problems of the elementary-school principal are treated.

2. The program committee of this organization shall provide the best educational talent available for a full-day program at the yearly meeting.

3. The Association shall exert every influence to have principals study special phases of their problems with great care and to send the results of their work in the form of an article to an educational periodical.

4. The Association shall endeavor to lead graduate students to choose problems of the elementary school for their major graduate work and to plan to return to the elementary schools after taking higher degrees.

5. The Association shall present to each member a monthly review of the problems that are being studied by other elementary-school principals.

6. The Association reserves the right to issue a Yearbook which shall contain the results of studies made by special committees.

7. In every way the Association shall stimulate the talent of all educators to a deeper study of the problems of the principal.

8. Each member of the Association is pledged to give the best of his ability to his daily work and the best results of his special studies to the entire profession.

The officers of the organization are: president, Leonard Power, Port Arthur, Texas; first vice-president, Catherine Blake, New York City; second vice-president, Ide Sergeant, Patterson, New Jersey; third vice-president, M. J. Kneisley, Seattle, Washington; receiving secretary, Mary W. Reisse, Philadelphia, Pennsylvania; corresponding secretary, J. Bracken, Duluth, Minnesota; treasurer, Courtland Davis, principal, J. E. B. Stuart School, Norfolk, Virginia.

The membership fee is $2.00. The $2.00 membership fee is payable after the membership fee to the National Education Association has been paid. Otherwise the membership fee is $4.00, $2.00 of which will be sent to the National Education Association. LEONARD POWER, *President*

THE ANNUAL MEETING OF THE KINDERGARTEN UNION

The Twenty-eighth Annual Meeting of the International Kindergarten Union was held at the Hotel Statler in Detroit, May 2-6. Matters of more than usual importance were considered, both by the speakers on the program and by those who participated in the business meetings. Among the addresses were the following: "Kindergarten a Factor in Democratic Education," by Randall J. Condon, of Cincinnati, Ohio; "The Responsibility of the School for the Child's Health," Dr. Arnold Gesell, Yale University; "Health Standards in the Modern Kindergarten," by Professor Patty S. Hill, of Teachers College; "Educational Measurement in Detroit," by Stuart A. Courtis, president of the Detroit Teachers College; "The Project an Adaptation of a Life-Method of Thought and Action," also by Professor Hill. A number of committees made reports, including reports on supervision, on college curricula, on child study, on testing kindergarten and primary children, on kindergarten extension, on co-operation with the National Education Association, on the project method in kindergarten education. Steps were taken to improve state organizations and to bring about closer relations with the National Congress of Mothers. The president of the Convention was Miss Nina C. Vande-

walker, of the Bureau of Education at Washington, and the secretary, Miss Edna D. Baker, of the International Kindergarten College, Chicago.

THE SUMMER MEETING OF THE NATIONAL EDUCATION ASSOCIATION

The regular summer meeting of the National Education Association will this year be held in Des Moines, July 3–8. President Hunter and Secretary Crabtree have prepared an excellent program and there is the added interest of the first gathering under the reorganization or delegate plan. Des Moines will entertain in hospitable fashion.

The general theme of the meeting is the American program of education. This will be considered in a series of symposiums, each confined to a single viewpoint, as that of the principal, the classroom teacher, the college, and the normal school. Several important standing committees will report. Among the notables to appear are Vice-President Coolidge and Judge Towner.

THE READER'S GUIDE

SIGNIFICANT ARTICLES

HORACE MANN STUDIES IN EDUCATION

"The Horace Mann Studies in Elementary Education," the first instalment of which appeared in the *Teachers College Record* for March, 1919, are being continued from time to time. Under date of January, 1921, Charles F. Smith and Elbert K. Fretwell describe a very interesting experiment in the organization of clubs for young boys. In the third grade the boys called themselves Eaglets and arranged four degrees as follows: Egg, Fledgling, Flier, and Hunter, each with its appropriate achievements. The fourth-graders were the Silver Eagles; the fifth-graders, the Golden Eagles; and the sixth-graders, the Wolf Pack. This modification and extension of the boy-scout idea to younger boys contains great possibilities and deserves wide imitation.

In the number for March, 1921, Miss Marie Hennes contributes an account of project teaching in advanced fifth grade. The pupils were led at the very outset in September to organize their own program of work. They set up specific aims and arranged for the distribution of time. Among the things learned were how to make a budget, how to use a check book, and how to write letters. The most satisfactory application of the project idea seems to have been to the study of current events, with the corresponding development of subject-matter in civics, history, geography, and science. A number of testimonies from the children indicate that they had a lively sense of the value of the experiment.

THE PANAMA CANAL AS AN EIGHTH-GRADE PROJECT

Worth McClure and Emma D. Stone, of the Gatewood School, Seattle, Washington, report in the *Elementary School Journal* for April, 1921, the attempt of some children in the eighth grade to make a model of the Panama Canal. The work grew out of the study of commercial and industrial geography and required an elaborate "engineering" staff to direct the project. The girls, it seems, became especially interested in studying the vegetation, while the boys were working on the locks. The whole seems to have been rather in the nature of a by-product than one of the principal factors of the course.

A PROJECT IN ENGLISH COMPOSITION

A newspaper clipping a few months ago gave rise to a project in letter-writing in a school located in Michigan. Mr. George S. Lasher, of the University of Michigan, who gives the account, says that the clipping told how a mother and her fifteen-year-old daughter were injured while on their way to the husband and father, who was seriously ill at their home in the South. The report of the accident contained so much human interest that the pupils in one of the classes in the school were touched by it and desired to write letters to the injured girl. Mr. Lasher also describes at some length the making of a book about Chicago, by a class of pupils in the University High School, when he was a teacher there. His accounts are accompanied by a running comment on the value of such work. The article is to be found in the *Bulletin* of the Illinois Association of Teachers of English for April 1, which is to be obtained from Professor Harry G. Paul, 322 Lincoln Hall, Urbana, Illinois.

SETTING UP SCHOOL STANDARDS

Speaking with special reference to English but in the light of general principles, Mr. C. E. Douglass, newly elected assistant superintendent of schools in Baltimore, Maryland, says, with regard to school standards, that they are to be determined by three considerations, namely, educational aims, the demands of society, and the kind and degree of mental abilities of the students. The important educational aim is not knowledge nor mental power, but behavior. Hence the English sanctum must be defended against depredations of both intellectual aristocrats and intellectual acrobats. Democracy demands that we make good citizens of all, and the war has left us with a growing conviction that intelligence can be measured with a sufficient degree of accuracy to make possible a reasonable forecast of one's range of achievements. Recently one of the more progressive among educators has declared that by and by we shall give credit to graduates of high school and college in proportion to their relative attainments. To do this we must add to tests of intelligence more rational measures of achievement. Mr. Douglass' article may be read in full in *Education* for April.

SUPERVISED STUDY OF HISTORY

One of the very best of the periodicals issued by state teachers' associations is the journal of the New York Association, published at Rochester. A sample of the suggestive contributions in this magazine is the outline on "Supervised Study of History," by Mabel E. Simpson in the April number. After arguing the need of revision of the teaching of history, Miss Simpson presents some of the elements of method in supervised study. She quotes from Dr. McMurry the main factors in study and recognizes the project-problem method as a means of motivation. She would use varied types of lessons, and urges teachers to make careful preparation for that. Finally, she turns to the elements of supervised study which involve content. The teacher must know the course of study, must train the children to regard the textbook as an instrument or tool, and must make intelligent use of collateral reading. This last point is illustrated by means of the work of a class in community civics, which gathered much valuable material among the dusty archives of the city hall.

THE NEW EDUCATION

In the *Nation* for Wednesday, May 4, appears the first of a series of articles on the new education, by Evelyn Dewey, entitled "Its Trend and Purpose." Miss Dewey analyzes the critics of our educational practice into two classes, those who complain that things are not as they used to be and those who complain that they are. The former bewail the passing of hard work, the training of the memory, and attention to the individual. She thinks it is a fact that in our modern system there is too much dealing with children in the mass. There are, however, far more sweeping changes necessary because of three great factors in modern civilization, namely, increase in scientific knowledge, the resulting industrial system, and our democratic form of government. The first makes specialization necessary. Nobody can know everything. Education, therefore, must consist rather in learning to learn. Instead of merely reading from books, pupils must be able to use them and to go beyond them. There must be the opportunity for that kind of concrete experience which used to be possible in the farm and village life of the old days. It must be of such a character too as to give opportunity for the development of initiative. Democracy demands the opportunity of participation on the part of everyone.

A REAL BOOK[1]

This is a real book. A review of it can have but one justification—to get people to read it. To pile it high with praise will not have the desired effect. Nobody will accept the reviewer's estimate. Everybody makes allowances for reviews as he does for newspaper headlines. A reviewer might grow hortatory and urge teachers to get the book on the pain of a great loss in failing to read it. But that is an old attitude and teachers no longer revere

---

[1] *A Project Curriculum*, dealing with the project as a means of organizing the curriculum of the elementary school, by Margaret Elizabeth Wells, Ph.D. J. B. Lippincott Co., Philadelphia and London, 1921.

authorities. An analysis of the contents might serve as basis for a study in comparative book anatomy. But the book is a living thing. Let us see what the book does and how well it does it.

.The book, in spite of its forbidding title, tells a very interesting story about a most interesting educational experiment. The author, Miss Wells, planned and, with the aid of student teachers, carried out the experiment in the Training School of the State Normal School at Trenton, New Jersey. She evidently started out to do something real in the school. She accomplished this by arranging that the children of the first three grades should visit the state fair held at Trenton. With this common experience insured to all the pupils, the fair became a topic of conversation and discussion. Then it was decided to have a fair in the school. Of course it was a children's fair, but a real one, none the less. Older people would call it "playing fair." So would the children, under the influence of their elders. But the children had the kind of a fair that they would create and manage.

After the fair had been held, it was impossible to go back to the formal curriculum. So the first grade was led to play family, the second to play store, the third to play city. And they played, and they played, and they played, until the school year was over. The leader of the whole experience and the author of the book says: "Thus ended the happiest year the writer has ever spent in the schoolroom; and she has reason to believe that nearly 100 per cent of the children were just as happy." If you want to know what the children did the whole year, you will have to read the book.

There are 335 pages in the book. One hundred and thirty-four pages are given to the account of how the children played fair, and then family, store, and city. Then follows (so much for anatomy) a section devoted to "Theses Underlying This Curriculum and an Evaluation of Each." This section covers 65 pages and carries us to page 201. The theses set forth in formal fashion the principles on

which the experimenter-author rests her defense for allowing the children to have a fair and play family, store, and city for a whole year. They form a good defense, especially for meeting a faculty requirement for a doctor's degree.

There is a third section to the book covering pages 202-28. This amounts to a collection of quotations from authorities on education with comments by the author and her final formulation of ten working principles for teaching. If you want to know what these principles are, you will have to read the book.

Section 4 follows. This is a very interesting analysis of the results, achievements, outcomes of the experiment viewed as a curriculum as compared with other more traditional or conventional curricula. This section, with section 1, which describes the experiment, constitutes the heart of the book and the author's contribution to educational literature. There follows a valuable appendix of materials produced and used in the school and a useful index.

This is not only a real book, it is a very significant one. It records achievement. The reviewer wishes to say what he thinks is significant in the experiment described.

First, the year's work in the school maintained the organic unity of the school life and the extra-school life of the children. This is the fundamental principle on which the curriculum of the elementary school should be based. School life is not to copy, nor to tell about, extra-school life. It should rather continue, enlarge, and re-enforce outside life. The unity of the curriculum in the child's experience is not to be secured by an artificial plaiting of the strands of the traditional school subjects, by correlation and the like, but precisely by the opposite procedure. The unity is there already, resting on the organized family and community life into which the child is being incorporated. The school does not introduce children into society. They are already there when the school gets them and they remain there after the school has them.

Not to destroy but to expand and illuminate this outside life is the chief function of the school. To be successful in this work, the school must take the position of the child's developing experience within a given social situation, work with that experience so as not to introduce conflict, confusion, failure, but rather unity, order, success, and joy. This is what Miss Wells did in her experiment. Check me up and see for yourself.

Again, the dualism between play and work was removed. Educators have spent decades establishing the meaning and legitimacy of play in the world of·children and, finally, of grown-ups. It was necessary to do so in order to get rid of false notions and values. But we have reached a point where the distinction between work and play is increasingly hard to maintain and is practically valueless. Children live their lives in an adult world, working their way into it by the use of their immature powers and the materials they can manipulate. But there is nothing unreal or artificial in their work, which we call play. The experiment of Miss Wells may be called playing family, store, city, and the like. In reality it was living and reliving family, store, and city in terms of the children's powers and interests.

Lastly, the experiment, just because it was so well carried on and carefully reported, shows how all the traditional school subjects come in when such a large and inclusive kind of life is carried on in and out of school. This is one of the most valuable parts of the book and will amply reward the teacher who seeks help in organizing work of this type. It will go far also to persuade critics of the project-method that their fears are, in part at least, groundless. Children will probably learn more in the same time by the new methods than by the old—and some very valuable things which they can learn in no other way.

We are going to have a new elementary school, a new curriculum, a new technique, a new life. Miss Wells has made a fundamental contribution toward this new school.

WILLIAM BISHOP OWEN

THE NEW BOOKS

Brightness and Dullness in Children. By Herbert Woodrow. Philadelphia: J. B. Lippincott Co., 1920. Pp. 322.

A very clear and readable book on the use of intelligence tests.

Child Life and the Curriculum. By Junius L. Meriam. Yonkers-on-Hudson: World Book Co., 1920. Pp. xii+538.

A full account of the work of the experimental school at the University of Missouri and an exposition of the principles on which it is based.

The Elementary School Curriculum. By Frederick G. Bonser. New York: Macmillan Co., 1920. Pp. 466.

Principles for the selection of materials and practical applications, with emphasis on the project point of view.

The Essentials of Good Teaching. By Edwin A. Turner. With an Introduction by Lotus D. Coffman. Boston: D. C. Heath &·Co., 1921. Pp. xiv+271.

A general analysis for use in normal schools.

Essentials of English for Higher Grades. By Henry C. Pearson and Mary F. Kirchwey. New York: American Book Co., 1920. Pp. x+469.

Modern exercises in composition are interspersed with applied lessons in grammar.

The Fundamental Principles of Learning and Study. By A. S. Edwards. Baltimore: Warwick and York, 1920. Pp. 239.

A compilation based upon the best modern authorities but not well displayed.

The Horn-Ashbaugh Speller. By Ernest Horn and Ernest J. Ashbaugh. Philadelphia: J. B. Lippincott Co., 1921. Pp. 105.

A method speller, containing a selected and graded list.

How to Measure. By G. M. Wilson and Kremer J. Hoke. New York: Macmillan Co., 1920. Pp. 285.

An elementary treatment intended to be used in the giving of diagnostic lists by classroom teachers.

Lessons on the Use of Books and Libraries. By O. S. Rice. Chicago: Rand, McNally & Co., 1920. Pp. 178.

A textbook for pupils in higher grades and secondary schools. Useful for teachers.

Methods and Results of Testing School Children.
By Evelyn Dewey, Emily Child, and
Beardsley Ruml. New York: E. P. Dutton
& Co., 1920.
A description of the lists used in an investigation
of certain New York City schools.

The Nation and the Schools. By John A. H.
Keith and William C. Bagley. New York:
Macmillan Co., 1920. Pp. 364.
A study in the application of federal aid to educa-
tion in the United States.

New Voices. By Marguerite Wilkinson. New
York: Macmillan Co., 1920.
An introduction to contemporary poetry.

Outstanding Days. By Cheesman A. Herrick.
Philadelphia: Union Press, 1920. Pp. 282.
Selections relating to the anniversaries.

A Project Curriculum. By Margaret E. Wells.
Philadelphia: J. B. Lippincott Co., 1921.
Pp. ix+338.
The first account of a full curriculum for the
early grades on a project basis.

Project Work in Education. By James L.
Stockton. Boston: Houghton Mifflin Co.,
1920. Pp. 167.
Largely historical. The author conceives of projects in the sense of matter as well as method.

Psychology for Teachers. By Daniel W. LaRue.
New York: American Book Co., 1920.
Pp. 316.
A very simple exposition with abundant exercises
both before and after each chapter, together with
selected references.

The Silent Readers, Grades Four to Eight. By
W. D. Lewis and A. L. Rowland. Philadelphia: J. C. Winston Co., 1920.
A series of readers containing chiefly short prose
selections arranged for practice and testing in silent
reading.

The Test and Study Speller. By Daniel Starch
and George A. Mirick. Boston: Silver,
Burdett & Co., 1921. Pp. 63.
A study and test speller based upon several
investigations. For Grades V and VI.

The Worker and His Work. By Stella S.
Center. Philadelphia: J. B. Lippincott
Co., 1920. Pp. 350. Illustrated.
A literary presentation of vocations. The selec-
tions are taken from contemporary books and maga-
zines.

IN PAPER COVERS

*Twentieth Yearbook of the National Society for
the Study of Education.* Part I, Second
Report of the Society's Committee on New
Materials of Instruction. $1.30.
Contains 250 brief accounts of classroom activities.

Part II, Report of the Society's Committee
on Silent Reading. $1.10.
Miscellaneous studies edited by Professor Ernest
Horn, chairman of the Committee.

Sample Projects. First and second series.
Edited by James F. Hosic. $0.50 each.
To be obtained from the Editor at 506 W.
69th St., Chicago.
Somewhat detailed descriptions of about thirty
projects in various subjects, together with outlines for
critical study.

*Lessons in Civics for the Six Elementary Grades
of City Schools.* By Hanna Margaret
Harris. Bulletin 1920, No. 18, Bureau of
Education, Washington, D.C.
A detailed and highly suggestive outline.

*Standard Requirements for Memorizing Liter-
ary Material.* By Velda C. Barnesberger.
University of Illinois Bulletin No. 26. $0.50.
Based on an examination of fifty courses of study.

*List of Books for Township Libraries in the
State of Wisconsin, 1920–22.* Issued by
C. P. Cary, state superintendent, Madison.

A Syllabus of High-School English. Department of Public Instruction, Bismarck, North
Dakota.

*Minimal Essentials in Composition and Gram-
mar for the Elementary School, Grades One
to Eight.* Fifth Report of the Inland Empire
Council of Teachers of English. Published
by Intermountain Educator, Missoula, Montana. $0.15.

*The Future of the Scarborough School, Scarbor-
ough School Aims, Educational Principles,
Subject-Matter and the Program of Studies,
Mental Measurement, English, Social Studies.*
A series of monographs by W. M. Aikin,
Scarborough-on-Hudson, New York.

*Course of Study in English for the Elementary
Schools of Detroit.* By Clara Beverly, Rege-
nia P. Heller, S. A. Courtis, and Committees
of Teachers. Detroit Board of Education.

The Journal

of

Educational Method

Volume 1   OCTOBER, 1921   Number 2

CONTENTS

THE NATIONAL CONFERENCE ON EDUCATIONAL METHOD
506 West Sixty-ninth Street, CHICAGO, ILLINOIS
$3.00 a year   Monthly Except July and August   35 cents a copy
Application for entrance as second-class matter has been made at the post-office at Chicago, Illinois,
under the Act of March 3, 1879

THE NATIONAL CONFERENCE ON EDUCATIONAL METHOD

An Association of Persons Interested in Supervision and Teaching

Officers of the Conference

President, C. L. WRIGHT, Public Schools, Huntington, West Virginia.
Vice-President, MARGARET NOONAN, Harris Teachers College, St. Louis, Missouri.
Secretary-Treasurer, JAMES F. HOSIC, Teachers College, New York City.

Executive Committee

THE PRESIDENT AND THE SECRETARY-TREASURER, *ex officio*.
C. C. CERTAIN, Northwestern High School, Detroit, Michigan.
MARGARET MADDEN, Doolittle Elementary School, Chicago, Illinois.
MARY E. PENNELL, Public Schools, Kansas City, Missouri.

Board of Directors

C. C. CERTAIN, Assistant Principal and Head of Department of English, Northwestern High School, Detroit, Michigan.

BESSIE GOODRICH, Assistant Superintendent of Schools, Des Moines, Ia.

J. M. GWINN, Superintendent of Schools, New Orleans, La.

KATHARINE HAMILTON, Assistant Superintendent of Schools, St. Paul, Minn.

JAMES F. HOSIC, Associate Professor of Education in Charge of Extramural Courses, Teachers College, Columbia University.

FRED M. HUNTER, Superintendent of Schools, Oakland, Calif.

WILLIAM H. KILPATRICK, Professor of Philosophy of Education, Teachers College, Columbia University.

MARGARET MADDEN, Principal, Doolittle Elementary School, Chicago, Ill.

F. M. McMURRY, Professor of Elementary Education, Teachers College, Columbia University.

MARGARET NOONAN, Professor of Elementary Education, Harris Teachers College, St. Louis, Missouri.

MARY E. PENNELL, Supervisor of Primary Grades, Kansas City, Mo.

J. A. STARKWEATHER, Assistant Superintendent of Schools, Duluth, Minn.

W. F. TIDYMAN, Director of the Training School, State Normal School, Farmville, Va.

JOHN W. WITHERS, Dean of School of Education, New York University.

C. L. WRIGHT, Superintendent of Schools, Huntington, W. Va.

Address applications for membership to the Secretary of the Conference, 506 West Sixty-ninth Street, Chicago, Illinois. The fee for active members is $3.00, for associate members, $2.00; $2.00 in each case is applied to the support of the Journal, for which each member receives a year's subscription. The editorial office is at 525 West One Hundred and Twentieth Street, New York City.

The Journal of Educational Method

VOLUME 1   OCTOBER, 1921   NUMBER 2

EDITORIALLY SPEAKING

TIMELY

The response to the first issue of *The Journal of Educational Method* is most reassuring. "There is a place for this new journal," says one well-known editor. "I will do anything I can to help it along," says another. "This first number is a very valuable contribution," is the comment of a school superintendent. In one large city every principal of an elementary school is enrolled in the Conference and will read the *Journal*. In similar fashion the faculty of one of the two best-known state normal schools in the United States has joined as a body. There seems to be a general recognition of the fact that in the long run it is method and not material equipment that makes the school. Method is, of course, greatly aided by equipment, but equipment without effective method is all but worthless. The numerous letters from editors of the excellent state and city periodicals scattered through the country, welcoming a serious journal of method in teaching and in supervision, which have been received, are particularly gratirying. What better provision for their professional reading could principals and their teachers make than a subscription to their state organ and one to *The Journal of Educational Method?* For the encouragement so warmly extended by our brother-editors, our best thanks.

PRINCIPLES VS. PATTERNS

For quick and easily obtained results use a formula. If you seek continued growth, inculcate ideas. Educational leaders are always confronted by those two alternatives. Some choose the former. They talk naïvely of "introducing" this or that procedure or newest educational wrinkle into their schools much as they do of installing a new heating-plant or a new system of accounting. "Supervised study" and the "socialized recitation" are notable examples. One principal announced gravely, "On November 18 we will begin supervised study in our school." Yet the report of one of the most thorough-going investigations of the plan of supervised study shows that it is only in case the teacher is fully alive to his opportunity and has adequate training in the technique of directing study that any appreciable good comes of lengthened periods and other devices employed in what is called supervised study. There is no substitute for working ideas. Those who attempt a short cut by the presentation of patterns instead of the inculcation of principles are deceiving themselves. Education of children requires something more than mere *training* of teachers. Fads are a poor substitute for philosophy. The best type of direction is genuinely intelligent self-direction.

A SUPERVISOR'S EXPERIENCE IN DIRECTING A TRY-OUT OF THE PROJECT METHOD

ROSE A. CARRIGAN
Supervisor of Shurtleff District, Boston, Mass.

It is always a great joy to speak about a matter concerning which one has a deep-seated conviction. It is therefore with very great pleasure that I shall recount a bit of personal experience in attempting to arouse a group of uninitiated teachers and to give each a whole-hearted purpose to develop a project activity in her own classroom. The story is by no means unique. Undoubtedly many progressive supervisors are today absorbingly interested in their own project of finding a way to introduce learning through projects into schools where as yet the method applied to education is either unknown or else doomed to vigorous opposition at the start. Those who believe that the *method* of teaching is highly important are already asking themselves the question, "How can we get the project method of learning launched in schools of the traditional type?" The purpose of my paper is to offer at least one answer to this question.

A REASON FOR MY GRIPPING INTEREST

My own deep-seated conviction regarding the value of the project method of instruction in our schools has grown out of my complete confidence in democratic living. Some one has called this democracy of ours "the great social experiment of civilization." Perhaps it is still in the experimental stage but certainly a subsequent stage of great positive achievement awaits it if we but provide for its direction competent, well-qualified leaders and supply these with loyal, right-thinking, happy followers. Failing of such provision, our great democracy stands in grave danger and imminent peril. The remedy lies within the power of school authorities and must be applied in schoolrooms of the present day. With us rests the great responsibility of providing the able leaders and intelligent followers who can stem the disrupting tide and carry this great nation on to future accomplishments for humanity, the greatness of which outdistances all powers of prediction.

Right and effective ways of democratic living cannot be acquired over night. Rather they are subject to the laws of habit-building. They grow with the child. They grow more beautifully when fostering and pruning are administered day by day by the understanding teacher who has been especially trained in the art of guiding, whose chief business is guidance. This, as I see it, is a strong argument *against* an autocracy and *for* a democracy in the schoolroom. Such democratic living in the school can be promoted by the project method of instruction. It is because of this feature of the work that learning through projects has held me with gripping interest. A great love of democracy and an unbounded belief in its possibilities for good tend to lead progressive supervisors to a try-out of the project method of instruction, a setting up within the classroom of democratic procedure under the expert guidance of the teacher.

WAYS IN WHICH THE PROJECT METHOD OF INSTRUCTION MAY BE INTRODUCED INTO SCHOOLS OF THE TRADITIONAL TYPE

Various ways have been suggested by which the project method of learning may be introduced into schools of the traditional type. Those which I shall mention are said to have been successfully used in Detroit. They have succeeded in Boston and have been introduced in other places. They are:

First, voluntary preparation by the teacher. Incentives may be provided through regular courses at normal schools and institute instruction such as Detroit offers.

Second, a lecture approach. This is a convenient means if teachers are organized into a club or an association. It has succeeded well in Detroit.

Third, a course of instruction offered for the upgrading of teachers, that is, for their improved professional preparation during service. This plan has been used effectively in Boston.

Fourth, by special appeal to individual teachers, who, in the judgement of the supervisor, are well adapted to introduce an innovation with success. This plan is common wherever experimentation has the sanction of the school community and the supervisory officers. It involves, besides a judicious choice of the teachers who are to make the try-out, a tactful setting forth of the aim to the teaching force, and such diplomatic promotion of the extension of the experiment as will prevent struggles which sometimes hamper the growth of a worthy cause.

Fifth, through grade meetings at which are displayed objective results of exceptionally fine projects worked out by the few who have shown early interest. In this connection the use of moving pictures illustrating certain steps in the project activity are most useful. To carry out this plan the full sanction of principals of buildings is necessary.

Sixth, through library and museum exhibits of tangible achievements. These may prove highly suggestive as the work progresses. They have been effectively used in Boston, Detroit, and other places.

Frequently it becomes necessary to undertake a definite campaign to enlist the favorable attitude of principals of buildings and the sanction and co-operation of school communities. In this connection a committee with which I was associated last summer recommended the following:

1. A judicious use of the press in reporting teachers' meetings of importance and current school projects. It might even provide for a school column carried on as a school project or a city or town project.

2. Demonstration and discussion of school projects on the occasion of parents' day.

3. Addresses before clubs, institutes, and teacher-parent associations.

4. Avoidance of criticism because of lack of balance or perspective in the work by giving proper place to such factors as skill in reading, writing, spelling, and arithmetic.

5. Project exhibits at county or state fairs.

A SUPERVISOR'S EXPERIENCE IN COMMU-
    NICATING THE PROJECT METHOD

My own approach to the introduction of the project method came about through a course of instruction which I gave in the fall of 1919 for the up-grading of teachers in the service. It was made possible by a regulation of the school board of our city. Teachers who have taught two years or five years receive their next increment in salary only by satisfactorily meeting a requirement of additional preparation. Part of this requirement is fulfilled by successful accomplishment in courses sanctioned or provided by the city school authorities. Courses offered at colleges of standing are, of course, among those which receive the city's sanction. Candidates for promotional credit are free to make their own choice of courses. I was requested by the assistant superintendent who had charge of promotional credit to give a course on the project method. I advertised not the project method, but the problem-project method, because I wanted to have it well understood that the course would include projects which might be purely intellectual. Now it happened that I once taught in our city normal school and that during the closing years of my work there my subject was methods in arithmetic. You will readily see, then, why some of the younger teachers who chose my promotional course came thinking I was going to give them some sage advice on how to get their classes to solve arithmetic problems. I mention this circumstance that you may realize how little disposition to investigate the project method was present the first night of our meeting. We began our course by getting answers to a little questionnaire, and I thereby found that, with the exception of one person, not a teacher in my class knew the slightest thing about the project method applied to education or had ever even heard of it. A later testimony of a member of the class, given after the close of the course at a meeting of prevocational teachers, was that the project idea seemed so foreign to this particular group of teachers at the start, that for the first few lessons they were wholly uninterested in the work and even tempted to give it up, but as the course progressed their growing enthusiasm was matched only by that of their own pupils, who were soon carrying

out purposeful activities with surprising zeal.

Very early in the promotional course the teachers adopted as their own project, the launching and carrying on of a project in each teacher's classroom. We discussed the possibilities, set a night for reports from each on preliminary happenings in their own classes, and when the night arrived we gave our collective judgments as to the wisdom of the projects which the children had expressed a desire to undertake. As a result, very many acceptable ones were soon in full swing. We met two evenings a week and consulted about all difficulties that arose in any classroom and shared the news of little successes. Experiences thus recounted gave courage to the faint-hearted. At each meeting I offered what counsel I could and was able besides to add a little to a clearer understanding of the fundamental philosophy of project work and the essential characteristics of its application in various specific situations. No reading was required, though a selected bibliography was given for use by such enthusiasts as might wish to read, but it was understood that the teacher's energy was needed for the experimental project going on in her classroom. It was not long before the group purpose was somewhat recast. It now became a purpose to make a genuine contribution to education in the form of a collaborated account in print of their own classroom experiences related to learning through projects. As a result several good manuscripts were written.

It will be seen from my account that the teachers who conducted this work so successfully were just the rank and file of teachers in a large city system. They were not a picked group, enamored of the project method or unmistakably characterized by college-degree ambitions. Yet they became centers of influence to nearby teachers. If time allowed, I could tell you how, in each school district where they taught, other teachers were inveigled into trying to follow their example. Most of the enticement came through their own pupils who pleaded in some such words as, "Please can't we have a civic league like Miss Ford's children?" or "Can't we have a milk campaign and gather booklets like Miss Harrington's class?" Sometimes the teacher was urged out of a mere *pretense* at project activity when children in a neighboring class where a *real* project was under way asked if they could not help her children to get material as they did not seem to know how to find it for themselves. And thus the leaven had begun to work.

A few of the projects undertaken may prove of interest. One fourth grade adopted a project in connection with its study of "Typical Regions and Centers Related to Boston" (a requirement of the course of study). The children called it, "Finding Out Who Are South Boston's Providers and Friends." The working out of this project brought about many visits to neighborhood stores, a canvass of household food and clothing for evidence of sources of supply, a classification of knowledge thus obtained, the making of individual and class scrapbooks, and much other self-directed activity productive of definite progress in work prescribed for the grade. The teacher, a tiny, gentle lady, reported night after night her utter amazement at what her children could do.

Another fourth-grade project was connected with the work required in the hygiene of food and drink. This was called, "A Milk Campaign." It culminated in a play, "The Milk Fairies." The teacher recounted an amusing incident of a little girl who tried to secure from the Whiting Milk Company a large milk bottle she had seen on the top of their building. She wanted one large enough to allow several children to enter. She made a number of visits to the store and finally the Company responded to the child's request by sending from the factory a large cardboard bottle which had doors that opened and closed. Her delight was unbounded, for had she not contributed much to the success of the play? The follow-up activity of the children accomplished a great increase in milk drinking by the members of the class. All either acquired newly or increased a milk-drinking habit.

An interesting fifth-grade project was built around a kind of slogan, "We live in the schoolroom five hours a day, why not make it a pleasant place in which to work?" This project connected definitely with the grade requirement in history concerning the stories of some of the chief settlements on the American coast and the lives of a few of our great American leaders. Learning directly connected with requirements of their course of study in English and science were by-products. The work brought about the formation of many committees which assumed various responsibilities such as fresh decorations for every holiday, letters of invitation, and letters requesting information. There were also many other accomplishments which could be checked off on the prescribed work of the grade. A lecturer from the Art Museum answered a request from the class for a lecture on the Pilgrims. At first she had asked the privilege of lecturing on a different subject because she had so few pictures of the Pilgrims, but the chairman of the committee refused to accept a substitute lecture; so she brought what pictures she could get and supplied his demand.

A sixth grade made an excellent magazine. This project improved the children's command of English to a surprising degree. The boy who had never exerted an effort in school in his life got himself elected chairman of the Joke Committee. The jokes steadily improved in point and also in their connection with school-life interests.

Another sixth grade formed a Junior Civic League, and much of their activity connected in vital ways with both community civics and personal hygiene. One parent, who had persistently refused to supply his child with much-needed glasses, yielded to the persuasive arguments of her classmates and the glasses were forthcoming. Dental care was given to every tooth in the room that needed attention.

Many more illustrations of the projects guided by these, until then, uninitiated teachers might be given. Those already mentioned, however, will suffice to indicate the types of activities which were launched in their classes in the first bloom of their interest in the possibilities of learning through projects.

CHECKING THE RESULTS OF STIMULUS

The first promotional course already described was a general course involving the fundamental philosophy and the principles of application. It was followed in the fall of last year by other promotional courses dealing with project work in specific fields of teaching, such as primary grades, manual arts, oral expression, and history. Previously, a stimulus had been created in the primary grades by the work of a small committee which had sought to bridge the gap between the kindergarten and the first primary grade. This committee had prepared a small pamphlet, published as a school document, which suggested projects for Grade I.

Prevocational teachers of shop and academic classes has been stirred to activity by the leadership of their zealous special supervisor and by the lecture appeal.

Recently the results of the various causes of stimulation have become strongly apparent. Teachers of every grade, the high-school group inclusive, have been showing marked interest in instruction through projects. Requests for lectures have been received from groups of high-school teachers, normal-school faculty, and others. Indications of progress in interest have been highly encouraging. I have thought that we should begin to take account of stock. Accordingly, with the consent of the superintendent, a questionnaire was sent to the elementary-school principals through the machinery of our Department of Educational Measurement. There is now under way a cataloging of our resulting information for ready reference. The responses to the questionnaire have revealed a wonderful harvest, an amazing growth in project activity. Sixty-seven school districts reported purposeful work carried on by the children. The accomplishments indicated in the reports received connected with grade requirements in geography, history, hygiene, nature work, arithmetic, and English. A few illustrations of specific projects undertaken are "A Japanese Tea Party," "A Spanish Party," "Following President Harding's Trip by Pictures," "The Building of Stockyards," "A Debating Society," "A Banking Business," "The Conducting of a Newspaper," and The Organization of an Anti-cigarette League.

It is not to be denied that care must be

taken in evaluating our reports. We must always allow for the too great eagerness with which some are ever ready to seize upon the new and attempt to promote it before making a sufficient study of the basic philosophy and fundamental principles which must govern its development. These are they who may label as project work something which is not genuine. They may put forward a perfectly good and long familiar type of problem work and call it a project, but it may fall short of the "great adventure," the typical unit of life-experience, the bit of democratic living which is brought about by our ideal project.

It will be seen that the account of my experience has dealt merely with the *launching* of the project method of learning in schools of the traditional type. No attempt has been made to offer suggestions of helps by the wayside, though these will most surely be needed after teachers have actually embarked on their interesting, I had almost said perilous, journey. I suppose all true adventures have their perils. Help, then, ready at hand, there must be, and supervisors must ever be prepared to apply it with art. Words of encouragement, a caution here and there, scraps of kind advice, even direct information will always be needed by teachers undertaking for the first time to teach through projects. Their need of inspirational help all along the way will be the same regardless of the type of appeal to which they have responded at the start. They may belong to the first class we have mentioned, those splendid volunteers who have sought inspiration in visits to normal schools or in institute experiences; they may have responded to the call as they listened to a lecture delivered expressly to arouse their willingness to venture; they may have caught the spirit while attending a professional course baited, perhaps, with a reward which made another appeal at the start; they may have been sought out individually as persons especially well qualified to make a success in experimentation and to cause the spread of improved methods, or they may have embarked on the enterprise because of some other appeal not herein set forth, but whatever it be that caught them, they will need inspiring help throughout their march from the traditional, formal type of teaching toward the ideal on which is fixed the hope of the supervisor who believes that child life is, after all, just life, that the child lives just as truly from his first to his fourteenth year as he does from his fourteenth year to his seventieth, and that differences in his response to environment at seven or fourteen or seventy are occasioned only by the varying amounts of his experience.

THE WIDER STUDY OF METHOD [1]

WILLIAM H. KILPATRICK
Professor of Education, Teachers College, Columbia University

"You recall our discussion of a month ago about the two ways of looking at method. That matter has ever since been a good deal on my mind, but there are several questions I wish to ask."

A second meeting of teachers

"Before you begin with the further discussion won't you tell me what was said before, I mean your conclusions; I wasn't here then and I haven't understood the references I have been hearing to the two problems of method. What are they?"

A review and summary is requested

"We concluded first of all that just as we need to study the curriculum to find out *what* to teach, so we need to study method to find out *how* to teach. When we came more closely to the question of method we found there were two problems of method: one long recognized, the problem of how best to *learn*—and consequently how best to *teach*—any one thing, as spelling; the other less often consciously studied, the problem of how to treat the learning child, seeing that he is willy-nilly learning not one, but many things all at once, and that we teachers are responsible for all that he learns. The first of these problems we called the narrow view of method; the second, the wider view of method."

"I begin to see what you mean. But why do you say 'narrow' and 'wider'? Do you mean to disparage the one and exalt the other?"

"By no means. The one is narrow because it considers only one thing at a time, the other is broader because it takes into account many learnings all going on at once. But there is no wish or willingness to disparage the narrow view. Some of us think the psychology of learning which undertakes to answer the first problem is the most notable single contribution that psychology has thus far to offer."

"Won't you say a further word about the wider view of method? I don't get exactly what you mean. The idea is so new I don't fully grasp it."

"Well, if the others don't mind hearing it again, I'll gladly explain how we saw it a month ago. As it seemed to us, any child during an educative experience learns not merely the one thing he is supposed to be engaged in, say a grammar lesson, but is also at the same time learning well or ill a multitude of other things. Some of them may be: how he shall study, whether with diligence or the reverse; how he shall regard grammar, whether as an interesting study or no; how he shall feel toward his teacher, whether as friend and helper or as a mere taskmaster; how he shall regard himself, whether as capable or not; whether or not he shall believe that it pays to try (in such matters as grammar); whether to form opinions for himself and to weigh arguments in connection; how he shall practically regard government (school, home, wider), whether as alien to him and opposed to his best interests, a mere matter of contrary superior force, or as just and right, inherently demanded, and friendly to his true and proper interests. This by no means exhausts the list, but it will give you some idea of what we had in mind in saying that many things are being learned at

The wider view of method is again discussed

8

once. You will also see how important some of these attendant learnings are, and I believe you will agree with us that whether they are well learned depends in great measure on how the teacher treats the children."

"You are right, I am sure, and I see, too, how important the recitation period is. The "socialized Isn't this what some people recitation" have in mind when they speak of the 'socialized recitation'?"

"Yes, undoubtedly, only I have not seen any attention called in connection with it to this central and underlying fact of many simultaneous learnings. The 'socialized recitation' by its emphasis on the social situation fixes attention upon an important source and matrix of simultaneous learnings. Think how many things go on in a properly conducted recitation and how favorable for learning are the conditions. The conscious presence of others engaged with us on a common problem gives stimulation or thought, furnishes occasion for the exercise of many kinds of social behavior, and provides the critical and approving situation so useful for effectual learning. Yes, the 'socialized recitation' is a noteworthy attack upon the wider problem of method."

"I begin to wonder whether these attendant learnings are not just as valuable The impor- as the learning that is general- tance of the ly more immediately in our concomitant consciousness. Are not our learnings practical ideals and attitudes built largely in this incidental way? Go back to the grammar lesson. Isn't the boy in just such everyday experiences building his actual ideals, I mean the ideals and attitudes he actually lives by? Isn't it in this way that he becomes accurate or slovenly in his thinking, efficient or not in attacking problems, courteous or dis- courteous in his dealings with others, honest or dishonest in doing his work? It begins to seem to me that it is mostly in these concomitant learnings that the important things of life are found rather than in the school subjects as we commonly think of them. What do you say?"

"Before we take that up I think it might help if I introduced some terms I Terms to heard at summer school last designate the session. The word con- differentiated comitant you used just now outcomes of was one of them. The terms an educative as I got them were primary, experience associate, and concomitant. The word 'primary' was used to refer to all the learning that belongs closely to the thing immediately under consideration: If I am making a dress, then the primary includes all the learning that comes from the actual making, such as increased skill in planning and cutting. The term 'associate' is usually found in the phrase 'associate suggestions' and refers to all those allied thoughts or ideas that come from working on the dress, but which if followed up then would lead me away from my dressmaking. I may thus be thinking whether the dress will wash, and so think about the dye used, and ask myself how such dyes are prepared. This in its place is a valuable and proper question, but I do not need to answer it in order to make this dress, and if I do try to answer it, I must for the time lay aside my dressmaking. The 'concomitant' learnings grow (in part at least) out of the dress-making, but do not belong so closely or exclusively to the dress as do the primary. I may thus say, 'I see it pays to be careful.' I learned this, perhaps in connection with making the dress, but it should remain with me as an ideal that will reach beyond dress-making. In general we may say that the concomitant learnings have to do with more generalized ideals and attitudes, while the primary learning has rather to do with specific knowledges and skills. The concomitant is typically of slower growth, requiring perhaps many successive experiences to fix it permanently in one's character. Prominent among concomitants are personal attitudes, attitudes toward one's teachers or comrades, attitudes toward the several subjects of study (as geography or history), attitudes toward one's self, such as self-reliance or pride or humility. Other important concomitants are standards of workmanship and the like, neatness, accuracy, or the reverse."

"I see what you mean, but why must you introduce more 'terms,' as you call them? If you people that study and read books would only learn to use everyday words, you'd be much more popular and do much more good. And why do you choose such outlandish words for your terms? Who ever uses such a word as concomitant? Why don't you choose a short word? But I didn't mean to offend you."

"You didn't really offend me. I suppose it was another case of 'pride going before **The use of** a fall.' I was proud of myself **terms** that I had made my meaning clear, for I confess I had trouble last summer in getting the idea. And you are in good company in wishing for simpler terms, for I remember the professor said that he felt he ought to apologize for such long words and he asked us to suggest shorter ones, only we couldn't. But you, in my judgment, are wrong in objecting to 'terms.' They help us to think. Why, ever since I got these distinctions I can see the things themselves much clearer. In fact I never really saw the things in my pupils until I got these distinguishing terms. I

tell you a name is the way to hold and spread an idea. When you talk about a thing and give it its proper name, you yourself have something to hold to, while other people begin to ask what is meant and to look for the thing back of the name. Without terms there would be little exact thinking."

"I suppose you are right. It sounds reasonable. At any rate, I can't argue against you. But I wish you would explain how you actually use these terms primary, associate, and concomitant."

"Principally they make me critical of my work. I mean they help direct my self-**The use of** criticism. I used to be con-**the designative** tent if my pupils didn't miss **terms** in daily recitation work and could pass on the term examinations. I thought that was all. Now I know better. That was being satisfied with the *primary* only. I never thought about the associate suggestions and but little of what I now call concomitants. It is not that I do not value the primary now, I do value it perhaps just as much as before, only differently, more intelligently, I believe. But I think a great deal more about the other two.

"It used to be that I was often impatient if my children asked questions suggested **Associate** by the lesson but not on the **suggestions** lesson. You see my eyes were glued on the course of study, and I thought of these questions only as mind wandering. I still am troubled to keep the class sufficiently intent on the matter at hand, but I feel differently about the outside questions and I act differently. Now I feel that I and my pupils are really succeeding when these associated suggestions arise. Properly used, they mean growth. We don't yield to the present inclination to follow them up, but we do notice them enough to see whither they invite us. Sometimes we write them down for future use. And I see a different attitude is already growing up in the class. They are more thoughtful. Associated suggestions noted in the past come up again in their right places, and James or Mary is proud to have foreseen the point. They feel differently toward me too. We seem to be working more sympathetically, and we really enjoy thinking things out together and connecting them all properly. I find that I respect my pupils more, or really the advance connections they see are remarkable. And they think more connectedly now, instead of less connectedly as I feared. Their organization is much better. You see I was beforetimes repressing rather than encouraging their natural inclinations to think.

"And as for the concomitants, I am now much concerned about them, particu- *Concomitants* larly as to what attitudes are being built and how I can help forward the better ones. I see now that I always valued those things, the ideals and attitudes of my pupils; but I didn't concern myself consciously and specifically about them. I somehow trusted to luck for them. I was a kind of fatalist about them. The pupils who were going to have good ideals were going to have them, and that was all there was about it. I scolded sometimes and criticized a good deal, but I now think that in so doing I did more harm than good. Now I know that each ideal and each attitude has a life-history of its own, each is built up just as truly as is any fact of knowledge or any skill."

"It seems to me that you are now contradicting yourself. Earlier you were *Are attitudes* speaking of these attitudes as *sought* being built incidentally. Now *directly?* you talk as if you seek them directly. Which is right?"

"So far as the child is concerned they are principally built incidentally, that is, in connection with other purposes of his. I as teacher, however, must be conscious of what he is doing and steer his various activities so that the proper ideals and attitudes shall actually grow up. I seek them directly, he achieves them—for the most part—indirectly. But at times we do talk matters over, because clear consciousness is often an important factor in building ideals."

"I understand you now on that point, but I wish to ask further. Do you then *Is each act to* judge each thing the children *be judged in* do under these three heads of *these terms?* primary, associate, and concomitant?"

"Typically, yes. Each study period, each recitation period, and each recess is in its own measure going to result in primary learning of some kind well or ill done, in few or many, rich or poor, associated suggestions, in good or bad concomitants. As teacher I am in some measure responsible and in so far I must know what is going on and adequately appraise the results. In the light of the results—so far as I do or could influence them—am I to be judged."

"Isn't it different now? If I understand you aright, we examine and promote *The primary* almost if not entirely on the *is now too* primary learning, and dis- *much stressed* regard the other two."

"Yes, I think we do. You see we can test the primary learning so much more easily than we can the others. The new scientific tests and measures of achievement even reinforce the tendency to pay exclusive attention to the primary, because they are so far for the most part confined to the more mechanical skills and knowledges. I sometimes fear their first effect will be to fasten the merely mechanical side of school work even more firmly on our schools."

"Well, you certainly surprise me now. You have always been eager for each new advance of science, as I have heard you say, and here you are decrying what you must admit is at least one of the most scientific steps yet taken in the study of education. I didn't expect it of you."

"The new tests are indeed a contribution of the very first value, but what I say The danger in is still true. So far as they the new tests measure achievement they are up to now largely confined to the more mechanical aspects of learning. A superintendent gives a series of tests in spelling, arithmetic, or reading. Sooner or later the teachers learn the records of their classes, and unless the superintendent is wise they will find themselves rated according to these records. If the superintendent could as satisfactorily measure the teacher's success in building ideals and attitudes, so that all the educational outcomes could be weighed, the situation would be different. But as matters now stand the superintendent is in danger of taking the teacher's attention away from the "imponderables," the ideals and attitudes and moral habits that cannot yet be measured in wholesale quantities, and of fastening that attention upon a part only of the educational output and that the most mechanical. This is no fanciful picture, I assure you. The danger is very real. Such considerations as this make me look earnestly for the day when we shall be able to measure the whole gamut of achievement. I believe that day will come and a great day it will be. Till then, however, I should advise superintendents to look carefully how they use the tests. Use them, but with a clear sense of their

limitations and dangers. In the meanwhile the greater reason for urging attention to the wider problem of method. We must make everyone see the value of the concomitant learning and of the associate suggestions. Every recitation period, every school exercise must be appraised under all three heads of primary, associate, and concomitant."

"If you made your expression even stronger, I should not object. When I The greater consider that while we are need to study stressing arithmetic, for exmethod ample, our children are forming at the same time the very warp and woof of their moral characters, I shudder to think of the consequences if our teachers see only the arithmetic and ignore the lifeattitudes being built. Fortunately, there is no necessary opposition between the two, rather the contrary; but nothing can excuse us for failing to consider those other outcomes that inevitably accompany every school activity."

"The wider problem of method seems to me now to be almost the same as the moral The wider problem of life itself. As I problem of now see it, our schools have in method is the the past chosen from the whole problem of life of life certain intellectualistic tools (skills and knowledges), arranged these under the heads of reading, writing, arithmetic, geography, and the like, and have taught these separately as if they would, when once acquired, recombine into the worthy life. This now seems to me to be very far from sufficient. Not only do these things not make up the whole of life; but we have so fixed attention upon the separate teaching of these as at times to starve the weightier matters of life and character. The only way to learn to live well is to practice living well. Our highly artificial study of arithmetic and geography and physics has too often meant that the child lived but meagerly in and through the school studies. The practice of living that has in fact counted most for him has too often been what he and his like-starved fellows could contrive for themselves apart from their elders. Educative indeed has this been, but not always wisely so. There is no cause for wonder that American citizenship disappoints. Democracy demands a high type of character. Our schools have not risen to the demand upon them."

"Do you mean that the wider problem of method especially concerns building for citizenship?"

"That is exactly what I mean. It has always been so. Without clearly distinguishing what they did, or rather how the results have been attained, each long-abiding type or ideal of civilization has contrived its answer to this wider problem of method in such fashion as to mold the type of character correlatively needed to perpetuate itself. The Spartan and the Athenian of antiquity differed from each other quite as much by reason of different methods of education as because of the different contents of the curriculum. The proverbial "hardening" of the former was

To each civilization its type of method

sign and result of the treatment accorded their youth. The slave of every age has by well-contrived processes been made lowly in spirit the more contentedly to bear his hard lot and lowly station. Civilizations have differed much as to whether the individual man should think for himself: those opposed to such thinking have always contrived such methods of treating their young as early habituated them to acquiescence in the officially approved opinions. Prussia, old China, Mahomet, the Jesuits, the older military discipline, all represent various efforts along this line. These have differed among themselves almost *in toto* as to the primary learning they have sought to inculcate; but they have been agreed markedly in the methods of inculcating the concomitants, the desired attitudes.

"We then in this country must study anew the (wider) problem of method in order the more adequately to devise the proper treatment of our young so as to fit them for democratic citizenship. The beginning of this wisdom, I believe, is to recognize the fact that the child learns many things at once. On this rock of simultaneous learnings shall we by proper effort rear the needed structure of an all-round character."

To America its appropriate method

AN EXPERIMENT IN CO-OPERATION
♦ II. READING WITH A PURPOSE
JAMES F. HOSIC
Associate Professor of Education, Teachers College, Columbia University

In the preceding article of this series a brief account was given of how certain selected schools in Chicago set to work to make definite improvement in the teaching of English. One of the important problems attacked was that of study reading. This was approached in the light of the principle that in good reading there is specific purpose to guide the process. The reader regards the ideas found as provisional and checks them up in the light of the whole, of the *aim* which the writer is seen to be carrying out. We will now review some of the steps that were taken in applying that principle.

THE TEACHERS STUDY THE PROCESS OF READING

In the first place, the teachers were invited to verify the principle for themselves. Various passages were read with these questions in mind: "At what point do I first see clearly what the passage is intended to do? Regarding the passage as essentially the answer to a question, how many and what chief points do I find? Is the answer full, clear, and reasonable, or do I feel impelled to verify my impression by reading again? Is any other answer possible? Have I ever been called upon to answer such a question? What answer did I make?"

The net result was, of course, fresh interest in the process of reading. Many observed their own mental activities in reading for the first time. These processes took on new dignity—were seen to be highly complex, involving far more than mere recognition of words. The work of the children had new meanings. Their behavior in reading had now hitherto unthought-of explanations. It became clear that learning to read means the formation of right mental habits, the conscious control of analysis and thinking. Using the current pedagogical gibberish, we might say that there was less teaching of books and more teaching of children.

One of the most tangible results was the ready consent on the part of almost all to the abandonment of that old reliable time-killer of the public school, reading aloud at sight in the lower grades. "Study first!"

became the slogan. Even if the children do whisper or vocalize at first, at any rate they know that they are not reading aloud. If we persist, we shall accomplish three very desirable things, namely, set up in the pupils' minds the ideal of careful study, greatly increase their speed in silent reading, and enable them, when they read aloud, to read with fluency and to give the sense. And to a gratifying degree all of these things undoubtedly happened. A curious and persistent fallacy is, by the way, the belief that children must above all things learn to read aloud at sight by trying to do it long before their experience with language or with the difficult art of looking ahead when you are pronouncing from the page enables them to deal with the sentence as a *simultaneous* as well as a successive whole. Nobody would require the tiny tot at the piano to perform for visitors or for a recital audience in this fashion. Sight reading in piano lessons is a private performance for many moons. But because reading aloud at sight is a performance which, after a fashion, can go on, and because it is something to do in the "recitation," when perforce there must be continuous vocal utterance on the part of somebody, it does go on, as all who make a practice of visiting schools can testify. Only a better knowledge of the psychology of reading and of learning to read will stop it. Such seems to be the conclusion suggested by our attempts to apply Thorndike's "Reading as Reasoning."

BEFORE TAKING AND AFTER TAKING

That what is needed is a better conception of the job may be illustrated by the following pair of lessons, conducted by the same teacher, with the same grade of children, using the same book.

The topic of the first lesson was "Polly's Pranks," an excerpt from a well-known book on birds. A child was called upon to read the first paragraph aloud. He stumbled over the word "cyclone" in the sentence, "When Polly got through with the work-basket, it looked as though a cyclone had struck it." Dutifully the teacher set herself to the task of securing the pronunciation of the word. She divided it into syllables upon the blackboard. She set up phonetic analogies; "Cy is like ci," she explained. She called out a choral response from the class. Then she required the boy to read the passage again. That the passage *suggested* anything to the reader, to the audience, or even to the teacher, there was not the slightest evidence. The recitation appeared to be a linguistic exercise pure and simple; pronunciation the sole end in view.

After an interval of a few weeks, however, during which the teachers of this school discussed the principles of reading after the manner indicated above, this teacher conducted a lesson on "The Tongue-cut Sparrow." "What a strange idea!" said she. "Tongue-cut! How and why would a bird have its tongue cut?" The sally elicited several conjectures, among which was the cheerful suggestion that the bird made too much noise and had therefore suffered the loss of the end of its tongue.

Then the teacher offered her own experience. Her brothers on the farm had caught a young crow and had tamed it. In the harvest time they conceived the notion of teaching the bird how to speak. So they loosened the membrane under its tongue and induced it to say something that sounded like "Vote for Bryan! Vote for Bryan!" The children smiled at the quaint

conceit, the significance of which they did not of course fully grasp, and turned to their books with avidity to discover, each for himself, the fate of the tongue-cut sparrow. And wonderful to tell, the teacher did not interrupt them while they were doing it. She let them get the whole story and then welcomed spontaneous remarks and discussion on the points involved, which she directed toward the clearing up of the children's impressions, making each certain as to what actually did happen, and thus sought to enable the reading to yield sound and true vicarious experience. Mechanical details were rapidly cleared up in the process of achieving this end.

LEARNING HOW THE PUPILS DO STUDY

The ideas about reading developed in conference, which began to work reform in the manner which has just been illustrated, were strengthened here and there by means of special study lessons in which the pupils tried out such methods as they knew and thus oriented the teacher as to their needs and her responsibility.

For example, a fourth-grade class was asked to study a selection from Thoreau called the "Battle of the Ants." Some finished in less than one-third of the time required by others. Individual differences were marked. In answer to the demand, "What did I say I would ask you when you had finished?" one boy rose and began at once to try to reproduce the thought of the first paragraph. Any other remark in a certain tone of voice would apparently have touched off the same response on the part of this youngster, who was evidently thoroughly habituated to a certain formal type of school exercise.

Others, however, were ready to answer the question which had actually been agreed upon, namely, "Just what did you do when you studied the lesson?" "I tried to pick out the main points," said one. "I read the piece through and then tried to see how much of it I could remember," said another. "There were some things I knew I did not understand," said a third, and "I made up my mind that I would ask the teacher about them." The passage this pupil had in mind proved to be that in which Thoreau compares the struggles of the ants to those of the Greeks and Trojans around the walls of Troy. Another pupil said that he suspected there was a story about Troy and he meant to look through the books in the library in order, if possible, to find it.

A SHIFT OF EMPHASIS IN TEACHING

As was to be expected, the teachers who discovered that few of their pupils had knowledge of good methods of work began to give specific training in how to study. They showed the children how they themselves went about it. They set up different procedures and familiarized the pupils with the uses of each They sought to build up definite *ideals* of method and of efficiency, seeking all the while to discover and satisfy individual needs

Perhaps most noticeable was the shift of emphasis in their questioning. There was a tendency to get away from minute questions of fact, such as "What does it say in that passage?" and to ask instead questions requiring thought, as "Why did it happen? How do you know?" and the like. The questions, moreover, especially at the outset and near the conclusion of the study of a selection, tended to be more inclusive, to deal with the thing as a whole, to set up and check by reference to certain purposes for which the reading should be done. For instance, a group which had come to a good understanding of the story of Hawthorne's "Pine-Tree Shillings" was asked, "Do you like the mintmaster? Would you be glad to have him as a relative of yours? Why? If you wished to tell this story to the friends at home tonight, what main steps in the story would you have to recall?"

In answer to the last question the pupils of this sixth-grade class readily analyzed the story into the following steps: (1) situation, the colonists need a convenient form of currency; (2) pine-tree shillings are agreed on and Captain Hull is made mintmaster; (3) Captain Hull becomes very rich by putting away his commission, the twentieth shilling; (4) Captain Hull promises his daughter in marriage to Samuel Sewall; (5) at the wedding the captain surprises everybody by giving his daughter as her dowry her weight in pine-tree shillings

How these methods of study began to be applied to other subjects and how the questions of proper materials and of treatment appropriate to them came into focus and were disposed of, our next instalment will relate.

ONE PHASE OF THE TECHNIQUE OF THE PROJECT METHOD OF TEACHING

MARGARET E. WELLS
New York City

A question frequently asked by teachers eager to aid in the development of the project method is, "How large should a project be?" Thereby hangs a tale.

This is one of the most pertinent, most vital, and perhaps most troublesome questions to be solved by the educator. Indeed, if trying to answer it offhand, one would say, "There can be no answer to this question. The project should be as large as it happens to be, as initiated by the child or the group of children. It must comprise as much as is necessary for its own maximal functioning as an educative medium."

Such an answer is simply evading the issue and cannot satisfy the lay teacher, for whom, after all, it is necessary to establish a sort of working basis for the immediate use of this developing concept of education. Since our normal schools are not always handling specifically the content and method of the elementary-school curriculum which the apprentice will have to deal with when she assumes the responsibility of her own schoolroom, she must often rely upon other instrumentalities for guidance and help. In other words, there is a decided conflict at present, in almost every locality, between the *what* and the *how* of the teacher's childhood and normal-school experience and the *what* and the *how* of her teaching in the rapidly approaching change of school practice which this newer concept of education is bound to bring with it. For this reason the question which opens this discussion must be answered. The answer has to do primarily with organization; next, with motives—"drives" toward a definite end; third, with the

necessary planning and adjustment in order to attain the end set up—in order to perfect the project, so to speak.

Let us suppose, for purposes of discussion, that we accept the principle that the project should be as large as it happens to be when initiated by the child. What will happen, in a school of thirty or forty pupils, under the care of one teacher, with perhaps occasional help from special supervisors of music and art? Suppose Willie's project to be the building of an American fleet while John is engaged in constructing a delivery wagon, and Mary is making a new outfit for her doll while Jane has conceived the notion of baking some cookies for a coming entertainment. Would not the teacher have to be omniscient, omnipresent, and omnipotent to keep the school wheels moving at all, not to speak of using the project as a vehicle for teaching the tool subjects? It is the glowing descriptions of the working out of some one or other of such miscellaneous, detached projects as these, by a "project-inspired" teacher, who may have had the most favorable equipment and other conditions, which often dismays the teacher seeking to become "project-inspired."

Now, what are the handicaps under which the teacher inexperienced in project teaching labors when she puts her hand to the plow? Perhaps the greatest is her own lack of practical acquaintance with the world of doing—her habit, in these days of factory production and division of labor, of accepting things as they are. Moreover, when all is said and done in spite of the privilege that may be granted her of encouraging her children to carry out their detached, accidental projects, she must cover a certain amount of subject-matter as outlined in the course of study.

As to the first of these points, it never can become as easy and natural to teach by the project method as to follow the established modes, until the normal schools "suffer a sea-change" and send out their graduates with a knowledge of the world of things, a stock of experience in the world of doing, and the courage to gather further information as needed which comes from actual experience in developing projects.

As to the second, some plan must be formed to insure the transmission of the social inheritance and to prevent endless duplication and overlapping, without throttling the child's initiative and denying him free opportunity to find himself. Such factors as content, grading, sequence, organization, drill, development of skills, habits, attitudes, appreciations, and originality must be provided for in developing a technique for the project method.

To allow children to initiate their own projects, whether small or large, as oases in the desert of the required course of study, has some value. But a consideration of the child's immature interests and habits and of the variety of defects in home environment shows that our teaching can never become "100 per cent project" without the teacher's finger in the pie of initiative.

One of the great values of school life is that it makes the child one of a group, the group being at least as important as the individual. If this can be conceded, why not encourage individual projects, many of them absolutely child-suggested, as parts of a group project? If the children are sent to school in order that they may acquire the social inheritance under the guid-

ance of a mature mind, why not allow the teacher to determine the use of a large, interesting unit of life as a group project for the grade? This may be done so tactfully, so deftly, that the children will adopt and develop the idea almost as spontaneously as if it were their own. And the general idea, once adopted, will give ample opportunity for purely self-suggested individual and small-group projects, indeed, will generate them so rapidly that the teacher has merely to guide to a wise choice among the rich suggestions of the children. Moreover, this predetermination of the phase of life to be studied in each grade will avoid the over-cultivation of some parts of the field of knowledge to the total neglect of others, and can be made to bring about that "review with interest" which is the essential of drill.

By using large units of life as basic projects, mass or class or group teaching is called for at frequent intervals in launching the successive phases of the unit project, while the minor projects which grow out of this phase, being knit together by their common origin and aim, are much more easily handled by a teacher with only one pair of hands than such a heterogeneous collection of projects as are named in the earlier part of this paper. Co-operation is spelled in large letters, unselfishness becomes of paramount importance, group censorship rather than teacher censorship becomes the disciplinary agency.

After an intelligent launching of the project, the children following more-or-less unrecognized suggestion by the teacher, a natural unfolding follows and the teacher's pondering over ways and means to motivate becomes a thing of the past. Indeed the child is more likely to show and to increase initiative when it is a case of the next step, and the next, and the next, than he is when the selection of projects is a hit-or-miss affair. As in life itself the doing of one thing suggests another and the doing of this opens the possibility of doing something else, so when we move a large life-project bodily into the schoolroom the sequence and organization of subject-matter, the need for discipline, and the need for drill largely take care of themselves.

Moreover, if a curriculum be built up of large life-projects significant to all, the same or very similar fundamental projects being found in the same grade throughout the city, we overcome one of the most serious objections that have been urged to the use of projects as anything more than mere relaxation or sugar-coatings in a city system, namely, that it would make the matter of promotion or transfer difficult, if not impossible.

So it would seem that not only will the developing project-technique be furthered by the building up of a curriculum consisting of long-range social projects arranged in such a way that each grade will build upon the preceding, but the teachers now in service will thereby be helped to master any of the difficulties involved in the change from the old to the new.

In the working out of such a scheme, we shall probably discover more, or perhaps different, school essentials for socialized living, and shall demand social measuring sticks or tests, in addition to those we now have for the more formal necessities of living, such as reading, writing, and arithmetic. May the day speedily dawn when we shall be able to diagnose the social ills of the school and apply the necessary remedial teaching as we now are learning to handle reading, spelling, and arithmetical ills!

PLANS FOR TEACHERS' MEETINGS

EMMA AMES BOETTNER
Assistant Supervisor of Grammar Grades, Baltimore County, Maryland

I. Purpose:

Teachers' meetings are organized to provide a means whereby comparatively large groups of teachers may profit to the maximum through suggestions obtained by coming in contact with:

1. An intelligent discussion of teaching problems and the *emphases* of the county for the current year.
2. A wide range of classroom experience, gathered together through discussion of concrete types of activities.
3. Needed revisions.
4. Need for growth on the part of teachers.

5. Final outcomes of instruction.
6. The latest developments in the *field of method* and classroom technique—*vital issues of immediate interest.*
7. Bibliographies of current articles and recent publications—worthwhile material for professional reading.
8. Discussion of reprints or mimeographed material to direct attention to possible solutions of significant problems.
9. Samples or descriptions of valuable materials—exhibits of projects worked out by classes, etc., posted at the office of the super-

visors and discussed during meetings.

10. Demonstration lessons to illustrate effective methods of teaching.

II. Types of group meetings:

1. Intergrade meetings where specific classroom problems, related to two or three grades, are discussed in detail; the plans outlined later in this paper showing the type of procedure.

2. Meetings of special groups of teachers to discuss common problems. For example, a meeting of eighteen teachers of Grades IV and V was held at the supervisor's office to discuss the difficulties of teaching industrial arts. As these teachers had no previous experience in teaching the subject-matter or the making of the projects, the supervisor gave specific help in working out the directions upon the actual projects desired, as the weaving of a bag or the making of a book.

3. Special meetings at individual schools where a problem of significance to that school is discussed. A meeting of this type was conducted at each of several large schools last year. The teachers of the school met the primary supervisor and me to discuss the results of the October Survey in Reading and Arithmetic, securing information regarding the graphing of the results for each grade and also for the school. Suggestions for informal tests and remedial work were given. Through these meetings developed the realization by each teacher of the relation of the work of her grade to that of the other grades throughout the school.

4. Meetings of supervisors in charge of special subjects, as music and drawing.

5. Committee meetings where constructive work on some problem is outlined. An example of this type of meeting would be that of the committee on history texts. This committee met three times for conference with the supervisor, finally submitting a report at the regular grade meetings in April.

6. Demonstration meetings, held in certain schools, the classroom teacher planning the day's work in close co-operation with the supervisor, to meet the specific needs of the visiting teachers.

7. General meetings in which a specific class problem is discussed.

III. How to conduct meetings:

1. Meetings should be conducted upon a democratic basis because the teachers then have a vital interest and feel that they are contributing to the common good of the school system. We should apply the same principles of good teaching here that we wish the teachers to put into practice. The meetings might well be similar to round-table discussions, with a maximum of teacher participation, guided always by careful, clear thinking on the part of the supervisor.

2. Programs for teachers' meetings should be drafted in such terms as to be a means of informing the

public and the authorities regarding the work of the supervisor and teachers. Since our work next year will follow up the work of Mr. Clark and Mr. Calkins at the Institute, our *objectives* might reasonably be: (a) problem-solving in arithmetic and geography; (b) increased ability in writing and spelling (because of felt need).

3. With these points in mind, the following tentative suggestions are presented for use in the programs of the meetings which I hope to conduct during November and January of the current year.

a) Geography:

(1) List five points which you consider important in the teaching of geography by the project method, emphasizing the fundamental idea of purpose. You will receive for discussion at the next meeting the tabulated summary of your suggestions.

(a) Discussion of mimeographed material called "Geography Project" by M. L. Warren (adapted from article in *The Journal of Educational Method*, September, 1921).

(b) By what standards should the results of the project method be judged and what tests should be employed? Give specific instance from your own experience to show that

more learning took place in a definite period when work was based upon the fundamental principles underlying the project method.

(2) As a result of the work with concrete problems in regional geography, given by Mr. Calkins at the Institute, how have you stimulated and assisted your pupils in careful analysis and quick, original, clear thinking with regard to reflective problem-solving?

(a) What means have you used to get pupils to (i) define the problem clearly; (ii) keep the problem in mind; (iii) make many suggestions; (iv) evaluate each suggestion carefully; (v) organize the material.

(3) Economical and effective study habits.

(a) The relation of supervised study and the socialized recitation to the project method of teaching: (i) discussion of how pupils may be guided to discover problems for study and investigation in connection with a content subject like geography; (ii) review mimeographed suggestions received at last meeting, "Necessity for Setting Up Thorough-going Technique in Study Lessons in History." Draft a similar set of suggestions for geography.

(4) What type of a plan book might the teacher keep for project work? Illustrate from geography.

b) Arithmetic:

(1) How has your use of the Thorndike *Arithmetic Texts* been influenced by the suggestions given by Mr. Clark? Please review the inclosed summary of Mr. Clark's work at our recent Institute. Bring this summary to the meeting for discussion.

(2) Be prepared to discuss the bearing of the following factors upon the question of problem-solving in arithmetic. Give concrete instances to illustrate your points.

(a) The origin of thinking is in the pupil's own experience of some difficulty that troubles him. (He must know what the question is.)

(b) Consideration, from the pupil's own past experiences, of some plan that will solve the problem. (Must know what facts you are to use to answer it.)

(c) Suspended judgment until the plan is carefully examined and criticized. (Must use facts in right relations.)

(3) Thorndike says: "We should find an abundance of problems which will exercise the intellectual powers well and at the same time prepare the pupils more fully and directly to apply arithmetic to the problems they will really encounter in life."

(a) Draw up a set of standards by which problems might be judged. Do this in a number of clear-cut principles (not less than six), each principle followed by a few sentences to make illustration concrete. These standards will be collected at the meeting.

(4) Mention instances in your teaching which show that remedial work to meet individual differences has resulted in any of the advantages following:

(a) Saves time of pupil.

(b) Is more efficient.

(c) Provides plenty of work for pupils.

(d) Children have more incentive to progress.

(e) Does away with discipline problem.

(f) Gives bright children

increased opportunities.

(g) Gives dull children increased opportunities.

(h) Children feel responsibility.

(i) Parents realize responsibility rests upon pupils.

(j) Makes children work harder.

(k) Excellent for drill work.

(l) Accomplishment of children shows that it pays.

(5) Questions about the details of learning in arithmetic, the probable answers of which we should be considering:

(a) What constitutes sufficient practice for the necessary skills?

(b) What is the most desirable length of review periods?

(c) How much practice at the time of initial teaching should a new topic receive?

(d) What specific skills, information, and knowledge of principles do children possess when they come to the seventh grade?

(e) Is there a definite relation between speed and accuracy in computation? Does increasing either increase the other?

(f) What activities have you used to teach the facts and processes, avoiding the development of the "tool" without sufficient teaching of its use?

(g) What definite objectives should be set up for pupils and teachers, in terms of specific abilities, to be acquired in relation to actual human needs?

c) Penmanship:

(1) Come prepared to discuss penmanship in regard to:

(a) Essential points to be emphasized in developing ability to write.

(b) Length of writing periods from standpoint of hygiene and efficiency.

(c) Use of definitely established scales and standards toward which to work.

(d) Frequent testing.

(e) Special help from teacher to meet the varying capacities of children. (Provision for individual differences by group teaching and individual instruction.)

(2) Analyze the important elements that enter into writing in terms of such outcomes as habits, skills, knowledges, attitudes (interests and ideals).

(a) If *progress lies in abilities acquired*, how may this analysis help in the follow-up or remedial work with which you are planning to remedy the situation for those pupils who are below standard in speed and quality?

d) Spelling:

(1) Read carefully, in the course of study, the suggestions for teaching spelling in the grammar grades, pp. 150–57. What additional recommendations would you make regarding the best method of helping the pupil to secure a "spelling consciousness," making for accurate spelling ability?

(2) These recommendations will be given to a committee on spelling. The members of this committee will use your recommendations to plan definite methods of teaching spelling. The following topics are suggestive:

(a) Sources of words to be taught.

(b) Use made by pupils and teacher of spelling-text for the grade.

(c) Economical ways of learning and teaching spelling.

(d) Number of words taught in one lesson.

(e) Type of spelling lessons: teaching lessons, testing lessons, column vs. dictation procedure.

(f) Plan of review: Value of using for testing such a scale as Ayres' "Measuring Scale for Ability in Spelling."

(g) How the dictionary should function.

(h) Incentives for arousing pupils' interest in spelling.

BIBLIOGRAPHY FOR "TEACHERS' MEETINGS"

Books that would help teachers:

THORNDIKE, *New Methods in Arithmetic.*

This book will be used by our teachers as a basis for constructive work as related to the new tendencies in organization in arithmetic.

Sixteenth Yearbook.

This gives G. M. WILSON, "A Survey of the Social and Business Uses of Arithmetic," pp. 128–42; F. N. FREEMAN, "Handwriting," pp. 60–72; H. C. PRYOR, "A Suggested Minimum Spelling List," pp. 73–84.

WILSON and HOKE, *How to Measure.*

The best and most helpful book that our elementary school teachers would use. It gives much material upon pupil diagnosis—ability and difficulties. See analysis of aims of geography teaching, pp. 205–7.

COURTIS, *Standard Practice Tests in Handwriting—Manuals.*

A desk copy of the pupils' manual would prove helpful to the teacher, as it gives specific suggestions for classroom procedures. The teachers' manual is also valuable.

TIDYMAN, *The Teaching of Spelling.*

Definite recommendations for securing better teaching of spelling.

HORN-ASHBAUGH, *Spelling Book*, Grades I—VIII.

A carefully compiled list of words, with good suggestions in the general directions to teachers and pupils. The procedure, adapted from these suggestions, is being "tried out" in Baltimore County.

STARCH-MIRICK, *Study Speller*.

Another good list of words, with helpful suggestions that might be used to supplement procedures followed.

O'BRIEN, *Silent Reading*.

Our teachers will find this particularly helpful in following up the intensive work in silent reading stressed last year.

Eighteenth Yearbook, Part II.

This gives HORN's "Principles of Method in Spelling" and MONROE's "Principles in Arithmetic."

BONSER, *Elementary School Curriculum*.

Contains many practical suggestions for the teacher.

STUDENT REACTIONS TO THE PROJECT METHOD[1]

For the past two years we have been conducting experiments with the project method in the subject of history at the Horace Mann School for Girls, Teachers College, Columbia University. The special fields selected for this experimentation were Modern European History in our ninth year and Contemporary Social Problems in the tenth year of our senior high school.

As a teacher of history and civics for many years I have come to feel that neither of these subjects is doing for our young citizens what the Committee of Seven said they should do. That report, issued in 1899, has come to be looked upon by many of us as the Old Testament of the history teacher. It contained much that was and still is excellent. For instance under the caption "Training for Citizenship" we note the following as objectives in history: "the power to gather information"; "training in the handling of books"; "an understanding of the relation between cause and effect"; "the scientific habit of thought"; "the cultivation of resources within themselves"; "and so to develop historical-mindedness as to materially influence the character and habits of the pupil."

Now the thoughtful teacher of experience knows that these objectives, splendid in themselves in training citizens—not embryo historians—are seldom realized from the study of history as it is generally taught in our schools today. It was, therefore, the main purpose of our experimentation with the project to see what could be done to realize these citizenship objectives.

We took our general method from John Dewey. "The true starting-point of history is always some present-day situation." This meant, of course, the abandonment at the start of chronological order and the covering of our field by the selection of class projects.

In modern European history we have used such projects as: (1) The progress of labor and how it affects us today (the Industrial Revolution). (2) The Irish Question: causes and possible solutions. (3) How did France become a permanent republic? (4) Why is Japan one of the leading nations of the world and what have been her relations with the United States? (5) How did constitutional government come to England? In Contemporary Social Problems we have discussed and worked out such typical projects as: (1) How do we elect a president of the United States? (2) What are the possible solutions of the negro problem? (3) The past, present, and future of the prohibition movement. (We closed this project with a formal debate on, "Should the eighteenth amendment be repealed?" (4) What has been the effect of immigration on the United States and what should our present-day policy be toward the immigrant? (A Naturalization Court was staged by the class in the auditorium.)

Both of these classes were organized in a democratic manner with chairman, secretary, and activities committees, determined by our

[1] Part of the facts in this article have appeared in the Teachers College Record and are reprinted by permission

needs. It is "our" class; the responsibility is divided, the teacher is "not dethroned"; and we do not spell "socialized" with capital letters. Civic notebooks are kept by each student; a special shelf is reserved for us in the school library for reference books; a clipping bureau has been established; and one day of the week is given over for current events, a prolific source of future projects. Each project is organized roughly as we progress, and then put in final form as the "Irreducible Minimum." So much for the purpose, method, and general machinery.[1]

During the past term these groups have been observed regularly by my Teachers College class of mature students, composed for the great part of teachers of some experience and training in history. And it is the object of this paper to record the reactions of this group of college observers and also the reaction of the pupils of the classes themselves.

I asked both of these groups to give careful thought to this question: "What do you consider to be the good and the bad features of the project method?" The answers in all cases but one were handed in without any name attached. From the replies I have listed the following, avoiding unnecessary repetitions, but giving in their own words the pupils' conclusions for and against the project method as I have interpreted it in my teaching procedure with them.

I will first give the answers of the Horace Mann pupils. In nearly every instance there was a majority vote of the class favoring the statement as given.

Good Features:

1. We have overcome the difficulty of getting enough references by going to many different sources for enough material so that everyone may be prepared each day.

2. We learn how to organize materials for

[1] The method of setting the projects, the materials used, pupil charts and summaries, as well as typical answers to test questions are given in fuller detail in the November, 1920, issue of the *Teachers College Record*, Columbia University.

ourselves and do not have everything prepared for us by the teacher.

3. We do our arguing and discussing on the basis of "light not heat," and are becoming more broadminded.

4. We gain more lasting information because we have rooted it out for ourselves.

5. It trains us logically—to think clearly and to get our ideas over to the class.

6. The girls have attained an independent attitude of studying and we are getting along much faster.

7. Our discussions are usually the most helpful part of our lessons.

8. Getting and putting things together from the library has helped us a very great deal, not only in history but in everything.

9. Our interest in current literature has been stimulated.

10. We learn how to do things, how to work out our own problems.

11. We learn to thrash out questions for ourselves, instead of relying on textbooks.

12. The girls are more interested and will work harder. They will remember what they learn because they choose the subject and build it up themselves.

Bad Features:

1. We are not yet able to curb unnecessary discussion.

2. We talk too much about "the project method" and what we are going to do next.

3. The home-work assignments are indefinite, although we are improving in this respect.

4. Too much time is spent on one project.

5. It is hard to get references that bear directly on the point of discussion.

6. There is a tendency to wander off the track when becoming interested in something else.

7. We do not do our home work regularly.

8. Too much of the work is carried by a few pupils.

9. The girls who do not do outside reading can get away with it without anyone noticing it.

10. Too much time was spent on the negro problem, but that difficulty has been successfully met in our last project, on prohibition; but the matter still can be improved.

11. We could not go to college on the project method because we never can limit ourselves to

any length of time, therefore we could not cover enough ground. (Class about equally divided in its opinion on this last statement.)

From the answers handed in to me by my observers from Teachers College, who have followed the work daily from the beginning of the spring term, the following expressions were compiled. In order to get a general response, both pro and con, I asked the group of regular observers to vote on each statement and have appended their answers, giving the "Yes" vote first in each instance.

Advantages:

1. Tolerance of the opinions of others, open-mindedness, and good will. (7–0)

2. Self-reliance, i.e., ability to go and gather useful information. (7–0)

3. The beginning of a scientific and critical attitude toward material. (7–0)

4. General orderliness: (very good [4]; good [3]. Discipline shifted from teacher to group itself: self-government.

5. A get-together spirit and ability to co-operate. This is a remarkable feature. (7–0)

6. Good followship and good leadership. (7–0)

7. Acquiring the power to participate in worthwhile constructive discussion. (7–0)

8. An aroused and increased interest. (7–0)

9. Wholehearted activity stimulated in pursuit of knowledge. (6–1)

10. Remarkable facility in using parliamentary procedure as an instrument in conducting class affairs. (7–0)

11. The teacher is "not dethroned." Is in center of the group as adviser and guide instead of dictator. (7–0)

12. Responsibility for the conduct of the work felt to rest on both teacher and pupils. (7–0)

13. Life situations approximated. (6–1)

Disadvantages:

1. Loss of time in ground covered due to parliamentary discussion. The latter, however, felt to be distinctly worth while; a question of relative values. (7–1)

2. Loss of time due to needless discussion, but the class is conscious of this fault and is trying to overcome it. (8–0)

3. A lack of continuous and severe mental work. (3–4)

4. The slower student seems to demand more definiteness in the daily assignments. (7–1)

5. Getting beyond the depths of the pupils so that they talk about things without clearly understanding them. (2–6)

6. Certain required subject-matter slighted. (1–7)

7. Non-participation on part of some members of the class is greater by this method. (3–5)

8 Encourages the expression of opinion not founded on sufficient knowledge. (3–6)

These replies furnish the evidence as to the success and failure of our particular application of the project method. I have purposely arranged these lists so that the dangers and difficulties not successfully overcome should stand last, and consequently leave the stronger impression. For to every one of us who believe in the project method here lies the challenge and here our opportunity.

R. W. HATCH

HORACE MANN SCHOOL
TEACHERS COLLEGE

THE CLEARING HOUSE .

AN AMERICAN LEGION REUNION

I. Reminiscences of France given, pictures and souvenirs shown, also entertainment enjoyed. Children as soldiers and Red Cross workers returned from France.

II. Teacher's Aim:

A. Ultimate.

1. To learn and appreciate the great things the French have contributed to civilization.

2. To appreciate interdependence of France and United States.

3. To interest the children in French history to the extent that they continue their reading outside of school—Napoleon, Joan of Arc, *Tale of Two Cities*, Lafayette.

4. To cultivate the reading and study habit.

5. To appreciate problems which confronted the government and to create respect for the government.

B. Immediate.

1. To give rational knowledge of France.

2. To show the effect of natural surroundings (climate, soil, minerals, and location) on development.

3. To create an atmosphere of "France" in the room while studying France.

4. To raise problems which will be solved by children—for example, "Why do the French drink so very much wine?"

III. Material:

A. Books: Tarr and McMurry, Book II; Atwood, *New Geography*, Book II; Carpenter, *Europe;* Carpenter, *How the World is Clothed;* Smith, *Commerce and Industry;* Cressy, *The Story of*

Food; Monroe-Buckbee, *Europe and Its People;* Allen, *Europe;* Chamberlain, *How We Are Clothed;* Williams, *Paris;* Marian M. George, *Little Journeys to France and Switzerland;* National Geographic Magazine; Bradley, *Touring Europe in an Automobile;* "Biographies of Great Artists," Bonheur; *Great Buildings of the World; Children's Classics in Dramatic Form, Book V;* "History of Napoleon"; Dickens, *Tale of Two Cities; History of Lafayette;* Canfield, *Home Fires in France; Notes from a French Village,* pp. 1—26; *La Pharmacienne,* pp. 259—61; "Jean Valjean" (dramatized), *Dramatic Reader, Book V; Book of Knowledge.*

B. Pictures: Rosa Bonheur, Millet, Corot, and Pictures from *National Geographic Magazine.*

C. Maps.

D. Newspaper clippings.

E. Victor record, "The Marseillaise."

F. Songs: "The Marseillaise"; "Somewhere in France Is a Lily"; "Joan of Arc"; "Long, Long Trail."

IV. Procedure:

A. *Raising of Project*—A boy brought a shell which his brother had picked up from a battle field in France. The children were intensely interested in the shell and in what the boy told of the things his brother saw in France. Other children were eager to bring souvenirs which they had at home and to tell of the things their friends and relatives had seen in France. In consequence it was decided to pretend they were their brothers and friends and to have a reunion of all the returned soldiers—to tell of the interesting things they saw in France (it was decided to say very little about war scenes), to show the things brought back, and to prepare some entertainment for the day.

B. *Exploration.*—Problems.

1. How did the soldiers get to France?
   a. Ports from which they sailed in United States.
   b. Ports in Europe at which they landed.
   c. Drill in proper pronunciation of names of French ports.

2. What soldiers of the French Republic were seen fighting who did not come from France? Map study of French possessions, descriptions of French from Algeria, Tunis, Morocco, Sudan, Sahara, and other French possessions. Use of block outline map, showing French possessions over the world.

   What other possessions could have sent soldiers? Corsica, Madagascar, French Guiana, St. Pierre Miquelon, Somaliland, French Indo-China. What products did these islands send to help the French soldiers?

3. Many of the soldiers did not get to see Paris. What impressions were received by the ones who were fortunate?
   Paris as seen by the soldiers:
   a. Beautiful parks and boulevards.
   b. Louvre.
   c. The tomb of Napoleon. Study "History of Napoleon."
   d. Versailles.
   e. Eiffel Tower.
   f. Notre Dame.
   g. Suburbs—Malmaison, Fontainebleau.
   h. Shops.
   i. Royal Opera House.
   j. Jeanne d'Arc as seen in front of Pantheon.
   k. Champs Élyssées.

4. Why did the French peasants have so much money at the beginning of the war?
   a. Thrift of the French peasants.
   b. School savings banks in France. Problems in arithmetic.—Ex.: A French boy attends school eight years in the grades. He saves 18 francs (using 19 cents as a franc). Each succeeding year he saves one more, 19 francs the second, 20 the third, etc. By the time he is through, how much would he have in our money?

   How could he have more than that? (By the bank paying interest). Study of interest as presented in Thorndike. Each child is given a blank check, is taught how to make out a check, writes a check for $100 which he places with the "Woodland Bank." He figures interest simple and compound on his $100. Thorndike problems and those made by the class solved. Problems in changing soldiers' money to French.

5. Why was the water in France tested before the soldiers used it for drinking? Study of impure water, germs, value of boiling water before drinking. Is the same result found from freezing the water? Kansas City water. Ozark project as contemplated.

6. Why did the soldiers see so much wine-drinking in France? Study of sanitary conditions; sewerage in rural France; reasons for im-

pure water. Why did the foreign population in the United States object to prohibition?

Study of grape-raising and wine-manufacturing as an industry. People employed in manu-facturing, amount made, consumption, etc. The Eighteenth Amendment.

7. Some of our soldiers saw the king of England. How many saw the king of France? Picture of new President Millerand shown. Tricolor made and hung with the Stars and Stripes. Current events about new cabinet, length of office of president of France, Élysées Palace, residence, Premier Aristide Briand. Ex-premier's trip to Africa. History of France —monarchy to republic. Louis XIV, XVI, Napoleon, characters of interest in France. General Joffre. Jean d'Arc. Historical events.

8. How do battle fields now appear? Battle fields marked out on map. Pictures shown of them as they are to day. Reconstruction in France; new territory added. Clearing fields of shells; danger from unexploded shells, etc.

9. What difference did our soldiers see in the methods of transportation in France and at home? Trains, boats, trucks, etc. Why did they see *small* freight cars and engines?

10. What did the soldiers see in rural France which amused them? Experiences of American Red Cross workers, as given by Dorothy Canfield Fisher in *Home Fires in France*.

11. Why do some of the soldiers have an "A" on their sleeves? (Army of Occupation). Where did they occupy Germany? Where did the Germans enter France? Was it easier to enter from that direction than from any other? Study of frontier of Belgium, northeastern France, and of southwestern France. How has the location of France helped its people to be a wonderful nation?

12. Why did the boys bring so very many silk aprons, silk handkerchiefs, silk patterns, and other articles of silk from France? Study of silk industry as learned by some of the soldiers who visited Lyons and St. Étienne.

13. What were some of the copies of masterpieces brought by Americans? (Show pictures.) What have the French contributed to art?

  a. Love and appreciation of art. Love for the beautiful. Cultivation of art instinct in children. (Educating talented children at expense of government.)

  b. Pictures of Corot, Bonheur, Millet, Lebrun.

  c. Study of artists, important pictures shown and told about to class. Feature stories written for Room 2 *Monitor* about certain pictures.

  d. Game: Who can find the most pictures by French artists in Woodland Building?

  e. Tribute paid to Miss Buchanan for valuable collection of pictures; letters written to her.

  f. Louvre—gems of the Louvre.

  g. Visit, after study, to city art gallery.

14. Why were many of the convalescent soldiers sent to southern

France? Climatic conditions in southern France. Climatic conditions in southern France as compared with northern France. Where were some of the convalescent camps?

What soldiers from the United States found a climate in northern France similar to that they were accustomed to in the United States? What conditions did they find?

15. Why have the Germans looked longingly at the French territory along the Belgian border? What trouble has already been caused by this situation? History of the acquisition of Alsace-Lorraine. What did the intelligent soldiers expect to find when they found coal deposits? Is this true in France?

16. What was being done in the square beds into which the flats off the coast of Brittany have been divided? Study of oyster industry.

17. In visiting with the *poilu*, at what occupation did they find most of them had been engaged? What do they raise on their farms? (Wheat, flax, sugar beets, etc.) What did the doughboys think of their farming methods? Pictures of old implements, also of modern tractors and implements used in reconstruction.

18. From what place does some of the best china in the world come? Why? Study of manufacturing of china in Limoges. What material is required for the manufacturing of china? Do we have such material in Kansas City? Why?

19. Where in France did the boys find the opportunity for mountain-climbing? Study of the Alpine district, Mont Blanc. What did they see the people doing there? Show pictures.

20. One soldier went the length and breadth of France by boat. How did he do it? Study of rivers and canals used in transporting food and ammunition. What is the "missing link" in France?

21. What newspaper did the boys enjoy most while with the A. E. F.? (Two pages of *Woodland Monitor* devoted to feature stories.) Some of the stories are feature stories written about French peasant life—stories taken from French artists' pictures. All write stories, the best in penmanship and theme written on paper. Copies of "The Stars and Stripes" brought and read.

22. What were some of the French words used by soldiers at reunion? *Bon jour, vive la France, pardon, parlez vous, bon ami, merci, madame, monsieur, mademoiselle, s'il vous plait, adieu.*

23. Why did so very many soldiers return to America in such splendid physical condition? Study of foods, exercise, diet, etc.

24. How to entertain soldiers after they have had a good time visiting about France. Sketches—Jeanne d'Arc, Jean Valjean, *The Diamond Necklace*; songs.

C. *Plans and drills in preparation.*— The problems are made out by teacher (some suggested by children, some worked out by the whole group). Some are given to individuals to work out, and some to small groups. Some are worked out before the reunion, others prepared to give the day of the reunion. Friday, two weeks from the day the project began, is selected for the day of reunion. All work is directed toward that aim. Much drill is found necessary for the success of the "reunion."

1. Sentence forms, use of complete sentences, subject, predicate, number, etc. Drill on verbs.
2. Elimination of "baby blunders."
3. Use of adjectives in describing things seen in France.
4. Because of use of such sentences as "He fought *noble*," it was found necessary to learn use of adverbs. (Study from language books).
5. Attempt to enlarge vocabulary, use in conversation of "isolated," etc.
6. Drill in spelling.
7. Drill in penmanship, to be able to write letters and articles for school paper.
8. Songs: "La Marseillaise," "Star-spangled Banner" (alto and soprano), "America" (learned by all), "Somewhere in France," "Joan of Arc" (by groups). Groups selected to prepare and give sketches from "Jeanne d'Arc," "Jean Valjean," and *The Diamond Necklace.* "Jeanne d'Arc" is read in class and characters impersonated, tried out, and selected. The other two are prepared at home by groups; best scenes selected for "reunion."

The Reunion.—Room is decorated with red, white, and blue. Stars and Stripes with Tricolor displayed. Posters, cartoons, and border depicting French scenes are placed around room.

1. At 9:45 soldiers (Room 2, 47 strong) gather, greeting each other with French words; Boy Scout suits or Red Cross aprons worn by many children.
2. Soldiers tell in what division they were, where they landed, and show in what drives they saw action.
3. "America" sung, flag salute given.
4. One group tells of all the soldiers from the French Republic that they saw. They tell of the use of camels. They show on block outline map the routes used in coming to France.
5. Soldiers who visited Paris show pictures and describe beauties of Paris.
6. One *poilu* tells of his government —president, premier, and cabinet. His sister tells of the present conditions in her country.
7. A group of Red Cross Hut workers tell of rural France. Information from Dorothy Canfield Fisher's *Home Fires in France.* A nurse recently returned shows pictures and tells of the battlefields as they are today. A tourist who visited France before the war describes the beauties of France before the war. She shows pictures (taken from *National Geographic Magazine*).
8. Souvenirs are exhibited on large table. The children tell what they are, where they were found, and experiences with French country people. They describe implements used for farming; also show pictures of tractors being used there now.
9. A group show the silk *souvenirs de France* and tell of the silk industry in France as they saw it.

10. Greatest pictures of French artists shown.
11. Boys tell of experiences and what they learned of oyster industry in Brittany.
12. Dramatizations given.
13. Paper read.
14. "La Marseillaise" played on victrola, then sung by children.
15. Original dramatizations given representing things seen in France.
16. Four boys tell of a motor trip through France.
17. Some girls show perfume and soap which they brought back, and they tell how it is made.
18. A Frenchman explains why in his country they drink so much wine.
19. Songs by groups: "Somewhere in France Is a Lily," "Joan of Arc," and "Long, Long Trail"; "Star-spangled Banner."

ROXANA M. ADAMS.

TEACHERS' TRAINING SCHOOL,
KANSAS CITY, MO.

AS REPORTED

THE N. E. A. AS A REPRESENTATIVE ASSEMBLY

All reports seem to indicate that the reorganization of the National Education Association has proved effective. At the Des Moines Meeting there was a new sense of individual responsibility. Many attended the meeting as appointed delegates representing local bodies, and their presence took on a new dignity in consequence. The business of the Association proceeded smoothly and with no evidence of the factional differences which threatened to destroy the society's usefulness.

One serious difficulty remaining is to find a time of meeting when all can attend who might wish to do so. As it is, the summer sessions of the normal schools and colleges detain a very large number who would enjoy participation in the meeting and who would have much to give. Among other suggestions, that of holding the annual convention late in August has been made. This would have advantages, but it would find many leaders already at their desks preparing for the year's work. Why not choose a time, say the Christmas holidays, when a large number of affiliated societies could join and thus make the meeting in a large way an educational clearing-house?

The next annual meeting will be held in Boston in July, 1922.

THE PROGRAM OF THE NATIONAL COUNCIL OF PRIMARY EDUCATION

The National Council of Primary Education was organized in 1915 through a rather spontaneous assembling of primary and kindergarten leaders. It was agreed to work toward a three-fold goal, a greater use of activities in the primary school, greater freedom of method for the teacher, and closer co-operation with the kindergarten and the grades above.

The first of these purposes has led to a study of the extent to which activities are being used in early education, the form which these activities take, and the extent to which children are permitted to initiate activities. The culmination of this study has been the publication of the report of an investigation led by Miss Annie E. Moore, of Teachers' College, under the title, "What Constitutes an Acceptable Day's Work in the Primary Schools?" In this report the question is raised and data, consisting of observations in many types of schools, are given, but the answer is left open for further discussion. This report has been spread broadcast over the country and is stimulating widespread interest. The observations consist of detailed accounts of the day's work in both very formal and very free types of programs and is therefore full of suggestion to classroom teachers and supervisors

In seeking the second purpose, it is realized that freedom of method must depend in large measure upon the kind and extent of the teacher's professional training. With a view to raising the standard of professional interest and in line with our stand for self-initiated activities, informal local groups of teachers have been organized for the sake of the happy influence of greater social contact and for intimate discussion of immediate professional problems. These gatherings, being voluntary, avoid the perfunctory tone so often present in grade and association meetings and allow the opportunity for digestion and assimilation of the lectures and discussions of more formal gatherings. In general these social gatherings tend to dignify the field of primary education and impress the public with its importance and, incidentally, also to overcome the somewhat general impression that anybody can teach primary work and that those who know enough are soon promoted to higher grades.

The third goal is being reached through the social commingling of kindergarten and primary teachers and a mutual exchange of ideas. The Council's influence has undoubtedly been a factor in the increasing demand for movable furniture and other equipment which permits the greater use of activities and bridges the gaps which heretofore existed between kindergarten and first grade. A list of minimum essentials in primary furnishings may be found in the *Fourth Council Report*.

So far the studies undertaken have been centered in the first grade, since conditions there are fundamental, but the findings are full of suggestion for all early education. Other studies are in progress which will in due time broaden in scope. The Council's work will not be complete until, through a general awakening of interest in the general public and among the entire teaching corps, the best practice of the best schools becomes the common practice of all schools.

ELLA VICTORIA DOBBS,
*Chairman, National Council
of Primary Education.*

UNIVERSITY OF MISSOURI

LIBRARIES IN EDUCATION

The following statement of principles is urged for adoption by the National Education Association and other educational societies:

1. All pupils in both elementary and secondary schools should have ready access to books to the end that they may be trained (a) to love to read that which is worth while; (b) to supplement their school studies by the use of books other than textbooks; (c) to use reference books easily and effectively; (d) to use intelligently both the school library and the public library.

2. Every secondary school should have a trained librarian, and every elementary school should have trained library service.

3. Trained librarians should have the same status as teachers or heads of departments of equal training and experience.

4. Every school that provides training for teachers should require a course in the use of books and libraries, and a course on the best literature for children.

5. Every state should provide for the supervision of school libraries and for the certification of school librarians.

6. The public library should be recognized as a necessary part of public instruction, and should be as liberally supported by tax as are the public schools, and for the same reasons.

7. The school system that does not make liberal provision for training in the use of

libraries fails to do its full duty in the way of revealing to all future citizens the opportunity to know and to use the resources of the public library as a means of education.

Committee: J. I. Wyer, director of New York State Library, *chairman;* Walter Brown, librarian of Buffalo Public Library; Annie S. Cutter, Public Library, Cleveland, Ohio; Lucile F. Fargo, librarian of North Central High School, Spokane, Washington; H. A. Hollister, high-school visitor, University of Illinois; Florence M. Hopkins, librarian, Central High School, Detroit, Michigan;

Willis H. Kerr, librarian, State Normal School, Emporia, Kansas; C. G. Leland, superintendent of libraries, Department of Education, New York City; O. S. Rice, supervisor of school libraries for the state of Wisconsin; Mary C. Richardson, librarian, State Normal School, Geneseo, New York; Alice Tyler, Library School, Western Reserve University, Cleveland, Ohio; Harriet A. Wood, supervisor of schools and public libraries for the state of Minnesota; Adeline E. Zachert, director of school libraries for the state of Pennsylvania.

THE READER'S GUIDE

SIGNIFICANT ARTICLES
A SYMPOSIUM ON THE PROJECT METHOD

One of the most important of the recent articles dealing with method is the symposium in the September number of the *Teachers' College Record*. This is made up of contributions from five persons, Professors Kilpatrick, Bagler, Bonser, Hosic, and Mr. Hatch of Teachers' College, and embodies the main points of a discussion carried on at the annual meeting of the Elementary Section of the Alumni Association of Teachers' College. The general topic was "Dangers and Difficulties of the Project Method." Among the dangers feared by Professor Bagley were less permanent retention, less actual transfer, weakened respect for race experience, lack of provision for organization of knowledge, underestimate of the need and value of control and guidance of children, and lack of perspective. He believed, however, that these dangers would ultimately be realized and overcome. Professor Bonser emphasized the dangers of misinterpretation and neglect. The idea may be taken in too narrow a sense, or children's passing interests may be overvalued, to the neglect of the race inheritance.

To avoid these and other dangers, an adequate scholarship must be brought to bear. Professor Hosic contended that much that is desirable in education can come only through projects. We must simply be true to the principles of democracy and of the newer educational psychology. Mr. Hatch gave an account of the reactions of pupils in the Horace Mann School to the project method and also of a class of observers from the college. Professor Kilpatrick defined project as a unit of purposeful experience and described each of four types. He found great value in the project as a means of bringing children and the race experience together. It provides for much broader outcomes of learning than more formal methods. Most of the objections urged against project-teaching seem to spring from misconceptions as to what is meant by it. There is no intention, for example, of simply turning children loose to follow their bent. Drill may properly be included, as well as most other forms of useful learning. The task before us is to work out an adequate technique, upon which a good beginning has already been made. Indeed, the whole outlook for a sound development is most favorable.

MOVEMENT IN HANDWRITING

How scientific studies may bear upon current school practices is well illustrated in the *Journal of Educational Psychology* for May. Reporting recent investigations made by means of a special camera, Professor Frank N. Freeman contends that the attempt to teach the so-called muscular movement, especially in the lower grades, is a "flat failure." There is comparatively little correspondence between the degree of arm movement and the degree of excellence attained. He shows also that less importance is to be attached than is commonly done to a level wrist and other phases of orthodox position. In a brief summary he sets forth the conclusions which his investigations seem to warrant with regard to position, to movement, and to speed changes. In general these are opposed, not so much to current practices, as to laying undue stress on position and movement and expecting too much regularity in speed.

PROFESSIONALIZING THE PRINCIPALSHIP

There is evidence to show that the office of principal of an elementary school is growing in dignity and importance and requires more and more of special training and fitness. Data of this kind were collected by Worth McClure, of the Gatewood School in Seattle, and were published in the *Elementary School Journal* for June. Replies from seventeen cities, supported by the testimony of certain college professors of education, indicate that principals are being freed from teaching, get better salaries, are more often supplied with clerical assistance, are recognized as experts in the making of courses of study, frequently appear on educational programs, write educational articles, bear responsibility as community leaders, and receive appointment and promotion more and more because of professional training and qualifications. The writer seems none too sure that managerial functions do not absorb the major portion of the principal's attention at present, but rightly hopes

these may be subordinated to leadership of the teachers.

WHY IS A SCHOOL?

In view of the natural tendency which men in general have to follow tradition instead of making a fresh analysis, Professor Smith's article on "A Theory of the School" in the *Journal of Experimental Pedagogy* for June is to the point. The writer remarks that some one has collected sixty-seven definitions of education; he will add the sixty-eighth, namely, that a school is a place for realizing impossible ideals. It serves to lessen the imperfections of life. But it should not, therefore, attempt to do what can be better done elsewhere. It cannot, for example, take the place of a good home. One of its chief functions is to maintain and hand on the best national traditions. These ideas are not so novel as the writer seems to think, but they are worthy of fresh emphasis from time to time.

HOW TO MEASURE [1]

Since its beginning, standardized and scaled mental measurement, both in and out of the schools, has evolved with phenomenal rapidity. Yet at no time has such rapid progress occurred as during the last three or four years. In view of this rapid evolution there are those who feel that no book dealing with mental measurement is justified unless it makes substantial original contributions or, at least, reports recently developed techniques. Those who feel thus will be annoyed by this book by Wilson and Hoke, for anyone who has read one or more of the previous books on educational measurement will find little in this one that is novel.

Whether or not such critics are right does not especially interest me. I am interested, however, that those who read the book shall understand that the techniques for the practical uses of mental measurement in education

[1] How to Measure, by G. M. Wilson and Kremer J. Hoke. New York: The MacMillan Company, 1920.

have been carried far beyond what is indicated in this book. The mention of two such lines of development will suffice. In the first place, methods have been evolved for combining the results of several tests, thereby permitting many practical uses otherwise impossible. In the second place, much progress has been made in the interpretation of certain tests in the light of others, as, for example, the interpretation of educational tests in the light of intelligence tests. Both of these very significant developments are practically ignored in Wilson and Hoke's book.

In view of the fact that most of the important centers for distributing test materials have for sale sample packages of tests, together with full instructions for applying and scoring them, there are those who feel that it is unjustifiable to take up a large percentage of a book merely in compilation—merely in reproducing the tests and describing the routine procedure for applying and scoring them. Because of the frequent improvement in tests such a book will be short-lived inevitably. Those who feel thus can expect considerable annoyance in reading this book.

Now that I have forewarned those who are looking for original or novel ideas and stimulated the protective mechanism of those who are annoyed by routine, let us consider the bias of still another group of critics. There are those, and their number is very large, whose knowledge of the principles, practices, and possibilities of mental measurement in education is substantially zero. They desire a book which takes nothing for granted, which gives as clearly and simply as possible only the first simple steps from the selection of a single test to remedial prescriptions based upon the results from that single test. Those who feel thus will be greatly pleased by this book by Wilson and Hoke. In simplicity, clearness, and practical helpfulness it is at least the equal of the best books in this field and is better than most, and in its up-to-dateness it is the superior of all.

WM. A. McCALL.

THE NEW BOOKS

The Organization and Curricula of Schools. By W. G. Sleight. New York: Longmans, Green & Co., 1920. Pp. 264. $2.00 net.

To establish a point of view rather than present details is the author's aim. Though written for English training colleges, the book is informing to Americans as well.

The Redirection of High-School Instruction. By H. G. Lull and H. B. Wilson. Philadelphia: J. B. Lippincott Co., 1921. Pp. 286.

An attempt to discover and organize the functional elements in high-school instruction.

L'education des enfants anormaux. By Alice Descœudres. Neuchatel: Delachaux et Niestlé, 1916. Pp. 434.

Deserving of attention from any interested in the problems of education of defectives. The author is a highly successful teacher in classes for special children in Geneva.

The Socialized Recitation. By Charles L. Robbins. Boston: Allyn and Bacon, 1920. Pp. 100.

A clear exposition of principles and certain specific illustrations.

The Teaching of Geography. By Mendel E. Branom and Fred K. Branom. Boston: Ginn & Co., 1921. Pp. 292.

Reflects the current interest in social methods and problem attack. Numerous references, mainly to the periodicals, are added to the various chapters.

The New Methods in Arithmetic. By Edward L. Thorndike. Chicago: Rand, McNally & Co., 1921.

A very concrete and stimulating presentation of the theories embodied in the author's series of arithmetics, published by the same house.

The Measurement of Silent Reading. By May Ayres Burgess. New York: Russell Sage Foundation, 1921. Pp. 163.

A monograph to accompany the author's Silent Reading Scale, also published by the Sage Foundation. This is one of the simplest of the reading tests now available.

Empirical Studies in School Reading. By James F. Hosic. New York: Teachers

College Bureau of Publications. Pp. 174. Cloth, $2.50. Paper, $2.00.

A scientific basis for the evaluation of method in literature and literary reading-books. Over eighty pages of stenographic reports of lessons are included.

Problem-Solving or Practice in Thinking. By Samuel Chester Parker. Reprinted from the *Elementary School Journal.* Address the Department of Education, University of Chicago. $0.40.

Making a High School Program. By Myron W. Richardson. Yonkers-on-Hudson, New York: World Book Co., 1921. Pp. 27. Kraft binding. $0.75.

A practical scheme for organizing the semester's program in any high school.

The Project Method. By John Alford Stevenson. New York: Macmillan Co., 1921. Pp. 305. $1.80.

Devoted mainly to a critical survey of various definitions of the project method and to the author's own distinctions. A few concrete applications are included.

Psychology for Normal Schools. By Lawrence Augustus Averill. Boston: Houghton Mifflin Co., 1921. Pp. 362.

An attempt to select and simplify those phases of psychology likely to be grasped and used by first- or second-year normal-school students. Study apparatus and reading references are appended to each chapter.

The Principles of Teaching in Secondary Education. By Herbert H. Foster. New York: Charles Scribner's Sons, 1921. Pp. 367. $1.75.

Differs from most recent works in this field in that the discussion is confined to teaching as such and does not attempt to deal with other problems of high-school education.

Arithmetical Essentials, Book I. By J. Andrew Drushel, Margaret E. Noonan, and John W. Withers. Chicago: Lyons and Carnahan, 1921. Pp. 304.

Special emphasis is laid on presenting the situations in which the various processes have their actual uses.

The Alexander-Dewey Arithmetic, Elementary, Intermediate, and Advanced Books. By Georgia Alexander. Edited by John Dewey. New York: Longmans, Green & Co., 1921.

The authors of this new series have attempted to give greater reality to the processes to be mastered by means of "socialized recitations" and problems drawn from daily life.

Junior High-School English, Book I. By Thomas H. Briggs, Isabel McKinney, and Florence Skeffington. Boston: Ginn & Co., 1921. Pp. xiv+395.

This volume, the first of a series of three, is for the seventh grade.

Effective English Expression. By Edward H. Webster. New York: Newson & Co., 1920. Pp. 323.

A simple high-school text in which the author aims to arouse specific purposes in the minds of the pupils.

Business English Projects. By W. Wilbur Hatfield. New York: The Macmillan Co., 1921. Pp. 303.

A high-school text in a new vein. Suggestive as to possibilities in the grammar grades.

A Study of Poetry. By Bliss Perry. Boston: Houghton Mifflin Co., 1920. Pp. 396. $2.25.

A companion to the author's well-known *Study of Prose Fiction* and like that intended both for college classes and for general reading.

A Study of the Types of Literature. By Mabel Irene Rich. New York: The Century Co., Pp. 540.

Intended as a textbook for the fourth year of high school. Numerous complete selections are included and are accompanied with questions for study and lists for wider reading.

Poems of the English Race. By Raymond Macdonald Alden. New York: Charles Scribner's Sons, 1921. Pp. 410.

Pieces chosen primarily for their interest and arranged chronologically under the two divisions of narrative and lyrical poetry.

One-Act Plays by Modern Authors. Edited by Helen Louise Cohen. New York: Harcourt, Brace & Co., 1921. Pp. 342.

THE JOURNAL OF·
EDUCATIONAL
METHOD

Edited by JAMES F. HOSIC

Volume I   NOVEMBER, 1921   Number 3

Published by the WORLD BOOK COMPANY, at Greenwich, Conn., for
THE NATIONAL CONFERENCE ON EDUCATIONAL METHOD

$3.00 a year   Monthly except July and August   35 cents a copy

Application for entry as second-class matter at Greenwich, Connecticut, pending

THE NATIONAL CONFERENCE ON EDUCATIONAL METHOD

An Association of Persons Interested in Supervision and Teaching

---

Officers of the Conference

President, C. L. WRIGHT, Public Schools, Huntington, West Virginia.
Vice-President, MARGARET NOONAN, Harris Teachers College, St. Louis, Missouri.
Secretary-Treasurer, JAMES F. HOSIC, Teachers College, New York City.

Executive Committee

THE PRESIDENT AND THE SECRETARY-TREASURER, *ex officio*.
C. C. CERTAIN, Northwestern High School, Detroit, Michigan.
MARGARET MADDEN, Doolittle Elementary School, Chicago, Illinois.
MARY E. PENNELL, Public Schools, Kansas City, Missouri.

Board of Directors

C. C. CERTAIN, Assistant Principal and Head of Department of English, Northwestern High School, Detroit, Mich.
BESSIE GOODRICH, Assistant Superintendent of Schools, Des Moines, Ia.
J. M. GWINN, Superintendent of Schools, New Orleans, La.
KATHERINE HAMILTON, Assistant Superintendent of Schools, St. Paul, Minn.
JAMES F. HOSIC, Associate Professor of Education in Charge of Extramural Courses, Teachers College, Columbia University.
FRED M. HUNTER, Superintendent of Schools, Oakland, Calif.
WILLIAM H. KILPATRICK, Professor of Philosophy of Education, Teachers College, Columbia University.
MARGARET MADDEN, Principal, Doolittle Elementary School, Chicago, Ill.
F. M. McMURRY, Professor of Elementary Education, Teachers College, Columbia University.
MARGARET NOONAN, Professor of Elementary Education, Harris Teachers College, St. Louis, Mo.
MARY E. PENNELL, Supervisor of Primary Grades, Kansas City, Mo.
J. A. STARKWEATHER, Assistant Superintendant of Schools, Duluth, Minn.
W. F. TIDYMAN, Director of the Training School, State Normal School, Farmville, Va.
JOHN W. WITHERS, Dean of School of Education, New York University.
C. L. WRIGHT, Superintendent of Schools, Huntington, W. Va.

Address applications for membership to the Secretary of the Conference, 525 West One Hundred and Twentieth Street, New York City. The fee for active members is $3.00, for associate members, $2.00; $2.00 in each case is applied to the support of the journal, for which each member receives a year's subscription. The editorial office is at 525 West One Hundred and Twentieth Street, New York City.

The Journal of Educational Method

VOLUME I   NOVEMBER, 1921   NUMBER 3

EDITORIALLY SPEAKING

WHAT'S IN A NAME?

As was to be expected, some of our contemporaries are more or less puzzled by our use of the words Educational Method. "Method is the way teachers proceed, isn't it? Why then do you include in your journal articles which evidently are intended primarily for those who supervise teachers?" Why indeed? Because if supervision is ever to come into its own it must have "methods" too. And it is precisely because the principles of method that should guide the supervisor are the same as those which should guide the teacher that the discussion of the two functions should proceed side by side. If supervision were merely scientific management or inspection or bossing the job, then truly it would have but little in common with the art of teaching. But since it has to do with constructive leadership and guidance as well as organization and coördination of effort of those who are or should be seeking to improve, the analogy is a true one. There is besides this justification, namely, that example is more powerful than precept. Supervisors who know how to stimulate and direct effective group activity among their teachers actually de-

velop good teaching methods by doing so. The term Educational Method is a fit one to designate the entire body of principles which underlie all modern school practice.

INTERNATIONAL RELATIONS

Much interest attaches to the appointment by the National Education Association of a committee whose chief immediate function is to organize and conduct an international conference on education. There are great possibilities in the idea. Americans will do well to enter into the conference, however, with two very definite purposes, first, to be more eager to receive than to give and, second, not to propose any joint enterprises which we are not fully resolved to carry out to the bitter end. Our self-assurance is amusing and sometimes annoying to Europeans, who pardon it as characteristic of youth and immaturity. As for starting things and then going off and leaving them, that practice is thought by many of our friends abroad to be our established custom. A few good plans consistently followed up for many years would do much to improve our reputation abroad.

Annual meeting of the National Conference on Educational Method, Chicago, Ill., February 28 and March 1, 1922

HOW THE TEXTBOOK MAY AID THE TEACHER IN GETTING PROJECTS TO GOING

Margaret E. Noonan

Professor of Elementary Education, New York University

The term *project* as it has come to be used in the field of education has two aspects. First, it is a term used to define or describe a *method* of acquiring facts, skills, habits, ideals, or interests, a *method* of modifying behavior, or conduct. From this aspect it emphasizes learning through meaningful, or purposeful, rather than through purposeless activities. Purposeful acts may, however, result in modifying behavior in either a desirable or an undesirable direction. Activities in which one engages with the utmost wholeheartedness may modify behavior in a bad direction if the facts, habits, or ideals that are established are socially undesirable. For instance, a bandit holding up a train may be pursuing wholeheartedly an activity that is purposeful but that is undeniably non-social and consequently not an educative project. It would be a great mistake to assume that wholehearted or purposeful activity, *per se*, is the key to the solution of the problem of preparing for the development of truly social beings in our democratic society. Very definite social objectives in facts, habits, ideals and attitudes that are to be realized as the end of all activities and relationships in school life must be held in mind in all discussions of the project as a method of organization, and all school activities must be judged valuable or otherwise in accordance with the degree in which they lead to the realization of these social objectives.

In order to evaluate the textbook in getting projects going it is important to consider both requirements for the *educative project:* the content presented in the text, as well as the method of organizing such content. It may be argued by some that the function of a textbook is to present content only and that any discussion of method in connection with a textbook is irrelevant. Every textbook, however, does present *some* method of teaching. The subject matter, or content side of every text must be presented in some organized fashion, and since the order in which facts are organized is an important element in method, every textbook does emphasize a method and every variation in the textbook organization of content in relation to the learner's experience is a variation in method. The project method demands an organization that takes as its basis, or starting point, an activity clearly related to the learner's present life needs and purposes. It demands that this relationship be clearly shown, not implied, so that the learner may (1) enter wholeheartedly into the activity, (2) determine in the light of this relationship the proper steps to be taken in carrying out the activity to its conclusion, (3) appreciate the amount of emphasis, practice, or drill each step should receive, (4) have a clear indication of the goal that is to be reached.

Any textbook that organizes its subject matter around activities that are closely related to the purposes of the learner at the stage of development for which the text is designed, that shows the relationship of the facts to be learned, or of the habits or skills to be acquired, to this activity, and that sets up a definite and specific goal in the light of this activity seems to be pointing the way to securing purposeful activity. On the other hand, every textbook that organizes subject matter, however valuable, in such a manner as to ignore these principles is encouraging purposeless activity. I am aware that in the hands of a skillful, well-trained teacher the latter kind of a textbook may be made valuable, but the rank and file of teachers too frequently follow the organization suggested in the text, which at present is usually some logical scheme that appeals to the author but that is so remote from the mind of the learner that he is not likely to see any connection with his own aims and purposes.

The inability to see the value of textbook content on account of the current method of textbook organization of content is more marked among immature learners in the elementary school than among more mature students. Nevertheless, I was greatly impressed recently with the enthusiasm shown toward the study of educational psychology by a class of college students preparing for teaching, who used as a textbook a psychology whose subject matter is organized about problems the solution of which college students can appreciate as having significance for a teacher. Their interest in the subject and the amount of work done by the class in addition to the assigned work far exceeded what I had found in previous classes, where the text employed had followed the more usual organization of psychology texts—discussions in order of sensation, perception, imagination, memory, reasoning, and the like. I am not implying that a psychology textbook organized on a topical basis has no value. Its chief value, it seems to me, is as a reference rather than as a textbook. I believe that there is a distinct place for two kinds of books for class use. One should be of the encyclopedic kind, compiled by authorities on the subject matter involved, and designed to be used only for reference, another arranged by students of educational methods and intended for textbook use.

Professor Harold O. Rugg, in a recent discussion entitled "How Shall We Reconstruct the Social School Curriculum," expresses the opinion that one of the reasons why the old correlation movement failed to be effective in securing the organization of related materials in one body of subject matter rather than in separate compartments was "because there were no systems of textbooks in which the correlation was worked out."[1] It seems to me that the advocates of the project method will be equally handicapped in their efforts to improve classroom teaching until the writers of textbooks show an appreciation of the importance of the organization of subject matter from the standpoint of activities that are meaningful and vital to those for whom the text is designed.

Recently I spent some time going through arithmetic texts for primary

[1] Rugg: *The Historical Outlook*, May, 1921, Vol. XII, No. 5.

grades evaluating the activities suggested from the standpoint of purposes appealing to primary children. I was forced to the conclusion that children who used the texts examined would undoubtedly develop the attitude that arithmetic has little value in their lives. "Write figures from 1 to 20," says a text. What for? How is a child to know when he has written his figures satisfactorily? What is the goal in accuracy or perfection desired? There is nothing in the text to indicate. "To write digits till one's chubby hand aches and then to be told to take one's sponge and rub them out seems very hard," Emmy Lou once remarked.[1] The pity of it is that the majority of "Emmy Lous" become so accustomed to doing things in school the purpose of which they cannot understand that they become too stultified even to question, "What for?"

Purposeful activity always has some very definite goal to be attained. Furthermore, the goal it represents is a possible one, and you should know when you have reached it. When, for example, a child sets out to make a wagon, he wants a wagon that is made well enough to run when pushed, or one that a child can ride in, or one in which he can transport something—a wagon that is made well enough to be satisfactory for some definite purpose. The particular purpose he has in mind determines just how accurate and how careful he must be in making the wagon. But in following such directions as, "Write figures from 1 to 20," he might go on writing figures day after day and never know when he had written them satisfactorily enough. In carrying on

to completion many projects which appeal to children as meaningful, writing figures from 1 to 20 is involved. The degree of accuracy that is necessary, however, differs with each project. The particular goal to be reached may demand the writing of *one* figure half a dozen times until it is satisfactory for the purpose, or may be satisfactorily attained by the first writing.

As I proceeded in my examination of arithmetic texts I found, "Draw a line six inches long." "With a ruler measure the top of your desk." "Measure the width of the door." "Measure the length of the blackboard." Just measuring for the sake of measuring! "Count the pieces of chalk in the chalk box." "Count all the panes of glass in your schoolroom windows." "Count all the objects in the room." This meaningless counting and measuring may be defended by some teachers on the ground that children like to do it. Professor Dewey, in discussing the meaningless activities in which children are asked to indulge, says: "I frequently hear deadly devices extolled on the ground that children take so much interest in them. Yes, that is the pity of it. The mind cut off from worthy employ must take relief in what is left."

Outside of the school and away from school a child engages in counting and measuring not in order to carry out artificial activities but because of some worth-while purpose. He measures in order to make a house, or a box, or a cage, or a card, or something that he wants to use in a definite way. He measures with just the degree of accuracy that is necessary in order to get

[1] George Madden Martin, *Emmy Lou.*

the result that he is after and the degree of accuracy varies, of course, with his purpose. To measure accurately to a quarter of an inch when a measure to the nearest inch would be satisfactory, as it frequently is in life situations, is certainly a waste of time and an inefficient method of measuring. Measuring everything in the classroom for the sake of learning to measure and with no other purpose not only encourages meaningless activity but also develops inefficient habits of measuring. If a child is measuring in order to make cards necessary for playing a game, or to make tickets of admission to a play, he has some real reason for measuring and he not only knows the degree of perfection necessary in his measuring, but also knows when he has accomplished a satisfactory result. Such activities should be used as the basis of organization for acquiring knowledge and skill in measuring.

The use of significant projects as a basis for organization of subject matter means a distinct reorganization of the material of present-day texts. It means that children's experiences must be taken into consideration in our organization to a much greater extent than at present. A child's experience with time, for example, does not come in any such orderly fashion as the order given in many textbooks suggests. He can appreciate, because of his experiences, the fact that a week is made up of seven days long before he has a basis in experience for "sixty seconds make a minute" or "sixty minutes make an hour."

There will be, I think, two arguments

advanced against the organization of subject matter in texts around projects. One will be advanced by those opposed to projects as a method of teaching on the ground that the utilization of children's purposeful activities as a basis for organization will necessitate the omission of content that should be taught because of social demands. But any content that is socially desirable is so because it is a part of significant social activities. In so far as these activities are a part of the world in which children move as well as adults, children's interest in them will be limited only by their ability to comprehend them. A more pertinent objection that may be made against the organization of textbooks about significant projects will come from the advocates of the project as a method of teaching. Their objection to selected projects in textbooks will be that projects to be really significant as a means of setting up purposeful activity should originate with the learner and that a text organized about projects destroys the very essence of purposeful activity by determining the activity that is to be used in securing the desired content. Professor Dewey's discussion of this point is illuminating to me. He says: "There is no ground for believing that the teacher should never suggest anything. The wise teacher is very much more likely than the child to know what his own interests and impulses mean. But the suggestion must fit in with the child's dominating mode of growth."[3]

It seems to me that many of children's most purposeful activities are suggested by other children, by parents, by teach-

[3] Dewey, *School and the Child*.

ers, or by other adults. The activity of going to school *at all* is suggested by others, but that does not mean that the child does not enter into it wholeheartedly.

I believe that if all textbooks were organized exclusively on a project basis, and the projects used were ones which children of about the same stage of development had really initiated and carried through, there would be more rather than less *initiation* of purposeful activity on the part of children than we have at present. It seems to me much better to have children following a text and carrying on activities the purpose of which they can understand, even though the activity was suggested by some one else, than to have them doing things the purpose of which they cannot understand and which have no significance in their lives.

THE GRADING AND PROMOTION OF PUPILS

CHARLES B. WILLIS
Principal of the Alexander Taylor School, Edmonton, Alberta, Canada

Much attention has been paid to the problem of the grading and promotion of pupils during the last few years, and rightly, since it is intimately connected with questions of school costs, medical treatment, curricula, school plant, etc. *Laggards in Our Schools* by Ayres and the many comments in school surveys on age-grade tables have given us one side of this by pointing out the existence of the problem. Little has been done, however, on the other sides of it—correction and, more important still, prevention.

This problem and its solution is essentially a recognition of the problem of individual differences and provision for them, with the necessity of class teaching also being taken into account. The many measurements made of performance and intelligence by Courtis, Terman, and a host of others all tend to point out the great range and variety of such differences. The tendency in the past has been to consider differences in class work and in progress made through the grades as due largely to differences in health, attendance, etc., rather than to differences in natural ability.

At present educators are satisfied that the great range in progress made by different children is due largely to differences in ability, and especial importance must be attached to this difference since it is the factor which is least easily changed—in fact practically does not change at all. If a child is lacking in application to study, it is usually possible for the teacher to secure better effort, and even "school attitude," which has been shown by Pressey, writing in the *Elementary School Journal*, to be very important, may be changed, but native intelligence seems to be the one thing which the teacher cannot influence or improve. At the same time, it must be borne in mind that very few people make use of their maximum of ability and hence nearly all of us may hope to surpass anything we have done so far if we will only make full use of what nature has given us.

In passing, it might be said that school progress does correlate much more highly with mental age than is indicated by Pressey's results. He worked with only one grade, Grade VII. The differences in mental level were slight compared with the whole range of differences possible, but no doubt practically the whole range of differences in school attitude were present. Naturally differences in scholarship found were caused more by the great differences in school attitude than by the comparatively slight differences in mental level. His experiment shows that differences in class work within a grade, where differences in mental level are comparatively small, are due, to a very considerable extent, to differences in school attitude.

Up to the present the measurement of intelligence has been largely in the hands of trained psychologists, who could measure very well indeed but who were usually satisfied with locating a few feeble-minded children and recommending an occasional extra promotion. The results that have been obtained from the use of the measurement of intelligence as applied in most school systems are disappointing in the extreme, because workers have been content to measure, tabulate figures, and make graphs, and have stopped without doing any follow-up work of value. Of course this work is that of the school administrator rather than that of the psychologist, but so far the work of the psychologists in mental measurement has been almost totally fruitless.

An account of what has been done in one school system might give a better idea of the possibilities of mental measurement follow-up work. The Alexander Taylor school has about five hundred and fifty pupils in seventeen rooms. Grades I–VIII, and three other small schools, containing in all nine rooms, send nearly all of their pupils to Alexander Taylor at the end of Grade V. It is compulsory to attend school until the age of fifteen years. The course of study and the grading is very much like that of some of the eastern states. About a third of the pupils are foreign—Hebrew, Russian, German and Austrian, mainly. The school year contains 190 to 195 days.

During the last four years the intelligence of nearly all of the children in the school has been measured. The average I.Q. is about one hundred for the English-speaking, non-foreign part of the school, though most of the schools of the city must exceed this level considerably. As in practically every school on the continent, many of the pupils of average intelligence had, through irregular attendance, sickness, careless grading, poor teaching, etc., lost a year; many others who were bright had not reaped any advantage in the way of extra promotions from ability and so had in many cases grown lazy and indifferent, so much so in fact, that they were very often not recognized as bright by their teachers; finally some who were slow had been carried along to grades where they were not capable of doing the work. The following table of mental age and grade shows the condition that existed September 1, 1920, after the promotion, etc., of those who were present at the end of

June. Only the English-speaking children of English descent are taken in in this table.

Mental Age	Grade									Total
	1	2	3	4	5	6	7	8	9	
4	2	....	....	....	....	....	....	....	....	2
5	5	1	1	....	....	....	....	....	....	7
6	4	7	2	....	....	....	....	....	....	13
7	3	19	9	....	....	....	....	....	....	31
8	....	12	21	8	1	....	....	....	....	42
9	....	2	4	19	4	2	....	....	....	31
10	....	....	2	8	20	6	4	....	....	40
11	....	....	....	1	7	14	14	6	....	42
12	....	....	....	....	1	11	18	4	2	36
13	....	....	....	....	....	2	11	17	7	37
14	....	....	....	....	....	....	5	15	8	28
15	....	....	....	....	....	....	1	6	8	15
16	....	....	....	....	....	....	....	3	6	9
17	....	....	....	....	....	....	....	1	....	1
Total	14	41	39	36	33	35	53	52	31	334

This gives a correlation between mental level and grade of .92, a much higher figure than Pressey got. If the fact that all in one grade were not equally far advanced were taken into account, this figure would no doubt be slightly changed and would probably be somewhat higher.

The follow-up work based on the condition found here consists of: (1) extra promotions for some pupils; (2) retardation or demotion of others; (3) proper placing of new pupils; (4) especial care taken to make sure that, as pupils enter Grade I and come up through the grades, the condition at present existing will not be repeated.

Many pupils who were below the grade their mental age would appear to warrant were given extra promotions either by being left only a half-year in each of two successive grades or by being promoted from, for example, Grade VI in June to Grade VIII in September. During the school year 1919-20, seventy-three pupils in the Alexander Taylor School received extra promotions. Only one of these pupils failed of promotion at the end of June, 1920. From September 1, 1920, to March 1, 1921, about eighty-five pupils have been given extra promotions on the basis of intelligence, class work, etc. Of these all but three or four are doing satisfactory work.

Pupils who come in from other schools are placed by taking account of their former standing and their mental level. Some are moved up a grade, others down a grade, and still others saved from demotion when they do not appear to be doing satisfactory work but the mental test shows the probability of their soon doing so. A mental level of about 12 years 9 months to 14 years 3 months is considered about right for Grade VIII at the beginning of the school year, September 1; 11 years 9 months to 13 years 3 months for Grade VII, etc. Since the test was first used it has been the important or deciding factor in about 110 extra promotions and has been a means of saving about 100 children from demotion or non-promotion. Few mistakes, in fact practically none, have been made by promoting too rapidly, but doubtless many have been made by our being too cautious.

The over-age in the school has been cut down from 42 per cent to 29 per cent, counting as over-age all pupils who are more than 7 years 3 months of age when they begin Grade I or more than 14 years 3 months when they begin Grade VIII, etc. In other words, the average time required to complete eight grades has been cut down by slightly over one year. Very careful standard tests show that the work of the school has improved about 7 per cent at the same time as the grading, and, in addition to this, the classes are more closely grouped around the median scores. (The scores made are for Grade VI about the same as or somewhat better than the standards set by Courtis and others for Grade VII, etc.) On a test in arithmetic given last spring by the provincial inspector, one of the Grade VIII classes in the Alexander Taylor school scored the highest of any Grade VIII in the city and the other Grade VIII in the school was very little lower. Definite, pointed supervision, applied as follow-up work after standard tests have revealed class weaknesses, has more than balanced the effect of rapid promotion on class attainment.

It must be kept in mind, however, that energy, persistence, regularity of attendance, class work, health, school attitude, etc., are important factors to be considered in grading. Intelligence is probably as important as all the other factors combined, and, since it is practically beyond the influence or control of the teacher and changes relatively little, is more basic. The teacher may overcome defective application on the part of the pupil but can scarcely overcome the handicap of defective mentality. If a pupil is not doing well in class, the reason should be found and proper remedies applied. If poor work is due to a lack of ability and the pupil is really doing as well as he can, he is encouraged and made to feel that he is coming on all right, but if he is found to be bright and lazy, steps are taken to bring about a change. Often the simple statement that he is not doing well, though he is bright and capable of good work and must do better, is sufficient to produce considerable improvement. It is well to remember that few pupils attain at all nearly to the success

their mentality would warrant. This, no doubt, accounts for the occasional case where a pupil of average ability does excellent work or a pupil of poor ability does average work.

At present the following are being used as guide lines to aid, not as rules to be slavishly followed. Pupils who have completed Grade VI in June may be promoted to Grade VIII in September: (1) if mental age, September 1, is 14 years 3 months or above and they are in the upper 69 per cent of the class in the June tests; (2) if mental age is 13 years 9 months to 14 years 2 months and they are in the upper 31 per cent of the class; (3) if mental age is 13 years 3 months to 13 years 8 months and they are in the upper 7 per cent of the class.

Grades III, IV, and V are treated similarly except that in Grade VI 12 years 9 months is substituted for 14 years 3 months in Grade VIII, etc., and the six-month interval used for Grade VI is cut to 5 months for Grade IV and to 4 months for Grade III. (Common sense is needed in applying these standards. Common sense here has the usual meaning, uncommon sense.)

The following regression equation has been developed to indicate the probable marks in Grade VIII of a pupil who is skipped from Grade VI:

$$M = .2025X + 2.5276Y + 2.2686Z - 9,$$

where M is the Grade VIII marks, X is the Grade VI marks, Y the I.Q., and Z the spelling marks in Grade VI. For an explanation of the method of developing this, any good work on educational statistics may be consulted. It is, of course, not useful except in the system where it has been developed, but if a number of cases are taken a similar equation may be developed for any system.

The brighter pupils who enter Grade I in February complete Grade I and Grade II in one and one-half years; the duller ones are given a go▉▉rounding by putting one and one-half years in Grade I.

Skipping grades is, however, at best only a makeshift. The grading, from the time pupils enter school, should be handled so that pupils do not get behind the grade they should be in. To obtain all the advantages and none of the disadvantages of skipping grades, school systems with large schools should provide an eight-year course of study for pupils of I.Q. about 93–107, the average pupils; a nine-year course, with less academic and more manual work, for pupils of I.Q. about 78–92; and a seven-year course, somewhat enriched, for pupils of about I.Q. 108–122. Pupils above 122 I.Q. and below 78 I.Q. might well be given special ungraded classes. It seems obvious that a child who will require nine years in public school would do better to take one-ninth of the course per year than to fail once, take one year's work twice, and cover the other years' work at too rapid a rate for his understanding. Pupils should not of course enter Grade I until their mental level is at least 6 years 0 months, regardless of their actual age.

The feeble-minded are not at all the important school problem they have been painted. (Like nearly all schools of five hundred to six hundred pupils, we have ten to fifteen of them all the time.) They usually give little trouble but make very little returns for the money spent on them. A little school work of a drill nature in reading, writing, etc., and manual work can be taught them. The girls had best be looked after by a good, kind, motherly woman, not necessarily a teacher, who will teach them a little housework, sewing, etc. They should, of course, be segregated after the age of puberty. The feeble-minded are a very minor part of the problem of school grading and their detection one of the less important uses of the mental test.

The pupils in a school system should be measured by means of the National Research Group Intelligence tests, published by the World Book Company, Yonkers, New York, as early in September as possible if they have not been tested before. This, together with supervision by means of standard tests, should be the chief function of the superintendent in small cities; in large cities, a special director of measurements and supervision should take care of this work.

Pupils could then be given extra promotions, etc., on the basis outlined above or, if the seven-, eight-, and nine-year course of study were in effect, could be placed in one of these that would, without skipping or failure, allow them to finish Grade VIII at the mental age of 14 years 0 months to 15 years 0 months. In extreme cases, some skipping or failure might be needed. Careful grading gives more and better education at less cost.

About 5 per cent to 10 per cent of any average class should be held back. There is a conflict in high-school work between the high standards necessarily required for entrance to professional schools, such as medicine, law, etc., and the lower standards that are necessary if the high school is to give education to the majority of the children, not deny it to them as at present. The standard for entrance to the professional schools might be raised above what it is at present to bar out inferior people. A mental test should also be given and a fairly high standard required. A lower standard or easier courses might be made use of for pupils who simply wished to benefit by a high-school education. Schools should be made to fit the pupils, not pupils expected to fit the schools.

On account of the small number of pupils and the lack of money and clerical assistance, little work of value can be done in a single school and the experimental work that is done does not give very reliable results. A city with ten or twenty large schools offers a very rich field for work of this nature. The work of grading and supervision is almost totally ineffective without such a scientific basis. In this short account, many things have been passed over rapidly and all and sundry are warned not to interpret and extend these ideas in their own way and then blame the writer if their own mode of handling is unsatisfactory.

MIND-SET AND LEARNING [1]

WILLIAM H. KILPATRICK [2]

Professor of Education, Teachers College, Columbia University

"I wish I understood these 'laws of learning.' Everywhere I go some one refers to them. They sound

A meeting of teachers

very imposing—and mysterious—but do they really amount to anything? How did the world manage to get on so long without them?"

"Well, you may be interested in the laws of learning, but I'm not. I don't

Do teachers need psychology?

see the use of teachers worrying their heads about psychology. Teaching has to do with children, real live children; but psychology is as dead as other things that live only in books. Teaching is hard enough and dry enough without having to learn psychology besides. If I went to summer school, which I don't intend to do, I'd study photography or something else interesting, but you'd never catch me in educational psychology. Besides, when I go off in the summer I don't want to be always reminded of my work. September to June is enough for me."

"Yes, we all know how you feel on such matters; but I believe one reason

The study of education makes teaching more interesting

why you find teaching dry and hard is exactly because you don't study it. At summer school last year I found out so many new things about children and how they learn, and heard so much of the plans and experiments of the other students, that I could hardly wait for school to begin again. I was so eager to see those

---

[1] The reader must fully understand that Professor Thorndike is in no wise to be held responsible for my popular commentary and elaboration of what is more succinctly—and scientifically—presented in his *Educational Psychology* (Teachers College Bureau of Publications). It has seemed necessary to give this account in order that the reader may more easily follow certain further discussions.

[2] All rights reserved by the author.

things in my pupils and to try some experiments of my own. You will perhaps say I have always liked teaching. So I have in a way, but teaching the same way year in and year out was getting to be pretty monotonous. Now it's a different thing. I have more interesting things to watch than you can imagine. But I must admit that I don't seem to see all my psychology as clearly now as when we were discussing it in the class. More difficulties have arisen than I ever dreamed of. For one thing the psychology seems more complicated, not only when I watch for it in my pupils but also when I try to straighten it all out in my mind. There's nothing I'd like better than for us to talk it over, but I warn you I'll raise many questions. For I want to know."

"If psychology or anything else will keep teaching my brats from being **Does psy-** humdrum, I'll say, "Yes, **chology fit all** let's study it." I am willing **children?** to listen awhile and see how your discussion starts off, but I tell you beforehand I'm skeptical of it all. You don't know my pupils. Psychology may help your nice well-dressed children who come from good homes, but it takes something stronger for mine. My first step with each new class is to put the fear of God in their souls. After that I can sometimes do something with them. Perhaps I might even use psychology then, if I knew enough about it."

"Where shall we begin? Some one suggested the laws of learning."

"That's my first question: why do you say 'law'? I know you don't mean that we have to obey Thorndike or

whoever first made those laws, so why say law?"

"A law of learning is like any law of nature. Newton didn't *make* the **The meaning** law of gravitation; he *dis-* **of the term** *covered* it. As I understand **"law"** it, a law of nature is nothing but a statement of an observed regularity. Galileo discovered certain laws of falling bodies, but bodies fell afterwards just exactly as they had fallen before. They didn't pay any attention to Galileo. He only told what they do, regularly do, always do, so far as he could tell. The laws were merely exact statements of how bodies fall."

"Well, if that's all I don't see the use of laws. Why bother with them?"

"The use is this: if we know what to expect of falling bodies, we then know how to act where falling bodies are concerned."

"That's nothing but common sense, isn't it? Where does the science come in?"

"Science is itself nothing but common sense, common sense more careful of itself. Science is based on experience just as common sense, but it has more exact ways of measuring and of telling. In particular it tries to include many experiences under one statement. A law of nature is merely a very inclusive, very careful, and very reliable statement of what to expect."

"That sounds reasonable, but apply it to our topic. What is a law of learning?"

"A law of learning would be nothing but a very carefully made and very inclusive statement of how learning takes place."

"Give us one of your laws of learning. I'd like to know how learning takes place. Perhaps I'd know better how to make my pupils learn."

"I'll give you the Law of Readiness: When a bond is ready to act, to act gives satisfaction and not to act—"

"Now there you go with your outlandish jargon. Why don't you use everyday English. Bond! What is a bond?"

"That is the trouble about trying to be exact. As a matter of fact I fear I have over-simplified it now. I think, though, we'll have to begin further back. We'll have to get some preliminary terms or give up the effort to use understandingly the laws of learning."

"Go on. Only don't give us too many."

"Let's begin with S➡R and build up from there. S stands for stimulus,

The symbol S➡R or perhaps, more exactly, for situation acting as stimulus; and R stands for response. Any act of conduct is a response (R) to some sort of situation (S). I hear a child crying (S), I stop and listen (R). I meet a friend on the street (S), I say 'good morning' (R). My friend sees me and hears me speak (S), he responds in like fashion (R). He notices that I stop walking (S), he stops (R). I see that he is within hearing distance and attentive (S), I speak commending his address of last evening (R). He hears me speak (S), the meanings of my words arise in his mind (R). He appropriates my meaning (S), his face flushes and he feels gratification (R)."

"You haven't said a word about bond or connection. Please explain that. I told you I'd raise many questions."

"Notice the next to the last instance given: He hears me speak (S), the meanings of my words arise

The term "bond" in his mind (R). If he had not in the past *learned* the meanings of these words, my voice would have struck in vain upon his ears. The meanings could arise in his mind only because in the past he had learned to associate thenceforth these meanings with these sounds. That is, his past experience had built up somewhere in him—in his nervous system, in fact—such connections or bonds that when a particular sound is heard (e. g., my spoken words *magnificent address*), its appropriate meaning arises as a thought in his mind. Each such language connection or bond has to be learned, that is, built up by and in experience."

"But not all bonds are built up or learned, are they?"

"No, that is what I was about to say. My friend flushed with pleasure (R),

Innate vs. acquired bonds when I commended his address (S). His being pleased at commendation and his flushing in connection were not learned; these responses are innately joined. Each one of us is born with many such responses already joined by strong bonds to their appropriate situations."

"What is the arrow in S➡R? Is that the bond connecting S and R?"

"Yes. It is usually better to think of the situation (S) as being sized up or received by one nerve structure (or mechanism), the response (R) as made by a second, and the arrow as a third nerve structure that carries the stimulation from the structure (or mechanism)

S to the structure (or mechanism) R. There are some difficulties in so simple a statement, but we shall not go far wrong so to take it."

"Do you mean that this S➡→R holds of everything we do? Everything?"

"That is exactly what I mean. All conduct of whatever kind is so de-**All conduct can** scribed. Of course some **be described** situations are very simple, **in terms of** while others are very com-**S➡→R** plex. And similarly with responses, some are simple, others exceedingly complex. The bonds also vary. Some are so simple, definite and 'strong' that as soon as the stimulus comes the response follows with almost mechanical promptness and certainty. You know how it is if one is struck sharply just above the knee cap, the knee flexes in spite of anything we can do to prevent it. Other connections or bonds are so weak, so little formed, that the least little interference will prevent the response. If I ask a third grade pupil what is 2 x 2, he will say 4 at once. If I ask 7 x 6, he may tell me 42, but he is likely not to feel very sure of it. If I ask 8 x 13, he is almost sure not to know. Now it isn't a question of knowing 42 as a number in and of **Readiness** itself, it is precisely a question of having **discussed** or not having built a bond that joins 42 to 7 x 6, so that: thought of 7 x 6 (S) is followed by 42 (R). The arithmetic connections or bonds have to be built in order to be available for use. I wonder if the word 'learn' doesn't begin to take on a more definite meaning?"

"I see that S ➡→ R does join up with arithmetic and language; but does it fit all learning—geography, for example, or composition?"

"Most certainly. If one should ask about the capital of North Dakota. some will answer at once; others will hesitate, making perhaps several guesses; some won't know at all. The presence or absence of the bond and its strength if present tells the tale. So with composition work. One child will leave a straight margin to the left of the page, another will write as if there were no such thing. The difference is the presence or absence of the appropriate bond. One child will join with *and's* many short sentences. Another will consciously avoid it. So with morals. One boy in a tight place (S) will lie out of it (R). Another in the same tight place (S) will tell the exact truth unflinchingly (R). Everywhere it is a question of what bonds have or have not been built."

"Now tell us about readiness and satisfaction and annoyance. I have them fairly clear, but there are still some difficulties."

"And others of us know nothing about them as yet."

"Readiness is easier to see than to tell. I like to think of it as connected with the degree of stimulation needed at any given time to bring about a given response, the greater the readiness, the less stimulation is needed. Suppose a small boy and a heartless experimenter. One hot day the boy begs for ice cream, boasting recklessly that he can eat six helpings. The experimenter dares him to do it, saying that he will furnish the ice cream. The contest is on. Situation: a plate of ice cream before a small boy on a hot day. Response: the boy falls with alacrity upon the cream. Readiness is high. The second helping finds, if possible, even greater readiness. But toward the end of the third plate readiness sharply declines. The fourth sees readiness reduced to the zero point and even below. Readiness then is a condition of the neurone measuring the degree of its craving for activity."

"That is clear so far, but are there not other causes of readiness or unreadiness?"

"Indeed yes. Fatigue, due to extended exercise, is a common cause of unreadi-

Conditions making for readiness or unreadiness

ness. (The case above was different. It was not so much exercise. of jaw or palate nerves as it was fullness of stomach that reduced below zero the readiness for ice cream.) Preoccupation with something else of an opposing kind may also bring unreadiness, as when fear or sorrow cause unreadiness for mirth. A most important source of readiness is set, one's mental attitude at the time."

"I wish you would tell us about set. I have heard so much about set and purpose that I just must straighten them out. What is the connection between set and purpose? But first, what is the difference between set and readiness? They seem much alike to me."

"They are much alike and sometimes confused, but I believe we can make a

"Set" and "readiness" discriminated and related

clear distinction between the two. Set is broader than readiness. Readiness is best thought of as belonging to one response bond (possibly a compound response bond), while set refers to the mind acting more or less

as a whole (or for our purposes, set more precisely belongs to an aggregate of bonds that for the time being have practical charge of the person or organism.)[1] The term mind-set-to-an-end brings out perhaps more clearly what I have in mind. The emphasis here is on one controlling end which seems to possess the mind. The organism is bent or set upon attaining this end (typically an external end). The practical relations between set and readiness are here most interesting. A boy gifted in baseball is anxious that his team shall win in the match next Saturday. We may say that he is 'set' on winning the match. This set reaches out to many allied and auxiliary response bonds and makes them *ready* for the part they may possibly play in attaining the end in view. The boy's ear will be 'wide open' to hear any useful 'dope' on the game. His eye will be 'peeled' to see the curves of the opposing pitcher. This effect is general, the mind-set-to-an-end in fact makes more ready all one's inner resources (response bonds) that by previous inner connection seem pertinent to the activity at hand. Nor is this all. Simultaneously with passing on readiness to pertinent bonds, this set also makes unready all those response bonds whose action might interfere with attaining the end in view. The same thing that made our baseball boy ready for the necessary practice during the preceding week made him correspondingly unready for anything that might interfere with that practice. Every teacher knows that little study is given to books just in advance of any engross-

[1] There is still a slightly different sense in which the mind set makes one see everything as "roseate" or makes one "blue."

ing contest. Some college teachers say no serious study is possible till after the Thanksgiving games."

"You have struck something live now. But you seem almost to make a thinking being out of mind-set. It entertains ends. It seems to know what will help and what will hinder action to these ends. I don't see what becomes of the person—his self, I mean."

"Your inquiry raises a real difficulty, but it is a difficulty rather of language than of fact, I believe. Suppose a little girl walking by a toy shop. Her shoes have been hurting her feet. All at once her eyes fall on a fairy vision of a doll. Her heart (aggregate of S ➡ R bonds capable of forming a mind-set) responds at once. She wants the doll. A set for possessing the doll is in possession of the girl. Shoes are forgot, by-standers vanish. She and the doll for one brief moment make up the whole world, but in another moment the mother is included: 'O Mother! I want her so much. Please get her for me.' Then that world enlarges to include in succession shopkeeper, price, money, possible sources of money, Father, Uncle George. A formal analysis will perhaps make clear the life history and action of this psychological set: (i) there must be available for stimulation certain end-setting-up S ➡ R bonds (here the doll-appropriating response and, likely enough, bonds for doll-carriages, ice cream, etc.); (ii) something (here the chance sight of the doll) stimulates one such available S ➡ R bond; (iii) a response follows, wherein an end is set up (here the strong wish for the doll); (iv) from this

The action of the mind-set

'set' the spread of 'readiness' through previously made connections to allied and auxiliary S ➡ R bonds (here become 'ready' the bonds for asking Father or Uncle George); (v) a similar and simultaneous spread of unreadiness to such other S ➡ R response bonds as might thwart or unnecessarily postpone the doll-appropriating activities (the pains from the shoes are forgot); (vi) then follows the auxiliary action of the most ready of the allied S ➡ R bonds ('O Mother, please get her for me'). Thus instead of using the mysteries of self and thinking to explain what has here gone on, we must, I think, ultimately explain from the inside and along these lines what a self is and how thinking proceeds. But that's another story."

"Well, we have to admit that psychology is not as dead or dry as I said. But how are you going to use all this? What bearing has it on your laws of learning that you began to talk about?"

"Possibly when we take them up our digression will be justified. Suppose we begin now? Thorndike gives three major laws, those of Readiness, of Use and Disuse (or Exercise), and of Satisfaction and Annoyance (or Effect). The Law of Readiness follows well what we have been discussing: *When a bond is ready to act, to act gives satisfaction and not to act gives annoyance. When a bond is not ready to act, to be forced to act gives annoyance.* Think what we have been saying about readiness, and see if this law does not sound reasonable."

"Why, yes indeed. That boy and the

The three Laws of Learning

The Law of Readiness

ice cream—as long as the ice-cream-eating bonds were ready to act, he got satisfaction from his eating. And the less ready he became, the less satisfaction he got from his eating. I suppose if he had been compelled to eat all six plates, it would have proved very annoying. Yes, this law is clear, but I have been wondering if it isn't a kind of definition of what is meant by satisfaction and annoyance. What do you say?"

"The question is a very interesting one. I am inclined to agree with you. But probably we had better not go into that discussion just now. Fix attention on readiness as a state of the neurone (or nerve structure) which disposes it to action, then this law throws its light on the meaning of satisfaction and annoyance. Probably our general experience has something else to add in any particular case. I am inclined to say that this law partly defines and partly joins things of which we have otherwise independent knowledge. Let us now go to the Law of Satisfaction and Annoyance."

"You skipped the Law of Use and Disuse. Do you wish to keep the order you first gave?"

"So we did skip it, and I believe it is best to take the other first. Before taking it up, consider what we are about. Some S ➡ R bonds we bring into the world with us; others and the great majority we acquire after we get here. Of the innate bonds some fit our civilization and need to be maintained; others don't fit so well, and need to be changed or killed off. Acquiring new bonds or changing old ones is what **Learning defined** we mean by learning. Perhaps our commonest work is strengthening or weakening bonds."

"What do you mean by strengthening a bond? When is a bond strong and when weak?"

"We strengthen a bond when we change the connection between any S **Strengthening bonds** and its R so that the response (R) will more likely follow the stimulation (S) or will follow more promptly or more definitely. Weakening is merely doing the contrary; though often people speak of weakening a bond when they really mean strengthening a substitute bond. Of course, pedagogically, this is usually the best way of weakening an undesirable bond."

"Can all bonds be changed? Or are there some beyond our influence?"

"There are some bonds practically beyond the power of education to modify. These we call reflexes. They belong especially to certain more mechanical actions of the body. Education too has limits fixed for it by nature. Of course then when we are speaking of learning we restrict ourselves to modifiable bonds."

"We are ready now to state the Law **The Law of Satisfaction and Annoyance** of Satisfaction and Annoyance (or Law of Effect): *A modifiable bond is strengthened or weakened according as satisfaction or annoyance attends its exercise.*"

"When we had this last summer our instructor led us to repeat many times: 'Satisfaction strengthens, annoyance weakens.' And then he would have us repeat the whole law. So that in the end we fixed it strongly in mind. It is a great law, all right. I never dreamed when I first heard it how much help it can give the teacher. But the more

I watch my children learning, the more I believe that this law is the very bottom on which our learning rests and upon which we must base our school procedure."

"Let's go on and see how this law tells us what to expect in our teaching."

"I believe I see already how it all is going to work out. Mind-set-to-an-end is purpose. If the child has a strong purpose, this as mind-set pushes him on to attain his end. This mind-set makes ready his inner resources for at-taining the end. When he succeeds, these ready neurones and the success both mean satisfaction; and satisfaction means strengthening the bonds used. He learns by doing. His purpose helps him learn. It must be so. Mind-set, readiness, success, satisfaction, learn-ing—they follow just this way. Am I not right?"

"You have certainly caught the clue. We'll follow it up next time."

(*To be continued*)

AN EXPERIMENT IN COÖPERATION
III. Reading as Study

JAMES F. HOSIC

Associate Professor of Education, Teachers College, Columbia University

At the outset of our experiment, the reader will recall, it was agreed that we should endeavor to make the train-ing in reading bear fruit in all of the pupils' use of books. The need of im-provement in ability to deal with the printed page in history, geography, and arithmetic, as well as in literature, was remarked by everyone. The problem of generalizing habits of study reading and of securing intelligent application to various kinds of reading tasks was clearly recognized and was included in the program.

STARTING THE DRIVE

In the early weeks of the enterprise visits to reading classes and to classes in other subjects confirmed the suspi-cion of the leaders that the majority of the teachers were not making persistent efforts to train the pupils in study or to make the reading lessons the basis of generalized habits capable of being adapted to new but similar tasks. The question, *How* will you do this? or the equally pertinent question, How *did* you do it? was seldom heard, much less a reference to the fact that the methods of reading were being learned largely for the sake of applying them in the other studies.

The teachers were asked to observe the methods of the pupils and to begin systematic instruction in the art of study. Some frankly confessed that they themselves had never analyzed their study procedures and therefore felt unequal to the task of guiding the children. To show how inadequate the equipment of some of them was I will cite the extreme case of the teacher of history who had her pupils pass to the board in rotation, each writing from memory a sentence from the text. There was no analysis, no consideration of problems, no selection of items of importance, merely the memorizing of sentences one after the other as they appeared in the book—"only this and nothing more."

At the other extreme of course were those who knew how. These set the pupils to looking for the meanings of chapters, sections, and passages as wholes. With books open in class they went through the unit of subject matter step by step, thinking the writer's thoughts after him, discovering his purposes, interpreting his suggestions, contributing of their own experience, debating moot points, and making such applications of the ideas as they could.

THEORY AND THE FOLLOW-UP

All of the teachers were urged to read or reread Professor McMurry's *How to Study*, and in some of the conferences his principles were discussed and illustrated. Attention was called also to Mr. Lyman's outline of a program in "Assimilative Reading," based on Professor McMurry's book, which appeared in the *School Review* for October 1920. This outline, although written for the Junior High School, was seen to include much that should be taught earlier.

Dependence was not placed, however, entirely on group conferences and professional reading. Both the principals and the special supervisor engaged in a persistent "follow-up." It was doubtless this room-to-room visitation, with informal chat, a bit of teaching, a suggestive question, and an occasional complete lesson which made the theory discussed in conference effective in actual practice. Without the discussions

the specific help would have been in some instances misinterpreted, but without the classroom visits the discussions would have been too often without tangible results at all.

The kinds of opportunities that presented themselves may be illustrated by the following. A teacher remarked that her history class made very slow progress and evidently needed something which she had not as yet supplied. In an actual recitation it appeared that no use had so far been made of the author's own analysis of the content. The headings had not been either noted or challenged. Examination of them soon discovered the fact that they were not to be trusted. They were sometimes inaccurate or even misleading. Why have them at all? This question led to the discussion of how ideas are organized, and set the pupils to writing headings for themselves and so to dealing with questions and problems instead of merely with statements of fact. The pupils learned, in a word, how to do something constructive with the text instead of passively accepting its words and trying to present them unchanged and unassimilated at the hour of recitation.

On another occasion in a more elementary class the topic for reading was Gutenberg and the invention of movable type. The pupils were reading the very brief paragraphs of which the account was composed one at a time and answering questions put by the teacher, evidently with a view to getting the text translated into the pupils' own words and so brought surely into their comprehension. There was apparently no large question in the pupils' minds nor any guiding purpose which would tend to interpret and organize the piece as a whole.

When the first part was completed, the supervisor begged to be allowed to set a task for the class. He asked the children whether they could do something hard. They responded willingly. Indeed they could! Very well then, would they read the whole of the second or concluding part of the lesson and be ready to tell what it was about and why the writer had a Part I and a Part II. This they did, explaining that the first section was necessary to relate how another had by accident discovered that wet blocks would imprint characters on paper, while the second was devoted to an account of Gutenberg's practical application of the idea.

By accident the supervisor happened upon the beginning of this same lesson in another room. Here the teacher introduced the study by raising the question as to who really invented printing. She said there might be an honest difference of opinion. The lesson would contain some facts that they might consider. Would the pupils read with the idea of deciding to whom the credit for this most useful discovery really belonged? Needless to say the pupils read the whole account without interruption and were so eager for the fray that they could hardly restrain themselves till the discussion should begin. It was cleverly directed by the teacher, and resulted not only in much rereading and clearing up of not-understood passages together with a definite fixing of the main facts in their relations in the minds of the children but also created some sense of the value of with-holding judgment until the case has been adequately considered, presented a method of gathering data and holding them in mind, and probably also aroused an interest in the main question sufficient to furnish "drive" for further reading when the opportunity should offer.

THE PROBLEM OF FINDING MATERIAL

These two lessons are excellent examples of two widely different conceptions of the task of teaching children to read. The former was obviously more formal and mechanical. It was also far more superficial and narrow in its range of values. The fact that it is exceedingly common explains in large measure why there is general complaint that children and even the youth of high school and college do not know how to study. Their teachers have had a wrong or inadequate conception of their job.

The fault lies in part at the doors of the makers of books for school children and also in part at the door of those who choose the books which the children are required to use. Any one who will examine a score of school books selected at random but representing both prescribed, or "regular," and supplementary texts will easily verify the statement that those who write for children seem often to think only in separate sentences and frequently fail to secure a reasonable degree of unity in their paragraphs or perhaps even in the piece as a whole. In a word, the writers themselves do not adequately consider the organization of their material and hence prove the enemy rather than the ally of the teacher who would train her pupils in connected thinking.

Books of a scientific or informational character appear to be the most objectionable from the point of view of style and organization. This may be due to the fact that the story form embodies an organization more easily grasped because of the concreteness of the events of which it is made up. In any case the selection of books suitable for training in general informational reading—not the reading of excerpts but the reading of whole volumes—is a difficult task.

WAYS AND MEANS: A READING INDEX

The English Centers determined to make a point of such reading in the intermediate grades. The course for those grades was separated into two parts, first, silent reading of informational material, and, second, study, oral reading, and dramatic expression of literary material, the emphasis being divided about equally between the two. This set everyone to looking for worthwhile books and selections, the larger wholes preferred.

In order to enable each seeker to contribute to the common fund of knowledge of the most valuable material, a plan for a Reading Index was devised and each teacher was provided with a few cards upon which she could conveniently report the results of her experience. Ordinary library cards were used, printed on the face and back as indicated in the sample forms which appear below. In order to avoid making the task seem too arduous, only ten or twelve cards were given to each teacher at first, but many were glad to use a larger number when they saw the possibilities of the scheme. Some were eager to revise.

X——— SCHOOL

READING REPERTOIRE *(obverse)*

E. M. D. Grade 3

Title: "Polly Flinder's Apron"	
Author: Madge A. Bingham	
Book: Howe Third Reader	*Page* 1
Classification: (a) *Form*, Story	
(b) *Subject Matter*, A dream	
Comment: This piece gives play of fancy and calls to the children's minds memories of their own dreams, which they are glad to tell. The information conveyed is negligible.	
Teacher: A——— B———	*Room:* 102
Key other side	(Over)

KEY *(reverse)*

Grading: E = easy M = medium D = difficult
Classification
A. Form: 1. Prose 2. Poetry 3. Drama
B. Subject matter:

1. Adventure	7. Humaneness
2. Art	8. Humor
3. Biography	9. Ideals
4. Child life	10. Nature—out-of-doors
5. Fancy	11. Patriotism
6. History	12. Travel—life in other lands

Comment: Reason for teaching

The filling out of these cards had a positive influence on the teacher herself. It brought out forcibly the fact that lessons in reading should be carefully selected. They should fit into some logical scheme in order that they may provide the opportunity for not only a varied and well-balanced experience in reading but also for acquiring a definite body of knowledge. Moreover, by means of it each teacher was compelled to consider what chief purpose each piece should serve and was thus placed in the best possible frame of mind for preparing to do her part in the classroom activity.

No one will be surprised to learn that not a few teachers had never consciously considered what peculiar values a certain piece might afford nor planned to present it in the light of unique and definite purposes. In such hands truly reading may be little more than ready recognition of words, not a means to a liberal education.

Since others may be interested in the selection of informational reading books other than texts made up of miscellaneous short selections for the pupils of the intermediate grades, a few of the titles most often commended are here set down. The reader is asked to note that the list does not represent a consensus of opinion arrived at after several years of winnowing, but rather a body of first impressions. Not all teachers had access to collections sufficiently varied to permit them to judge the value of some of the books named. The list may, however, serve to illustrate the nature of our problem and the partial solution of it at which we arrived.

MATERIAL FOR INFORMATIONAL READING

Grade 4

Wonders of the Jungle—Ghosh
A Visit to the Farm—Large
Home Life Around the World—Mirick and Holmes
Wilderness Babies—Schwartz
Jack, the Fire Dog—Wesselhoeft
Grasshopper Green's Garden—Schwartz
Thirty More Famous Stories
Among the Meadow People
Stories of Great Americans for Little Americans

White Patch—Patri
Little Pioneers—Warren
Ten Boys on the Road from Long Ago
Animals at Home—Bartlett
Lolami, The Cliff Dweller
Stories of Country Life—Bradish
The Sandman—Hopkins
Children of the Arctic—Peary
The Dutch Twins—Perkins
Five Little Strangers—Schwartz
Four Old Greeks—Hale
Big People and Little People of Other Lands—Shaw
America First—Green
American History Story Book—Blaisdell
Child's Book of American History—Blaisdell
For the Children's Hour—Bailey—Bk. III
Glimpses of Pioneer Life—Livingston
Stories of American Life and Adventure—Eggleston
Stories of Illinois—Pratt
Tales of Long Ago—Terry
Safety First for Little Folks—Waldo
Early Sea People—Dopp
Story of Ab—Nida
Later Cave Men—Dopp
Travelers and Traveling—Tappan

Grade 5

Great Inventors and their Inventions—Bachman
Stories of Woods and Fields
Old Settler Stories
Wood Folk at School—Long
Krag and Johnny Bear—Thompson-Seton
Colonial Stories
Children of History
Kwahu, the Hopi Indian Boy
A Boy on a Farm—Abbott
Story of Glass—Bassett, etc.
True Story of Benjamin Franklin—Brooks
Cave, Mound, and Lake Dwellers—Holbrook
Our Country's Flag—Holden
A Little Brother to the Bear—Long
The Magic Forest—White
Later Cave Men—Dopp
Heroes of Everyday Life—Coe
Ten Little Indians—Wade
Hans Brinker—Dodge
Children's Classics—Stevenson
Children's Plays—Skinner
Our Holidays

Boys and Girls of Colonial Days—Bailey
Camp and Trail in Early American History—Dickson
Days and Deeds of One Hundred Years Ago—Stone and Fickett
Indian Child Life—Eastman
The Iron Star—True
Lake Michigan and the French Explorers—Morton
Makers of Our History—Faris
Real Stories from Our History—Faris
How We Travel—Chamberlain
Travels of Birds—Chapman

Grade 6

American Book of Golden Deeds—Baldwin
Stories of Brave Dogs—Carter
Makers of Our History—Faris
Fighting a Fire—Hill
Stories of Animal Life
Story of Christopher Columbus
Stories of the Great West—Roosevelt
Toward the Rising Sun
Under Sunny Skies
The Wide World
Lobo, Rag, and Vixen—Thompson-Seton

Secrets of the Woods—Long
Bird Stories—Burroughs
Pioneers of the Mississippi Valley—McMurry
Adrift on an Ice-pan—Grenfell
Black Beauty—Sewell
American Indians—Starr
Home Life in All Lands—Morris
Around the World in the Sloop Spray—Slocum
Lives and Stories Worth Remembering—Kupfer
Heart of a Boy—DeAmicis
Heidi—Spyri
Heroes of Every Day Life—Coe
Lisbeth Longfrock—Poulsson
Mexican Twins—Perkins
Nuremberg Stove—LaRamée
Some Merry Adventures of Robin Hood—Pyle
Stories of the Spanish Main—Stockman
Tad and His Father—Hullard
American Hero Stories—Tappan
Lincoln: The Man of the People—Mace
Stories of Thrift for Young Americans

Material for literary study was much more easily found. The difficulty there was chiefly one of method—but that is another story.

A COURSE OF STUDY IN GEOGRAPHY FOR THE FOURTH AND FIFTH GRADES

Elizabeth Breckinridge
Principal of the Normal School, Louisville, Ky.

An organization somewhat different from that of the traditional course of study is attempted in this paper. The idea or purpose back of the organization has been to try to show how the course of study may be made to contribute to a better understanding among teachers of the principles of project-teaching. The first step was to decide, as carefully as possible, upon the objectives for each of these grades—the knowledges, skills, habits, appreciations and attitudes that should be the outcomes of the study. The next question was to decide on worth-while projects which, when analyzed, it is found will give the training necessary for the attainment of these objectives.

FOURTH GRADE—WORLD GEOGRAPHY

Grade Objectives:

1. An acquaintance with the earth as the home of many peoples.
2. Knowledge of the conditions of life in the warm, cold, and temperate regions of the earth.
3. A sympathetic attitude toward all peoples and all classes in the various regions and countries studied.

4. Appreciation of the services rendered us by the different peoples of the earth.

5. An understanding of how our work and products are of value to the different peoples of the earth.

6. Appreciation of the beauty of the world as expressed by its plant life, its mountains, oceans, streams, etc.

7. Knowledge of the necessary place geography.

8. Formation of proper habits of study, which includes an intelligent use of the globe and maps.

From the study of local history and geography in the third grade the children have gained an idea of the sources of the home food supply, of means of travel and transportation, of topographical features, and of some of the conditions which have controlled the growth of Louisville. An attempt is made in the fourth grade to organize these experiences of the children and develop the idea of the earth as the home of peoples who, on account of their environment, have different occupations and different modes of living.

The "children's projects or activities" indicated below are suggestive only of the types of responses that may be expected of children as a result of a certain approach to the subject. A different approach might bring different responses. "The one essential of any project is that the person or persons engaged must be working wholeheartedly in an undertaking for which there has been purposeful planning." It is also well to remember that the desired outcomes in terms of knowledges, skills, attitudes, etc., should be kept in mind by the teacher from the first step to the last.

THE CHILDREN'S ACTIVITIES OR PROJECTS

I. The children tell of the places they have seen or read about and show any pictures they have of these places. Familiar places are located on the globe. The question is asked, "Where are we?" Louisville is located, and the direction and distance from the places visited are noted. The children recall the people that they have known who have traveled around the earth. "How long did it take them?" "How did they go?" "Where did they stop?" are some of the questions asked by the children. The more significant ones that cannot be answered at once serve as projects to be worked out and reported upon later. The children collect railway and steamship guides to aid them in the solution of their questions. All routes are traced upon the globe and upon maps. To substitute "geography" for "literature" in Dr. Aydelotte's recent statement, geography "has meaning for a student only so far as the student has questions in his mind."

II. One approach may be to have children trace to region of production some article of common use. This is in answer to their question, "Where does it come from?" They study pictures of the region—lantern slides and moving pictures, if possible—and museum material. If the situation is such as to encourage children to ask questions, they'll not be slow about asking them. They'll want to know how the people build their houses, why they do not build them of wood; what they eat; how they keep warm; what they do to make a living; how they travel; how many people live in this region; what they send us; what they get from us; how they get the furs, etc.; in fact, their questions will include every topic usually studied under "surface," "climate," "drainage," etc., found in many of our courses of study to-day. With this difference, that here the desired knowledges, skills, habits, etc., are gotten in response to a felt need expressed by the children in their questions instead of being imposed upon them by an outside authority. In working out the answers to their questions the children should have access to all the books and illustrative material, pictures, museum exhibits, etc., available. They will probably want to reproduce on the sand table or dramatize certain phases of the life in this region. To help answer some of their questions concerning the surface features of the distant region a study is made of the surface features in the home environment that bear a resemblance to those in the distant region.

III. The study may again be introduced by pictures, or by the idea of trade or exchange of products. Children may go to a market and note foods not grown at home, or they may trace to region of production some articles of clothing, e. g., rubber. Whatever may be the approach the teacher should so plan the situation that the pupils will feel a real whole-hearted desire to know more about this region and that they will express this desire in such questions as, "Where do the foods come from?" "How were they brought here?" "How were they raised?" "Why do not these foods grow here?" "What does rubber come from?" etc.

IV. For method of procedure see suggestions above.

THE KNOWLEDGES, HABITS, SKILLS, APPRE- CIATIONS AND ATTITUDES INVOLVED

I. Acquaintance with the globe as the symbol of the earth.

A. An understanding of the fact that we live on a round earth; that an idea of its size may be gotten by the time required to travel around it; that its surface is divided into masses of land and bodies of water, called continents and oceans. History: A knowledge of the stories of Columbus, Magellan and Drake. Modern means of travel as compared with those of the early explorers.

B. Habit of relating geographical facts to the globe and maps.

II. Knowledge of the cold regions of the earth.

A. Knowledge of the people and their occupations.

1. Homes: Winter house; material used; why this material, necessary for its being round or dome-shaped; summer house; compared with our tent life; how made.

2. Food: How obtained, weapons used.

3. Clothing: How skins are secured, how prepared, etc.

4. Transportation and communication: how sledges are made, how drawn, etc.

5. Trade or exchange: the products imported and exported.

6. Extent and centers of population.

B. An understanding of how the life of the region is influenced by geographical location.

C. Appreciation of the efforts of the people to overcome the handicaps of physical environment.

D. Knowledge of the more important types of plant and animal life.

E. Appreciation of the dependence of the different regions of the earth upon each other.

F. Effective habits of study, including ability to collect and organize data in answer to a question and the intelligent use of maps, globe, pictures, and other illustrative materials.

G. Knowledge of the essentials of place geography.

H. Skill in making graphs; making product maps; coloring outline maps to illustrate location of products or some other phase of the work; collecting pictures and other illustrative material.

III. Knowledge of hot regions of the earth.

The knowledges, habits, skills and attitudes desired as outcomes of this study are similar to those outlined above. The experiences that the children will have in trying to answer *their own* questions about the region will enable them to attain the desired objectives in terms of knowledge, habits, etc.

IV. Knowledge of life in temperate region.

The details of this study will be worked out later. It is recommended that strikingly different types, e. g., the hot and the cold regions, be selected for the first study of the year.

The study of "World Geography" affords abundant opportunity for the children, through their reading, to enter vicariously into the life of the various regions of the earth. As Dr. Bobbitt urges: "The geographical readings should be such as to permit our children imaginatively to travel through the various cities and countries and regions of the earth, . . . and through this reading experience they will acquire knowledge and appreciation of the world such as can never be obtained from the most perfect memorization of the facts supplied in our textbook geographies." [1]

---

[1] Bobbitt, Franklin, *The Curriculum.*

FIFTH GRADE—STUDY OF NORTH AMERICA
WITH EMPHASIS ON THE UNITED STATES

"Emphasis may now be placed upon questions which lead to a more intensive study of the geographical controls of activities, and consequently to more restricted parts of the earth's surface. . . . In the study also of each important industrial material produced in the United States, there are included questions of exports, imports, and foreign trade routes and relationships, so that contact is relatively constant with the world as a whole." [1]

Grade Objectives:

1. Knowledge of the large relief features of North America and of the facts concerning the distribution of industries and vegetation.
2. Knowledge of the more important industries of the United States.
3. An understanding of the dependence of an industry upon geographic environment.
4. Knowledge of the processes used in some of the more important industries.
5. Appreciation of the interdependence of different sections of a country and of different countries.
6. Appreciation of the dignity of labor.
7. Understanding of the reasons for growth of certain cities.
8. Knowledge of the essentials of place geography.
9. Effective study habits, including the ability to use illustrative material, reference books, maps, globe, charts, etc., intelligently.

THE CHILDREN'S ACTIVITIES OR PROJECTS

I. Study may be introduced by some current event or by a succession of pictures of significant regions, or the children may tell of the places in North America that they have seen or read about. The class discussion and the pictures should suggest many problems to the children, e. g.,

"Why has North America so many kinds of places and so many kinds of workers?" If given an opportunity to find the answers to their own questions they will consult textbooks, reference books, pictures, maps, the globe, newspapers, magazines, etc. The teacher will need to see that all of the materials needed for solutions of the problems are available for the children. The teacher will also need to see that the children so interpret the material that it will show its bearing on the solution of the problem. In other words, with every step the children should keep the goal in mind, namely, the answer to their question.

II. A. The children may recall their experiences on the farm at some previous time, or their school excursions to the country. Class discussions together with a visit to a flour mill, tobacco factory or some local industry will serve as a stimulus to them to ask many worth-while questions. As indicated above, they should be given the opportunity to answer their questions. This will afford training in the best habits of study. The teacher should see that the necessary materials, books, charts, maps, pictures, etc., for the solution of the problems are available.

B. The following brief account of the work of a fifth grade class will indicate one method of procedure. The children were given the opportunity to tell what they would like to know about lumbering. Some wanted to know one thing, some another. When they were asked how they would set to work to find the answers to their questions, they replied, "Go to the library." "Consult books in the room cabinet." "Hunt for pictures in the magazines." "Talk to people who know." After several days of reading and collecting pictures the class was brought together for an informal discussion. The children on this occasion had many questions to ask; some were suggested by the pictures found but not understood, others arose from reading not yet completed. These questions served as a motive for further study.

One afternoon the entire class with their teacher went to the woods "to play lumbermen." On this trip the children had opportunity to observe some of the native trees of Kentucky, how trees prevent washing of soil on a hillside, how quickly fire spreads in a forest and how

[1] Bonser, Frederick Gordon, *The Elementary School Curriculum.*

difficult it is to put it out. (They had concrete experience with their camp fire.) Many children brought back twigs and branches to use in their sand table work. One boy, who was working on transportation, hunted all afternoon for branches suitable for making a corduroy road.

The study closed with the children's planning, writing and giving quite an ambitious three act play, of five scenes, entitled, "Christmas in a Lumber Camp."

The knowledges, habits of study, appreciations, in fact, all of the outcomes desired for this study were gotten by these children and no one would doubt their "wholehearted activity" throughout.

THE KNOWLEDGES, HABITS, SKILLS, APPRECIATIONS, AND ATTITUDES INVOLVED

I. Position of North America.

A. Account for importance among the continents.

1. How have location and size contributed to the importance of North America?

a. Advantages of position with respect to surrounding bodies of water, being in three heat belts?

2. How has coast line influenced the development of North America?

a. Extent of coast line, opportunities for trade.

3. How have the surface features contributed to the growth of North America?

a. Value of the plains to man.

b. Value of the mountains to man in production of lumber, mineral resources, etc. Effect of north and south trend of mountains.

B. Ability to use reference books, maps, charts, etc., intelligently.

C. Knowledge of location of important places.

D. Effective habits of study.

E. Appreciation of the natural beauty of our country.

II. Leading industries of the United States.

A. Agriculture.

1. Chief crops raised in Kentucky.

2. How Kentucky ranks as a wheat growing state; as a corn state; as a tobacco state, etc.

3. The industries in Louisville that are dependent upon agriculture.

4. Do we in Kentucky need all of our agriculture products; if not, what do we do with the surplus?

5. The dependence of the people in Kentucky upon other sections of the United States for food.

6. Location of the great wheat sections of the United States; of the great corn section; cotton section, sugar section, rice section, etc.; and the more important geographic reasons for their production.

7. The value of our agricultural products to us and to the peoples of other countries.

B. Lumbering.

(The following outline is taken in part from the course of study of the Elementary School, University of Chicago. I have seen it, however, in more detail than indicated here, worked out in our own school with excellent results.)

1. The uses of lumber.

2. The native trees of Kentucky.

3. The location and extent of the forest land in Kentucky.

4. The value of the Kentucky forests as a source of fuel and lumber; as a means of protection against floods; as an element of beauty.

5. Important industries in Louisville dependent upon lumbering.

6. How the Kentucky trees are gotten to the mills.

7. The more important processes in the manufacture of lumber.

8. Location and distinguishing characteristics of the forest regions of the United States.

9. National forests—number, how secured, value to the country.

10. Extent of forest land to-day as compared with forested area when early settlers came to America.

11. Enemies of the forests.

12. Methods of lumbering in southern forests; in northern forests.

13. Location of important shipping centers for lumber.

The method used in teaching other industries is similar to that used in the case of agriculture and lumbering. Care should be taken that the children do not get the idea that only one product is produced in a section. Some current event may help to decide the order in which the industries are studied.

After the United States, problems relating to Canada, Mexico, Central America, Panama and our island possessions are studied. As Dr. Bonser expresses.it, "Each is approached through some tie of vital relationship to us in meeting some need. The survey of the important questions of geographic control, in determining the activities and conditions of its peoples, is relatively brief for each region, but, after so much detailed study of particular occupations and of our own country, the essential elements are obtained with relative ease." [1]

BIBLIOGRAPHY

Branom, Mendel E.—The Project Method in Education.

Branom, Mendel E.—The Value of the Project-Problem.

Method in Elementary Education, Elementary School Journal, Vol. 18, p. 618.

Stevenson, J. A.—The Project and the Curriculum. School and Home Education, March, 1919.

Branom, Mendel E.—The Project Method in the Teaching of Geography, Vol. 16.

Courtis, S. A.—Measuring the Effect of Super-vision in Geography, School and Society, July 19, 1919.

Lull, Herbert G.—The Relation of Project-Problem Instruction to the Curriculum, School and Society, Feb., 1919.

Courtis, S. A.—Teaching through the Use of Projects, or Purposeful Acts, Teachers College Record, March, 1920.

Kilpatrick, William H.—The Problem-Project Attack on Organization, Subject-Matter, and Teaching, N. E. A. Proceedings, 1918.

Kilpatrick, William H.—The Theories Underlying the Experiment, Teachers College Record, Vol. 20, p. 99.

Taylor, W. S.—Project Methods in Teacher-Training Courses, School and Society, Oct. 26, 1918.

Bonser, Frederick Gordon.—The Elementary School Curriculum.

Hennes, Marie.—Horace Mann Studies in Elementary Education V, Teachers College Report, March, 1921.

The Teaching of Geography, History, and Civics, Course of Study, State Department of Education, Trenton, New Jersey.

The Course of Study in Geography for the Elementary School, University of Chicago.

Course of Study in Geography, Horace Mann School.

Course of Study in Geography, Topeka, Kansas.

Course of Study in Geography, Speyer School.

Course of Study in Geography, Baltimore County, Md.

MOTIVATING THE OUTSIDE ACTIVITIES OF A JUNIOR HIGH SCHOOL

MATIE P. BABER

English Teacher, Enslow Junior High School, Huntington, W. Va.

The opportunity of making one-third of the waking hours of one-fourth of our population either the happiest or the most miserable period of their lives lies in the hands of a very few people, those of the Junior High School teachers in this newly established division of our educational system. Also the problem of making the slowly awakening adolescent youth look forward with joy to from eight to ten years more of active, investigating, growing and developing school and college life, or to make of him a helpless driven creature, disliking his

[1] Bonser, Frederick Gordon, *The Elementary School Curriculum.*

environment and counting the days when he may get away to develop and live his life without the restrictions and carping criticisms imposed upon him by one of his fellows whose only claim to authority is that of a few more years of existence and a little greater book knowledge, lies in the hands of the few fortunate people who have the destiny of the adolescent youth of our land in the making.

Recognizing the restless, changing period in our youth at this time, the faculty of the Enslow Junior High School, Huntington, W. Va., have attacked the problem of so motivating the outside activities of our school as to develop the social side of their school life to meet the need of the boys and girls of every class of society. This we consider our democratic duty to our community.

We have in this school children from all classes of society, from the children of the highest officials of our state, to the son and daughter of the poor widow who works with her bare hands at the most menial labor to keep her children in school. Could you tell in the classroom or social activities the difference between these two? Not at all. You may see them side by side in the receiving line at the Alumni party (not reception), or the widow's son may be contributing a solo for the entertainment of the visitors while the son of wealthy parents may be dipping ice cream behind the scenes. Social distinctions and personal affairs are all swept away in the one effort to contribute to the enjoyment of the group. How do we bring it about? Simple enough. The teacher is an example of living democracy before and with the children.

At the beginning of the school year the seventh, eighth and ninth grades are organized and officers elected, consisting of president, vice-president, secretary and treasurer. All the activities of these classes must be decided upon by the individual classes. The home-room teachers of these classes are present at these meetings, though only in an advisory capacity. A period or two in the English department is given to the instruction of the usages of parliamentary law and the president insists upon a strict observance of the simpler forms. By the time these boys and girls finish the ninth grade they can and do conduct a public meeting in a correct and self-possessed manner which would put to shame the average man or woman of affairs.

After an activity has been voted upon, a committee is appointed to take the matter before the "Board of Control," which consists of the principal, vice-principal, two members of the faculty, and one member from each of the three classes. Here the activity is permitted or prohibited as the judgment of the body decides. Refusals rarely occur. since this is a well-known check upon thoughtless or unreasonable requests.

The seventh and eighth grades are permitted one party and one picnic each per year. The teachers enter into these activities with the same enthusiasm as the children, and they would be missed from the fun as much as the most popular member of the class. But since the ninth year will in all probability be the last school year for a small per cent of our boys and girls, they are permitted more class activities because we wish to acquaint them as far as possible with the social observances which will make them at home in any sensible environment. Their first party occurs on or near Hallowe'en or Thanksgiving, and every one is requested to be ready to contribute something for the entertainment of the whole group. Committees on plans and arrangements are appointed with a teacher as a member (not a chairman) of each committee. Special invitations are sent to the teachers of the other classes and they are considered as special guests. By this time the home-room teachers have discovered who are the leaders and who the retiring backward people in the class, and a quiet word is spoken in the ears of the leaders that they see that certain people have good times. They do not fail us and "wall flowers" are unknown at our parties.

During the winter months an Alumni party is held in order to still the clamor of former students for an opportunity to return, and to give our ninth grade boys and girls an opportunity to play host to a group of people some of whom they have never seen. No young matron who is entertaining in her own home for the first time could be more anxious to please than are these young people who for the first time undertake a real social responsibility. While this affair is never allowed to become a formal one, activities are chosen with special regard to the older people rather than in accordance with their own personal inclination. Invitations are sent to all former teachers and principals and in the words of one of the latter, "Formality is thrown to the winds when we enter Enslow Auditorium, and we are all young again."

The final party during the last month of school, to which parents are frequently invited, is filled with anticipation of life at senior high school, tempered with regret at leaving the scene of three years of happiness and growth. A picnic and "hike" are also enjoyed during the last month of school.

Special friendships between the boys and girls, while not unduly encouraged, are met with a sympathetic understanding on the part of the teacher. They know that wholesome companionship meets with the approval of the teachers, who can usually put an end to any sentimentality by a few sensible sympathetic words, or at least prevent its doing any special harm. Parents are encouraged to open their homes to the friends of the boys and girls and secure their confidence at this critical period.

So much for the purely social activities. Our public entertainments are another feature which we have worked out for the purpose of giving our students a sense of self-confidence and power when in contact with the public, either singly or in groups. At the beginning of the school year plans are made by the faculty for special public entertainments. These usually consist of a "Minstrel" put on by the general talent of the school, "the public-speaking plays," put on by that department, which is a story in itself, and an "Operetta" put on by the music department, which is the big event of the year. In the minstrels some of our most overgrown awkward boys have developed behind their black faces a self-possession and ability which has enabled them to take leading parts in other activities.

The interlocutor in one of our minstrels developed such dramatic and musical talent that he was later chosen as a leading character in a public-speaking play and as the hero in the Operetta which was given that year. That boy, who came from one of the humblest homes, was chosen for the leading rôle in a play and musical given at the senior high school last year, and he says that it was the encouragement and incentive given him in his three years at the Junior High School that has determined him to complete a college course, though he must work his way inch by inch in order to do it. These entertainments interfere in no way with the regular routine of the school work with the exception of one half day which is given for dress rehearsal for the "Operetta," which is allowed that the children may not be overtired from the three full house performances, a matinee and two evening performances. The work for all these affairs is motivated. The music department has a problem which makes music a joy, and an incentive and purpose in working out notes and exercises. The Public Speaking and English departments are responsible for the dramatics, the Home Economics department sees to the costumes, the Manual Arts attend to the stage setting, the Art department looks after the posters and advertising, and the Commercial department attends to the ticket sales and to the business end of the project. Aside from the initiative power and ability developed in the boys and girls, the school has made $1,500 in the past three years with these school activities, the public has enjoyed wholesome and instructive entertainments, the school has secured a piano, victrola, a library of several hundred volumes, besides several other pieces of smaller equipment, and a sympathy and

understanding has grown up between the teachers and students that could have been secured in no other way.

But after all perhaps the weekly assembly has been the best means of giving every boy and girl a chance to discover his latent powers and an opportunity to express them. At the beginning of the year each teacher is assigned a certain date for which she is to be responsible for the assembly program. The teacher usually selects a subject, project or unit around which the program is built. An effort is made to use different children each time, so that all may have a chance to appear at some time during the semester.

Some of the projects worked out last year were a review of the "Women's Movement in America," which was given just after the national election. A number of girls impersonated the leading American women from colonial times to the present, giving in the first person the things which they had achieved for their country as a proof of their fitness for the new duties of citizenship. Another teacher worked out contributions which the negro race had made to America. The lives of Booker T. Washington and the poet Dunbar were reviewed, a number of negro folk songs sung by the glee club, and some victrola numbers of famous negro quartets were given. For "good English" week an English teacher worked out a "good English" program in which every child either from the floor or from the platform had a part. This program gave a great impetus to the movement for better speech. These assemblies were grasped by the teachers as an opportunity to work out special classroom problems which had apparently been unsolvable. One English teacher who had a homogeneous group of border line children was in despair for a problem to interest them and secure a maximum of effort. She hit upon the device of a simple dramatization for assembly, and found undreamed-of ability when the children really awoke to effort.

Every department is willing to assist in the simple preparations for these assemblies, the public speaking and music departments largely motivating their work through them. These programs were not allowed to interfere with regular class work, and children were placed largely upon their own responsibility and healthful rivalry was engendered among the groups for the success of their particular problem. These assemblies were held at 8:30 in the morning, but there were never less than eight to fifteen interested parents and visitors, some of whom remarked that they had paid fifty cents for an entertainment neither so entertaining nor so instructive.

We do not claim that all the credit for the improved conditions in our schools has been due to the motivating of these activities, but we do claim that they have been a means of self-expression which had led some of our adolescent boys to say that they were always glad to see Monday morning come, and to cause 90% of our ninth grade students to enroll for Senior High School when formerly 10% was the maximum to be expected.

Does this take extra time and thought on the part of the teacher? It most certainly does, but we are amply repaid by the knowledge that we have contributed something toward the making of better Americans, and by the lasting gratitude and friendships we have from the young men and women who are, we hope, better, stronger and happier because of helping hands and sympathetic counsel and comradeship at the most critical period of their lives.

FILMED GEOMETRY

CHARLES H. SAMPSON
Huntington School, Boston, Mass.

Can geometry be taught by means of the moving-picture film? I know of nobody who claims that such a subject as this can be absorbed visually. I do not myself claim that such a thing can be done. I say and wish to emphasize the statement that the combination of a good textbook and a good teacher can not be duplicated. But I do claim that there is a place for the educational film in the classroom.

I suppose geometry is about the last subject that one could expect to film. Whether it can be done successfully or not is for others to judge. I have tried to do it and think that I have succeeded. In any case, two thousand feet of visualized geometry is an interesting educational treat to watch. The future will demonstrate the permanent value of it.

Definitions, construction problems, and the various mathematical computations can be very well illustrated on the screen. These things are, after all, the most important factors to consider when one is thinking of practical values. Applied geometry does not require the demonstration of proofs.

This statement tends to create the impression that a film such as this is to be used only in the applied mathematics class; such, however, is not the case. There is, of course, a real opportunity to use it there, but the field is larger than this. Boys and girls in the grammar grades are more interested in the future than they themselves realize. It would be difficult to convince them by any reasonable amount of talking that the future subject of geometry was worthy of serious consideration. If the dormant interest in geometry can be aroused and if a geometrical moving picture can be made the agent to arouse that interest there is an object in having moving pictures in the classroom.

Some of the educators of the "old school" are inclined to assume, apparently without thought, that the modern teacher who believes in visual instruction is doing all that he or she can to produce a visual-minded generation of students. No thinking teacher has such a thought in mind. I am sure that most of us realize that the path of the present-day student is already too abundantly strewn with roses. Most of us are doing what we can to make the way harder,

not by putting obstacles in the path but by making the traveller do his own travelling. The educational film is not so much a teacher as an "interest-producer." It aids the teaching of the subject by injecting that element of interest which so many subjects lack.

Certainly there is no more difficult student to interest than those found in the evening schools. This is no fault of the student but rather the result of an existing condition. It is not easy to attend class after a day of hard work; it is difficult for one to keep awake to the values in the lesson. This last statement may be accepted literally. If the educational film can arouse and maintain interest in an evening class it has a place there. Interest promotes attendance and helps accomplish the desired end.

I do not hope to see moving pictures supplant the textbook in our schools. I do hope, however, that more attention will be devoted to visual instruction in the future than in the past. We begin to learn as children because of what we see. Is there any reason why the visual method of learning should be neglected as we grow older? I think not.

THE CLEARING HOUSE

A NEWSPAPER IN THE PRIMARY
SCHOOL

Project: The writing and publishing of a newspaper by the 3A Class of Lee School, Cleveland Heights, O.

I. How the Project was Initiated.

  1. Primary Supervisor told 3A teacher about a "Newspaper

Project" that had been worked out in the Primary School on Adelbert Road.

  2. Teacher visited Primary School, saw newspaper and discussed Primary School project with the 3A class at Lee School.

  3. 3A Class became interested in the

"Newspaper Project" and decided,—

(a) That they would like to publish a newspaper of their own.

(b) That they would like to exchange newspapers with the children in the Primary School.

II. Specific Purpose.

1. To write a newspaper that would meet the requirements of a good newspaper and would satisfy the demands of its "subscribers."

2. To publish the newspaper so that it would be possible for each child to have his own copy and so that copies would be available for friends and parents who were interested in the children's project.

III. Planning the Paper.

What constitutes suitable material for a school paper?

1. News items.
   (a) Daily observations in connection with various school activities.
   (b) School news.
   (c) News of the day.

2. Personals.

3. Material for a "funny page."
   (a) Jokes.
   (b) Riddles.
   (c) Funny stories.

4. Stories, letters, poems, and jingles written in connection with any of the social studies of the school.

5. Reports by teacher relative to pupils' progress, e. g.,
   (a) List of children having 100% Attendance Record for current month.
   (b) List of pupils having exceptionally good judgment.

(c) Honorable mention for work in oral English.

(d) Excellent work in Silent Reading.

(e) Class rank in arithmetic.

(f) Exceptionally good work in spelling.

6. Advertisements secured by pupils.

IV. Execution.

1. Preliminary step to work up enthusiasm, to establish standards, and to give weaker members of the group proper idea of procedure.
   (a) Children give items for contribution to newspaper, orally, using third person, when possible to do so; e. g., Jane Lewis reports:—

   Some time ago, Jane Lewis and her father and mother and little brother went to the Hollenden Hotel for dinner. Jane heard her father say to the waiter, "Jane and Bill." She wondered what he meant.

   At the end of the dinner, the waiter came in with a big "Baked Alaska" with "Jane and Bill" written in chocolate. Do you know what a Baked Alaska is? It is a brick of ice cream with whipped cream over it. They had a very happy time.

2. Class criticisms of oral contribution.
   (a) Was item an interesting one?
   (b) Does it represent child's best effort?
   (c) Its good points; its weak points.
   (d) Suggestions for improving contribution.

3. Writing news items.
4. Reading news items.
5. Class criticisms with view to accepting or rejecting items.
6. Differences of opinion as to desirability and advisability of publishing certain items submitted led to election of an Editorial Staff, who with teacher pass upon fitness for publication of items in question and offer suggestions to improve contributions.
   (a) Effort made to have contribution from every child in every issue of the newspaper.
   (b) Child's best effort accepted whether or not his contribution measures up to standard of other members of the group.

V. Selection of Name for Paper.
   1. Names suggested.
   2. Discussion as to suitability from standpoint of content.
   3. Adoption of name, "Breezy Bits from Portable Four."

VI. Plans for Publishing Paper.
   1. Inquiries made as to cost of printing paper. Price found to be prohibitive.
   2. Services of stenographer secured to make stencils.
   3. Copies of paper made by teacher on mimeograph, using stencils.

VII. Business Arrangements.
   1. Discussion of price to be charged for newspaper.
      (a) Three cents suggested inasmuch as that was price charged for Cleveland *Press* and Cleveland *Plain Dealer*.
      (b) Suggestion made that writing and publishing of "Breezy Bits" involved much work

by many people and that it was worth five cents.
   (c) Vote taken. Price fixed at five cents.
2. Election of two Business Managers, whose duties are
   (a) To sell papers.
   (b) To make change and keep account of money.
   (c) To attend to any correspondence arising in connection with the newspaper.

VIII. "Interests and Activities" in connection with and growing out of project.
   1. Furnishes means of motivation for various school activities because of opportunity given to report in their newspaper all interesting experiences in connection with these activities.
   2. Stimulates outside reading. Children read newspapers and magazines to see just what kind of material can be supplied to improve their paper.
   3. Demand for good oral reading when written contributions are presented to group for criticism.
   4. Provides training in both oral and written English through opportunity given children to talk and write on subjects about which they really know something and in which they are vitally interested.
   5. Need for letter writing.
      (a) Thank-you letters to friends and parents who helped to make the project a success.
      (b) Letters to arrange for exchange of newspapers with Primary School to whom they were indebted for the newspaper idea.
      (c) Letters acknowledging re-

ceipt of Primary School paper and expressing appreciation of it. ·

6. Outlet provided for written work in connection with other projects being carried on during the current month, e. g.,

   (a) Children made Lincoln books in February. Lincoln jingles appeared in February newspaper.

   (b) History work in March centered around the "Settlement of Marietta."
   The March newspaper contained the account of the journey to the Ohio country.

   (c) Pioneer life in Marietta formed the basis of the History work in April. Imaginary letters from the early settlers of Marietta to their friends in the east appeared in the April issue.

7. Need for technical work in English and spelling felt in order that this work might appear in proper form in accordance with the requirements of a good paper.

IX. Feelings, Attitudes, and New View Points Developed.

   1. Co-operation.
   All working together for a common purpose.

   2. Responsibility.
   The best effort of every member of the group required to make the paper a success and to make each issue better than the last.

   3. Good judgment.
   (a) In selection of material for contribution.

   (b) In criticism of contributions of other members of the group.

4. Service.
   Through the newspaper the children attempt to pass on to others some of the things from which they derived pleasure during the month.

5. The newspaper makes a connecting link between the school and the home and strengthens the bond between the two.

6. Gives the teacher a very effective way of getting certain needs and certain ideas "across" to the parents.

7. Gives the parent an opportunity to compare his child's efforts with the work of other children in his group. Reveals individual needs. Parent becomes conscious of child's strong points and of his weak points, and works with teacher to overcome difficulties.

BREEZY BITS FROM PORTABLE FOUR

(Excerpts from the paper)

Our slogan: Just the best that you can do,
Is the service asked of you.

REPORT ON TARDINESS BY ALEXANDER GINN

April 21. There has been no tardiness in Portable Four so far in April. If Donald Bowes helps we think we will have a good record.

April 22. Donald Bowes was late twice today.

A LETTER OF THANKS

The children in Portable Four gave Mr. McLane a copy of their March newspaper. The same day that he received his newspaper, he wrote the children a letter of thanks. They enjoyed his letter very much.

OUR HEALTH CHART

We have a Health Chart. We have pictures of Health Chores on the sides of the chart. The names of all the children are on the chart. When we do all the Health Chores for a week, Miss Kingsborough puts a flag after our names. Some of the children have flags after their names. How would you like to have a flag after your name? I would like to have a flag after my name because I am a good American and the good American tries to gain and keep perfect health.—*Ruthbelle Stone*

THE PARROT

On Friday, April 8, Miss Hughes came into Portable Four and brought a parrot. The parrot was very funny. It whistled and it said, hello and no and yes and polly. The children sang a song named "Polly's Bonnet" and the parrot sang too.

HOSTESS FOR THE KING'S HERALD

Ellen Duff was hostess for the King's Herald on April 9. She served ice cream and cookies. Among the guests present were Robert Campbell, Charles Flarida and Leslie Dole from Portable Four. They had a very nice time.

TWO GREAT EYES

One night when Jane Summers was in bed, she saw two great, big eyes. Jane's kitty had jumped up on her dresser and sat on it. Jane called her mother. Her mother came and took Mr. Pussy down and then Jane went to sleep.

A WHITE KITTEN

On Saturday, April 9, Jane Johnson got a kitty. The kitty is white with gray spots. It can stand on its hind legs. It sleeps in a basket under the kitchen table.

A SUNDAY CONCERT

On Sunday, April 10, Dorothy Allan had company. Dorothy planned a concert. Dorothy's father played a piece on the piano. Everybody had a good time.

REPORTED BY GERTRUDE HALL

On Wednesday, April 13, Gertrude Hall went to the Heights Theater. She saw the Top of the World. The part she liked best was canning fish by machinery.

On Saturday, April 16, Gertrude went to the Art Museum. She saw Alice in Wonderland. There were dolls in the show with strings tied on them so they could walk. Some ladies talked for the dolls.

WAITING FOR A WARM DAY

The children in Portable Four had two spelling tests from the Indiana Spelling List. Mildred Batchelor stood one hundred in both tests. She told her mother she stood one hundred and that her paper was almost as pretty as Ravella Leonard's. Mildred's mother was very much pleased and she said Mildred could wear socks when the next warm day comes.

THE PAINTED TERRAPIN

On April 15, Miss Hughes brought a turtle into Portable Four. It crawled along Miss Kingsborough's desk. Miss Hughes tried to make it turn around so the children could see its back leg. It was a stubborn little thing. It turned right around and walked forward. Miss Hughes turned it over on its back. The turtle tried to turn over but it couldn't. It was called a painted terrapin. It had thirteen squares on its back. It was two years old.

CLEAN-UP WEEK

April 16 to April 23 was Clean-Up Week. Some children in Portable Four saw brooms with clothes tied around the ends on the telephone poles. Signs on the brooms said, "Clean-Up."

The children in Portable Four celebrated Clean-Up Week by cleaning their desks and by washing the finger marks off the glass on the bookcase.

John Schreiner and Jane Lewis dusted the rugs on all the chairs in Portable Four.

Jack Crilly washed all the window sills and Gertrude Hall washed the tops of all the desks.

OUTSIDE READING

Jack Crilly is reading a very interesting book. It is called *Arabian Nights*.

Dorothy MacDonald is reading Grimm's *Fairy Tales*. She likes the story of Faithful John.

Jean Horton is reading *The Little Princess* by Frances Hodgson Burnett. She enjoys it very much.

Jane Lewis is reading a book called *In the Court of King Arthur*.

Robert Lewis thinks the boys and girls would enjoy the book he is reading. It is called *Under the Lilacs*.

SEEING EVERYTHING IN JAPAN

Andrew Eken says he is going to see everything in Japan and a great deal in China and Korea. We think he will have many interesting things to tell us when he comes back.

ON THE BLACKBOARD IN PORTABLE FOUR

Miss Kingsborough has the words, "Courtesy," "Good Judgment," "Responsibility" and "Co-operation" written on the blackboard. The boys and girls look at these words and they try to mind them. The children try to be polite. They try to do the right thing at the right time. They try to take care of themselves. The boys and girls try to work together and help each other.—*David Howatt.*

A SPEED TEST

The boys and girls in Portable Four are going to have a race on the multiplication tables. They have a big yellow sheet on which they will write down one hundred and twenty answers. They will have seven minutes for the race. They are going to invite their mothers to the speed test.

ROLLING DOWN HILL

On April 3, Deborah Cleaveland's mother took Deborah and her brother and sister over to Rockeferrer's. Deborah and her brother and sister rolled down a great, big hill. They picked spring beauties and dog tooth violets and yellow violets. They had cookies and crackers and Forbes chocolate to eat. Deborah had a very nice time.

SECOND GRADE ASKS THIRD GRADE TO CRITICIZE

On April 22, Mary Ellen Finfrock from Miss Henderson's came to Portable Four and read the children a story called "The Honest Woodman." After she got through she asked the children to criticize the way she read it. The children thought that she read it beautifully. They told her that she could improve by looking off her book.

AT ADELBERT GYMNASIUM

On Saturday, April 23, the boys and girls in Portable Four went to the Adelbert Gymnasium. They did a dance called "The Romans and the English." When it came time for the children to fall down, all the people laughed and clapped. Four girls had their pictures taken. Their names were Jane Lewis, Ellen Duff, Ravella Leonard and Helen Born. They were in the pulling position. The pictures are going to be in the *Plain Dealer.*

INTERESTING REPORTS

On Monday, April 25, Miss Dysinger brought the boys and girls in her room over to Portable Four. Miss Dysinger's children gave reports on ants, bees, lions and snakes. The boys and girls in both classes asked questions. Some of the questions were very difficult to answer. William Hyde knew a great deal about snakes. He brought some rattles from a rattlesnake. These are the children who gave the reports:

Jean Mellen   Ruth Beebower
Robert Mellen   William Hyde

A WALK IN THE WOODS

On Tuesday, April 26, Miss Harmon took the children out for a walk in the woods. When they went a little way they came to a pond. Miss Harmon said there were frogs in the pond. We have read about frogs and we know that frogs come from tadpoles. The tadpoles come from frog's eggs. The tadpole pushes his arms through his skin. By and by his tail is gone and then he is Brother Green Coat.—*Junior Deming.*

A PIONEER EXHIBIT

The boys and girls in Portable Four are going to have a Pioneer Exhibit. They are going to make things out of wood, paper, plasticine, clay and soap. Junior Deming brought two bears made out of soap. His mother ordered the soap on purpose for Junior to make different kinds of animals. Junior's father helped Junior make the bears and the whole family offered suggestions.

STUART'S WAGON

Stuart George made a wagon out of wood. It is a covered wagon like the pioneers' wagons.

ROBERT LEWIS' WAGON

Robert Lewis made a covered wagon like the pioneers' wagons. Miss Reed said the horse could be a little fatter. Robert said his horse was not going to the Ohio Country. It was coming back from the Ohio Country and that was why it was so thin. Robert is going to make a banner. It is going to say on it, "I have been to the Ohio Country."

The people in the east began to get jealous because so many of their best people went to Ohio so they made two pictures. One was a well dressed man riding a fat horse. He had a banner and it said, "I am going to the Ohio Country." Then they made another picture of a man riding a wreck of a horse. He wore shabby clothes. He carried a banner and it said, "I have been to the Ohio Country."

3A'S THANK 4A'S

Miss Barber's class made a set of arithmetic cards for the boys and girls in Portable Four. They made forty cards. There are four examples on each card. We like the cards very much. We thank Miss Barber and her children for making them for us.

HALF ASLEEP

The other night the telephone rang. A little girl's mother jumped and grabbed the clock. She said, "Hello, hello." Then she answered the telephone and took the clock with her. Pretty soon she dropped the clock. She was half asleep.

SKIPPING A ROOM

A little boy named Lawrence once skipped a grade in school. When he came home he told his mother that he had skipped a room. A few days later Lawrence's mother saw his brother Raymond skipping across the room. She asked him why he was doing that. Raymond said he was doing just what Lawrence did.

MORT'S DOG AT SCHOOL

One day, Mort's dog went to school. The dog could not get in. Pretty soon a little boy went into the school. He did not shut the door and the dog went into the school. The children were having arithmetic. The dog went up to Mort and licked his slate. The teacher said, "Mort Crowell, you take that dog home."

Mort took the dog home and locked him up in the corn bin. Then he went to school again. When Mort's grandpa went to get the corn the dog got out and went to school again. He went up to Mort and the boys and girls began to laugh.

The teacher said, "Mort Crowell, you take your dog home, and you stay with him."

LETTERS FROM THE EARLY SETTLERS OF
MARIETTA TO THEIR FRIENDS IN
THE EAST

Marietta, O.,
Sept. 9, 1788.

Dear Cornelius,

I am going to tell you why I left my home in Danvers and came to Ohio.

One day as I was going out to plant my corn, my little son said, "Oh, father, please let me go with you."

He took his rake and spade and we both were very busy. What do you think happened? I heard a familiar sound. I turned around and saw my son crying.

I said, "What is the matter, my son?"

He said, "The soil is so rocky that I can't get enough dirt to cover my corn."

I decided it was time for me to move to a place where there was enough dirt to cover my corn.

Yours truly,
JANE SUMMERS.

Marietta, O.,
Aug. 30, 1789.

Dear Phineas,

We heard a great deal about the Ohio country, and I find that all I heard about the rich soil is true, for here the tallest settler has to stand on his tip toes to pull an ear of corn. When we were back in Danvers we had to kneel down to pluck the corn.

We had great trouble with the buckwheat for the crows were determined to devour it. We had to watch it all day long. The rabbits and the squirrels were pests too.

Yours truly,
ELLEN DUFF.

Marietta, O.,
Aug. 18, 1788.

Dear Reuben,

We like Ohio very much. The crops grew very well during the spring and summer. One bad thing was that there were so many trees. Some of the trees we cut down with our axes and others we deadened by girdling them.

We have plenty of game. There are many rabbits here. There are lots of fish in the streams.

Your friend,
RUSSELL MOODY.

Marietta, O.
June 15, 1789.

Dear Frederick,

I used to think I was brave but now since I came to the Ohio country, I don't think I am so brave. There are wolves and terrible snakes here.

One time when I was coming home at sunset, a pack of hungry wolves followed me. I climbed a tree and spent the night there.

In the morning when I was ready to go home, I saw a calf that the wolves had devoured for their breakfast.

One night my friend was bitten by a copper head snake when he was asleep.

You are not even safe to walk around your cabin because you might find a snake coiled right up in your path. I wish you were here to help me fight these terrible foes.

Yours truly,
JANE LEWIS.

HAZEL KINGSBOROUGH
Cleveland Heights, Ohio

THE READER'S GUIDE

THE WAITING NICHE

A writer in the *Virginia Teacher* for July, Professor L. R. Drown, wants a philosopher to define the project method. He read the *Twentieth Year-Book*, attended the Atlantic City meeting of the National Society for the Study of Education, has surveyed some of the current books on the subject, and finds himself dissatisfied with the way things are going.

In the first place he wonders what is to become of the excellent work that has been done on the minimum (or is it minimal?) essentials of the course of study. This was tending toward the building up of a science of education. But some of the advocates of what they call project-teaching appear to seek equivalents for essentials in "amorphous immediate experience simply because the latter has firm grasp upon the attention."

Again, there is difficulty in the matter of subject-matter vs. method. Some enthusiasts declare the project is both. They appear, however, either not to know or to ignore the principles set forth by Dr. Dewey, who has shown how the two, subject-matter and method, are unified. They evade the responsibility of either using or replacing the substantial body of methods and philosophy already built up. As a result, teachers, with no criteria agreed upon, feel free to call any sort of exercise which appeals to them a project.

We must choose a philosopher, says the writer, and apply consistently the principles which he works out. The basis is already laid in the definition of Professor Kilpatrick, "a unit of whole-hearted, pur-poseful activity proceeding in a social environment." The problem now is, What worth-while modifications of present practice may this idea foster? These will relate to (1) the nature of purpose, (2) the laws of learning, (3) the curriculum as providing for activity and complete acts, (4) general discipline, and (5) desirable results in knowledge, skills, habits, attitudes, and ideals, measured by such objective devices as we have or can develop. All this will require considerable time. After ten or twenty years we may wisely take account of progress and shall no doubt be able to justify the project method.

STANDARDS OF TEACHING ABILITY

"Standards of Teaching Ability," a brief though highly suggestive article on the judgment of teaching ability, appears in the *Educational Review* for October from the pen of Stuart A. Courtis, Director of Instruction, Teacher Training, and Research for the public schools of Detroit. Mr. Courtis believes that at present our ignorance on the subject of what constitutes teaching ability is very great. We know very little, for example, as to whether sympathy or the lack of it will produce the best results in terms of rigidity of discipline. We must first define teaching ability wholly in terms of the changes to be produced in children; second, we must formulate standard tests for measurement of these changes; third, we must institute careful control studies of the relation between special qualities in teachers, nature of materials used, methods of use, etc., and how these qualities may be developed; last, we must devise tests for the selection of the capable and the elimination of the unfit among those

N. Y.: Doubleday, Page & Co., 1921.
Pp. xiv + 355.

Thirteen stories that high school teachers will
be glad to use in this new and convenient form.

Word Finder. By Hubert V. Coryell and
Henry W. Holmes. Yonkers-on-Hudson,
N. Y.: World Book Co., 1921. Pp.
viii + 150.

A spelling-dictionary to enable a pupil in the
elementary school to look up quickly the spelling
of a word he wishes to use.

The American Public School. By Ross L.
Finney. New York: Macmillan Co.,
1921. Pp. xiv + 335.

A history of American education written for
normal school students.

State Maintenance for Teachers in Training.
By Walter Scott Hertzog. Baltimore,
Md.: Warwick & York, 1921. Pp. 144.

An investigation of the principles involved in
the making of subsidies to prospective teachers.

Child Welfare. By Nora Milnes. New
York: E. P. Dutton, 1921. Pp. 243.

From the social point of view by the director
of the Edinburgh School of Social Study.

Mental Development and Education. By
M. V. O'Shea. New York: Macmillan
Co., 1921. Pp. xvii + 403.

Principles of teaching based on natural laws of
human development. Intended as a textbook for
teachers in training.

Right Royal. By John Masefield. New
York: Macmillan Co., 1920.

A long narrative poem on cross-country racing
in England.

Stories of the Day's Work. By Roy Davis
and Frederick G. Getchell. Boston:
Ginn & Co., 1921. Pp. 318.

Selections from American authors, chosen with
a view to arousing interest on the part of older boys
and girls in various occupations and developing
respect for honest toil.

Uncle Zeb and His Friends. By Edward W.
Frentz. Boston: Atlantic Monthly Press.
Pp. 224.

A series of incidents, mainly concerned with
animals, as told by "Uncle Zeb."

IN PAPER COVERS

Mathematics for the Seventh School Year.
By Raleigh Schorling and John R. Clark.

An experimental edition published by the
authors, instructors in the Lincoln School of Teachers College, New York City.

*Wilkins Prognosis Test in Modern Lan-
guages.* By Lawrence A. Wilkins. Yonkers-on-Hudson, N. Y.: World Book Co.
Specimen set, 10 cents postpaid.

*Report of the Division of Educational Tests
for 1919–20.* By Walter S. Monroe.
Bulletin No. 5, Bureau of Educational
Research, University of Illinois. 25 cents.

*Courtis Standard Practice Tests in Handwrit-
ing.* By S. A. Courtis and Lena A. Shaw.
Yonkers-on-Hudson, N. Y.: World Book
Co., 1921. Specimen set, 50 cents postpaid.

Syllabus in the Philosophy of Education.
With Questions for Discussion, Reading
References, and Topics for Papers. By
William H. Kilpatrick. Published by
Teachers College, Columbia University.

University High School Journal, Vol. II.

An English number of a periodical published
at the University of California. Contains a complete course in English for the high school.

Getting Out the High School Paper. By
Clara C. Ewalt.

A bulletin issued by the Cleveland School of
Education.

*A Scale for Measuring Habits of Good Citi-
zenship.* By Siegfried M. Upton and
Clara F. Chassell. Teachers College,
Bureau of Publications, New York.

Bibliography of Tests for Use in Schools.
Yonkers-on-Hudson, N. Y.: World Book
Co. Second edition, September, 1921.
294 titles. 10 cents.

Projects for the Elementary School. Series I
to III. Sample materials for Kindergarten and Grades One to Three, Grades
Four to Six, and Junior and Senior High
School. Extension Department, State
University of New Jersey, New Bruns-
wick, N. J. 25 cents each.

THE JOURNAL OF EDUCATIONAL METHOD

Edited by JAMES F. HOSIC

Volume I　　　　DECEMBER, 1921　　　　Number 4

PUBLISHED BY THE WORLD BOOK COMPANY FOR THE NATIONAL CONFERENCE ON EDUCATIONAL METHOD

$3.00 a year　　　Monthly except July and August　　　35 cents a copy

Annual Meeting of the National Conference on Educational Method, Chicago, Illinois, February 28 and March 1, 1922

THE JOURNAL OF EDUCATIONAL METHOD is published monthly, from September to June, by World Book Company, Yonkers-on-Hudson, New York, for the officers, directors, and members of the National Conference on Educational Method. The subscription price is $3.00 a year; the price of single copies is 35 cents.

Postage is prepaid by the publishers on all orders from the United States, Mexico, Cuba, Porto Rico, Panama Canal Zone, Republic of Panama, Bolivia, Colombia, Honduras, Nicaragua, Peru, Hawaiian Islands, Philippine Islands, Guam, and the Samoan Islands. Postage is charged extra as follows: For Canada, 25c on annual subscriptions; other foreign countries not named, 50 cents. All communications regarding subscriptions or advertising should be addressed to World Book Company, Yonkers-on-Hudson, New York.

Address applications for membership to the Secretary of the Conference, 525 West One Hundred and Twentieth Street, New York City. The fee for active members is $3.00, for associate members, $2.00; $2.00 in each case is applied to the support of the journal, for which each member receives a year's subscription.

The editorial office is at 525 West One Hundred and Twentieth Street, New York City.

Entered as second-class matter 8 December 1921 at the post office at Greenwich, Connecticut, under the Act of 3 March 1879. Acceptance for mailing at special rate of postage provided for in Section 1103, Act of 3 October 1917, authorized 8 December 1921.

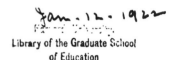
The Journal of Educational Method

VOLUME I   DECEMBER, 1921   NUMBER 4

EDITORIALLY SPEAKING

IF IT WORKS

The Project Method has its opponents—at least they object to the name. "What does it mean?" ask they. "Is it after all anything new? Has anyone the right to apply it to so wide a range of ideas and activities? Aren't we about to lose sight of the basic conceptions of reform in education which our generation has been devoted to in order to run after this fad, this passing fancy, which promises only disorganization and loose practices? Why not limit the application of the term to certain units of objective activity long familiar in agriculture and shop work, call it a device, and let it go at that?"

Such questions are natural and probably futile—except perhaps the first. The term Project Method is already in general use. Pick up any educational journal of wide circulation and see for yourself. The workers in the field believe that it stands for something of value to them, and whatever this is they mean to have. The Project Method is already a condition, not merely a theory.

It is not very hard to see how this condition has come about. Educational concepts have been multiplying so fast that the ordinary person can hardly be expected to keep them all in mind, much less act

in the light of them. Motivation, socialized recitation, supervised study, provision for individual differences, measurement of intelligence, measurement of achievement, educational sociology, science of human behavior, subjects in terms of knowledges, habits, skills, interests, and ideals, added to the ideas of Rousseau, Pestalozzi, Froebel, and Herbart, have flooded the market. There had to be consolidation or bankruptcy of thinking. The term project began to gather to itself one by one the favorite educational notions of our time. Problem was absorbed, socialization likewise, as well as economy of learning, education through experience, the school as life, larger opportunity, fuller participation, self-activity, ethical quality of conduct, concreteness, and many more. We seem on the way to a new unifying, a new synthesis, of our educational ideals. Considering the satisfaction and practical value attached to such a unification, it is no cause of wonder that a term which appears to promise this should be popular. It deserves to be.

Whether the ideas connoted by the term are all or even partly new does not greatly matter. The question is this, does this term give us a better grasp of them and does it enable us to organize and conduct our school work better in consequence? Time alone can tell. If the words Project Method do not serve a useful purpose in education, they will soon drop out. If they do, it is a waste of time to object to them. If they work, they work. The law of evolution holds even of educational terminology.

Thoughtful criticism is of course invaluable. The Project Method has, like all new and promising ventures, not been altogether fortunate in its interpreters. To mistake an outward form for the inner spirit is a blunder not confined, however, to the interpretation of this particular concept. Critics would do well to seek and exploit the best of the possible interpretations and not be offended by some book or article which perchance might as well not have been written. Criticism which seeks to improve the ideas and the practices for which Project Method stands is much needed and should be welcomed, but criticism which inquires whether we had better avoid the term is as good as wasted. The term we have and much hope of good from it. Its meaning is rapidly, perhaps too rapidly, evolving. Such is the way of the world. For the present at least the thing undoubtedly works. The question has passed the academic and entered the practical stage. Let us now inquire not, Shall we do this thing? but, How can we do it better?

THE FUTURE OF THE CONFERENCE

The National Conference on Educational Method was organized at Atlantic City with great enthusiasm. The point was made and appreciated that not since the Herbartians came together to discuss many-sided interest and apperception has there been a gathering of educators de-voted so wholeheartedly to the improvement of teaching by the application of certain far-reaching and fundamental principles of method. The chief unlikeness was the numbers which the latter-day conference called out because of its connection with the other meetings of the week.

As the months go by the need of the Conference becomes more and more apparent. The interest in method grows apace. There is evident a rapidly-growing tendency to break up the formality of school procedure and substitute freer and more spontaneous activities. The danger is that these shall not be guided by sound central principles. Sane and intelligent application of an appropriate philosophy of education reflecting the best current knowledge of society and of the laws of human growth can alone save us from vagaries.

To such a mission the Conference should wholeheartedly devote itself. A number of excellent leaders are already identified with it. These will doubtless attract others. Leaving to contemporary organizations the working out of solutions for problems of finance, equipment, and general administration, as well as the problems peculiar to selected groups of workers, the Conference should interest itself in the improvement of teaching, in *better* stimulation and guidance of children and youth.

All who teach or who train and direct those who teach will find in the Conference an opportunity for exchange of experience. Supervisors particularly, who, oddly enough have no organization peculiarly their own, may well make the Conference their clearing-house. The Chicago meeting of the Conference will no doubt have much to offer them, and it is safe to say that many of them will be on hand to participate in it.

SUPERVISION FROM THE TEACHER'S VIEWPOINT [1]

J. CAYCE MORRISON

State Education Department, Albany, N. Y.

A modern city school system is a very complex organization. The public schools imply equal opportunity to all children, which means the giving of equivalent instructional opportunity in all classrooms. Some one must be responsible for seeing that the instruction in each and every classroom meets an acceptable standard of excellence. *Making sure of this school service is supervision.*

Today the schools are required to teach health, train for better citizenship, instruct children to use profitably the leisure time of life, and drill them in better physical exercises. In addition, the school must teach reading, writing, arithmetic, spelling, history, geography, language, algebra, geometry, French, Spanish, chemistry, bookkeeping—the list is too long to enumerate; every parent and teacher knows the problem involved. Most or all of these subjects overlap one another; some one must be responsible for seeing that each subject is taught in such proportion that each child may have a well rounded and well balanced education when he comes to the end of his public-school course. Assuring that this ideal shall be achieved is *supervision.*

Teachers are not all of equal ability nor do they have equivalent preparation for their work. Every year, in the average school system, there are many young teachers just entering the profession; there is another large group experienced elsewhere but unfamiliar with the new environment and problems. Some one must be available to help these inexperienced teachers, or teachers new to the system, to find the materials they need, to become acquainted with their pupils and problems, and to fit generally and quickly into the work that is to be done. Then, too, teachers must always be students in order to keep abreast of the times. Some one must be responsible for organizing opportunities for teachers to learn, to grow, and for seeing to it that they do learn and do grow. This, too, is supervision.

To insure that all children have equivalent instructional opportunity, to coördinate properly all the instructional activities of the school, to provide every teacher with fullest opportunity to give her best possible service, and to organize conditions so that every teacher will continue to grow in service—these are absolutely essential features of any modern school system, they are cardinal points of school supervision.

Supervision, *i.e.,* the organization and improvement of instructional service, is one of the most important problems in present day public-school work. Much supervision has been unintelligent, much has lacked sympathy; there is a feeling abroad that a great deal of it has had an autocratic, dictatorial bearing. Even the wisest, most sympathetic supervisors are, today, looking for methods, for ways and means to improve their own work. This chapter reports an investigation designed to con-

[1] From a report of the Survey of the Elmira Schools made by the State Education Department, Albany, May, 1921. This phase of the investigation was made possible through the fine coöperation of the superintendent, assistant superintendent, principals, supervisors, and teachers of Elmira, New York.

tribute something to the knowledge and technique of expert supervision.

The poet wrote, 'O wad some Pow'r the giftie gie us, To see oursels as ithers see us!" It is good for supervisors to see themselves as their teachers see them. It is good for supervisors to know what of their method, their technique, has seemed valuable to teachers, what has made little or no impression, what teachers have wanted but have not received. To answer these questions, the Survey Committee undertook to find out what Elmira teachers thought of the supervision of Elmira schools.

At a meeting of the principals, assistant superintendent, and superintendent early in February, the chairman of the committee explained the purpose of this part of the investigation and the necessarily impersonal features of such a study. Principals agreed to take the matter up with their teachers and to ask each one to answer, to the best of her or his ability, the three questions. Endeavor was made to eliminate any feeling of obligation and to make this contribution voluntary in every way. The questionnaire follows:

TEACHER'S REPORT CONCERNING SUPERVISION

City .... Teacher's name ....

School .... Date ....

Grade ....

To Teachers: One of the most important questions confronting city schools at the present time is that of adequate supervision. The survey committee in approaching this problem has but ONE thought, that of assisting principals and supervisors to find the best means of helping teachers to improve classroom instruction. The committee believes that the best way of approaching this question is for principals and supervisors to know definitely what phases of their work have been beneficial to teachers, and what help teachers would like to have which has not yet been given.

When you have filled out this paper, please seal in the accompanying envelope and hand it to your principal, who will give it unopened to the survey committee. Your individual paper will be retained by the committee and the information you give will be used, without mention of name, and only as a part of the general survey report which will be given for the city at large.

Describe briefly, but as definitely as possible, the most valuable help you have received this year from

A. Your principal.

B. The assistant superintendent or any one of the supervisors (specify position).

On the opposite page, state any specific supervisory help you would like to have, that you have not yet received.

Sixty-two academic and vocational school teachers and 158 elementary school teachers contributed to the study. This was more than 95 per cent of the entire teaching staff. Each reply was read carefully and tabulated according to the following outline or classification of methods of supervision:[1]

OUTLINE OF SUPERVISORY METHODS

1. Personal conference
    a. Offering encouragement, suggestions and inspiration
    b. Pointing out teacher's errors or faults
    c. Offering new plans, methods
    d. Leading the teacher to recognize own weakness and to seek improvement
    e. Leading teacher to exercise initiative, to undertake new projects
    *f. Coöperation
    *g. Special assistance
    *h. Generally helpful
2. Teaching the class
    a. While the teacher observes

[1] For interpretation of the meaning of each item of the following outline, see "Methods of Improving Classroom Instruction," El. Sch. Jour. XX, Nov. 1919.

b. Supervisor discussing the purpose and methods of his demonstration with the teacher before and after the class period

c. Supervisor taking the class during or at the close of the period to correct errors noted during observation

3. Having teacher visit other teachers
   a. To observe good teaching
   b. To seek help on certain specific problems
   c. For specific purpose with results of visit checked by the supervisor

4. By directing professional study
   a. Suggesting reading
   b. Noting improvement through suggested reading and professional study
   c. By directing or encouraging normal, college, or university work

5. By improving classroom management
   a. Program
   b. Lesson plan and reports, "Preparation of outlines"
   c. Discipline, control
   d. Pupil activity
   e. Classroom appearance
   *f. Pupils' general mental attitude
   *g. General help

6. Teachers' meetings
   a. General
   b. Discussion of indirect problems of instruction
   c. Discussion of direct problems of instruction

7. By model or demonstration lessons
   a. Merely mentioned
   b. Followed by group or general discussion
   c. Preceded by teachers' preparations for the lesson and followed by supervisor's checking results on basis of conclusions reached in discussion

8. By contact with pupils
   a. Written tests
   b. Reading pupils' papers
   c. Questioning pupils in class
   d. School exhibits, competition
   *e. Individual work

9. By provision of materials, books, class aids

10. Use of standard measurements
    a. Without teachers' coöperation
    b. With teachers' coöperation

11. Letters or bulletins to teachers
    a. To meet needs seen by supervisor
    b. To meet needs proposed by teachers

*12. Miscellaneous

*13. No help

A more complete definition of each item or method contained in the original outline is given in the article referred to under 1 above. The items added are defined more clearly below.

1f. "Coöperation." The replies listed here indicated that supervisors had coöperated in some general way with teachers through personal conference.

1g. "Special assistance." These replies named some specific thing not otherwise included in the classification that the supervisor had done.

1h. "Generally helpful" included only those replies that were vague, and indicated that the teacher was not cognizant of having received any definite help, but was too polite to say so in writing.

5f. and 5g. are defined in the mere statement of the outline.

12. A few miscellaneous replies were grouped under this item.

13. A few teachers specified that they had received *no help;* these replies were tabulated under 13.

The following table shows the classification of supervisory methods used by principals which teachers had found generally helpful.

Interpretation of the table on p. 134 shows that teachers believed they had received most help from principals through the methods listed in order as follows:

1. Personal conference

5. Help in improving classroom management

* These items were added to the original classification.

CLASSIFICATION OF METHODS OF SUPERVISION USED BY PRINCIPALS

Showing the statistical tabulation of supervisory methods used by principals which teachers had found specially helpful. (See outline for meaning of 1a, 1b, 5a, 4c, etc)

Methods	Total Times Mentioned E H		Variations of the several methods															
	E	H	a E	H	b E	H	c E	H	d E	H	e E	H	f E	H	g E	H	h E	H
1	168	48	48	10	2	—	23	—	8	—	11	19	53	19	3	—	10	—
2	—	—	—	—	—	—	—	—	—	—	—	—	—	—	—	—	—	—
3	—	—	—	—	—	—	—	—	—	—	—	—	—	—	—	—	—	—
4	10	2	6	2	—	—	4	—	—	—	—	—	—	—	—	—	—	—
5	46	19	3	—	1	—	29	11	2	—	1	1	6	1	4	6	—	—
6	50	6	4	—	—	—	46	6	—	—	—	—	—	—	—	—	—	—
7	—	—	—	—	—	—	—	—	—	—	—	—	—	—	—	—	—	—
8	4	—	—	—	1	—	—	—	—	—	3	2	—	—	—	—	—	—
9	8	—	8	—	—	—	—	—	—	—	—	—	—	—	—	—	—	—
10	10	—	10	—	—	—	—	—	—	—	—	—	—	—	—	—	—	—
11	11	10	—	—	—	—	—	—	—	—	—	—	—	—	—	—	1	—
12	—	—	—	—	—	—	—	—	—	—	—	—	—	—	—	—	—	—
13	2	—	2	—	—	—	—	—	—	—	—	—	—	—	—	—	—	—

6. Teachers' meetings

11. Letters or bulletins to teachers

4. Direction of professional study

10. Use of standard measurements

9. Provision of materials, books, class aids

8. By principal's direct contact with pupils

Only the first three, Nos. 1, 5 and 6, were mentioned often enough to warrant their consideration as methods having any general or widespread and helpful use by principals throughout the school system. The ten teachers reporting "10. Use of Standard Measurements," were all from the same school. The use of No. 11 was also largely reported by teachers of the same school. Further analysis of the methods reported, according to the table, shows that elementary teachers reported that they had received most help from

1f. General coöperation, through personal conference

1a. "Encouragement, inspiration and suggestions" offered by the principal in personal conference

6c. "Discussion of direct problems of instruction" in teachers' meetings

1c. The principal's "offering new plans and methods" through personal conference

5c. Help in "discipline and control" of pupils

The academic and vocational school teachers reported that they had received most help as follows:

1e. From the principals' "Leading teacher to exercise initiative, to undertake new projects"

1f. From "general coöperation" through personal conference

5c. Help in "discipline and control" of pupils

Two teachers reported that they had received no help from their principal. No teacher mentioned any of the following methods as having been used by principals:

2. The principal's "teaching the class"

3. Visiting or observation of other teachers

7. Model or demonstration lessons

A few teachers did not answer the second question asked on the questionnaire. Many specified the help they had received from just one of the special subject supervisors or from the assistant superintendent. Others described help they had received from two or more supervisors. The analysis of replies was made in the same manner as described above. Help from the assistant superintendent was described by nearly fifty elementary teachers. The chief methods mentioned were:

1. The personal conference
2. Teaching the class
9. Provision of materials, books, class aids
7. Directing the teaching of model lessons
6. Organization of group "teachers' meetings"

Careful analysis of these replies disclosed characteristic features of the supervisory methods used by the assistant superintendent which had appealed to teachers as being most helpful to them. These features are best described in questions from statements by the teachers themselves.

"She (the assistant superintendent) is always ready to aid at any time either by ideas, model teaching or inspiration. Her great appreciation of work done is an added incentive to do one's best."

"Great help in introducing new reading method." "Help in devising different ways to teach backward children."

"Assistant superintendent inspires teacher. Her visits are spent teaching, which is of great help to the teacher."

"The assistant superintendent has given me definite criticism and definite suggestions for improvement."

"Assistant superintendent—Monthly grade meetings. The teachers of each grade organized under her direction, and held monthly meetings to plan and talk over their work."

". . . She is very helpful with methods of presentation and has a way of giving courage and hope when you are discouraged."

"The assistant superintendent gave a model lesson in reading to my 1B class that was a great deal of help to me. She has made the teaching of reading a real pleasure by providing the right kind of books and giving us a practical method of presenting the work to a class."

"By planning model lessons to be observed by all teachers of first grade." "The assistant superintendent has given me a new reading system, which I have tried for one term and found much easier and more efficient than the old one."

The above statements are fairly typical of the 40 odd statements concerning the supervisory help which had been received from the assistant superintendent.

There were special supervisors, each with an assistant for each of the four subjects: drawing, music, physical training, and writing. In the tabulation of replies only three methods were mentioned often enough to be considered. These were:

1. The personal conference
2. Teaching the class
5b. Preparation of outlines for the teachers to follow

A closer analysis revealed the fact that the most help had come from the supervisor's teaching the class and talking over the aims and methods of the work with the teacher. This method apparently had been generally followed by the supervisors of each subject.

The majority of statements tabulated under 5b refer to outlines of work to be accomplished, which were prepared by the supervisor and submitted to teachers.

The majority of the replies listed under method 1 stated that supervisors were generally helpful or that they encouraged or offered helpful suggestions. A number of teachers stated specifically what help had been received.

In brief, teachers had found most help from special subject supervisors in

(a) Their teaching the class so as to demonstrate what should be done.

(b) Their outlining of the work that the teacher was to do in the supervisor's absence.

(c) Their encouragement of teachers and suggestions as to improvement of the work.

Sixty teachers gave statements as to the kind of supervisory help they would like to have which they had not received. Classification of the help wanted from supervisory officers follows:

Twenty wanted supervisors to teach class. Two of these specified that they would want to discuss the model lesson with the supervisor.

Ten wanted more specific plans or methods given by supervisor, and

Six asked for better or more definite outlines of work to be done.

Five suggested the value of group meetings, where the assistant superintendent or supervisor might give more specific instructions.

Seven wanted specific help on some specified thing.

Three wanted supervisory help that would help them to grow.

The remaining 15 suggestions were widely scattered in their requests for additional help.

The following quotations from teachers' statements were typical of a group of replies that did not readily admit of classification in the outline followed in this report.

"My only complaint against supervisors is that they are indefinite. Most of them come in, watch work, say 'Go right on,' and leave. We never know how or where we stand."

"Supervisors should understand that there are many subjects to be taught other than the special subjects, and so should not demand more than their share of time."

"This is the day of specialists. Why not have several music, drawing, and physical training supervisors take entire charge of the work and relieve the grade teachers of trying to be all of these?"

"It would be a help to me if there were less frequent visits by the supervisors, giving one more time to work out one's own salvation."

These quotations are not typical of all the replies received but do express four viewpoints of the supervisory problems that were held by classroom teachers.

"We never know how or where we stand." Teachers know that the supervisor's work is to help improve the instructional work of the school. They want to know what of their work satisfies the supervisor and what can be improved. They want to see their work as others see it. A supervisor's program should be so organized that he will have time for personal interview with the teacher after each observation period. This personal conference should come, if possible, on the same day the class is observed.

"Supervisors should . . . not demand more than their share of the time." This is a matter of judgment. If the curricula and the supervisory program are well organized by the administrative head of the school, this criticism of supervision would tend to disappear. Evidently Elmira has practically solved the problem, for the criticism was voiced by only one teacher. It is a supervisory problem, however, to which supervisors must give attention.

A number of teachers voiced the wish that the special supervisors might teach all the work of the special subjects. This evidently is a crucial question not only in Elmira schools, but in city schools generally. *Is the special supervisor a teacher of a special subject or a supervisor of the teaching of a special subject?* Many classroom teachers gained their education and training before public schools were required to teach music, drawing, and physical training. In every city school system there are a few of these teachers who have not had or taken the opportunity to learn how to teach these special subjects as they should be taught. Such teachers resent having to teach a subject which they look upon as a "fad"; they would have the special supervisor do all the teaching of the special subject. Music, drawing, and physical training should be an integral part of the classroom work. The special supervisor should be a teacher of teachers, their inspiration, guide and help at every point. She should be an expert teacher of her subject, capable of demonstrating just how the new or difficult lesson should be taught. There is no longer any place for a classroom teacher in the elementary schools who cannot make music and art and physical drill an integral part of her daily work.

It is probable that the classroom teacher who complains because of the amount of supervision has wholly missed the reason for such supervision. She is very likely beyond the growing stage; she is in such a rut that any suggestion of improvement seems painful to her. And yet she must grow, must improve, or else there should be no place for her in the public schools.

This attitude on the part of teachers presents one of the most difficult problems for supervisors.

Summary.—One hundred fifty-eight elementary teachers and 62 high school teachers or a total of 220 coöperated in making this study. Each teacher was asked to tell as definitely as possible: (A) What supervisory help from her principal had been most valuable, (B) the most valuable help she had received from the assistant superintendent or any special supervisor, (C) what help she would like to have that had not been given her. Most teachers answered A and B; only 60 answered C.

Four supervisory agencies were mentioned in teachers' reports: the principals, the assistant superintendent, the heads of departments in high school, and the supervisors of special subjects. Analysis of supervisory methods used by principals showed that teachers had gained most help from principals, through suggestions, inspiration, and coöperation gained in personal conference, discussion of direct problems of instruction in teachers' meetings, and help in the "discipline and control" of pupils. Many of the references to coöperation from principals were vague and probably did not indicate any very definite or specific help. In the academic group, emphasis was placed upon the "principal's leading teachers to exercise initiative, to undertake new projects." This is a very high type of supervisory help. There was no suggestion from teachers that any principal had given help by teaching the class, by arranging for demonstration lessons, or by having teachers observe one another's work. The analysis of reports from each school showed the strength and weakness of the supervisory technique of principals.

The supervisory strength of the assistant superintendent lay in her ability: (a) to give teachers confidence in themselves; (b) in taking charge of the class and demonstrating to the teacher the methods or technique needed, the demonstration preceded and followed usually by conference between teacher and supervisor; (c) in helping teachers to choose or select new materials, books, class aids, etc. and in seeing that the supplies selected were secured for the teachers; (d) in organizing group "teachers' meetings" for planning work, discussing methods, and demonstrating the best methods of teaching.

The most valuable help received from the special supervisors of music, drawing, writing, and physical training had come through: (a) suggestions and criticisms received in personal conference; (b) the supervisor's teaching of the class to demonstrate methods of presentation; (c) the supervisors' preparation of outline of work to be accomplished. Academic teachers placed more emphasis on help they had received from department heads: (a) in improving the technique of teaching; (b) in preparing lesson plans and outlines of work together; and (c) in grouping children more nearly according to their ability.

Only 60 teachers attempted to describe any supervisory help they would like to have which had not been given. The small percentage answering this question may be due to: (a) the question coming last on the sheet; (b) a desire on the part of teachers not to appear critical; or (c) a general lack of understanding as to what additional supervisory help might have been given.

Two chief helps were requested by teachers:

(a) that the supervisor demonstrate by teaching the class; (b) that the supervisor's outlines, plans, or advice be specific. It seems a sad commentary that only three of 220 teachers should have requested supervisory help that would enable them to grow in their work.

THE PLACE OF THE PROJECT METHOD IN RELIGIOUS EDUCATION

FRANCES ROSE EDWARDS

St. Luke's Church School, Rochester, N. Y.

"No, I don't believe in all this talk about the project method," said one conscientious Sunday School teacher to me just yesterday.

"Don't you" I asked.

"No, I don't. It means that you are deceiving the children into thinking that they are running things when they are not."

This represents just one of the many vague conceptions of the project method which can be found floating around among Sunday School teachers who are at all informed regarding educational theories. Many of them are not, and perhaps it is just as well. To many the term "project method" seems to loom like a monster on the horizon, threatening all that they hold most dear, even including the Bible itself. It is indeed difficult for many of them to realize that they may be straining at a gnat, after having swallowed a whole camel.

Four years ago the project method first dawned on my horizon, and the most that can be said is that I realized dimly that there was a big idea back of it, and spent many troubled moments trying to fit it into the scheme of things, get at its essentials, and work it out. I firmly determined to seize the first opportunity to find out, and hence I formed a well-defined project of my own, namely, to determine the place of the project method in religious education. This soon resolved itself into four questions for study: 1. What is it? 2. What are its possibilities? 3. To what extent is it being used? 4. How can it best be introduced?

In answer to these questions I shall try to sum up the results, in so far as I have digested them, of class discussions, individual reading, special research, and attendance upon Sunday morning religious discussion groups, in as simple words as possible, from the viewpoint of the Church School teacher.

First, then, what is the project method? It is not a method, it is the Christian way of living, the way of the Kingdom, the way of fellowship and coöperative endeavor. What marks do we expect to find in the true Christian? Let us name a few, briefly. Perhaps we would state as the prime essential that fellowship which is the spirit of love, fellowship with God and with man. We expect the Christian to be a man with a purpose in life to the carrying out of which he devotes himself wholeheartedly. Moreover we expect him to be able to see results, to plan intelligently, and to modify his actions as he learns to judge results in the light of his experience. All of this takes rather a long time to say, and in this busy world we are constantly looking for short cuts. Consequently the term "project" has been used to express

this whole idea of what we call the worthy life, and to include all the processes of purposing, planning, executing, judging, appreciating. With this idea in mind educators have many of them tried to pigeonhole it, but this cannot be done, for it represents more than any technical terms. Those terms are not essential, except for convenience in understanding one another; and there they are helpful if a common definition has been agreed upon, just as the term "chair" is a useful term if we all know what a chair is.

Granted, then, that the project method represents our ideal way of living, what connection has this with our way of teaching in the Church School, with our conception of the Bible, with our relations with the children? What are its possibilities, if any, for us, or does it simply represent another manner of stating an ideal?

This brings us directly to the question of what we are trying to do in our Church Schools, anyway. There are many answers we can give: make Christians, teach the Bible, help children to be good—all more or less vague. In one Church School I remember that above the platform there was stretched a long printed strip of cloth, with the words, "The purpose of this school is the formation of Christian character." Perhaps that expresses our aim, if we use the term "character" as including not only the idea of being good, but of being good for something. How are we going about it? Well, we are teaching lessons about faith, and humility, and obedience, and loyalty. We are telling stories about men who have lived good lives. We are sending money to the heathen, we are even making scrapbooks for them, and clothes.

We do not seem to be getting very far. In our meetings we spend a great deal of time discussing modern young people—their irresponsibility and lack of principles. We are discouraged, and wonder whether it is all worth while, and then we feel ashamed of ourselves and determine to try doubly hard next week to give them what they should have.

Do we know what they should have? Instinctively we say, why of course we do. How ridiculous! Haven't we our course of study? But is it meeting the needs of the children? We have already confessed that we are not getting them. Let us think back a little. How much did the lessons which were taught to us mean? Frankly, I'll confess that I was more or less bored most of the time, but went because I loved my teacher. As for the lessons, I do not remember much about them. Somehow they did not seem to have much connection with life. Is not that one trouble, that we do not touch the real life of the child? Can there be something wrong with our methods?

Let us again think back. When did you learn the most about cake-making, the day that you all made cake in school, when you each stood behind your cupboard and mixed the ingredients just as the teacher told you, or that Saturday morning when Mother let you bake cake at home, and you looked up the recipe, and measured it all out, and put it together, set the pan in the oven and watched it bake so eagerly, only to find that it had fallen flat, which Mother said was because you had slammed the oven door when you had peeked in at it. Yes, it is the doing it at home that we remember. Ah, you say we were learning by experience, then. Is that the best way to learn? How often we say that, after all,

we tell children they must in the end learn for themselves by experience.

Have we ever tried to help them learn by experience, to place them in situations where they could learn? They are doing that wherever they come in contact with life now. We are trying to control their environment, though, and provide playgrounds for them, and direct their recreation. In some of the public schools the teachers who believe in the project way of life are experimenting and are trying to give the children an opportunity to learn through experience in doing, how to plan, and work together for a common purpose, and decide whether they have reached their goal. This they call, for short, the project method. It is the technical working out of the big idea.

That may be all very well for the public schools, but, as one Sunday School teacher said to me, they have time to experiment and their aims are not our aims anyway. Is there a difference between secular and religious education? What is that difference?

What is our idea of education? Is it always the same or does it change? As we look back we find that different ages have had very different ideas of what it means to be educated, and of how education should be carried on. In brief, education has probably at all times meant the passing on to one generation of the ideas which preceding generations have worked out as essential. Are these ideas, gained through experience, of how we should meet life essentially secular or essentially religious? In early days we find no distinction made; education was simply equipment for life in all its phases, which included habits and skill in doing things, and information, and attitude toward God and man. With the separation of Church and

State, the State undertook to develop primarily the knowledge and the skill needed for life, and the Church undertook to develop right attitudes. There is a common ground, however, where the two meet, for the State recognizes the need of right attitudes, and the Church realizes that information is a necessary basis upon which to build. In short, State and Church should work together to develop a full and complete conception of life, and the difference is one of emphasis rather than of kind. In this case is it not sensible to suppose that they should utilize similar methods?

What methods are being used in education? For a long, long period we simply herded children together, massed them, and told them what to do, and punished them if they failed. Later the school began to recognize the child as an individual, and to try to help him as an individual to develop. Still he was told *what* to do. How much effect does this have on most of us? Were not our school lessons a more or less mechanical performance? Which ones meant the most to us? Probably those which we entered into wholeheartedly. Then why not give more opportunity for such participation? That is just what the schools are trying to do. The teacher and the children work together to carry out plans which the children help to form.

If this way of doing things can be carried over into the Church School, will it not mean that the children are practicing at living the Christian life? What could be better for them than this actual attempt to work out ideals in their everyday contacts?

All very well, but can this be done? Is it being done?

A survey of the field shows that only to a small extent is wholehearted purpose-ful activity characteristic of Church School work. Is not this because we have not yet fully conceived the child in terms of personality, individuality? Just as on a clear night when we look at the crescent moon we may see the faint ring which indicates the completed circle, so when we see the child we must see him as he is and see also all that he may become. Only so can we meet him and coöperate with him in his facing of life situations.

Wherever we find successful work being done we shall find that it is being undertaken as a project and carried forward in that spirit. Where work is failing to produce results we shall find that it is largely because we have failed to provide situations which call forth the desired response. We have seen that the children need help in acquiring information upon which to base action, in forming habits, and in developing attitudes.

Let us take first the question of information. What are our courses of study doing for the children? They are providing stories, chiefly derived from the Bible, and superimposed, so far as the children are concerned, with typical informational questions. The Scribner Completely Graded Series and the Chicago Constructive Bible Studies represent two attempts to prepare graded courses, based primarily upon Bible stories. The Chicago Course in its senior department provides for life interests with its courses, "Christianity and Its Bible," "Social Duties from the Christian Point of View," and "Christian Faith for Men of To-day." It also considers the beginner and provides rather good material for the early classes. The Scribner Series represents in general about the same level of achievement, with some variations in courses.

On the side of the denominational courses the International Series as edited by those denominations which are using it represents the average of achievement. Perhaps one of its best courses is that for seniors entitled "The World a Field for Christian Service," as allowing more scope for individual initiative.

The Unitarian Beacon Series is a recent attempt to devise a course better adapted to the needs of the growing child. The fourth grade course, "World Stories," strikes the same note which is being stressed in planning new public school curricula. Here again the senior courses are especially noteworthy as providing life situations, or at least contact with life which might easily be developed.

The Christian Nurture Series of the Episcopal Church is the first attempt to bring together information, worship, and service, and unify them. This is a big step forward. The courses are uneven in development as yet, and the whole can be superimposed as readily as any of the older courses. The books are the standard textbook type, calling for question and answer to be written out.

On the informational side, then, no curriculum has been set forth which appeals to the child in terms of functions, life problems, using Biblical and other material to illustrate and help the child to judge values in accordance with standards determined by others as well as those which he has so far evolved from his own experiences. Far less has any course been developed which would provide for activity as an integral part of the work, although the Christian Nurture Series attempts to do this.

To give the child opportunity for expression, programs of social service and missionary activities have been devised, again superimposed, unrelated, and too often exploiting the child, for the sake of the object. This same holds true in worship, which is generally quite remote from the child's experience, in the way in which it is conducted.

That departments of religious education are alive to the situation is shown by official statements. In the 1920 bulletin, "Religious Education for the Presbyterian Church in the United States of America," we read: "The Curriculum Committee is working toward the provision of such material, so coördinated and adapted to the developing needs of the children and youth as shall constitute a comprehensive plan for the Presbyterian Church both on the instructional and expressional side."

Again, in the pamphlet entitled "Principles and Methods of Missionary Education," issued by the Congregational Educational Society, we read: "Project teaching has become a well-known and valuable educational method and has been successfully applied in the field of missionary education. The missionary project is an enterprise more or less extended and involved according to the age of the participants and in which the elements of study and service are blended."

In some schools we find the students actually bearing responsibility for running the school, sharing in the planning, and carrying out of plans. How are you to be sure that they will not upset everything? On the other side, how can you ever expect them to develop responsibility if they never have any experience?

The extent of purposeful activity is limited in many ways. The Church is strongly conservative and inclined toward the use of authority rather than freedom for discussion. Especially with children does it believe that they must be told what to think, rather than taught how to think. Another great difficulty is found in the lack of adequate equipment. One favorable aspect of this situation is that the churches will not have to break away from the idea of desks, as for the most part these have never been provided. Then the great lack is that of a proper curriculum. Just as Miss Wells has experimented with unifying purposes for the elementary school, so some one is needed who can experiment with a curriculum for the Church School which shall provide a purpose large enough to include worship, knowledge, and activity along service lines. This involves a knowledge of the needs of the child at each period in his development, which in turn depends upon ways of testing and measuring religious growth. The whole field of religious education has just been opened, and much pioneer work must be done in it before satisfactory results can be attained.

Meanwhile, if one wished to initiate purposeful activity and provide for cooperative effort along some lines, how best could one go about it? In many lines of endeavor the caution holds true, "Be radical in thought but conservative in action." In the first place, avoid all mention of the term "project." If this is advised in public school circles, how much more essential is it in the Church School! Talk with individual teachers of the needs of the classes, the problems to be met, the value of help from the children. In planning work for the year, offer a class a choice in courses, let them choose the one they desire. They will study it with a definite purpose. When

an appeal for money comes, or for service, present it as such. Make it possible for the children to obtain information as to the need, then let them decide to undertake certain responsibility, and carry it through. Interest one teacher in testing her class to discover progress. Perhaps she may work out some way of testing. She may make some contribution to knowledge of the needs of that age. At least her own eyes will be opened. She will be alert to meet needs. Discuss with teachers the possibilities of interesting parents. Perhaps an exhibit of work might be suggested. Teachers might find that children could coöperate in preparing such an exhibit. Little by little wholehearted purposeful activity could be started along various lines. Then some literature might be circulated as to what is being done elsewhere, as to methods, technique, and a desire for meetings to discuss problems together created. Sharing administrative responsibility with older students might result naturally, if teachers and children have worked together for exhibit or some other purpose.

The working out of plans in common will lead to growth, a more vital school, an added realization of responsibility on the part of the teachers, and a desire to keep abreast of the tide, and on the part of the children a new value attached to the Church School and its week-day activities, which through experience will result in the development of a finer type of Christian men and women, who through practice in living together have learned to carry the Christian attitudes into all the relations of life. They will be citizens of the Kingdom, walking in the way of the Kingdom.

MIND-SET AND LEARNING

(Continued)[1]

WILLIAM H. KILPATRICK

Professor of Education, Teachers College, Columbia University

"Are we ready to continue our discussion, and shall we begin where we left off?"

"Please, before you go further, give a short summary of what was said last time. Several of us here today were not present then, but have been attracted by the reports that have gone out. Give us the gist of your discussion."

"We covered a good deal of ground, but I'll try to sum it up. We agreed that teachers should study the psychology of learning for the double reason that with it they could teach better and that understanding better how learning goes on, they would get more satisfaction from their teaching. The symbol S➟R opens, as it were, the door to the psychology of the learning process. Any act of conduct consists of some sort of response (R) to some stimulating situation (S), as I hear a shout (S) and turn to listen (R). All conduct can be so described. The symbol is best conceived in terms of physiological psychology: the stimulation (S) takes place because in the nervous system there are mechanisms, so to speak, especially suited to receiving such stimulation; and other mechanisms appropriate for responding. Any particular response (R) follows appropriately a certain stimulus (S), because there is also in the nervous system a specific nerve structure path or bond (neurones and synapses, to be more specific) connecting the initial sensory mechanism with the final motor response. These paths or bonds may be thought of somewhat as the systems of wires connecting different telephone instruments. Talking at one end corresponds to the stimulus, hearing at the other end to the response. My friend hears me talk because at my request the various switchboard operators have appropriately joined the intervening wires. Now in the case of the human telephone exchange system—our whole aggregate of nerve structure—we bring into the world with us at birth some of the connections between S and R already made, as when a missile flies close to the eye (S), the eyelid closes (R). Other connections we make only after (certain kinds of) exercise; as I may, after learning, strike a baseball (R) when I see it coming (S). This making new connections between S and R (or changing old ones) is what we mean by learning.

"One very interesting fact was noted about the action of the mechanisms that have to do with receiving and conducting stimulations and with making responses: at some times these mechanisms are more ready to act than at others. Repeated exercise may result in fatigue and the mechanism may then fail to respond to a stimulus that would in the beginning have sufficed to bring a prompt response. Certain mental attitudes also will cause readiness or unreadiness. If

The discussion continued

A short summary

Readiness

[1] Continued from the November number. All rights reserved by the author. The account here given is, as the informed reader will at once see, largely based on Thorndike and Woodworth.

I am very angry with a man, I am unready to laugh with him, but I am—alas—only too ready to hear evil of him. If I am very anxious to succeed at golf, I am easily brought to think about golf **Mind-set** strokes, golf clubs, golf records, and the like. This fact of mind-set needs to be distinguished from simple readiness. Suppose I, being thus interested in golf, am entering eagerly upon a tournament with high hopes of success. In such case my mind is said to be *set* on the end of playing to win. If anything postpones the start I am restless: my mind-set acting within urges me on. Such a mind-set radiates, as it were, a wave of readiness to all my conduct mechanisms that are likely to be needed in my play. And just as truly the same set radiates unreadiness for any thwarting activities. My mind-set thus contemplates some end, urges me from within to put forth efforts to attain this end, makes ready for action my various mental and physical resources that may be used in action, and at the same time makes unready for action any mechanism that might by its action interfere with attaining my end. The value of the mind-set in making thus for effective effort is, as we shall presently see, no greater than its value in making for effective learning.

"The laws of learning are concise statements of the conditions under which learning takes place. Everything **The laws of** so far is in a way preparatory **learning** to them. Thorndike recognizes three principal laws of learning, those of Readiness, Exercise (Use and Disuse), and Effect (Satisfaction and Annoyance). The law of Readiness connects the fact of readiness as described above with the facts of satisfaction and annoyance: *When*

a bond is ready to act, to act gives satisfaction and not to act gives annoyance. When a bond is not ready to act, to be forced to act gives annoyance. The especial significance of this is to be seen in its connection with the law of Effect (Satisfaction and Annoyance): *A modifiable bond is strengthened or weakened according as satisfaction or annoyance attends its exercise.* It follows at once that learning (strengthening a desired bond) will take place more easily if the bond is in a high state of readiness. Indeed if a bond is so unready to act that annoyance attends its exercise, unlearning (or weakening the bond) rather than learning (or strengthening the bond) may be expected."

"Does this explain the value of interest in learning? I have always believed that **Interest and** interest helped learning, but **learning** now I seem to see more in it than ever before."

"Exactly so; to take interest in doing anything is to have a mind-set towards it. That means, as we saw, an inner urge to engage in that thing and readiness in sense and thought for whatever helps it along."

"Why say 'readiness in sense'? Do you mean that my eye actually sees things I am interested in better than it sees others? I thought the eye was like a mirror or camera and saw everything in front of it."

"The *eye* does see everything in focus before it, and, as a mere mirror, sees them indifferently; but *you* don't see them that way. *You* pick out from all the things in front of your eye certain ones to pay attention to. When I say 'you pick out,' it would be more exact to say that your mind-set at the time, your various readinesses, pick out the things significant to these readinesses. Don't you know that a girl on her way to buy a hat will see the shop windows of the milliners more certainly, more readily in fact, than the windows of the hardware stores? Her eyes, as bare optical instruments, may see the hardware windows, but that seeing meets no response within. Actual and effective seeing is selective according to the mind's set at the time. So with hearing and all the rest."

"Then the working of interest is a scientific fact, and not mere sentimentality. I had got the idea that really hard-headed thinking ignores interest. Haven't we been told that?"

"Possibly you have heard something like that, and some sentimentalists have brought just reproach on a good cause. But it is true beyond a doubt that interest is a significant factor in mental life and a positive help to learning."

"It seems, too, that you don't oppose interest to effort. I thought some people hold that you have to choose between interest and effort, that you can't have both."

Interest and effort

"You are certainly right that I don't oppose interest to effort. Exactly the contrary: interest is the natural, indeed the only basis of effort; the stronger the interest, the stronger, if need be, will be the effort."

"You gave the law of Effect as if it were scientifically established. Is it not true that some psychologists reject it? It seems to me I've heard about some rats learning a path quicker if they were punished for going wrong than if they were rewarded for going right. What does this say about the effect of satisfaction?"

Satisfaction and learning

"There are two replies to be made to that. First, the law of Effect includes, as its statement shows, both satisfaction and annoyance. Whether the rats learned faster by punishment or by reward matters not to this law; either learning was by effect. The fastest learning, other things equal, is where both are used, satisfaction when they go right, annoyance if they go wrong. The other reply is that among psychologists Watson alone, so far as I have heard, denies the law, and he gets little if any backing in his contention. It is true that some very good psychologists have questioned whether the law as stated is ultimate. They do not deny the law as a fact, they merely propose to explain it by appealing if possible to more fundamental considerations."

"Suppose any one denied the law, could he consistently use punishment?"

"If this law is not true, punishment has no place in the learning process strictly considered. The fear of punishment might be used to secure practice, and so in this indirect way affect learning, but to be consistent, one who denies this law would have to deny that the pain attached to going wrong helped the rats to learn more quickly the way out."

"I wonder if everyone understands the word satisfaction in the same sense. Do you mean by satisfaction pleasure and by annoyance pain?"

"No. I do not mean to make satisfaction the same thing as pleasure. Sometimes they may be the same thing, more often not. If I had to choose single words as synonyms I'd use success and failure. Indeed Woodworth uses these words instead of satisfaction and annoyance."

"Well, won't you please leave off this hair-splitting and arguing! If the laws you talk so much about are of any service please go on and explain how we can use them."

"Very well. Take the very specific case of John who has not well learned his number combinations. Suppose he is called on in class for 7 x 9. He hesitates; it might be 72, or 56, or 63. Which it it? He tries them in this order. When he says 72, the teacher looks unimpressed, certain pupils quickly raise their hands, one or two actually snicker, the teacher says 'No.' Now this response of 72 did not bring satisfaction because it did not succeed. He saw by the words and manners of teacher and fellows that 72 was the wrong response. The failure brought annoyance, and the snickers served to increase it. When he ventures 56, he is by reason of the previous attendant annoyances the more anxious to find it right. This very anxiety increases the annoyance of failure. When finally he says 63 and it succeeds, his satisfaction is all the greater by reason of his previous failures and their attendant annoyances. Now the law of effect says that next time he will be less likely than he was this time to say 72 or 56 and more likely to say 63. If this happens often and consistently enough, he will eventually say 63 at once without fail.[1]"

How the law of Effect works

"I heard a speaker say that the trouble about some punishment is that it makes a boy regret that he was caught, not regret that he did wrong. Just what did he mean? What difference does it make?"

"The trouble is one of misplaced annoyance and it makes all the difference. Go back to our law of Effect. If a response is made to a certain situation with annoyance, when that situation comes around again we shall be less disposed to respond in that way. If this keeps up long enough, we simply won't respond at all to that situation with that response. A boy meets a certain temptation, he yields, does wrong, is caught at it, and is punished. Here the situation (S) is meeting the temptation, the response (R) is two-fold, doing the wrong and letting himself get caught. The punishment provides annoyance; but with which part of the response is the boy annoyed, at having done wrong or at getting caught? It depends upon the boy and what he thinks. If he regrets (is annoyed at) having done wrong, then he will next time be less likely to repeat the wrong. But if he regrets (is annoyed at) being caught and no more, he will next time take greater pains not to be caught, and no more. The effect of the punishment on his character education depends exactly on the thing at which he feels annoyance, whether on having done wrong, on having got caught, or even (if he is a husky young fellow) at having submitted to being punished. It is all important that satisfaction and annoyance be attached appropriately."

Misplaced annoyance

"Well, you've scored on that application of the law of Effect, for that's an important matter."

"Now tell us how a mind-set influences

---

[1] To show the actual working of "effect" here it may be pointed out that no such factors as practice or recency will serve to explain the subsequent advantage of the response 63 over the response 72 and 56. It cannot be practice, for 63 was used no more frequently than 72 or 56. Nor will recency suffice. If the next occasion for responding to 7 x 9 should arise in a few moments it might with some pertinence be argued that 63, being the last used, is appreciably more "recent" than either of the others and so would have the advantage. But when the next occasion comes twenty-four hours later, recency can no longer be claimed, for the intervals elapsing since the use of all three are too nearly the same. The response 63 would on this basis have no appreciable advantage over the others. The "effect" of the response seems unavoidably an essential factor. See Woodworth *Psychology* (1921) p. 391 ff.

learning? And does readiness cóme in? And what are the connections between the laws of Readiness and Effect?"

"This is what we have been all the time leading up to. Suppose a girl has asked her mother's permission to make a dress 'all by herself' and her mother has at last consented. What do you say? Any mind-set?"

Mind-set and learning

"I should say so, there is a very definite mind-set. I remember something like this when I was young, and I was nearly wild with enthusiasm and determination. I was bent on showing them all that I could make a dress. I chose a party dress, because I had been invited to go to a more important party than usual and I thought I had no suitable dress. Yes, there is a definite mind-set."

"And what about an inner urge?"

"What do you mean by an inner urge? Is there also an outer urge? And are the two different?"

"Let me answer that. I know the difference. Sometimes I find a boy bent and determined to do something, say make an airplane. Then the urge is inside the boy. I may try to discourage him, others may laugh at him, he may find difficulties, but as long as he feels that way inside he will persist in spite of all outside interferences. That's an inner urge. But suppose the boy's father tells him to mow the lawn, and the boy does it only because his father makes him, the urge here is outside. With an outer urge one will let up at the first opportunity. If any interference comes along, he will try to take it as an excuse to stop. This girl had a strong inner urge to make the dress. A strong mind-set to accomplish an end means exactly a strong inner urge. Am I not right?"

"Exactly right. But now tell us what else this girl's strong mind-set means besides an inner urge?"

"You called it further back a mind-set-to-an-end. I should say it means a clear and definite end in view, a strong purpose with a clearly defined end. Here the end was to make a dress that would fit and be becoming, and call forth favorable comments from all who saw it and wonder that so young a girl should make such a success. The strong mind-set means setting up this sort of end."

"And what about readiness or unreadiness?"

"I know; it was just what we had before. The mind-set makes this girl ready to see and examine dresses and styles and patterns and fabrics, and to hear people talk about such matters, and to read *Vogue* and the *Delineator*."

"Yes, it will make ready for action all the mechanisms in the girl's mental make-up that might have to do with making the dress. But what about unreadiness?"

"We had that too. It makes the girl unready to do anything else. I dare say she is more or less of a nuisance about the house till the dress is finished, for she won't want to be called on to mind the baby or to set the table or even to be told it's bed time. Yes, all the mechanisms whose action might interfere will be distinctly unready to act."

"What does all this mean for thinking? Does this girl think?"

"Certainly she thinks. She has to choose the style in which she will make the dress. That takes thinking and a great deal of it. I guess she'll run everybody in the house nearly crazy looking and passing judgment, unless she is one of the kind who somehow already knows her own mind. Then she has to choose the material, and watch the price so as not to exceed her money. After that it will be the pattern and how to lay it on, how to cut it out, etc., etc. Yes, she has to think."

"An important matter is what guides her thinking? What tells her what to think? It is the end in view that guides. Here it is exactly the kind of dress she wants to make that guides her thinking. In this case it is a party dress. Her purpose to make this party dress guides her thoughts at least in a large way all the time. Some smaller purposes, specific subordinate ends I suppose you would call them, guide at other times; but all have to fit together."

"You say all have to fit together. Is this what some call organization?"

"Exactly, this is what is meant by organization. Everything she does, buying, planning, cutting, sewing, all have to work consistently together or she will not have the kind of dress she wants. I should say there is opportunity here for the best kind of organization. How to organize her efforts is part of what she had to learn, and an important part."

"But are you not leaving out the most important thing, the learning? I can see how the girl's purpose means a definite end in view and an inner urge to attain that end. I can see too how these things mean an efficient organization of effort—in fact the whole thing seems to be working for efficiency of action. But I don't yet see where learning comes in. Can you explain more clearly?" .

"All we need is to apply our previous reasoning. Learning mainly comes by the law of Effect. Any movement of mind or body that succeeds (or brings satisfaction) has for that reason a better chance of being used again. Similarly any movement that

fails has a smaller chance. This better (or less) chance of being used again we call learning. The greater the feeling of success or failure (satisfaction or annoyance) the more definite the learning.[1] Now if the girl has a strong interest in making the dress, what she does by way of planning or execution that makes manifestly for success brings great satisfaction. Wherein she fails, she feels annoyance. This success (satisfaction) fixes in her nervous system the success-bringing movements. The annoyance in like manner tends to cut out the failure-bringing movements. When the girl has finished her dress, each step that helped make it a success is more firmly fixed in her (as a habit or skill or memory), and each step that hurt will less likely be used again. And not only are the separate steps thus fixed (or dropped out), but so likewise are the connections of one step with another. The organization as an effective whole is fixed in the girl's mental make-up. The stronger the purpose and the more definite the success (or failure) the stronger and more definite the learning."

"You have said nothing about the factor of readiness here. Does that play any part?"

"Yes, indeed. The readiness we discussed as growing out of the mind-set not only prepares each pertinent mechanism for use but accords satisfaction when used. We then have, as it were, satisfaction coming possibly from two sources, first, from the readiness of the mechanisms used and, second, from the resulting success. This fact means the possibility of better learning."

"How does consciousness help? Does it have any part in the learning process as here described? I have heard some say that this too is an important factor."

[1] Except in some extreme cases where such factors as consternation or paralysis of action interfere with the learning process.

"Indeed it is an important factor. Its function here is at least three-fold: first, to connect more surely and definitely the various responses with their several appropriate stimuli, second, to attach satisfactions or annoyances more precisely where they severally belong, and third, by emphatic attention to heighten the satisfaction or annoyance felt. It is for these reasons, among others, that we are most anxious that pupils think while they act and con-sciously intend the several steps they take."

"I have to admit that you have proved your case. I was skeptical at first. But now I see no escape. If the laws of learning are true, purposeful activity is the way to utilize them. It should make teaching both more effective and more interesting thus to understand the working of educational psychology. Readiness, mind-set, action with satisfaction, these do indeed give a different outlook upon teaching."

AN EXPERIMENT IN COÖPERATION
IV. Oral Composition

JAMES F. HOSIC

Associate Professor of Education, Teachers College, Columbia University

One of the two purposes which the leaders in the English experiment were firmly resolved to accomplish was to improve the speaking of the children in the selected centers and at the same time develop a method of doing this which other schools might successfully employ. The need of improvement was most keenly felt in connection with the work of classes in subjects other than English. As in the matter of reading, the complaint was voiced that the use of the vernacular as an everyday instrument of communication was too imperfect. The pupils spoke indistinctly, inadequately, inconsecutively, not merely incorrectly.

The seat of the difficulty, it was suspected, would be found not primarily in poor teaching but, as was the case with the reading, in a wrong conception of the job. The composition work actually going on was indeed found to be largely of the traditional sort, namely, practice in writing, with much emphasis on correctness in grammar and mechanics. This carried over but slightly into the various activities of the school day for the two very obvious reasons, first, that children do not often communicate with each other in writing and, second, that learning how to avoid mistakes in the mechanics of writing does not go far toward the development of power in well-planned, forceful speaking. In a word, the situations met with in the composition classes were not the situations constantly recurring in almost all other classes. The emphasis in composition was falling in the wrong place.

SETTING UP NEW IDEALS IN COMPOSITION

The first step to be taken in the movement for more satisfactory composition teaching evidently was to set up new ideals. The teachers must come to cherish different aims. Speaking must largely replace writing in the composition hour. The children must be shown what good speaking is, and must come to think of their composition work as practice in doing well what they had occasion to do all day long. This meant care in the choice of topics for composition and a rational conception of standards of performance.

During the opening conference in each school the fact was brought out that there was a general feeling of dissatisfaction with the oral English of the pupils. The attitude of the teachers was found to coincide with that of the principals and supervisors. Everyone became conscious of how general this attitude was. In this way the necessary "mind-set" was assured. The workers were ready to try out new plans.

These were worked out in conference through discussion. To have handed out ready-made directions would not have sufficed. In the first place, the teachers would not have understood and appreciated them so well as they did after informal consideration; in the second place, the contributions of the teachers themselves would have been missed; and, in the third place, the opportunity to set a good example of informal teaching would have been lost. It should be steadily borne in mind that the whole experiment had to do with methods of supervision quite as much as with methods in English. We sought to improve English teaching through improved procedures in supervision. From beginning to end no one was allowed to forget that we were attempting to develop and illustrate methods of improving the work of a school, not only in English, but in other subjects as well.

Two points emerged from our discussions: first, it was agreed that children tend to express themselves in concrete particulars and, second, that they like to talk about their own affairs. These two facts suggested the choice of narrative based upon experience as the type of composition to be stressed, the basic activity from which other activities should grow. It was definitely decided that for one entire semester great emphasis should be placed upon oral compositions of this type.

OUTLINES FOR GUIDANCE

The course of study in English in force in the Chicago schools was unfortunately not sufficiently detailed to provide adequate guidance for work in composition. The sections on that subject had been prepared, moreover, largely from another point of view. The new endeavors had not long proceeded before the need of supplementary outlines was apparent to all. A committee was appointed, therefore, to prepare them, a committee consisting of one superintendent, one principal, three teachers, and the English specialist. The committee decided not to write an elaborate course in oral composition for use indefinitely, but to prepare a simple program to assist teachers in making a beginning of the work in the classes *as they then were*. The course of study was conceived of as an instrument of supervis'on fitted to do a particular thing at a particular time and, in the nature of the case, soon to be superseded, inasmuch as the work of the centers would pass into succeeding phases.

Readers of these articles, though not able to use this brief course in their own work, may care to see it.

ORAL ENGLISH

Suggestions for teachers in the English Centers, second semester 1919.

Note:—Develop ability in the language period; call it into exercise in *all* other classes.

I. Aims as to technique—growth in power of expression.

A. First cycle—kindergarten and grades 1 to 3.
  1. Willing attempt by each pupil to say something clearly to the class—something that the speaker believes the class will be glad to hear (audience motive).
  2. Better English sentences.
B. Second Cycle—grades 4 to 6.
  1. As above—see cycle 1.
  2. As above—see cycle 1.
  3. Proper sequence of sentences —ability to talk connectedly.
C. Third Cycle—grades 7 and 8.
  1. As above—see cycle 1.
  2. As above—see cycle 1.
  3. As above—see cycle 2.
  4. Proper subdivisions of the thought—topical organization—if demanded by the speaker's purpose.
II. Aims as to subject matter.
  1. To employ only subject matter of lasting value to the pupils.
  2. To draw upon first-hand experience rather than memory of books. The reading done should be *investigative*.
  3. To group subjects or projects about centers of interest so as to build up useful bodies of knowledge and opinion and form positive attitudes.
III. Suggestions as to possible topics.
  A. Personal Experiences and Current Events, including visits, play, anniversaries, etc., etc.
    1. In cycle 1, home, school, neighborhood.
    2. In cycle 2, ditto, but extend the horizon as far as the experience of the pupils permits.

  3. In cycle 3, train definitely in reading and reporting accounts in the periodicals; train also in discussion and further investigation.
B. Occupations.
  1. In cycle 1, accounts of what others do for us and discussion of how we may help them; e. g., parents, public officers, food producers and purveyors, and others in the child's range of observation.
  2. In cycle 2, a wider range and more general view; e. g., farming, lumbering, mining, manufacturing, transporting —what is done and why, and how we profit by it.
  3. In cycle 3, from the personal standpoint—vocational guidance; the advantages and disadvantages, the preparation required, remuneration, chance of promotion, etc. (Note the variety of forms of English expression, such as debate, dramatization, etc. possible.)
C. Health.
  1. In cycle 1, for personal habits.
  2. In cycle 2, as in cycle 1 plus sanitation, ventilation, and other social phases in home, school, and neighborhood.
  3. In cycle 3, as in cycle 2 plus exercise, emergencies, climate, occupations, civic aspects.
D. Applied science and the world of nature.
  Select appropriate topics from the Chicago Course of Study which are not otherwise treated in the given cycle, such as

seasons, animals, natural phenomena, etc.

E. Our city, state and nation.

F. Thrift.

IV. Methods.

1. Develop specific and definite purposes in taking up the various
topics—organize "projects."

2. Let the pupils help in the planning.

3. Teach each child how to perform
his part—select his particular
phase or item, think how to listen
to and help his classmates, how
to ask questions, converse, etc.
Remember the children are in
need of mastering little by little
the practical art of communication.

4. Employ theory—principles—only
as guidance to actual practice.
Help the pupils discover and state
principles for themselves; then
make sure that the principles—
a very few and very simply stated
—are positively understood and
learned for all time.

5. Supply the correct form when
errors are made, but reserve instruction and drill for class work
or individual treatment.

6. Limit each speaker as to time and
help him to plan by selecting a
specific topic, a phase of the
subject which can be presented
briefly. Avoid vague and sweeping topics; insist on concrete and
personal handling.

7. Use the textbook only when it
bears upon the aims you have in
view—a means to your end.

V. Helps.

Leonard: English Composition as
a Social Problem.

Sheridan: Speaking and Writing.

Mahoney: Standards in English
Composition.

Hosic and Hooper: A Child's Composition Book (grades 4-6).

Hosic and Hooper: A Composition-
Grammar (grades 7 and 8).

Klapper: The Teaching of English.

O'Shea and Kellogg: Series of
Textbooks on Health.

Barnard: Course in Civics for
Philadelphia.

Note:—Outlines on written English
and on the use of literary motives
and subject matter to follow.

COMMENTS ON THE COURSE IN ORAL ENGLISH

With regard to the outline for the organization of oral English in the elementary
school, please consider the following comments:

1. The *course* is intended to be *suggestive*
but not *limiting;* that is, while it maps out
pretty definitely the things to be aimed
at and the kinds of things to be done, it
still leaves opportunity for choice and
initiative on the part of the individual
teacher.

2. The course is intended as a *minimum
course.* Undoubtedly the aims which are
mentioned for the first time in the second
cycle can, to some extent, be realized
earlier. The same is true with regard to
the third cycle. There is no desire to
hamper anyone with regard to these aims.
It seems worth while, however, to set up
aims that really are to an appreciable
degree attainable so that we may have the
satisfaction of definite success.

3. Observe the *arrangement by cycles.*
This is intended to keep up the continuity
of effort through a sufficiently long period
to accomplish the aims which are set up. .

The greatest weakness of our English work is its lack of continuity.

4. Note the attempt to make the course cumulative, so that what is begun is continued for the remainder of the course. Such habits as are involved in the learning of English require a considerable time for their development and, what is more, they readily die out if they are left without exercise. Each teacher according to the present scheme will see to it that things that are once learned are kept in use. This means, of course, the best and clearest understanding by each teacher of all that has been done with the pupils before she receives them.

5. Note that the securing of *suitable topics* for composition is regarded as of equal importance with the setting up of right aims in the matter of language development. It is believed, first, that the composition period is too precious a time to spend in talking merely for the sake of talking. What is talked about ought to be as valuable in itself as in any other recitation in the school day. This does not, of course, mean valuable in a narrow sense. When one child has told the others, for example, how he celebrated Valentine's Day, he has enlarged their knowledge of that very interesting phase of life. He has, moreover, made it possible for them to celebrate Valentine's Day more satisfactorily than before. The result is genuine individual and social progress. "Valuable," then, means valuable in the sense of (1) creating or strengthening right attitudes and ideals, (2) giving useful knowledge, or (3) strengthening habits through the strengthening of motive. Second, it means that *real situations* are created for the cultivation of language ability. It is only in this way that language ability can be cultivated. If pupils use language in purely artificial situations in the school, they will use language of a very different character in the natural situations outside of the school. We are driven, therefore, to the enterprise of establishing situations for the use of language just as real in the school as obtain anywhere. The psychology of this is imperative. In simple terms, you cannot really teach the technique of language except through the actual communication of ideas that are worth while both to the person who utters them and to the persons who hear them.

6. A set of *centers of interest* have been selected from which topics may be drawn. It is believed that each of these represents a good deal of useful material that is not now being taught in other studies. Of course the situation will vary from room to room in this regard. Moreover, there is opportunity for teachers to choose according to their own knowledge or taste. It should be observed that all of these fields of interest are capable of being exploited by the younger children and also by the older. The teacher must in each case find the level of the child's actual and potential experience. In other words, she must use what has already come into his life or what he can put there by the imaginative reconstruction of the experience he has had.

7. Speaking more in detail with regard to the outline itself, the following is offered:

a. By "personal experiences in the home, school, and neighborhood" is meant brief concrete accounts of happenings in the life of the individual or of his group. Typical titles are "What We Do at Home on Saturday," "The Most Interesting Place I Ever Saw," "How I Made—," "How I Earned a Dollar," etc. In the highest grades pupils should actually read

Current Events, The Literary Digest, the daily papers, etc., and should give well organized reports of what they have read. It will be necessary here of course to train pupils, first, in picking out the right thing to read, second, in reading it analytically or reflectively, and third, in preparing an orderly report of it which is reasonably clear and concise. In all this work there is a fine opportunity for training pupils in courteous, clear-cut, thoughtful questioning and discussion, leading to sound judgments. Such work is probably as important as any that can possibly be done for the pupils who are about to leave the elementary schools. If the field of civics is chosen, the topics should of course be those not already provided for in the regular work in history and civics. By this is meant not the course on paper, but the course as actually carried out in the school. Here again the teacher must see to it that she keeps reasonably within the range of the children's horizon and that they are encouraged to talk about what they actually know or can find out for themselves. Formal reproductions of what the books say are not intended. The younger children may be led to think about their city, what advantages it provides for them, and what services they can render to it. This should all, of course, be kept distinctly in the concrete and personal. Generalizations are almost, if not quite, meaningless and futile in the case of the younger children. This does not mean that pupils are not to learn definitely what is important for them to learn. It merely means that a child in the early years does not think very much in abstract terms. This is an obvious truth which the makers of our textbooks have not yet apparently discovered. Even

in the case of the older children, the number of general conclusions reached should be few and they should be based upon the children's own investigations and reasonings. The danger to be avoided is that we shall have our children repeating words instead of thinking out on the basis of actual experience, opinions and principles.

8. Each person must put a *common-sense interpretation* upon the terms used in the outline. For example, in the first cycle the word *freedom* has been avoided, inasmuch as it often means nothing more than babbling and wandering. It is believed that the pupil who is conscious of trying to do something for his audience will attain freedom as rapidly as it is possible for him to do. The term, *better English sentences*, means simply progress from where the pupil is in the direction of where he ought to be. Obviously a sentence is not a good sentence if it is not clear, if it has ungrammatical expressions in it, if it contains words that are mispronounced, or if it contains vulgar slang or words that are no words. It is probably impossible to go further in defining just what better sentences for a given class ought to mean. The teacher's business is to know exactly where the pupils are and then to push them on as rapidly as circumstances will permit in the direction in which they ought to go.

9. *A word about grammar*. There are two extremes with regard to grammar. One person would throw it out. Another would have a stiff course in it. The truth probably lies somewhere between these extremes. Note that much grammar should be learned through the early years just as other things are learned, namely, by the pupils' informal contact with it. For

example, if a child begins a proper name with a small letter, his teacher should simply say, "John, you have begun a proper name with a small letter" and show him how to write it. This is merely calling a spade a spade when the spade is there. If this were done, the children would gradually build up the principal grammatical concepts just as they do other concepts. When the fifth grade is reached, it will be possible occasionally to indulge in informal lessons leading to generalizations. These should bear upon subject and predicate, the inflections of words, and the like. Such work is directly a part of the composition work and is easily recognized by the children as merely a way of improving their speech. Even in the seventh and eighth grades there seems to be no excuse for a formal isolated and technical course in English grammar. Just as the teacher tries to secure sticking to the point, otherwise called unity, in composition, so she should try to secure grammatical organization and correctness. Grammar, in other words, is but a part of that body of principles of good composition which the children should gradually master.

10. Understand that this outline of oral English is *only a part* of what should constitute the course in language and composition in the elementary school. Undoubtedly children gain a great deal of language power through story-telling, dramatization, and other literary exercises. Such work is relatively easy to plan and execute and is sometimes allowed to monopolize the whole of the language time. It has seemed best to defer the outlining of this type of work until after the more practical or matter of fact type has been well started. Later an outline of work in

composition dealing with literary material will be furnished.

11. Note, finally, that work in *written English* is easily handled in a school where the work in oral English is well organized. The preparation for writing a paper is not unlike the preparation for giving a short talk. Moreover, it is comparatively easy to put on paper what you already have clearly in your mind. There are few people, on the contrary, who can actually compose readily in the act of writing. It is for this reason among others that the outline of written composition is deferred. Later such an outline will be provided. It is not intended of course that no written work shall be done in the meanwhile, merely that the emphasis for the present shall be placed upon oral English, and that we shall make a concerted attempt to organize it along the same line in the various schools.

The comments included in the course will doubtless enable the reader to put the proper interpretation upon what precedes. The arrangement by cycles met with instant approval. It was so obviously in harmony with the actual experience of the workers that it was welcomed as setting up really attainable aims and as avoiding the stupid practice of pretending that certain results are to be reached in a single year when every observer knows that they are not and can not be.

To the objection that the outline is too indefinite it may be answered that at the stage of the experiment in which the outline was written and circulated, each teacher was supposed to be experimenting and hence deserved the utmost freedom. No one on the committee, moreover, would willingly have prepared a detailed list of topics, for example, in advance of the reports of the teachers in the various schools. It was better, *for the time*, to be content with giving such suggestions as could be made to each teacher personally when it appeared there was need of suggestion. A much more detailed course in composition did, however, in due time take shape and in it appeared the results of the experiments of scores of teachers who had been stimulated by the general plan of attack which has just been described.

SELLING A CITY ITS SCHOOL SYSTEM

J. A. STARKWEATHER
Assistant Superintendent of Schools, Duluth, Minn.

For the last few years, in all parts of the country, many persons have been dissatisfied with present education. This dissatisfaction arises from the changes in the conditions of living produced by modern society. The public in general is dissatisfied but is not altogether sure of the cause. The ardent supporter of the most classical and the ardent supporter of the most practical are equally sure that something is wrong,— what is it? The demand of the times is for leadership, leadership which offers to the public such education as will be suitable to their needs combined with a selling campaign which will put before them its value. Our Duluth schools set as their ideal this aim: "Give to each individual pupil in the school system that educational equipment which will best fit him to take his place as a useful member of society." With this basic philosophy we set about the matter of taking the public into our confidence. We had many conferences of the administrative force and finally agreed upon a program of activities to acquaint the public with the actual school work as it is carried on in the schools day by day. The organization was as follows: An executive committee consisting of four people with the duties of publicity, statistics, exhibits, and organization.

The executive committee was chosen from the members of a general committee, each of whom was chairman of a subcommittee. The subcommittees were: the committee on night schools, the committee on kindergarten and elementary schools, the committee on junior and senior high schools, the committee on industrial education, the committee on teachers, and the committee on music and physical education. With this working organization we began our active campaign.

Each chairman made a report to the general committee of the things which he thought were vital to the interests of the committee he served. These facts were gone over carefully by the general committee and finally the material was turned over to the publicity committee for preparation for the newspapers. The latter committee made some interesting discoveries in regard to newspapers and school publicity. The editors were not keen about publishing school material because they thought the people were not interested. The publicity committee learned that material previously sent to newspapers had consisted of long, dry-as-dust articles of a technical or philosophical nature which the public did not read. The committee found, however, that as soon as live material was sent, editors were only too glad to publish it. For live material we found the following things to be practical: (1) pictures of children, (2) names of children, (3) informal stories about activities in which many people engage, (4) articles popular rather than technical. The picture in this article and its explanation illustrate the point. Every article should be illustrated by a picture showing some activity or person. The article should be brief and cover not more than two points. One point is even better than two. The Sunday newspapers may publish longer articles providing they are furnished with suitable pictures which catch the eye and carry a message of things in which people are interested in regard to their own children or in regard to the activities of present day life. Needless to say it is not wise to start upon a plan of school publicity unless the things you are doing are worth advertising.

Our executive committee decided that the subcommittees represented the various phases which we wished to explain to the people of the city. These were listed as follows:

1. What we mean by "Industrial Art" and why we teach it.

2. What Duluth is doing for special pupils, such as the blind, deaf, those of low mentality, the anemic and tubercular.

3. Methods of primary education.

4. The theory and practice of the Junior High School.

5. A study of teachers' salaries with a view to increasing them to proper standard.

6. The place of music in the public school and in the community.

7. The meaning and service of night school.

In order to get these things before the people in the most satisfactory way, the publicity committee asked the chairman of each subcommittee to furnish stories and pictures of the work in which he was interested. The publicity committee arranged with the newspapers to have something ready for publication in every Sunday issue. The newspaper men counted on these stories and came regularly to the office for them. A good example is the following account of the "movies."

SCHOOL MOVIES ARE COMPLETED; GIVEN TEST RUN

METHODS OF DEVELOPING PUPIL, PHYSICALLY AND MENTALLY, WILL BE SHOWN ON SCREEN

The success attained by instructors in the Duluth public schools in their efforts toward laying the basis by which the youth of the city may become good citizens is convincingly shown in motion pictures taken of work in the various schools which were given a test run in the offices of the board of education yesterday afternoon.

The work of filming the activities of the Duluth school children was under the supervision of J. A. Starkweather, assistant superintendent of schools.

CHILDREN'S WORK SHOWN

In keeping with the general belief that stories of children create the greatest interest, the pictures are devoted chiefly to subjects pertaining to the work done by the little tots. In the first reel, the little girls are seen in company with their teachers fashioning articles of feminine apparel and toys in the kindergarten room. In another room the boys are shown erecting toy houses, bridges and moulding pottery from clay. Augmenting the children's activities in the kindergarten rooms is a drill the routine of which is similar to the familiar proverbial "London Bridge is Falling Down."

A feature episode which illustrates methods employed as a means of and assisting in the proper expression of thought is the staging of a child play. The pupils play the various roles before scenery of their own invention.

The manual training department makes an appeal to the pupil mechanically inclined. Electricity, wood-working and kindred subjects are taught. For the girls, instructors in needlework are seen supervising the fashioning of dainty hats, scarfs and other articles.

DULL PUPILS PROVIDED FOR

For the pupils who are not as apt as their companions a separate department has been created. The work done consists of basket weaving, rug and carpet making.

One scene which prompts the spectator to feel that the work in the local schools is planned along the lines of equality to all pupils is the classroom where the deaf and dumb are taught to communicate with one another in the best manner nature has provided.

The instructors in this department are experts, and, according to results obtained, their success has been remarkable.

FULLY EQUIPPED PRINT SHOP

Among the interesting pictures taken of pupils in the advanced classes are those of the school printing shop, fully equipped with type and presses necessary to the composition of a school publication. As in the other departments practical instructors are seen instructing the pupils in how printing is done.

A modern garage and machine shop where the pupil is taught the automobile trade, the operation of lathes and welding processes is also shown.

To the girls in the higher classes is afforded an opportunity of learning home nursing. Interest is chiefly centered on the sickroom, where two pupil nurses give a demonstration of how the sick should be cared for. The rapidity with which they perform their duties is an indication of the thoroughness of the course.

As a climax to the film is the depiction of a school fire drill in which pupils are seen to leave their classrooms in perfect order and go through the smoke and fire to the open. Mr. Starkweather said that when the fire drill picture was taken it took less than a minute to empty the school building housing 800 pupils.

The pictures will be shown for five days in the New Garrick Theater starting May 23, Mr. Starkweather announced yesterday.

The Board of Education authorized the publicity committee to issue three numbers of an official paper which stated the position of the Board on matters to put before the public. Enough copies were made to enable us to send one to each family in the city. It would require too much space to reprint these papers here. They covered the points mentioned in the objectives we set for accomplishment. Some of the matter printed in these papers is reproduced here.

In order to help carry over the study of methods in elementary education, we planned and widely advertised a "Visit the School" week. This was most successful. Many buildings had a 95% attendance of parents during the week, which was an hitherto unheard-of thing. A register of visitors was kept and the total number of individuals who visited the schools during the week was found to be 6,411. Having a school population of 17,000 pupils, we considered this a good representation. In most schools, parent-teachers associations were already organized from which committees were appointed to arrange programs to acquaint the parents of each district with the methods of education carried on in each school. This was done by having various classes present a regular recitation for the benefit of the mothers. Classes in geography, arithmetic, or reading, or whatever subject seemed most desirable were conducted.

In order to acquaint the business men with what we were doing, the Commercial Club appointed an educational committee. The supervisor of each department of the public schools appeared before this committee and explained in detail the theory and practice of his work. The Superintendent gave the final summing up before the

These girls all made their middy blouses. This is a class in 8th grade sewing at the Lincoln Junior High School. The average time spent in making the middy blouses and skirts was twenty-eight hours. The average cost for skirt and blouse was $3.56. In times of high cost of living, ability to make one's own clothes is a great saving in the family budget.

Club. As a result of these meetings the Commercial Club published a pamphlet at its own expense giving unqualified endorsement of the methods of the public school system. This pamphlet included in summarized form the theory and explanation which had been given by each supervisor. Copies were distributed to the members of the Commercial Club and others.

As a grand climax the Board of Education authorized the executive committee to take a moving picture film of the activities of the public schools. The committee wrote a scenario based upon the philosophy of education represented by everyday classroom practice. Four thousand feet of moving picture films were taken, representing the activities as they were actually carried on in the public schools. The pictures were made in the rooms under regular classroom conditions. No special set-ups were made except in the case of outdoor activities where a number of rooms were combined, but even in this nothing was shown which is not a part of the regular school curriculum. These films represented every school in the city. During the time that the pictures were being taken they were widely advertised by the newspapers and also, of course, by the children themselves. The pictures were exhibited in one of the downtown moving picture theaters. The receipts were divided between the moving picture house and the Board of Education. Ten thousand children from the public schools and six thousand adults saw these pictures during the week they were exhibited. They have since been shown in several of the buildings as part of an educational program for parents and teachers, and also as a means of impressing on the younger students the desirability of going on to the Junior High School. They have also been shown in various parts of the country with considerable success. They represent an unusual method of advertising, and there is nothing else we could have done which would have equalled it in effectiveness.

In order to present work of the Junior High Schools in addition to what was shown in the pictures, exhibitions were placed in downtown store windows for two weeks before the close of school. This covered the activities of the various departments such as home training, manual training, industrial arts, and so on. The storemen said they had never before had windows which attracted more attention than those which carried the message of the Duluth schools to the people.

Previous to our campaign our tax rate for school purposes was about 13.8 mills. The year following this campaign, through legislative enactment which received active support of Duluth citizens, the tax rate was raised from 13.8 mills to 20 mills.

WHEN THE I. Ds SCORED

PRUDENCE A. NICHOLAS ✓

Des Moines, Iowa

Did you ever walk into a classroom radiantly enthusiastic for your subject, and then walk out again with gloom and depression on your fair brow? Did you ever enter that room confidently certain of your ability to interest "anybody" in the assignment for the day, and then leave as abjectly miserable as a tax on soda water? Did you ever try to put over a story poem which has been popular for generations and find it welcomed in much the same way that a Yank welcomes an army bean? Were there eyes that looked and saw not; ears that heard and heeded naught; brains that wouldn't crank up but kicked back and broke your spirit? This accumulation of uneasy circumstances together with a certain impenetrable atmosphere influenced us so greatly that we quite easily fell into the habit of calling that strangely assorted, ill-favored class the I.Ds. The "I" stands for the product of a certain African pachyderm, while the "D" denotes the crowning central edifice on the capitol at Washington.

Not once in a blue moon could one find such a class. Gathered from the ends of the earth they seemed. It was almost impossible to find a common appeal. Three boys were old repeaters, who tolerated school because there wasn't anything else to do. There was Charles, a non-thinker, a non-producer, a non-everything. Even his disposition was negative. And Zeke, he of the flat-boat feet and floating-raft mind—floating with the current and never arriving anywhere. As to the raft, well, rafts are wooden, aren't they? Then there was Bert with a full set of Hun ancestors, a "me and God" attitude, and a really likeable side which he succeeded in hiding most of the time. Frank was more nearly normal, except that he was careful not to take his imagination out of its tissue paper.

One supercilious youngster, son of an Army captain, informed us early in the game that he didn't expect to get much. The Eastern schools which he had just left were so superior to the Mid-West brand. He carried about with him an air of aloofness that was maddening. A great, over-grown, long, thin, bashful boy hailed from St. Louis. His vocabulary consisted of "yes" and "no," seldom vocalized, however, but always decorated with intense apoplectic blushes. But then, there never was a thirteen-year-old boy who could be himself with legs too long and pants too short! The remaining boy was the blond better half of a pair of twins. The girl was pretty and pleasant but not over-burdened with intellectuality. Her chum Mary was the most aggressive member of the class, having had the supreme courage once to suggest a picnic. Nita of the bovine eyes, two drab frightened little sisters, a girl with movie queen ambitions, and our Erma constituted the list. Erma was from an obscure Kentucky town and was overwhelmed and dazed by the multitudinous intricacies of a "taown" school.

It was to this array that we tried to teach Miles Standish. For days and days we tried to teach Miles Standish. Tried—the word took on new meaning. It involved a display of colonial relics, groups of pictures of the times, a set of crayon drawings, questions finally answered by the teacher in desperation, and at last, a dramatic monologue in which teacher figured as director, orchestra, usher, and leading lady. No dent of interest appeared on the serene placidity of the class. Not a flicker of an eyelash, not a solitary sigh of life, not a token of response. Still we labored.

One day when purple despair was about to engulf us, the little god who watches over teachers who think they have done their best, literally yelled (I heard him!) right out in class, "Quitter! Why don't you wake these kids up? Why don't you think up something for them to do?"

"Do," we screamed, "We've done everything!"

"That's the trouble," he bawled, "you've done it all yourself. Get busy. Isn't there anything that THEY can do?"

We were up on tiptoe in a minute. Ideas began to come and as they came, we talked. "Children, would you like to do something different?" There was an almost imperceptible change of expression. "Wouldn't it be fun for the boys to build some little log houses for Priscilla and Miles Standish, and wouldn't it be jolly for the girls to dress some dolls to represent the characters in the story?"

I was reminded of a dangerous railroad crossing judging from the way they stopped, looked, and listened. A few seconds later these apathetic children emerged from their lethargy and came stumbling, pushing, hurrying up to the table desk where they leaned and hung over the book racks, eager to question and plan.

"I'll bring the nails." "We've got a saw." "We can go out tonight and get some branches for logs." These and sundry other remarks from the boys. The girls offered dolls, material, and time. At last here was something our little Kentucky girl could do. She knew how to sew. "Say, Miss," she said shyly, "I reckon I can tote one of them dolls home tonight and make it a little Miles Standish suit, if you all is willin' for me to."

And so, before the zeal could waver, committees were appointed; they met on the spot; the project was launched. This was the first of innumerable consultations and hours of hard, happy work before and after school. There were adjustments to be made of misfits on committees, a few complaints of slackers to be investigated, and at least a semi-daily inspection of the progress being made. Our assembly room was on the top floor and the youngsters worked in the basement. We contemplated asking the school board to put in an elevator. (You know one can *ask* the school board for anything). There were three groups of boys working in three different parts of the basement. They were making a house for Priscilla, one for Miles Standish, and one group was building a church. The girls sewed at odd moments in the recitation rooms or Domestic Science Department. We literally walked miles trying to keep tab on every activity at once, but the results justified the expenditure of every ounce of energy. When the other departmental teachers began commenting on the marvelous change in the I.Ds, we knew the objective was already won.

One noon I came upon St. Louis sitting flat on the basement floor, his attenuated legs half covered with twigs and chips. He was faithfully working to complete the church on time. When we entered, he looked up, smiled, and uttered the first full sentence he had had the courage to deliver. This was just the beginning of longer bursts of oratory later on. Zeke and Bert voluntarily instituted a continuous prodding process in order to keep everyone active. There was daily evidence of much thought and planning. The girls came up to the mark wonderfully. Our little Kentucky maiden outdid herself. She cut out tiny patterns and with infinite pains and unbelievably fine st'tches made the most cunning little garments for Miles Standish. "Clad in doublet and hose and

boots of Cordovan leather," says the poem. Erma confessed that "boots of Cordovan leather" were almost too much for her, but she had experimented until the results she produced were marvels of ingenuity. Besides dressing Priscilla and the Indians and other varied characters in the story, the girls had manufactured diminutive curtains for the windows, neat little braided rugs, table covers, etc. The boys added simple chairs, tables, and shelves in soft wood for the houses, and benches and pulpit for the church. How they did read and discuss that text to find out what to do! Nice old Zeke in his zeal found a worn leather-backed memorandum book. His clumsy fingers, grown skillful with ardor, cut three small sections through the binding and all. He came proudly bringing them up, like three grains of sand in his big Sahara hand, and announced that they were the books "prominent three, distinguished alike for bulk and for binding, Bariffe's Artillery Guide and the Commentaries of Cæsar—and between them was standing the Bible." They gave just the right air when placed on the tiny shelf. When some one suggested moving the table, Frank, who had arranged the simple furniture, objected, saying that it must be "a table of pine by the window," and so it remained. In the church they put some very realistic pews and a wee pulpit, while on top was the "howitzer planted high on the roof—a preacher who speaks to a purpose." And horror of horrors, on a pole in front was the head of the brave Wattawamat, an old doll head bloody with raspberry juice and red ink!

Then, as is ofttimes writ, came a day when our erstwhile solemn, stolid Charles stumbled into class shaking with silent laughter. The other boys had been quite all right until this unforeseen spectacle arrived. They too succumbed to some secret humor and giggled and snorted in a helpless chorus. When asked for the cause of this mirth, the blond twin came quickly to the desk and whispered that it was a secret but that they would tell later. More than once that hour we suspended operations entirely until the masculine builders could control their risibilities. At recess down we flew to the basement. Being urged to look, we looked. As a final touch of realism there on the door of one log house was carefully stretched and fastened a skin. We looked more closely. Could it be? It could have been and was the silvery skin of a too adventurous mouse sacrificed in the name of Literature. We all shouted together. No one was ever able to tell me the how of the capture. Every time one started the tale, he was overcome by some mental vision of the scene itself and was unable to go on.

How friendly they all became! How freely they talked together, praising and criticizing each other in much more extreme terms than we felt at liberty to use. And all to such good purpose.

The final date arrived at which auspicious time the exhibit was to be made, the story reviewed, and all things connected therewith finished. Teacher was to be surprised; she was to be led into the classroom with eyes closed, and was then, at a signal, to open them upon the finished spectacle adjusted according to the best judgment of the class. It was their own idea and teacher

played the game. There on the sand-covered table was the Standish house and the church and a tiny Plymouth Rock looking more like the original than Plymouth Rock itself. The Puritan dolls and the Indian runner were grouped in appropriate positions. Crowding closely around were eager-eyed youngsters gazing with pride on the results of their combined labor. Little lumps tried to gain a foothold in teacher's throat. And we had called them the I.Ds! When teacher had inspected, praised, and questioned, her attention was attracted to something under the table. A quiet voice explained that the two successful committees, finding that committee number three had failed to finish Priscilla's house on time, had decided that, in all justice, it should be exhibited in its incomplete state. A card tacked on read "Unfinished by ———," with names attached. Mr. Eastern Culture's cognomen was among them. It had its effect.

Did it pay, this social problem? Time and energy and patience in large amounts had been consumed. We knew and the children knew that we were repaid a hundred times. They knew and understood the story; they liked the swing of the poetry; they could quote therefrom; they had lived it all. They had become acquainted, the barriers were down, they were receptive. The advance was not brilliant, but they improved correspondingly in all branches. And think what it did to Charles! Charles chuckled! Then, too, there was that mouse. There's something in that! I.Ds— We deserved that name ourselves.

THE CLEARING HOUSE

A SILENT READING PROJECT—
FOURTH GRADE

I. *Aim.*—To teach silent reading that the children may read more intelligently for information, develop a taste for the finest and best in literature, and cultivate habits and appreciations leading to a better use of their leisure hours, thereby enlarging their experience and giving them greater control of conduct in the society in which they live.

II. *Situation.*—A group of five portables with no facilities for a school library at the present time; many homes meagerly supplied with reading material.

Pupils are always glad to see each other when they return to school in the fall. To help create this atmosphere of good fellowship, one period of the day is used by pupils and teacher to talk over summer vacation experiences. Each pupil is given a chance to contribute to the group so as to draw in even the shy and diffident child.

III. Questioning.
    1. To find out what children read during the summer. List on blackboard.
    2. To ascertain aims in reading:
      a. For pleasure?
      b. For information?

IV. Books we have in school that pupils have enjoyed reading:
    Silent Readers—Winston, Bolenius, supplementary readers, geography, history, etc.

V. Problems to be solved.
    A. How we may obtain more reading material for our class.
      1. From Public Library.
      2. Ask Library assistants to suggest good books.

      3. Obtain supplementary readers from Board of Education.
      4. Bring books from home.
      5. Bring magazines from home:
        St. Nicholas.
        Youth's Companion.
        American Boy.
      6. Teacher provide reading material if she can.
    B. When reading at home, when and how do you like to read?
    C. Which kind of reading do we use in school more frequently?
    D. Which kind do you enjoy listening to?
    E. How find out best readers in this class?
    F. Which kind of reading shall we use in this class? (We had just a little silent reading last half of previous year.)

VI. Test children for speed and comprehension.

VII. Group children according to ability into
    A. Slow group.
      1. Teacher lead children to a conscious purposing through a selection of right materials.
      a. To increase rate of speed. Advantages: more interest and pleasure on part of child.
      b. To obtain thought.
      c. For word and phrase drill.
      2. Rewards for improvement.
      a. Choosing of stories to read silently or to group.
      b. Admittance to
    B. Advanced group:
      1. Reproduce stories read.

2. Help others with difficulties.
3. Teacher a "handy-man" in both groups.

VIII. Dramatization.
  1. Before other classes.
  2. Before Parents' Club.

IX. Library Corner.
  1. Choose pupil librarian by ballot.
  2. Use of table before school.
  3. Use of table when other work is finished.
  4. Formulate rules to be followed when other pupils are at the table.
    a. Silence in Library.
    b. Rights of others.
    c. Proper use of books.
    d. Orderly arrangement of books.
    e. Unselfish attitude—others having same choice of books. (Abuse of privilege means loss of same.)

X. Home Reading.

XI. Frequent tests to ascertain increase in speed and comprehension.
  1. Children keep own record.
    Slogan: Break my own record.

XII. How the process may carry over into
A. English.
  1. Book reviews.
    What ought we to tell in giving a book review?
    a. Author.
    b. Title.
    c. What story is about.
    d. Tell part and read part.
    e. Tell whether you liked it or not, and why.
    How may class help in game?
    a. Ask questions.
    b. Give suggestions.
  2. List books, magazines read at home.
  3. Letters.
    a. Of thanks to Librarian.
    b. Ask for suggestions and talk at our school on Public Library.

c. To Library Extension Bureau, State Department of Education.
d. Comparison of statements on points to be investigated in silent reading, calling for arguments given with clearness and force.
4. Reproduction of short stories and current events.
5. Dramatization.

B. Geography.
  1. Better understanding of printed page.

C. History.
  1. Better understanding of social relations.

D. Arithmetic.
  1. Intelligent reading of problems more than half solves them.

E. Art.
  1. Posters and signs for Library Corner.
  2. Make booklets for clippings.
  3. Bulletin board for current events.

XIII. My Criteria for Judging Work.
  1. Has it led children to a better use of leisure hours and given them greater power over the printed page?
  2. Has it given satisfaction with opportunities for "possible leads?"
  3. Has there been conscious purposing in a natural situation, with opportunities for selection, organization, judging?
  4. Has it given every child a chance to participate in group activities?
  5. Has it imposed responsibility upon individual and group?
  6. Has it increased their love for the beautiful in nature, art, literature?
  7. Has it developed habits, attitudes, and appreciations most helpful in effecting desirable controls of conduct?

FANNIE B. NESSLE.

A DEMONSTRATION LESSON

The following demonstration lesson was given in Duluth as an illustration of how an industrial art subject may furnish the motive for study in several other fields of learning.

Just ten days before the demonstration lesson was given the supervisor called at the building, and after a conference with the teachers in regard to the work they were doing, requested that they put on a demonstration lesson for the other teachers of the city. This was agreed upon and the outline below is a copy of the one followed by the teachers in the preparation of the lesson and also given to the teachers at the meeting.

The study of India took eight days of actual schoolroom work. The outline given to the teachers was an outline of the work which the children did in those eight days. The demonstration lesson showed the result of that eight days' teaching. The work was done in a district of the city in which facilities for home study are limited. The demonstration lesson showed remarkable results, particularly in the oral and written English which was secured from the pupils through this method of studying a subject in geography and history. Every child in the class was able to stand before the group of teachers and talk to the point about the subjects studied. All the teachers remarked about the choice of words these children used in their oral description of the Taj Mahal. The phraseology of such magazines as the *National Geographic* and *Everybody's* was at their command.

The arithmetic material involved problems of proportion, because in making a miniature of the Taj Mahal the pupils looked up the measurements of the building and minarets. They even determined the height of the trees which they placed in front of the building. The trees were made from yarrow dipped in green stain. The Taj Mahal was made of clay. The lake consisted of a piece of glass over blue paper.

All the teachers agreed, however, that the most remarkable results of that week's work were the oral and written English and the stimulus the children received for investigation and research in order to be able to talk intelligently to the class and to the visiting teachers. The outline follows:

Franklin School, Tuesday, April 19—3:30 p.m.

Grade.—6A.

Subject.—The Study of India.

Project.—Making a model of the Taj Mahal.

Purpose:

1. To arouse interest in the study of India.
2. To teach how to gather and use source material.
3. To increase skill in the manipulation of illustrative material and the study of design and proportion.
4. To furnish an apperceptive basis for abstract thinking.

Subjects related to the project: industrial art, reading, English, geography, history, and arithmetic.

Source Material:

Stoddard's Lectures, Vol. 4.
National Geographic, March, 1921.
National Geographic, September, 1916.
Atlantic Monthly, March, 1921.
Munsey's.
Encyclopedias.
Book of Knowledge.
Stereoscopic Views of India.
Carpenter's *Asia*.
Century Book of Facts.

Industrial Art:

1. The children became interested in the Taj Mahal while studying architecture in the 6B grade and decided to make a model of the building for the industrial art work while studying India.
2. Discussion of the architecture.
   a. Comparison with Greek and Roman buildings.

b. Characteristics.
  1. Dome.
  2. Minarets.
  3. Use of color by means of semi-precious stones, mosaics, and tiles.
c. Comparison with buildings in America and in Duluth.

Reading:

Socialized recitation to demonstrate the use of source material.

English:

1. The Three Great Moguls: Style of architecture used by each.
2. Setting.
  a. Time built.
  b. Place.
  c. Occasion for building it.
  d. Ground surrounding it.
3. The Building Itself.
  a. Exterior.
  b. Interior.
4. Comparison with other buildings.
  a. Mosque of St. Sophia at Constantinople.
  b. Dome of Cathedral in Florence, Italy.
  c. National Capitol at Washington.
  d. State Capitol at St. Paul, Minnesota.

History:

1. Early trade routes to the East (maps, charts, etc.)
  a. Land.
  b. Water.
2. Wealth of India.
  a. Precious and semi-precious stones and gems.
  b. Spices.
  c. Tea.
  d. Silk.
3. Early industries.
  a. Glass making.
  b. Stone cutting.
  c. Metal Work.
4. Fall of Constantinople, 1453.
  a. Need of an all-water route.
  b. Development of explorations — Diaz, Vasco da Gama, Columbus, Magellan.

5. Government.
  a. Early Tribal—Moguls.

Geography:

1. Physical Features.
2. Climate.
  a. Winds.
  b. Rainfall.
  c. Temperature.
3. Products.
  . Wheat.
    Rice.
    Cotton.
    Tea.
    Silk.
    Pearls.
    Lumber.
4. Famines and their causes.
5. Religions.
  a. Brahmanism.
  b. Buddhism.
  c. Mohammedanism.
6. Government—Under England.

Arithmetic:

1. Learning to draw and construct to a scale.
2. Computing the area of surfaces.

Auditorium:

1. Purposes.
  a. To unify school procedure—both classroom and building.
  b. To increase interest in classroom work and to learn to recognize fine work.
  c. To provide an opportunity for the children to participate in a school activity for the benefit of others.
  d. To make classroom problems and projects take on new importance in both children's and teacher's eyes.
  e. To encourage research work.
  f. To start new interests.
  g. To help remove self-consciousness.
  h. To cause responses that lead to further activity.

AS REPORTED

THE SECOND ANNUAL MEETING OF THE NATIONAL CONFERENCE

Plans are being made for the second annual meeting of the National Conference on Educational Method, which will be held in Chicago on Tuesday afternoon, February 28th, and Wednesday forenoon, March 1st. The Tuesday afternoon meeting will be held in one of the leading hotels and the Wednesday morning meeting in Fullerton Hall of the Art Institute, which has been engaged for the purpose. It is hoped that there will be a large attendance of those who are interested in the particular purposes which the Conference is attempting to serve.

The program, while not yet complete, can be outlined somewhat as follows:

At the Tuesday afternoon meeting several speakers will describe briefly the newest aspects of the work in method and supervision in their schools. There will also be a discussion of the technique of reporting educational activities, particularly projects. It is felt that if others are to profit by one's experience, he must be able to describe it so as to bring out the principles involved as well as merely the external activities. He must, in a word, be able to interpret it to others.

At the Wednesday morning meeting there will be a series of discussions of the next steps in our forward movement. This discussion will turn upon such pertinent problems as the sane development of the newer phases of method in teaching and supervision, the refining of methods of study, and the like.

The second annual conference will resemble the first in the concreteness of the discussions; as far as possible reference will be made altogether to actual experience. The program ought to enlist the enthusiasm of many workers not yet enrolled.

THE ENGLISH COUNCIL IN CHICAGO

Among the organizations which are devoted to the development of particular subjects, the National Council of Teachers of English has had an enviable reputation for its forward look and systematic methods. The eleventh annual meeting held in Chicago during the Thanksgiving recess appears to have been up to the usual standard. The principal subjects discussed were The Movement for Better Speech, The Equipment of the Teacher of English, and The Application of Scientific Method to the Solution of English Problems.

Of the committees which will be active during the next year, the most important probably is that which has undertaken an investigation under the chairmanship of Professor Allen Abbott of Teachers College into the possibility of measuring the qualifications of teachers of English. By arranging a series of tests and trying these upon large numbers of English teachers who have attained high rank in the profession, the committee expects to be able to offer something far more definite in the way of standards than we have had. This will enable those responsible for the admission of prospective teachers to our training institutions to turn away some who can never hope to be effective. Another result that should follow from the work would be a better distribution of emphasis in the work itself.

INVESTIGATION OF THE CLASSICS

The National Committee on the Teaching of Latin and Greek in the Secondary Schools of the United States is directing a sweeping investigation into the teaching of Latin in the high schools. The work is subsidized by one of the large foundations and will proceed in the light of the most recent scientific methods of investigation. For example, before pupils are tested as to their ability in the school subjects, they will be examined as to their general intelligence. Every effort will be made to avoid the fallacies which have too often led to mistaken judgments such as, for example, ignoring the presence of a selected group. Since one of the principal phases of the investigation relates to the value of the study of Latin as training in English and another to the possibility of the transfer of improvement in certain mental powers, the work of the Committee has a very general interest. Any who would like to keep up with its work may write for information to Mr. Mason D. Gray, East High School, Rochester, N. Y.

REORGANIZATION OF ELEMENTARY EDUCATION

One of the most interesting passages in the *Addresses and Proceedings of the National Education Association* for 1921 is that relating to the report of the Commission on the Reorganization of Elementary Education. Speaking for the Commission at the meeting in Des Moines, the chairman, Miss Margaret S. McNaught, State Commissioner of Elementary Schools, Sacramento, California, stated that several definite phases of the work of the Commission were completed and the results about to be published. These include a volume on *Intelligence Tests and School Reorganization* by Professor Terman and others, a detailed study of adult education with special reference to immigrant education by Miss Elizabeth A. Woodward, a report on the delinquent child in the public school by Miss Olive M. Jones, a thesis on minimum essentials by Miss Abbie Louise Day, and a bulletin on the *Teaching of English in the Elementary Schools* by Miss Theda Gildemeister. For information about these reports and the work of the Commission in general, those interested may write to the Secretary of the National Education Association, Washington, D. C.

THE CALL TO SERVICE

The call to service in the National Education Association has never been clearer than now. There are important tasks ahead—big, challenging tasks that call for the best effort of the organized teachers of the Nation. The call is to educators of all classes and ranks. Adequate elementary education must be provided for every American child, which means that there must be enormous improvement, particularly in rural education. Secondary education must eventually be made a vital, universal opportunity for every boy and girl. Higher education—general, professional, and technical—whether under public or private auspices must be helped to grow both in quantity and quality until it is able to meet full and ready-handed the problem of training the leadership of our democracy. Libraries for rural communities as well as urban must be built up to keep alive the high purpose and the spirit of intelligence which schools exist to create. The ideals of educated men and women must more and more be made the ideals of our whole people. All this will require leadership. Our Association must help to provide that leadership. It will require professional unity—in locality, State, and Nation. Our Association must enlist the profession and help obtain that unity. The right development of education in America will require far-reaching changes in the methods and ideals of revenue raising. It is for the National Education Association through study and publicity to light the way. Public sentiment must be quickened to see education in the perspective of its true importance. Our program of service includes all of these things. Let us join hands to make this year the greatest in the history of professional organization among teachers. Let us work shoulder to shoulder for the growth of the National Education Association and the realization of its program of service.

CHARL ORMOND WILLIAMS
President, National Education Association.

THE READER'S GUIDE

IS THE RATING OF HUMAN CHARACTER PRACTICABLE?

In the *Journal of Educational Psychology* for November Professor Harold Rugg of the Lincoln School of Teachers College, Columbia University, begins an important series of articles based upon his experience in checking up on the use of the Army rating scales. He was statistician to the Committee on Classification of Personnel in the Army in 1918 and had opportunity to study the working of the rating scales in some of the large camps.

Professor Rugg opens his series with the question, "Can human character be rated on point scales accurately enough for practical uses in education?" and answers, "Yes, if the rating is done under sufficiently rigorous conditions," but adds that these conditions are not attainable in the public schools. He supports this position with a survey of the development of point scales and a body of data drawn from his experience in the Army. He concludes that it was very improbable that an officer was located within even his proper "fifth" of the entire scale by "official" rating.

IF I WERE TO DO IT OVER AGAIN

Miss Gladys Steinkraus writes very frankly and happily in the *Journal of Education* for November 3 on the theme suggested by the above title. Three years ago she gave up teaching in order to be married. In looking back she sees teaching more clearly as a real profession. If she were to do it over again she would treat her work as something big; she would be more free in making suggestions to her superiors; she would have a more sensible working schedule and would thus lead a more normal life. Her confession will

no doubt arouse a responsive chord in many minds, even of those who are still at it.

ONE VIEW OF THE PROJECT METHOD

Among those who have made the attempt to define and illustrate the meaning of the project method is Mr. J. A. Stevenson, whose volume *The Project Method of Teaching* was recently published by Macmillan. Mr. Stevenson approaches his task by way of a survey of the various uses to which the term "project" has been put, particularly in the fields of agricultural education, home economics, and various trades and industries. He finds approximately twenty definitions or descriptions of the project. His own is as follows: "A problematic act carried to its completion in a natural setting."

He sets up four pairs of aims to distinguish the project method from some other methods and particularly to bring out its potential values. These are: (a) reasoning *vs.* memory of information, (b) conduct *vs.* information for its own sake, (c) natural setting for learning *vs.* artificial setting for learning, and (d) the priority of the problem *vs.* priority of principles. The project, declares the writer, provides for the first of each of these pairs and is the only concept in common use which is adequate for unifying them. The third, namely, a natural setting for learning, is the great contribution which the project method is making to education. A careful examination of 42 textbooks in common use disclosed 14 methods of teaching, no one of which can meet the four desirable standards mentioned above.

The author's treatment proceeds to a comparison of his own definition with that of various others, compares problem with project, discusses certain implications of the project method and the relation of the project to the curriculum, and concludes with a rapid survey of various applications of the project method to school work. A bibliography of some ten pages is added.

The discussion of the project method in education is so recent that it is perhaps ungenerous to find fault with so plausible an analysis as this of Mr. Stevenson. It may be pointed out, however, that his concept is less inclusive than it should be. Other writers on the subject frankly admit that the term "project method" covers a new synthesis of educational ideas, almost all of which have seen service. Among these are self-activity, the school as life, favorable conditions of learning, socialization, concreteness, and experience. It is perhaps both truer and simpler to say at once that the project method, if looked at from the teacher's standpoint, is an attempt to embody in the activities of children the most useful principles of modern educational psychology on the one hand, and the most significant principles of socialized or democratic group activity on the other. It makes central the element of purpose, which in the case of the group is common. It emphasizes participation in planning and in judging results as well as in overt activity. It leads on to related activities and develops a wide range of associated and concomitant ideas and emotions.

But while it is true that the project method does involve many familiar concepts, it calls for a new emphasis and a new technique. The development of conscious purpose in experience has not generally been placed first in the list of aims which the teacher should seek to reach, nor has it been generally recognized that this purpose, once in mind, controls every phase of the activity of the pupil. We have commonly had the assignment, which may be nothing more than a clear statement by the teacher of the nature of the task which is to be undertaken. In practice it has been too frequently far less than this. Only recently, moreover, have we sought to develop methods efficient in bringing about genuine group cooperation. Here also purpose is the central feature. The aims to be realized must be common to all members of the group and must be known to be common.

Unless a deeper meaning were read into the expression "problematic act" than Mr. Stevenson seems to do, we should not have a concept of purposeful experience in mind when we speak of the project method. The term "natural setting" does not help us a great deal for the reason that whether a setting is natural or not depends on the attitude of the learner rather than on the external surroundings themselves. School affairs may be as "natural" as any others. Indeed, it is the ideal of the project teacher so to interpret school life that its values will be apparent to the pupils.

As a presentation of various ideas now current, this new work on the project method has distinct value. It helps to define the problem of method and it does present certain criteria. But it can hardly be said to be a satisfactory and complete analysis.

THE NEW BOOKS

The Value of School Supervision. By Marvin Summers Pittman. Baltimore: Warwick & York, 1921. Pp. x + 129.

A report of results obtained by means of the "zone plan" of supervision of rural schools.

The Selection of Textbooks. By C. R. Maxwell. Boston: Houghton Mifflin Co., 1921. Pp. x + 139. Price, $1.35.

A handbook for administrators.

The Psychology of Learning. By William Henry Pyle. Baltimore: Warwick & York, 1921. Pp. 308.

A very clearly written summary of the established facts, with directions for numerous experiments and a bibliography of scientific investigation.

Education in Theory and Practice. By Gilbert H. Jones. Boston: Richard G. Badger, 1919. Pp. 396.

Intended as a general introduction to the study of education.

Scales for Measuring Special Types of English Composition. By Ervin Eugene Lewis. Yonkers, N. Y.: World Book Co., 1921. Pp. vi + 144. Price, $1.20.

The "types" are: order letters, letters of application, social letters, narrative and problematic, and simple narration.

Elementary Geography; Advanced Geography. By Frank M. McMurry and A. E. Parkins. New York: Macmil'an Co., 1921. Pp. vi + 322, illus., maps, and pp. viii + 501, illus., maps.

A new series written with intent to relate the subject closely to children's present interests and needs and to cover the essentials, while providing for individual differences.

Youth and the New World. Essays from the Atlantic Monthly. Edited by Ralph Philip Boas. Boston: Atlantic Monthly Press, 1921. Pp. ix + 320.

Story, Essay and Verse. By Charles Swain Thomas and Harry Gilbert Paul. Boston: Atlantic Monthly Press, 1921. Pp. xi + 394.

Selections from contemporary writers whose work appeared in the Atlantic Monthly.

Charm. By Catherine T. Bryce. Boston: Atlantic Monthly Press, 1921. Pp. 18.

A "better-speech" play.

Here and Now Story Book. By Lucy Sprague Mitchell. New York: E. P. Dutton & Co., 1921. Pp. xiv + 360. Price, $2.00.

. Experimental stories written for the children of the city and country schools.

Mon Petit Livre Français. By Clara S. Dolton. London: Longmans, Green & Co., 1921. Pp. vi + 86. Price, $0.65 net.

A text for children in the primary grades.

IN PAPER COVERS

Statement of Principles and Procedure Affecting Grades VII–XII in the Reorganized Plan of Secondary Instruction with Special Reference to Grades VII–IX. Prepared by the Board of Superintendents. School Document No. 2, 1921, Boston Public Schools.

Report or Survey on Intermediate Schools and Classes. Submitted to the School Committee of the City of Boston by the Board of Superintendents. School Document No. 19, 1920, Boston Public Schools.

Facilities for Foreign Students in American Colleges and Universities. By Samuel Paul Capen. Bulletin; 1920, No. 39, Bureau of Education, Washington, D. C.

Statistics of State Universities and State Colleges. For the Year Ended June 30, 1920. Bulletin, 1920, No. 48, Bureau of Education, Washington, D. C.

Part-Time Education of Various Types. A Report of the Commission on the Reorganization of Secondary Education, Appointed by the National Education Association. Bulletin, 1921, No. 5, Bureau of Education, Washington, D. C.

The Visiting Teacher. By Sophia C. Gleim. Bulletin, 1921, No. 10, Bureau of Education, Washington, D. C.

Higher Education, 1918–1920. By George F. Zook. Bulletin, 1921, No. 21, Bureau of Education, Washington, D. C.

Report of the President on the Program and Development of the National Education Association of the United States. By Fred M. Hunter. Published by National Education Association, Washington, D. C., October, 1921.

English in the Elementary Schools. Bulletin No. 21, Chicago Board of Education, Sept., 1921.

THE JOURNAL OF EDUCATIONAL METHOD

Edited by JAMES F. HOSIC

Volume I   JANUARY, 1922   Number 5

PUBLISHED BY THE WORLD BOOK COMPANY FOR
THE NATIONAL CONFERENCE ON EDUCATIONAL METHOD

$3.00 a year   Monthly except July and August   35 cents a copy

Annual Meeting of the National Conference on Educational Method, Chicago, Illinois, February 28 and March 1, 1922

THE NATIONAL CONFERENCE ON EDUCATIONAL METHOD

An Association of Persons Interested in Supervision and Teaching

THE JOURNAL OF EDUCATIONAL METHOD is published monthly, from September to June, by World Book Company, Yonkers-on-Hudson, New York, for the officers, directors, and members of the National Conference on Educational Method. The subscription price is $3.00 a year; the price of single copies is 35 cents.

Postage is prepaid by the publishers on all orders from the United States, Mexico, Cuba, Porto Rico, Panama Canal Zone, Republic of Panama, Bolivia, Colombia, Honduras, Nicaragua, Peru, Hawaiian Islands, Philippine Islands, Guam, and the Samoan Islands. Postage is charged extra as follows: For Canada, 25c on annual subscriptions; other foreign countries not named, 50 cents. All communications regarding subscriptions or advertising should be addressed to World Book Company, Yonkers-on-Hudson, New York.

Address applications for membership to the Secretary of the Conference, 525 West One Hundred and Twentieth Street, New York City. The fee for active members is $3.00, for associate members, $2.00; $2.00 in each case is applied to the support of the Journal, for which each member receives a year's subscription.

The editorial office is at 525 West One Hundred and Twentieth Street, New York City.

Entered as second-class matter 8 December 1921 at the post office at Greenwich, Connecticut, under the Act of 3 March 1879. Acceptance for mailing at special rate of postage provided for in Section 1103, Act of 3 October 1917, authorized 8 December 1921.

The Journal of Educational Method

VOLUME I   JANUARY, 1922   NUMBER 5

EDITORIALLY SPEAKING

OUR PUBLISHERS

All of our friends will be glad to know that the task of promoting and publishing the *Journal* has been undertaken by the World Book Company, the central office of which is at Yonkers-on-Hudson, New York. This company has an enviable reputation for issuing well-printed books and large facilities for selling and marketing. There is every reason to believe that through the efforts of the company our circle of readers will rapidly enlarge. It has, indeed, already reached gratifying proportions. The *Journal* remains the official organ of the National Conference and within its general management and editorial control. Business communications should be addressed to the World Book Company, Yonkers, N. Y. Communications for the editor of the *Journal* or Secretary-Treasurer of the Conference should be addressed to 525 West 120th Street, New York City.

MASSACHUSETTS LEADS

If ye editor is correctly informed, Massachusetts is taking more active steps to develop modern methods of teaching than any other state. At least she has the first project society which has reported and she is the first to attempt to coördinate the activities of all of her teacher-training institutions in that field. It is the custom of Mr. Wright, the director of elementary and secondary education and of teacher training in the state, to call the entire personnel of the faculties of the several normal schools into conference early in September of each year. In 1921 a chief topic of discussion was educational method and Professor W. H. Kilpatrick, of Teachers College, was engaged to give a series of lectures on the project method. Commissioner Wright is now planning a systematic follow-up. Miss Elizabeth Fisher, of the Lowell Normal School, will visit each of the other normal schools in turn and conduct conferences for the discussion of the problems of method which are arising in the progress of the work in each school. She will also address the student body, giving to each group of students the advantage of her impressions gained from observing the work of various schools. The country needs the stabilizing which fundamental ideas in education give, and at present the most far-reaching conception of method is undoubtedly that suggested by the term "project" as used by its most thoughtful interpreters. No doubt other states will emulate Massachusetts now as they have often done in the past.

WANTED: SCIENTIFIC STUDIES

If the discussion of educational method is to get beyond the introductory stages, we must have more accurate data upon which to base conclusions than we now have. This applies quite as much or more to supervision as to teaching. Indeed Mr. Courtis's account in *School and Society* of a year or two ago remains almost alone in its field. He gave, it will be remembered, the results of testing schools in which the work in geography had been unsupervised, supervised in a general way, and supervised in detail, with a follow-up from room to room. Many are confident that the newer methods of work, which enlist more fully the pupils' energies and awaken their powers, do actually achieve both more and better results. In a word they attain economy. But we should be in a more satisfactory position if we had a larger array of verifiable facts. Do children learn to spell better when they learn by the project method? Let us find out.

This *Journal* will welcome well-written accounts of experiments involving rational attempts to measure the effects of newer methods, side by side with articles of a theoretical character and informal accounts of teaching experience. We wish to publish quantitative studies which bear upon the value of method. Who will help?

STANDARDS FOR RATING PUPILS

H. G. Masters

Principal, Beechview-Beechwood Schools, Pittsburgh, Pennsylvania

Little attention has been given to formulating standards that would serve the teacher as a guide in rating pupils. At present the teacher is forced to rely upon standards that are the result of her own experience. These are individual standards and represent the teacher's personal reactions to the problem. The inevitable result is that there are as many standards as there are teachers putting "marks" on report cards. A pupil, under these conditions, may consistently throughout his school life do work worthy of a grade of "good," and yet be rated all the way from "unsatisfactory" to "excellent." Much of the criticism from parents and pupils may be laid to this lack of a uniform rating standard.

The organization of these schools is such that it was more convenient to have the teachers work in two groups. The general plan was to have each group work out a set of standards. The principal, acting as chairman of each group, was able, in some measure, to guide the discussion along parallel lines. In this way radical differences in the two sets were avoided.

Each group having completed its work, the two united in a series of meetings to select the best from each set of standards and mold these into a composite set that would represent the best thought of the group as a whole. There still remained, however, some moot points to be cleared up and a committee of three, one each from the primary, intermediate, and grammar grades, was appointed to work with the principal in arranging "Standards" in the present form.

Copies of the "Standards" were placed on the bulletin boards and in each room.

They were discussed at one of the weekly assembly meetings. The teachers set aside a study period for a discussion of how the "Standards" were to be applied, the object being to put before the pupils, in as concrete a way as possible, what the faculty considered the outstanding characteristics of pupils being rated with any one of the letters in use. The pupils quickly realized that here was a measuring rod, something concrete by which they could measure themselves and upon which they could base an argument for a change in rating. The teachers, likewise, found in the "Standards" a basis upon which to make a rating in the first instance and to justify it later if necessary. Both pupils and teachers accepted the "Standards" as the basis of settlement of any question arising in connection with "marks" on the report card.

Pupils in grades four to eight graded themselves, using the "Standards." These grades were later compared with the semester marks given by the teacher. The results of the comparison show that in 12% of the cases the teacher's rating was higher than the pupil's; in 61.2% of the cases the teacher's rating was the same as the pupil's; in 26.8% of the cases the teacher's rating was lower than the pupil's.

So far the "Standards" have justified their existence. But much more needs to be done before they will have attained their greatest value. Objectives in subject matter must be worked out and socialized. These must be so simply and clearly written that the pupil may read with understanding. He must be able to mark off his progress on this "simplified" course of study and be his own judge as to whether or not he has earned promotion. It means a dual course of study: one in simplified form for parent and pupil, another in great detail and highly socialized for the use of the teacher and school officials.

STANDARDS FOR RATING PUPILS
BEECHVIEW-BEECHWOOD PUBLIC SCHOOLS

	E Pupil	G Pupil	F Pupil	U Pupil	P Pupil
A.	1. Recitation (oral and written) clear and concise.	1. Recitation (oral and written) clear and concise with help.	1. Recitation (oral and written) fairly clear with much help.	1. Recitation (oral and written) indefinite or careless.	1. Recitation (oral and written) shows little idea of subject matter.
	2. Asks intelligent questions.	2. Asks majority of questions intelligently.	2. Asks some intelligent questions.	2. Seldom asks intelligent questions.	2. Asks and answers very few questions.
	3. 90% of work done correctly.	3. 80% of work done correctly.	3. 70% of work done correctly.	3. 60% of work done correctly.	3. Less than 60% of work done correctly.
B.	1. Thorough, prompt, and shows initiative.	1. Thorough and prompt with some help.	1 Requires urging and much help to follow directions.	1. Forced preparation.	1. Makes no preparation.
	2. Makes up work lost during absence.	2. Shows some initiative.	2. Shows little initiative.	2. Can follow few directions.	2 Cannot follow directions.
		3. Makes up some of work lost during absence.	3. Does not make up work lost during absence.	3. Does not make up work lost during absence.	3. Does not make up work lost during absence.
C.	1. Receives criticism well and corrects mistakes.	1. Receives criticism and corrects most mistakes.	1. Accepts criticism and corrects some mistakes.	1. Inattentive to criticism and does not correct mistakes.	1. Indifferent and listless.
	2. Attentive and enthusiastic in every phase of school activity.	2. Attentive and enthusiastic in every phase of school activity.	2. Lax in attention and enthusiasm but willing to coöperate.	2 Lacks enthusiasm and coöperation.	2 Lacks enthusiasm and coöperation.
D.	1. Marked ability to apply knowledge.	1. Ability to apply knowledge.	1 Requires help to apply knowledge.	1. Has little ability to apply knowledge.	1. Has very little ability to apply knowedge.

A. Knowledge of subject matter.　　B. Preparation.　　C. Attitude.　　D. Application.

THE PROBLEM METHOD[1]

Principal of the Chicago Normal School, Chicago, Illinois

Educational thought is subject to frequent shifts of emphasis. Now it is the curriculum that is criticized. Again it is the method of teaching that receives chief attention. All at once we are discussing the organization and administration of the schools. These shifts are unsettling. Just as one has his own system worked out, he has to square himself with the new demand. No teacher wishes to be behind the times. Everyone is ambitious to know and use the latest and best in theory and practice. Professional pride and the desire for professional advancement conspire to keep one alert and moving. In spite of popular tradition, the modern teacher neither is nor is permitted to be stationary, conservative; education is in a flux. Change is everywhere dominant. It is hard to keep one's feet on the ground. Even the direction is lost sight of. Some one is always arising to challenge every effort and to dispute every result. It is a wonder that anyone retains his courage and confidence.

All this, however, is but evidence of growth. The past three decades in American education have wrought wonderful changes. The whole conception of what education is has been broadened and defined. All tradition has been subjected to scrutiny and examination. Nothing has been allowed to escape. A new theoretical basis has been laid for our practice. New aims, new standards, new methods, new values have been stated. Progress in all related sciences has compelled progress here. New concepts, new technique, new terminology have been introduced. Education has gained the right to be classed as a profession.

This change and growth has begun to reveal certain definite and discernible tendencies. Fundamental lines of development are giving stability and meaning to the process. Social life, for example, is accepted as the test of value of any curriculum or method. The method of testing processes by their results has been carried over into this realm. The school is an institution designed to insure social continuity and social progress. There is a vast deal to be done in the way of embodying the new points of view in concrete form. But the method of experiment is relied on to give us this result. We are confident, not that we have achieved finality, but that we have arrived at a method of progress.

In the midst of all this change, we draw back when a new organization, a new method is proposed. We have seen too many devices have their day. We are suspicious of panaceas. We have learned only to unlearn too many educational slogans. The doctrine of interest, the Gary system, the theory of concentration, the doctrine of correlation, where are they? Is it strange that the teacher becomes blasé, suspicious, conservative, and contemptuous? Storm-tossed, with the earth and sky mingled together, our greatest need would seem to be stability and a guiding star.

Just now we are asked to accord hospitality to another newcomer, the Problem

[1] This article originally appeared in the Chicago School Journal.

Method, or the Problem-Project Method, if· you please. We shall have to take account of it, whether we will or no. Just how seriously we should consider it, we have a right to inquire. Perhaps we can assure ourselves of the right answer by an examination of its scientific credentials. Where did it come from, how does it happen to be here, what claims does it make, on what are its claims based? This article will attempt to answer some of these questions. No effort will be made to expound the method either in outline or in detail. It will be sufficient to trace it to its origin in certain scientific and practical tendencies of the day. Perhaps we can then judge how much likelihood there is that it has come to stay, as much as anything really stays.

The Problem Method, or Problem-Project Method, is the formulation for educational use and application of results gained in five fields of thought and activity. These are: (1) Modern Philosophy, (2) Modern Logic, (3) Modern Psychology, (4) Modern Science, (5) Modern Industry. These fields overlap, of course, but it is aside from the purpose of this article to trace their mutual relations and interdependence. Corresponding to these five sources, we find five outstanding moments, factors, elements, as you will, that form the basic structure of the method. These are: (1) The Philosophy of Experience, (2) The Logic of Purpose, (3) The Psychology of the Act, (4) The Method of Science, (5) The Processes of Industry. Let us consider each briefly. They may seem formidable garbed in their technical terminology, but they are really very simple. If only we can make them seem so!

1. *The Philosophy of Experience.* The term experience in philosophy and educa-

tion is fundamental. It cannot be defined. We all know what it is. It is the all-inclusive term for all that we are aware of. It applies to the whole or to any part of the content of our lives. A sensation, a thought, a feeling, a resolve, an ideal, a wish, a hope, a party, a battle, a football game, a map, anything and everything that we know of we classify as experience. The experience philosophy takes the point of view that the most effective control of life is to be had from the control of the inner life, *i. e.*, experience. It thus takes radical issue with the behavioristic school that would ignore, if not deny, the inner life, and would seek the control of life from the study of outward behavior. Perhaps it would be truer to say that the experience philosophy includes both the inner and the outer under the concept of experience. For education, two positions taken by this philosophy are fundamental. The first is that *experience can be controlled*. We have control of anything when we can wield it to accomplish our purposes. We can control our experience so as to bring about desired results in our experience. We can direct our present experience so as to bring a future experience that we foresee. This is all rather abstract, but still clear and simple. By having the experience of planting a seed under certain conditions we can have later the experience of seeing the plant, the flower, the fruit. Education is the enlargement and control of experience.

There are two kinds of experience: (1) direct experience and (2) indirect experience. Direct experience is produced by the object or situation being present to stimulate us. We have direct experience of a battle when we are in it. We have direct experience of an orange tree when we see, touch, handle the tree and fruit.

Indirect experience is produced by communication. We read about a battle and try to imagine ourselves there. We study about the orange tree, see pictures of it, buy the fruit, and construct an image of it. But the object or the situation is not present to the senses. Indirect experience approximates direct experience. It is like it in quality but differs in degree and completeness. We read about the Parthenon, see pictures of it, compare it with other monuments, but there is an added sense of reality when we actually behold it. The relation of direct and indirect experience is this: *Indirect experience is possible to us only as direct experience has given us the elements of the communicated experience.* I can understand the geography of Africa, which I have never seen, only to the degree that my direct experience has made me able to understand and image a tropical climate, a sandy waste, wild animals, dark-skinned men, and the like. *Indirect experience is valuable to us only as what is communicated enables us to enlarge and control our direct experience.* We read that phosphate rock will restore soil. We purchase and use it in a worn-out field. We receive a great increase. Indirect or borrowed experience has controlled our action but has resulted in an enlarged and direct experience. The second fundamental position is that *experience is social*. The individual has it. It is peculiar to him. But it is social at the same time. It is gained in coöperation and communication with others. Others are a part of his experience. They make it possible. They join with him to create it. Others have elsewhere and at other times had and handed over to him their experience in word, institution, custom, invention, and the like. Coöperation and communication are the social activities resulting in the

enlargement and control of individual experience. Education should consciously carry on these activities so as to maintain the continuity of individual experience. The classroom group provides the opportunity. The socialized recitation is this social process made into a conscious method of instruction.

2. *The Logic of Purpose.* The second fundamental moment or factor in the problem method is the standpoint of modern logic. The essence of this position is that thought should be studied as a function rather than as a structure. It asks what thought does. It inquires under what conditions it arises, how it goes on, what results it produces. Our older books on method were built on the inherited structural logic that goes back to Aristotle. They laid great stress on induction, deduction, reasoning, questioning, defining and the like. Functional logic emphasizes the fact that thinking takes place in the presence of a problem. It describes how the mind proceeds to solve this problem. The problem forces the forming of a purpose. Thinking seeks the realizing of this purpose by forming a plan and trying it out. If it succeeds, the problem is solved, the purpose is accomplished, the plan is proved true. This functional logic, it may be said, is but the refined exposition of the method of modern science, particularly biological science. Aristotle's logic was based on the scientific procedure and results of the century preceding him. Modern logic is based on the scientific procedure and results of the last century. For education the vital point is that problem, purpose, and thinking are seen to be indissolubly linked. No problem, no purpose, no thinking. Add that problem, purpose, and thinking belong to experience, not to behavior, and that all

three involve social coöperation and the connection of the second fundamental moment with the first becomes at once apparent.

3. *The Psychology of the Act.* The third fundamental moment in the problem method is the psychology of action. This psychology is based on the anatomy of the nervous system. This nervous system consists of a series of five elements—sense organ, sensory nerve, brain, motor nerve, muscle. A complete act involves all five. Reflex and instinctive acts do not require thinking. Habitual acts may dispense with thinking. New situations, however, cannot be met by reflex, instinctive, or habitual reactions. The new problem requires thought for its solution. The brain suspends the activity of the series of the five elements until the right action is thought out. Once thought out, the series is restored and the act follows. If the right result follows, the problem is solved. But it takes a complete act to get a complete experience. Only the complete experience can test the value of the thought. That is why we "learn by doing." The problem, therefore, calls for a new form of action and thinking is the means of establishing this new form of action. Modern functional logic and modern biological psychology coincide in their emphasis on the relation of problem, purpose, and thought.

4. *The Method of Science.* The fourth moment in the problem method is the method of modern science. As indicated above, this procedure has furnished the basis of modern logic. But the scientist is not studying logic. He is solving problems. These problems are objective. They are practical, arising in the field of industry; or theoretical, arising in the prosecution of research. The method of procedure has been learned by experiment. Experiment always starts with a problem. It may be a problem to the student, as in high-school physics, or a problem to the world of science, as the isolation of an ion. The success of the scientific procedure or method has dictated the method of instruction in the sciences. Therefore we have the laboratory. The problem method is established in science instruction. Only recently have the teachers of science recognized that in the earlier years the pupil's problem was the starting point for the teaching of elementary science. This is the step forward taken by the movement in general science. The example of the sciences, therefore, has contributed practically to the theory and practice of the problem method. It might not be too much to say that science has been the chief source of the movement.

5. *The Processes of Industry.* The fifth moment in the problem method has been contributed by industrial processes. Industry, that is, manufacturing, the trades, the domestic arts, agriculture and the like, have definite practical problems to solve and definite purposes to accomplish. The problems and purposes are clear and tangible. The schools have learned how to imitate industry. The manual training shops, the cooking laboratories, state their curricula in the form of problems. The pupils make a chair, a table, a gas engine; they print a pamphlet; they make bread, bake potatoes, can peaches; they design and make a dress. The problem and the purpose of the activity are definite and clear. The procedure is learned as a means to an end. The solution has the practical, objective test of the result obtained.

The problem method is, then, no mere device. It is not a new formula of success.

It is an effort to make available for school procedure the results of modern philosophy, modern logic, modern psychology, modern science, and modern industry where they coincide in making the problem the starting point for purposeful activity, for thinking. It attempts to make school procedure tally with the theoretical and practical procedure of the world. It aims thus to connect the school with life.

COERCION AND LEARNING [1]

WILLIAM HEARD KILPATRICK

Professor of Education, Teachers College, Columbia University

"Ever since our talk on mind-set and learning I have been wondering how coercion would affect learn-

The teachers meet again

ing. Wouldn't there be a contrary mind-set which would interfere with learning? And if so, how is it that we do find children learning under teachers who use coercion? Our reasoning last time on the influence of purpose on learning seemed clear and was convincing to me, but I can't go on and straighten out the effect of coercion."

"Before we begin on something new, suppose we summarize our conclusion on mind-set and learning. We'll

A review

then be in a better position to see and perhaps solve the problem you raise. For it is a very real and very important problem.

"Perhaps our best plan will be to present a tabular statement of how a strong mind-

Mind-set and learning

set acts. Suppose a boy who 'likes' mathematics is brought face to face with a certain difficult problem. The teacher says this is an unusually hard problem, he doesn't know whether any member of the class can solve it or not, though they have now enough mathematics to solve it. He'd like them to try, but he is not very hopeful. The boy feels in this a definite challenge. He proposes to solve that problem and 'all by himself.' He attacks it, but it doesn't yield at once. He redoubles his efforts. We have then a clear case of study and, let us suppose, of eventual success under the influence of a very strong mind-set-to-an-end. We find accordingly

1. *A definite end in view.* The boy is definitely determined to solve the problem all by himself.

2. *An inner urge to attain this end.* The teacher has not required the problem, but the boy is strongly urged on by himself from within to solve it.

3. *Readiness in all the boy's pertinent inner resources.* All his knowledge and skill, all his available ideas, are in a state of readiness. They rise up, as it were, earnestly desiring to be used.

4. *An unreadiness for thwarting activities.* He has real difficulty for the time being to enter wholesouledly into his other lessons. He can hardly cease thinking about the problem.

5. *The end defines success for him.* He won't count it success unless he solves the problem beyond a question and by his own unaided efforts.

6. *Success attained brings satisfaction.* The stronger the mind-set and the more difficulty in finding the solution, the greater will be the satisfaction of success.

7. *Satisfaction means fixing the responses that brought success.* When he finally sees the solution, the way out of the difficulty, the satisfaction attending will by the law of Effect fix in him the success-bringing steps."

[1] All rights reserved by the author.

"Do you mean by 'fixing the success-bringing steps' that he will remember the solution?"

"Yes, I mean that and more. Solving the problem means seeing the elements of the problem in a certain appropriate relationship. Now the satisfaction of success will fix in him this relationship. It will be almost impossible for him to forget it. Moreover his mind will in sheer pleasure at hard earned success play back and forth over the main success-bringing step, so that exercise with renewed effect will fix this yet more strongly in his mind. Each time he shows his solution to an appreciative listener, this fixing process will again be repeated. And there is yet more. This present success will make him more inclined to attack the next challenging problem he meets. And he will for the same reason find it easier next time to get into the spirit of seeking; the mindset to study having this time brought success will the next time more readily call into play the boy's available mathematical resources for solving such a problem."

"Is this why purposeful learning is so much advocated now?"

The function of purpose "Yes, only there are still other reasons for wishing to utilize the child's purpose. There is in the first place more likelihood of success. The strong inner urge will mean stronger efforts. Then there is greater probability of a good organization resulting. The definite end makes it easier to form an effective organization, because there is something to guide the steps. This is more evident where the effort to attain the end involves the assembling and uniting into one whole of many obviously different steps. The third reason for wishing the strong purpose is the one above described,

that the learning better takes place. The learning not only comes quicker, but it is more abiding when it does thus come. The satisfaction following success effects that by the law of Effect."

"You have not said anything about annoyance. Does that not enter into the situation?"

"Yes, but negatively. The steps that lead nowhere bring annoyance and for that reason they tend to drop out, to be not repeated next time. This is the other half of the law of Effect."

"Doesn't the satisfaction of such success affect also the associate suggestions and the concomitant learning that we discussed in October?"

"Indeed it does, but we must leave that now while we go back to the matter of coercion."

"Before you do that I have one question. We have always known that the capable **Why study this question?** child learned readily and the more so when he was interested. I don't see that you have told us anything new. What I want is some way to get learning from the mediocre boy who isn't interested. Have you helped us with him?"

"There is certainly nothing new in saying that the capable boy who works with strong purpose will learn. As you say, we've always known that as a fact. But to see wherein and how the learning takes place is another matter. For most people such an insight is new. If we can see more intimately and exactly into the learning process as it goes on under differing conditions, perhaps we'll know better how to direct the process. We have seen how learning takes place when a boy is deeply interested. Now we propose to see what happens and *how* it happens when a boy acts under coercion.

Between these two extremes are included most instances of learning. If we understand the extreme cases, possibly we'll know better how to handle the intermediate cases. We certainly have in the notion of purposeful learning no patent automatic process, no get-learning-quick scheme. On the contrary, we think any widespread appreciable improvement in school work will probably require long study on our part, but we believe that psychology suggests the point of attack and we propose to follow that leading."

"Won't you please take a clear case of coercion and carry through the whole discussion?"

"Before you do that I have one more question. What does coercion mean? Must there always be another person to do the coercing or might impersonal circumstances coerce? Might one even coerce himself? I wish you'd make this clear."

"To say what meaning a word shall have is not easy. Different people see things differently, and differing situations sometimes require differing senses of meaning. But if there is possible doubt we must say what meaning we propose to use. Let's begin with the clearest case of coercion, which is certainly where one person coerces another into doing something he wouldn't otherwise do. Suppose a boy has planned to go swimming with the other boys and his mother in spite of his tearful pleading forbids, and 'forces' him, as we say, 'against his will' to stay at home and mind the baby. Suppose further that before he will yield she has to threaten punishment and even after the other boys have gone she has to speak sharply to 'make' him treat the baby decently and care for her properly. What, now, are the characteristic elements in this

The meaning of coercion

instance of undoubted coercion? As it is an extreme case, we may expect the elements to stand out in unusual relief. First, in point of time we find a mind-set already occupying the stage of action. This mind-set would, unless thwarted, result in a certain line of conduct, here in going swimming with the boys. Second, there arises some interposition, felt by the one coerced to come more or less from the *outside*, which sets up the essential coercion, namely, a state of affairs that thwarts the activity already under way and *against the will* of the coerced directs experience along another and, under the circumstances, *unacceptable* line. Third, the one coerced *accepts but against his will* the new line of conduct because he fears a threatened and still more unacceptable alternative.

"This is of course an analysis and description, not a logical definition. The italicized words must have been experienced in order to be understood; but having been experienced their meaning is fairly definite. With these understood, the essential elements of coerced activity stand out."

"It seems to me, then, that whether you call any such experience a case of coercion depends upon the attitude of the one concerned, whether there arises in him a contrary set which inwardly rejects while there is outward yielding."

Coercion is a matter of attitude

"Yes, I think you are right, and the more definite the inner rejection, the clearer is it a case of coercion."

"Might it not happen that what began as a clear case of coercion would cease to be such because the coerced changed his mind, the inner attitude shifting from rejection to acceptance?"

"You are quite right, and the possibility

of this is a matter of great practical importance for the educator."

"Would you also not need in this discussion to say whether you were thinking of the one who did the coercing or the one who felt coerced?"

"Perhaps so, but our instance given above was in terms of the attitude of the one coerced. Whether he learns or not is our concern, so we have given our analysis and discussion in terms of his attitude. We have in our past discussions seen clearly that the attitude of the learner affects his learning. That's why our discussion is here so given."

"Have we sufficiently answered the question as to whether coercion must come from another person or might proceed from circumstances?"

"I think so. This inner attitude of rejection is most easily and most typically aroused by persons, possibly because their motives are both complex and hid and are accordingly the more easily mistaken, and resentment is thus more readily stirred. Resentment, I may add, seems a typical accompaniment of coercion. The young and hotheaded may entertain feelings of resentful and rebellious rejection against mere impersonal circumstances, where older and calmer persons would accept such thwarting as inevitable. To the one group this kind of thwarting would be coercion, to the other not. But the two undoubtedly merge into each other in intermediate cases."

"Can, then, a person coerce himself?"

"With the discussion as given the question is for us now one of fact. Do we see anyone rejecting with inward rebellion what he imposes on himself? If yes, then one may coerce himself. The cases that seem most like it may, however, upon re-flection turn out to be the coercion of circumstances rather than of one's self. The question thus becomes rather academic than useful."

"Well, may we not go on to something interesting? When you people get to splitting hairs, you never know when to stop. It gets so tiresome to the rest of us. Are we never to take up the effect of coercion on learning?"

"It is too bad to spend so much time on what may seem unnecessary. We are, however, now ready to go on with our topic. Shall we take an illustration and follow it through with the same steps we used at the outset?"

"By all means. An illustration always helps."

"Suppose, then, John has lately been so much interested in football that he has slighted his lessons. At length the teacher in desperation tells him that he must stay away from practice that afternoon and work some problems he has repeatedly missed. As soon as he can work them he may go. To make a clear case, suppose John feels rebellious the whole time but doesn't dare actually to rebel. Our problem, then, is to find out what kind of learning will go on, and how it will take place."

An instance of coercion

"Shall we take into account only the learning of the problems or shall we consider all the learning that takes place? I mean shall we ask about all the simultaneous attendant learnings that we discussed in our September and October meetings?"

"Eventually we must take account of all, because they are all taking place, but for our immediate purposes let's begin with the problem solving."

"Well, if the boy is going to be rebellious the whole time, he won't learn much. Anybody knows that. I don't need to study psychology or pedagogy or pedaguese or anything else to tell me that. Why don't you ask something that people want to know?"

"Yes, we went over the same point earlier with learning through interest. The main results in the clear cases may already be known, but if we can find out how the rebellious attitude works to prevent the learning, we have learned something new; and perhaps then we'll know better how to manage rebellious cases. Shall we go on?"

"Yes, for gracious' sake do."

"Well, consider John. He stays because he's afraid not to stay, and he studies at least after a fashion. Is there any mind-set?"

"Certainly, he is dead set against the whole performance and, as you said, this contrary set continues throughout."

Opposed
mind-sets

"Is that all? Is there any other mind-set? Remember, he can get out with the boys only if he will convince the teacher that he can work the problems. Does this mean anything?"

"Yes, it probably means that he will try to convince the teacher, and so will study the problems."

"Then he will have a mind-set on the problems?"

"To a degree, yes, but he may try to convince the teacher by some kind of bluff, or it may be even by cheating. But whatever the means he adopts for convincing the teacher, he will have at least some temporary mind-set for that."

"Why do you say his mind-set for the study or for the cheating, as the case may be, will be temporary?"

"Because he is really intent on getting to the football. That's the end for him.

The study and fooling the teacher are only means. For the football he has what we called an *inner* urge. For what he does to convince the teacher there is only an *outer* urge."

"What is the effect of the rebelliousness?"

"It acts, as it were, on the side of the football urge. The two work together. They are almost parts of the same thing."

"Yes, I see that, but what is the effect of the rebellious spirit on these temporary sets? Doesn't the feeling of opposition keep him from trying to persuade the teacher?"

"I don't think so. I was wondering if this rebellious feeling of opposition doesn't work against the boy's studying, but in favor of his fooling the teacher."

"I believe you are right. The teacher undertakes to force the boy to study. To get ahead of the teacher would avoid the study and so afford an outlet for the boy's spirit of opposition. Yes, the rebelliousness works against study, but for getting ahead of the teacher."

"But suppose the boy is in the end forced to study, is there or is there not any set for the problem solving?"

"Well, let's see. Suppose one of the problems involved a long subtraction. Will the boy remember throughout that he is subtracting, or will he forget and either begin adding or have to go back and ascertain anew what he is trying to do?"

"Certainly if he is to solve the problem he must in some measure have a mind-set that puts his mind on it. In such case he probably would go ahead consistently in his subtraction."

"But the contrary mind-set roused by the coercion would interfere with this mind-set, wouldn't it?"

"Yes, as a rule the contrary mind-set

interferes to some extent with his attention to the arithmetic, at times so much so as to prevent anything but a very mechanical sort of attention. In other cases there would be less interference. In still others he might really give pretty good attention to the arithmetic."

"Would it not depend on the strength of the contrary set and on the degree of rebelliousness, as to how much interference there would be?"

"Exactly so."

"This discussion sounds very reasonable, but I thought we were to hear about the psychology of learning under coercion. You seem to have overlooked that."

"Suppose we take the seven definite steps in purposeful learning under a strong favorable mind-set as given above, and discuss the effect of coercion under those heads."

"All right. In that case we had a strong mind-set-to-an-end that favored, as you say, the learning. How is it here?"

"We have here also a strong mind-set, but it is opposed to his staying in or studying. We find also a certain temporary and relatively weak mind-set for the problems. The stronger the rebelliousness that attends the opposed mind-set, the weaker this mind-set for arithmetic is likely to be."

1. "What about the definite end in view?"

"There is one main end, to get to the football. There may be a kind of subordinate end to solve the prob-
In coercion
diverse ends
lems, but there may be in place of this a plan of deceiving the teacher."

2. "What about the inner urge?"

"The inner urge is to get to the football. There may be a derived and temporary inner urge to deceive or otherwise cheat the teacher, but any urge for the problems would in this case be typically outer. It will let up as soon as the external pressure is removed."

3 and 4. "What about readinesses and unreadinesses?"

"Each mind-set will have its own system of readinesses and unreadinesses; and
Resulting
unreadiness
these will greatly interfere with each other. So long as the contrary mind-set is acting—especially so long as the rebellious feeling is present—it will be psychologically impossible for good arithmetical thinking to go on. The thoughts just won't come with the necessary fullness and freedom. Under such circumstances it would be only relatively mechanical work that could result."

"Won't there be actual readiness for thwarting activities? Don't pupils under such conditions actually take to a kind of sabotage, as they say in labor discussions?"

"There certainly is likely to arise readiness for thwarting activities, and sabotage is not an inapt phrase to describe many of them. But often an older and homelier word is even more apt."

"You mean cheating, I suppose, and you are certainly right. Many children have
Tendency to
deception
under unwise management found arising within very great 'readiness for thwarting activities.' In answer to such readiness, hitherto and otherwise good children may find a natural if unholy satisfaction in 'beating' the teacher?"

"Yes, here as elsewhere the law of Readiness holds: Where a bond is ready to act, to act gives satisfaction."

"And does this satisfaction fix the cheating habit in these children?"

"Yes, unless there is some counteracting annoyance. Only we mustn't say they will surely cheat under all other conditions. The rule of no general automatic transfer holds here as well as elsewhere."

5. "And what is success for this boy?" "It all depends on the ends set up. The main success, if success there be, will

Ambiguous success

be getting out with the other boys. There may be the subsidiary success in his efforts at cheating, or the milder success at the problem solving."

6. "And what about the satisfaction which attends success?"

"Each success carries its own satisfaction, the amount of which depends on the strength of the corresponding mind-set. If the boy can beat the teacher, considerable satisfaction; he has got out and he did it by his own contrivance. If he solves the problems and so gets out, the main satisfaction may still be in getting out. The satisfaction in the problem solving as such is lessened in the degree that he has felt resentfully that his work has been under compulsion."

7. "What, then, shall we conclude about the learning that results from coercion?"

"First, in so far as the opposed mind-set begets unreadiness for the problem solving,

Coercion gives a less promise of success

in that degree the necessary thoughts are unlikely to arise. There is then danger that psychologically he will be unable to do a good job of thinking. In other words, his chances of successful solution (as the teacher counts success) are lessened in the degree that the boy feels opposition and rebellion.

"Second, the satisfaction that results from successful problem solving (supposing he does succeed) is likely the smaller,

Less satisfaction

both on account of the lack of readiness for the necessary effort because of his opposition to the coercion, and also by reason of the overshadowing feeling of satisfaction that he has at length escaped coercion.

"Third, since the satisfaction is small there is small learning. The law of Effect[1]

Less learning

must play its part. There may even have been built up a growing distaste for the whole subject of mathematics. If so this is merely the negative side of the same law."

"Do you mean that the annoyance of the whole proceeding may disgust him with

Aversion may result

mathematics? It isn't the mathematics that is at fault, it was his own previous idleness or lack of attention to duty. Won't the annoyance thus serve to keep him from being idle again? Why do you pick out the mathematics to suffer?"

"It all depends upon the boy's own reaction. If he lays the blame on his idleness, he will less likely be idle next time. If he blames the teacher and the dryness of mathematics, then he may build an aversion to both. Which he will likely blame, you know as well as I; but the law of Effect will work in any case."

"Do you conclude that coercion has no place in school?"

"No, I wouldn't say that. I think

The place of coercion

it has a place. But I would say that if my coercion is of such kind as to arouse a strong feeling of active resentment, then I

---

[1] As we saw in the November issue: When any response is made, the tendency so to respond is strengthened or weakened according as the response is attended by satisfaction (success) or annoyance (failure). If this is continued often enough and consistently enough, an effective habit or aversion is in time built. The stronger the satisfaction or annoyance the sooner is the habit or aversion built.

need look for little useful learning to result directly, and there are other possible results to be positively feared. If at any particular time teaching is my aim I must at that time either avoid coercion or I must so use it as not to arouse the contrary set that spoiled, as we have just seen, the most of John's learning."

"But haven't we heard of children who practised piano playing under coercion and later came to love their playing? What about them? And what about holding up standards? Isn't that necessary and isn't it coercion?"

"Those are questions that we must face, but we'll have to postpone them to next time."

(To be continued)

AN EXPERIMENT IN COÖPERATION
V. Classroom Technique in Composition

JAMES F. HOSIC

Associate Professor of Education, Teachers College, Columbia University

Once a general policy as to the work in composition had been laid out, the task before us became that of developing an effective classroom technique. This required, to a degree, the breaking of new ground, although much guidance was to be had from the books of reference mentioned in the outline course of study which had been prepared by a committee and printed for distribution by one of the school presses, as was related in the article next preceding this one. Books alone cannot, however, work a reform; personal contacts are indispensable. And so it proved in this case. School conferences, followed by much visiting from room to room, were necessary to turn the trick.

What may happen when too much dependence is placed on the printed word comes out clearly in an incident which occurred outside of the group of schools constituting the English centers. A teacher in the eighth grade, following as she believed the plan of procedure advised by Mr. Sheridan, held her pupils for six weeks strictly to the rule of "three grammatical sentences," no more, no less. Then she flew the signal of distress, complaining that the children's speeches were halting, stilted, and uninteresting.

It developed, however, that a boy who had appeared more inhibited than the others really had a capital story to tell about an exciting experience through which he had passed while spending some months with his uncle on a ranch in the West. The class was asked to select the most important part of the speaker's composition and settled at once upon the sentence referring to the charge of a wild bull. The pupils were encouraged to ask questions and they soon elicited numerous valuable details, even to the shrill whistle which had successfully summoned aid and which was finally reproduced, to the general satisfaction of the class and the surprise of the neighbors. At last the boy stepped to the front of the room and in a series of terse and forceful sentences told a short but really thrilling tale of adventure on the sagebrush plains. He did what the teacher had hoped for but did not know how to get. She had made the attack too formal.

At the other pole were the practices of those who cherished the ideal of "freedom," which, being interpreted, means not rational control but merely childish babbling on. With this view all is well if only the pupil talks. When he pauses he should be encouraged to "tell us a little more," though what he is saying may have no semblance of beginning, middle, or end. This is the doctrine of "practice makes perfect" without the qualification of "judicious" to save it. Possibly some of the bores who speak in public but never know where to begin or when to quit could trace the beginnings of their style to those primary grades in which they had "freedom" of utterance.

Some children are undoubtedly shy when they enter school and are slow to respond when invited to speak. The solution lies, however, not in calling out rambling reproduction of stories or in temporary neglect, but in asking the child to tell *one* thing he does to help his mother or *one* thing his pet does. Such a request can be complied with, and it has the priceless value of tending directly to expression in complete sentences and to the development of the "sentence sense." Even pupils who are ready, confident, and fluent may well be stimulated in this way.

LIMITING THE SUBJECT

In any case the secret of starting children on the way toward speaking to the point in good, clean-cut sentences, as Sheridan and Mahoney have pointed out, lies in aiding them to select at first small and definite subjects or aspects of subjects.

The following are good illustrations:

When the members of a class in the second grade were asked to tell something of their recent experiences, one small girl responded, "Last Sunday we went to Lincoln Park. We saw a big snake. It was coiled up. It looked like a rug." In a similar situation another child in a third grade said, "Last night I had to go to the store for my mother. It was raining. But I didn't get wet. I had my mother's umbrella."

Let him who thinks such achievements as these on the part of little children of only average ability and limited linguistic background too commonplace to be worthy of notice ask himself whether speaking thus connectedly on a small subject and speaking in complete and separate periods is not likely to carry over helpfully into the recitations in the subjects other than English, and whether such a sense of form and sequence is not a good foundation for a more elaborate superstructure to be erected later.[1] At all events those who were engaged in the work of the centers became more and more convinced of it. For the tendency toward connected and more comprehensive answers became ever more marked in all classes. Monosyllabic replies and amorphous collections of run-on sentences were less and less in evidence. The small and definite subject was found to be the thing to begin with in any class, no matter what the grade, in which habits of good speaking had not yet been formed.

THE USE OF TITLES AND REVISION
ON THE SPOT

As soon as possible, certainly by the beginning of the third grade, the pupils

[1] No one, of course, will fail to realize how much such small happenings meant to the children.

were encouraged to think of suitable titles for their compositions. The title tends to hold the speaker to his point—indeed, it helps him to know definitely what his point is. It helps the audience, moreover, both to listen thoughtfully and to make suggestions for the improvement of the speech. On one occasion a fourth grader chose for his title, "The Christmas Turkey." He began by saying, "I got up very early Christmas morning," and then proceeded to tell about the big turkey that was put into the oven to roast. When he had finished, his classmates hastened to inquire why he had mentioned his getting up so early, whereat he replied that he had wanted to see the turkey placed in the oven. "You should put that in," said they, and he did.

Such discussion of speeches and appropriate revision on the spot were found to be essential to improvement. As soon as the speaker had finished, the question was raised, "What did he try to do?" followed by, "Did he do it?" or "Could he do it better and if so, how?" By focussing attention on one main quality at a lesson, by a persistent follow-up from day to day, and by permitting speakers from time to time to say it again, taking advantage of the suggestions offered while they were fresh in mind, decided progress was made.

The process is not unlike that of the time-honored revision of written work, but it requires greater tact. Only the more courageous pupils should be put through the ordeal the first time or two. The procedure easily becomes formal, of course, and the teacher must be on guard against mere routine. Needless to say a quick ear for effects is required, and discriminating judgment as to the possibilities in each instance. The fact that so few teachers have had similar training themselves is a real handicap. Nevertheless the technique of oral revision can be learned—if there is guidance and encouragement at hand.

One of the chief problems of oral composition is that of finding your story. Learning what to say and what not to say became one of the main objectives of the children's work. For example, a boy in the third grade sought to tell about a picnic. He presented the usual string of commonplaces, to the effect that he rose in the morning, had his breakfast, went by wagon to the picnic grounds, had lunch and returned. "So nothing happened!" exclaimed the teacher. The boy stood crestfallen for a moment and then looked up with animation and said, "Oh, yes! We went fishing." Here was a lead. A judicious follow-up brought out the fact that the speaker's brother had seen his float go under, had boasted of the catch he was about to make, and had pulled hard on his line, only to land at last a large bundle of brown paper. Being advised by the class to call his story "The Fish We Didn't Catch," the pupil then told the incident without waste of words.

The same method elicited from a Polish boy in the fifth grade the following narrative: "Last night I bought the meat for supper. When the package was handed to me, I put it under my arm and started home. The package slipped out from under my arm and dropped to the walk. Before I could pick it up, a dog grabbed it and ran away with it. I had to buy another piece of meat. So last night the meat cost twice as much as it should have done. That dog must have thought that I was a millionaire." Many of the members of this class displayed a similar sense of values and put in an interpretative touch which raised a plain narrative somewhat above the merely commonplace.

ATTENTION TO STYLE

The pupils were quick to recognize and condemn monotonous imitation of style. The attention of the members of a second grade was called to the fact that each speaker began his story like the one before him. Couldn't they avoid this? Assuredly they could. The next speaker took time to collect herself and then opened with a new pattern. Those who followed were obliged to do likewise or meet with adverse criticism.

In the upper grades attention was directed somewhat to the choice of the right word. "John *walked* through the door just now," remarked the teacher. "How else might he have come?" "Run, jumped, dashed, crept, sidled, backed, slid, bounced, or burst," cried the pupils. "Which of these words will best express the meaning?" continued the teacher, and so the discussion went on. With the purpose of the speaker as the chief criterion, rational decisions were rendered and the process of criticism made to seem both clear and sensible.

AS TO GRAMMAR

But what to do with grammar? Could English be called worthy which did not include instruction in the nature and functions of the "parts of speech," phrases, clauses, etc.? The following incident will illustrate in part the answer that was made to these questions. After three or four speeches had been heard in a seventh grade class, one concerned with an automobile accident in the country was selected for study. The speaker had begun with the sentence, "One day we were going to the country, when it rained." "What was the important thing this boy had to tell?" asked the teacher. "How the rain made the road slippery and caused the accident," the pupils replied. "Very well, then, notice his first sentence. Can you improve it?" "Yes," they responded. "Put the important part in the important place and say, 'One day when we were going to the country, it rained.'" "You mean," said the teacher, "that you would put the principal idea in the principal clause and the subordinate idea in the subordinate clause." And thus a spade was called a spade and a grammatical concept was brought into a functional relation.

WRITING FOLLOWS SPEAKING

Following in the wake of the oral composition, the written composition gave little trouble. Knowing well what they wanted to write, the pupils had little trouble in writing it. Composition was regarded as primarily a process of thinking, and writing as a process of transcribing what has already been thought. Just as reading is at first mainly finding on the printed page the familiar words of spoken discourse, so writing, as far as children are concerned, is mainly a process of putting speech on paper.

In our experiment it was so defined. Writing was taken to mean merely the mechanical process of expressing speech in graphic form. At first and especially in the earlier grades only that which had first been spoken was written. This policy enabled the writer to give almost his whole mind to the new and difficult medium and the outcome was highly gratifying. Mistakes of any kind in mechanics became more and more exceptional. We were all convinced that the royal road to good mechanics is through well-organized oral work as the foundation.

This seems to be particularly true of the so-called sentence sense. Those who have not seen the process are sometimes incredulous. One such said, "But how can you teach the sentence until you have writing, with the use of capitals and periods?" "Oh," replied one of the initiated, "when the pupils speak, you can hear periods dropping on the floor all about!" It does appear to be true that the sentence as a unit is much more easily apprehended in oral than in written composition. There is, moreover, the immediate reaction of the class, and social disapproval shows up the bad construction at once and emphatically.

Many will think the program which I have just sketched too simple. Why not fill the pupils' minds with literary stories and get long and beautiful compositions as a result? The answer is that you must have a good foundation before you build an ornate superstructure, and besides, telling beautiful stories which have been told to you is only a small part of an effective life. The work which I have attempted to describe was aimed at growth in power of expression in workaday situations and it succeeded. Stories have their place, however, in the language development of little children, as we at no time allowed ourselves to forget.

A REFRESHING SUMMER SCHOOL

JAMES M. GRAINGER

State Normal School, Farmville, Virginia

Summer school! Ordinarily the words connote a hot season of confinement within the halls of a "higher institution of learning," where distraught but ambitious teachers, already frayed to a frazzle, further deplete their powers by wildly pursuing four or five courses, sometimes more— usually lecture courses of the type made in Germany. They do it because the school authorities back home require it and they have a mistaken notion that such flagellation is immensely beneficial and is necessary for professional growth.

The teacher usually comes out of such an experience with a sense, perhaps, of having superficially "covered a lot of ground," and she may have got a smattering of information and a medley of new suggestions and tricks of the trade. But her energies have been dissipated rather than conserved.

Mind and body have become exhausted. No really sound growth has taken place and no initiative remains for carrying into practice the new ideas she may have caught on the fly. When she returns to her school, she settles back into the same old rut, sadder but not much wiser for the experience. Next summer she goes and does likewise again.

The summer sessions of the Normal School at Hyannis, Massachusetts, however, are conceived and carried out in accordance with a sounder theory of the function of a teacher's vacation—the theory of *re-creation*. "Old Cape Cod" is justly famous as a summer playground of America and undoubtedly does the nation an invaluable service in this capacity. No one nowadays doubts the importance of true recreation among the essentials of the balanced life. But to the teachers of Massachusetts and other states who have attended the summer sessions of the Cape Cod Normal School at Hyannis during the past twenty-three years, the Cape has afforded recreation in a deeper sense. For through the regenerating influence of this remarkable vacation school thousands of teachers have been made over in mind and spirit and renewed in courage to serve their state in the high vocation of training American citizens.

Beyond question, the location of the Hyannis summer school on one of the most delightful sections of the New England coast gives it an immense advantage. The cool ocean breezes playing across the Cape from day to day bring just enough fog and rain to set off the many days of perfect "Hyannis weather" that are strung like jewels across the summer months. But the features which really distinguish Hyannis from the general run of summer schools and give it character are not physical. They have their root in the philosophy of life and of education underlying the institution and in the spirit in which the work and play are organized and administered under the leadership of the principal, Mr. W. A. Baldwin.

Some of the radical ideas in the subsoil of the school are axioms often heard in educational discussion but seldom applied in school: Education is life. Life is growth. Life and growth require breathing—not only *in* but also *out*. They require both activity and rest, work and play. Growth is not explosion. It is a gradual evolution and takes time. Sound growth is conditioned by all sorts of weather, sunshine and rain and wind—a variety of experiences in favorable combinations.

And strange to say, Principal Baldwin insists that teachers are really only human beings who grow just like all the rest of us. Those who come to summer school are usually very ambitious, but they should not dissipate their energies in too many kinds of work and should undertake only so much work as can be well done with a certain amount of deliberate daily application for a reasonable period of time. Many and varied courses are offered at Hyannis every summer, under able instructors; but no student can possibly undertake more than two. For instead of the brief hurried lecture periods usually found, each class meets for a "double period" of an hour and a half every morning and requires two hours or more of outside preparation daily. These long periods enable instructor and students to accomplish far more than the usual brief periods and with a greater sense of satisfaction, because they give the time allowance necessary for real thinking. Since only two of these double periods can be scheduled in the forenoon, with an intermission for the daily chapel or morning exercises, and there are no afternoon classes, it is obvious why no student can undertake more than two courses in one summer session. Students usually find that a single course of this kind gives them all the work they can do well, if they are to take advantage of the many opportunities that the sessions always offer outside of class work.

Another conserving and unifying influence in each session of the school is the "watchword." For years it has been the practice of the principal to select a term which would express a prominent or fundamental idea in the educational thinking of the year and to propose this to the faculty and students as the watchword for the work and the play of the summer session.

One summer the watchword was "seeking after truth," again it was "democracy," and again "participation." In 1919, the summer after the war in Europe, it was "reconstruction," and addresses at morning exercises, the faculty meetings, and class work were all directed toward the consideration of educational readjustments necessitated by the war.

In 1920 the watchword was "Americanization." On the first day of the summer session Principal Baldwin explained the significance of the word for the nation and for the state of Massachusetts, where the overwhelming proportion of foreign-born population made Americanization the crying need. But the problem concerned the native-born as well, and was seen to be as broad as the nation, on the one hand, and as specific as the daily living of the individual citizen or the smallest child in school, on the other. Mr. Baldwin urged that students and instructors should tie up their thinking during the session with the great fundamental need suggested by the watchword.

From that hour "Americanization" became the center of interest around which all of the various activities of the session revolved, the problem which all sought to solve, the project which united all in a common effort. Every undertaking took color from the patriotic purpose of the whole community. At the daily assemblies, or morning exercises, which were always anticipated with interest as an essential event of each day, addresses and informal talks were given by members of the faculty, local ministers, and visiting educators on the manifold aspects of Americanization. The class work likewise was consciously directed toward discovering and showing how the various kinds of educational work may contribute to the making of better Americans.

The largest classes in the school dealt with the training of teachers for Americanization work among foreigners and were conducted by instructors from the State Department of Education as a part of its state-wide Americanization program. This work, of course, carried out directly the purpose of the watchword, in one of its aspects. To no less extent the courses in psychology, pedagogy, and special methods in the main branches of kindergarten, primary, and secondary education and supervision, each found new meanings and applications in the patriotic impulse, while a number of the courses treated institutions or procedures which are peculiar to American education and therefore definitely significant in Americanization. Among these were the junior high school, the continuation school, practical arts and evening schools, the project and problem methods, the socialized recitation, and that ingenious Yankee development, mental measurements. All of these were pointed constantly toward serving the peculiar needs of America in education at the present time. It is much to be able to say for the watchword of the session that it unified all of these varied interests.

Furthermore, Hyannis does not preach American and practice—German methods! To exemplify the underlying principle of the truly American type of school procedure, free and equal self activity and participation on the part of each individual, the classes were conducted in the most democratic fashion. The instructor eschewed the pedagogical despot imposing his own ideas or those of the learned authorities on the minds of his students. He chose rather to serve as a helpful leader seeking after truth along with his students. Many of them were themselves teachers of great ability and wide experience, and, if effectively drawn out, each was capable of making some contribution to the thinking of the group. Hence the instructor, instead of delivering lectures on which the students took down voluminous notes, encouraged class discussion in which the experiences of the students were brought forward and interpreted in the light of the best educational thinking of the day. For we learn best not by experience alone nor by thinking alone, but by a continuous interplay of experience and thinking about that experience. Since most of the classes were purposely small, it was possible for each student to participate in his own way in this democratic sharing of ideas—and he was expected to do so. This procedure had the double advantage of requiring everyone to work out his own salvation and of enabling each to seek, with expert guidance and the help of many sympathetic minds, the solution of his own individual problems in Americanization.

From this it will be seen that the work of the school is so conducted as to take full advantage of the rich personal contacts and relationships which are among the most valuable experiences in such an institution. Among the students the percentage of graduates from colleges and normal schools is unusually high and there are always numbers of able and progressive teachers, principals, and superintendents from Massachusetts and the surrounding states present. Dr. John Dewey, at one time a member of the somewhat cosmopolitan summer faculty, said that he found the students here better equipped for the work he required than any class he had taught. Hyannis "is a real school" as the catalogue insists; but the aim of its work

is not cramming of the mind—or the notebook—with a rehash of scrambled facts and ideas. It aims to promote deliberate purposeful thinking about practical educational problems of the day, and thus "to meet the needs of the teachers of an evolving Democracy."

Summer work conducted under such circumstances brings regeneration, growth, and social efficiency.

But the studies and classroom work make only half of a summer session at Hyannis. The other half is play. For in the Hyannis scheme of symmetrical living, work is deliberately balanced with educative recreation. Under the discerning leadership of the principal, students and faculty merge into one big beautiful family, living and growing together in helpful comradeship. Everywhere there is evidence of happy coöperation in intelligent service. This is what has come to be known as "the Hyannis spirit." In this spirit the classes seek earnestly to solve the problems of individuals and of the state and the nation in education. And in this spirit everybody joins freely in the enjoyment of the various forms of social recreation and outdoor sports, directed by the student committee on recreation. Sometimes the recreation grows directly out of the work, as in nature study walks, games and dancing, and dramatization. But instead of the majority sitting on the bleachers to watch a few players, as in the modern commercialized school and college athletics, everybody takes part in the kind of sport he most enjoys. Though hardly typical of American sport at the present time, this plan of recreation is distinctly the democratic plan and will prevail when American sport outgrows commercialism and becomes truly Americanized.

During the session of 1920 the influence of "Americanization," the watchword of the session, was quite as evident in the recreations as in the class work. Early in the first week the entire school was effectively organized for recreational activities. The method was very simple but particularly instructive. Each person made a list of the various activities in which he would like to join. These were tabulated by a student committee, elected for the purpose, and groups were formed for carrying on each kind of recreation. These groups elected their own leaders who should see to it that everyone could find ample arrangements and congenial companions for the enjoyment of his favorite recreation. By this democratic organization everyone was enabled to form enjoyable friendships with people of like interests and to get full benefit of the ideal location of Hyannis for outdoor pleasures.

At the Normal School Beach and elsewhere hundreds enjoyed the delightful waters of the "South Shore" every sunny afternoon. Everybody went swimming. Sailing parties and boating, both by day and by moonlight, also attracted great numbers. Groups of nature lovers on excursions or hikes discovered for themselves the flowers of the locality, such as the star-like Sabbatia and the wild orchids; they studied the birds, insects, and water creatures or admired the scenery which has made Cape Cod an artists' paradise. Beautiful secluded spots for quiet meditation were found by pensive individuals, while those more sociably inclined went on automobile trips to historic Plymouth of the Pilgrims, to Provincetown, to the government fisheries station at Woods Hole, or to other places of special interest. Everywhere cameras were in evidence as one of the best means of recording, for future enjoyment, the pleasures and associations of the day. Of course tennis, baseball, basket-ball, and other athletic games each brought out its quota of enthusiastic devotees, as in every summer school. They were in charge of special committees which arranged match games and tournaments.

Regular weekly socials were held by the whole school family besides many class picnics, beach parties, clam bakes, and other gatherings of smaller groups. They contributed largely to the enjoyment of the happy personal relationships of the summer. A few of these socials were held in-doors but the out-doors was preferred and especially the seashore, where frequent camp-fires in the evenings lit up circles of faces shining with the pleasures of singing and story-telling in the open. The big weekly socials were under the direction of the faculty. A new committee took charge each week and enlisted the help of student leaders. These socials differed according to circumstances and the places where they were held. One, a big Fourth of July picnic, occurred on the seashore at the colony of tent-houses where many of the school people live during the summer sessions. Besides the usual games, folk-dancing, and supper on the beach, a beautiful little pageant of the Pilgrim story was enacted on the shore of Lewis Bay by the class in physical education. Other socials took place on the school campus, "under the willows," or inside the buildings. Ridiculous applications of mental measurements and psychic phenomena featured one, a minstrel show impromptu marked another. At each of these social gatherings new talent developed and new and delightful ways of having good times together evolved. Everyone realized afresh in his own experience the immense value of play in education.

"This has been the most wonderful social experience of my life," exclaimed an enthusiastic teacher from Worcester, after one of the school socials. And she voiced the sentiments of hundreds who, through the socials at Hyannis, have got new light on how to live and how to make a school a center of social growth and progress. The only wonderful thing about the Hyannis social life is that it is absolutely free from anything like class distinctions. All participate. Actually to encounter such a condition in real life is, to many teachers, a refreshing experience, even in America.

Hyannis has power to rejuvenate those who catch her spirit because, having accepted the principle that education is growth and growth must come from within the organism, she lives by it. Activities prescribed according to preconceived notions of the faculty are replaced by those which spring from the actual needs felt by the students. It has always been the policy of Principal Baldwin to encourage all sorts of worthy undertakings which the students want in connection with the summer school, to urge each student and instructor to participate freely in such as he can carry on happily and effectively, and to link up the class work and the recreations naturally with these activities. Thus the so-called project method, now widely advocated in educational circles, has long prevailed at Hyannis. The "watchword" converts the whole session into one big project, each class finds its own projects, and each individual his. It is like electrifying street-car service. Instead of being dragged along by the teacher, the classes advance naturally and spontaneously by motive powers

discovered within themselves. They have a sense of real value in the work they do because they see how it contributes directly to their needs.

Among the many projects carried out during the summer of 1920, four will serve as examples of different types of instruction through service performed in this way. First, a school paper, to which practically all members of the school family subscribed, enabled those interested in writing, especially the students in English, to get valuable experience in composition and to use their ability for a practical purpose. Second, a school concert, organized under the direction of the music department, brought together and exercised much musical talent for the pleasure of the whole school. Third, students who wished to express their gratitude for what Hyannis had done for them carried out a campaign to raise contributions for the Student Loan Fund, which helps worthy students to take the course in the Normal School. The campaign gave valuable experience in a type of organized effort much used nowadays, and by raising several hundred dollars served a worthy purpose in recruiting for the profession and making it possible for a number of young people to be trained for teaching. Fourth, a school pageant was composed and staged to give expression to the conception of Americanism which the summer's study of the subject had developed. The work was done chiefly through committees elected from the English, the music, and the physical education classes, but it was so arranged that the entire school was drawn into the actual presentation. The effectiveness of the pageant in uniting a community and expressing its ideals was only one of many lessons learned through this project.

Actual participation in school work carried on with the motive power such projects supply gives teachers a new joy in the service which they become assured they can render by tying up school work with life outside, and a new faith in the efficacy of teaching as a life work. That this joy and this faith are sadly needed in the teaching profession today is clearly attested by the recent withdrawal of thousands of teachers into more lucrative occupations. No doubt this hejira found its immediate occasion in low salaries, high costs, and war-time opportunities to perform services of undoubted usefulness elsewhere. But lack of faith in teaching itself as an effective way to spend one's life had more to do with it. For faith makes the difference between doleful drudgery and joyful service. Changing standards and a disquieting scrutiny into the aims, materials, and methods of education in recent years have helped to undermine both the confidence of the public, whence come the salaries, and the very faith of many conscientious teachers in the work of the schools. "Where there is no vision, the people perish." Until faith in the practical efficacy of teaching is restored, the profession will remain poorly supplied with devoted workers. To renew the teachers' faith in themselves and their great mission, summer by summer, is recognized as the inspiring project of the summer sessions at Hyannis.

"The education of the young child," writes Principal Baldwin, "means to us at Hyannis to encourage such activities each day as the best present development of the child demands." And summer students at Hyannis have learned that this is also his guiding principle for the education of those older children who come to his school summer by summer to be recreated. "Except ye become as a little child"—only to become a pupil and get the pupil's point of view is a kind of rebirth, but the means of growth also must be supplied. To this end the school seeks to do three things for its summer students: (1) it seeks to guide them in such thinking, and studying, as will be vital and helpful to them as thoughtful teachers; (2) it seeks to give them an opportunity for true recreation and to show them how to find and use such opportunities elsewhere; (3) it seeks, through the kind of life they lead there as serviceable members of a democratic school community, to make them better citizens in the great democracy. These are the things which "the best present development" of the children demands. To spend a summer at Hyannis means, all in all, to live fully for a season on a high plane.

A thoughtful Boston teacher has written recently, "Last summer I came to Hyannis for the first time, and I know now that my experiences there have done more toward making me a better American than any other single influence in my life." Hundreds of others will give the same testimony. Consider the influence exerted by all the thousands of teachers who have attended the Hyannis summer school during the past twenty-three years and have gone back better citizens themselves, to make better citizens for Massachusetts and for America. To paraphrase Dean Swift, "Whoever can make two good citizens grow where only one grew before deserves better of America and does more essential service to his country than the whole race of politicians put together." The Normal School at Hyannis is really the most serviceable means on the Cape for true recreation.

THE WORK OF
THE BOSTON MILK EDUCATIONAL COMMITTEE
AND THE NEW ENGLAND DAIRY AND FOOD COUNCIL

W. P. B. LOCKWOOD

*Head of the Dairy Department of the Massachusetts Agricultural College and
Managing Director of the New England Dairy and Food Council*

Our nation, with other nations of the world, when she found herself in a world war, began to question how she was to feed her armies and her people at home so as to keep them in good health. She had already told us that in 1912 about five per cent of the children in American schools were more than seven per cent below the accepted averages of height and weight for their age. This number was rapidly increasing during the years from 1912 to 1918 and 1920, when from twenty-five per cent to thirty-three per cent of the school children of the United States fell below this accepted average of physical development and health condition. During these same years Dr. E. V. McCollum of the Johns Hopkins University brought before scientific people the results of intensive experiments and studies showing that certain foods promoted growth and health, thus acting as protective foods.

He has proved beyond doubt that butter fat contains growth substances not found in other food fats except egg yolk, that a second essential substance for maintenance of health is found in all natural foodstuffs, and that the addition of certain leaves and seeds of plants produces great improvement in development and health. He says that as the result of very numerous trials he has become convinced that there are two lines of procedure by means of which satisfactory diets can be made up. These diets are formed by the combination of those parts of the plants which are storage organs, with liberal amounts of the leaf of the plant or by use of such mixtures along with milk or egg; milk is better than egg.

To help bring this message of Dr. Mc-Collum's before the public the Boston Milk Campaign Committee of trained workers, coöperating with the Massachusetts State Department of Health, Boston Department of Health, Massachusetts Agricultural College, Federal and State Department of Agriculture, Boston Dietetic Bureau, Boston Chapter of the American Red Cross and other agencies, began its work three years ago.

The influence of this undertaking was felt in a permanent increase in the use of milk in establishments where talks, posters, and literature had been given. One large company, realizing the need of the use of more milk by its workers, gave a ten ounce glass instead of an eight ounce one and reduced the cost from four to two cents per glass. The company reported a one hundred per cent increase in sales during the year. The active efforts of the committee ceased, however, on account of lack of permanent organization and financial support. The results of the work already done showed the advisability of more work in Boston with the possibility of extending the enterprise to other New England cities and possibly to the country and town schools.

In June, 1920, a group of interested people met to start the organization to functioning in a more general and larger way and on a permanent basis. The result was the organization of the New England Dairy and Food Council, working through the Boston Milk Educational Committee, formerly the Boston Milk Campaign, the purposes of which are as follows:

A. To collect and disseminate information relative to the food value, health value, and economy in the use of milk and dairy products and other food products.

B. To collect and disseminate information concerning the production, distribution, and consumption of milk and dairy products and other food products.

How can this be done? First, it is essential to reach the children and, through them, the parents; and second, it is also essential to reach the mother, father, home keeper, or young man or woman directly.

To reach the children entails two objects: first, to impress the child that there is happiness and success in health and that health, first of all, means supplying the body with material for its growth, repair, and fuel to keep it in running order.

As stories never fail to interest children, it again becomes an effective method of teaching the rules of the health game to impress upon small children what milk will do for them and to show older boys and girls that it is reasonable and logical to supply the body with the right material if we expect a normal, healthy body. The New England Dairy and Food Council has such stories for use called "The Quest for the Fountain of Health," "The Milk Fairies," and "The Milk Way Is the Health Way."

"The Quest for the Fountain of Health" is illustrated by colored pictures or colored lantern slides. This story tells us about Peggy and Paul, a girl and boy of ten or twelve years of age, who are very unhappy because of the lack of robust health. So they both start out to seek for the Fountain of Health. The robins whom they meet by the roadside are taking their morning baths, and drinking plenty of clean, cold water. Next, they meet the good Mother Hen with her Chicks, who are eating bread and milk. They find Tabby Cat washing her face and paws before eating her mid-morning lunch of milk, and Sport, a collie dog, is taking his exercise out of doors. He invites the children to the Food Pageant. There Peggy and Paul become acquainted with Captain Milk, who leads the group of muscle-building foods, and with Captain Milk, leader of the energy foods, bone and tooth-building foods, and also leader of the growth and health foods. But, not satisfied with what all these friends have told them, the children go on. Later, they meet Wise Old Owl, who advises them to rest and watches over them until they are ready to go on. Next they meet Bossy Calf, who feels very sure that the Fountain of Health is her Mother. She sends them across the green field where they are greeted by Buttercup, The COW, the Foster-Mother of all the world, with these words:

Welcome, little boy and girl,
I'm glad you've come to me,
For I can tell, you need my help
If strong you want to be.
The many friends you've found today
Have done their very best
To help you on the road to health,
But you must do the rest.

The second story, which never fails to interest the smaller children, is the "Milk Fairy Story." The little school boy and school girl enjoy hearing about Johnnie who does not like milk. One day, exhausted by playing soldier with his boy friends, his mother sends him out to lie down in the shade to rest and to cool off while she prepares his dinner. Then, as he drops off to sleep, the tree nearby turns into a large bottle of milk and fairies come to him, each represented by dolls attractively dressed, who bear the names of Sugar, Fat, Captain Protein, Mineral Twins, Water, and the Magic Twins or Vitamines. Each in turn tells Johnnie his name and what he will do for him if he will only drink milk. Then as Johnnie awakes from his dream, he is called in to dinner and his reward for asking for milk and telling his mother of his dream is a very surprised and happy mother, who is delighted that her boy is going to drink milk.

The third story, "The Milk Way Is the Health Way," used for older boys and girls, is illustrated by charts or lantern slides. The boys and girls are told that their bodies are human machines and need food for construction, repair, and fuel for running. The lesson teaches that certain foods supply material for muscles and flesh, others for teeth and bones, others keep the body warm and create energy, while still others promote growth and health. Growth foods are essential, as each boy and girl realizes when he reads the charts showing the number of pounds that should be gained yearly at different ages. Milk, the All-Round Food, plays its important part with vegetables, fruits, starchy, sugar, and fat foods and protein foods. Another way of measuring the value of milk with other foods is by graphic illustrations of the calorific returns of milk compared with coffee, also by the picture "A Race for Life," two boys starting the day with their breakfasts, one of coffee and bread and butter; the other, a dish of cereal and a glass of milk. The drawings show most

clearly which boy is the winner. "The Two Dogs," showing the difference in growth of the one fed wisely and the other fed unwisely, never ceases to tell its lesson. Thus the message comes home that "our bodies are made from the foods we eat. What kind of a body do you want?"

The second means of spreading the word of the food value, health value, and economy in the use of milk and dairy products is to reach young men and women, mothers, fathers, and home keepers directly. This message tells of the body construction, muscles, bone, alimentary canal and its process of handling food; then, the part that the protein foods, energy foods, mineral foods, and health promoting foods play in the repair and upkeep of our bodies. Dr. Howe, of the Forsyth Dental Infirmary, Boston, has added greatly to this message by giving us the use of a set of lantern slides, telling of his experiments which show the effects of foods on the teeth and bone structure of the body. Then, too, it is of interest to many money spenders to know that certain foods give greater return in nourishment for the same amount of money. This is shown by the New York A. I. C. P. charts and pictures comparing milk and cheese with other foods, the best division of five dollars spent in food for a good return in health, and again by the comparison of nourishment in clear soup, with a stew of meat and vegetables and a milk soup. Through these pictures there is proof that one should understand the importance of certain foods; that milk plays a very prominent part and surpasses in its power any other one food; that old and young should eat more milk because it is palatable, easily digested, and all parts are used by the body. It is a good

Foods which contain Vitamines, MILK, EGGS and GREEN VEGETABLES
Children in play, "The Quest for the Fountain of Health"

muscle builder, and energy and growth-giving food, and a good tooth and bone builder.

In addition to interest in these stories and messages, a great deal of interest is always shown by young and old in the lantern pictures on the care of the cows, improved farm conditions, the care and handling of milk by the producer, dealer, and consumer, and the methods of delivery in different countries.

It is worth while to note that in many of the schools the talks are followed up by similar lessons in language, hygiene, and drawing of posters and charts. There is a stimulation among the children to purchase milk in the schools where it is sold. It is a well-known fact that children like to do what they see others doing. Reports are given of children who never liked milk and had learned to like it because their playmates had milk to drink at school. One teacher reported that where fifteen bottles of milk were sold at first the number soon increased to sixty. Teachers likewise report that the school work of the last part of the morning is made easier, as the children do not show signs of fatigue. The talks influenced many principals and teachers to decide to serve milk in their schools, as they realized the value of educational food work and the need of milk as a food for growing children.

There are also two mechanical exhibits which tell their own story. The milk bottle exhibit, telling briefly the story of milk coming from the cow to the consumer, is attractively presented through colored pictures. The mechanical cow exhibit tells that the cow is an economical producer of human food, taking food that people cannot eat and making it into milk which is used as milk, butter, cheese, or ice cream. This exhibit moves:

1. The Cow puts her head down in the manger, then raises it.

2. She chews all the time.

3. Milk is represented as coming from the teats.

4. Milk is represented as flowing from pail to factory.

5. There is a continuous procession of products, milk, butter, ice cream, etc., from factory to American homes.

6. There is a continuous procession of people going from their homes to work.

7. The Milk Story is told on a roll 56 inches long.

Still another means of teaching the milk story is by the pageants, "The Milk Fairy Play" and "The Quest for the Fountain of Health," given by children at the summer playgrounds, open air schools, and at fairs. These plays aim to teach children and parents the health value of milk and its important place in the diets of all people. Costumes for these plays are gladly furnished by this organization.

Such statements as the following are coming to our attention very frequently. A mother made the following remark: "My child never liked milk and would not drink it until it was served in the schools. She now drinks a good quantity and is doing better work at school."

One mother came to the office for a sample set of literature. She was very much interested—said her child had brought home some splendid leaflets on milk. Mothers wondered why other schools in their town were not distributing the literature.

A principal writes: "Last year, the literature you sent me was a great spur to the homes. The reason I am ordering so liberally is because I wish to send something into every home about once in two months this year."

Such testimony of our work makes us feel that we are of real service to the schools and the community in making children and adults realize that certain foods do promote growth and health, protect the body, and that the selection and use of these foods help to build sound bodies and minds—both essentials for the foundation of success and happiness in life.

THE PROJECT METHOD AS APPLIED
TO PRIMARY ARITHMETIC

GRACE V. ROWLAND

State Normal School, Hyannis, Mass.

If one uses the project method in teaching, there must be activities "going on" in the schoolroom and they should be of such a nature that they are the expressions of the children's interests guided by the teacher and leading to a definite end. I say "guided" because one would not let an activitiy that is not educative be found in school even if it is the expression of the children's interests. The teacher will offer abundant opportunities for the development of the native capacities of the children along the lines of greatest growth. She will also create such an atmosphere that the children themselves will suggest activities in which they wish to engage, and here again her ability to guide in proper fields of activity will be taxed. She will be able to help the children select the best activities—those making for the greatest growth and development. In this kind of teaching—based upon project work—the children and teacher are living together and planning activities as groups of people do outside of school. The pupils are living in a democratic group (their class) and are learning to meet real situations right in school—just as they do in their home life and later in the larger groups of community, state, and nation.

This article is chiefly concerned with the application of this kind of work to one important part of a curriculum, namely, arithmetic. There are several ways in which the idea may be applied, but here we will consider only two of them: first, where arithmetic is a necessary part in the working out of a project and, second, where the arithmetic work itself takes the form of a project.

Let us first consider a number of purposeful activities which may occur in the primary grades and see how arithmetic played a necessary and important part in their development.

ACTIVITY I.

Situation—A second-grade class are interested in getting up a concert to which they wish to invite the first grade.

Planning and Executing	Subject Involved
a. Discussion of what will be done at the concert. (This includes songs, stories, etc.)	Language
b. Singing over songs, choosing those which they think the company will enjoy.	Music
c. Deciding what whole class, choruses, quartets, or soloists will sing.	
d. Deciding that programs are needed and making them out.	Language
e. Proposal to make programs for all; discussion of style, size, etc.; deciding upon style of cover.	Drawing
f. Making of several sample covers (volunteer individual work); choosing of the final cover; discussion of method of reproducing it; all making from dictated directions the final rectangle (shape and pattern of cover); planning size of inside sheet, etc.; making this by following dictated directions, similar to those above.	Handwork / Arithmetic

g. Making cover design.   *Drawing*

h. Finding need for material to *Language*
fasten cover and inside sheet
together; discussion of suita-
ble and inexpensive materi-   *Arithmetic*
als; hearing reports of groups
who have tried out one kind
of material and various ways
of tying same; choosing the
least expensive and yet attractive kind.

i. All figuring number of yards of *Arithmetic*
material needed for 75 pro-
grams; (possibly deciding
number of spools needed);
planning method of cutting
material so as to save waste;
cutting.

j. Writing programs.   *Writing*

k. Putting programs together and *Handwork*
tying them.

l. Concert.   *Music*

ACTIVITY II.

Situation.—The children of the first
grade wish to save money to buy
thrift stamps.

Planning and Executing   Subject Involved

a. Discussion about cost of one *Arithmetic*
stamp; place where one buys
stamps; what a child needs to *Language*
do when he goes to office for
one; where his money goes
and when he gets it back.

b. Study of thrift stamp book *Arithmetic*
combinations and sums which
make a quarter; individuals
bringing money saved and
class helping each to see how
much more he must save before he can buy a stamp.

Continued study of book,
counting number of stamps
to be bought before one
can have book filled.

ACTIVITY III.

Situation.—A third grade wish to have
a garden. (Outline here presupposes

situation where there are many gardens
planned by a supervisor. A plot with
plans for individual beds is given to the
teacher.)

Planning and Executing   Subject Involved

a. Deciding, as a class, upon the *Language*
kind of a garden; choosing of
kind of seeds for individual
beds.

b. Watching man plow and har- *Nature*
row the garden; study of the
reasons for this.

c. Laying out the boundaries of *Arithmetic*
the big garden, the paths and
individual plots.

d. Laying out on schoolroom floor *Arithmetic*
a diagram of the size of the
individual bed, *i. e.* 8' x 4';
measuring string to mark off
same in garden; finding number of rows possible for planting, number of stakes needed
for all rows; measuring and
cutting twine for same.
Winding string around stakes
ready for garden use.

(The rest of the activity—
planting, care of garden, etc.
is omitted in this account as
enough has been suggested
to show how arithmetic necessarily came into the project.)

ACTIVITY IV.

Situation.—A fourth grade class wish to
have a picnic after school some Friday
in June.

Planning and Executing   Subject Involved

a. Deciding when and where to go. *Language*

b. Planning how lunch is to be
carried so that each can do
his share; decision to let each
take his supper and all help
plan a class treat.

c. Finding cost of most popular *Arithmetic*
treats suggested, *e. g.*, ice
cream, lemonade, peanuts,

etc.; deciding reasonable amount to assess each member; discussion of possible guests and added assessment thereby incurred; deciding upon one treat within cost of what class wishes to pay.

d. Choosing committee to order *Language* amount of cream decided upon and selecting another group to collect assessments from children and turn over same to chairman of "ice cream committee"; decision to have all other class members divide themselves into groups for serving cream and gathering up plates.

e. Collecting dues and paying bills. *Arithmetic*

f. Picnic.

These simple but interesting projects show occasions of wholehearted and purposeful activities which consequently have been educative. Let us consider their results in knowledge gained in the field of arithmetic.

ACTIVITY I.

Arithmetic facts learned: inch and half inch; using both in construction; adding and subtracting without reduction; multiplication of small numbers; measuring, using feet and yards. ·

ACTIVITY II.

Arithmetic facts learned[1]: counting by ones to twenty-five, by fours to twenty, and by fives to twenty-five; learning combinations of twenty-five, e. g.—two dimes and one nickel, five nickels, two dimes and five pennies; adding to any sum below twenty-five enough to make twenty-five.

ACTIVITY III.

Arithmetic facts learned: measuring, using feet and yards; finding perimeter; changing inches to feet and feet to yards; multiplication table (probably of six, since it takes six inches to go around a common garden stake).

ACTIVITY IV.

Arithmetic facts learned: multiplication of numbers of two and three figures without reduction; subtraction, addition, and division with and without reduction; use of pounds, quarts, gallons, and dozen, with fractions of each.

Two chief attainments in arithmetic which life requires of most of us are accuracy and speed. We very readily see that the first skill is necessarily an aim and achievement on the part of the members planning these activities. Accuracy was essential to their judging of what courses to take, e. g., what treat to buy, what length of string was needed, what number of pennies, nickels, or dimes was needed before one could get another thrift stamp, etc. As far as these projects are concerned, the children's attitude and interest are such that they will use what accuracy and speed they can in their work, but not sufficient practice in any one kind of activity is *here* given to insure speed. One fundamental element to be kept in mind is the fact that a multitude of preceding and succeeding projects and games carefully planned will accomplish this. Drill work itself may take the form of a purposeful activity or project.

We have already seen a few instances of projects involving necessary and valuable arithmetic work along with other subjects, and now let us consider some which are almost entirely arithmetic activities.

[1] Note. Some of the very quickest ones will learn these facts (after much repetition), but most will only be able to give combinations, etc., with use of coins.

ACTIVITY I.

Situation.—A third grade wishes to make cards for second-grade seat work.

Brief description.—Discussion of kinds of cards to be made and consultation with teacher of second grade to see if certain cards would be suitable. Planning kinds of examples.

Facts involved.—Construction of cards (x inches long and x inches wide); review facts in addition or subtraction.

ACTIVITY II.

Situation.—A fourth grade wishes to keep weekly individual records of gain in speed of silent reading (as shown by tests given by teacher).

Brief description.—Discussion of kinds of records, decision as to kind to be used; keeping records; figuring individual gains; comparing gains as individuals and as groups.

Facts involved.—Construction of individual record sheets (using small fractions of inches); rapid counting; addition and subtraction with and without reduction.

ACTIVITY III.

Situation.—A first grade wishes to play circle bean bag (like regular game only two circles of varying sizes drawn on the floor are used instead of the bean bag board).

Brief description.—Explanation of game; choosing of sides; keeping of score by official score keeper and then by all.

Facts involved.—Making figures (one to ten); adding all combinations whose sum is not greater than ten.

ACTIVITY IV.

Situation.—A second grade wants to learn to tell time so that each one may know when to get ready for recess or gymnasium or when to get milk for the lunches.

Brief description.—Reading Roman numerals, telling hours, etc.

Facts involved.—Reading Roman numerals; number of hours in a day, minutes in an hour, etc.; telling hours, half hours, quarter hours, minutes.

These activities were wholehearted, purposeful ones in which children felt the "inner urge" to engage, and in each case there was a definite end in mind. There were opportunities for developing accuracy and speed as in other projects. Moreover, in the eight projects briefly outlined, much interest and consequent effort would be apparent. The children love to "plan things," make things or play games, and as we have seen, each of these centers of interest necessitated the learning of important facts of arithmetic or the review of them.

And so we see that these projects have really been occasions of group activities such as we find all through our lives. The children worked together and played as they do out of school. In the course of these projects they learned through experience with quantities many arithmetical facts. Aside from these primary facts there were many other elements in their growth, e. g., greater power of initiative, of judging values, of organizing themselves, of solving vital problems which one may meet every day (and so carry knowledge outside of school), greater satisfaction in helping others, thoughtfulness for the needs of others, etc. The intelligent teacher will often and regularly check up results to see what she is accomplishing and how economically she is doing it.

To some it may seem that all this makes for a rather "wishy-washy" kind of arithmetic, but practical experience proves quite the contrary. As Dr. Kilpatrick said the other day, we have "better arithmetic and a living child."

THE CLEARING HOUSE

EDUCATION AS "ACTIVITY LEADING TO FURTHER ACTIVITY"

In the spring of 1921 it was decided to devote the first hour every morning, in a second and third grade classroom in a public school system, to a period of self-initiated activity with a view to comparing the efficacy of such an informal procedure with the prescribed routine of the previous formal daily program. Such experimentation resulted from the conception of education as preparation of the child, through the medium of actual experiences, for an active and intelligent part in a democracy. Believing that knowledge acquired through personal experiences is of greater immediate value and permanency than subject matter administered from an adult point of view, we attempted to unify the curriculum with the life of the child and to psychologize the subject matter involved. Realizing, too, that children learn more readily and intelligently, and require less repetition in learning when individual interest and curiosity are aroused without the exertion of effort, we stressed constructive work and play over subject matter as such.

Needless to say, in order that conditions might be provided suggestive of expressing life situations, some seemingly radical external changes in the classroom were essential. The seats and desks were unscrewed and arranged in horseshoe formation to provide more available space for work and play. All nutritive materials and equipment that might serve as occupational and constructive incentives, or stimuli offering new experiences, were taken from cupboards and high shelves and placed within ready sight and easy reach of the children. We searched for materials that suggested group participation rather than individual activity. Physical apparatus such as balance beams, slides, and trapezes were installed

or borrowed from the kindergarten. The influence of environment was shown when a dark cloakroom was transformed into a cozy library. No new reading material was introduced, but the sudden interest in reading was quite amusing. In short, the children were encouraged, through the provision of normal outlets, to make fruitful use of the energies that were purely distressing in the formal classroom.

The first hour in the morning seemed the most logical time in the daily program for such a period, as the child, bringing his plans from home, is then at the height of his interest and enthusiasm. Short periods of self-elected work preceded the actual introduction of the experiment in order that the transition from the relatively formal to the less formal procedure be gradual and natural. Nevertheless, when the children were told that an hour each day was to be devoted to "noisy work time" (as distinguished from quiet occupational seat work) their joy was unbounded. They were given complete freedom in their choice of classroom materials and were told that they could talk or move about as they wished—the only stipulation being that they were not to annoy or interfere with the rights of others. We suggested also that they occupy their time with something both purposeful and worth while. The results of the experiment were most gratifying. We soon discovered that the remainder of the daily program must be more flexible, as the morning hour invariably furnished the key-note to the vital interests of the children, and the entire day's work might therefore profitably hinge around these life interests. Situations frequently arose which necessitated the urgent and immediate acquiring of formal subject matter. It is quite true that certain interests occupied so much time and attention that other interests of equal importance were necessarily omitted. But is it not better to carry one line of interest and effort as near completion as possible, and have the children experience the satisfaction of accomplishment, than to scatter the attention through the attempt to follow various interests in dutiful adherence to ten and fifteen minute periods according to time schedule? Accurate daily records for each child were kept throughout the entire experiment that he might judge for himself whether or not he had made the best use of his time.

This particular phase of work offers a wealth of opportunity for the development of the individual child's character. Many times over we noted the following moral qualities expressed: unselfishness, self-control, helpfulness, patience, consideration, respect, and courtesy. Growth was manifested by their increased intellectual curiosity and their capacity for sustained interest. They experienced the sense of achievement resulting from their ability to initiate and carry out projects to self-determined ends. They learned to appreciate the rights of others, to coöperate intelligently, and to discriminate. The children became more skilled in the use of materials because they could experiment individually in their manipulation. Each member of this miniature democracy was cognizant of the fact that he had equal rights with the other members; for did he not have the privilege, if dissatisfied with the work in a certain group, to start out for himself? And could he not place his grievances before the justice of the entire community in the "town meeting"? These get-together meetings at the close of the morning hour served as a check upon each individual, for then he was held responsible (through an oral report to his classmates) for his actions and the worth of his choice of work. It was in this gathering that he was guided in learning to give and take constructive criticism. The making and discussing of plans at this time afforded the teacher excellent opportunities of guiding, of helping to improve the oral language of the children, and of stimulating their interest to further activity. The achievement of democratic motivation was evidenced in the development of independence, the unfoldment of originality, and the evolution of leadership (through the power of self and group direction).

Perhaps the most valuable result of the entire experiment was the teacher's awakening interest in child study, her appreciation of the significance of the child's ever-present interests and capacities, her respect for his individuality, and her realization of the infinite possibilities of the informally organized classroom.

ROWNA HANSEN
Duluth, Minn.

HOME LIFE IN LOUISVILLE IN 1800 AND 1921—HEATING, LIGHTING AND VENTILATION

While studying the history of Louisville, a class of 3A children was encouraged to ask any questions they wished about the people who first settled the city. Many questions arose, among them the following: "How did the pioneers keep their cabins warm?" "If there were no matches, how did they start their fires?" "How did they see to get home?" "How did they light their cabins?"

These questions were used as a basis for science work and provided excellent opportunities for both oral and written English, reading, and spelling. Our work was outlined under three heads: (a) how the pioneers heated their cabins; (b) how the cabins were ventilated; (c) how they were lighted. Under heating we studied (a) the kinds of fuel burned, (b) how to build a fire, (c) what a fire needs to make it burn, and (d) how fireplaces, stoves, grates and furnaces keep us warm. We compared the present with pioneer times and found out some of the inconveniences our ancestors experienced in meeting their needs.

Experiment.—The children built a fire as the pioneers did. They struck arrowheads together. The friction made sparks, which fell upon the straw and caused it to burn. The effort required in making sparks showed the children how much harder it was to start a fire in this way than to use a match.

A written language lesson followed the discussion of this experiment.

Example.—"One of the boys brought some dry grass. Another child brought two arrowheads. The arrowheads were made of flint. Flint is a very hard stone. We struck the pieces of flint together and made sparks. The sparks fell on the dry grass and it began to burn. This is the way the pioneers started their fires."

The children then attempted to build a fire in a sand pan. They brought paper and small pieces of kindling from home. The sticks and paper were placed close to the bottom of the pan, leaving no place for air. They touched a match to the paper, but the wood did not burn. They wondered why. One member of the class said the fire would not burn because it had no air. I told them there was a way we could find out if this were true. We made an experiment by putting a lighted candle into a closed box. All air was shut out and the candle did not burn. When the holes were opened so the air could get in, the candle burned all right. This established the fact that a candle needs air in order to burn.

Conclusion.—If a candle needs air to make it burn, a fire needs air for the same reason.

The children drew a diagram of the box on the board and wrote a paragraph describing the experiment. The written work was preceded by oral and board work.

Language.—"To-day we built a fire in the sand pan. We laid the paper flat, put our sticks side by side upon the paper and lit it. Our fire did not burn. We wondered what was the matter."

After the experiment described above, the children wrote the following:

"Miss Burks brought a chalk box which had a hole in the top and in each side. There was a glass door to the box. There was a candle inside the box. Miss Burks put corks into the holes, lit the candle and closed the door. The candle went out. She took out one cork and lit the candle again. It went out. When she took out all the corks, the candle burned. That was because it had air."

After making the experiment to show that a candle needs air to make it burn, the following paragraph was developed:

"Yesterday we found out that a candle needs air to make it burn. We built another fire in the sand pan. We crumpled the paper and laid the sticks across each other, so that the air could get underneath. This time the fire burned all right. The pioneers put their logs upon andirons so that the fire could have air to make it burn."

At this point a trip was made to the engine room so that the class could see how the furnace worked and compare our elaborate heating system with the simple one of early days. This part of the work was summarized in an oral language lesson. Temperature was studied in connection with the heating. This necessitated learning to read the thermometer, and finding the effect of heat and cold upon the mercury.

Experiment.—We dipped the thermometer into hot water and the mercury quickly rose to the top of the tube. We then dipped it into ice cold water and the mercury went down into the little ball. The thermometer was put out doors and then brought into the warm schoolroom. The same thing happened. The warm air made the mercury rise, the cold air made it drop.

This question was put to the class: "Why do we need a thermometer in the room?" and several children answered, "To know when the room is too hot or when it is too cold."

Oral and Written Language.—"We dipped

our thermometer into hot water. I could see the mercury going up. We put the thermometer into ice cold water. The mercury went down into the little ball. The warm air makes the mercury go up, and the cold air makes it fall. We need a thermometer in the room so that we can tell whether the air is too warm, or too cold, or just right. Mr. Brown told us that the temperature ought to be 68 or 70 degrees."

Ventilation was next studied under two heads: the need for ventilation and the dangers if neglected. The need for ventilation was illustrated by the story (Pages 4-6-8) in *Good Health*, by Jewett. The children read these stories silently, discussed them, and told them to the other groups.

In order to show that breathing sends something into the air, a simple experiment was performed. Lime water was put into a perfectly clean bottle. The children saw that the water was clear. A child breathed into the bottle through a tube and the lime water became cloudy. From this experiment the children concluded that we breathed something into the air which was impure. Impure air ought to be purified. The next question was, "How is this to be done?" It is to be done by ventilating our rooms well.

Written Language.—"When we breathe, the air in the room becomes impure. When the air in the room is bad, it makes us sleepy and we do not want to work. We can make it pure by letting the fresh air in."

Some of the children also wrote a short paragraph describing the experiment of breathing into lime water.

In order to create a sentiment against sleeping with closed windows, one of the student teachers made a chart which was divided by a line into two columns. At the top of one column there was a cut-out window, with real curtains blowing in. Over this column were these words, "Come in, the Air is fine." At the top of the other column was a picture of a closed window. The names of the children who slept with open windows were written in the first column, and the names of those who did not were placed in the Closed Window column, until they could honestly say they were sleeping with open windows. The names were then transferred from the Closed Window column to the Open Window column.

In answer to their questions about lighting, the children found out how the pioneers lighted their cabins by reading Pages 124-125 in *Pioneer Life*. The answer to the question, "How do they see to get home?" was found on Pages 18-19 in *Polly the Pioneer*. They then compared lighting in pioneer times with lighting at the present time, and the advantages and disadvantages of each. They modelled crude lamps and made dipped candles. Before making the candles they read and discussed the story, "Candle-Making at the Coolidges" in *Everyday Life in the Colonies*. They then wrote a letter to some friend or relative, telling how they made the candles. This is one of the letters:

Dear Mother:

To-day we made some candles like the pioneers' candles. Our teacher melted paraffin. We cut pieces of heavy cord about four inches long. We looped this over a pencil and twisted it. We dipped the cord into the hot paraffin, lifted it out and let it cool. We did this until our candles were about as big as Christmas candles. The pioneers made their candles this way.

Your loving son,
JOHN.

The care of the eye was studied as a part of the lesson on lighting. It was discussed from the standpoint of, "Which is the best light—candle, gas, or electric light?" "How should the light strike the paper?" "How can we keep the eye well?" Each unit of work was summarized by a written lesson, previously developed in class.

ELIZABETH BRECKENRIDGE,
Louisville, Ky.

AS REPORTED

PROGRAM OF THE SECOND ANNUAL MEETING OF THE NATIONAL CONFERENCE

Two sessions of the National Conference on Educational Method will be held in Chicago during the meeting of the Department of Superintendence. The first will convene in the Pine Room of the Stratford Hotel on Tuesday afternoon, February 28, at two o'clock and the second in Fullerton Hall of the Art Institute at nine-thirty on the following morning, Wednesday, March 1.

The speakers and their topics on Tuesday afternoon will be: 1. The Possibilities of the Project Method in the Ordinary Classroom, Supt. Fred M. Hunter, Oakland, California; 2. Some Experiences with the Project Method in the Training School, Principal E. A. Hotchkiss, City Training School, Kansas City, Missouri; 3. Criteria of Project Teaching, Miss Bessie B. Goodrich, Director of Elementary Education, Des Moines, Iowa, and Mr. R. F. Franzen, Head of the Bureau of Measurements, Des Moines.

On Wednesday morning the following will be the speakers and their topics: 1. Method in Curriculum, Professor William H. Kilpatrick, Teachers College, Columbia University; 2. The Next Step in the Development of Effective Methods of Supervision, Miss Elizabeth Hall, Assistant Superintendent of Schools, Minneapolis, Minnesota; 3. Supervision Without a Supervisor, Mr. T. W. Gosling, Superintendent of Schools, Madison, Wisconsin; 4. A New View of Teacher Rating, Mr. Stuart A. Courtis, Director of Instruction, Teacher Training, and Research, Detroit, Michigan.

On Tuesday afternoon steps will be taken to elect five members of the Board of Directors. The new Board will afterward elect the officers of the Conference in accordance with the constitution.

All friends of the Conference are asked to extend the notice of the meeting and to urge those who are interested to arrange to be present.

JAMES F. HOSIC,
Sec'y-Treas.

THE JUNIOR RED CROSS

Mr. James N. Rule, Director of the Junior Red Cross, has resigned to become supervisor of science teaching for the state department of education of Pennsylvania. He is succeeded by Mr. Arthur W. Dunn, formerly specialist in civic education for the Bureau of Education. Mr. Dunn has recently issued a new pamphlet on school correspondence. This is now confined to exchange with schools in other countries.

THE HYANNIS PROJECT SOCIETY

During the last two summer sessions the State Normal School of Hyannis, Massachusetts, has provided opportunity for the study of the Project Method under the leadership of Miss Elizabeth Fisher, teacher of education in the Lowell Normal School. In order to keep in touch with each other the members of these classes have now organized a Project Society, the first meeting of which was held at the Hotel Bellevue in Boston, December 3.

During luncheon various members contributed bits of pleasantry and reports of experience. Afterwards an address on "The Present Status of the Project Movement" was given by Professor James F. Hosic of Teachers College, Columbia University. Principal W. A. Baldwin of the Hyannis Normal School was present and spoke briefly of the relations of the summer students to the school and of the Hyannis spirit, which he believes will grow.

The following resolutions were passed:

Resolved, That as an association and as individuals this organization shall promote the project method in education, especially by enlarging our own understanding of it and by sharing with others our viewpoint as to its advantages.

Resolved, That the association seek to take full advantage of the opportunity for inspiration and guidance which will be afforded by the National Education Association, whose annual meeting will be held in Boston in July, 1922.

The question of affiliation with the National Conference on Educational Method was discussed. There appeared to be a unanimity of opinion in favor of establishing such relations whenever the National Conference shall have provided a mode for doing so.

AN INVESTIGATION OF EDUCATIONAL FINANCE

The American Council on Education has secured the sum of $170,000 from the Commonwealth Fund, the Carnegie Corporation, the General Education Board, and the Milbank Memorial Fund to be used in the investigation of educational finance, and has selected a commission to conduct the investigation made up as follows: Samuel P. Capen, director of the American Council on Education, Washington, D. C., ex officio; Ellwood P. Cubberley, dean of the school of education, Stanford University; Edward C. Elliott, chancellor of the University of Montana; Thomas E. Finegan, state superintendent of public instruction, Harrisburg, Pennsylvania; Robert M. Haig, associate professor of business organization, Columbia University; Victor Morawetz, attorney at law, New York City; Henry C. Morrison, formerly state superintendent of public instruction of New Hampshire, professor of education, University of Chicago; George D. Strayer, professor of educational administration and director, Division of Field Studies, Institute of Educational Research, Teachers College, Columbia University; Herbert S. Weet, superintendent of schools, Rochester, New York.

Dr. Strayer has been selected as chairman of the commission and director of the investigation. The aims of the commission as so far announced are: to study in typical states and communities current programs of public education, how these programs are carried out, and the present and prospective costs involved. It is proposed also to look into the relation of educational expenditures to other public expenditures, methods of securing revenue for the support of education, the possibility of effecting economies, and possible sources of revenue which have not been tapped. A try-out will be made in New York State in order to develop a working method.

Among the well-known educators who have been employed to give assistance to the commission are: Dr. Albert Shiels, formerly director of educational research in the public schools of New York City and superintendent of schools in Los Angeles, California, and Dr. Carter Alexander, until recently deputy state superintendent of public instruction, Wisconsin, and formerly professor of secondary education in Peabody College for Teachers.

THE READER'S GUIDE

THE NEW GEOGRAPHY

As was to be expected, the Great War has greatly stimulated interest in the subject of geography. Within a few months several volumes have come to the reviewer's desk which, taken as a whole, reflect certain striking tendencies in organization, emphasis, and method.[1]

Two of these books, *Teaching Geography by Problems* and *The Teaching of Geography*, are treatises, of 306 and 292 pages respectively; *Teaching the New Geography* and *The Essentials of Geography: A Manual for Teachers* are condensed handbooks to accompany the corresponding series of elementary school geographies prepared by their authors, the Frye-Atwood and the Brigham and McFarlane; and the others are the two volumes making up a new series for the elementary school by McMurry and Parkins.

From the prefaces in the last-named we learn that the authors would emphasize the human side of geography, that they accept the regional as the basic treatment, that they seek to develop the problem attitude on the part of the pupils, that they would have the pupils use the textbooks to a considerable extent as a source of material for the working out of original problems, and that they aim to appeal to genuine intrinsic interests, beginning always to develop a topic on the basis of the pupil's own experience. With greater or less enthusiasm in regard to each of these points all of the authors under consideration profess similar convictions. If one should add to this analysis reference to simplicity and concreteness of presentation, greatly enlarged and improved facilities for the use of maps, pictures, supplementary reading, first-hand

observation, and varied means of expression, he should have what is evidently to be regarded as the "new geography."

The aspect which stands out most strikingly in the books we are considering is the problem or project method. Smith devotes all his space to it. The brothers Branom announce as a subtitle, "The Project, or Active, Method." Dr. Atwood and Miss Thomas declare themselves unreservedly in favor of the problem method and show how to use it. Brigham and McFarlane, though more cautious, accord this method an honorable place and are careful also to illustrate it at length. McMurry and Parkins would have the text of their books regarded as a series of problems with their answers and they state numerous problems which the pupils are left to answer for themselves.

In contrast to the mere memorizing of definitions, facts, and locations, which was—and is—much too prevalent, this increased emphasis on rational processes in the study of geography is highly gratifying. The subject is now in a fair way to come into the place it should rightfully occupy.

This consummation will be greatly aided by the new stress on the human element. What man is doing to his environment and what it in turn is doing to him, these are the facts that really matter. The study of them naturally brings with it nearly or quite all of the knowledge of physiographic processes, of the influence of the heavenly bodies, of boundary lines, capitals, and centers of population, of industry and commerce, which children can assimilate.

There is another and deeper significance attaching to the new point of view. Geography

[1] The Teaching of Geography, by M. E. Branom and F. K. Branom, Ginn & Co. Teaching Geography by Problems, by E. E. Smith, Doubleday, Page & Co. Teaching the New Geography, by Wallace W. Atwood and Helen G. Thomas. Essentials of Geography: A Manual for Teachers, by Albert P. Brigham and Charles T. McFarlane, The American Book Co. Elementary Geography; Advanced Geography, by Frank M. McMurry and A. E. Parkins, The Macmillan Company.

ceases to be merely a study of man in his physical environment and becomes a study of man in his relations to other men everywhere. It takes on a genuinely social character and becomes one of the chief means of overcoming insularity and provincialism and of stimulating a lively sense of our interdependence with other, even the most distant, peoples. It may easily lead to higher and nobler conceptions of service and of world amity and peace.

All of this and much more besides is suggested by even a rapid examination of a series of recent volumes on geography that, with all of the texts and helps to which they refer, make possible, even in the case of the teacher with limited experience, a type of learning in the class in geography which is undoubtedly cultural in a true and vital sense.

SIGNIFICANT ARTICLES

SUPERVISORY POLICIES

Everyone will be glad to see an appreciation of the good work done by Superintendent C. P. Cary in his long career as head of the Wisconsin State Department of Public Instruction. Such an appreciation has been prepared by Mr. Carter Alexander, until recently Assistant Superintendent in Wisconsin, and the article is published in *School and Society* of December 10.

The principal points made by Mr. Alexander are: first, the members of the staff of the Department were chosen and directed on a professional basis; second, a truly professional theory of supervision was put into actual practice; third, the aim throughout was to do the square thing, only secondarily considering what the law would permit; fourth, as far as possible the work was done openly and above board; fifth, the administration was fearless; and sixth, as far as possible the work was done impersonally.

These criteria for measuring the merit of the Department are supported by numerous details too extensive to be reviewed here.

They will no doubt be regarded as sufficient to establish the writer's contentions. The last part of the article is devoted to explaining why the Department fell and what its future is likely to be. As might be supposed, the principal cause of the Superintendent's failure to be reëlected was purely political. The various charges brought against him, such as lack of coöperation with educational agencies, were apparently without foundation. Whether the work of the Department in the future is good or bad will depend on whether political influence conducts and controls it or not.

TEACHING TEACHERS TO "MOTIVATE"

An interesting account of a course for prospective high school teachers as given in Tufts College will be found in *Educational Administration and Supervision* for November. The writer, Professor Waples, explains that the teacher in training appears to be lacking in an understanding of the kind of technique that will secure desirable responses on the part of the pupils. He therefore organized a course dealing with principles of motivation, the technique of motivation, and measurement or estimate of results. The class was asked to examine certain standard texts in order to discover what teaching methods are now being advocated. They then made a classification of types of interest. The practice exercises consisted of demonstrations of individual students, the method being supplied by the instructor, and demonstrations of the way in which the method was selected by the student himself. Finally, sixteen standard tests and scales were examined. The conclusion of the writer is that while there were a number of undesirable features in the course, there were also several assured values. The students came to realize the necessity for psychological organization of material and at least half the class made marked advance in ability to do this. A greater awareness of individual differences was developed and greater respect for the principles of educational psychology as an aid to teaching method. In addition, the students gained in confidence. The final test of the value of the course will be, however, the success of the students in their actual teaching.

THE CASE AGAINST MYTHS AND FAIRY STORIES

We have been accustomed to encomiums of myths and folk stories as material for reading by little children. It is somewhat startling, therefore, to note in *Education* for November the following title: "The Case Against Myths, Folk-Lore, and Fairy Stories as Basal Reading for Children." The writer, Gilbert L. Brown of the Northern State Normal School, Marquette, Michigan, made an examination of reading material commonly used in lower grades and found folk-lore employed. The assumption is that this sort of reading is in harmony with the culture epoch theory. Mr. Brown points out the now well-known fact that there is little support for the culture epoch theory and that therefore heredity does not prescribe the specific subject matter of education. The defense of fairy stories is, of course, psychological. Here the argument is for the training of the imagination, but since the imagery of fairy tales is fancy, and not congruous with normal human experience, such stories should occupy but a small part of the time of the children. Emphasis should be placed rather upon reading better adapted to arouse and direct new and permanent interests.

DIFFERENTIATED COMPOSITION SCALES

The experiment in English composition which was begun at the University of Minnesota in 1917 has resulted in the publication of a series of three scales for exposition, narration, and description, in each of which structure, mechanics, and thought content are measured separately. The zero point taken is that provided by the Nassau County Extension of the Hillegas Scale and the method of deriving the steps on the scale is that adopted by Dr. Hillegas in the original Hillegas-Thorndike Scale. An account of these new scales will be found in the *Journal of Educational Administration and Supervision* for December. It is from the pen of Professor M. J. Van Wagenen of the University of Minnesota, who says that specific qualities of themes can be graded by these scales with at least as much accuracy as general merit has been measured by the scales which have preceded them.

THE CASE FOR THE LOW I. Q.

What many have been thinking, Mr. John L. Stenquist of the Bureau of Research in the Public Schools of New York City says in plain terms in the *Journal of Educational Research* for November. He points out that there are many fallacies in the present-day conception of intelligence tests. Many are narrow and academic in scope, being based largely on school success. There are, in fact, many other kinds of intelligence than are now being measured by tests of that name. This is brought out by means of a host of illustrations drawn from a study of mechanical ability which was ascertained through a series of simple tests in assembling common articles and in picture matching. The author submits that such ability as is measured by these tests may prove of greater value in certain aspects of life than the ability measured by the more abstract tests. He thinks it unpardonable to attach a stigma to pupils scoring low in the so-called intelligence tests. There is ample opportunity for them to live useful and happy lives.

THE NEW BOOKS

The American Spirit in Education. A Chronicle of Great Teachers. By Edwin E. Slosson. New Haven: Yale University Press, 1921. Pp. x + 309.

One number of a series of fifty volumes, each by a master in his field. The whole series should be accessible to teachers; it supplies a background indispensable to breadth and personal culture.

Health Education and the Nutrition Class. A Report of the Bureau of Educational Experiments. By Jean Lee Hunt, Buford J. Johnson, and Edith M. Lincoln. New York: E. P. Dutton & Co., 1921. Pp. xviii + 281.

An account of extended investigations carried on in a New York public school.

An Introduction to School Music Teaching. By Karl Wilson Gehrkens. Boston: C. C. Birchard & Co., 1919. Pp. viii + 132.

A manual covering the lower grades and high school.

Project Work in Education. By James Leroy Stockton. Boston: Houghton Mifflin Co., 1920. Pp. xiv + 167.

Historical and analytic. The author suggests a new study, to combine elements of several old ones.

How to Teach the Primary Grades. By Nellie Cooper. Chicago: A. Flanagan Co., 1920. Pp. 304.

The favorite devices of a primary supervisor.

Story Hour Readings. By E. C. Hartwell. New York: American Book Co., 1921. Fourth Year, pp. 367, illus.; Fifth Year, pp. 400, illus.; Sixth Year, pp. 400, illus.; Seventh Year, pp. 416, illus.; Eighth Year, pp. 432, illus.

Completing the popular "Story Hour Series." Prominent features are the use of current as well as classical material and the grouping of the selections.

English for Immediate Use. By Frederick Houk Law. New York: Scribner, 1921. Pp. xii + 372.

A book to supply practical as opposed to special literary needs. Exercises oc upy a large amount of the space.

The Teaching of English. A New Approach. By W. S. Tomkinson. Oxford University Press, 1921. Pp. 230.

Stress is laid on debate, to be followed up, however, by reading of classic literature.

IN PAPER COVERS

Address of the President of the United States at the College of William and Mary, Williamsburg, Va., October 19, 1921. Government Printing Office, Washington, D. C.

Opportunities for Study at American Graduate Schools. By George F. Zook and Samuel P. Capen. Bulletin, 1921, No. 6, Bureau of Education, Washington, D. C.

Present Status of Music Instruction in Colleges and High Schools. Bulletin, 1921, No. 9, Bureau of Education, Washington, D. C.

State Laws and Regulations Governing Teachers' Certificates. By Katherine M. Cook. Bulletin, 1921, No. 22, Bureau of Education.

Monthly Record of Current Educational Publications. Index, February, 1920–January, 1921. Bulletin, 1921, No. 31, Bureau of Education, Washington, D. C.

A Preliminary Study of Standards of Growth in the Detroit Public Schools. By Paul C. Packer and Arthur B. Moehlman. Detroit Educational Bulletin, No. 5, June, 1921.

Measuring Classroom Products in Berkeley, Sections 1 and 2. Directed by Cyrus D. Mead. University of California, Bureau of Research in Education, Study No. 1, 1921.

The Marking System of the College Entrance Examination Board. By L. Thomas Hopkins. Published by the Graduate School of Education, Harvard University.

Price List and Circular of Information, Bureau of Educational Measurements and Standards. Kansas State Normal School, Bulletin No. 10, 1921.

Guide Book for Foreign Students in the United States. The Institute of International Education, Bulletin No. 5, New York, 1921.

Junior Red Cross—A Program. Washington, D. C., November, 1921.—*Organization for Action,* Supplement 1, Sept., 1921.—*School Correspondence.* Supplement 2, Sept., 1921.

A $1,000 Trip Through Europe

Contest open to every member of the National Educational Association

After an expenditure of $450,000 and three years of effort on the part of America's leading Educators, Compton's Pictured Encyclopedia has been completed. Dr. Harding, the Managing Editor, says: "I feel quite justified in claiming that we have given you the very best work of reference and educational inspiration ever prepared for children of common and high school ages." Now that the epochal New Work has been completed, Professor Searson says: "Your biggest problem is to bring this New Work to the attention of the school people in the quickest possible way;" and Dean Ford, the Editor-in-Chief, states: "The Department of Superintendence is just the group whose competent opinion of Compton's Pictured Encyclopedia would be welcomed by the whole staff."

The Trip to Europe will include a Pilgrimmage to Oberammergau and the Passion Play; also principal points of historical and educational interest in England, Belgium, Germany, Italy, Switzerland and France, including a visit to the Battlefields.

The contest is just to show you—without cost or obligation—what we have achieved in Compton's Pictured Encyclopedia

ANYTHING that we might tell you of Compton's Pictured Encyclopedia would be inadequate. Only when you have turned the pages and have seen for yourself can you appreciate the importance to the Educational World of this New Work. Therefore, the only aim of this contest is to put the New Work into your hands for a personal inspection.

Every member of the National Educational Association is eligible to compete for one of the following awards:

$1,000 Trip through Europe

$500 Trip to Alaska via the Canadian Rockies

$250 Trip to any of our National Parks

If for any reason the trip is not desired, winner will receive the equivalent in money

100 Honorable Mention Prizes
A complete set of the New Work

Each entrant is to write a 500 word discussion on "The Practical Educational value of Compton's Pictured Encyclopedia" with especial reference to its use in the socialized lecitation and the problem project method of instruction.

All discussions must be in our hands by April 20th, 1922, in order that the Awards may be made in time for the trips to be taken this summer. The following prominent educators have been appointed as judges:

WM. C. BAGLEY, Professor of Education, Teacher's College, Columbia University.

MARION L. BURTON, President of the University of Michigan, Ann Arbor, Michigan.

H. B. WILSON, Superintendent of City Schools, Berkeley, Calif.

A Vital and Valuable Educational Movement

The Practical Educational Value of Compton's Pictured Encyclopedia must be apparent to every thoughtful school man and woman. It is an altogether new type of work designed for the daily use of boys and girls of school age.

It is up-to-date — every word written entirely since the World War.

It is progressive—especially adapted to use in either the socialized recitation or problem project method of instruction.

It is accurate—edited by sound scholars of recognized world-wide authority.

It is intensely interesting—composed in clear, vivid style, which brings the very heart of each subject into brilliant relief to catch and fix the attention of the reader.

It is complete—injecting into the difficult technical portions of each subject the same spice of connected interest as exists in those outstanding "wonders" and "marvels" to which books for children usually confine themselves.

"It is really pictured"—containing thousands of illustrations selected from over a half million photographs gathered from all parts of the world, with an "idea" in every picture and a picture for every idea that needs a picture.

To enroll in this contest, simply mail the coupon on this page, or, if you attend the convention in Chicago, February 27th to March 3rd, we urge a visit to our attractive and interesting exhibit in Booths 86 and 87, Leiter Building, where enrollment blanks may be had.

As soon as your entry blank is received these beautiful volumes will come direct to you by express —all charges paid. Read them, enjoy them, review the thousands of beautiful illustrations and note the hundreds of new features of vital educational value. Then write your dicussion. The 500 word limit will seem all too short.

After the Awards have been announced you need only reverse the cover on our packing box and return the books to us *at our expense.*

Just Mail this Coupon

Take the first step now toward the Trip to Europe, or one of the 102 other really worth while Awards which we have listed. Mail the coupon today while the matter is fresh in your mind.

F. E. COMPTON & CO.
58 E. Washington St., Chicago, Illinois

THE JOURNAL OF EDUCATIONAL METHOD

Edited by JAMES F. HOSIC

Volume I   FEBRUARY, 1922   Number 6

PUBLISHED BY THE WORLD BOOK COMPANY FOR
THE NATIONAL CONFERENCE ON EDUCATIONAL METHOD

THE NATIONAL CONFERENCE ON EDUCATIONAL METHOD

An Association of Persons Interested in Supervision and Teaching

Officers of the Conference

President, C. L. WRIGHT, Public Schools, Huntington, West Virginia.
Vice-President, MARGARET NOONAN, School of Education, New York University, Washington Square, New York City.
Secretary-Treasurer, JAMES F. HOSIC, Teachers College, New York City.

Executive Committee

THE PRESIDENT AND THE SECRETARY-TREASURER, *ex officio*.
C. C. CERTAIN, Northwestern High School, Detroit, Michigan.
MARGARET MADDEN, Doolittle Elementary School, Chicago, Illinois.
MARY E. PENNELL, Public Schools, Kansas City, Missouri.

Board of Directors

C. C. CERTAIN, Assistant Principal and Head of Department of English, Northwestern High School, Detroit, Mich.

BESSIE GOODRICH, Assistant Superintendent of Schools, Des Moines, Ia.

J. M. GWINN, Superintendent of Schools, New Orleans, La.

KATHERINE HAMILTON, Assistant Superintendent of Schools, St. Paul, Minn.

JAMES F. HOSIC, Associate Professor of Education in Charge of Extramural Courses, Teachers College, Columbia University.

FRED M. HUNTER, Superintendent of Schools, Oakland, Calif.

WILLIAM H. KILPATRICK, Professor of Philosophy of Education, Teachers College, Columbia University.

MARGARET MADDEN, Principal, Doolittle Elementary School, Chicago, Ill.

F. M. McMURRY, Professor of Elementary Education, Teachers College, Columbia University.

MARGARET NOONAN, School of Education, New York University, Washington Square, New York City.

MARY E. PENNELL, Assistant Superintendent of Schools, Kansas City, Mo.

J. A. STARKWEATHER, Assistant Superintendent of Schools, Duluth, Minn.

W. F. TIDYMAN, Director of the Training School, State Normal School, Farmville, Va.

JOHN W. WITHERS, Dean of School of Education, New York University.

C. L. WRIGHT, Superintendent of Schools, Huntington, W. Va.

THE JOURNAL OF EDUCATIONAL METHOD is published monthly, from September to June, by World Book Company, Yonkers-on-Hudson, New York, for the officers, directors, and members of the National Conference on Educational Method. The subscription price is $3.00 a year; the price of single copies is 35 cents.

Postage is prepaid by the publishers on all orders from the United States, Mexico, Cuba, Porto Rico, Panama Canal Zone, Republic of Panama, Bolivia, Colombia, Honduras, Nicaragua, Peru, Hawaiian Islands, Philippine Islands, Guam, and the Samoan Islands. Postage is charged extra as follows: For Canada, 25c on annual subscriptions; other foreign countries not named, 50 cents. All communications regarding subscriptions or advertising should be addressed to World Book Company, Yonkers-on-Hudson, New York.

Address applications for membership to the Secretary of the Conference, 525 West One Hundred and Twentieth Street, New York City. The fee for active members is $3.00, for associate members, $2.00; $2.00 in each case is applied to the support of the Journal, for which each member receives a year's subscription.

The editorial office is at 525 West One Hundred and Twentieth Street, New York City.

Entered as second-class matter 8 December 1921 at the post office at Greenwich, Connecticut, under the Act of 3 March 1879. Acceptance for mailing at special rate of postage provided for in Section 1103, Act of 3 October 1917, authorised 8 December 1921.

The Journal of Educational Method

VOLUME I   FEBRUARY, 1922   NUMBER 6

EDITORIALLY SPEAKING

SPREAD THE NEWS

If the letters which come to the editorial desk may be taken as a trustworthy indication, the *Journal of Educational Method* has found its place in the field of educational journalism and is assured of long life and much influence. The lengthening subscription list argues for the same opinion. In a few months our circle of readers has widened to include almost as great a company as is appealed to by some journals of many years' standing.

Having won our spurs, so to speak, we feel justified in asking our friends to spread the news, to tell others how good the going is. Marketing costs disproportionately in the distribution of most products. Let us scale down the cost in this case and put the savings into an improved product. If the supervisors, teacher trainers, and progressive teachers who have cast in their lot with us will but pass the word along, the thing will be done. Lend a hand and have a larger part in developing an organ of experience, experiment, and practical philosophy in the field of educational method.

LIMITATIONS OF THE PROJECT

When the *Journal of the National Education Association* gives of its much-sought-for space room for an article on method the reader takes notice. Here must be an utterance regarded as of extraordinary significance. And so it is. Professor W. W. Charters, of the Carnegie Institute of Technology, discourses of the "Limitations of the Project," and, in doing it, presents an issue which no one interested in the progress of education can afford to overlook.

On the surface this is nothing more than the problem of definition. In reality, however, it is a matter of point of view and of an ideal to be set up and striven for. What is a project? Merely an objective activity carried to completion, whether under compulsion, externally directed, or no? Or is it an act which claims to be an act, a *complete* act, precisely because it does involve the essential subjective as well as objective factors? If it is only the former, then we have merely, as some say, a new device, but if it is the latter, then we have a philosophy of method, capable of unifying and giving point to the scientific studies in the psychology of learning through experience which have opened up a new world to the student of method.

The word "project" is, of course, of no great consequence. Anyone is certainly under obligation to suggest a better term if he can. But the idea of a unifying conception, embodying the floating tendencies toward better teaching, which are so markedly characteristic of our time, *is* worth fighting for. It holds out the hope of a better theory to guide our practice. Upon what a sound historical basis the idea rests, Principal Owen's article in the January issue of the *Journal of Educational Method* clearly shows. Not a new discovery but a new and invaluable synthesis of discoveries, this is what the Project Method really is. Why try to emasculate the idea and so put off the day when we may count upon the aid of a central organizing viewpoint in education?

SUGGESTED STUDIES IN THE FIELD OF MENTAL TESTING

Arthur S. Otis

Director, Department of Test Service, World Book Company, Yonkers-on-Hudson, N. Y.

The writer has recently received a number of requests for suggestions as to researches and minor studies to be made in the field of mental tests by teachers, superintendents, and others. It has seemed worth while, therefore, to publish a list of such researches in order that they might be easily accessible to the large number of teachers and administrators.

The studies listed below, of course, in no sense whatever include all that would be interesting and profitable to undertake even in the field of mental tests with which this paper deals, and no mention will be made of the many interesting studies which could be made in the field of educational tests.[1]

In enumerating these studies, we shall begin with the simpler ones which are suitable for those who are not in a position to undertake extensive or comprehensive researches, involving the expenditure of a large amount of time or requiring a considerable knowledge of statistics. Those studies suggested at the end, however, are of the more comprehensive type and might serve as subjects for theses. The following investigations are discussed:

1. Comparison of the general mental ability of a single grade with that of the other grades.
2. Comparison of the mental ability of pupils and brightness of pupils with teachers' estimates of mental ability and brightness.
3. Comparison between scores in the group and individual administration of a group scale.
4. Experimental reclassification.
5. Comparison between the index of brightness and progress through school.
6. Permanency of the I. Q. or percentile rank.
7. Determination of the correspondence between scores in two or more tests.
8. Determination of what constitutes the difference between brightness and dullness.

1. Comparison of the General Mental Ability of Pupils of a Single Grade with that of the Other Grades.

The comparison of the mental ability of one group of pupils with that of other groups is hardly to be considered a research within itself, but is a project which is very often necessary in preparation for further investigation such, for example, as the relative degree of efficiency of different teaching methods. This investigation

---

[1] A list of thirteen suggested research problems, dealing largely with educational tests, is given in Bulletin No. 33 of the Bureau of Educational Reference and Research, University of Michigan, dated December 1, 1921.

requires that the methods be tried out on classes whose general level of mental ability is the same, so that the factor of mental ability may not vitiate the determination of the relative efficiency of the teaching methods. It may be desirable, however, to compare different classes of the same grade in a school in mental ability so as to determine whether these differ appreciably, either in order that different types of instruction may be given to the different classes, or that the classes may be equalized in mental ability, so that the same instruction will be equally suitable for both classes. A brief description will be given, therefore, of the method of making a comparison between the mental ability of groups for whatever purpose it may be desirable to make this comparison.

For doing this a convenient method would be to arrange the test papers of the pupils of each class in order of magnitude of score and to find the median score of each class by means of the accompanying table. This is a convenient measure of the "central tendency" of the mental ability of the group, and groups may be compared, therefore, by means of the medians. That group may be considered as having the greater mental ability which has the higher median score.

TABLE

For Finding the Upper Quartile (Q_3), Median (M), and Lower Quartile (Q_1) Case Among Any Number of Cases.

The first line of the table is read thus: If there are 20 cases in all, consider the 15th as the Upper Quartile, the 10th as the Median, and the 5th as the Lower Quartile case. The score obtained by the Lower Quartile case is the Lower Quartile Score, etc. By noting the manner in which the columns progress the table may be extended indefinitely.

Number of Cases in Group	Upper Quartile Case	Median Case	Lower Quartile Case
20	15	10	5
21	16	11	6
22	17	11	6
23	18	12	6
24	18	12	6
25	19	13	7
26	20	13	7
27	21	14	7
28	21	14	7
29	22	15	8
30	23	15	8
31	24	16	8
32	24	16	8
33	25	17	9
34	26	17	9
35	27	18	9
36	27	18	9
37	28	19	10
38	29	19	10
39	30	20	10
40	30	20	10
41	31	21	11
42	32	21	11
43	33	22	11
44	33	22	11
45	34	23	12
46	35	23	12
47	36	24	12
48	36	24	12
49	37	25	13
50	38	25	13
51	39	26	13
52	39	26	13
53	40	27	14
54	41	27	14
55	42	28	14
56	42	28	14

The second consideration in the comparison of groups is the comparison of heterogeneity, or, in other words, the determination of the relative degree in which scores of the different groups are scattered. The degree of heterogeneity of a group may be measured in terms of the Inter-Quartile Range (I. Q. R.), which indicates the range covered by the middle 50 per cent of scores. Thus, if the middle 50 per cent of scores of one group covers a range of 55 points, and the middle 50 per cent of scores of another group covers 60 points, the second group is said to be more heterogeneous than the first.

To find the median score and the upper and lower quartile scores of a group consisting of any number of pupils, consult the accompanying table. Thus, if the group contains 21 pupils, the lower quartile, median, and upper quartile scores of the group will be the scores of the sixth, eleventh, and sixteenth individuals when these are counted in the order of magnitude of the scores, beginning with the lowest score.

There is still another purpose for comparing the mental ability of groups and that is to discover the "overlapping" in mental ability between successive grades. Ideally, pupils should be graded in school in such a way that there shall be very little, if any, overlapping in mental ability, which means that practically all children in the sixth grade, for example, would have degrees of mental ability above those of any pupils in the fifth grade, etc. Even in a case of ideal grading, a pupil in the sixth grade may have a mental ability less than that of some pupil in the fifth grade, because of inadequate educational opportunity in the case of the sixth grade pupil, causing him to be retarded educationally, or because the fifth grade pupil by virtue of extra effort is able to do better than would normally be expected from one with his mental ability.

In most schools, however, where tests are used for the first time, it is found that there are very many sixth grade pupils who have mental ability lower than that of many of the fifth grade pupils, and in the majority of cases this appears to be due to inadequate methods of promotion, by which dull pupils are promoted faster than their ability and achievement warrant, and bright pupils are held back to a slower rate of progress than that of which they are capable because of the lack of provision for extra promotions, etc.

A convenient and vivid way of determining the amount of the overlapping of mental ability between grades will be as follows: First, arrange the papers of each grade in order of score and find the median of the

grade. That score which is midway between the norm for the fourth grade and the norm for the fifth grade may then be taken as the proper dividing line between fourth grade mental ability and fifth grade mental ability, and similarly the proper dividing line between the mental abilities of the other successive grades may be determined. The scores may then be tabulated so as to show for each grade separately the number of pupils attaining scores from 0 to 9, from 10 to 19, etc., or better, using smaller intervals of score such as 0 to 4, 5 to 9, etc. These tabulations will disclose at a glance the number of pupils in the fourth grade, for example, whose mental ability is above the dividing line between the fourth grade and fifth grade mental ability, and also the number of pupils in the fifth grade whose mental ability is below this dividing line. The same comparison may be made of the overlapping between other adjacent grades.

If this overlapping is very great, as, for example, when more than half of the pupils of any one grade have scores outside of the range of the mental ability normal for that grade, it would be very desirable to reduce this overlapping in any convenient manner in order that the pupils of any one grade will be as homogeneous as possible.

It is, of course, not desirable to demote pupils, and for this reason most of the adjustment must be made by means of extra promotions of bright pupils. This may have the effect at first of slightly reducing the average mental ability of the several grades, and consequently reducing slightly the grade standards of achievement in the school subjects. This, however, may be atoned for by gradually raising the standards year by year, and it is far better that the grade standards of achievement in a school should be slightly less than those of other schools than that the pupils should overlap greatly in ability. In other words, it makes very little difference whether a group of pupils doing a certain grade of school work happens to be called the high fourth or the low fifth, so long as the group is homogeneous and is making good progress. But, on the other hand, it is extremely undesirable that for the sake of preserving the conventional standard of achievement in the several grades a state of affairs is perpetuated in which the heterogeneity of mental ability in each grade is so great that the efficiency of instruction is materially impaired.

In order to correct for overlapping, therefore, a good plan would be to allow all dull pupils to remain in the grade where they are found, but to give extra promotions to all pupils whose mental ability is above the dividing line between the grades in which they are found and the grade above. Since, as has just been explained, the standard of achievement in the grade above will be slightly lowered, the probability of these pupils succeeding after extra promotions is greater than would otherwise appear, and it is entirely possible that the efficiency of instruction which may be used in homogeneous classes will be so increased that this slightly lowered standard of achievement in the several grades may very quickly be brought up to standard.

A second and more scientific method of correcting the defects of overlapping is to divide the pupils of a grade into two or more classes on the basis of score. Thus, for example, when the scores of the pupils of a grade have been arranged in order, those pupils making the upper third of scores may be placed in one class, those

making the middle third may be placed in another class, and those making the lower third of scores may be placed in a third class. Each of these classes will then be much more homogeneous than the grade as a whole or than a class in which high and low mental ability are indiscriminately mixed.

It should be realized in this connection that the ideal method of grading and classifying is that the pupils of each grade should have degrees of mental ability completely within the limits set by dividing lines, as explained above, and that in addition they should be divided into three or more groups on the basis of brightness, as measured by the Index of Brightness, the Intelligence Quotient, or the Percentile Rank. Since this procedure, however, would in most schools cause a very great amount of shifting, it is not generally desirable to attempt to make such a classification suddenly, but if the form of classification suggested above, made on the basis of mental ability, be adopted initially, this form may gradually be changed to the more ideal form as the overlapping of mental ability between grades is slowly reduced by means of extra promotions.

2. *The Comparison of the Mental Ability and Brightness of Pupils with Teachers' Estimates of Mental Ability and Brightness.*

After a teacher has had a class of pupils under her instruction for a period of a month or two, she should have formed a fairly adequate opinion as to the degree of mental ability and of brightness of her pupils. And yet in most cases where the pupils of a grade are tested, certain pupils are found to make high scores whom the teacher had never suspected were capable of so doing, and conversely, some pupils make much lower scores than the teacher supposed they would make. The value of mental ability tests, however, is greatest if these are given when, because of brief acquaintance with them, the teacher's judgment of their degrees of mental ability is wholly inadequate, as, for example, at the beginning of the school year, when it is most desirable that the pupils should be properly classified. In order to determine the degree to which the results of tests of mental ability given at the beginning of the year, or indeed at any time of the year, agree with the mature judgment of the teacher when she has become well acquainted with the pupils, it is of interest to have the teacher make estimates as carefully as possible of the relative degrees of mental ability and of brightness of her pupils, as independently as possible of the tests, and then to compare these estimates with the test results. If the tests have been given at the beginning of the year, the comparison will be most valid, of course, if the estimates are made by a teacher who has not seen the test results. Or if they have been seen by the teacher, she should attempt to be as little influenced by them as possible in making her estimates. If the tests are to be given after the teacher has become acquainted with the pupils, she should make her estimates before the tests have been given.

In order to compare scores with teachers' estimates of mental ability, the latter may be expressed conveniently in terms of rank. Thus, for example, the teacher may place at the head of her list the name of that pupil whose mental ability she considers to be furthest developed regardless of his age. She may place next the name of the pupil whose mental ability she considers to be next furthest developed, etc., ending

with the pupil whose mental ability appears least developed regardless of age. After the scores have been found, these may be arranged in order of magnitude, and the rank of each pupil in score may be found and placed beside his rank in the teacher's estimate of mental ability. The discrepancy will be at once apparent. Thus, for example, it may happen that the child whom the teacher ranked as highest in mental ability may have a score which ranks fourth in magnitude among those of her pupils. Any case of great discrepancy should be carefully investigated by the teacher for the purpose of discovering upon what grounds she ranked the pupil either higher or lower than his test score seemed to warrant, and in all cases where the score is lower than the estimate the teacher should, if possible, re-examine the pupil in order to determine whether he has done his best in the examination. If the pupil's rank according to score is higher than his rank according to the teacher's estimate, it can hardly be considered that he did more than his best in the test, and the fault is likely to be in the teacher's estimate. In either case, the teacher should endeavor to correct her estimate by reconsideration of the available evidence with a view to justify the higher score, or to discover any possible error in the score, due to either nervousness or failure on the part of the student to properly understand the directions on the test so that the final test scores and estimates may agree fairly well. When this has been done, the purpose of the testing will have been largely attained and many interesting facts will no doubt be brought to light in the process. Thus, for example, it may be found that a pupil who the teacher thought could not do well in school does after all have the mental ability to do very well and only lacks stimulation and encouragement, which may be given in many cases by extra promotion. Again she may find that some pupil who, because of very engaging manners and alert expression of the face, has seemed to her to be very bright, after careful re-examination will be found not to have the mental ability estimated by the teacher, so that the teacher will know better what to expect from this pupil in the future.

In a similar manner the degree of brightness of pupils (the relation between mental ability and age) may be estimated by the teacher separately or in conjunction with estimates of mental ability. These should then be compared with measures of brightness obtained by the IB, CB, IQ, or PR. This comparison may be made by comparing ranks in a manner similar to that described above for comparing estimates and measures of mental ability. Such a comparison is very likely to disclose the fact that the teacher in some cases has not adequately taken into account the age of the pupils, and for this reason has overestimated their degrees of brightness. Thus, a fifteen year old pupil in the sixth grade who is small of stature and who does very good sixth grade work may be rated by the teacher as fairly bright, possibly above the median brightness of pupils of her class, whereas if she had realized how much the ability of this fifteen year old child was below that of the normal fifteen year old child, she would have given a very much lower rating in brightness.

Discrepancies in these ratings of brightness should also be carefully studied by a reconsideration of the grounds upon which the estimate was made or by giving re-examinations if this seems best.

3. Comparison between Scores in the Group and the Individual Administration of a Group Scale.

As has been indicated above, it is frequently desirable to give second examinations to pupils whose first scores do not accord with teachers' estimates of mental ability. For this purpose a second group test is often found sufficient. Any nervousness on the part of the pupil or failure to understand directions in the case of the first examination may be entirely absent on a second examination, in which case the pupil may make a score in the second examination very much more in accord with his mental ability. If, however, a second group test does not yield an explanation of the discrepancy, an individual examination should be administered. For this purpose it is customary to use the Stanford Revision of the Binet Scale. There is a slight disadvantage in this, however, since the correspondence between Stanford-Binet Mental Ages and scores in the several group tests has not been carefully established as yet. An investigation of this correspondence is suggested below. For this reason it may be found more advantageous for the teacher to examine the pupil individually, using one of the examination blanks on which he has already taken the test. The questions may then be asked of the pupil orally and his answers compared with those which he gave on the test blank. This form of comparison is very illuminating, since it can be determined just what questions he was not able to answer in the group examination but which he is able to answer when asked orally in an interview. Needless to say, the teacher should be very careful in giving such an individual examination that all nervousness on the part of the pupil is eliminated before beginning the examination.

For this purpose introductory remarks may be of value, such as the following: "On looking over your test paper, John, I thought that you had not done your best. Do you think you did?" The child will undoubtedly say that he did not and the teacher may then say: "Well, now let me ask you some of these questions again so as to give you another chance." This should elicit from the child his very best effort. In giving this individual examination, the teacher should give every encouragement to the pupil and conceal as far as possible any mistakes which he may make of which he is not conscious. If it should be found that the pupil is still unable to answer correctly those questions which he missed in the group examination, the score may be taken as an accurate measure of his mental ability. If, however, he is able in the individual examination to answer correctly those questions which he missed in the group examination, it would appear that the score was not an adequate measure of his mental ability, in which case the teacher may either revise the score according to her best judgment or may administer the Stanford-Binet Scale, or the Herring-Binet Scale.[1]

This shows the need for an investigation of the relation between scores in a group test when administered to pupils in groups, and scores in the same test when administered individually and orally. For this purpose a large number of pupils in a wide range of grades should be tested by both forms of a group examination, such as the National Intelligence Tests or the Otis Self-Administering Tests of Mental Ability:[2] Higher Examination or Intermediate Examination, administering one form to the pupils in groups and later administering the second form to the same pupils individually and orally, observing, let us say, the same time limits as indicated for the group examination. The scores made in the group administration should then be compared with those made in the individual administration for the purpose of determining what score a child is most likely to make in the individual examination who has made any given score in the group examination.

4. *Experimental Reclassification.*

In the description of study No. 1, methods of reclassifying pupils into three or more classes within a grade on the basis of mental ability or on the basis of brightness have been explained. When such reclassification has been made it is very desirable that those pupils who are given extra promotion should be very carefully followed up to determine their degree of success in the higher grade, both as to quality of school work and as to the effect upon the child. Similarly when classes are made more homogeneous by the division of grades upon the basis of either mental ability or brightness, the efficiency of teaching should be carefully investigated in order to determine whether there has been an improvement. When the pupils of a grade are divided into bright, normal, and dull classes on the basis of measures of brightness, these classes may be given school work of different degrees of intensity. The bright pupils should be given much more difficult problems to solve and more of them and should go more deeply into the content subjects.

[1] The Herring Revision of the Binet-Simon Tests is a new individual mental ability examination, published by the World Book Co., Yonkers-on-Hudson, N. Y.

[2] A new series of group tests for grades 9 to 13 and 4 to 8 respectively, published by the World Book Co., Yonkers-on-Hudson, N. Y.

On the other hand, the dull pupils should be given problems commensurate in number and difficulty with their degree of ability, and may be given only minimum essentials in the content subjects in order that at the end of the school year they shall appear to have covered the same ground as the brighter pupils, and in order that they may be promoted into a dull section of the next grade, in which again they will be given school work commensurate with their ability and where their effort may be spent with the maximum of result.

When such an experiment is undertaken in classification, it is especially desirable that the school work of the pupils be carefully studied in order that adjustments may be made by shifting pupils from one class to another where classification does not appear to be adequate. It would be very desirable to investigate the attitude of the pupils in the various classes to determine the psychological effect of such classification upon them, both as reflected in the quality of their school work and as exhibited in their attitude toward pupils in other classes. It would be very desirable also to investigate the attitude of parents toward having their children thus classified in order to throw light upon the subject of classification. It is indeed quite likely that the best results may be obtained by so designating these classes that no distinction between them is apparent, and also by conducting the instruction in such a way that differences of instruction are as inconspicuous as possible—not for the purpose of deceiving the pupils so much as for the sake of avoiding any discouragement which may come to a young pupil from the feeling that he is incapable of the same achievement in his school work as that of which his fellows are capable.

5. Comparison Between Index of Brightness and Progress Through School.

There are, of course, several purposes for which the results of intelligence tests are used and the efficiency of the tests must be judged, therefore, separately according to the use to which the results are to be put. Thus, if we wish to find the best test of predicting a child's ability to progress in school, the various tests must be compared for this specific purpose, whereas, if it is proposed to use the results to predict the quality of school work which a pupil may do, the tests must be compared specifically in this regard. Of a number of tests, one may be superior for one purpose and another for another purpose.

Let us suppose it is desired to choose the best one of several tests in mental ability for the purpose of determining pupils' ability to progress in school. For this there are two methods of making such an investigation. The first one is to administer several tests to the same group of pupils and keep careful record of their progress during the next one or two or three years, and afterward compare their progress through school with the results of the initial tests. A second method which, while not so accurate, is necessary in order to save waiting, is to compare the results of the tests with previous progress made in school. It will be realized, however, that even though the results of tests administered in the sixth grade may correlate quite well with the progress which the pupil has made in the grades from one to six, it does not follow necessarily that the results of the same test administered in the third grade will be equally prognostic of the progress which the child will make in the next three or four grades. Whichever method is used, it must be kept in mind that it is necessary to compare the pupils' progress through school not with their scores, but with their measures of brightness as expressed in terms of IB, CB, IQ or PR which are derived from their scores. The relative values of the several tests in determining pupils' ability to progress in school may be found by comparing the coefficients of correlation between ability to progress in school and measures of brightness obtained by means of each of the several tests.

It should be realized in this connection that numerous studies have been made in which a coefficient of correlation is found between scores or measures of brightness obtained by a single test and ability to progress in school or the quality of school work or teachers' estimates of mental ability, etc., and that while these are of some value in themselves, it is by no means proper to make comparisons between one test and another unless both tests were administered to the same children and were compared with identical measures of school progress, etc. The reason for this is that mental ability tests do not differ greatly in efficiency and the coefficient of correlation between measures of brightness obtained by tests and progress through school is very markedly affected by several different factors. First of all, the coefficient of correlation thus found is very materially affected by the degree of heterogeneity of the group. If calculated in the case of a select and homogeneous group the correlation will be very low, whereas if calculated in the case of an unselected and very heterogeneous group the correlation will be much higher for the same test. Again, schools differ very widely in the number of extra promotions which are given and in the amount of retardation of dull pupils, so that if the study is made in a school where practically no extra promotions are given and most children are allowed to progress regularly one grade per year, the correlation will be very low, whereas if the same study is made in another school where careful attention is given to extra promotions for bright pupils, the correlation for the same test may be much higher. Again, if the study is being made of the correlation between test results and teachers' estimates or school marks, the amount of the correlation for a single test will depend very largely upon the care with which the estimates or the marks have been made. Therefore, if it is desired to compare several tests as to efficiency for any purpose, these must be tried out upon exactly the same pupils and exactly the same criterion must be used in every case.

6. Permanency of the IQ or Percentile Rank.

A number of studies have been made recently to determine the permanency of the IQ. So far as these pertain to the lower ranges of mental ability these studies are of great value, but in so far as they deal with the upper ranges, their value is questionable, for reasons given below.

The Intelligence Quotient was invented for the Binet Scale. It is obtained by dividing the Binet Mental Age by the chronological age (not over 16 years). Whenever it is desired to express a degree of brightness in terms of an Intelligence Quotient, the score of the pupil, by whatever tests it may be obtained, should first be transmuted into terms of a Binet Mental Age. Now, Binet Mental Ages are generally considered to represent approximately equal steps in mental ability. That is, the steps between Binet Mental Ages of 13 and 14, 14 and 15, 15 and 16, 16 and 17, etc., are presumably approximately equal steps in mental ability. On the other hand, however, it is universally appreciated that in any given individual the growth of mental ability becomes retarded after the chronological age of about 14 years, so that the increment of mental ability of any given individual between the ages of 14 and 15 is slightly less than the increment of that individual between 13 and 14. His increment of mental ability between 15 and 16 years of age is still less and the increment between 16 and 17 years, if indeed there is any growth between these years at all, is still less. If the reader will follow out carefully the implications of these statements, he will see that the Intelligence Quotient of an individual as customarily derived cannot possibly be expected to remain constant. Thus, if it is a fact that the increment of growth of mental ability between the ages of 15 and 16 is less than that proportional to the increment of chronological age, the Intelligence Quotient must of necessity decrease slightly. On the other hand, if the increment of growth between the ages of 15 and 16 *is* proportional to the increment of chronological age, then the growth of mental ability does not stop suddenly at the age of 16, which means that if 16 years is used as the denominator in figuring the Intelligence Quotient of a single individual, first at the chronological age of 16 years and then at 17 years, the intelligence quotient at 17 must of necessity be greater than that at 16. It may be seen, therefore, that no matter at what age the growth of mental ability begins to slow up, the Intelligence Quotient of a single individual must either decrease slightly just before the age of 16 or increase after the age of 16, or both. It cannot be otherwise unless we suppose that mental ability develops regularly up to the age of exactly 16, that is, with equal yearly increments, and then suddenly

ceases altogether. This, of course, is an impossible supposition.

It should be clear, therefore, that any attempt to investigate the permanency of the IQ in the upper ranges which does not take account of these facts cannot yield valid results, for when changes in IQ which must of necessity occur in the upper ages, by virtue of the reasons set forth, are thrown into the same group with IQs derived in the lower ranges, the result can be nothing less than confusion, for any stability of the Intelligence Quotient in the lower ranges is entirely lost sight of because of the introduction of necessarily variable IQs from the upper ranges.

This whole difficulty could be simply and easily remedied by a slight modification in the present method of finding Intelligence Quotients. Thus, instead of dividing the Binet Mental Age which the individual attains by his chronological age, this should be divided by the Binet Mental Age which is the norm for his chronological age. In that case, it will easily be seen that a child whose mental ability develops in such a way that he attains at each chronological age exactly that mental age which is the norm for his chronological age, his Intelligence Quotient will remain exactly 100 throughout the development of his mental ability, and in a similar way it may be shown that the IQ of a bright or dull child may be expected to remain constant, since this method automatically takes account of the slowing down in the growth of mental ability in the years following the age of 14 and sets no arbitrary point at which mental ability must be assumed suddenly to cease developing.

If an investigation is made, therefore, of the permanency of the IQ, the IQ should in all cases be obtained by dividing the Binet

Mental Age obtained by the individual by the Binet Mental Age which is the norm for his chronological age. This amounts to exactly the same thing as finding the "Coefficient of Brightness" as provided in the 1919 edition of the Manual of Directions for the Otis Group Intelligence Scale: Advanced Examination, a method which has been adopted among others by Monroe and Buckingham for use with the Illinois Examination.

The really important question is this: Will a pupil maintain the same percentile rank (among children of his own age) throughout his growth of mental ability? This is a very reasonable condition to expect, for there is no makeshift in the method of obtaining percentile ranks such as that in the determination of Intelligence Quotients by dividing by the chronological age up to 16 and arbitrarily calling all pupils 16 who are over 16 years of age. It is suggested, therefore, that an investigation be made of the permanency of the percentile rank of individuals by testing the same pupils at different ages and converting test scores into percentile ranks.

In making this investigation it may be realized that it is not adequate to find the median or average percentile rank of a group when first tested and the median or average percentile rank of the same group in the second testing, and to compare only these medians or averages since the percentile ranks of some children may increase and of others may decrease and the median or average of the group may remain the same. Such a comparison would be of incidental value in showing whether the percentile ranks of the group as a whole seem to rise or fall, but if the median percentile rank of a group should either rise or fall, the presumption would be that there was

some error either in the norms or in the table for finding percentile ranks.

On the other hand, however, it is entirely conceivable that pupils may actually change in percentile rank as they grow older, either because their development of mental ability has become less than is normal for their ages, or for some reason has speeded up. An investigation of the permanency of percentile rank may, therefore, serve a double purpose, first, as a check upon the accuracy of the norms and tables for finding PR, and, secondly, to see whether all pupils develop mentally according to the same type of curve of growth.

Since the units of the percentile rank scale are of unequal value, that is, the interval between 50 and 55 on the scale is much less than the interval 90 to 95, it is not possible to compare directly the change in one portion of the scale with the change in another portion in which the units are of different magnitude. For this reason, the median change in percentile rank should be given separately for all individuals whose percentile rank according to the first testing was between 50 and 60, and separately for those whose percentile rank according to the first testing was between 60 and 70, etc. A statement of the median amounts of change of percentile rank either upward or downward of pupils whose initial percentile ranks fall within each interval of 10 points will be exceedingly illuminating and throw much light upon the possibility of prognosis of future degrees of brightness of pupils making any given percentile rank at any given stage of their mental development.

7. *Determination of the Correspondence between Scores in Two or More Tests.*

Requests are frequently sent to the writer for tables for converting scores of one test into terms of another, such, for example, as expressing scores in the Otis Advanced Examination in terms of scores in the Army Alpha Intelligence Examination. Numerous studies have been made for the purpose of finding the coefficient of correlation between two tests, but these do not seem to have been followed up by an investigation of the correspondence between scores. By correlation between scores is meant the degree to which high scores in one test imply, or are accompanied by, high scores in the other test, and similarly the degree to which low scores in one imply or are accompanied by low scores in the other. By the determination of the correspondence between scores is meant the determination of the score in one test which most probably measures the same degree of mental ability as the given score in the other test. It might be found, for example, that the correlation between the Advanced Examination and the Army Alpha is .80, but this does not tell us what score in the Advanced Examination corresponds to a score of 135, for example, in Alpha.

The method of determining the correspondence between scores in two tests is as follows: Administer both tests to the same group of individuals, using as heterogeneous a group as possible. Next make a distribution of the scores of the group in each test. Find the 5 percentile, 10 percentile, 15 percentile, 20 percentile, etc., score in each test. It may be assumed roughly that the 5 percentile score in one test corresponds to the 5 percentile score in the other, and that the 10 percentile score in one corresponds to the 10 percentile score in the other, etc. This method may be refined somewhat, however, by plotting on a sheet

of cross section paper the 5 percentile scores in two tests, one being measured horizontally and the other vertically, and plotting the 10 percentile scores, 15 percentile scores, etc., in the two tests in a similar manner, and then drawing a smooth curve as nearly as possible through these points.[1] The most probable form of this "curve" will be a straight line, but it is not proper to assume in advance that it is straight. By means of this smooth curve the correspondence may be found between scores in the two tests. For any point on the curve the score in one test on the horizontal scale below the point corresponds to the score in the other on the vertical scale opposite the point.

If the two tests which are being compared are given on the same day, it will be readily appreciated that some practice effect is likely to carry over from the first to the second test which will render the score in the second test somewhat higher than would have been the case if the first test had not immediately preceded it. In order to eliminate this extraneous factor, it is necessary to give one of the tests first in half of the cases and the other test first in the other half of the cases. It may be well, then, to find the correspondence separately for each of the two groups in order that the effect of practice may be ascertained. The true correspondence between the tests may then be assumed to be what may roughly be called the average of the two lines, obtained as described above.

On the other hand, if the second test is given, say, in two or three months, due allowance must be made for this fact in finding the correspondence between the scores, since obviously a score in one test

[1] This method has been described and illustrated in an article entitled "The Reliability of the Binet Scale and Pedagogical Scales," *Journal of Educational Research*, September, 1921, page 125.

cannot be assumed to be the equivalent of a score for the same child in another test taken after his mental ability has developed somewhat. To make allowance for the growth of mental ability between testings, find the line showing the correspondence between scores, as described above, and then subtract from the second score the normal amount of score gained in the length of time which has elapsed between testings, as shown by the table of norms.

Caution must be noted at this point. The reader should appreciate that if two tests are administered to the same pupils, a pupil making a given score in one test will not necessarily make the corresponding score in the other test. In fact, if a plot is made of the scores in the two tests as for the purpose of finding the correlation in two tests, it will very readily be seen that a pupil making a very high score in the first test tends to make a score in the second test somewhat lower than that corresponding to his score in the first test, and a pupil making a very low score in the first test tends to make a score in the second test somewhat higher than that corresponding to his score in the first test. It is hardly within the scope of this article to explain the reason for this, but it may be said briefly that high scores for any particular group tend to be an error upward and low scores for any particular group tend to be an error downward. Investigation of the correspondence between scores in the various group tests and the Stanford Revision of the Binet Scale is especially needed, particularly in the upper ranges of these scales where the scores are in excess of norms for any chronological age and where comparison by means of age norms is consequently impossible.

8. What Constitutes the Difference between Brightness and Dullness?

This is not a statistical research but a psychological one. Let us suppose we have before us two pupils, each making the same score in a mental ability test. We say, therefore, that they have the same degree of mental ability. Let us suppose, however, that while this mental ability is just normal for a ten year old child, one of these children is 12 years old and one is 8 years old. We, therefore, say that the first child is dull and the second child bright. Now, there is some fundamental difference in the quality of mind between these two children and this difference is by no means understood. Any investigation throwing new light upon the differences in quality of mind between two such children will be a distinct contribution to psychology. It is suggested, therefore, that an investigation be made of the mental characteristics of very bright and very dull pupils having the same degree of mental ability, for the purpose of discovering if possible what fundamental quality of mind differentiates bright pupils from dull ones having the same mental ability. Indeed, in the present state of our knowledge one may hardly make a suggestion as to what might be discovered, so that the field may be considered as almost virgin soil for future investigation.

The writer will be glad to know of anyone who wishes to undertake any of these researches and will be glad to give any help which he can to the investigator. It is especially requested that an account of any of these researches which are made be sent to the writer, care of the World Book Co., Yonkers-on-Hudson, N. Y.

COERCION AND LEARNING
(*Concluded*)[1]

WILLIAM HEARD KILPATRICK
Professor of Education, Teachers College, Columbia University

The teachers meet again "Let's go on with our discussion of coercion. I am anxious to get my ideas straight about coercion and a love for playing the piano."

"Very well. Only let us first recall our main line of thought so that we may not lose connection. We agreed **A summary of the effect of coercion** by a kind of definition that the presence of an aroused contrary mind-set is the sign and accompaniment of what we call coercion. The normal and legitimate effect of such a contrary mind-set we concluded is to bring unreadiness for the coerced action and to lessen—in any event —the satisfaction accompanying the successful completion of‘ this action. This unreadiness and accompanying lessened satisfaction would mean by the psychological law of Effect less of learning in connection with the coerced activity.[2] From this we further concluded that if we wish a child to learn best we should as far as feasible avoid arousing the contrary mind-set."

"Well, isn't it inevitable that if you force anything on another you do arouse opposition, and isn't this feeling of opposition just what you mean by a contrary mind-set? If this is so, then doesn't coercion, however you define it, necessarily prevent learning? How can one ever learn to play the piano through compulsion, still less learn to like it?"

"Not so fast. You are ignoring certain necessary qualifications to your statements.

Coercion does not prevent all learning The typical result of forcing conduct upon another is, true enough, to arouse opposition; but there are many possible degrees of such opposition. Some are so weak as hardly to mean a contrary mind-set. More to the point, however, we never have said that an opposed mind-set destroys or prevents all learning in connection. On the contrary, human responses are always mixed. We pointed out explicitly in the case of the boy kept after school to work his problems that he had at least two mind-sets, one of opposition to the teacher, the other much weaker as a rule but still present, to solve the problems. When he succeeds in solving the problems he feels some satisfaction. This satisfaction may come from either of two sources. He feels satisfaction first at getting out. The more exclusively his satisfaction as he finishes is centered consciously on getting out, the less in probability does his success fix any mathematics in his mind. The second satisfaction arises from the success attending his efforts at the mathematics. He may, it is true, have felt his resentment and opposition so keenly that he wouldn't even try to solve the problems. If so, no effort, and therefore no chance for success or satisfaction, and consequently no possible learning. But if

[2] Thorndike's Law of Effect may be freely stated: When any response is made, the tendency so to respond is strengthened or weakened according as satisfaction or annoyance follows.

he did try at all and did make any sort of success, then there will be some satisfaction and consequently some learning."

"You do admit, then, that coercion can bring learning?"

"Certainly. We have all the time said that coercion might and usually would bring some learning. Our point has been that in so far as coercion arouses and maintains a contrary mind-set, it tends to reduce and lessen the learning we wish."

"Then coercion is merely a poor way to get things learned?"

"It is that, true enough, but it may be worse than that. We have in this whole discussion been ignoring all **Coercion and** those accompanying learnings **concomitants** we discussed in September and October. In any actual case before us they have to be considered. Coercion may teach on the side, as it were, many undesirable things. For instance, many boys who have been badly managed in school conceive such a distaste for school that they leave it as soon as the law allows, to the hurt both of their own future and of society at large."

"Well, may we not go back to the piano playing? I think I see now how a girl may **Piano play-** learn to play from compul- **ing under** sory practice on the piano. **coercion** Isn't it just like the boy kept in after school,—the girl will as a rule give at least *some* attention to her practice and if she succeeds even a little bit, she will have some satisfaction arising from her success. So she will learn at least a little."

"Yes, that is exactly the case. Of course the more she puts her soul into what she does, the more likely she is, first of all, to succeed, and also the greater will be her satisfaction in what she accomplishes, and

consequently the better will be her learning."

"I find myself confused a little just here. I thought the question was not whether the girl will learn to play a piece from enforced practice. That I never doubted. The question I asked last time was whether the coercion if persisted in by the mother wouldn't result in a fondness for piano playing in the girl. And if this is so, it seems to contradict your analysis."

"You mean, then, to ask whether coercion can create a fondness. And if yes, how can we reconcile this with the effect of annoyance, which would be expected to create an aversion?"

"Yes, or you might put it, whether coercion can build an interest. I should certainly expect from your line of argument that an aversion and not a fondness would result."

"What are the observed facts? Does coercion build fondness or aversion?"

"I think I can answer that. Of course I haven't kept any statistics, as some of you would say; but my experience as a music teacher through a good many years is this: if a girl has talent and if she is begun right so that she feels herself succeeding, she will learn rapidly. If she does learn rapidly and keeps on growing in her music and if people praise her playing, she will grow more and more fond of her music. But if she has no talent, she won't learn very rapidly and will easily get discouraged. Then when people don't praise her playing, she will begin to look for praise and satisfaction along other lines. For such a girl a strong fondness for the piano will seldom, if ever, develop."

"But you said nothing about coercion and its effect."

"I don't think much about that with my pupils. It may help or it may hurt."

"I wonder if we haven't now the essential facts before us. If a girl has no talent for playing she will sooner or later find it out. If she is normally sensitive to what people say, she will gradually leave off playing for others. In such case the coercion couldn't help, it might hurt. If a girl has talent but doesn't know it, a certain amount of coercion—skillfully applied—may overcome an initial objection to practising until her success, which is probable from her talent, brings satisfaction enough to build a fondness. In such cases the coercion may help."

When coercion can help

"Why say 'may help'? Why not say 'does help'?"

"Possibly you are right, but I must believe in every case that so far as the child feels the coercion to be coercion, the desired learning is lessened. I admit the need for getting the child to put forth the necessary initial effort, but I can not admit that coercion is always the best way to secure this needed effort. Remember that coercion naturally lessens both the chance of success and the accompanying learning. Perhaps some other way than coercion might arouse the effort without at the same time incurring the hurtful effect almost bound to follow in some measure from coercion. In other words, as a teaching instrument coercion is always in some measure an evil. In a particular case it may be the best available instrument. If so, use it. But know all the time that it carries with it evil possibilities."

"Do you refer by 'evil possibilities' merely to the lessened learning or to the bad concomitant learning?"

"To both. We can never lose sight of either. If we decide to use coercion in any particular case, we must decide only after a full survey of all the probable results."

"You do admit, however, that coercion does sometimes build an interest."

"I must admit it. The facts as well as my own theory demand it as a possibility."

"Would you mind recapitulating your position on this point?"

"I am glad to do so. Building interests is perhaps as important a work as education can undertake. Whether it is feasible to build an interest along any given line depends first of all on the native capacities of the person."

"May I interrupt you? Do you refer here exclusively to some specific talent, such as a talent for music?"

"No, although some pronounced capacity or talent may be the dominating factor. I mean, however, to include other instances where the activity involves many different satisfactions as, for example, what we popularly call 'manipulation,' 'inventiveness,' 'social approval,' and the like."

"Haven't you now so broadened your conception as to take in all conceivable activities?"

"Yes and no. There is practically no activity to be shut out entirely. The Hindu fakir who daily tortures his body has actually built up in himself this repulsive practice as an interest."

"It may be an aside, but would you mind saying a further word about building interests? I mean without special reference to coercion. If I correctly understand you, there are first some necessary prerequisites and then an appropriate procedure."

"I myself reckon two necessary prerequisites for an abiding interest: first, **Prerequisites for building an interest** enough capacity for the activities involved to bring continued satisfaction; and second, a growing activity. The first may refer more specifically to one dominant talent, as for mathematics or music, or it may contemplate only a combination of more ordinary powers. But there must be the possibility of continued satisfaction from the exercise of the activity. The second prerequisite, that of the quality of growing, it seems is not equally necessary for all people; but on the whole the interest will not be abidingly gripping unless it continually faces at least some element of novelty."

"These I understand to be the prerequisites. Now what about the procedure?"

"The essential of the procedure is our old law of Effect, Exercise with satisfaction. We must somehow get vigorous action along the desired line and of a kind that brings a high degree of satisfaction. Suppose we say it in tabular fashion:

The procedure for building an interest

1. Get the activity going with zest,— if possible in the face of obstacles that challenge all but the last reserves of power.

2. See that success attends.

3. If possible, let there be approval from those whose approval is valued.

If the two prerequisites have been met and this procedure can be followed, I believe you will with practical certainty see an interest growing."

"You seem to think that overcoming hindrances is a help to interest. Isn't that contrary to general opinion?"

"Perhaps so, but I am sure of my ground. Granted an initial mind-set in that direction, there are few things so interesting as overcoming a difficulty that calls for all but the last ounce of available energy. Of

Overcoming hindrances

course if difficulties of this sort keep on confronting us, we have to be sustained by a belief that the end is worthy of the effort. Approval of others helps just here; it steadies our faith in the end."

"What do you mean by an interest when you speak of building an interest? Your last remark seems to me to imply the presence of interest, but not of *an* interest, as I understand the term. Interest is there, but it seems to be fleeting, found only in overcoming and the like. I thought you were to build up a permanent interest in some end that would supply interest to the necessary means."

The meaning of an interest

"Your distinction is well made and properly made. We do contemplate building an interest that will carry its own drive. Unless it comes about that the end, or the working with and toward the end, carries its own drive, arouses an inner urge, is desired for its own sake—unless these things happen, no interest has been built. Now what I mean is this: if one does put heart and soul with very great endeavor in working for some end, especially for some difficult end, if one sees himself succeeding, if one hears meanwhile the plaudits of those whose praise counts with him,— then not only is there interest in overcoming and in being approved, but you may be reasonably sure that an interest will in time be built which will of its own pull carry the person on without plaudits, perhaps even against jeers, without even present signs of success, but with many and varied efforts in a real struggle to achieve the end that is called for by the interest. Such an interest becomes as it were an intrinsic source of effort, capable of lending interest to auxiliary causes."

"From this discussion on building interests I see now more clearly than before how coercion fails. But

Virtues as moral interests

couldn't we go further? Wouldn't these two discussions have important bearings in the field of moral education?"

"Just what do you have in mind?"

"Are we not, in the realm of morals, mainly concerned with building what might be called moral interests? For example, with · building up in the child interests in honesty and fair play and consideration of others? If I understand rightly, honesty is indeed the best policy, but the man who acts honestly merely from policy is not really honest. Do we not wish to make him love honesty for its own sake, and isn't this substantially the same thing as the interest you have just described?"

"Yes. We wish these moral virtues and other social interests enthroned in the hearts of each one so that they are, so far as one's feelings at the time go, their own justification for being. Of course we wish more in the way of understanding the why of them and more in the way of loving our fellow men and so on; but you are exactly right as to their psychological character. They are interests to be built in the hearts of the young."

"And would the same procedure hold for these as for the others?"

"Yes, so far as these are interests, they are to be built in the same way. But some of them are broad generalized ideas and would accordingly demand first the procedure necessary for making such generalizations. That, of course, is another story."

"Would the same limitations on coercion hold in building these interests as hold, say, in building a fondness for piano playing?"

"Yes, and perhaps in effect even more strongly. In piano playing we have the possibility that great natural capacity for music may bring success in spite of the lessened efforts due to the coercion. In this way we have the possibility that the opposed mind-set will disappear under these favorable conditions and an interest accordingly come to be built. There are even good grounds for supposing that strong native capacity and initial interest are usually found together. The coercion might in such cases serve to cut off rival activities. The native ability would do the rest."

"Might not the same thing hold in the realm of morals? Are there not born moral geniuses, just as there are born musical geniuses? I fail to see why the same discussion would not hold unchanged."

"It would probably hold unchanged if we were content to have as many people incompetent in morals as in music. We are for the most part willing—indeed more than willing—to leave the making of music to the gifted few. But everybody needs morals, especially—as the humorist said— does the other fellow. So we must try to build moral interests often in mediocre native ability."

"You mean then that we may use coercion in morals where we don't in music?"

"No. Coercion is just as hurtful in one as in the other. We saw that coercion, if skillfully managed, might in music cut off thwarting interests and give the natural interests a chance to develop. In the same way, skillfully applied, it may help in morals, but remember that morals must be built even where there is no pronounced moral capacity to help us."

"I wish you would illustrate this. I don't quite follow all you have said."

"Suppose at home some evening the younger children persist in making so much noise that the older children cannot study and their parents cannot read. What should we do and why?"

A moral situation

"That's easy. I'd tell them to stop. If they didn't I'd send them to bed. Coercion or not, I certainly would not allow any of my children to ruin everybody else's happiness and I'd do it for their own good as well. Spoiling children does what the word says, it 'spoils' them."

"Well, that is what most people would do and for the same reasons. But let's examine the matter a little. There are several ways of sizing up this situation. We may consider the rights of the parents and the older children to reasonable quiet and the attitudes of the younger children toward these rights. So stated, we have strongly suggested an educational situation. The younger children either don't understand or don't appreciate or won't respect the rights of the others. Each of these failures is a matter within the realm of education. A diagnosis should accordingly be made to locate the exact defects, and the proper educational procedure followed to correct them. Am I right?"

"You may be right, but you haven't told us what to do. Would you punish the children or not?"

"Certainly not until I had made an educational diagnosis and not then unless I could see in reason that the proposed punishment promised to supply the needed educational stimulation called for in their particular cases."

"Don't you believe wrong-doing must be punished?"

"As you ask it, no. The sole reason the parent can properly have for punishing a child is the foreseen educative effect that is to follow."

"What about spoiling a child? Isn't it a real danger?"

"Yes, but it is brought about by bad education. I understand a spoiled child to be one who thinks his wish furnishes sufficient grounds for getting what he wishes and who is moreover disposed to make things uncomfortable till he gets it. Now both of these attitudes can come in only one way: he has tried them with such uniform success that they have been fixed in him. They can be removed only by reversing the process. He must learn by the action of satisfaction and annoyance that his wish is not sufficient, that others have rights which he must take into account, and that making himself a nuisance is not a socially satisfactory way to secure ends. It may take time and patience on the part of his elders for him to learn these things, but there is no other course available."

Educational diagnosis and treatment

"And what is the psychology of the procedure?"

"There are two possible ways of procedure: one is to attach annoyance to the children's wrong behavior, the other is to see that satisfaction attends the right. Of course both at times may be combined."

"You refer in the first to the use of punishment?"

"Yes, and it is best available when the annoyance will be attached uniquely to the wrong doing. Otherwise there is danger that wrong aversions may be built up, say to the mother for interfering, or to the home as a place where unpleasant things happen, or to the older sister for complaining, or to duty as a

Punishment and its limitations

disagreeable word that figures whenever pleasures are curtailed. It is this ambiguous effect of punishment, and indeed of all coercion, that makes it so unreliable an agency for moral betterment. If the attendant annoyance happens to be misplaced, mis-education takes place."

"The second possible procedure then is more satisfactory?"

"It promises better in every way, though it is less handy for the unthinking to apply than the 'shut-up-or-be-sent-to-bed' procedure."

"Do you recognize any proper place for coercion other than those already mentioned?"

"We didn't say explicitly, I believe, that coercion may at times be properly used to prevent the exercise of certain undesirable practices and consequently prevent the formation of undesirable habits. But even here a positive régime of building good

interests instead is, if feasible, far more desirable."

"Are there then no other uses for coercion? None whatever?"

"Oh yes. Coercion may properly be used as an emergency measure to prevent damage to one's self or to others or to valuable property. In themselves these are not educational measures, though we can never forget that they have educative effects, usually mixed, some bad and some good."

"You seem then to count aversion always as an evil but sometimes as the least of the evils confronting one."

The conclusion "I think it has always attendant evils. Usually these evils outweigh its good. Occasionally the reverse is true. The constant use of coercion, however, is a sign of bad teaching somewhere."

AN EXPERIMENT IN COÖPERATION
VI. Standards in Composition

JAMES F. HOSIC

Associate Professor of Education, Teachers College, Columbia University

Concerted attack on the problem of how to improve the speaking and writing of the children in the experimental schools brought us soon to the problem of standards. What constitutes good composition in a certain grade in school? What range of excellence may be expected? How does oral composition differ from written? These were questions that must be faced but with insufficient data for answer.

Composition, especially oral composition, is in fact a new subject in the elementary schools. "Language" or "English" has held the stage. Attention has

too often been divided between exercises aimed at correctness in grammar and mechanics and development of vocabulary through analysis of poems or other literature. Witness the textbooks and the courses of study. The direct approach through expression of the pupil's own experience, as in the plans of Sheridan and Mahoney, is comparatively novel.

We were of the opinion, moreover, that the attempt to set up standards for ourselves would react most favorably on the work, giving the teachers a better grasp of it and deeper interest. We hoped to measure our results in the end by published scales and make comparative studies, but this we afterward decided not to do for the sufficient reason that none of the scales available distinguished between composition as such and proof-reading. These we kept separate.

ORAL OR WRITTEN?

Since our method was to place oral composition first, both in time and in importance, we naturally leaned toward standards in speaking rather than in writing, but decided to collect examples of both. The teachers were asked to preserve from time to time the speeches of the children and also their written papers. In the earlier grades it was necessary for the teachers themselves to write out what the child had spoken, often from his dictation. In the middle and upper grades the pupils could do this for themselves. In some instances a stenographer was employed. In this way a collection of compositions was built up in several schools and the study of them began.

It was soon evident that, except possibly in case of the upper grades, there was no real need of setting up two sets of standards in composition. The pupils wrote as they spoke. (They were not permitted to write first, then memorize and speak—the sure road to bookish formality.) Besides, there was more immediate need of guidance for the practice of speaking, since this was first stressed, hence the decision was readily arrived at that all the schools should be asked to select sample compositions to serve as oral standards.

SELECTING THE STANDARDS

The enterprise proceeded *by schools*. Each school group needed to know its own state, what its pupils were doing. Each group would profit by the experience. To begin with the assumption that all schools should or could reach the same standards would have been a serious blunder; there is too much assurance that they can't and shouldn't. By organizing the work of each school separately we gained, moreover, the immeasurable advantage of variation in method and range in performance. Each person had a chance to make his maximum contribution. The individual was not lost in the crowd.

On certain items there was general agreement. We would choose narrative of experience as the type of composition. This, as has been explained, was the type which we depended upon to form the basic habits of good speaking—the sentence sense, holding to the point, etc. We would collect examples of the work as the pupils themselves left it, not as dressed up by the teacher. We would ignore the mechanics of writing, defined as all the new activities involved in putting speech on paper. The problem of mechanics would be met by means of a separate set of standards. We would judge merit with reference to the closing weeks of the grade.

The degrees of merit were to be as follows: Poor, Fair, Good, Excellent, and Superior. Fair was taken to mean that degree of merit which at least seventy-five per cent of the pupils could equal or excel by the end of the grade; Superior, that degree reached occasionally by pupils of extraordinary ability, often through treating a subject of unusual possibilities. The other degrees were to be relative to these. There was no marking in per cents or on a numerical scale. Particularly it was understood that compositions were to be selected as representing what the pupils actually did, not what in some Utopia they might be expected to do. How hard it was to hold to this common-sense principle will be understood by all who have observed the inflated and over-ambitious aims in English which in courses of study are too commonly set up. The feeling of justice and satisfaction which resulted was, however, worth many times the effort required.

The administrative procedure followed in the different schools varied. Commonly the principal appointed a committee of five to prepare a bulletin giving notice of the compositions wanted, how they were to be selected, when handed in, and the like, and, when the material was at hand, he assisted in having the samples typewritten and the standards mimeographed. Hearing the compositions read proved superior as a means of reaching a judgment of merit to reading them oneself. All the committees testified to the value of the discussions of merit and demerit to those participating in them. The exchange of impression was greatly broadening and enlightening to everybody.

A SET OF SCHOOL STANDARDS

The following set of standards selected at random from among those collected in the early stages of the work will serve to illustrate. These, it should be said again, were intended, not to indicate a distant goal of achievement but what was actually happening at the time. The contrast with the ambitious literary efforts of exceptional children sometimes offered as examples of school work is startling enough not to require comment.

A glance at these standards is sufficient to discover the possibility of improvement. For one thing the difference in merit between neighboring samples is not equally obvious. There is, moreover, no indication as to why the committee considered a certain composition good, say, but not excellent, nor why it was an advance over the good composition of the preceding grade. That the pupils of the upper classes would eventually show greater superiority over the earlier was of course expected. This was a satisfactory beginning, nevertheless, and provided some useful material for study even by the pupils themselves, who suggested changes, some of which were clearly desirable. From several such collections, as later revised, an annotated scale for the whole city was finally derived.

ORAL COMPOSITION STANDARDS OF THE X——— SCHOOL

GRADE 1

Superior

Our kitty's name is Browny. She plays with my little brother all day. When I come home from school I roll a ball on the floor. Kitty runs after it. She catches it in her mouth. Then she lets it go again and it rolls back to me.

Excellent

One day I found a bicycle. It was under some papers in the alley. I brought it home. When I come home from school, I change my clothes and go riding on the bicycle.

Good

My doll's name is Mildred. She has blue eyes and brown hair. She is a big doll. When I come home from school I play with her.

Fair

Yesterday my brother and I went out. We played tag.

GRADE 2

Superior

My grandpa brought a cat home. My mother gave it some milk in a saucer. She put it by my bed. This morning when I went to get up, I stepped in the dish and broke it.

Excellent

The cat next door looks like a squirrel. He runs like one. He can go faster than a squirrel.

Good

Our bird used to open the cage and jump out. He opened it with his foot. He used to fly into the parlor. His bathtub was on the window sill. He flew into it. When he was flying around he broke his leg with a piece of string.

Fair

Our dog is a Scotch terrior. He is black and white. All he does is bite my hair.

Poor

We had a little dog. It was named Trixie. It died.

GRADE 3

Superior

FISHING

All of a sudden I felt a terrible jerk on my rod. I saw flopping alongside of the boat a great big Black Bass. "Hey, Dad!" I yelled, "help me, help!" My father got up to get the rod, but the oar of the boat hit him in the chest. My fish got away. That was the end of my fishing for the rest of the week.

Excellent

A FISHING TRIP

I caught a fish. Do you know where I caught it? I caught it in the fish bowl. It was a gold fish.

Good

A GOOD LAUGH

Last Sunday we went to a show. We saw a coach with four dogs pulling. Inside sat a monkey. When the coach stopped the monkey came out. When the show was over, the monkey went up with the curtain. Everybody had a good laugh.

Fair

OUR CAT

We have a cat. I named him Bobby. He is black. He has one white whisker and one gray paw. He comes in bed with me every morning.

Poor

We had a ball game. We had sides. Our side lost.

GRADE 4

Superior

A GOOD LAUGH

One night my father and mother went to a party. My father dressed so that he had two fronts and not any back. He walked frontwards and backwards and nobody knew which side his face was on. Everyone had a good laugh and he surely took the prize.

Excellent

A PUNISHMENT THAT I DESERVED

My brother and I had a fight. My mother told me that I could not have a fight. But I did so. My brother won the fight. I lost. I got hurt in the fight. My mother saw me crying and said, "That is just what you deserved, because I told you not to fight."

Good

A GOOD LAUGH

One Hallowe'en we had a party. We put a little flour on each chair. We set down to supper, and when we got up, to the surprise of the guests they had flour on the back of them. We all had a good laugh. The reason that we put flour on the chairs is because it comes off easy.

Fair

A FUNNY EXPERIENCE

One afternoon when I came home from school I saw our duck with a live mouse. I was watching the duck and before I knew it the duck swallowed the mouse and that was the end of the mouse.

Poor

THE LOST CENT

I went down to my aunt's house. And I only had 14 cents with me. I was down at my aunt's house. I lost two of my cents. I could not go home till I found them. Then I found the two of my cents. I went home and had some good fun with my dog.

GRADE 5

Superior

TEACHING HIM A LESSON

It was a cold winter night when my brother decided to put on his warm bedroom slippers instead of his cold winter leather shoes. He put them on and sat down to read. He was not seated long before he heard our big collie dog bark. He said without looking up, "Be quiet Nelly." But Nelly would not stop, because where were the shoes? No other place but in the center of the room. She pulled one shoe after the other in front of my brother, and barked still louder, as if to say, "Put your shoes away." My brother got up to scold her, but when he saw the shoes he laughed and said, "Well, Nell, you know more than I do."

Excellent

A SCARE

My! but I was frightened when that lady came out with a whip. It was on Hallowe'en and I was putting soap on the door of an apartment building when all at once a lady came out with a buggy-whip. When I saw her I ran down the stairs. Say! she was mad. You bet I never went to that place again.

Good

AN ACCIDENT

I thought my father would be killed. Last night my father took our car out of the garage. He wanted to save his battery so he cranked it. He had the lever in third and our Buick started backwards. There was a garage in back of ours. Our car went through its door. It did not hurt the other man's car but ours has a big dent in the back.

Fair

AN AWFUL SCARE

One day, when we were at the beach, my brother asked me if I wanted to get on his back and he would swim. I got on his back and he began to swim. When we were out deep he went under and threw me off. When I came up, I said that I would never go swimming with him again, and I never did.

Poor

A QUEER THING I BELIEVE

When I was small I used to believe in Santa Claus. I thought he came in the chimney and fixed everything for us, but still I was a little puzzled because if he came in the chimney, his beard wouldn't be white, it would be black when he got in.

GRADE 6

Superior

QUEER THINGS I USED TO THINK

When I was small, a boy told me that if I pulled a horse's hair and put it in water for two days it would turn into a two-headed snake. One day I was watching some horses when I thought of what the boy had told me. Then I went up to one of the horses and pulled a hair out of his tail. Then I went home and put it in a pan of water. Two days later I looked in the pan of water and much to my surprise it was still a horse's hair.

Excellent

QUEER THINGS I USED TO THINK

When I was small I was very fond of balloons. One day my father bought me one. When I was playing with it, the string broke, and up in the air it went. I was told by a boy that it would land in China, or Japan. So when I saw it go up I said, "Send my love to the boys in Japan."

Good

SANTA CLAUS IS GONE

Last year I lost faith in Santa Claus. That Christmas I was not very tired but I had to go to bed early. I did not go to sleep, I was wondering why Mother did not go to bed. I was going to find out. I got up and went to the dining-room and there I found her trimming the tree. I never believed in Santa Claus again.

Fair

A GIFT FOR CHRISTMAS

When I was small I asked for a sled. Christmas came and I got the sled. It started to snow. I thought I would take a slide. Instead of sliding on the sled I slid on my nose. I told my mother I would not have another sled as long as I live.

Poor

QUEER THINGS I USED TO THINK

I used to think that there was bogymans. When I was going to the store I would walk behind a man. The big boys were the ones that said there was bogymans.

One day my mother said there was no such things.

GRADE 7

Superior

QUEER THINGS I USED TO THINK

When I was small I used to think that if I stuck a dead dog with a pin he would jump up. The next day I saw a dog lying asleep on the street. I jabbed a pin into the dog. I jabbed it in with all my might because I wanted him to wake up and get alive. He got alive all right. The first thing I knew I was minus a part of my trousers.

Excellent

AN EMBARRASSING MOMENT

One day in school my teacher was explaining a sentence to me. I was anxious to return to my seat so I retreated backwards toward it. Instead of sitting in my seat I sat down with the girl behind me! Seeing my mistake it did not take me long to return to my seat. Shouts of laughter greeted me on every side.

Good

AN UNUSUAL PRESENT

I have not received very many unusual presents but the one I have enjoyed most was the one that I received when I was in the country. We had not been in the country a very long time when one day my father said, "I am going away today and when I come home I will have a present for you."

I was more than overjoyed and waited very patiently until my father came home. When I saw him coming I ran to meet him. He carried under his arm a large wooden box. To my surprise when he opened the box I saw a cute little black pig. I never enjoyed any present as well as I did this one.

Fair

TOO MUCH WATER

It had rained the night before this mishap. My mother had a tub in the yard to catch the water for her rubber plant. A man was coming in the yard. I walked backward and sat in the tub of water. I began to cry, but seeing it was of no use I stopped and went into the basement to my mother. I started to cry again. She said I would have to stand in the sun till my dress dried because she did not have time to change it. Nobody knows how miserable it is to be wet.

Poor

ALMOST AN ACCIDENT

One day when I was about three years old, my mother was entertaining a literary club. In the midst of the program I started down stairs. I slipped and fell! My mother rushed to the scene of accident! Everybody held their breath! But I escaped without injury.

GRADE 8

Superior

A BAKING EXPERIENCE

I have always been teased at home about my cooking. Every time I baked or cooked anything Daddy was going to have his life insured.

One afternoon I was home alone and, as I had nothing to do, I decided to bake bran muffins. I went into the kitchen, put on a large apron and began to mix my muffins. How carefully I stirred them and how carefully I measured the ingredients! As I mixed those muffins I thought of the big, brown, fluffy muffins I would surprise the family with.

I put them into the oven and busied myself while they baked. Every few minutes I would look at them. They had been baking fifteen minutes and had not even begun to rise.

I began to worry. What was the matter with them? I was sure I had put soda in the mixture.

Maybe the oven was not hot enough, so I turned up the gas. I waited ten more minutes and still they did not rise.

Maybe they were not supposed to rise. I left them in until I was sure they must be done. How disappointed I was when I took them from the oven! They were very heavy and when I broke one open, lo and behold! it was soggy. I tasted it and it had a queer salty taste. Then I knew something was wrong. I knew I had the correct measurements, so I examined the ingredients. I looked at the flour, then at the milk, and I found them both perfect. Then I looked at the baking soda. I looked at the package and to my astonishment "Cream of Tartar" stood out in big black letters. So that was it! I had used cream of tartar instead of soda.

What was I to do with them? I tried to feed them to the dog, but he refused to ruin his health. I wasn't going to let the family tease me, so I emptied the dozen of muffins into the garbage can.

I cleaned up the mess in the kitchen, and when mother came home her kitchen was as she had left it. To this day the family never found out about those muffins. Between the dog and myself it will always remain a secret.

Excellent

DON'T COUNT YOUR CHICKENS BEFORE THEY'RE HATCHED

When I was small I considered a quarter a great amount of money. One day my father gave me a quarter for taking some weeds out of the front lawn. I thought myself a millionaire. I could see myself in an ice-cream parlor with a soda and a bag of candy. I could also see myself watching a thrilling picture at the movies. I could do all this then on a quarter, as things weren't so expensive.

I went merrily on my way, each minute putting my hand in my pocket to see if it was still there. When I was in front of the show I put my hand in my pocket once again to draw the money out. But alas! the quarter was gone. My dreams all vanished. I examined my pocket only to find a hole in one corner. I went home tearfully.

"I thought you were going to the show," said Mother.

"So I was," said I, then I burst into tears and poured out my story of woe.

"Well," said Mother, trying to make me stop crying, "that will teach you a lesson, never to count your chickens before they're hatched."

Good

HASTE MAKES WASTE

One day the teacher kept me and some other boys after school for looking out of the window at the trains pass on seventy-fifth street. After she had kept us about a half hour she said, "Now you may go home if you are through looking at the trains." We said we were. We started to go home and of course were in a hurry after staying so long.

When we got into the hall we thought we would make more time if we slid down the railing. We had gotten down two landings all right so thought we could make the next. I looked down the hall and saw Mr. B——— coming towards us at the other end of the hall. I thought he wouldn't see me so started to slide. When I was about half way down I heard his voice. He said, "Come back here and try that over." There was nothing else to do but go back. When I got back he said, "Go up stairs and walk down." If I had walked down in the first place I would have saved time. So I experienced the saying, "Haste Makes Waste."

Fair

ALL THAT GLITTERS IS NOT GOLD

One day mother said, "Darling, you will have to go to the store."

"All right," I replied.

As I was walking to the store unconcerned and not thinking of anything, I happened to look up, and behold! I saw a beautiful shiny quarter lying on the sidewalk. I ran to get it and I was thinking of the things I could buy with a quarter. But, much to my surprise, I saw that it was nothing but a shiny piece of tin. After that I learned the proverb, "All that glitters is not gold."

Poor

DO NOT COUNT YOUR CHICKENS BEFORE THEY ARE HATCHED

One Saturday morning while I was sitting on the back porch a lady asked me if I would cut her grass. I said, yes. I got finished about twelve o'clock. I then went home for dinner. After dinner I was going to the store, when I saw some boy friends playing football. They asked me if I wanted to play. I said, yes. We played about an hour. I then said, all of you come up to the store with me and I will buy you some candy and pop. We went into the drug store. All of the boys wanted pop and candy. I wanted soda and candy. I put my hand into my pocket to get my fifty cents, but alas it was gone, and my hopes were shattered.

PROGRESSIVE METHODS IN PUBLIC SCHOOL KINDERGARTENS

HELEN B. ROYCE

Kindergarten Department, Norwich, Connecticut

"Of course it is wonderful, but entirely out of the question for us. We haven't the equipment! We haven't the room! Think of our large classes, with only two teachers at the most! It is of no use to try this sort of work in public schools. Where would we get the materials?" So the comments ran as hundreds of teachers observed the work at Horace Mann School during the recent summer session. The writer was sorely tempted to break the rule of silence in her eagerness to refute such statements. She therefore welcomes this opportunity of assuring her fellow teachers that this type of work can be done successfully— even under adverse conditions—in public schools, provided the will to do it is there.

Speaking from personal experience she will endeavor to show how it has been done in two kindergartens, at least, with the hope that other teachers may be encouraged to try the methods they have admired but felt were not possible for them.

Observers do appreciate, to some extent, the value of this type of work, call it project, free, or socialized, as you will. But one can never wholly realize its inestimable worth until one has put it into practice and realized through personal experience its true values. A comparison of results with those attained under former methods will show a big gain as regards both the children and the teacher, whose "rejuvenation" naturally reacts to the good of all concerned. As the work goes on, one discovers unsuspected powers and abilities in the small pupils, and realizes how other methods have limited their development and growth—in more ways than one.

The kindergartens of which I shall speak were housed in ordinary public school rooms, furnished with the usual chairs, square piano, and long tables. (These old style eight-foot tables however, can easily be cut in half.)

The room used by the larger class is only twenty by thirty feet in size and has to yield parts of its inadequate floor space to wardrobe cupboards holding materials and supplies.

The kindergartner has charge, unassisted, of a group not exceeding thirty children, each morning. Her afternoon work calls her to another building, on the opposite side of the city, where, with the help of an untrained assistant, she endeavors to meet the needs of a class that may number forty-five. In spite of these conditions, successful project work has been done for the past two or three years.

Long ago the writer, at her own expense, began to add to her equipment books, puzzles, nature materials, dolls, small toys, and toy animals. The dolls and animals were well worth the cost, as they proved of great value in stimulating creative work with the small Froebelian blocks then in use. Later the kindergarten was equipped with the enlarged fifth and sixth gifts in bulk, but we have never attained the blessing of the Patty Hill floor blocks. With the enlarged blocks, however, came a need for larger dolls and toys that should be of proportionate size.

For years we tried to secure, as part of our annual supplies, these "outside" materials or money for their purchase. As the constant dripping wears away the stone, so our continued pleas for this necessary equipment finally overcame opposition. Every kindergartner in town now may spend ten dollars each year for toys, dolls, or whatever is needed outside of the antiquated supplies still listed in kindergarten catalogues. This is not a munificent sum but it can be made to go a long way, and we hope, ere long, the first grade teachers will similarly be encouraged to add to their stock of vital materials. Last year, at one school, the money was spent for a large grass rug (secured at a bargain price). This rug made available the use of an otherwise impossible floor for building purposes, games, and dramatizations. It has been a great help, and not the least in the way when not in use. It hangs, rolled up, under the blackboard ledge, supported by cloth straps finished with brass rings which slip readily over the hooks there provided. The children take entire charge of the rug and handle it easily.

We keep the enlarged blocks in painted wooden boxes, fitted with casters. These are convenient, serviceable, and easily moved.

Floor space being so limited, it is impossible to leave incomplete building projects from day to day. Therefore, we secured a wooden top for the sand table, which offers a considerable amount of space for individual or group building projects. This top is easily handled and when not needed takes up very little space, as it rests upright against the wall. By its use, buildings may be left as long as desirable and still not be in the way. Among projects initiated

and carried out by the children may be mentioned the building of a mill—which led to the addition of a freight platform, train, track, tunnel, and houses for employees, with the various workmen concerned, and the construction of a complete fire station, fully equipped. Both these projects lasted two weeks, growing from day to day, and would have been out of the question had no space other than the floor been available.

The Kindergarten Children Visit the Deer in the Park

Cupboards for the children's unfinished individual projects, such as aeroplanes, hammocks and the like, may be materialized from egg or orange boxes placed on end, if one has room to accommodate them. The children can make and hang curtains. But nothing is quite so satisfactory as the permanent low cupboards, which we are just securing after years of effort. Persistency pays!

Our work benches were old kitchen tables. By sawing off the legs these were easily made of the right height. Low shelves made of laths found in the school cellar provide space under the tables for the larger pieces of wood. Small pieces are kept in a wooden cracker box. We have not yet been successful in having good, soft, workable wood provided for us, but that has not prevented the work. A visit to several grocers will result in securing empty boxes for school use. When one of these has been changed into a cart, bird house, or other toy, let the youngster who made it visit the grocer and display the metamorphosis of his box, and the grocer's interest in saving the best wood among his discarded boxes will be assured.

Andrew Begins a Bird House
Laurel Hill Kindergarten, Norwich, Conn.

Candy stores have shallow wooden boxes, not stout enough for every purpose but available for many. They make splendid doll carriage, wagon, and wheelbarrow bodies. The covers are good for table tops. Split into narrow strips (easily done with a knife), the wood is just right for ladders, arms of doll chairs, etc. The sides of boxes are splendid for aeroplane wings, and a section with dove-tailed end makes a most attractive back for a doll's chair. Cigar boxes split too easily to be of much use, but the boxes as they are make good wagon bodies, doll bedsteads, and nail receptacles. Our boys put in partitions and have very serviceable boxes with places for six sizes of nails. Spools are useful, particularly

for doll house furniture. Ask your dressmaker to save them. The children will bring them in, too. It is possible to use the ends for wheels, but they are difficult to saw. We use all sizes of wooden button molds for wheels and other purposes. An old wooden curtain pole sawed into half-inch sections provides excellent wheels for small carts, ladder trucks, and autos.

For larger cart wheels it may be possible to secure discarded bobbins from a mill. Our manual training department contributed odd pieces of wood. Every carpenter shop has a pile of trimmings and waste wood containing just the sort of pieces needed for chair and table legs, cart handles, and similar purposes. The friendly foreman is glad to tie up a bundle or two for the children's use.

Our first request for tools met with opposition. The "powers that be" could not see what part tools had to play in the education of little children. We were sufficiently convinced of their need and value to make the initial purchase ourselves. A beginning can be made with a hammer, saw, and some nails. But let it be a good saw. Do not buy cheap tools. They are a handicap to an expert workman and almost of no use to a beginner.

After several months had elapsed, a glimpse of the kindergarten workshop with children busy therein was sufficient proof of the value of this style of equipment and now every kindergartner in town may have a set of good tools for the asking. Our set is not elaborate. It has grown from year to year and comprises several saws and hammers, a plane, a small vise, screw driver, awl, nail set, brace and several bits, tack puller, measure, compass, sand paper, screws, and nails of various sizes. The vise is only of use in holding the smaller pieces of wood. In sawing boards or larger strips, the children rest wood on a box. They are delighted to help each other by sitting on or otherwise steadying the board to be sawed.

We are careful to establish standards of good workmanship. The children learn to choose nails with reference to their suitability, to be economical of all materials, and to use tools and brush in proper manner. Do not be afraid of paint! If children have neither apron nor overalls, this need will stimulate a cutting and sewing project of apron making. A few drops of turpentine poured on fingers will quickly remove all traces of paint, which even an adult acquires when wielding the brush. We have used ten-cent paint but are to try an inexpensive wood dye this year.

The necessity of using box wood and other waste material has some advantages. The children are far more likely to continue their toy making at home if they learn the possibilities in the readily obtained materials. But not for one moment do we cease striving to have suitable wood provided—to use in conjunction with cast off pieces. Just as good paper is provided to insure every advantage to the pupil as he draws or writes, so should adequate constructive materials be given to him.

All sorts of cardboard boxes will prove useful. In visiting different stores one learns to what extent paper cartons have replaced wooden containers. These, particularly the heavier ones, make splendid doll houses, barns, garages and other buildings. Windows are easily cut with a jack knife, by both boys and girls, and the ease with which the cardboard boxes may be obtained makes their use popular. Pieces of old shoe leather make admirable hinges for the barn door.

In connection with this work do not be discouraged if some children do considerable observing before initiating any projects. Some of the most original, thoughtful construction in one class was the work of a boy who seemed for a long time wholly lacking in initiative. His last toy, a one-man trolley car with twelve double seats, trolley arms, cash box and other fittings, was a project of six weeks' duration and then not completed when school closed.

Hammock, hat, bag, and rug weaving can successfully be carried on with homemade looms. Ours were originally pad backs, donated by the upper grade children. Two of these pieces of cardboard may be joined with brass fasteners, for larger looms. Some of the children cut their own notches. Last year we found it possible to have inexpensive beaver-board hammock frames prepared at a carpenter shop. These are, of course, more durable, but the weaving on the cardboard looms is quite as successful and satisfactory. The use of cardboard permits the making of looms of any size and shape desired. Expensive weaving materials are unnecessary. Though we have some cotton roving, we prefer for nearly all purposes the easily obtainable strips of cloth. The children bring in pieces of their dresses and suits; Mothers' Clubs or Parent-Teacher Associations gladly donate scraps. The children like to cut the inch-wide strips (on a fold or stripe) and sew some of the strips together, learning the importance of fastening the thread well each time. But we do not insist on their preparation of all such material. If much white cloth is donated, it is an easy matter, with Twink or Rit, to change it into attractive and serviceable colors. Heavy twine can be used for stringing looms, but cotton warp is inexpensive.

New cloth for aprons, costumes, and doll dresses is not available, but clean cast-off garments often furnish pieces sufficiently large for such uses.

Lacking oil-cloth or boards for clay modeling, squares of heavy paper may be used to protect tables, or perhaps your storeroom will reveal a supply of the once popular slates, as did ours.

We asked our manual training department to make teeter boards for us. Even a small room will accommodate one if the board is removable so that it can rest upright against the wall. And it serves other purposes, too! It makes a splendid bridge for the use of the Three Billy Goats Gruff, and, properly placed and braced, a usable slide. If you can not hang swing ropes from your ceiling, use a door frame. The children love being in motion without exertion (the initial stage of the auto enthusiast perhaps), and after a period of strenuous application will run to the swing for a moment or two of relaxation. Through use of the swing one exceedingly timid boy gained courage which seemed to free initiative and ability previously not functioning.

Have you wanted a garden and bewailed the lack of space, or tools to cultivate it? Even a three by twelve-foot plot will permit of a class garden, in the planting and care of which every child may share, even though small groups work at one time rather than the class as a whole. The children will bring spade, rake, and hoe. Our garden furnished two hundred radishes and about forty medium-sized heads of lettuce last spring; we anticipated in the fall the joy of cosmos and marigold blossoms, a small yield of potatoes for ourselves, and sun-flower seeds for the birds. If you have no out-door space, use your window boxes for seed planting, even though the resulting growth may be less decorative than the plants usually found therein. Ask your community or other clubs to save one evening's discard of the waxed-paper cups used so generously at such places. These, with a hole punched for drainage, make excellent flower pots, continuously serviceable for weeks.

School orchestras may be organized even though ready-made instruments are lacking. Small tin kettle covers make good cymbals; a round hat or oatmeal box is quickly converted into a drum; clappers are easily fashioned from a shingle; a ten-cent rattle will furnish several bells which can be fastened singly to sticks, and small pebbles in a securely closed box are effective rattles.

Lack of space for keeping materials and partially completed articles out of sight may deter the extremely orderly teacher from introducing project work. We use window sills, desk, and piano at times as repositories for all sorts of things in the making. But is not a workshop bound to show signs of its activities and its workmen, and would any good teacher sacrifice such wonderful opportunities for development in her desire to preserve a spic and span room? The children "tidy up." They are wholly responsible for cleaning up their own scraps, sawdust, etc., and for putting away materials.

Perhaps you are saying "Anyway, we can never keep records. It is utterly impossible with so many children." Nevertheless, fairly complete records may be kept even with large classes.

Hectographing individual record cards takes much time. We used them, each covering twenty school days, when our enrollment was small. It certainly is easier to keep track of the children's activities in a small class. When numbers increased, we gave up the cards but not the recording, simply using a blank book, arranged for the purpose, instead. One set of headings was written at top of second and next to last pages. By cutting an inch from the top of the intervening sheets, one heading served for all and preparation of individual cards was thus avoided. (We do not like the book as well as the cards but it does save time for the busy teacher). It is not always possible to record every child's occupations during the period of self-initiated work, but it is possible to make a note of new developments and to see what is going on, for later recording, even with a large class. For our record of social and moral traits a book with headings in column at the left side of second page, with remaining sheets cut to show headings, gave ample space for data concerning each child.

Records are so vital, in this type of work especially, it is better to let something else go than to attempt to do without them.

To the teachers who are organizing their rooms on a social basis for the first time, may I suggest the wisdom of proceeding slowly? Evolution is safer than revolution. Win the approval and support of principal and supervisor by showing them what this sort of curriculum does for the children. Do not be afraid to advertise its good points. Many of us are critical of values until we see results. If you can not get what you want and need, at once, do not give up wanting it. Persist in the determination to give your pupils the best educational opportunities and eventually you will succeed.

There is always a possible usable substitute for the unattainable, if one only searches. It is not so much the possession of adequate materials and environment as the determination to put this method into use, against any odds, that brings results. "Where there's a will there's a way." No matter what obstacles have to be overcome, the results achieved will more than repay the teacher's efforts. Good results do come, in public schools, even though conditions are not ideal. As an instance of development the following record may be of interest.

When Edwin came to kindergarten he was selfish, lazy, unwilling to coöperate, untidy in work and person, unimaginative, dependent, and interested solely in play apparatus. His early records show many play activities, each of brief duration, in the one period daily. Compare these with the later records of sustained interest in the chosen task through nearly every period, which resulted during the year in the following completed projects: a freight boat, a motor boat, two wheelbarrows, ladder truck with two ladders, cart, two automobiles, three bird houses, crocheted reins, and a doll hammock. In addition he repaired the kindergarten doll furniture and helped many playmates in their toy making. He developed marked initiative, became a leader, generous and extremely helpful (at everyone's call for assistance), neat and careful, imaginative, and very industrious, as his list of toys shows. The power of the project in sustained application was surely proven. There, as in many instances that might be given, were "purposeful planning, execution, and judgment."

Little Angelo came at four years of age, destructive, quarrelsome, with no respect for property or person, the victim of an unrestrained temper. The first four weeks he demanded rather more than his share of the teacher's attention. But soon he succumbed to the lure of "invitational" material. With the making of his first project—two sticks crossed, nailed, and pronounced an aeroplane—Angelo began to change for the better. The joy of creating and owning something made him respect other's work and property. Before long, as he became master, in a small way, of tools and materials, he became master also of himself, and the outbursts of temper ceased altogether.

tice in America's most progressive schools.

A few of the children's projects are shown in the accompanying illustrations made from photographs. Others have included the following: Four pieces of fire apparatus were built following a trip to a fire station. During the process of construction, two of the boys made two trips each—on their own initiative, to study engine and chemical wagon more closely. The doll furniture is largely the work of girls, who enter just as enthusiastically

A Good Drying Day
Hobart Avenue School, Norwich, Conn.

Ironing Day
Hobart Avenue School, Norwich, Conn.

If one could only take and display character photos of children before and after a year of life in the socially organized kindergarten, the most skeptical of conservatives would have to grant the value of such schooling. The finished projects tell much, but sometimes the crudest, simplest article made by one child represents more real growth than the elaborate toy of another.

The less tangible results are the vital ones, but, in the writer's opinion, no other methods ever gave such opportunities for growth, mental and physical as well as moral, as those now governing the prac-

into the carpentry work as the boys. A child's chair was made a year and a half ago by a colored boy for his baby brother, and is still in commission. Clay candlesticks did duty at several Parent-Teacher meetings. An auto was made in October, improved in November, brought back in January for a new license, and in April for repairs and paint.

The children wash and iron the doll clothes. Our Sterno not only heats the irons but cooks apple-sauce and jelly for winter treats. A fair in behalf of the Chinese Famine Sufferers instigated all sorts of individual and group projects.

THE CLEARING HOUSE

A LESSON IN CONSTRUCTION WORK

Teacher:—Let us have a little exhibit this afternoon of the booklets. The first row carry yours up and place them on the blackboard. Next row follow quickly.
(All booklets placed on blackboards.)

T: Well, what do you think of them? Sylvia, what do you think of them?

Sylvia: I think they are awfully pretty.

T: Henry, do you like them?

P: Yes, ma'am.

Gordon: I like them very well, but I think they would look better if I took mine away.

T: Show us yours.
(Pupil goes to blackboard and points out his booklet.)

P: That's the best one there.

T: Do you like Gordon's, children? Yes, I don't think Gordon's hurts our exhibit at all.

P: It makes it better.

Tom: Mine isn't good.

T: What's the matter with it?

Tom: It is lopsided.

T: Put on just a little bit crooked. All right. Sit down, class. We will take a little time to talk about these now. What are you going to use yours for, ————?

P: To put kodak pictures in.

T: That is what we had planned to use them for. I wonder how many of these booklets are going to leave Chicago this summer. Where is yours going, Sylvia?

Sylvia: Mine is going to Michigan.

P: Niagara Falls.

P: Toronto.

P: California.

T: Where is yours going?

P: Florida.

T: And yours?

P: Montana.

T: Nearly all going out of town, aren't they?

How are you going to carry yours?

P: I am going to have an envelope and a suitcase.

T: What is apt to happen to these booklets if we carry them so far?

P: They would get dirty.

T: What would you suggest making for them? You want them to look just as pretty and clean when you bring them back in September as they do now. What shall we do?

P: Make an envelope.

T: How many think that is a good idea? Yes. When you bring them back to your relatives in September and you open up your little books to show your snapshots, they will be nice and clean. What sort of envelope would you suggest? The envelope will have to protect the book, won't it? What kind of paper shall we use?

Elizabeth: Strong paper.

T: Why strong?

P: So it won't tear easily.

T: Is that true, class?

Class: Yes.

T: What else can you say about that paper?

P: Dark, so it won't get soiled.

T: Is that true?

P: If it falls into some water it might dye the book.

T: You mustn't let it fall into the water. I wonder if somebody could go to the cupboard and find some paper that is strong and that is dark. Those are the two things you said it must be, Stanley.
(Pupil goes to cupboard and selects blue paper.)

T: What do you think of this?

Class: No.

Elsie: I think it is a little bit too light.

T: Well, see if you find a piece that you like better. (Pupil selects brown paper.)

T: How many of you like this blue paper?

Who prefers the brown? The browns have it.

P: Why can't we have what we want?

T: Suppose somebody wanted purple, why couldn't he have that? Remember I told these children to go to the cupboard and pick out the paper that would suit the purpose best. What shape envelope should we have?

Class: Square.

T: Why?

Class: Because our books are square.

T: Yes. What size?

Tom: Four inches square.

Elisabeth: Five.

T: What do you say?

P: Four and a half.

T: What do you say?

P: Five inches.

T: Yes, so there will be an inch on each side of the envelope. Why won't a four-inch envelope suit?

P: Because you would have to tug to get the book out.

T: What about six inches?

P: Too big.

T: What about five inches?

Class: Just right.

T: How many would like a five-inch envelope? Yes, I think that would be best. It would give it just room enough. How much paper will we need?

P: A six-inch square.

T: Just think. How much paper do we need to make our envelope five inches square?

P: Ten inches square.

Gordon: Eleven inches square.

P: You would have to have something to turn over.

Wallace: Six by seven inches. Then you will have to turn over a flap.

T: Six by seven inches. Would that make our five-inch square envelope? Somebody isn't thinking.

Elisabeth: Eleven inches long and eight inches wide.

T: That is pretty good. Why eleven inches long? How much do we need from there to there?

P: Five inches.

T: Correct. How much from there to there?

P: Six inches.

T: Why?

P: If you are going to make your envelope a square——

T: But that doesn't allow for what?

P: The flap.

T: How much do we want for the flap?

P: A half-inch.

T: Yes, that would be enough. Would you like a half-inch?

P: Half an inch at the top and half an inch at the bottom.

T: Do you need a flap at the bottom?

P: No, ma'am, but you do at the sides.

T: What are we going to have down here at the bottom?

P: A crease, a fold.

T: Yes, a fold. Well, how much of a flap? Ten inches for the envelope and one inch for the flap. That would make how much?

Class: Eleven inches.

T: Now how wide should our paper be?

P: Seven inches.

T: Why?

P: Because five inches across the envelope and an inch on each side for the flap.

T: That would be all right, but I am wondering if we could change that and save a little paper.

Joseph: A half-inch.

T: Do you think that is better, Lyle?

Lyle: Yes. (Brown paper passed to class.)

T: Take your brown paper and cut an oblong—how long?

Class: Eleven inches.

T: And how wide?

Class: Six inches.

T: Yes. Children we will have to finish these on Monday. We cannot go on today. Who knows how to go ahead and finish the whole thing? We all ought to. We will have to wait until Monday, though.

MY PROJECT-PROBLEM

My children were cultivating a bad habit of selecting books to read that were uneducative and very trashy. The majority of the children were Italians, of the extremely poor type, who were unable to buy good books for their own use and were therefore in the habit of borrowing books without any opportunity for selection. This question arose in my mind, "What must I do to interest these children in reading better books?"

One day while we were out playing on the school ground, our attention was turned to an injured bird. Immediately we decided that we would care for it until it was well. Then little voices said, "It is a sparrow," others, "It is a wren." Of course I was asked, "What kind of a bird is it?"

I had a number of bird books of my own in the room and knew the children would be unable to find the necessary material to work on at home, so I asked them this question, "Can't you find out what kind of bird it is by looking it up in my reference books?" It was impossible to get those children out for the rest of the recess period, for each wanted to read about birds.

A discussion soon followed and through our discussion and reading matter we decided that the bird was a wren. Our bird study became in earnest, for we learned about the habits of birds, their plans of building nests, their choice of places for nests, how to recognize them by their singing or chirrup, the value of birds, whether or not they were useful or destructive, and, last, but not least, how to defend our birds.

Lively interest was felt in the reading and composition writing which followed. Then building of bird-houses began, and the making of clippings from magazines and papers.

Soon the books on my shelves had been read and the children began to ask for more. The big question came up, "Can't we give an entertainment and raise some money to buy more books?" This was the beginning of our plan for a school library.

Our entertainment was given. All grades from the first to the ninth became interested in it. Each grade contributed toward the performance. I gave the children books and they selected a play of their own, revising parts of it with my assistance. We had a free orchestra, sold ice cream and candy, and charged admission to the entertainment. From this we planned our arithmetic lessons, finding out the amount received, expenditure, and gain. The pupils were all anxious to know how many books we could buy with the proceeds. We worked this out by considering the various costs of the books. Here is where our long and short division problems came into action.

Then after the buying of books we had an excellent chance to find the average cost of books, using comparison, addition, multiplication, etc.

We did not forget our birds in winter time, for crumbs of food were saved and placed on a board fastened on the window sill, which served as a tray. We brought from home suet and bones with little bits of meat clinging to them and suspended these in a tree where they could plainly be seen by the children.

Snowy weather came. One of the boys constructed a sled with sails and gave it to me. Then other boys began to make other things. Help was received through a book on inventions and constructions which they discovered in our new library. The sleds were used on the school ground, where much pleasure was derived from them, as well as more knowledge of measurements, distance, and direction.

Soon the school board became interested and gave us a splendidly equipped playground, including swings, see-saws, giant stride, sliding boards, and a game of volley ball.

ANNA SEARFOSS

AS REPORTED

SECOND ANNUAL MEETING OF THE NATIONAL CONFERENCE ON EDUCA-TIONAL METHOD, CHICAGO, ILLINOIS, FEBRUARY 28 AND MARCH 1, 1922

PROGRAM

First Session, Tuesday, February 28, 2 p.m.

Pine Room, Stratford Hotel

1. THE PRESENT STATUS, James F. Hosic, Associate Professor of Education, Teachers College, Columbia University.

2. SUPERVISION WITHOUT A SUPERVISOR, T. W. Gosling, Superintendent of Schools, Madison, Wisconsin.

3. PROJECTS IN THE TRAINING SCHOOL, E. A. Hotchkiss, Principal of the Teacher Training School, Kansas City, Missouri.

4. CRITERIA OF PROJECT TEACHING, Bessie Bacon Goodrich, Assistant Superintendent of Schools, and Raymond Franzen, Director of Measurements, Des Moines, Iowa.

Second Session, Wednesday, March 1, 9:30 a.m.

Fullerton Hall, The Art Institute

1. THE NEXT STEPS IN DEVELOPING MORE EFFECTIVE METHODS OF SUPERVISION, Elizabeth Hall, Assistant Superintendent of Schools, Minneapolis, Minnesota.

2. METHOD AND CURRICULUM, William H. Kilpatrick, Professor of Education, Teachers College, Columbia University.

3. A NEW VIEW OF TEACHER RATING, Stuart A. Courtis, Director of Instruction, Teacher Training and Research, Detroit, Michigan.

4. POSSIBILITIES OF THE PROJECT METHOD IN THE ORDINARY CLASSROOM, Fred M. Hunter, Superintendent of Schools, Oakland, California.

THE STUDY OF CURRENT EVENTS IN BOISE

A good example of how the modern school turns important happenings to good account is reported in a recent number of *The Capital News*, published in Boise, Idaho, and sent in to the *Journal* by Mr. P. J. Zimmers, superintendent of schools in that city. Pupils in every grade from the first to the twelfth were active and almost all of the school subjects found a place.

The method of attack varied in different classes. In the first grade, for example, the teacher held up a picture of a battleship and asked, "What is it?" This led on to the question of cost, relation to taxes, etc. Much good material for oral composition was found in the study. Reading lessons were made up. The Conference on Disarmament was illustrated and dramatized.

In the intermediate grades the peace project was made the foundation for much work in arithmetic. Sample problems were: If a home can be built for $5000, how many could be built for the price of one battleship? If one student spends $750 for a year at college, how many could go to college for the price of one battleship?

In the fifth grade children learned at home the monthly expense of the family and found how many families in Boise could live as well as they do now for the cost of one gun. Slogans were written out in the penmanship class. In hygiene the children discussed such topics as pestilence and tuberculosis which follow the exposure incurred in trench warfare.

In higher classes still more difficult studies were undertaken, such as the amount of coal needed for the ships of the Navy as compared with that needed for the schools of Boise. It appeared that the supply used by the Navy between April, 1919, and April, 1920, would heat the schools of Boise for 1500 years. History classes in the high schools studied the real purpose and personnel of the Conference and such detailed features as the program of Secretary Hughes and the interests and policies of Japan.

The result of such activities has been, of course, that all the children are eager for more news of the Conference.

SECOND ANNUAL MEETING OF N. A. D. S. S. T.

The second annual meeting of the National Association of Directors of Supervised Student Teaching will be held in Chicago during the time of the meeting of the Superintendents' Section of the N. E. A. The following program has been arranged and the invitation is extended to all who are interested in these discussions to attend the sessions, which will be held at the Palmer House, corner State and Monroe streets, on Monday and Tuesday forenoons, February 27 and 28, 1922.

PROGRAM

Monday, February 27, 1922, 9:00 a. m.

1. Administration of Student Teaching in the Teacher-Training Institutions of the United States. E. I. F. Williams, Professor of Education, Heidelberg University, Tiffin, Ohio.

2. The Case Method for the Study of Teaching. Wm. P. Burris, Dean of the College for Teachers, University of Cincinnati.

3. The President's Annual Address. A. R. Mead, Professor of Education, Ohio Wesleyan University, Delaware, Ohio.

4. Discussion of Certain Papers Given at the Atlantic City Meeting of N. A. D. S. S. T.

Fiske Allen, Director of the Training School, Eastern Illinois State Teachers College, Charleston.

5. Graded Units in Student Teaching. H. C. Pryor, Head of Department of Education, Northern Normal and Industrial School, Aberdeen, S. Dak.

6. Open Discussion of Papers Given.

Tuesday, February 28, 1922, 9:00 a. m.

1. Preparing Teachers Through Preparation. H. L. Miller, Professor of Education and Principal of University of Wisconsin High School.

2. Methods of Making Assignments for Student Teaching. H. R. Douglass, Professor of Secondary Education, University of Oregon.

3. Student Teaching and the Junior High School. H. C. Foster, Head of Department of Education, Michigan State Normal College, Ypsilanti.

4. Essential Factors in the Supervision of Student Teaching. H. W. Nutt, Director of Training School, University of Kansas.

5. Importance of Aims of Education in Teacher Training. H. G. Swanson, Professor of Education and Director of Demonstration School, State Teachers College, Kirksville, Missouri.

Special. Arrangements are being made for a luncheon at noon on Tuesday, the 28th, at which time a discussion of some of the more important tendencies in Teacher Training will be given by Dr. Wm. C. Bagley.

ROBERT A. CUMMINS, *Sec'y-Treas.*,
University of Southern California,
Los Angeles, California.

THE READER'S GUIDE

AMERICAN EDUCATION

Of two recent volumes dealing with the history of education in America, one is for the general reader and the other for students in normal schools.[1] Because of the difference in purpose there is little ground for comparison between the two. The first is certainly the more readable, which suggests a query as to why textbooks, particularly textbooks in education for normal schools, need to be reduced to a bareness of treatment that repels rather than invites.

Mr. Slosson writes as a layman, but as one who has investigated his subject. In the matter of higher education he has a wealth of first-hand knowledge, obtained by a series of visits, the results of which he reported in his *Great American Universities*. His familiarity with the colleges leads him to give proportionally much larger space to describing them than would ordinarily be expected. Possibly he knows his audience and places his emphasis accordingly. It could hardly be accidental that almost all of his illustrations are of college buildings or of men prominent in the college world. The frontispiece, however, is a portrait of Horace Mann.

The most serious lack of perspective is in the treatment of the growth of high schools. This is easily the outstanding feature of public education in the last fifty years. The reader of Mr. Slosson's book will not get this impression, nor will he have more than an inkling of the character and size of the present high school population nor of the development of its course of study to the point where it is suited to the requirements of all the children of the community.

The scientific movement in education is scarcely touched. The replacing of an obsolete descriptive educational psychology with a psychology of activity has made possible a completely new statement of educational aims and of educational methods and is the basic cause of the nation-wide transformation of elementary school work and reorganization of the seventh, eighth, and ninth grades which is in progress. A British reader would not suspect this, if he had read no other account of recent educational movements in America than that of Mr. Slosson.

Nevertheless the book is delightful. There are no lapses of style or false notes. The stream of thought flows smoothly on and the reader finds himself borne steadily forward, without undue effort, unwilling to lay down the volume till the end is reached. Many passages are memorable. Neatly turned sentences and unhackneyed phrasing give a fresh and illuminating sense of the significance of events already familiar. Much of the appeal of the work is no doubt due to the biographical element. The subtitle, "A Chronicle of Great Teachers," apprises the reader at the outset that he will hear more of men than of institutions. Except for the advanced reader or the technical expert, this point of view is undoubtedly best. After all, "Institutions are the lengthened shadows of great men."

Professor Finney's book is by contrast commonplace. He has intentionally written down to his readers and hence will not inspire them. There is lacking also that gripping sequence which leads the reader on. The order of chapters is in some parts puzzling. Wishing to present European backgrounds, the author interpolates chapters on Rousseau, Pestalozzi, Froebel, and Herbart; the connection, however, is not close. Professor Cubberley has done the thing very much better in his

[1] *The American Spirit in Education*, by Edwin E. Slosson, Yale University Press; *The American Public School*, by Ross L. Finney, The Macmillan Company.

Public Education in the United States—a book, by the way, which Mr. Slosson does not seem to know.

As a simple outline upon which to build a course in American education for beginners, *The American Public School* will prove of value. The author is undoubtedly right in thinking that the elaborate surveys of education in ancient and medieval times which were once inflicted upon students in normal schools were of little use. He has made a commendable selection of the facts really worth teaching. All teachers should know them. Students using his book would enjoy the more literary treatment of Mr. Slosson and should read *The American Spirit in Education* straight through for its total effect. It is full of both sweetness and light.

SIGNIFICANT ARTICLES

THE LINCOLN SCHOOL

In the *Educational Review* for January will be found an article on "Education as Viewed by the Lincoln School," contributed by Dr. Otis W. Caldwell, the Director. The substance of the article was originally presented as a Commencement address before the school and is now adapted to a wider audience. Among the principal points emphasized are the fact that thoughtful parents wish their children to have an education which will fit them for something more than merely making a living; that this education must come by doing and being; that therefore the pupils should be allowed to participate in the conduct of school affairs, and that the school subjects should be reorganized on a more vital basis. Dr. Caldwell thinks that there are signs that the education which the school is providing is an improvement upon the older traditions.

HIGH SCHOOL INTERESTS IN DETROIT

The latest number of the *Detroit Educational Bulletin* published by the Board of Education in that city, contains a wide range of articles.

Among those of more general interest are the following: "The Education Outlook," by the late Frank V. Thompson, Superintendent of Schools in Boston; "Comparative Values of Different Methods of Civic Education," by Professor David Snedden of Teachers College, Columbia University; "Problems and Solutions in the Classification of School Children," by Miss Jennie B. Boyer of Detroit Teachers College; and "Speech Improvement—The Program in Practice," by Mr. C. C. Certain, assistant principal of Northwestern High School, Detroit, Michigan, managing editor of the *Bulletin*.

METHOD OR ORGANIZATION?

Shall we think of projects in terms of method or in terms of organization? Mr. W. S. Dakin of Hartford, Conn., prefers the latter. Writing in the *Journal of Education* of December 1, Mr. Dakin reviews succinctly the current tendencies with regard to the so-called project method. He thinks it a serious effort to coordinate and put into actual practice: (1) better motivation of work in fundamental subjects; (2) economy of time by intensive study of large units; (3) indirect teaching of facts through the use of the tool subjects in solving problems; (4) correlation of fundamental subjects with informational, constructive, and cultural exercises; and (5) class coöperation in the preparation and discussion of lessons.

Much good, Mr. Dakin says, would result from considering the project as a means of reorganizing our courses of study, of readjusting relations between the three R's and other subjects, and of shifting the emphasis from memorizing to doing. To prevent haphazard skipping from one high spot to another, projects should be selected from the courses of study as now organized. As a plan of teaching, the project may call into play all the basic methods, including drill. The pupils ought to take part in the selection of the aim and the development of the general plan.

Not the least important of Mr. Dakin's

suggestions is his statement that the introduction of the project plan will require a higher type of supervision. Neither mechanical checking of progress nor the use of tests and scales will suffice. The supervisor must actually help the teacher in evolving her plans.

MEASUREMENT IN EDUCATION

It is significant of the tendency of the times that Professor Edward L. Thorndike of Teachers College should be called upon to deliver the annual address at the opening exercises of Columbia University in September on the subject of "Measurement in Education." Professor Thorndike spoke appropriately on the use of measurements in determining fitness for entrance to college. He summarized the results of investigations which showed how inadequate the older systems were, and commented upon the progress that is being made at Columbia College, Brown University, and elsewhere to apply objective measures. A summary of his address will be found in the *Teachers College Record* for November, 1921.

MARKS AND MOTIVES

One of the best means of keeping in touch with education in England is the *Educational Times*, edited by Mr. Frank Roscoe of London, Secretary of the Teachers' Registration Council, who is remembered by many as a visitor to the National Education Association a few years ago. In the January number of this magazine we find an article on "Marks and Motives," by A. F., which contains many suggestions useful to American teachers. The main idea is to provide better motives than those which school marks afford. One device is to divide the class into two groups known as Romans and Carthaginians and, pitting these groups against each other, to reward the victors with some much sought for privilege. The writer believes that a system can be built up in such a way as to dispense with marks altogether in the upper grades.

THE PROJECT IN GEOGRAPHY

A somewhat comprehensive exposition of the possibilities of the project method as applied to the teaching of geography appears in *Education* for January from the pen of Fred. K. Branom, instructor in geography in the Chicago Normal College. After setting forth the principal aims of teaching geography, Mr. Branom asks, "How may the teacher succeed best in teaching geography?" His answer is, "Through projects." He then proceeds to show somewhat in detail what he understands by projects and how they can be carried out. His survey of the character of the problems which are now being presented will be welcome to all who are interested in new methods.

THE NEW BOOKS

The New World Problems in Political Geography. By Isaiah Bowman. Yonkers, N. Y.: World Book Co., 1921. Pp. 632. Price, $6.00.

A most informing survey of the "new world" by the Director of the American Geographical Society. Profusely illustrated. Excellent maps.

The Teaching of History in Junior and Senior High Schools. By Rolla Milton Tryon. Boston: Ginn & Co., 1921. Pp. vi + 294.

A valuable presentation of the newer point of view and newer material for classroom use.

Psychology and the School. By Edward Herbert Cameron. New York: Century Co., 1921. Pp. xiv + 339. Price, $2.00.

A popular treatment for beginners. Fairly comprehensive, clear, and well printed.

The Parent and the Child. Case Studies in the Problems of Parenthood. By Henry Frederick Cope. New York: Geo. H. Doran Co., 1921. Pp. 184.

Useful for all who are concerned with the care and training of children.

The Parish School—Its Aims, Procedure, and Problems. By Rev. Joseph A. Dunney. New York: Macmillan Co., 1921. Pp. xx + 326.

A distinctly progressive view of Catholic schools for the general reader.

Contemporary British Literature. Bibliographies and Study Outlines. By John Matthews Manly and Edith Rickert. New York: Harcourt, Brace & Co., 1921. Pp. viii + 196.

Suggests the desirability of a similar volume dealing with American writers.

Producing in Little Theaters. By Clarence Stratton. New York: Henry Holt & Co., 1921. Pp. 258, illus.

Both educators and general readers will find this book delightful and informing.

Modern Junior Mathematics. By Marie Gugle. New York: Gregg Publishing Co., 1920. Book One, pp. x + 222, price 80 cents; Book Two, pp. xiv + 239, price 90 cents; Book Three, pp. xiv + 246, price $1.00; Teachers Manual, pp. 27, paper, price 25 cents.

A course complete in three books for seventh, eighth, and ninth grades.

The Common-Word Spellers. By Ervin Eugene Lewis. Boston: Ginn & Co., 1921. Book One, pp. x + 150, illus.; Book Two, pp. viii + 184.

The two books cover the eight grades. Both choice of vocabulary and method have been modernized.

A Guide to the Teaching of Spelling. By Hugh Clark Pryor and Marvin Summers Pittman. New York: Macmillan Co., 1921. Pp. 141.

A book of concrete suggestions reflecting modern scientific studies.

Elementary English, Spoken and Written. By Lamont F. Hodge and Arthur Lee. New York: Charles E. Merrill Co., 1920. Book One, pp. 324, illus.; Book Two, pp. 484, illus.

IN PAPER COVERS

Preparation for Teaching History and Citizenship in Grades I to VI. A Manual for Normal Schools. Massachusetts Department of Education, 1921, Bulletin No. 6.

Studies in Education. Society of College Teachers of Education, Monograph No. X, Baltimore, Md., 1921.

Bridging the Gap. By James F. Hosic. The English Bulletin, Vol. I, No. 4, 1921.

Otis Group Intelligence Scale. Manual of Directions for Primary and Advanced Examinations. Revised edition. Yonkers, N. Y.: World Book Co., 1921.

Miller Mental Ability Test. By W. S. Miller. Yonkers, N. Y.: World Book Co., 1921.

Report of the Commissioner of Education for the Year Ending June 30, 1921. Washington: Government Printing Office, 1921.

Topics in Elementary Geography. By C. P. Sinnott. State Normal School, Bridgewater, Mass., 1921.

The Secret of Thrift. A Manual for Teachers, beginning with Grade VII. By Clifford B. Upton. Issued by American Bankers' Association, New York, 1921.

Detroit First-Grade Intelligence Test. Ay Anna M. Engel. Yonkers, N. Y.: World Book Co., 1921.

Recent Publications of the Department of the Interior, Bureau of Education, 1921: *Part-Time Education of Various Types,* Bulletin No. 5. *Pharmaceutical Education,* by Wortley F. Rudd and P. F. Fackenthall, Bulletin No. 11. *The Housing and Equipment of Kindergartens,* Bulletin No. 13. *Education of the Deaf,* by Percival Hall, Bulletin No. 14. *Special Features in the Education of the Blind During the Biennium 1918–1920,* by Edward E. Allen, Bulletin No. 16. *Educational Boards and Foundations, 1918–20,* by Henry R. Evans, Bulletin No. 17. *Education in Homeopathic Medicine During the Biennium 1918–1920,* by W. A. Dewey, M. D., Bulletin No. 18. *Educational Survey of Wheeling, West Virginia,* Bulletin No. 28. *The Work of the Bureau of Education for the Natives of Alaska,* Bulletin No. 36. *Educational Work of the Boy Scouts,* by Lorne W. Barclay, Bulletin No. 41. *Business Training and Commercial Education,* by Glen Levin Swiggett, Bulletin No. 43. *Educational Work of the Girl Scouts,* by Louise Stevens Bryant, Bulletin No. 46.

THE JOURNAL OF EDUCATIONAL METHOD

Edited by JAMES F. HOSIC

Volume I   MARCH, 1922   Number 7

PUBLISHED BY THE WORLD BOOK COMPANY FOR
THE NATIONAL CONFERENCE ON EDUCATIONAL METHOD

$3.00 a year   Monthly except July and August   35 cents a copy

THE NATIONAL CONFERENCE ON EDUCATIONAL METHOD

An Association of Persons Interested in Supervision and Teaching

Officers of the Conference

President, C. L. WRIGHT, Public Schools, Huntington, West Virginia.
Vice-President, MARGARET NOONAN, School of Education, New York University, Washington Square, New York City.
Secretary-Treasurer, JAMES F. HOSIC, Teachers College, New York City.

Executive Committee

THE PRESIDENT AND THE SECRETARY-TREASURER, *ex officio*.
C. C. CERTAIN, Northwestern High School, Detroit, Michigan.
MARGARET MADDEN, Doolittle Elementary School, Chicago, Illinois.
MARY E. PENNELL, Public Schools, Kansas City, Missouri.

Board of Directors

C. C. CERTAIN, Assistant Principal and Head of Department of English, Northwestern High School, Detroit, Mich.
BESSIE GOODRICH, Assistant Superintendent of Schools, Des Moines, Ia.
J. M. GWINN, Superintendent of Schools, New Orleans, La.
KATHERINE HAMILTON, Assistant Superintendent of Schools, St. Paul, Minn.
JAMES F. HOSIC, Associate Professor of Education in Charge of Extramural Courses, Teachers College, Columbia University.
FRED M. HUNTER, Superintendent of Schools, Oakland, Calif.
WILLIAM H. KILPATRICK, Professor of Philosophy of Education, Teachers College, Columbia University.
MARGARET MADDEN, Principal, Doolittle Elementary School, Chicago, Ill.
F. M. MCMURRY, Professor of Elementary Education, Teachers College, Columbia University.
MARGARET NOONAN, School of Education, New York University, Washington Square, New York City.
MARY E. PENNELL, Assistant Superintendent of Schools, Kansas City, Mo.
J. A. STARKWEATHER, Assistant Superintendent of Schools, Duluth, Minn.
W. F. TIDYMAN, Director of the Training School, State Normal School, Farmville, Va.
JOHN W. WITHERS, Dean of School of Education, New York University.
C. L. WRIGHT, Superintendent of Schools, Huntington, W. Va.

THE JOURNAL OF EDUCATIONAL METHOD is published monthly, from September to June, by World Book Company, Yonkers-on-Hudson, New York, for the officers, directors, and members of the National Conference on Educational Method. The subscription price is $3.00 a year; the price of single copies is 35 cents.

Postage is prepaid by the publishers on all orders from the United States, Mexico, Cuba, Porto Rico, Panama Canal Zone, Republic of Panama, Bolivia, Colombia, Honduras, Nicaragua, Peru, Hawaiian Islands, Philippine Islands, Guam, and the Samoan Islands. Postage is charged extra as follows: For Canada, 25c on annual subscriptions; other foreign countries not named, 50 cents. All communications regarding subscriptions or advertising should be addressed to World Book Company, Yonkers-on-Hudson, New York.

Address applications for membership to the Secretary of the Conference, 525 West One Hundred and Twentieth Street, New York City. The fee for active members is $3.00, for associate members, $2.00; $3.00 in each case is applied to the support of the journal, for which each member receives a year's subscription.

The editorial office is at 525 West One Hundred and Twentieth Street, New York City.

Entered as second-class matter 8 December 1921 at the post office at Greenwich, Connecticut, under the Act of 3 March 1879. Acceptance for mailing at special rate of postage provided for in Section 1103, Act of 3 October 1917, authorized 8 December 1921.

The Journal of Educational Method

VOLUME I   MARCH, 1922   NUMBER 7

EDITORIALLY ¡SPEAKING

MORE CRITERIA FOR JUDGING THE PROJECT METHOD

The professors of education are determined that the classroom teacher shall not become confused as to what is meant by the "project method" if they can help it. The latest attempts at guidance are found in the *Elementary School Journal* for January and the *Educational Review* for February, the writers being respectively Professor Parker, of the University of Chicago, and Professor Horn, of the University of Iowa. Professor Parker would make the matter very simple and plain. He would accept the dictionary's definition of a project as "something of a practical nature thrown out for the consideration of its being done." His definition then would read as follows: "A pupil-project is a unit of practical activity planned by the pupils." The illustrations which follow the definition portray classes of fifth grade children making castles—purely imaginary or in imitation of historical ones—to illustrate feudal life. One class composed a poem called "Our Castle in the Sand-Pan." Professor Parker also offers specific accounts of how projects are worked up in the Francis W. Parker School in Chicago, and would evidently define many of the accounts of school activities found in the *Twentieth Year Book of the National Society for the*

Study of Education, Part I, as projects inasmuch as they offer opportunity for practical planning.

Professor Parker notes three important movements in the new education, namely, motivation, problem solving, and project teaching. The three, however, he says, should not be confused. They are distinctly separate, or rather, project teaching is a subdivision of problem solving, inasmuch as it involves practical planning. Thus it will be seen that his distinction turns on the meaning of the word "practical." If, as he seems to feel, everyone will understand this word in the same sense, and if we will agree to this as the principal criterion of project teaching, we shall have no further cause for dispute.

That the sailing is not to be quite so plain seems evident from the second article, that by Professor Horn. He also would undertake to clear up confusion. He reminds us that projects originated in agriculture, manual training, and domestic science. Such projects were highly practical problematic activities taken in their natural setting and involving the use of concrete materials, usually in a constructive way. They could be distinguished from other school activities in that: (1) they were organized more directly about the activities of life outside the school; (2) they were more concrete; and

(3) they afforded a better test of working knowledge. The chief objective on the part of the teacher was efficiency in performance. Other subjects began to use similar methods, even, for example, in the translation of the famous passage about Cæsar's bridge. There was a fair amount of agreement as to the fundamental characteristics of the project.

Confusion, however, has arisen. Some have introduced the subjective element, insisting that the pupils shall initiate school activities as well as carry them on. Less emphasis, too, is placed on identifying projects with the activities typical of adults outside the school. Professor Horn would insist upon social utility as the main criterion of the project. It must represent a body of subject matter of known value in life outside the school; it should seek not merely to interest the child, but to develop the interests that he should have. School policies should demand a sharp and systematic attack on social objectives of value, should regard the technique of teaching as special to each subject and even to the parts of subjects, and should make definite provisions for thorough learning through practice, drills, summaries, and reviews.

By way of comment upon these two articles, it is perhaps sufficient to remark that when the authors have agreed as to which is confused, there will be time enough to consider the relation of the position of the winner to the position which he attacks. It is not entirely clear that there is as much confusion in the minds of teachers generally as the authors seem to think. Possibly those who have not settled upon a technical meaning for the word "project" may find it easier to accept it as designating a fundamental concept of method than as referring to some type of organized or objective activity. Certainly when pupils discuss the making of a castle to illustrate medieval life they probably think it worth doing. The project presented a situation demanding reflective thinking. Not least of all it offered the opportunity for the pupils to judge of the success of their work when it was completed. What Professor Parker calls "practical planning" would seem to provide—at least by implication—for most, if not all, of the essential elements found in the more inclusive definitions of the project.

Professor Horn's plea for a return to something in the past will probably be ineffectual. The pendulum swings, it is true, but never, in school work, directly back. If the subjective element which he decries is not present in his so-called "projects," then they offer only opportunity for learning in a formal sense, no matter how far they may approximate activities of social value in themselves, or *resemble* real projects.

REORGANIZATION OF COURSES IN EDUCATION
IN THE NORMAL SCHOOL

W. F. TIDYMAN

Head of Department of Education and Director of Training School, Farmville, Virginia

For many years the usual courses in education have been given in the State Normal School at Farmville. These included psychology, general and special methods, history of education, principles of education and management. The selection and arrangement of these courses have received continued study, and carefully considered changes have been made from time to time, aiming at adapting them to accepted educational principles on the one hand, and to local needs on the other. In spite of these efforts at progress and adjustment, there has been a growing dissatisfaction with the old courses, due it would seem to the confusion resulting from the overlapping of topics, and to the conviction that the old organization violated fundamental pedagogical principles. The outcome has been a thoroughgoing reorganization of courses. The problem and the tentative solution constitute the burden of this paper.

The situation before reorganization was attempted may be shown concretely in connection with Course III, the two-year course preparing teachers for work in the grammar grades. In addition to Introductory Psychology, required of all students in the first quarter, the following courses were offered: Grammar Grade Methods, Methods and Management, Principles of Education, and History of Education. The Grammar Grade Methods course included brief treatments of the fundamental subjects, emphasizing these topics: aims of education, the selection and organization of material, and methods of teaching. The Methods and Management course consisted of a careful treatment of the types of teaching, and problems of class and school management. The main topics were: aims of education, the selection and organization of material, methods of teaching, and management. Similarly, the Principles of Education and History of Education courses treated from somewhat different points of view the topics: aims of education, the selection and organization of material, methods of teaching, and management.

In this plan of organization the same topics were taken up from three or four points of view in as many different courses. The outcome of this succession of fragmentary and incomplete treatments was, necessarily, confusing for teachers and pupils. It may be well to point out again that we were following the traditional and accepted practice in these matters. The inherent difficulty in the situation is apparent at once to anyone familiar with recent discussions of principles underlying the organization of material. Material was organized in subjects upon the basis of similarity in source or character—the logical scheme of organization—rather than upon the basis of the student's needs or the teacher's problems. Thus material from history, psychology, experimental pedagogy, and other sources was put into separate courses.

The key to the situation seemed to lie in a new organization of material upon the basis of the teacher's activities. Accordingly, the teacher's work was analyzed and the following fivefold classification of duties was made: (1) the determination of aims and values; (2) the selection and organization of material; (3) the presentation of material or method; (4) class and school management; (5) extra-school activities.

This classification of the work of the teacher served as the basis for the new organization of courses. Five courses were planned as follows, and they appear in the curriculum in the following order: Introduction to Elementary Education, Grammar Grade Curriculum, Grammar Grade Methods, Class and School Management, and History and Principles of Education. The first course, Introduction to Elementary Education, serves to acquaint the student with the work of the teacher, the fundamental aims of education, and the place and value of education in a democratic society. In this course, also, provision is made for a study of community life, its forms and processes of organization, and opportunities for leadership. The second course, Grammar Grade Methods, develops the fundamental principles of the selection and organization of material, and shows their application to the several subjects. Scientific methods of curriculum making are emphasized, and the results of scientific investigations in the several subjects are made available. The third course, Grammar Grade Methods, embraces what in the past has been included in general and special methods. It acquaints the student with the common types of teaching, and the technique peculiar to the various subjects. The fourth course, Class and School Management, treats such managerial duties of the teacher as are separable from methods of teaching. Such, for example, are initiating routine, preserving hygienic conditions in the classroom, securing the coöperation of boards of patrons, and the organization and support of education in Virginia. The fifth course, the History and Principles of Elementary Education, comes toward the end of the senior year, after all the other work in education and in teaching has been completed. It serves to summarize and unify the knowledge and experience gained in the students' previous work. Modern tendencies in education are studied in connection with their historical beginnings.

This general program was followed in outlining the work in education in all curricula, although certain changes were made to adjust the work to the different curricula, and to groups within the same curriculum. The 1921–1922 catalogue of the Normal School contains detailed outlines of curricula, showing the adaptations to Kindergarten-Primary, Primary, Grammar Grade, and High School courses, as well as brief statements concerning each course.

A few remarks by way of explanation and criticism of the reorganized courses may not be amiss. These are being followed this year for the first time,—they are still in the experimental stages. We feel, however, that we are moving in the right direction.

The psychology courses were left undisturbed in their primal position. It is possible, however, that further study will show that the Psychology of Childhood and the Psychology of Adolescence, if not Introductory Psychology, may be placed later in the course. The Missouri survey supports this position.

The distinct advantage of the reorganized courses lies in the thoroughness and economy of time and effort resulting from the clear and definite division of work. Definite topics are allotted to each course for thorough and final treatment.

The courses are arranged in a natural sequence. Introduction to Elementary Education and the curriculum courses usually precede teaching, methods and management courses usually parallel teaching, and History and Principles of Education usually follows teaching.

No restrictions are placed upon the instructor as to the source of material. At his discretion he may select material from psychology, experimental psychology, experimental pedagogy, sociology, history, or any other field. The old organization of material around subjects has been accepted for so long that there is some difficulty in getting suitable textbooks for the courses as planned. This is especially true of the Introduction to Elementary Education and the curriculum courses. However, with new books in these fields appearing, the difficulty will soon be overcome.

THE SUPERVISOR AND THE PROJECT METHOD [1]

This report represents the composite thought of twenty-six principals, five superintendents, and three supervisors. The group selected for its problem the following:

"How may the supervising officer help the classroom teacher to use the 'project' method and how may he supervise the work in the most helpful and coöperative way?"

The problem falls into three large divisions, namely:

I. What are the supervisor's responsibilities?
II. What is to be expected of the teacher?
III. What kind and how much supervision is most helpful?

Each of these topics was discussed and outlined in a general way in the group meetings. Committees were then appointed, who took the suggestions as made in the group meetings as a basis and went into the topic more thoroughly. Their findings were embodied in a report to the group.

These reports were adopted by a majority vote and appear in this summary.

I. What are the supervisor's [2] responsibilities?

A. He should have a thorough knowledge of the project method.

On the surface it is almost a barren platitude to say that the supervisor who succeeds with the project method must have a thorough knowledge not only of the philosophy of the method but also of the practical application of it. Yet this is much more than a platitude. In the face of the doubts and reluctance with which conservative teachers give up old methods, the supervisor's first duty is knowledge. Without it he cannot take even the first step in introducing the newer method into his school; with it, he possesses the only means of intelligently convincing his teachers.

This is not the place to urge the necessity of mastering the literature of the subject, although one will find in it enlighten-

[1] A report prepared by a committee of students in the summer session of Teachers College, in a course conducted by Professor James F. Hosic. The chairman was Mr. H. G. Masters, Principal of Beechwood-Beechview Schools, Pittsburgh, Pa.

[2] The term "supervisor" is used throughout the article to include superintendent, principal, and supervisor as such.

ment and inspiration. The important thing is to become grounded in the principles that underlie the conception of method. It is necessary to caution against the danger of a too narrow view of the project. A narrow view of the project restricts it too much to the first type described by Professor Kilpatrick. The teacher who has not been grounded in the theory of the method, in her first attempt to work with it is usually inclined to think of it as a means of teaching children to make something. The dominant idea is to show material results. The supervisor or principal finds this his first chief difficulty. If he is not careful to broaden the conception to include other types, his teachers probably · will become discouraged with meager results. Nothing is more important than that a body of teachers in the early stages of their acquaintance with the method understand that projects in enjoyment, appreciation, problem solving, and development of skill, if they be purposeful, are as much projects as making a dress or building a sailboat. For the beginning teacher to know this, the supervisor must know it, and his knowledge must be more than a perception of the fact,—it must be an all-pervading conviction.

He must have not only a knowledge of the many ramifications of the project, but also an intelligent grasp of the practical results obtained in other communities. But much more than reading results, as reported, is needed. Projects should be seen in the process of development. Visits to classrooms in neighboring communities where the project method is being used successfully should be arranged. The practical working out of these projects should be studied, not with the prejudiced eye of a partisan, but with the sane

judgment of a practical administrator. If the supervisor possesses a clear comprehension of the project as a broad inclusive principle of classroom method, and a grasp on the results which actually can be obtained by it, he is in an unassailable position to introduce it into his school.

B. He should create among the teachers a desire to use the project method.

The supervisor must bear in mind, when he plans the introduction of the project method into his school, that he has as many different individualities before him as he has teachers, and must proceed on that basis. He has stepped back into the classroom again with his teaching staff as his class. Some of the teachers will be conservative, some over conservative— just plain "sot agin" anything newfangled. Some will be receptive and still others over enthusiastic. It will be his task to enthuse the conservative and restrain the over enthused. In other words, he has a project before him and as a working example of what he proposes to do, it should be worked out projectively.

It would seem to be advisable to call a meeting of the teachers as early in the year as possible, at which time a general discussion of the school work should be taken up. The "project method" should not be thrust forward at once, as to do so might produce a contrary "set" on the part of some which might be very difficult to overcome. Time is not pressing. It would be preferable to proceed slowly and keep going, than to proceed rapidly until some unforeseen difficulty were met upon which the whole project might be wrecked. Rather draw out criticisms of the present condition of the school work and methods and thereby produce a condition of healthy dissatisfaction. From this proceed to select work which has been observed where the teacher, without calling it "project," has used the "project method" and achieved noticeable results. Bring these before the teaching group and attempt to draw out the question "Why?" The teachers now being interested, the supervisor can begin to talk "project method," definitely connecting the term with the work already accomplished. He will find that the teachers have all done some of this kind of work and are on familiar ground, from which they will enter willingly into an interesting discussion, thereby producing a common bond. This may require several meetings.

It would be well at this stage to group the teachers according to their interests and have them form projects. Many of them will adapt themselves readily and some very excellent material will be produced. Of this the best and most readily adaptable to the situation at hand may be worked out in the classroom and produced from time to time before the group as a whole as a demonstration lesson. If these lessons are followed by conferences where difficulties are solved and outstanding good parts are brought forward strongly, the movement will soon be in full swing.

It now behooves the supervisor to observe closely the progress of the several "projects," to see that the weak teacher is given opportunity to observe others and benefit by demonstration lessons, and that she has the experience of actually carrying on the work in her own room.

C. He should have a thorough knowledge of the teacher's problem.

This knowledge is necessary along two lines,—material and organization. Material may be considered as either permanent or transient in its nature. The former is that type of material which may be used in many undertakings and should be in the school as a part of the permanent equipment. Such material would include reproductions of famous pictures, reference and story books, specimens of materials—metals, rocks, etc.—exhibits of industries or manufactures, models of machines, boats, etc., which are a perennial source of interest to pupils. The supervisor should know where these materials may be obtained. Many of them can be secured from State and Federal bureaus. Advertising agencies also furnish abundant and valuable material. The amount of this material will increase with each succeeding project.

If the material is not already in the possession of the school, or cannot be obtained from a library or museum, then the supervisor must find some other source of supply. It may be that a Parent-Teacher Association, a Civic League, a Chamber of Commerce, or some other body of interested citizens will purchase the equipment. Supplying the funds with which to buy the needed equipment would in itself make a very fine project for the school and would produce a more lasting impression than if the money were received as a gift.

Transient material is that type of material which will be needed for only one project, or for a short time. It may be donated or loaned by the pupils, teachers, or friends of the school.

How to adapt the project to the course of study will be a real problem to the teacher. How to include all the essentials and not expand beyond the limits fixed by the course of study are problems that will be met early in the teacher's preparation for using the project method. The supervisor's knowledge of the course of study and the field to be covered by the proposed project must be sufficiently thorough to enable him to assist the teacher in making these adjustments to the arbitrary limitations as set up by the course of study.

The social aspects of the pupil-group will determine in large measure the kind of class organization that will be most effective. The group may be one that must be held rather firmly to the matter in hand, or one to which may be given a considerable amount of freedom, or finally the members may have progressed so far along the road toward a sense of a social responsibility that some form of class organization is desirable. The important thing is that the pupils be given full freedom to work out their problems, only stopping short of the place where freedom becomes "license" or when the value of the teacher's leadership is in danger of being weakened. Here it is that the supervisor who, by longer acquaintance with the group, has a clearer knowledge of its characteristics, may by wise council and guidance be of great assistance to the teacher in determining the type of pupil organization that is most likely to be successful.

D. The supervisor should have rich resources from which to suggest ways and means to the teacher.

In helping the teacher to realize her rôle in the project method, the supervisor should make it clear that one important duty is to have a fund of clear-cut, vital questions ready for use in setting the field for purposeful activity. The supervisor should appreciate the teacher's inexperience in that kind of preparation and be ready with a number of suggestive questions in the subject under discussion. The average teacher will have difficulty in bringing forward live issues that will stimulate purposeful activity on the part of the pupils and may fail unless given aid.

II. What the supervisor may expect from the teacher.

A. The supervisor may reasonably expect the teacher to be ready and willing to do the following:

1. To investigate the project method by informing herself, through available literature, of the arguments advanced both for and against it.

2. To examine the course of study for possible "leads" in subject matter best adapted to the needs of the children.

3. To keep abreast of the times, and to be alert to any situation that may present itself as a means for "purposeful activity."

4. To experiment in a wholehearted manner.

5. To receive constructive criticism in the right spirit and to confer with the supervisor in planning and executing the project.

6. To confer with and to visit other teachers who are using the project method successfully.

7. To make sure that her work has a psychological basis.

8. To have the work judged by scientific measurements and tests.

9. To keep a simple record in order to check the amount of work accomplished in relation to the course of study.

B. In order that the project method may be carried on successfully, the supervisor may expect the classroom teacher to possess the following attributes or characteristics:

1. She must be sympathetic. She should believe in children's purposes and activities and provide a definite place on the program to express these purposes; she should

be interested in their interests, enter into their activities, and live through their experiences with them; she should appreciate their viewpoint.

2. She must be a leader. As a leader she must assume the responsibility of knowing the goal, of keeping the class to the purpose; she must direct their activities and guide them to a successful conclusion, and provide for illustrative material.

3. She should be broad in her views, have a thorough knowledge of the course of study, recognize leads in many directions, develop leadership, recognize initiative and provide for promoting it; she should make provision for the exceptionally bright child and at the same time take care of the slow child, create a democratic situation with social control, have command of subject matter and organize it so as to conform to the children's plans.

III. What kind and how much supervision is most helpful?

The suggestions for this section of the report were obtained from a questionnaire. Forty-three replies were returned. These were tabulated and formed the basis for the following:

A. The kind of supervision that is most helpful:

The highest type of helpful supervision is that of strong, sympathetic leadership which results in helpful coöperation, constructive criticism, and stimulating discussion with the teachers in group meetings and individually. The supervisor should observe, suggest plans and materials where needed, lead the teacher to the best literature on the subject, should help in adapting the project to the course of study, should demonstrate if necessary, and should commend and encourage the teacher and pupils. In the use of the project method it may be

necessary for the supervisor to guard against waste; and a method of testing and judging results should be worked out by the supervisor and the teacher.

B. The amount of supervision needed will depend upon the ability and experience of the teacher. If she has both of these qualities, she should be permitted to develop the project along her own lines without interference from the supervisor. However, he should keep in sufficiently close touch with it to know how logically and how intelligently it is being developed and to show his interest in it. But if the teacher has limited experience and ability and is too diffident to ask for help, the supervisor should tactfully assist when he deems it necessary. The time and number of visits depend upon the stage and length of the project. Under the project method as well as under the formal method, the amount of supervision depends upon the need of the teacher and the amount of time the supervisor can give to her.

BIBLIOGRAPHY OF PROJECT TEACHING

(Courtesy of Librarian Eggers of the North Side Branch of the Carnegie Library for the use of the Pittsburgh, Penn., Public Schools.)

ADAMS, M. G. Home Project Work in Vocational Home Economics in Secondary Schools. *Jour. Home Econ.*, 10: 358, 1918.

BIGELOW, G. I. Course of Study and the Program in the Project Method. *Teach. Col. Record*, 21: 327, Sept., 1920.

BOWMAN, C. A. Graphic Aids in Analysis. *Indus. Arts Mag.*, 9: 56, 91, Feb.-Mar., 1920; 10: 9, 49, Jan.-Feb., 1921.

BRANOM, M. E. Value of the Project-Problem Method in Elementary Education. *El. School Jour.*, 18: 618, Apr., 1918.

BRANOM, M. E. Problem Method of Teaching Geography. *Jour. Geog.*, 19: 233, Sept., 1920.

BRANOM, M. E. Project-Problem Method in History. *Hist. Out.*, 11: 107, 1920.

BRANOM, M. E. Project-Problem Method in the Teaching of Geography. *Jour. Geog.*, 16: 333, May, 1918.

BRANOM, M. W. Project Method in Instruction.

CHARTERS, W. W. Projects in Home Economics Teaching. *Jour. Home Econ.*, 10: 114, Mar., 1918.

CLARK, A. B. Another Experiment in Problem Teaching. *Eng. Jour.*, 8: 218, Apr., 1919.

COURTIS, S. A. Teaching Through the Use of Projects or Purposeful Acts. *Teach. Col. Rec.*, 21: 139, Mar., 1920.

DAVIS, E. Inquiry into the Nature of the Project Problem. *School and Society*, 12: 346, Oct. 16, 1920.

DENNIS, L. H. Home Project Work in Secondary School Agriculture. N. E. A., 1916: 622.

EATON, E. ST.J. Some Applications of the Project Method in High School. *Sch. Sci. and Math.*, 20: 443, May, 1920.

FOULKES, T. R. AND DIAMOND, T. Argument for Larger Projects Suggestive of Community Activity. *Manual Tr.*, 21: 5, Sept., 1919.

FRITZ, J. A. How a Project Was Worked Out in a 1-B Room. *Kind. and First Gr.*, 4: 20, Jan., 1919.

GARBER, E. Teaching Chemistry by the Project Method. *Sch.Sci. and Math.*, 21: 454, May, 1921.

GETMAN, A. K. The Home Project—Its Use in Teaching Vocational Agriculture. *Univ. of State of N. Y. Bul.* 712, June 15, 1920.

GREEN, J. L. English Project Motivated by History. *Eng. Jour.*, 9: 557, Dec., 1920.

GRIFFITHS, N. W. Four-year-old Child and the Project Method. *Kind. and First Gr.*, 5: 187, May, 1920.

GRIMSTEAD, W. J. Project Method in Beginning Latin. *Class. Jour.*, 16: 388, Apr., 1921.

HATCH, R. W. Teaching Modern History by the Project Method. *Teach. Col. Rec.*, 21: 452, Nov., 1920.

HENDRICKS, B. C. Projects as a Teaching Unit in High School Physics. *Sch. Sci. and Math.*, 21: 163, Feb., 1921.

HENNES, MARIE. Project Teaching in an Advanced 5th Grade. *Teach. Col. Rec.*, 22: 137, Mar., 1921.

HIGGINS, L. D. Cutting Off a Limb, a Project. *Teach. Col. Rec.*, 17: 38, Jan., 1916.

HIGGINS, L. D. Home Project Work in Utah. *Jour. Home. Econ.*, 12: 67, Feb., 1920.

HORN, E. What Is a Project? *El. School Jour.*, 21: 112, Oct., 1920.

HOSIC, J. F. Outline of the Problem-Project Method. *Eng. Jour.*, 7: 599, Nov., 1918.

HYDE, M. Projects in Literature. *Eng. Jour.*, 9: 401, Sept., 1920.

JACKSON, L. L. Project—Sinning and Sinned Against. *Ind. Arts Mag.*, 7: 138., Apr., 1918.

JILEK, A. L. Project Method in Teaching Civics. *El. School Jour.*, 21: 216, Nov., 1920.

KILPATRICK, W. H. Problem-Project Attack in Organization, Subject-Matter and Teaching. N. E. A., 1918: 528.

KILPATRICK, W. H. Project Method. *Teach. Col. Rec.*, 19: 319, Sept., 1918.

KRACKOWIZER, A. N. Projects in Primary Grades.

LANE, C. H. Aims and Methods of Project Work in Secondary Agriculture. *Sch. Sci. and Math.*, 17: 805, Dec., 1917.

LARKIN, M. J. M. Project Method Tested. *Kind. and First Gr.*, 5: 271, Sept., 1920.

MINOR, R. The Supervision of Project Teaching. *Ed. Admin. and Sup.*, 5: 357, 1919.

MINOR, R. Problem Teaching: How to Plan It. *Jour. Geog.*, 19: 61, Feb., 1920.

MINOR, R. Project Teaching in Grade Six. *El. Sch. Jour.*, 20: 137, Oct., 1919.

MOORE, J. C. Project Science, Progressive. *Sch. Sci. and Math.*, 16: 686, Nov., 1916.

NOLAN, A. W. Problem of Summer Teaching in Connection with Project Supervision. *U. S. Educ. Sec. Sch. Circ.*, No. 7, Nov. 15, 1920.

NOLAN, A. W. Project Methods in Teacher Training in Vocational Agriculture. N. E. A., 1918: 275.

PARKER, .B. M. Sixth-grade Science Projects. *El. Sch. Jour.*, 20: 279, Dec., 1919.

RANDALL, J. A. Project Teaching. N. E. A., 1915: 1009.

RICH, F. M. A Few Live Projects in High School Mathematics. *Sch. Sci. and Math.*, 20: 34, Jan., 1920.

SNEDDEN, D. Project Method of Teaching Home-Making. *Ed. Admin. and Sup.*, 5: 94, 1919.

SNEDDEN, D. Project as a Teaching Unit. *Sch. and Soc.*, 4: 419, Sept. 16, 1916.

STARK, W. O. Problem of Discipline in the Project Method of Learning. *Educ.*, 41: 310, Jan., 1921.

STEVENSON, J. A. Project in Science Teaching.

Sch. and Home Educ., **38:** 110, 1919. *Sch. Sci. and Math.*, **19:** 50, Jan., 1919.

STEVENSON, J. A. Project and the Curriculum. *Sch. and Home Educ.*, **38:** 146, 1919.

STEVENSON, J. A. Problems and Projects. *Sch. and Home Educ.*, **38:** 209, 1919.

STEWART, R. M. Project as a Method of Teaching. *Sch. Sci. and Math.*, **20:** 594, Oct., 1920.

STOCKTON, J. L. Project Work in Education.

SWEENEY, E. L. Problem-Project Method in Primary Grades. *Kind. and First Gr.*, **5:** 177, May, 1920.

TALLMAN, L. New Types of Class Teaching. *Rel. Educ.*, **12:** 271, 1917.

TAYLOR, W. S. Project Methods in Teacher Training Courses. N. E. A., 1918: 276. *Sch. and Soc.*, **8:** 487, Oct. 26, 1918.

TIPPIO, W. A. A Project in Girls' Physics. *Sch. Sci. and Math.*, **21:** 425, May, 1921.

TRAFTON, G. H. Project Teaching in General Science. *Sch. Sci. and Math.*, **21:** 315, Apr., 1921.

TRYBOM, J. H. Application of the Project Teaching; Elementary Manual Training. *Man. Tr.*, **22:** 29, Nov., 1920.

TOWNE, M. E. Developing a Class Project. *Ind. Arts Mag.*, **9:** 442, Nov., 1920.

VON HOFE, G. D., JR. Giving the Project Method a Trial. *Sch. Sci. and Math.*, **16:** 763, Dec., 1916.

WADE, E. B. Utilization of the Chance Projection in Science Teaching. *Sch. Sci. and Math.*, **20:** 775, Dec., 1920.

WAKE, W. S. Project in General Science. *Sch. Sci. and Math.*, **19:** 643, Oct., 1919.

WELLS, M. E. A Project Curriculum.

WHITCOMB, F. C. General Project Method of Teaching the Industrial Arts. *Ind. Arts Mag.*, **9:** 131, Apr., 1920.

WHITNEY, H. J. Project Teaching of Manual Training. *Man. Tr.*, **22:** 57, Sept., 1920.

WOELINER, R. Project Analysis. *Man. Tr.*, **21:** 159, Jan., 1920.

WOODHULL, J. F. Project Method in the Teaching of Science. *Sch. and Soc.*, **8:** 41, Jan. 13, 1918.

WOODHULL, J. F. Projects in Science. *Teach. Col. Rec.*, **17:** 31, 1916.

WOODHULL, J. F. Science Teaching by Projects. *Sch. Sci. and Math.*, **15:** 225, 1915.

SUPER-NORMAL CHILDREN—A STUDY

E. RUTH PYRTLE

Principal of the McKinley Junior High School, Lincoln, Nebraska

The tendency in the best modern education is to study the individual differences in children and as far as possible to make the course of study and daily school program fit these individual differences. Many schools are taking care of the various types of children—the super-normal, the sub-normal, the motor-minded, etc.,—by special classes suited to the needs of these children.

The first group to receive special attention in Lincoln, Nebraska, was the super-normal or brighter group. This group, called the Preparatory School, was started by Superintendent W. L. Stephens in September, 1909, in the McKinley building under the supervision of the principal, Miss E. Ruth Pyrtle. Each year following for eleven successive years two or three groups of 25 pupils each were sent to this school.

The preparatory school was established to give pupils who are capable, both mentally and physically, a chance to do more intensive and extensive work than the regular course of study provides. Leading educators everywhere are convinced that there is a great deal of waste in education, both in subject matter and in time. The arguments in favor of saving time in the elementary course are well set forth in the report, "Economy of Time in Education,"

Government Bulletin No. 548. On page 40 this important bulletin says:

"One of the conspicuous causes of waste in elementary education is the attempt to give the same preparation to all, regardless of wide differences in aptitude and the character of the life to be led. Classifying the grades above the sixth as secondary will facilitate a differentiation in the upper grades which will permit some pupils to make more direct preparation for business or the industries than is now possible, while others continue to follow the more strictly academic program as far as may be necessary in preparation for managerial positions or professional life. Without accurate and detailed accounts of the results of actual trial under such an organization, positive assertions as to economy of time could not be made, yet the probability that time would thus be saved would be strong. But enough communities have made progress in this important field to place the matter beyond the stage of mere probability. Worcester, Indianapolis, Baltimore, Lincoln, Harrisburg, and Rochester by maintaining special classes for exceptionally capable children have shown that it is possible for able pupils to save one year between the sixth grade and the twelfth, and with other advantages to themselves besides the saving of time."

Plan of Selecting.—The school was made up of pupils from every sixth A and seventh B grade in the city. The superintendent requested that about 10 per cent of the enrollment of these grades be recommended, selecting those whose records were highest and who were physically capable as well as mentally so. To the parents of those selected by the principals the superintendent sent the following letter:

"To the Parents:

In our public-school system there are some pupils who can, without jeopardizing health, accomplish more than their classmates but who, being able with little effort to keep pace with the rest, are satisfied and fail to develop the powers which are latent within them. While the average and less capable are gaining the ideal of hard work, these few are gaining the idea that all things

can be had without effort. This idea is likely to follow them through life and to make them really less effective than some of those of smaller natural gifts who have gained the habit of intense application.

It is our purpose to select from the pupils who have completed the sixth A grammar grade those who have shown unusual capacity. With the consent of the parents these pupils are to be gathered into what is known as the Preparatory School, where during the next two years they will be permitted to complete the regular work of the seventh and eighth grades, and the work of the first year of the high school, so that when they enter the high school it will take only three years for graduation. This plan will save a year's time, but the most important consideration is that these pupils will learn to exercise their exceptional powers instead of settling down into contented mediocrity.

Occasionally after a pupil enters this school, we find it advisable that he should not attempt to do all the work of the first year of the high school. In this case he will be permitted to carry such part of it as seems best to the parent.

Inasmuch as —— is one of those receiving the highest standings in scholarship in —— class, —— is entitled to membership in this school for such length of time as —— shows that —— is able to carry the work successfully. Are you willing for —— to become a member of the Preparatory School, which is conducted in the McKinley Building, corner 15th and M streets?

An early reply will be greatly appreciated. I shall be pleased to answer any questions relative to the plan.

Respectfully yours,

————————

Supt. of Schools

Course of Study for the Preparatory School.—The course of study was the same as that in the regular seventh and eighth grades except that music and art were omitted and one year of regular Freshman high-school work was done during the two years in Preparatory. To get this additional work done the Preparatory student found it necessary to study one and one-half hours, on the average, outside of the regular class hours. The high standard of health exhibited indicated that the program was not too heavy. Besides this extra work many of these pupils became proficient in music and art because of the private work done in these lines.

The advantages gained through the Preparatory School may be summarized as follows:

Summary of Advantages.—

A. Better work done, because more intensive.

B. Fewer pupils in room, so better instruction.

C. Same teacher for four successive semesters.

D. No waste of time waiting for slow pupil.

E. German or French and Latin languages acquired at psychological language age.

F. Punctuality and attendance averaged 98 plus, which indicates that good habits were established, also that good health was prevalent.

Since the Preparatory students came long distances, averaging one to four miles, they got more fresh air and outdoor exercise than they otherwise would. This perhaps accounted in part for the high standard of good health. None dropped out or failed because of poor health. Very few wore glasses—not one in twenty.

It is the policy of the preparatory school to make classroom instruction concrete and connect life in school with commercial and industrial life outside. To assist in this, speakers from outside have talked to the pupils regularly on such topics as "Banking," "Geography—Weather Forecasting," "Gardening," "Bird-Study," "Right Living," "Newspaper Cartoons," "Cigarettes," etc.

Careful records were kept of the progress and achievements of these children by classroom instructors, by supervisors, and by the superintendent. It was most gratifying to note the high standing of these pupils in high school and in the University. The individual record of each member can be followed throughout his school course. The life record since leaving school would be most valuable study. Owing to crowded conditions—acute housing conditions—in 1919, the superintendent did not have a class selected. These conditions still exist and the plan has not been resumed.

Would that we could measure the value to the individuals served, and to society, of having the individual in school do the type of work suited to his needs and his native capacity!

PSYCHOLOGICAL AND LOGICAL[1]

WILLIAM HEARD KILPATRICK

Professor of Education, Teachers College, Columbia University

"What do these terms 'psychological' and 'logical' mean? I know what each means when it stands alone, but when they appear thus contrasted, they seem to have specialized meanings. Am I right?"

"Yes, I think you are right. As contrasted terms they were introduced, I believe, by Professor Dewey."[2]

"I know it; that's where I found them. But I wish we might talk it over. I believe it would help me at any rate."

"The clearest idea I can get is to think of the 'psychological' as the order of actual experiencing and the 'logical' as the way we arrange what we learn from the experience."

"I don't quite understand. Won't you please explain?"

"Suppose we illustrate. Take government, for example. When did you first begin to learn anything about government?"

"Do you mean the very first, when I was a child?"

"Yes."

"Why, I can hardly say. The earliest that I recall is when I wanted to go on a picnic with my older sister. My mother wouldn't let me and I cried. I think she punished me. At any rate I learned that there were some things I couldn't do without my mother's permission."

"Suppose we take that as a beginning, though it certainly was not your very first. You had in this an experience of being governed and you learned something from it."

"Yes, and the next time I knew better what to expect."

"You mean that what you learned grew out of one experience and prepared for a succeeding experience along the same line?"

"Yes, that's true, though I hadn't said it to myself just that way before now."

"And is this always true, that each experience leaves some result of learning and that this resulting learning in turn prepares, in part at least, for the next experience?"

"You have in mind a succession of experiences along any one line, like government?"

"Yes, and I mean to ask whether in such a case there always is a succession of experience and result,—E_1 R_1 E_2 R_2 E_3 R_3 E_4 R_4 . . ."

"I believe you are right. If I understand you, E_1, E_2, E_3, etc. mean successive experiences of government, and R_1, R_2, R_3 refer to the successive results learned respectively from these experiences."

"Yes, and each R grows out of the E preceding and prepares you in some measure for the E succeeding."

"I am getting lost. You are going too fast for me. I see the different experiences all right. Every time Mother or Father or teacher made me do something, or set up a rule, or punished me for breaking a rule, that was an experience of government. They are the successive E's. That's clear. But what are the R's?"

"Well, let's see. By the time you began

[2] See *Child and Curriculum*, pp. 25–28; *How We Think*, pp. 61–63; *Democracy and Education*, pp. 256–261.

school, had you learned at home what you as a six-year-old might and might not do?"

"Yes, I was pretty well adjusted, you might say, though I would sometimes break over."

"Had you learned all this at once, as the result of just one experience?"

"No, it took a great many experiences to teach me. I remember that for quite a while I kept running away, till finally I learned that I had to have permission before I went out of the front gate."

"Did, then, your first experience of running away teach you nothing about government?"

"Oh, yes. I learned that I couldn't run away without being called to account. Eventually I learned to ask permission."

"And after that another round of experiences, perhaps in connection with your brothers and sisters, taught you something about others' rights and the need to respect them."

"Yes."

"So each experience (E) does leave some deposit of learning (R), and each such R does make you look out differently—in some degree—upon the future?"

"Yes, that's clear. I see that each R not only grows out of a preceding E but also helps us face some succeeding E."

"I should like to ask here about the successive R's. Does R_3 sum up R_1 and R_2, or what?"

"Let's answer that by another illustration. Suppose a child, say three years old, is first introduced to dogs by playing with a white, playful little fellow. As he plays (E), he builds up in himself a notion (R) of what a dog is and what to expect. When his mother says that Grandmother has a dog, he expects the same kind of small white playful dog. But suppose Grand-

mother's dog turns out to be black, though small and playful. What will he now think when he hears that Uncle John has a dog?"

"He will think that Uncle John's dog is small and playful, but he will be in doubt as to the color."

"Does his notion (R_2) after playing with Grandmother's dog reject R_1, his former notion of dog?"

"No. In part R_2 confirms R_1. He thinks even more firmly that a dog is small and playful; but in part it changes R_1. He now thinks a dog may be white or it may be black."

"And will the like process continue when he meets large dogs, yellow dogs, fierce dogs, and so on?"

"Yes, it must so continue. I see now that each succeeding R in some measure utilizes all the preceding, but it may correct their deficiencies."

"Isn't it in these different and contrasting experiences that the child comes to notice the different things about a dog?"

"Yes. Suppose Fido hurts his foot and goes limping about, what effect on the boy?"

"Why, he will become more conscious of Fido's feet than before and he will also see how all four feet must work together if Fido is to run well."

"Let me say it a little more explicitly. As the child has from time to time need to think, now of foot, now of tail, now of forelegs, now of eyes, he comes to separate these out of the total notion of dog and for the purposes of thought gives them, as it were, a kind of separate existence. This we may call differentiation of parts. Moreover, while the child is differentiating out any one part, as the foot because of the lameness, he is at the same time seeing how this part is connected with the rest: Fido needs all four feet for normal running. This we may call integration or coördination. ·Now I assert that differentiation and integration go hand in hand."

"Yes, that's clear. Now does not this have some effect on the successive R's?"

"To be sure. They become thus ever more complex. They have more and more recognizable parts and the parts are seen to be joined together in ever new ways."

"From what you are saying the separate parts seem to become known after the child has a notion of a dog and not before?"

"Yes."

"But is not this contrary to what we have been taught about going from the simple to the complex?"

"Do you mean that a child should build his idea of a dog as he builds a block house, one block or one element at a time?"

"Well, why not?"

"Let's try it and see how it would work. Shall we begin with the feet to build our idea of a dog. Does the child first learn the feet of the dog, and then the legs, joining the latter to the former on top? And does he then learn the body, and join this to the already waiting legs and feet? And does he next add the ideas of tail and head? Does he take each such successive step with no notion of the whole dog till he has thus built it up?"

"That's absurd! You are making fun of me."

"Not of you, but of that way of building up an idea. It *is* absurd, isn't it?"

"It certainly is, but now I am lost, I am afraid, entirely. How does the child build an idea?"

"Go back to the differentiation we discussed. The child saw the lame foot and so saw foot and feet more clearly than ever before. This differentiation was bringing

into clearer relief what was less clearly present before."

"Yes, I see that much."

"But the notion of the dog was all the while a notion of a whole dog even from the first."

"Certainly."

"But it was not so with building the house. The first block didn't make a whole house or anything like it."

"I think I see now. The boy's first experience was of a whole dog and he got a notion of a whole dog. This notion was at first simple enough—and inadequate— but it became more and more complex and more and more adequate as more and more parts or characteristics were differentiated and integrated. However, the notion under consideration was all the time and at each time that of a whole dog."

"Exactly so."

"Well, what has all this to do with 'psychological and logical'? Have you forgotten that? What is the good of all this anyhow? What is going to come from it?"

"We do seem to have gone pretty far afield. Suppose we try to collect it all together. Imagine as regards government a very long series of experience and learning-result closely worked out, stretching from earliest babyhood up to the knowledge of the most learned scholar in the realms of thought. We may picture it in this fashion: $E_1 R_1 E_2 R_2 E_3 R_3 \ldots E_{10} R_{10} E_{11} R_{11} \ldots E_{50} R_{50} E_{51} R_{51} \ldots E_n R_n E_{n+1} R_{n+1} \ldots$ In this the E's mean successive experiences of government and each succeeding R is the learning result that followed that experience. In every case R grows out of a preceding E and prepares, in some measure, for a succeeding E. Let's look at this series and ask some questions about it. We'll suppose we have before us the growth of the conception of government in a well taught person who comes at length to be a great authority in the subject. I ask first: Is each R made from its preceding E by conscious intent or not?"

"I should say not with conscious intent. Surely as a child he didn't intend to learn. He didn't think about that. He learned, to be sure, but he didn't consciously mean to learn."

"Probably as a child he did not consciously intend his learning,—though often his parents meant he should learn,—but how about his later years?"

"If he is to become a conscious student of the subject, there certainly will come a time when he intentionally studies his experiences in order to draw from them their lessons. Even if he were not to be a scholar, he might still as a man of affairs take conscious note of what was going on so as to profit by it. So the later R's are made with more or less conscious intent."

"Can his parents or a teacher help this process?"

"Certainly. They can help the boy draw proper conclusions. I suppose in line with our previous discussions they will wish him to be purposeful in his experiences in order that he may better learn. They will also in all probability 'set the stage' or 'load the dice' ,or otherwise contrive that he have fruitful experiences."

"What do you mean by fruitful experiences? Are some more fruitful than others?"

"Why certainly. In fact if parent or teacher or somebody didn't help the child, he would never catch up with what the race during untold centuries has been learning. This means, of course, wise oversight of the boy's experiences."

"Suppose the E's are the right kind,

that is, purposeful on the boy's part and fruitful of result, what about the successive R's? How will they differ from each other?"

"As we have already seen, each R in turn is itself more or less of a whole, summing and supplementing and correcting the preceding. They grow continually more and more differentiated within and at the same time more and more fully coördinated. They are also, I suppose, more consciously organized—we might say more and more logical. Not only will each be more carefully drawn as a conclusion from the preceding experiences, but I think each formation of the conception will be more and more consciously made, organized on more and more rational grounds. This is what I mean by saying it would grow more and more logical."

"Let's go back a minute. How different is any E from its R?"

"If I understand you, they are different kinds of things. Any E is a bit of life itself, actual experiencing, while the R is a result in the mind, an ordering and arranging of what is learned from the experiencing. E is life, R is what is learned from life so arranged as to control better the next experience (a new E) along this line."

"Even a child profits from his experiences, then?"

"Certainly. You might say, if you wish, that each time of life has its own learning, its own arrangement of learned results, its own logic. These successive R's differ as regards organization in degree, but little if any in kind or function."

"You apply the term logical to each learning result. Do you do this deliberately?"

"Yes, I think the essence of logical arrangement is effectual organization of experience. I find this in substance—

perhaps I had better say 'in germ'—in the learning of even the youngest child. The very essence of learning is for control of subsequent experience. So I am willing to say that each R from the first is for its stage logical."

"Am I to infer that by analogy you apply the term psychological similarly to each experience?"

"Yes, just as the result (R) is organized logically, so is the learning experience by its very nature arranged psychologically, that is, for learning. Perhaps the definition here lies as much in the contrast as in the terms themselves."

"I am not quite clear as to your use of the word logical. Do I correctly understand you that when the words logic and logical are used in their ordinary sense, they refer to the higher reaches of systematic organization, the kind we expect of well-disciplined minds? But when logical is used in contrasted connection with psychological, both terms vary with the development of the person: to each psychological age and experience its own logical arrangement?"

"Yes, that's the way I understand it."

"Won't you state, then, succinctly the difference between the psychological and logical order? I think I know, but I am not sure."

"The psychological order is the order of experience, of discovery, and of consequent learning. The logical order is the order of arranging for subsequent use what has already been learned."

"I have heard people discuss whether we should arrange a course in science, say, psychologically or logically. I think I see dimly what they mean, but I should like to see it more clearly. Can you help me?"

"I think so. Go back to our long series written down above, stretching from $E_1 R_1$ up to $E_n R_n E_{n+1} R_{n+1} \ldots$ Let's ask, first, what is the difference between a scientist and a teacher of science,—between what a scientist and what a teacher of science should try to do? Where on this scale would the scientist as such live?"

"I suppose toward the end."

"Suppose we say he now has reached R_n and no one has gone further. Then he will try to push ahead and learn still more. He will use his R_n to map out an experiment or a series of observations (E_{n+1}) from which by careful reasoning he will hope to draw some new conclusions. If successful he will arrange his results in a form to stand criticism and present them as R_{n+1} to the world. This is what the scientist as such would do."

"Yes, I see that."

"Now by contrast suppose a teacher of science who has gone through the whole series up to and including R_n; how will he try to bring his son, say, up to R_n?"

"How old is the son and how much does he already know?"

"Why ask these questions?"

"Because he must begin where the son is."

"Do you mean that each learner is at a certain stage on this series and must begin there if he is to advance?"

"Yes, surely. How else could it be done?"

"I agree with you, but is it always so done? What about our textbooks, in physics for example?"

"What do you mean?"

"Is it not true that most textbooks take the latest results of science (R_n) and try to state them simply, then divide this material into thirty chapters and assign these in turn as lessons?"

"I hadn't thought of it that way, but I believe you are right."

"Suppose the child has reached a development indicated by R_{10}; is Chapter I (the first thirtieth of R_n) the same as R_{11}, and Chapter II the same as R_{12}, and so on?"

"Why no, that would be like building that block house, wouldn't it, a block at a time, and like getting the notion of the dog by beginning with the feet and then adding the legs?"

"I think it would be much like it. And what notion would the child have of physics after a few lessons like this? Do you from this see the difference between the logical and psychological order?"

"I begin now to see. The logical order is taking a mental organization fit for grown-ups, chopping it into pieces, and giving it piece at a time to the child to learn. I suppose the idea is that when he gets all the separate pieces he will then have a whole. But isn't it absurd? It is in fact like building up the notion of the dog by getting first the separate notions of feet, legs, body, tail, and head, and then putting these together. I am glad you gave me that illustration."

"Isn't geometry frequently so taught?"

"Yes, always so, unless there is special preparation for the ordinary geometry book. And that's one reason why it often proves so difficult. Of course Euclid's book was for much more advanced students."

"Isn't it true that when R_n is thus cut up into pieces and assigned as so many lessons, memorizing the formulation is about all the child can do?"

"This is often so. The child's E's, then, are not real experiences, only efforts to memorize statements of the results of somebody else's experience. Under such conditions thinking, real thinking, the thinking of discovery and exploration, is pretty well prevented."

"And if the child doesn't experience, if he has no true E's, he will have no true R's, no really self-organized learning results. Am I right?"

"I think so. I see no escape from that conclusion."

"But are you not going too fast? Do you mean that the child must himself rediscover all that the race has found out? That's impossible!"

"I don't mean to leave the child without help. His process will be immensely shortened by having as a guide some one who knows the field. He is thus saved the costly blind alley wanderings. But he must himself face the essential problems if he is to organize in himself the solutions. On no other basis can he come to have an effectual grasp of the solutions as instruments of further thinking along this line. We can give him information, that bichloride of mercury is a poison. He can use this information and save himself from being poisoned; but neither chemistry nor medicine can be taught merely by giving such information. Where knowledge and wisdom and power are sought, there must be much actual facing of difficulties. Experience in a field is necessary for anything like mastery of the field."

"I am not clear on one point. A while back we spoke of the child's having from the first a notion of a whole dog. That seemed clear then. But I fail to see the similarity between that and his work with the science. Do you mean to assert that he has from the first a notion of the whole science and that this undergoes differentiation and integration as we saw in the case of the dog?"

"Yes and no. We do not say that the notion of physics as a science was born the day the child first realized that a stone unsupported will fall, any more than we think the notion of biology was similarly born the first day he saw the dog. But any vital and natural experience has a unity that makes it a whole, whether it be of a falling stone or of a lever or of a syphon. And the child forms a notion of the experience which for him at the time is a whole, however much his more sophisticated elders may feel it as of necessity only a part of a larger whole. Later, if the child is fortunate he will have further fruitful experiences in this realm. Each such will be a whole, but oftentimes will join itself with previous experiences; and the new notion will supplement and correct the old ones. Differentiation and integration will in this manner arise, and at length what you and I call the science of physics will be born. If the boy be so inclined and is still fortunate, this likewise will undergo differentiation and integration and logical articulation with successive experiences until mayhap the existing limits of the science are reached. Throughout, if the process be normal, each experience (E) is a whole and each successive R is for our pupil, student, and scholar at that stage likewise a whole, however partial and lopsided that particular R may later appear. But the thirtieth part of R_n is to the novice not a whole, nor is memorizing it or otherwise 'learning' it likely to be felt as a vital and whole experience of physics (though it may be felt as a real experience of bad teaching). Nor is 'learning,' in this fashion, all the chopped up parts of R_n a valid way for building in the boy the organization R_n. That can be done only by following the psychological as herein sketched."

"You are pretty hard on the logical order when used for learning. I judge you don't approve of grammar as most of us learned it."

"I certainly do not. It exactly illustrates what I mean to condemn."

"Wouldn't you on the whole mistrust definitions?"

"Yes. If I hear that a teacher requires his pupils to memorize many definitions, I have my doubts at once as to that teacher's insight."

"One further question. What does 'psychologizing subject matter' mean?"

"It refers to the work of the teacher in preparing for the learning of his pupils. In terms of our discussion it means to take a science as the scientist knows it (as R_n) and 'unscramble' it into such a series of $E_1 R_1$ $E_2 R_2 E_3 R_3 \ldots$ as will lead the learner from where he now is through successive experiences (E) and learnings (R) until he comes to a firm grasp of the science itself. It means to make a path of psychological order from the learner's present state up to a state where he has much experience well organized."

"One last question. You have spoken as if this applies only to science. Does it apply also to our ordinary school subjects?"

"Indeed it does. I may by elaboration say that high school science should certainly begin as general science and that be preceded by many experiences preparatory to it—not 'deferred values,' mind you, but experiences in which children live here and now. Geography should be so taught. In our best schools English grammar has already been so made over that little of the nth degree logical is now left. The older grammars were atrocious examples of teaching by the strict logical order. Civics is now being remade thus into citizenship. History teaching is probably scheduled for a similar transformation. Many causes are at work to make over the school subjects more and more into the psychological order. In fact our best thinkers now conceive the curriculum itself as a series of experiences in which by guided induction the child makes his own formulation. Then they are his to use."

"We have much to think over, but I believe it is worth it."

AN EXPERIMENT IN COÖPERATION
VII. The Question of Grammar

James F. Hosic

Associate Professor of Education, Teachers College, Columbia University

Traditions die hard. As a matter of fact they generally have a kernel of truth in them, no matter how much exaggeration of emphasis custom and hearsay may have added to it. So it is with the tradition of the linguistic aspects of the study of English in the schools. Beginning as an offshoot of the study of Latin, the study of English grammar early secured a place of honor in the elementary schools and to this day the pedagogical conscience is likely to be tender in regard to it.

In our experiment the first troubled spirit to broach the subject made the man higher up the point of reference. "The high schools complain that we do not teach enough grammar. How shall we meet this criticism?" Now, the well-known tendency of most teachers to underestimate the previous training of their students is not an entirely convincing reason in the minds of grammar-grade teachers for ignoring criticisms from above. The pupils suffer and they come back to their former teachers to say so. Those teachers face a condition, not merely a theory.

The answer which the leaders made to the query, "WHAT about grammar?" was, "Wait, and see. Let us consider first what the pupils in the grades actually need in the way of instruction in English grammar to enable them to improve their speaking and writing. Possibly when we concentrate in the right way upon the essential topics, the high school teachers will be better satisfied. So far as the instructors in foreign languages are concerned, they must expect to teach a good deal of grammar. That is what they are paid for."

THE PROOF OF THE PUDDING

Presently something happened. One of the district superintendents called the principals and upper grade teachers of a certain territory into consultation about English teaching with the principal and English teachers of the high school which serves that territory. The high school teachers were asked to voice their sentiments in the matter of grammar and they did so in no uncertain terms. Pupils coming to high school were notoriously deficient in this respect.

Then the principal of our experimental school was invited to explain just what his teachers were doing with grammar. It wasn't a formal study—merely a handmaiden to speaking and writing. There was no attempt to cover a treatise on the subject, however elementary. "We thought so," was written on the faces of the high school group.

And then the superintendent did an uncanonical thing. He called for the records in English of pupils who had come from the various schools. "And lo, Ben Adhem's name led all the rest." When it came to actual performance, to the *use* of English, the graduates of the school which was making no effort whatever to conform to demands for formal instruction in grammar, but which had earnestly striven to develop an effective course in composition, especially oral composition, made the best showing by the testimony of the high school itself.

The sequel was startling. Impressed by the incident which we have just described, the principal of the high school requested his English teachers to visit the experimental school and endeavor to catch the secret of modern, informal methods in composition. The teachers went—with what feelings may be imagined.

Investigation in other quarters tended to confirm the impression which this experience gave. Pupils going to high school from the experimental schools were being remarked upon for their ability to meet the actual demands of speaking and writing which arose in the English classes and elsewhere. Scholasticism received little comfort from our enterprise, though none of us were so sanguine as to hope for its early and complete disappearance from strongholds in which it has so long been entrenched. "Should not a *gentleman* know all of these things?" quoth he.

WHAT GRAMMAR TO TEACH

None of us assumed, of course, that there is any virtue in *avoiding* instruction in grammar altogether. Just as a few fundamental principles of effectiveness—of rhetoric, if you please—are a distinct aid to him who would attain to clearness and force, so some facts and principles of correctness as determined by current usage are of value to one learning to obey the conventions of the vernacular. Grammar constitutes a part of the science of the art of expression in words but as such has its natural limitations. The question to raise is, "What knowledge of grammar does in fact enable the speaker and the writer to improve?" Almost equally pertinent are the questions, "*How* is such knowledge best acquired, and when?"

In accordance with our general plans and point of view, we of the English centers regarded all of these as open questions. That children make certain types of grammatical errors more frequently than others is now scientifically determined. It is not known, however, to what extent teaching the rules governing correctness in such matters will work improvement. Some reputable writers seem to assume as an axiom that ascertaining what errors in grammar are most frequently made automatically selects the topics for chief emphasis in systematic grammatical instruction. We assumed nothing of the sort. Instead, we asked each teacher to investigate the matter for herself and presently to report upon what grammatical instruction she found worth while in her grade. Ultimately committees were formed to organize the findings in the various schools, and at last a central clearing house committee was asked to put the several reports into one.

The following brief outline as thus prepared for the Chicago Course of Study was the result:

ESSENTIALS OF GRAMMAR

Grammar is to be taught with a definitely practical aim, not as an end in itself. That aim should be:

1. To help in the formation of habits of correct English.
2. To assist in the mastery of the sentence as a unit of oral and written English.

The teaching of grammar must grow out of the needs of the children in so far as their attempts at expression indicate those needs. Such suggestions as follow must not be misconstrued to mean the formal grammar of definition, classification, and subtle analysis. The course to be effective must be coördinated with the work of composition, i. e., primarily with the speech of the children. Only in the highest grades may the simpler, more obvious facts of grammar be so employed as to aid in the interpretation of literature.

GRADES I–IV

Correct errors of speech as they appear. Attempt the elimination of the characteristic errors of the class in hand, such as, double negative, wrong form of pronoun, incorrect uses of the verb. The common errors are so many and so well known that it is unnecessary to list them here; moreover they vary somewhat in different districts. It is advisable for the teacher to list those most prevalent in her own class and then work persistently to overcome them.

Contrive games and three-minute drills to give children practice in the correct use of words they commonly misuse.

GRADE V

In this grade the teacher should gradually and carefully introduce a small amount of grammatical nomenclature; that is to say, she may begin to call a spade a spade. She must not require definitions nor formal pointing out of parts by the pupils. She may accustom them to her distinction of *common* and *proper nouns*, with reference to the capitalization of the latter. The terms *verb* and *adjective* may well be used in criticism of their speech, e. g., that the *verb* is wrong when they say "I seen" for "I saw"; that a narration might be more interesting if instead of saying that one "went across the street" a verb were used that gave more of a picture, as dashed, crept, sneaked, or wabbled.

If such a procedure is judiciously followed throughout the grade in connection with the children's composition, they will gain a fair acquaintance with a terminology which is useful at the time by way of economy and which serves as what might be called the foundation of some measurably formal instruction later.

Notation: Guard against "action word." Call it a verb.

GRADE VI

The "sentence sense" has been developed through five years of oral composition. If they have been taught rightly, the children have been consciously "speaking in sentences." They should be taught enough about the relationship of *subject noun* and *predicate verb* and about verb forms to assist them to understand the *agreement of verb with subject. Present and past tenses* may be taught by way of helping the child who says "I ask him to go" to correct his speech.

Note. Whatever of grammatical content is taught here must be the natural outgrowth of the children's endeavor *to use English.*

GRADE VII

With the composition of the pupils as the basis of the study, the idea of parts of speech should be amplified to include in this grade:

1. Adverbs: Distinguish from adjectives for the sake of usage.
2. Pronouns: Case forms for subject, object, and possessive—purpose as above, correct usage.
3. Verbs: Participles, also proper contractions; e. g., show why "he don't" is incorrect.

In sentence structure consider:

1. Phrases: To place them most effectively in composition, or to help in the interpretation of literature.
2. Subordinate clauses: To use them as a means of more accurate or graceful expression.

GRADE VIII

The task of the eighth grade is to organize the material that has been informally handled in the earlier grades and to amplify further the ideas of sentence structure and of parts of speech. The basis of the material of instruction is, as before, the pupils' use of language. This being the case, the outline which follows is not given as direction for the order in which the topics should be considered, but as a summary of the grammatical knowledge which the pupils may be expected to assimilate in the *course of the year's work in composition.*

Note carefully the suggestions for the previous cycles. Discover whether the pupils of the seventh grade have the abilities indicated. Develop or re-develop them as necessary.

I. Parts of Speech.
1. Nouns: common and proper, singular and plural, possessive.
2. Pronouns: case forms of personal and relative pronouns as subject or object; correctness of reference (*who* and *which*).
3. Adjectives: recognition, for effectiveness in use; comparison, for correct form.
4. Verbs: tense, voice, noting principal parts of troublesome verbs (use dictionary).
5. Adverbs: distinguished from adjectives by form and use.
6. Prepositions: to secure correct idiomatic use.
7. Connectives: treated very simply, not for classification, but with the purpose of enlarging vocabulary and securing more accuracy of speech.

II. Sentence Structure.
1. Simple Sentence: classified according to purpose as declarative, interrogative, imperative, exclamatory.
2. Essential Elements of Simple Sentence:
(*a*) Subject, simple and complete.
(*b*) Predicate, simple and complete.
(*c*) Modifiers, classified as to use, not form.
3. Complex Sentence: function of subordinate clause, clearness, variety, economy of words.

4. Compound Sentence: value in summing up or in balancing statements.

Note. None of these topics should be treated exhaustively. The purpose of the course is fulfilled in the realization that there is a law of language, the basis of correct speech; in the recognition that there are greater force, flexibility, and variety to expression.

Briefly, the children should pursue the course with the conscious purpose of learning how to make better sentences.

Two features of this outline are worthy of notice. In the first place, grammar is related as closely as possible to composition. Indeed, it is described as a part of the course in composition. In the second place, the purpose to be served by instruction in each topic is definitely indicated. Attention is to be called to phrases, for example, not to insure the ability to distinguish or classify but to cultivate the power to construct better sentences.

This is the spirit of the whole outline and is to become the "conscious purpose" of the pupils whose course in grammar is suggested by it. Grammar is to be, not a subject apart, pursued for its own sake, like the science and mathematics now happily being superseded, but a guide to improvement in the art of communication, an aid to him who would obey the conventions of the vernacular current in his time and so economize the attention of his auditors.

HIAWATHA'S WEDDING FEAST
Dramatized by Seven-Year-Old Children

ETHEL M. GREEN

State Normal School, Milwaukee, Wisconsin

The play was given by the second grade of the Milwaukee State Normal School. It represented the product of about two months' work, not more than a half hour each day, however, having been given to the study. A part of that time was devoted to costume-making in the regular art period and for the making of pipes, bows and arrows, tomahawks, and other things needed in the play. During the regular gymnasium period some time was given to learning the Indian dances needed in the play, and at the regular music period to learning songs to be sung, and at the regular literature period to learning the poem and arranging the play. During the regular reading period some time was spent in reading Indian stories for the purpose of enjoyment and of getting information concerning Indian dress and habits that might be valuable in working out the play. Two half-hour periods were devoted to writing letters to a school supply company inquiring the cost of red clay to be used by the children for modeling the pipes. A little time was taken to calculate the cost of materials.

In addition, the children at home on their own initiative spent some time collecting Indian relics, such as · bowls, tobacco pouches, horn, etc., and in making such things as spears, tomahawks, etc., that were needed in the play.

A little extra time was spent by individuals who had been selected by the class to confer with teachers in various departments on particular problems. For example, the music department was asked to write the music for the words that Chibiabos sang; the physical training teacher was asked to help with certain Indian dances; and the head of the art department was asked to help with the stage scenery.

The children themselves chose the particular part of the story to be dramatized. They had played "Hiawatha's Childhood" without costumes, and the entire story of Hiawatha had been read to them many times: After much discussion they agreed upon the "Wedding Feast."

On the stage was a wigwam which had been brought by one of the children, and stretched on the back wall was a large poster of pine trees, expressive of the lines, "Dark behind it rose the forest." There was also a large hollow log.

> "And Osseo when he saw it,
> Gave a shout, a cry of anguish,
> Leaped into its yawning cavern,—".

The stage setting was arranged to harmonize in color with the costumes which the children had made. Their suits were of khaki cloth, fringed and decorated brightly with Indian symbols. Their moccasins of brown cloth were also brightly decorated, and their headgear was adorned with gay colored feathers made of paper.

At the beginning of the play Hiawatha, Minnehaha, and old Nokomis were busy about the wigwam in preparation of the feast. Some of the guests had arrived and were squatted in Indian fashion on either side of the stage. An Indian yell was heard in the distance. It came nearer and nearer.

Then from the piano below the stage came Indian dance music; at the side entrance to the stage there was a tremendous Indian yell, and in came a procession of thirty or more children in full Indian costume. They came in the stooping, sneaking, alert manner characteristic of the Indian race. They encircled Hiawatha and Minnehaha, dancing the Indian snail dance, winding about them, then unwinding, keeping time to the music, and finally seating themselves in Indian fashion in a large semicircle on the stage.

Then the feast began. Old Nokomis and Minnehaha set large bowls before the guests, and gave them spoons. These bowls were borrowed wooden bread bowls which the children had chalked white. The spoons were made of black cardboard. The guests began to eat. Of course they were only pretending.

Then the children spoke to the audience.

1st Speaker:

"You shall hear how Pau-Puk-Keewis,
How the handsome Yenadizze
Danced at Hiawatha's wedding;
How the gentle Chibiabos,
He the sweetest of musicians,
Sang his songs of love and longing;
How Iagoo, the great boaster,
He the marvelous story-teller,
Told his tales of strange adventure,
That the feast might be more joyous,
That the time might pass more gayly,
And the guests be more contented."

2nd Speaker:

"Sumptuous was the feast Nokomis
Made at Hiawatha's wedding;
All the bowls were made of bass-wood,
White and polished very smoothly,
All the spoons of horn of bison,
Black and polished very smoothly."

3rd Speaker:

"She had sent through all the village
Messengers with wands of willow,
As a sign of invitation,
As a token of the feasting;
And the wedding guests assembled,
Clad in all their richest raiment,
Robes of fur and belts of wampum,
Splendid with their paint and plumage,
Beautiful with beads and tassels."

4th Speaker:

"First they ate the sturgeon, Nahma,
And the pike, the Maskenozha,
Caught and cooked by old Nokomis;
Then on pemican they feasted,
Pemican and buffalo marrow,
Haunch of deer and hump of bison,
Yellow cakes of the Mondamin,
And the wild rice of the river."

5th Speaker:

"But the gracious Hiawatha,
And the lovely Laughing Water,
And the careful old Nokomis
Tasted not the food before them,
Only waited on the others,
Only served the guests in silence."

6th Speaker:

"And when all the guests had finished,
Old Nokomis, brisk and busy,
From an ample pouch of otter,
Filled the red-stone pipes for smoking
With tobacco from the Southland,
Mixed with bark of the red willow,
And with herbs and leaves of fragrance."

While the sixth child was speaking, old Nokomis and Minnehaha gathered up the bowls and spoons. Then Nokomis filled the pipes and the guests began smoking. The pipes were of red clay, and had large bowls and long handles. Nokomis said:

"O Pau-Puk-Keewis,
Dance for us your merry dances,
Dance the Beggar's Dance to please us,

Pau-Puk-Keewis Dancing at the Feast

That the feast may be more joyous,
That the time may pass more gayly,
And our guests be more contented!"

Then Pau-Puk-Keewis danced to piano music such a dance as he thought might have been danced at the feast. The gymnasium teacher had taught him the dance. He was dressed as he thought Pau-Puk-Keewis might have been dressed, even to the plumes on his head, the fan of turkey feathers, and the tails of foxes on his heels.

Then Nokomis said:

"Sing to us, O Chibiabos!
Songs of love and songs of longing,
That the feast may be more joyous,
That the time may pass more gayly,
And our guests be more contented!"

Chibiabos sang in sweetest tones:

"Onaway! Awake, beloved!
Thou the wild-flower of the forest!

Thou the wild-bird of the prairie!
Thou with eyes so soft and fawn-like!
If thou only lookest at me,
I am happy, I am happy."

All the children joined in singing the last line, "I am happy, I am happy." After this some one said:

"O good Iagoo,
Tell us now a tale of wonder,
Tell us of some strange adventure,
That the feast may be more joyous,
That the time may pass more gayly,
And our guests be more contented!"

And Iagoo answered:

"You shall hear a tale of wonder,
You shall hear the strange adventures
Of Osseo, the Magician,
From the Evening Star descended. . . .
Once, in days no more remembered,
Ages nearer the beginning,
When the heavens were closer to us

And the Gods were more familiar,
In the Northland lived a hunter,
With ten young and comely daughters."

At this point Iagoo stopped and smoked. He had decided when we were working out the play that, even though he could tell the whole story, it would be too long. The audience might get tired, and the Indians at the feast might get restless. Then, too, the children had planned to dramatize at some later date the story Iagoo told, and the audience would not care to hear the story twice. All the other children did not know his plan, and some begged him to continue. He smoked in silence for a while, then said:

"There are great men, I have known such,
Whom their people understand not,
Whom they even make a jest of."

To these last words many of the Indians responded:

"Does he mean himself, I wonder?"

Then old Nokomis said again to Chibiabos:

"Sing to us, O Chibiabos!
Songs of love and songs of longing,
That the time may pass more gayly,
That the feast may be more joyous,
And our guests be more contented!"

And Chibiabos sang:

"When thou art not pleased, beloved,
Then my heart is sad and darkened,
As the shining river darkens,
When the clouds drop shadows on it!
When thou smilest, my beloved,

Then my troubled heart is brightened,
As in sunshine gleam the ripples
That the cold wind makes in rivers."

After this he sang again the first song, ending with:

"If thou only lookest at me,
I am happy, I am happy."

All of the guests joined in singing these last lines, then rose and danced an Indian war dance, and left the stage, stepping to the music in Indian fashion and chanting, "I am happy, I am happy."

Some of the values derived from the work I have described are as follows:

The pupils gained in the formation of certain social habits, such as that of working earnestly and joyfully together to attain a definite end, of giving help and of taking criticism in the right way. They gained in ability to take the initiative and in the habit of looking for better ways of doing things.

Through planning this play, and through doing all the things necessary to carrying out the plans, such as making costumes, having the words Chibiabos sang set to music by the music department, requesting the gymnasium department to teach the dances needed, through memorizing the lines, and through the actual playing of the story, the children obtained a rather thorough appreciation of this particular portion of *Hiawatha*. I think they gained also, as a result of the work, a better appreciation of music, drawing, manual arts, and dancing as actual means of expression.

PREPARING NATURE STUDY TEACHERS

JAMES S. GRIM

Instructor in Nature Study, Keystone State Normal School, Kutztown, Pennsylvania

In order to determine what students in some other normal schools of the United States were doing in their nature study work, it was suggested that each member of our nature study class (170 in all) write a personal letter to a teacher of nature study with the request that she hand the letter to an interested student of hers for reply. Patterson's Educational Directory was used to secure correct addresses. Normal schools were selected on a geographical basis, care being taken not to send letters to many schools in one state to the exclusion of other states.

The letters were composed in regular school time under the instructor's supervision. The supervision did not extend, however, to details of composition, but was restricted to general problems of motivation. Each student wrote out her nature study reactions, her experiences in the course, in a direct personal way as though she were telling about them across the table to a stranger of like age and experience. In many cases pictures of the school, the campus, and nature haunts nearby were inclosed.

Replies soon began to come in. These were brought to class and read aloud and discussed. In a few instances the instructor herself as well as a student replied, but in most cases responses came from students only. A sufficient number of replies have been received to indicate that nature work in many teacher-training schools of the United States is not handicapped by a deadening uniformity. States maintaining uniform courses of study exhibit wide diversity in actual practice in this phase of school work.

Although many objections can be raised to the student-reaction method of discovering drifts and testing tendencies in educational aims, yet when sufficient data are at hand this method has some merit of directness. For what a teacher does counts more than what she may try, listlessly or otherwise, to do.

One would naturally expect that students, graduates of a high school, studying the possibilities of nature material for training purposes in the grades would have definite ideas as to principles, aims, and methods involved and that discussions of their experiences would revolve around such ideas. One would think, too, that there would be some basis of general accord or agreement in principle that would be an outstanding feature of the responses.

This lack of harmony prompts the query, Is it not possible to discover or suggest elements that should be common features in courses offered in every state? Or does local tinge require conflicting aims and discordant principles?

From a study of the student replies a basis for uniformity does not seem impossible. The basis is the child itself—the chief nature problem. So long as we emphasized content, objective nature, however fascinatingly presented, there were bound to be teachers of the book and lecture type, and textbooks for student-teachers were naturally filled with insect, bird, and flower material—books that are excellent elementary biologies but poor tools as helps in nature study.

It is difficult to shed pedagogical names. It is agreed that the phrase "nature study" is unfortunate unless qualified and intensified by present-day interpretations. To the student-teacher who has a lower grade child before her the phrase "nature study" does not connote elementary biology; the phrase has not yet, in a sense, taken on science implications. The science consists in the selection, organization, and presentation of nature tools that will evoke desirable responses.

The child problem is the only outstanding one that can be common in all courses of nature study. Knowledge of nature *in* the child rather than familiarity with nature outside is basic in value. A knowledge of outside nature to a teacher is useful only in its means of personal reactions. Racial tendencies, inheritances of various sorts, tendencies of different forms, constitute a nature equipment whose significance to a leader of child life has more profound value than informational facts about flowers, birds, and insects, a considerable body of which cannot be made to function in classroom practice.

It is difficult at times to control the nature leadings within a child by the use of pets, gardens, etc., but the work ranks high or low according to this reasoned control. For instance, sunlight can be taught most effectively when the teaching conforms to the principle of biological relationships of organisms to solar energy.

Like a leaf the child moves toward the light. It cries for the moon; it gazes at the stars; it delights in playing with fire; and in the olden days it worshiped the sun. Here is an instinct, a nature force, a tendency to move in response to pleasurable feelings.

It is the teacher's privilege to organize situations in harmony with it—situations that will develop into habits of hygienic light relations.

In preparing a teacher for this work through a project-problem on light, the chief aim should be habit formation and should turn on the securing of repeated light responses. Handwork, "cutouts," games, songs, outdoor walks, garden activities, expression work generally, are aimless and meaningless to the teacher who has not a clear-cut response program in mind. Observation of response development in children and the discussion of the principles of interpretative expressions induced by concrete situations is the very heart of a nature study course for teachers.

In view of this it is very easy to understand why some teachers, poorly equipped in knowledge of science, are doing excellent nature work and why some others well-trained in biology, physics, and chemistry are not meeting expectations.

Enthusiasm for outdoor life, while helpful, is not so important for a prospective teacher as enthusiasm for child life and a desire to know how to use common things to develop wholesome responses.

Emphasis on the direct needs of the child to satisfy its normal and biological cravings should be the basis of nature work in teacher-training schools generally. Naturally, there must be variations in methods and materials in the several states to secure worth-while results.

A few subordinate problems raised by the students of our class, in view of so many divergent expressions of opinion by fellow students in many scattered normal schools, were: 1. Is there a basis of agreement? 2. In what might this basis consist? 3. To what extent can an agreement be widely accepted?

LEARNING TO LEARN

CHARLES H. SAMPSON

Huntington School, Boston, Massachusetts

The old idea of learning seemed to require that the student be attentive enough to absorb knowledge by listening. The teacher did most of the work in class. It was true, of course, that the student had something to do outside of class. The result was that the teacher became efficient as an explanatory medium of the truths of the subject that he was teaching but the student, unless somewhat exceptional, lost much because he could not, under the circumstances, bring the best of himself to the surface.

Unless a student learns to learn by doing, he is likely to suffer keen disappointments and possible failure, this, not because his native ability is below average but because he does not know how to use the abilities that he has.

Let us consider a class in college preparatory algebra, for example. The point can be illustrated here as well as anywhere. How can a student best learn algebra? There is only one satisfactory way that is applicable to all classes of students who have the ability to learn it at all. He must learn to learn it; he cannot generally absorb it as a result of mere teaching even though it be exceptionally well taught.

Let us suppose that a certain number of problems are assigned in the subject of fractions for a given lesson. The part that the teacher should play in the accomplishment of the solution of these problems resolves itself into a first-class explanation of the processes and methods involved and the reasons for doing this or that. He may well do a few problems further to illustrate the methods that he has been explaining if

by such procedure he can fix the application of them. Then the student must play his part; he must do the problems himself if the result is to be as desired. This requires work on his part rather than on the part of the instructor. Here is the whole trouble: the student does not want to work. He finds it difficult to get the idea that learning is the result of work. Merely to listen is not necessarily to learn.

A good way to conduct any recitation is to divide it into two parts, one of which is a teaching proposition, the other, a learning one. The first part is, of course, to be used by the teacher, the second part by the pupil, except for such supplementary aid as the instructor may find necessary to give. If students could see the advantages of attacking the job which is theirs during their half of the period as a game to be won, how simple and effective would be this task of instilling knowledge. A visitor to a class conducted after this fashion might find the teacher doing nothing during the second half of the period, but if he found all of the students working as though their lives depended on the result of their labors, he could rest assured that there was nothing the trouble with the method in that class.

During this latter half of the period instructor is nothing more nor less than a helper in time of trouble. A certain detail of the explanation may not have been entirely clear; let him explain and straighten out the difficulty. "Is this the correct answer to the first problem?" says John quietly. "No, John, there is a slight error there (pointing it out). See if you can get the correct result now." The chances are that John will succeed in a moment or two. He is learning to learn. Delightfully inspiring it is to see boys and girls playing the game.

"Here are two of the most difficult problems that I have been able to find anywhere, and the pupil who solves them before the end of the period will get an 'A' for the day," says the teacher. The student who does not respond to this has something the trouble with him. American youth does not play that way. He may say that he does not care to accept the challenge that has been thrown at him, but in his heart he will want to get the answers to those problems. Eventually, practically every member of the class will be able to get that "A."

Such a method as this shows its results gradually. A gradual accomplishment, however, is almost invariably the most satisfactory one in the end. It is true here. Boys and girls who have actually learned to learn need have little fear of the college entrance tests.

The teacher who can teach by lecturing may well consider himself somewhat of a wonder. This sort of thing gets by in college because there is no "comeback." In the preparatory classes for college, however, one may lecture his head off and yet not accomplish the desired end because he has no check at all on what his students are learning to do for themselves. Let us as teachers teach our students to learn.

THE CLEARING HOUSE

COST AND CONSERVATION

A good project for the seventh and eighth grades is learning to read the meters and compute the cost of electricity, gas, and water used in the home.

Launching the Project: Electric lights are burning when class enters room. Request a student to turn off the electric current. By class discussion bring out the following points:

1. Why not let lights burn all day?
2. Who determines the cost per month?
3. How does he decide the amount?
4. What other conveniences about the house?
5. How does each of these get to the house?
6. Does each convenience cost same?
7. Why have meters?
8. Does anyone else read meters except the representative from company?
9. Would it be well to have a check on reading?
10. Would you like to read the meters at your home and compute cost?

Students will be instructed to go home, locate their meters, make a drawing of the figures on the faces; also notice the shape of the meter.

Method of Procedure:

1. Drawings to be placed on board. Students describe outside appearance and location of meters. Learn to read dials.
2. Interpretation of terms. Students will go to the textbook and reference books to find what they can about meters, for the purpose of learning how the meter measures. They report information found.
3. Computing cost. Learn rates charged by company. Find amount consumed as indicated by two meter readings. Find cost of same.
4. Drill in reading and computing cost of several readings.

Practical Application:

Class work out a chart on which readings are to be recorded. Each student makes a chart.

Each student reads meters on Thursday and Monday evenings. All read meter on same day that company's representative reads it. Compute cost for month. Bring company's bill from home and check amounts. Pupils should be encouraged to continue checking readings each month.

The idea involved is, conservation of energy. Electric lights, often burning when not needed, are requiring energy which is supplied by coal. Our natural resources are decreasing with each generation.

A SEED SALE

Situation: A class of second grade children had become interested in a Junior Red Cross membership drive and wished to earn its dues of forty-five cents by selling seeds.

Activities: The children gathered seeds from home gardens. Each child made an envelope according to his own ideas. The best envelope was selected by the class, its owner was asked to explain how he made it, and many more were made like it. Then each child decorated an envelope. The decorations were discussed by the class and the most attractive designs were repeated many times on other envelopes.

The class advertised the sale well. Many children brought to school advertisements cut from magazines and newspapers. These were read to find out how to write an advertisement. The class observed that a good advertisement tells where and when to buy an article, and how cheap and how good it is. With these four points in mind, they set about writing advertisements, first learning to spell the words, then practising them on the board, and finally writing the advertisements on large pieces of unprinted newspaper. They cut large baskets and vases of flowers, printed their names beneath them, and hung them about the room. The large advertisements or posters were hung in the halls. Children were chosen to go to the different rooms and explain the purpose of the sale, telling a little about the work of the Junior Red Cross Society.

When the seeds were in the envelopes ready to be sold, the question arose, who should sell them? It was decided to play buying seeds with toy money in order to find out who would make good salesmen. In this manner several good clerks were discovered, but when the real sale took place there was such an unexpected rush that the little sales people became confused and the teacher had to do most of the selling herself.

One hundred and three packages of seeds were sold and many disappointed customers were turned away.

PROVIDING AN AUDIENCE FOR ORAL READING

In the fourth and fifth grades the following plan is in use in the Franklin School, Port Arthur, Texas. In this school there are four classes of each half grade, eight fourth grade, and eight fifth grade classes. Each teacher of academic work (reading, writing, spelling, language, arithmetic, and geography) has all of the academic work of a Low and all of the academic work of a High class for one grade. There are four teachers for each grade.

The teachers are requested to arrange their programs in such manner that reading will come at the same time for two teachers. The teachers are paired off before programs are made. To be specific let us use actual class numbers. Classes 29, 30, 31, and 32 are all Low Fourth classes. Classes 33, 34, 35, and 36 are all High Fourth classes. The teacher of academic work for class No. 29 has academic work for class No. 33. Class No. 30 and class No. 34 are taught by the same teacher. The third teacher teaches Class No. 31 and Class No. 35; in like manner 32 and 36 are taught by the same teacher.

Classes 29 and 30 have reading at the same time daily on their program. Today is preparation day. In each class from five to ten children are working with the teacher preparing material to be read tomorrow to the children of the other class. They are mastering the difficult words. They are making every effort to do their best tomorrow. While they are preparing, with the active assistance of the teacher, the other members of the class are reading silently. They are provided with ample material from the school library, with story books from home, and with magazines, railroad and steamship folders, and catalogues of mail order houses. What they have read during the silent reading period will be carefully checked during the language period.

The morrow arrives. It is a great day for each class. Those who prepared yesterday go with their teacher to the room of the other class. Class 29 is being entertained by children from class 30. Class 30 is being entertained by children from class 29. The children who are reading have an audience. The audience does not know what is going to be read. It is not going to find fault. It is expecting a good story, well read. During the language period, after the readers have returned home, the class will talk about the stories that were read. They will also criticize the manner in which they were read.

Let us step into the room of class 29. A child from class 30 steps forward. He announces the title of his story. Perhaps he gives a brief synopsis of it before beginning. He must do all that he can to hold his audience. Each member of that audience has on his desk a book. If the reader fails to interest him as much as the book, he will not listen to the reader but will read from his book.

All of the audience wait until the title has been announced and the story begun before anyone opens a book. Then we see a few books being opened and read. The story is a good one, light applause follows, and the entire audience attends to the title and beginning of the next story. This time not a book is opened. The audience is held while a boy reads from the Boy Scout magazine the story of "Yellow—Clear Through" by P. L. Anderson. At the end of four minutes the teacher calls time. By a show of hands the audience requests another minute. Five minutes is the final limit of time to be given to one

reader. At the end of the minute the audience votes to continue the story day after tomorrow. The reader takes his seat and a girl then reads about "Queen Mab and the Cherry Blossom," by Margaret Tod Ritter in the "Every Girl's Magazine." This time the girls vote to have the story continued. The third child to read is a boy who is large for his grade and somewhat backward. He could not do well in any standard reader for his grade, but the teacher has chosen for him an easy story, "From a Japanese School Reader," in *John Martin's Book* for February. This is the story he has longed for. He has had four days of careful preparation—we learn later. He reads without an error. The tale is full enough of interest to compensate the audience for the monotonous manner of reading. It is completed and the boy returns well pleased.

Do not think that all stories are from magazines. They are from many sources. One teacher has gathered together twenty-five different kinds of readers and story books from which to read. The school takes all magazines that are published for children.

The plan is useful for the poor reader or the lazy reader who comes before his audience not properly prepared. The audience leaves him by all reading silently, and the teacher stops him when she sees that he cannot hold a majority of the audience.

Each child under this plan reads orally to an audience at least twice a month. He reads to his teacher two or three times for each time he reads to the audience. Each time he reads he is on his feet for at least two or three minutes. The plan affords more reading. The reading is better motivated. Some parents complain because the children do not read every day. When invited to a reading lesson, however, they do not complain but go away well pleased with the accomplishments of their children.

By assigning the teachers in pairs classes 33 and 34 work together with the same teachers who have classes 29 and 30. The plan has proved so successful that from an experimental beginning with two classes it has spread to all of the classes. Some third grade teachers are using it. In a smaller school the children of one grade could read to the children of another grade.

LEONARD POWER,
Principal, Franklin School,
Port Arthur, Texas

INDIAN MUSIC—A CHILDREN'S PROJECT

It was also a normal school student's project. She had been asked to prepare a series of lesson plans for teaching English composition, unified in idea, and covering several weeks of class time. Her own interests were so strongly musical that somewhat unusual possibilities suggested themselves. It was decided that she should find music—folk music preferably—sufficiently expressive of an experience within the children's range as to make them wish to compose suitable words.

Indian music was found to meet these requirements. The grade selected for the experiment was the fourth. The class was a heterogeneous one in a recently organized school. It was regarded as decidedly below grade in English, and it certainly had no enthusiasm for composition.

The objective we had in mind could not properly be reached without an acquaintance with Indian life. This was carefully presented in the usual way, including various problems that the children themselves proposed. When the topic "Indian music" was reached, the first song was sung by the teacher. Then she played some songs on the piano, asking the children to suggest the idea or feeling expressed, and confirming—usually—their guesses by singing the words. Finally she played an unusually expressive selection which the class at once decided was storm music.

"Sing it," they demanded.

"I cannot sing this one," she replied; "I have no words."

"We must have words," they cried.

"There is only one way to get them," she suggested.

They saw the opportunity and went to work. First the whole selection was played again and they organized the ideas it expressed,—the rolling of the thunder, the beating of the rain, etc. Then came the line by line composition, with much discussion and trial of various renderings and with growing critical appreciation. There were opportunities for the teacher to list vocabulary possibilities and to make other suggestions that exercised their selective powers. Over and over they sang it to test each new line. When at last it was completed, they experienced the kind of creative joy that poets know.

The subsequent history of this group amply justified the experiment. They showed a real zest for rightly motivated composition, and an attitude toward criticism that looked toward a passion for perfection. They often wished to spend more time in revision than their teacher had anticipated, so that the sense of satisfaction experienced by the various persons concerned in this project became cumulative.

SARAH J. McNARY,
State Normal School,
Trenton, N. J.

A CORRECTION

Miss Elizabeth Breckinridge, Principal of the Louisville Normal School, desires us to say that the article on "Home Life in Louisville in 1800 and 1921—Heating, Lighting, and Ventilation," which appeared in our January issue, should have been accredited to Miss Minnie Burks, a teacher in her school. We are glad to make this correction.

AS REPORTED

EDUCATIONAL STANDARDS

Teachers and school officials everywhere will be interested in the standards adopted by the New England Association of Colleges and Secondary Schools at a recent meeting in Boston. The standards are as follows:

1. The purpose of the school should be to develop in each individual to the fullest possible extent the knowledge, interests, ideals, habits, and powers whereby he will find his place and use that place to shape both himself and society toward ever nobler ends.

The presence of such an effective purpose in a school will be shown by the intellectual attainment of the pupils, their courtesy, industry, respect for authority, sense of personal responsibility, initiative, and habits and powers of ready and effective coöperation.

A public high school especially should be in close relation to the community which it serves. With due allowance for local conditions, the efficiency of the service of the school will be revealed by its drawing power as shown by the percentage of the school population enrolled in the school, and by its retentive power as shown by the percentage of entrants who complete the course.

2. The instruction shall be on a high level, as measured by present standards and as shown by satisfactory results in pupils. Such results will consist not only in the mastery of subject matter but also in the interest and attention of the pupils and in the acquisition by them of correct habits of thought and study.

3. The program of studies shall be unified, coherent, well-balanced, susceptible of effective administration, and adapted to the purpose of the school.

4. The requirement for graduation from a secondary school shall be the completion of at least fifteen units, normally based upon the completion of eight years of elementary school work or the equivalent. Fractional units may be counted toward this total.

Definition: A unit represents a year's study in any subject in a secondary school, so planned as to constitute approximately one-fourth of a full year of work for a pupil of normal ability. To count as a unit, the recitation periods shall aggregate approximately 120 sixty-minute hours. Time occupied by shop or laboratory work counts one-half as much as time in recitation.

5. Teachers shall give evidence of adequate preparation in subjects to be taught.

6. Teachers of academic subjects beginning service in New England in September, 1922, or thereafter, shall have satisfactorily completed at least four years of study in institutions of collegiate grade, or the equivalent. In the opinion of the association five years of such study is desirable.

7. Teachers of academic subjects beginning service in New England in September, 1924, or thereafter, shall have had professional training equivalent to twelve semester hours.

The following types of courses are recommended as meeting the spirit of this requirement: general introduction to education, educational psychology, principles of secondary education, teaching of particular subjects, observation and practice teaching, history of education.

8. Teachers of special subjects (such as music, drawing, manual training, domestic science) beginning service in New England in September, 1922, or thereafter, shall have had at least two years of study beyond the secondary school, with special courses in the subject to be taught.

9. Satisfactory evidence of successful

298

experience may be · accepted in partial fulfillment of standards 6, 7 and 8.

Note: It is understood by the association that standards 5 to 9 do not apply to teachers in service in New England previous to September, 1922.

ESSAY BY AMERICAN SCHOLARSHIP HOLDER IN FRANCE

The French Government offers to American college women through the American Council on Education certain scholarships and fellowships in lycées and écoles normales. Miss Marjorie Howland, formerly of Vassar College, one of the young women appointed this year to a scholarship in the Lycée de Versailles, is the author of the following brief essay. Mr. Firmin Roz, of the Office national des Universités et Écoles françaises, writing of the work of the American scholarship holders, says:

"La Directrice du Lycée de Versailles nous a déjà adressé un très intéressant rapport sur l'organisation du travail des boursières américaines dans son établissément. Elle nous a même communiqué le premier devoir de chacune d'elles sur ce sujet: 'Définissez la simplicité, l'élégance et la coquetterie. Illustrez vos définitions par trois portraits.' La Directrice nous a prévenus que ce devoir était une seconde rédaction refaite d'après les indications du professeur et revue par lui. Vous trouverez ci-joint un extrait de la composition française de Miss Marjorie Howland qui nous a paru assez intéressant pour vous être signale. Il y a quelques légères retouches du professeur."

Miss Howland's essay follows:

La Simplicité

Pour une personne qui vient d'un pays où il y a tant de luxe, tant d'extravagance en toutes sortes de choses, c'est un vrai plaisir de trouver en France la simplicité. Le portrait de la jeune fille du lycée français est peut-être le meilleur exemple que je puisse trouver de cette simplicité qui m'a tant frappée partout. La jeune fille française n'arrive pas à son lycée

avec deux ou trois malles remplies de costumes pour toutes sortes d'occasions magnifiques. Elle sait qu'elle n'est venue à son lycée que pour étudier, et que les robes de soie n'y seront pas nécessaires. Quelques petits tabliers pour la classe, une robe de dimanche, voilà tout; elle n'a pas besoin de grandes malles. La coiffure d'une jeune Française, comme son costume, marque aussi la simplicité; mais c'est la vie qu'elle mène à son école que je trouve la plus intéressante à propos de la simplicité. Elle se lève à six heures et demie, fait sa toilette dans une chambre qui est à peu près chauffée, fait ses prières; elle exécute quelques mouvements de gymnastique, mange un petit déjeuner léger, et puis, elle s'en va en classe. Pendant la journée, nulle récréation, excepté quelques minutes après le grand déjeuner. Et pendant l'après-midi, nulle sortie, excepté pour aller à la classe; l'étude seule remplit les heures. Le soir vient; c'est le temps de sa récréation, mais quelle récréation simple! Des jeux dans le salon de son pavillon, la lecture, peut-être; puis, il est temps de se coucher. Ainsi la vie d'une jeune Française à son lycée témoigne à une Américaine de la simplicité de la vie française, et je crois que l'Amérique a beaucoup à gagner à ces leçons.

THE REORGANIZATION 'OF MATHEMATICS IN SECONDARY EDUCATION

THE FINAL REPORT OF THE NATIONAL COMMITTEE ON MATHEMATICAL REQUIREMENTS

The complete report of the National Committee on Mathematical Requirements is in the press and will, it is hoped, be ready for distribution in April. It is published under the title, *The Organization of Mathematics in Secondary Education*, and will constitute a volume of about 500 pages. The table of contents given below indicates its general character.

Through the generosity of the General Education Board, the National Committee is in a position to distribute large numbers

of this report *free of charge*. It is hoped
that the funds available will be sufficient
to place a copy in every regularly maintained high school library and also to furnish a copy free of charge to every individual who is sufficiently interested to ask for
it. Requests from individuals for this
report are now being received. Those who
are interested in receiving the report are
urged to send in their requests as early as
possible, addressing them to J. W. Young,
Chairman, Hanover, New Hampshire. If
the number of requests received exceeds
the number of copies which the Committee
is able to distribute, the earlier requests
will be given preference.

The table of contents of the report is as
follows:

FOREDOOMED TO "FLUNK"

For grading the members of a school or college class there is one method that would never
find adoption among producers in non-aca-
demic fields. It fixes in advance what proportion of the class shall receive highest rank,
what proportion the next highest, and so on
down, including the proportion that shall fail.
For example, if the teacher has a class of sixty,
he determines in advance that the highest
twelfth, say, shall receive the mark Excellent;
that the next three-twelfths shall receive the
mark Good; the next four-twelfths, Fair;
the next two-twelfths, Poor, while the remaining two-twelfths shall fail. That is to say, before he has read the final examination papers
or has made up his marks for the term's work,
he knows that of these sixty pupils, five will
take high honor; fifteen will receive the rating
Good; twenty, Fair; ten, Poor, while the ten
lowest will fail to receive a passing grade,
no matter what they have accomplished.
With the advantages always found in
mechanical systems, this method seems to
bewitch a certain type of teacher and
superintendent.

Yet who can picture a Deerfield onion grower
or a Rogue River orchardist undertaking to
grade his products in advance by any such
method? Only a crazy man would ignore the
difference between crop and crop. In cattle
judging, in fruit grading, in sorting manufactured articles, standards are standards year
in, year out. To condemn for discarding in
advance of inspection a fixed percentage of a
yield, regardless of the particular quality of the

season's run, would never occur to a practical man who must earn profits by sales.

Is the case different in school or college? No observant teacher can believe the quality of classes so uniform in successive years and so regularly distributed through the make-up of single classes that a rigid grading can be stencilled on them year by year without inaccuracy. Successive classes of boys and girls differ at least as much as successive runs of maple sap or alewives. This year the careful analysis of pupils' work may result in one award of honor and ten failures; next year the same method of individual rating may result in ten awards of honor and one failure. Yet from the Pacific coast to the outskirts of Boston, teachers individually or by whole staff may be found employing this inflexible method and praising it as impartial. Even in the bluest days of earlier New England, such election and rejection by forerunning decree were never commended to the use of men.—*The Boston Herald.*

THE READER'S GUIDE

THE NEW PSYCHOLOGY

Since the publication with Professor Thorndike of a series of studies in formal discipline, the teaching world has looked to Professor Robert S. Woodworth of Columbia University for unusually helpful treatment of the practical problems of psychology. More than an ordinary welcome, therefore, will be accorded his latest work entitled *Psychology—A Study of Mental Life.*[1] This is a much more ambitious work than the same writer's *Dynamic Psychology*, published by Macmillan three years ago. That book was made up of a series of popular lectures delivered at the American Museum of Natural History in New York City. The *Psychology* is a complete college textbook.

It differs in many respects, however, from the texts already available. There is, to begin with, a notable difference in style. Professor Woodworth writes with a simple, even homely directness that will appeal very strongly to college students. When one considers that the psychology class in college is made up of young people who only yesterday were in the high school, he realizes that a prevailing fault of college textbooks is the over-mature and abstract quality of the vocabulary used in them. This difficulty Professor Woodworth has

almost entirely overcome. No doubt some of the more puristic will be a bit shocked by his informality, not to say colloquialism.

Still more striking is the order of topics and chapter headings. After a preliminary chapter on what psychology is and does, the subject is opened with a study of reactions. In this way the student is introduced at once to the modern behavioristic point of view. There follows a series of chapters on native and acquired traits, including instincts and emotions. Then, as though to give the physical basis to explain the reactions so far described, appears a chapter on "Sensation." Chapter XII, entitled "Intelligence," strikes one as the first of the kind in any American psychology. Certainly it is unconventional to put perception near the end of the book. Undoubtedly our author has given more thought to the order in which the reader can best attack the subject than to the logical development of ideas. In other words, the point of view of the teacher has prevailed over that of the merely scientific.

A third very important feature of this new *Psychology* is the exercises. Here Professor Woodworth has applied the modern material of tests and scientific examinations. Such directions as "Pick out the true statements

[1] By Robert S. Woodworth. New York: Henry Holt & Co., 1921.

from the following list," and "Rate the images called up according to the following scale," represent a new type of practice that ought to prove a delight in the actual work of the classroom.

Of all the textbooks offered to the student world, certainly those dealing with the mental processes ought to be most skillfully prepared. Teachers in training as well as those in service will find in Woodworth's *Psychology* the book they have been looking for as a means to attaining a working knowledge of psychology, thoroughly sound and at the same time agreeable in its presentation.

SIGNIFICANT ARTICLES

A BRIEF FOR THE CASE METHOD

Professor W. P. Burris, of the University of Cincinnati, believes that the most important advance to be made in methods for the training of teachers is to introduce the case system into schools of education and normal schools. In *School and Society* for February 4, 1921, he recounts the history of the case method as applied to the teaching of law, and argues that its complete success there is evidence that it would be equally effective in the study of education. Objections there may be, but none that could not be overcome. He would, of course, continue the use of practice schools and other current means. In order to make his suggestion definite, he offers an elaborate plan for the making of a record of a school exercise. This includes a report by an observer and stenographic notes to be taken by a clerk.

It is interesting to note that President Lowell of Harvard University devotes several pages of his last annual report to the same topic, using, however, the term "problem method." He perceives a close connection between the project method as now advocated and the case system

used in the Harvard Law School since 1871.

PROJECTS IN CITIZENSHIP

Doubtless many will agree with Mr. R. W. Hatch, instructor in Citizenship in the Horace Mann School of Teachers College, that formal instruction in history and civics does not seem to result in effective habits of good citizenship on the part of the pupils. In the *Historical Outlook* for February he offers a series of concrete suggestions for projects intended to develop a sense of reality and effective ideals of group coöperation. Among his suggestions are those of meeting the problem of courtesy in the classroom through a town meeting, the arranging of a school congress, naturalization, and clean-up week. Mr. Hatch would group projects in citizenship under the following types: (a) projects involving extra-curricular activities; (b) incidental projects; (c) projects in classroom instruction.

EXTRA-CURRICULAR ACTIVITIES IN JUNIOR HIGH SCHOOLS

In *Educational Administration and Supervision* for January appears an interesting report on extra-curricular activities in junior high schools, compiled by students in Teachers College under the direction of Professor Thomas H. Briggs. The report opens with a definition as follows: "Extra-curricular activities are those legitimate activities not provided for in the curriculum." They will vary in different schools. Such activities are justified because they offer the best opportunity to help pupils to take their places as members of social units and because through them the school may utilize the spontaneous interests and activities of adolescents. Thirteen principles of administration are laid down for the guidance of those who have charge of extra-curricular activities, and at the end appears a list of such activities and an appropriate bibliography. The article as a whole is of very great value to any who have to do with extra-curricular activities.

THE NEW BOOKS

Opportunities of Today for Boys and Girls. By Bennett B. Jackson, Norma H. Deming, and Katharine I. Bemis. New York: Century Co., 1921. Pp. xviii + 274. Illus. Price, $.85.

A reading book devoted to vocations.

The Mechanism of the Sentence. By A. Darby. Oxford University Press, 1919. Pp. 210. 6/6 net.

A summary of facts for the information of teachers.

The Psychology of Arithmetic. By Edward L. Thorndike. New York: Macmillan Co., 1922. Pp. xviii + 314.

All of the school subjects need such an analysis as this.

Civic Science in the Home. By George W. Hunter and Walter G. Whitman. New York: American Book Co., 1921. Pp. 416. Illus. Price, $1.40.

What every boy and girl—to say nothing of their parents—need to know.

A Manual of the Mechanics of Writing. By Raymond Woodbury Pence. New York: Macmillan Co., 1921. Pp. xxiv + 211.

Primarily for college students, but valuable also as a desk book for the literary worker in general.

The Alexander-Dewey Arithmetic. By Georgia Alexander. Edited by John Dewey. New York: Longmans, Green & Co., 1921. Elementary Book, pp. xiii + 224, illus.; Intermediate Book, pp. xv + 256, illus.; Advanced Book, pp. xvi + 288, illus.

The work of a progressive educational thinker and a progressive supervisor of elementary schools.

Community Civics for City Schools. By Arthur W. Dunn. Boston: D. C. Heath & Co., 1921. Pp. x + 582. Illus.

This, with the companion volume on rural schools, represents a remarkable advance in specific teaching of vital as opposed to merely formal knowledge. The illustrations are numerous and to the point.

Community Civics and Rural Life. By Arthur W. Dunn. Boston: D. C. Heath & Co., 1920. Pp. xii + 507.

History as a School of Citizenship. By Helen M. Madeley. Oxford University Press, 1920. Pp. 106.

An account of dynamic teaching. Stress is laid on "action teaching," discussion, source work, and individual exploration.

New Geography, Book One. By Alexis Everett Frye. Boston: Ginn & Co., 1920. Pp. x + 264 + viii. Colored plates.

New Geography, Book Two. By Wallace W. Atwood. Boston: Ginn & Co., 1920. Pp. iv + 304 + xvi. Colored maps, plates.

Done in the best of the book-maker's art. The illustrations are especially striking.

Yosemite and Its High Sierra. By John H. Williams. San Francisco: John H. Williams, 1921. Pp. 193. Illus.

A charming book. Every geography teacher will wish to have his pupils see it.

Readings in Evolution, Genetics, and Eugenics. By Horatio Hackett Newman. Chicago: University of Chicago Press, 1921. Pp. xviii + 523. Illus.

A source book for college students.

A History of the Perse School, Cambridge. By J. M. Gray. Cambridge: Bowes & Bowes, 1921. Pp. 161. Illus. Price, 10/6.

A well-written account of one of the most interesting of the English "public" schools.

How to Speak. Exercises in Voice Culture and Articulation, with Illustrative Poems. By Adelaide Patterson. Boston: Little, Brown & Co., 1922. Pp. viii + 158.

The Use of Projects in Religious Education. By Gertrude Hartley. Philadelphia: Judson Press, 1921. Pp. 91. Illus.

A much-needed guide to modern constructive methods in the church school.

Peeps at Many Lands. Egypt, by R. Talbot Kelly, and *The Holy Land,* by John Finnemore. New York: Macmillan Co., 1921. Pp. 173. Illustrations in color.

Sunday School teachers will wish this for their pupils, as will day school teachers of geography.

IN PAPER COVERS

The Intermediate School in Detroit. By Charles L. Spain, Arthur B. Moehlman, and H. L. Harrington. Detroit Educational Bulletin No. 6, 1921.

Viewpoints in Biography. By Katherine Tappert. Chicago: American Library Association Publishing Board, 1921.

English. A Course of Study for Use in the Elementary and Secondary Schools of Washington. State of Washington, Department of Education, Bulletin No. 37, 1921.

The Training School. By Frank L. Wright. Colorado State Teachers College Bulletin. Series XXI, No. 3, 1921.

Whittier Social Case History Manual. By J. Harold Williams *et al.* California Bureau of Juvenile Research, Bulletin No. 10, 1921. Price, 25 cents.

Principles of Supervision. By W. F. Tidyman, State Normal School for Women, Farmville, Va., 1919. Price, 25 cents.

Detroit Kindergarten Test. By Harry J. Baker and H. J. Kaufmann. Yonkers, N. Y.: World Book Co., 1922.

The Course of Study in the Work of the Modern School. By H. B. Wilson. Berkeley, Cal.: Course of Study Monographs, Introductory, 1921.

Arithmetic: Course of Study for the Elementary Schools. Monograph No. 1. *Home Economics:* Course of Study for the Elementary, Intermediate and High Schools. Monograph No. 2. *Nature Study:* Course of Study for the Elementary Schools. Monograph No. 3. *Geography:* Course of Study for the Elementary Schools. Monograph No. 4. *Penmanship:* Course of Study for the Elementary Schools. Monograph No. 5. The Public Schools, Berkeley, Cal., 1921.

A Little Book of Verse. Written by members of the Four B English Classes of Wendell Phillips High School, Chicago, Ill., 1919–1920.

Survey of the Writing Vocabularies of Public School Children in Connecticut. By W. F. Tidyman. Bureau of Education, Teacher's Leaflet No. 15, November, 1921.

Educational Survey of Elizabeth City, North Carolina. Bureau of Education, Bulletin, 1921, No. 26.

Music Departments of Libraries. Bureau of Education, Bulletin, 1921, No. 33.

Salary Schedules, 1920–1921. National Education Association, Bulletin No. 19, January, 1922.

Mimeographed Bulletin on *Reorganization of Work in Seventh, Eighth and Ninth Grades.* By H. B. Bruner and J. N. Hamilton. Oklahoma Educational Association, 1921.

THE JOURNAL OF EDUCATIONAL METHOD

Edited by JAMES F. HOSIC

Volume I   APRIL, 1922   Number 8

PUBLISHED BY THE WORLD BOOK COMPANY FOR
THE NATIONAL CONFERENCE ON EDUCATIONAL METHOD

$3.00 a year   Monthly except July and August   35 cents a copy

THE NATIONAL CONFERENCE ON EDUCATIONAL METHOD

An Association of Persons Interested in Supervision and Teaching

THE JOURNAL OF EDUCATIONAL METHOD is published monthly, from September to June, by World Book Company, at Concord, N. H., for the officers, directors, and members of the National Conference on Educational Method. The subscription price is $3.00 a year; the price of single copies is 35 cents.

Postage is prepaid by the publishers on all orders from the United States, Mexico, Cuba, Porto Rico, Panama Canal Zone, Republic of Panama, Bolivia, Colombia, Honduras, Nicaragua, Peru, Hawaiian Islands, Philippine Islands, Guam, and the Samoan Islands.

Postage is charged extra as follows: For Canada, 25c on annual subscriptions; other foreign countries not named, 50 cents. All communications regarding subscriptions or advertising should be addressed to World Book Company, Concord, N. H., or Yonkers-on-Hudson, New York.

Address applications for membership to the Secretary of the Conference, 525 West One Hundred and Twentieth Street, New York City. The fee for active members if $3.00, for associate members, $2.00; $2.00 in each case is applied to the support of the journal, for which each member receives a year's subscription.

The editorial office is at 525 West One Hundred and Twentieth Street, New York City.

Application pending for entry as second-class matter at the post office at Concord, N. H.

The Journal of Educational Method

VOLUME I   APRIL, 1922   NUMBER 8

EDITORIALLY SPEAKING

RESEARCH OR PROPAGANDA?

If scientific workers in education get a jolt now and then, they should reflect that they have themselves at least partly to blame. In their eagerness for practical results they too often commend to the general attention what should meet the eye only of brother scientists. They announce their conclusions with periods instead of with question marks. In the general reaction, of course the innocent and the guilty suffer alike.

Certain recent criticisms of intelligence testing illustrate the point. Undoubtedly great progress has been made in devising instruments for measuring the more general mental abilities, but undoubtedly also no one should suppose that the next decade will not bring enormous changes and improvements in them. Meanwhile the wise school man will make haste slowly. Far from putting all his eggs in one basket, he will overlook no factor which might influence his decisions in dealing with problems of classification and instruction.

The conservative investigator would not have it otherwise. Unfortunately, however, some investigators seem to forget their proper functions and, not content with announcing their findings, would have them instantly adopted and put to general use. Instead of seeking confirmation at the hands of the specialist, they seek a general following.

Common sense would seem to suggest that writers on education should pick out their audience and write for it, leaving no doubt as to whether they are presenting merely accounts of investigations or well-considered and tested programs and policies urged for general acceptance. One can hardly be an original searcher after truth and a successful disseminator of useful knowledge both at the same time. The former must usually content himself, for the time at least, with Wordsworth's "fit audience, though few."

THE N. E. A. IN BOSTON

There is a certain fitness in the return of the National Education Association to Boston for the summer meeting under the presidency of a woman. It was at Boston in July, 1910, that the late Ella Flagg Young attained the honor of being the first woman to head the organization. With her election began a period of strife which has continued almost up to the present time. The new delegate system bids fair,

305

however, to give the national body a new harmony and effectiveness. It certainly begins well. Miss Williams has made a favorable impression and should prove a good leader. The program at Boston will undoubtedly reflect her intelligent interest in the common schools and tend to keep the balance from swinging, as it constantly tends to do, too far toward provision for the few at the expense of the many. The National Education Association at Boston ought to carry on the great work so nobly instituted by Horace Mann.

SUPERVISION WITHOUT A SUPERVISOR

Thomas Warrington Gosling
Superintendent of Schools, Madison, Wisconsin

The Madison plan of supervision places upon the principals of buildings the primary responsibility for the direction of the work of the teachers under their charge. Though there are supervisors for the several special subjects, there is no general supervisor for the entire system. The general supervision vests in the superintendent of schools.

The Madison plan is not a protest against the trained supervisor. It is a temporary expedient adopted on account of special local conditions. When the present superintendent was elected to office, there was a vacancy in the position of supervisor. For two reasons the superintendent did not wish to make an appointment immediately. In the first place he wished to become acquainted intimately with the system in order to have first-hand knowledge of its needs and in order to determine the particular type of supervision which would be most helpful. An equally important reason for deferring the selection of a supervisor arose out of the conviction that no one person can do the work of the principals, and that whenever the attempt is made to put the full responsibility upon one person there is a marked tendency on the part of the principals to surrender initiative and to become merely disciplinary and clerical heads of their schools. This issue is a most unhappy one, for whenever principals give their chief attention to disciplinary and clerical matters, the teachers quickly become mechanized and they lose enthusiasm, the spirit of inquiry and of investigation, and the incentive to professional growth.

Now if there is ever to be adequate supervision, the work must be done mainly by the principals. This statement applies to large schools as well as to small ones. Principals are or should be in intimate daily contact with the teaching process in their buildings. For this reason they are in a strategic position for rendering a maximum of supervisory assistance. It follows from this situation that the most effective method of securing adequate supervision is to exalt the office of principal, to invest the principal with greater responsibility, and to expect in return a large measure of initiative, of leadership, and of helpfulness.

The Madison plan of supervision without a special supervisor has aimed definitely to make the various principals the real supervisory officers of the schools. To this end the superintendent has devoted a large part of his time to conferences with the principals, both in their buildings and at his office. Fortunately, the school system of Madison is not so large as to require the superintendent to devote most of his time to administration. He reserves a large part of both his time and his energy for supervision.

Under the Madison plan the principals make frequent reports, usually by the week, upon the work which they have done in their schools. These reports indicate to the superintendent the *problems* which the principals have been studying and the *solutions* which they have offered. The teachers have shared in the work of supervision to the extent that they have made suggestions for remedial measures in reading and in arithmetic and for changes in texts. Some quotations from these reports will indicate the method and the content. One principal, for example, reported upon a problem in the eighth grade as follows:

"The eighth grade children are having difficulty in picking out the worth while things to read in the daily papers. So I suggested to Miss —— that each day she mark the items of importance in the daily paper. Each child has his own paper, which he also marks, picking out what he thinks is worth knowing. Then the children compare their news with the news that is picked out by Miss ——. Miss —— says she can already notice an improvement on the part of the children in the items they select."

Another principal writes as follows:

"The pupils in the first grade have read the first part of several primers. By reading the first part of several primers of equal gradation instead of reading each book through first, the pupils have become more familiar with the work which they have found in many different situations.

"As the pupils now have a limited reading vocabulary and are beginning to feel a need of developing new words for themselves, I suggested to Miss —— that she introduce phonics. The pupils are beginning to see resemblances and differences between such words as 'fan' and 'man,' 'fat' and 'rat,' and with a little help from the teacher are able to acquire new words by combining familiar sounds."

A sixth grade music situation was reported upon as follows:

"*Problem.* Class is slow and unresponsive when a new song is to be sung by note.

Suggestion. Teacher helps too much. The class will never take the responsibility as long as the teacher takes it for them. They find it easier to memorize than to work it out. Make the class read the notes even if they have to *say* the syllables and then sing them."

The same principal, reporting upon a discussion with a teacher concerning a fifth grade lesson in language, reported as follows:

"I have looked over the B class papers for thought content with this outline in mind:

"1. Do the pupils have a mastery of the sentence idea?

"2. Has the 'and,' 'so,' and 'then' habit been formed?

"3· Does the beginning sentence tell what the paragraph is about?

"4· Are the other sentences related to it?

"5· Are things told in the way in which they happen?

"6· Did the writer put in anything unnecessary?

"7. Is there a good closing sentence?

"Some of the paragraphs are very good. I think it might be very profitable to have five or six (choose three good and three poor ones) written on the board and let the pupils correct, using the above outline. Correct one kind of mistake at a time. You might add to the outline:

"8· Which sentence could be improved?

"9. You may help re-state it."

"The principal," writes another head of one of the schools, "has concentrated this week on Miss —— of the science department. In a conference with her, after three or four visits, he made the following suggestions:

"1. That she be very careful in writing her quizzes on the board to use complete sentences, suggesting to her that possibly her method of omitting important articles or phrases from her questions would undermine the work of the pupils in the English department, where they were taught definiteness of expression.

"2· That the pupils be held to more complete statements in these recitations, where these recitations are supposed to be complete.

"3· That her lesson assignments be more definite, and that since these were ninth grade pupils, they be given definite questions to look up rather than the general type of assignment that seemed to have been the practice."

Occasionally, of course, a principal will miss the spirit of the new order and make a report like the following:

"No classroom supervision this week. Time wholly occupied with the routine of the building, receiving parents, and individual conferences with teachers."

A report like this sets a problem to the superintendent, a problem of supervision quite as important as any other.

The most important supervisory reports which have come to the office deal with the development of suitable material for the instruction of gifted children and with the three achievement tests which were given in December. We are making the effort in Madison to devise a system which will emphasize enrichment rather than acceleration. The brighter pupils are not segregated from the others, but are given additional opportunities for work beyond the minimum requirements. The stimulus which the principals are giving to this plan promises to produce excellent results. We call our device for enrichment the "Home Corner." Reporting upon this, one principal writes as follows:

"That our school was not functioning in the case of one boy, at least, is clearly evidenced by the following composition on 'A Busy Week':

Sundays I play. Nights of Sundays I have ice cream. Then school time comes. I don't like school but I have to go. So I go five days. Then my good play time comes. Then I am glad. I play all kinds of things.

"I was disturbed and distressed over this situation, but I was unable to solve the problem. Then came the introduction of the Home Corner, which solved not only this problem, but others as well.

"As soon as the Home Corner was suggested Miss —— began planning with her children as to how it should be furnished. They suggested a fireplace, table, chairs, flowers, magazines, a spinning wheel, a telephone, a phonograph, and a rug. Then came the question, 'How can we get them?' Louis (who wrote the composition), inattentive, indifferent Louis, offered to bring a table and chair which he had made out of dry-goods boxes. He brought them. We marveled at them. They helped us to understand Louis better, and they helped him to find a new interest in school. Later he brought a spinning wheel.

"What Louis had done inspired other children to try their hand at furniture making and in a few days our Home Corner was well equipped with chairs, stools, and tables. Very crude they were, but not so to the children. One table fell to pieces shortly after it was made. This created a problem in furniture repairing, which was vigorously attacked and successfully solved.

"The construction of a fireplace created the need for a few lessons in measurement and emphasized the importance of learning arithmetic. The making of the fireplace, that is, the actual cutting, sawing, and putting together, seemed at first almost too difficult for the third graders. It was suggested that some of the larger boys in the Opportunity Room be allowed to help. The suggestion was scorned. It was their problem. They wanted to solve it. They did. A fireplace was constructed which would do credit to boys much older.

"The girls brought flowers, and made sash curtains, and are now working on a rug. Every spare minute they spend in sewing carpet rags. They have some frames on which several small rugs will be made and these will be sewed together to make a large rug. The design for the rug will be worked out in the drawing class.

"Not only have the children been reached but parents as well. The box for the fireplace was furnished by a father, and he even sent a drayman to deliver it. Another parent furnished the paint to paint the furniture, and another became so interested in the wool project that he taught his little son to spin. The following composition describes the first steps in the project:

One day Julius Cramer brought some wool to school. We went down stairs to heat some water. We washed the wool in warm soapy water. Then we put it in the sun to dry. Alex made some wool cards for us. We had fun carding the wool. Louis brought a spinning wheel. We like to run the wheel and play we are spinning.

"As I have just stated, some real spinning was done, for Alex's father, who had spun wool in Sweden, explained the process so clearly that Alex succeeded in spinning a few strands of yarn.

"The children love to work in the Home Corner and work very hard to attain standards of scholarship so as to have the privilege of working there. Besides raising the standards of work, the Home Corner is teaching the children to be neat and economical, to take responsibility with confidence, to solve their own problems, and to be thoughtful and considerate of others."

In December the following tests were given in the schools: Woody-McCall Mixed Fundamentals, Form I; Thorndike-McCall Reading Scale, Form IV; and Monroe's Standardized Reasoning Test in Arithmetic, Form I. After the tests had been scored and the results announced, principals and teachers were asked to make individual reports upon their analysis of the results of these tests, and to make suggestions for the remedial measures which ought to be taken. These reports are doubtless the most important achievement made up to this time. In making the analysis upon the results of the Woody-McCall Mixed Fundamentals, one principal writes in part as follows:

"1. I made score sheets to find the distribution of pupils' scores and to ascertain which problems presented the greatest difficulties.

"2. I graded the problems according to our course of study to see how the results appeared as the work of a grade. For example, problems 1 to 16 inclusive, 18, 19, 20, 22, 23, and 26 are types of fourth grade work; problems 17, 21, 24, 27, 29, and 31 are types of fifth grade work; problems 25, 28, 32, 33, 34, and 35 are sixth grade types. I do not expect pupils to be proficient in problems in advance of their grade.

"3. I took a survey of the pupils who were below the standard for their grade to see what mental, physical, or social handicaps might account for erratic answers, or for poor work generally. For instance, a child whose physical condition is poor, or whose home life is not conducive to good work, would be apt to make erratic mistakes, and we may not be able to do much to correct the defect. I based my judgment upon what the apparently normal child should do.

"4. I made a graph of our results compared with the June standards, and a chart to show the pupils just how their work compared with others. Seventh graders sometimes do not mind if their work is careless until they see a fourth grader classed with them. I have found that this helps to create an interest.

"My conclusions are as follows:

"1. The fourth grade can afford to do more intensive work in some other subject, as reading, for instance, that is, provided the test in reasoning shows the same degree of excellence. Only two fourth graders were below the standard for June and they were very little below. The arithmetic may have been emphasized at the expense of something else. I'll watch for it but I doubt if that is true."

A fourth grade teacher, after making her analysis of the errors in the Woody-McCall test, makes the following valuable contribution:

"It seems to me that the manner in which these standard tests are given is unpedagogical and also unfair to the pupils. Problems testing fifth and sixth grade pupils are placed on the same sheet as problems that are to test the fourth grade pupils and no explanations are made.

"The little fourth grade pupil faces an array of examples that he does not understand, and of course thinks he must solve as many as possible. He becomes bewildered and discouraged and often makes mistakes in the problems he should solve, simply because the new and difficult work has thrown him off his balance. Why not give a test that will really test the pupil on the work he is expected to have mastered and give that test in a fair way, and then demand each grade to come up to the required standard?

"If, for instance, one desires to test a fourth grade on their ability to do the work of higher grades, it would be much fairer to give them those tests separately and tell the children that such is the case and they will enjoy the spice of racing against a high grade. But, under the present system of tests, the pupils don't know whether they are failing on a fourth grade example or whether the example belongs to a higher grade, and the result is a disturbed mind."

The reports submitted to the teachers on the Thorndike-McCall Reading Test called attention to the numerous children who are misplaced in their grades if the reading test is to be taken as a criterion of judgment. Both principals and teachers are giving careful study not only to the problems of the groups, but also to the problems of individual pupils. One teacher writes:

"The girl who reads orally so splendidly has not the power of concentration and of reproducing the thought of what she has read. Her knowledge of rudimentary mechanics helps her to read far beyond her comprehension. She reads words not knowing what they mean. For her I have given drill using simpler reading and calling for the content."

Many pages of material like the foregoing could be given to show the type of work which the principals and teachers are doing under the Madison plan of supervision. The sole purpose of giving these quotations is to show that when the principals and the teachers are required to make formal reports upon their work, valuable results can be secured even when a special supervisor is not at hand. The time doubtless will come, of course, when a special supervisor will need to be employed. When that time arrives the way will be prepared, because there will be a clear understanding of function. The special supervisor will be a helper, bringing to principals and to teachers the results of her studies and investigations, making constructive criticisms, and giving stimulus in many directions. The principals, however, having come to a full realization of the importance of their duties, will continue to be the immediate supervisory forces in the system. The expense of special supervision is heavy. The results of special supervision are very limited unless there is active coöperation with the principals.

We hear a great deal said about the next step in supervision. In my judgment the next step is to train principals in such a way that they will understand and practice the art of supervision; to give such principals the utmost of confidence and of responsibility; and finally, to hold these principals to strict accountability for the success of the work in their schools.

Principals who do not have the opportunity for creative activity grow stale on the job. They lose enthusiasm, and become mere mechanics in their trade. On the other hand, the opportunity for initiative, for responsibility, and for adequate expression of their professional ideals tends to make them real leaders in the work of the schools.

METHOD AND CURRICULUM—I[1]

WILLIAM H. KILPATRICK

Professor of Education, Teachers College, Columbia University

The relationships of method and curriculum are as complex as they are intimate. But few of the phases of the problem can here be considered. The discussion includes three main questions: What is the problem of method? What is the problem of the curriculum? What is the relation of method to curriculum? The greater attention in this paper is given to the first question.

These three questions in more or less conscious form come down to us from a remote past. Our tradi-

The traditional conception

tional conception of the nature of education has formulated them for us in a simplicity of terms that has great plausibility and still commands wide acceptance. It conceives the problem of the curriculum as: What do I wish these children to learn? The problem of method as: How bring it about that the children shall most economically learn the things counted desirable? So obviously inevitable do these questions appear that many of you are even now wondering why I should think of doubting their correctness or adequacy. The educational theory here implicit becomes explicit only in the procedure that tradition suggests for answering these questions, a procedure now everywhere giving way, to be sure, but still present as the background for many terms and for much actual thinking.

This traditional procedure was as follows:

First, list the learning needed by the adult. (This has generally been thought of by school people of the past as organized in separate subjects and as consisting mainly of information and skills.)

Second, analyze each subject into its successive logical subdivisions until logically simple elements are found. Then arrange these in reverse order for (synthetic) learning by the pupil. Thus for reading, the child formerly began with the separate letters, then went on in turn to syllables, separate words, phrases, isolated sentences (with little or no thought content), finally reaching connected discourse. The like process was followed in penmanship, the beginning being made with the separate constituent elements of which the letters were later to be formed. Grammar as taught by Lindley Murray or Roswell Smith showed the same process.

Third, for learning rely on drill: memorization for information and practice for the skills. Originally the customary motive force for securing this drill was fear, but of later years this has gradually yielded to milder methods.

Fourth, in time, often only long after school days, occasions would arise for using the acquired information and skill. It was somewhat naïvely assumed that when such occasions should

[1] The substance of an address made before the National Conference on Educational Method, Chicago, March 1, 1922. All rights reserved by the author.

arise the reasoning creature man would by rational exercise of his free will apply surely and effectually what he had learned.

Now in terms of our questions, the first of the four steps was clearly a matter of the curriculum and was so understood. The remaining three steps generally received no special name, they went without saying. The term method if used at all was reserved for devices used under the third step to secure more readily and surely the desired skills and information (often falsely called knowledge). It may be repeated that many of us have not yet outgrown this naïve and simple conception of the educative problem. Some who assert that there is no such thing as "general method," but only "special methods," as of spelling and the like, are thus largely debating bygone issues in terms of outgrown concepts.

But there are certain snags on which these naïve answers catch, certain difficulties which demand thoroughgoing reconsideration.

First, learning does not, as a rule, best go on with logically simple elements. Being logical ele-**The logically simple not satisfactory** ments they are likely to be devoid of the connectednesses that on the one hand call forth interest and endeavor and on the other make for those further connections that constitute true learning. More lifelike elements are demonstrably superior. No one in this country would now defend our old alphabet method of teaching reading, and like changes of attitude are manifest on all sides. One of the most recent illustrations is the demand of Professor Gray

that, in order to give children proper habits of eye movements, early reading matter should have a thought content appealing to childhood. This is not to deny the need of conscious practice to fix adequately certain responses, probably, however, after living connections have already been established. It is indeed true that many points of the psychology involved in this specific question yet remain to be solved, but the main contention is established. The logically simple is not necessarily or even probably the beginning point of learning. The traditional analysis of the learning process here breaks down.

A second difficulty facing the older learning analysis is that learning is never single. Many learn-**Learning never single** ings of necessity go on simultaneously. No child assigned to a task learns, well or ill, just that one thing. Suppose a boy is put to memorizing a poem. He learns more or less well the poem itself. Call this the first learning. But in his doing this he necessarily practices some procedure for memorizing the poem; he may this time improve over his past procedure; he may conceivably do worse than usual. In any event he is changed in some manner or degree as regards a learning procedure. Any such change for good or ill is a true learning. We have then a second learning. It is further true that while he is learning he sits in some posture, good or ill. This, too, is either an improvement or a deterioration or a repetition as regards the past. In either case he is changed in some manner or degree, in other words learning again takes place. In the same manner he learns to like or dislike this poem. In so doing he changes also in some degree or manner his attitude toward poetry. Moreover, the teacher who assigned the poem comes in for consideration and there results in consequence a change for better or worse of attitude toward him. The school in like manner may well be better liked or worse liked according to the change of attitude toward poem and teacher. These seven simultaneous learnings by no means exhaust the list, but they illustrate the contention. The old analysis of education thought only of learning the poem. The new point of view cannot in conscience ignore all the other learnings. In the aggregate they may far outweigh the value of the poem. Thus again does the older analysis break down.

The thought just presented may be reinforced by consideration of the correlative aspect of the learning experience, that of multiple stimulation. The environment in which this pupil works is not one single thing to stimulate him to one single reaction. The environment is multiform. An indefinite number of stimuli impinge upon him during this one study period. It is quite true that what does in fact stimulate the boy depends on his present nature and disposition, but even so the list is a long one. Let us say, to simplify matters, that the teacher's word of command puts the child to work memorizing the poem. But what about the tone and look with which the words are spoken? How often do they cause resentment that rankles long after the study period is passed. And what about the teacher's dress and the char-

Manifold stimulation

acter displayed? Emerson says, "What you are speaks so loud that I do not hear what you say." And what about fellow pupils? Their attentive attitudes, or contrariwise their hidden sly looks and secret signs? What a wealth of reaction is possible here. We pass by the schoolroom, its ventilation, its equipment, with their silent stimulations, and go on to the wider situation. The hopes and expectations of those at home, their admonitions, the praise or blame they last Friday measured out, do these in half remembered thoughts and feelings combine to provoke favorable or unfavorable reactions to the work at hand? And the city, does it care for poetry or only for gain and what the gain will buy — loud dress, jazz dancing, cheap movies, or worse dissipations? Do any of these things affect directly or indirectly the boy's reactions as he memorizes the *Rime of the Ancient Mariner?* And what of the nation that environs and interpenetrates the city and the school, does it in any degree influence this boy as he sits there forming his character by the reactions he makes? Are the pictures of Washington or Lincoln on the schoolroom wall entirely a vain show? Or does his nation's history speak to the boy through them? And how does he respond when they speak? As the boy and his environment are simultaneously multiform, so are his responses varied and each response in some measure makes or mars his character. During one half hour the differences may be slight. But add all such together and the boy has become the character that he now is. The poem is worthy of serious consideration, but who shall measure all those other character effects that you and I have hardly learned to consider, still less to control. When we reckon with the inherent complexity of our teaching task as shown by this analysis, the inadequacy of the former view becomes tragic, pitiably tragic, because the issues at stake are exactly the issues of life.

But the old analysis finds yet another difficulty. Some things cannot be assigned for direct learning. **Assigned tasks not all inclusive** The cardinal assumption of the old scheme was that the child should apply himself in succession to a series of set tasks; and learning these he would in time accomplish the enumerated course of study. To make this plan work, the course of study found itself shrunk almost entirely to information and skills, because little else can be assigned and specifically required. To this day promotion is largely based on the acquisition of these more formal objectives and — sad to say — current scientific measurement is at times in danger of strengthening the sway of these mechanical affairs. But life demands for rich and effective living more than information and skills. Not to mention wisely organized knowledge, it must have habits, ideals, and attitudes. Many of these cannot be assigned as specific tasks. Imagine a teacher in the fifth grade literature class saying: "By next Monday you must show that you appreciate the poem at least to point 14 on the Jones Scale of Appreciation of Poetry. If not, you'll stay in after school till you do." There are some things that cannot be assigned in this fashion, and of these some are ex-

ceedingly important. It might be said in extenuation of the older point of view that it did not overlook these indirectly learned values. It thought to secure them on its theory of *formal* discipline.

We, however, who no longer believe in an indiscriminate transfer must face consciously the problem of building the necessary ideals and attitudes. Some, I fear, find it more convenient to ignore all these. But life won't consent to such mutilation. There are very important traits to be acquired that cannot be assigned as set tasks. The teacher must care for them otherwise. The old analysis once again breaks down.

The last count I bring in the indictment against this older point of view is that merely to teach adult **Deferred values unsatisfactory** needed traits does not suffice. I cannot now argue the point, but it violates what the best ethics tells us as to the good life. Moreover, as every teacher knows, it violates the best conditions for learning. "Deferred values" as a rule require artificial motivation. Particularly do we find it difficult on such a régime to build the habits, ideals, and attitudes the very régime would itself most demand. Any plan that reduces the school to mere preparation for later life is bound to produce an unsatisfactory school.

On these snags and difficulties, then, does the traditional analysis of the educative process fail. Learn- **Failure of old analysis** ing does not best go on with "logically" simple elements. Learning is never one single thing, but inherently and inextricably multitudinous. Not everything can be assigned for direct learning. The effort to run the school on this basis degrades child life and almost inevitably makes a martinet of the teacher. The old analysis fails, fails miserably. It has gone irrevocably to pieces. Yet many among us seem to be hopelessly en- tangled in its outworn conceptions and terms, lacking breadth of view to see the situation and recover themselves from the wreck.

Let us now examine more closely the problem of method. Obviously from what has gone before there **Two problems of method** are at least two problems of method. One I have else- where called the narrow or abstracted problem of method. This for the pur- pose of effective attack chooses, prop- erly enough, to disregard (for the time, at least) the fact of multitudinous si- multaneous learnings and asks how any one specific trait is best acquired. The trait under consideration need not be simple, though the simpler ones have naturally received so far the most ade- quate treatment. One might thus study the best means of having pupils ac- quire any one of the following: spelling, silent reading, the idea of school prop- erty, the ideal of the proper care of school property, an interest in good literature, an interest in and determina- tion to uphold good government. Such studies are very useful. We stand ready to welcome all the light on them we can get. But we must not overlook the es- sential fact that no such learning as that contemplated in acquiring any one of these can go on by itself. In actual life no such simplicity exists. To act as if it were so is to mistake an abstraction for a reality.

This brings us then to the second problem of method: How shall we man- age our pupils, considering the mani- fold stimulation of the complex envi- ronment to which they are subject and their simultaneous multiple responses? It needs no argument to prove that the teacher dealing with even one pupil is always and inevitably facing this sec- ond problem of method. For purposes of thoughtful procedure the teacher must, as the scientist, make an ab- straction and ask, say, "How shall I teach silent reading?" This is the first problem of method, but after it has been answered and the teacher faces the class, the second problem inevitably arises. The teacher must practically solve both. I like to call the real situa- tion with all its simultaneous learnings the *total learning situation*. The scien- tist may by great care face in his lab- oratory an approximately simple learn- ing situation; but the teacher before a class always faces a total learning situa- tion. And, so far as forethought can extend its sway over them, the teacher's responsibility includes all the resulting learnings.

The total learning situation merits yet closer attention. Consider the mul- tiple respondings, such as **The total learning situation** we considered above in the case of the boy learning the *Ancient Mariner*. We have here clearly an instance of what James taught us to call focal and marginal attention. Here the focal attention was ostensibly on memorizing the poem, actually there was a continual shifting. Accompanying the focal attention, how- ever fixed or shifting, there was more or less of marginal responding. What is at one moment marginal may at the next be focal, and vice versa. It is well established that learning goes on most quickly in connection with focal attention, but this is not to deny learning to marginal responses. If the responding come often enough, it must, by the laws of learning, in time leave an appreciable effect, though of course any turning of focal attention to the response will hasten the process. For the purpose of fixing ideas let us for the time, in disregard of fluctuations, apply the term *focus* to the object of the predominant focal attention and *marginal* to all the other responses. Learning may come then either in connection with the focus or the margin. As regards

Focal and marginal learning

the focus, the learning may be the end, as with the memorization of the poem, or in connection with means to the end, as a better knowledge of words from memorizing the poem. Of the marginal responses some of the most important appear as suggestions of other and perhaps rival objects of attention. These cross-fertilizations of experience I have elsewhere termed *associated suggestions*.[1] If these rival suggestions be allowed unrestrained sway, achievement would cease. On the other hand, to ignore them entirely would be to cease to grow. A mean adjusted to secure the good of both is desirable. These, as with other marginal responses, seem to depend on the existence of partially formed mental complexes. (The term complex is here used innocently of Freud to mean about the same as "apperception mass.") The interaction of the focally aroused complex, especially some aspects of it, with others in the nervous system brings marginal responses. It would seem that exactly in these are built those complex aggregates we call ideals, attitudes, interests, points of view, and the like. While these can be brought to the focus, and should occasionally be brought there for conscious criticism, they seem inherently matters of marginal attention built up primarily on the margin, while a different type of things occupy the more abiding focus as ends of the agent's explicit endeavor. It is these explicit ends of endeavor that we can assign as tasks and for which we can and do hold one more directly responsible. But the other class of mental constructs seem to belong inherently to the margin as reactions to what is going on in the focus. These inherently marginal affairs must, it would seem, be learned indirectly. The significance of this fact for both method and curriculum is great. These marginal learnings cannot be set as tasks. They fit but hardly if at all in our older curriculum conceptions, and even our scientific measurers seem happier to forget them. To ensure their learning requires a nicer skill in teaching than was thought of in the old days. But they are worth it. They seem almost supremely important in life.

Let us now turn to the correlative stimulation side of this same analysis

Marginal stimulation

and see if closer consideration of that yields any additional view. The one agent in the schoolroom for securing ordinary voluntary focal attention is, of course, the teacher. This is possible

---

[1] In this Journal, October, 1921, p. 10.

because the child has in the past built a group of attitudes toward the general teacher-schoolroom situation. The stimulation which produces the marginal responses may be considered under separate heads according as it is more immediate, less immediate, or still more remote. Among the more immediate stimulations are, as has already been suggested, the tone and manner of the teacher, the observed responses of fellow pupils, chance happenings in room or street or even in the books. They may work for or against the focal interest. Among the less immediate stimulations is the general scheme of curriculum and management as it does or does not satisfy the "natural" aspirations of childhood and youth.

These aspirations are, of course, very numerous and complex. Any observing teacher knows that adequate expression of the higher reaches of child character will often if not generally inhibit in greater or less degree some lower inclinations that might otherwise be very insistent. The felt adequacy or inadequacy of the available self-expression most of all creates a general set, which in turn determines, for the adolescent at any rate, almost everything about the school.

The discussion of the remoter stimulation will have to be postponed with the remainder of the paper to the next month's issue.

(*To be continued*)

AN EXPERIMENT IN COÖPERATION
VIII. The Mechanics of Writing

James F. Hosic

Associate Professor of Education, Teachers College, Columbia University

"Divide and conquer," says the old adage. This principle we endeavored to apply to the teaching of composition. We realized that too often everything is attempted at once and nothing done. Worse yet, many seem never to reach the problem of composition itself, being content to instill the gentle art of proof reading instead. This is necessary, of course, in order that certain conventions may be obeyed, but it is no more composition than good dressing is character. Ideas clothed in appropriate words, which are marshalled in fit array, constitute the indispensable factors, and punctuation, spelling, and the like

are only their humble body servants, as it were.

All of which ought to be so obvious as not to require mention. It isn't, however, as common practices testify, hence our firm determination to be clear in our own minds as to when we were looking after the one and when we were looking after the other.

MECHANICS DEFINED

As already stated, our experiment soon convinced us that speaking and not writing should be regarded as the basic activity in composition. We learned, moreover, that so far as children are concerned there is little difference between a speech and an equivalent effort in writing. Bacon's distinctions of readiness contrasted with exactness holds only for those to whom writing has become an habitual mode of expression. The children wrote as they spoke—they often wrote what they had spoken.

In this practice we found our cue. Composition proper is that which is common to speech and writing. Mechanics of writing may be defined as all of the new problems which arise in the attempt to put speech on paper. So considered, mechanics includes manuscript conventions of all sorts, spelling, punctuation, capitalization, spacing of words, paragraph and other margins, and all other formal means of presenting words to the eye so as to enable the reader to gather their meaning with comfort and economy.

Spelling is so generally regarded as worthy of a place on the daily program of the elementary school that we deemed it wise to give to the spelling problem a place of its own in our scheme of committee work. The account of it will be reserved, therefore, for a later article in this series. What was done with the companion problems we shall presently see.

DEVELOPING A COURSE IN MECHANICS

The movement toward elimination of non-essentials in school subjects has done much to simplify the course in English. Courses of study in that subject are still likely, however, to be vague if not really over-ambitious. Nowhere is this more true than in regard to punctuation and kindred topics. "Teach the ordinary uses of the comma" is a direction not infrequently found in outlines devised as guides for teachers of grades as early as the fifth or even the fourth. Such a direction bears on its face the evidence that the course-of-study-maker is thinking of what writers in general need to know, not what a child of ten requires. He is indeed writing, but not with his eye on the object.

We began our campaign by securing general agreement to find out what marks of punctuation the pupils of the various grades could not possibly get along without. Here we sought to distinguish between the occasional need of the more adventurous and the steady demand of the rank and file. The former should be met on the spot through first aid, but with no attempt at systematic instruction. On the latter our course in punctuation would be based. We resolved not to make a class exercise of any matter of mechanics until it promised to figure constantly in the work of the class throughout the term and ever thereafter.

The procedure adopted for getting the facts was similar to that already set forth. Each teacher was asked to become an observer and recorder for her own class. Her results were to be reported to a committee, whose duty it was to compile a course in mechanics for the school. Later a sort of composite of these school courses was to be made to serve as guidance for the city as a whole, though the needs of the particular school and the particular class were always to be met willy-nilly.

The first reports of many teachers were clearly in need of revision. They were couched in the general terms which traditionally characterize attempts at course of study making, and were too sweeping to be lived up to. Attention was called to the fact that we were making specifications which we meant to live up to. For we had agreed that our standard should be habitual correctness in all written work within the limits set for each grade by at least seventy-five per cent of the pupils of that grade. It was necessary only to press the query, "Are you in fact willing that your pupils should be held to the standards which you are setting up?" to bring about an immediate retraction. School supervisors have much to answer for in accustoming teachers to false and impossible standards which no one really expects to reach. We were determined to seek only the attainable in such definite matters as the mechanics of writing, and consequently held ourselves to a modest outline, as the following composite finally arranged for the city as a whole plainly shows.

A MINIMUM COURSE IN MECHANICS BY GRADES

The writing of a composition involves two processes: on the thought or content side, organization; on the mechanical side, getting on paper the thought to be expressed. The simple fundamentals of mechanics should in large part be mastered (made automatic, that is) during the first six years of the child's school life. The time when they should be taught is determined by the time when they are needed. The need is developed through the activities of the pupils. From grade to grade the complexity of the thought to be expressed increases. Consequently there is increased complexity in the uses of mechanical aids to expression, which are Capitalization, Punctuation, and Manuscript Form.

GRADE I
Capitalization:
Child's own name.
Pronoun *I*.

GRADE II
Capitalization:
Names of persons.
First word in a sentence.
Punctuation:
Period—at the end of a sentence.

GRADE III
Capitalization:
Names of months.
Names of days of the week.
Names of special holidays, as Thanksgiving, Christmas, New Year, Easter.
Titles of compositions.
Punctuation:
Period in abbreviations, Mr., Mrs., Dr., St., and Ave.
Comma after salutation in the simple friendly letter, thus:
Dear Alice,

....
....
....
ANNA BROWN
Manuscript Form:
Letter as above. Letter and other composition must have margin (one inch) at left edge of paper with indention (half inch) of first line.

GRADE IV
Capitalization:
Titles prefixed to proper names, as Aunt Jane, Cousin John, King Midas.
Geographical names.
Names of peoples, as Indians, French.
Proper adjectives, as British, Swedish.
Punctuation:
Period in further abbreviations as they may be used by pupils in this grade.
Interrogation point.
Apostrophe in contractions, as doesn't, haven't.
Apostrophe in possessives as these occur in the children's composition.
Comma in the courteous close of letter as shown below.
Manuscript Form:
Title of composition in center of line.
Margin at left edge of paper persistently followed up; no margin at right edge, except sufficient allowance to insure no crowding of words at end

of line. No word broken at end of line in this grade.

Letter form extended to include the courteous close:

Dear Charles,

....
....
....

Your friend,

JOHN WEAVER

GRADE V

Capitalization:

First word in a direct quotation.

Important words in titles of story or book.

Punctuation:

Quotation marks in unbroken quotation.

Comma

before direct quotation.

to set off a noun in direct address.

after yes or no.

Apostrophe in plural possessive as need arises. (No formal teaching of columns of singular and plural possessives.)

Manuscript Form:

Nothing new in composition form.

Letter—Introducing heading:

465 Webster Avenue
Chicago, Illinois
April 12, 1921

Dear Amy,

....
....
....

Your cousin,

DORA COX

GRADE VI

Work for complete mastery of all points covered thus far in the course. Not much is introduced in this grade. The advance is chiefly a wider application of principles and practices already taught.

Capitalization:

Important words in titles of persons, as King of the Lordly Isles.

Punctuation:

More extended use of quotation marks, not taught as an abstract topic, but as the children may attempt in the course of writing an interesting story to divide a quotation; for example, "Mother, come and help me out," I cried. "I am sinking."

Hyphen at the end of a line where a word is properly divided between syllables.

Colon in letter form as shown below.

Manuscript Form:

Business letter introducing the formal address:

465 Webster Avenue
Chicago, Illinois
April 15, 1921

Marshall Field & Co.
121 North State St.
Chicago, Illinois
Gentlemen:

....
....
....

Yours respectfully,

ROBERT WELLS

Achievement at the end of sixth grade: The power correctly to arrange, capitalize, and punctuate an original theme of from six to eight sentences, or a friendly letter, or a business letter such as an application for a position, order for merchandise, etc.

GRADE VII

Capitalization:

In topical headings.

Teach here *outline form*, showing subordination:

I.
  A.
  B.
  C.
II.
  A.
  B.

Punctuation:

Comma where needed, with subordinate clauses
in a series.
in compound sentences.
to separate words in
addresses and dates.

Colon before an itemized list.

Manuscript Form:

Indention to indicate a new paragraph. In this grade is developed the idea of a paragraph as a division of subject, constituting a unit of thought.

GRADE VIII

The course is cumulative, and the eighth grade must be held accountable for all that precedes. The summary of requirements for this grade includes little that is new.

SUMMARY OF MECHANICS OF WRITTEN COMPOSITION

I. *Capitalization:*

  A. Pronoun *I* and interjection *O*.

  B. First word of a sentence.

  C. Proper nouns and adjectives.

  D. Important words in titles.

  E. Titles of relationship or vocation prefixed to proper names.

  F. In quotations as required.

II. *Punctuation:*

  A. Period:

    1. After a declarative or imperative sentence.

    2. After abbreviations.

    3. In letter forms as required.

  B. Comma:

    1. To set off a word in direct address.

    2. To set off the name of a city from the state.

    3. To separate the day of the month from the year.

    4. To set off an appositive with its modifiers.

    5. To separate items in a series.

    6. As required in compound and complex sentences.

    (*Note.*—Avoid the error of separating short complete sentences by commas.)

  C. Interrogation point.

  D. Exclamation point.

  E. Apostrophe:

    1. In possessives.

    2. In contractions.

  F. Hyphen—between syllables at end of line.

  G. Colon—before itemized list and in letter form.

III. *Manuscript Form:*

  A. Arrangement of composition:

    1. Title in center of first line.

    2. Margin at left edge of paper.

    3. Paragraph indention.

  B. Letter forms (see Grade VI).

Notes.—While the block system is used in typewritten letters in introduction and address, the indention of consecutive lines (three spaces) is preferred in both personal and business letters written in long hand.

Uniform capitalization of first and last words in the salutation is required, as: *Dear Sir:—My dear Sir:—My dear Mother:*

Only the first word in the courteous close is capitalized, as:

                    Yours very truly.

In the salutation in letters addressed to firms, the use of *Gentlemen* is preferred to *Dear Sirs*.

COMMENTS ON COURSE AND METHOD

Most children who see others writing desire to write also. Such help as the teachers might give in the earliest grades would be called out quite naturally by this demand. All were expected to have a care for building up good images of words, for large firm characters made with free movements, and for straight lines and good spacing. The simple device of giving each pupil at least a yard of space at the blackboard was alone almost sufficient to prevent the small, cramped, and indistinct hand too often seen on school blackboards. Hygienic ideals were invoked to establish this practice.

Teachers were urged to direct the attention of the pupils first of all to the composition as the expression of certain ideas with a certain purpose, and to make swift corrections of mechanics in the sight of all herself rather than to start unsettling and time-consuming discussions of usage, especially as regards spelling, of which more hereafter. Meticulous fault-finding is a poor occupation at best; it certainly should not be established as a habit in the composition class.

For the middle and upper grades

carefully planned dictation exercises were advised as a means of helping pupils to overcome deficiencies. Such exercises were to be given with the full knowledge of the pupils as to precisely what was to be learned. The selections used, moreover, were to be simple, on the plane or a little above the plane of the pupils' own efforts. Isolated dictation exercises recurring at regular intervals regardless of particular needs have happily gone out of fashion and we took the utmost pains to avoid reviving them.

RESULTS

It is not possible to state in relatively exact quantitative terms just what per cent of improvement our classes made as compared with previous classes of the same grade. That the improvement was considerable there could be no doubt. Everyone conversant with the situation remarked upon it. Incorrectness ceased to be the bug-a-boo of written composition and yet mechanical matters were receiving less attention than formerly. The secret lay in two facts. First, when the pupils wrote they knew exactly what they wanted to say and could give their undivided effort to saying it in good form. Second, the teachers concentrated their instruction on a few essentials constantly needed and easily fixed them as habit. This was far better, all will agree, than tilting at windmills in the traditional Quixotic fashion. Organization guided by facts won.

THE PROJECT METHOD IN HIGH SCHOOL [1]

Little seems to have been written on the project method of teaching in the senior high school and college. Most of the sample projects offered and the illustrations used are for the primary, intermediate, and grammar grades. Indeed the statement was made by one of the professors at Teachers College that the method was not adapted to high school use.

Six high school teachers organized into a group to attempt to decide if the project method could be used profitably in our high school work. We saw that there would be many administrative problems in its use in high school which would not exist in a grade where the work is all in the hands of one teacher, and that close correlation of the various branches about one project would be impossible in the average high school whose faculty is organized as it is now.

We decided also that group work would be harder to manage in high schools than in the grades, for in many high schools it is practically impossible to find any time, in school hours or out, when a class can get together outside of the class period. Then, too, if a teacher has from four to seven classes a day, and each class is working on its own project, he must keep abreast of them even if they go far beyond the confines of his textbook and of his previous knowledge. This will offer him a problem

[1] This report is the result of a group project carried out by a committee of which Miss Edith L. Hoyle, of Ann Arbor, Michigan, was chairman.

of time and endurance which will need some careful administration on the part of the teacher himself. We did not, however, believe that these difficulties, if they are such, make the use of the method either impossible or impracticable for the classroom teacher.

It seemed to us that if we could get a whole-hearted purpose on the part of the pupils to carry forward a project, the planning, carrying out of the steps, and organizing and judging results would not be especially difficult with high school pupils, for the projects would be very largely of the problem type, that is, gaining some desired knowledge. The important thing, then, was to make the knowledge truly desired.

Of the six members of our group, four taught English, one mathematics, and one American history. We, therefore, confined our questioning to those three subjects and sought for some "approaches" which would be apt to awaken a whole-hearted interest on the part of the pupils. It seemed to the group that, of the three subjects considered, it was hardest to see how mathematics might be taught by the project method. The same forms, formulas, and problems must be mastered and solved, but evidently from a new viewpoint. The teacher's first problem would be to get the pupil to want to learn algebra, geometry, or trigonometry. Individual differences would have to be taken into consideration from the very outset, and time would be gained by giving careful attention to that at the start. Some pupils may be led to see the necessity of a really complete mastery of elementary mathematics in their prospective work as civil engineers, draftsmen, archi-

tects, or chemists. To others, especially the girls, these reasons might make no appeal. But perhaps they are planning to go to college and must make college requirements and be able to pass college freshman mathematics when they get there. It will take some very clever individual work on the part of the teacher to launch this first step in the term's project, that is, getting his pupils to want to know the subject matter and to be eager for the work. That should be the teacher's first project, and he should not be satisfied until every pupil is won.

No end of small projects may be used to awaken the pupil's interest in different parts of the course. At the beginning of some particularly hard section, a practical problem could be given the class which they could work out by the knowledge they have up to that point, but which would involve a long process. When they have done the work necessary to obtain the answer, let the teacher work it for them by the short cut method of the new chapter. Then give them some more problems of a similar nature. The mastering of that chapter will become a purposeful act on their part if for no other reason than to save themselves work.

In *School Science and Mathematics* for January, 1920, Mr. Frank Rich suggests the construction by the pupils of some simple musical instrument such as the chromatic zither for teaching the value of the knowledge of roots. The zither is an instrument all strings of which have the same tension but different lengths. The tuning is done by changing the length of the string and not the tension. When the instrument is tuned and these lengths compared, we find a certain definite relation between them which can be expressed algebraically. Each string is some power or root of the "key" string.

All sorts of practical projects can be undertaken in trigonometry, such as making instruments to turn off angles and with which the pupils can measure distances across a river, swamp, or street without crossing it, or with which the height of a building or hill can be calculated. In fact in all three subjects proficiency in any one chapter or set of chapters may itself be made a project.

By this time some doubting Thomas is asking, "What is the use of all this bother? Why not just go ahead and assign the lessons?" The purpose is to help the pupil see the use of his work and hence make it a purposeful activity to him—something which the preaching of "mathematics for mental discipline" did not succeed in doing for us when we were in high school.

In the discussion of the project method for American history for the junior or senior high school year (eleventh or twelfth grade), we felt that the first point to be settled was whether in using that method the chronological order should be followed or not. The decision reached was that there would be no particular advantage in setting aside the chronological order of the story as a whole up to the end of the Reconstruction Period, about 1875, and no particular advantage in following it after that date. However, the chronological order need not be strictly adhered to any of the time. If, for instance, in studying the results of the War of 1812 the need for protecting our infant industries introduced the tariff issue, and the class became interested in the tariff question, that is surely the time to follow it through its McKinley heights, its Underwood depths, and its Fordney rehabilitation. Having finished the story of the tariff, so far as it has been written, we would turn back to the rest of the results of the War of 1812. After the Reconstruction Period there are few things of importance but that are open questions of today and should be taken up when needed for current event work.

Can approaches be found for launching projects in American history which will bring about whole-hearted purposing on the part of the pupils? We found them easy to work up. We have just mentioned the War of 1812; let us take that as an example of how an approach might be made. These advanced high school pupils already know the general story. Ask them what caused the war and who won it, and the chances are that the answer will be that the impressment of American seamen caused the war and that the United States won it. Of course neither answer is a satisfactory one for a student of American history to give. Tell them, then, of seeing a Canadian textbook some years ago which said that our object in declaring war on England was to gain Canada, and that we were completely defeated by English and Canadian troops. It would need nothing more to get a whole-hearted purpose on the part of the pupils to find out whether that Canadian textbook was right or not, and in so doing to learn the true history of the affair.

A newspaper clipping to the effect that the United States is an empire in all but name might be used to introduce a careful study of our method of obtaining territory and of governing it. A debate on the ratification of the Treaty with Columbia would take the class into a very careful study of the debatable method of obtaining the Panama Canal Zone.

The approach will be easy to find in American history, and the wise teacher can easily see that the problem be made into a project.

We felt that the most suggestive thing we could do in the field of English literature was to see what approach one could get in some one rather heavy piece of literature, which approach could be followed up by a real project. We chose Burke's *Conciliation* as one of the hardest selections in the usual list of required readings. Let us suppose that the class has become interested in the discussion of some current problem, say the Philippine demand for independence. They are discussing what the United States should do, and they outline on the board the principles which they believe should guide the United States in her treatment of the Philippines. A parallel might be drawn then between the United States in 1921 and England in 1775, and we could turn to Burke to see what he said should be England's attitude toward her American colonies, and see if he said any of the things the class had just said for the United States, or if he had said anything which they had not thought of which might well apply. Differences of opinion as to his meaning would lead to a careful analysis to find the important point and the supporting evidence. There would have to be a summary of these points in order to compare them with the brief state-

ments the class had made on the Philippine situation. This would lead to a *felt* need for outlining, which would be secondary to the pupils' real aim, finding out Burke's meaning in answer to their question. To get a clear, brief statement of the meaning is the only legitimate excuse for outlining a piece of literature anyway, so why should a pupil do it if he does not *care* what the piece means?

Fortunately we do not have to confine ourselves to such hard reading for the average pupil as is Burke. Hardly any teacher allows the liberty of choice in reading that is allowed by the college entrance requirements or the course of study. The important question then is, "With what shall we start?" And the answer is, "With something that is at the child's level and that he will understand and enjoy, *regardless of what it is*." The writer once undertook to get a small high school to sing at assembly exercises, but failed to do so. In conversation afterward with one of the boys, she asked him why he didn't like to sing at school and he said that he didn't like those old songs, he had known them ever since his mother used to sing him to sleep with them. She asked him if there were any songs he did like, and when he said that he liked all the popular songs she told him to bring one of them to school and they would learn it. He brought "Shy Ann" and wrote the words on the front board. The next morning while the whole high school was lustily singing "Oh! oh! hop on my pony, there's room here for two dear, and after the ceremony"—the teacher was praying that no member of the Board of Education would go by.

But they sang! And gradually better music was introduced, new song books were purchased, a glee club was organized, and music, real music, came into that school.

We believe that exactly that sort of thing can be done in literature under the project method of approach. One might well start with periodicals, beginning with those the pupil likes, *regardless of what they are;* gradually better ones may be brought in. From periodicals it is an easy step to contemporary books; books take them to the library, and once there they may be led back to the masters. Here the course of study should guide, but *freedom within any list should be allowed.* If by such a scheme a love of good reading could be developed, more good books would be read in the end than by assigning them at first to a pupil who disliked them and read them only under compulsion.

That the project method would be of great value and assistance in teaching composition we were all agreed from the first. Without going into a tabulation of the various sources of topics that intrinsically lend themselves to the project method in composition, we wish to point out one that perhaps has been neglected—that of extra-class activities or organizations. They have a very definite value in that they are experiments in group living, and the interests and energies of the group are spontaneous and directed toward a common aim. Thus they are shot through with the social motive and with purposeful activity.

A concrete example of a situation in mind grew out of a discussion in a Senior class meeting as to the kind of picture to be presented to the school by the graduating class. In order to inform themselves more thoroughly about pictures and to make a discriminate selection, the members of the class agreed to write to an art dealer of the city asking him for a loan of pictures. The teacher who was acting as sponsor for the class brought to their attention the fact that the response would largely depend upon the effectiveness of the appeal and the general excellence of the letter. So strongly was the "inner urge" felt that the following day there resulted a sharp competition in the writing of the letters in the classroom. The letters were first read over by the teacher to "get a line" on the pupils' errors and deficiencies, which in a subsequent lesson formed the basis for purposeful drill. After the poorer letters were eliminated by the teacher, the remaining ones were turned over to a committee named by the pupils to make the final selection of the letter to be sent.

The letter brought the desired result; the pictures came and were placed on exhibition in the library. Numerous were the discussions outside of class, in the corridors, and on the playground as to individual preference. The teacher announced that there would be an opportunity for discussion in the classroom and suggested that they go into the matter more carefully. When the class met, the pupils decided—upon the advice of the teacher—to form into various groups for an intelligent study of the world's best known pictures, each group to report on its particular school of art—French, Italian, English, Dutch, American, etc., and on some masterpiece of that school. When the appointed day arrived each pupil was on his mettle, as he felt the responsibility to his group for an able presentation of their claim. The class as a whole was to judge the effectiveness of each group's appeal for its preference.

Thus it will be seen that, in addition to satisfying a felt need, the project furnished an opportunity for the exercise of certain skills and for enlarging the æsthetic experiences of the pupils.

Excellent results may also be obtained by projecting the activities of debating and dramatic societies, athletics, recitals, and the like into the classroom, if the teacher will keep in touch with these organizations and will be alert enough to seize on the situations as they present themselves.

Indeed, the various members of the group quite convinced themselves that the teacher who is filled with the project spirit, and who is willing to use his ingenuity to work out clever approaches, not only can use the project method in teaching mathematics, American history and English, but can use it to his great credit and to his pupils' everlasting advantage.

A SUGGESTED PROCEDURE IN SILENT READING FOR BRIGHT PUPILS

W. J. OSBURN

Director of Educational Measurements, State Department of Education, Madison, Wisconsin

The purpose of this article is to provide a tentative program for children whose reading ability is two or more years in advance of the grade in which they are located. There are three methods of dealing with such children: they may be promoted, or neglected, or supplied with additional work without promotion. The method which is in most general use is that of neglect. That the talents of bright children are withering away from disuse in practically every school appears unquestionable. Some of the children are marking time in dreary monotony while a few of the bolder spirits divert themselves by disorderly conduct. Surely America can ill afford thus to waste and smother its genius. The only encouraging thing about the present procedure is that any change is sure to make things better.

The policy of promoting all bright pupils until they reach the grade which corresponds to their intelligence level is also open to certain objections. In the first place it is impossible in some schools, and secondly, it often places mere children in classes with pupils who are much more mature socially. The promotion policy if fully carried out would permit some children to finish High School at the age of fourteen or even earlier. Such children are probably too young to be sent away from home to a college or university. The only other possibility is to provide a broadened course of study, something like that which follows.

Much attention has been devoted during recent years to remedial instruction for those who are weak in reading rate and comprehension, but little or nothing is available in the way of a technique which will develop other aims and values in silent reading. It seems wise, therefore, to assume that further training in such reading should be provided as a first step in broadening the course of study for those who are ready for such material. With such a purpose in mind the following suggestions seem to be at least worthy of a tryout.

As a necessary prerequisite for such a plan some means must be devised to discover where the child's chief interests are. Often the teacher will have located these interests from the child's reading and conversation. This information may often be supplemented by giving the children the following test. The questions may be given to a group of children either orally or in written form.

1. What indoor game do you like best?

2. What outdoor game do you like best?

3. What magazines have you read recently? Put a cross in front of the one you like best and tell why you like it.

4. What is your favorite book?

5. What occupation would you like to follow after you are through school?

6. What person not in the local neighborhood would you like to be like? You may give the name of some historical character if you wish.

7. If you had a million dollars and were perfectly free to travel, what foreign country would you visit? Why?

8. If you had a million dollars, name three things that you would buy for yourself.

9. If you had plenty of money and were free to go to any of the following,

which would you attend? (1) A Football Game; (2) Church; (3) The Movies; (4) A Political Convention; (5) An Art Gallery; (6) A Basketball Game; (7) Sunday School; (8) A Debate; (9) A Musical Concert; (10) A Baseball Game; (11) Grand Opera; (12) A Prize Fight; (13) Light Opera; (14) A Dramatic Recital; (15) A Dance.

10. If you had plenty of money and were perfectly free, how would you spend your summer vacation?

11. You will be given five minutes to write all the words you can think of. Write nouns only and take care not to repeat any of them.

Note to the examiner. — Explain what a noun is before the children begin on the last exercise. The words written during the latter portion of the five minutes will often disclose the type of the child's interest.

After the dominant interests are located, the following procedure is suggested. Provide books, magazines, etc., which fit each individual case so far as it is possible to do so. Local libraries are quite useful, particularly their newspaper files. In many cases the school district may be able to purchase some of the books. Many free bulletins are published on various subjects by the state and federal governments and by industrial concerns. These should be provided to fit the topics in which the children are interested. Sometimes the papers and magazines taken in the child's home may be used.

When the material is on hand the children are asked to look it over rather quickly in order to locate the articles or portions which seem pertinent. Where two or more children are working together, each should catalogue references for the other. The names of all articles, books, and magazines with sufficient directions for locating them should be written on cards and these cards should be assembled in a card tray provided for the purpose. The cards should be about 3 inches by 5 inches in size, and a pasteboard shoe box may be used for a tray. Special pasteboard trays may be purchased for a nominal sum. Guide cards should always be provided and arranged in dictionary order. Each child should be taught to file his cards in the proper way.

After the cards are assembled each child begins reading the references relating to his own topic for the purpose of discarding the material which is not relevant or valuable. When this process is completed he is ready to begin organizing the material that remains. This will include both outlining, summarizing and supplementing with the child's own thought.

The final step is the provision of some sort of an audience before which the child may report his findings. The audience may be another grade, a parent-teachers' association, the school society, a reading club composed of the bright pupils themselves, and the like. In every case some sort of an audience must be provided.

In order to stimulate and guide the work as suggested above it will be necessary in most, if not all, cases that some one furnish a list of guiding questions in relation to the topic or project which is being studied. The following series of questions will serve as a sample set so far as the subject of coal is concerned. It is assumed that the child is or can easily become interested in the topic. There are many tempting byways which the pupil may wish to follow up. He should be permitted to do so. If several pupils are working on this topic at once, one of them might be made responsible for each subsidiary question. Such questions are apt to arise in connection with the ventilation of mines, mine explosions, the origin and formation of coal, the use of water power, and the like. *The interest of the pupil should be the guide rather than the organization of subject matter.* The aim of the teacher should be to keep the children at work upon anything in which they are interested. No attempt should be made to compel the child to follow this list of questions or any list for that matter. Questions raised by the children are always given preference. The questions such as are proposed here are to be used only when questions are not forthcoming from the pupils. Similar questions and references can be furnished on each of the following subjects by the State Department of Public Instruction: copper, prime movers, silver, gold, slate, granite, marble, lead, zinc, leather, glass, petroleum, and a few others.

QUESTIONS FOR DIRECTING SILENT READING ON THE SUBJECT OF COAL

1. How does a coal mine look?
2. How is coal brought out of the mine?
3. How is coal weighed and sorted? What are coal breakers?
4. How is coal marketed?
5. What is a colliery? How is the coal moved and stored?
6. How is the roof of a coal mine supported?

7. How do the miners loosen the coal in the mine?

8. Why must coal mines be ventilated?

9. How are explosions prevented in coal mines?

10. Find anything you can which is interesting concerning Sir Humphrey Davy.

11. How are coal mines ventilated?

12. What is coal made of? How is water kept out of the mines?

13. How did ancient forests grow?

14. How can we tell that coal was once wood?

15. How did it happen that this wood turned into coal instead of rotting?

16. How long does it take for wood to turn into coal?

17. Is wood turning into coal now?

18. What is peat? Lignite? Bituminous coal? Anthracite?

19. How do these differ from each other?

20. What did people think of coal in the past?

21. How did they discover that it would burn?

22. How did people learn to burn anthracite coal?

23. Find out anything you can concerning the great fire in the coal mines of southern Ohio. How long has it been burning? How did it start? How much damage has it done? Will it ever be put out?

24. How is the amount of coal possessed by a country related to the prosperity of that country? To the ability of the country to make war?

25. How much coal does each of the following nations possess: England, France, Japan, Germany, and the United States?

26. Judging by the amount of coal which they possess, see if you can find other nations which are apt to become great industrially.

27. Where does Wisconsin get coal? Are there any coal mines in the state? If so, where?

28. What railroads bring coal to Wisconsin?

29. Find out anything you can about coal in Texas, Upper Silesia, and the Saar Valley.

30. How is artificial gas made?

31. How did people learn to use gas?

32. What other things can be made from coal?

33. How do prospectors search for coal?

34. How many large cities in the United States can you name which have grown up because coal mines are near them?

35. What substitutes can be used in the place of coal?

36. Is it likely that any of these will be used to any great extent in the future? Why?

37. To what extent is Wisconsin using a substitute for coal?

38. What cities are being particularly affected by the use of a substitute for coal?

References on Coal [1]

* Allen: *Geographical and Industrial Studies—United States, The New Europe, South America.* Ginn.

* Bishop and Keller: *Industry and Trade.* Ginn.

* Brigham: *Commercial Geography.* Ginn.

[1] The starred references are the more important ones.

* Fisher: *Resources and Industries of the United States*. Ginn.

* *Great American Industries and Minerals*. H. Flanagan and Company.

* Herrick: *A History of Commerce and Industry*. Macmillan.

Martin: *Story of a Piece of Coal*. D. Appleton and Company. New York.

Smith, J. Russell: *Story of Iron and Steel*. D. Appleton and Company. New York.

* *Stories of Industry, Book I*. Educational Publishing Company.

* Tappan: *Diggers in the Earth*. Houghton Mifflin Company.

* Williams: *Romance of Mining*. Seely, Service and Company, London.

Bureau of Mines; U. S. Geol. Survey Bulletins.

Mineral Resources of the United States. U. S. Geol. Survey Bulletins.

Around the World—Book III.

Information Readers—Book III.

All the Year Round—Book II.

Lights to Literature—Book V.

The Universal School Reader — Book IV.

American Inventions and Inventors.

Newspaper articles, especially those written during the war and during the Versailles Conference dealing with coal as related to the national welfare of France and Germany are very good.

It is hoped that some sort of technique similar to that suggested in this article can be worked out in such a manner that even an inexperienced rural teacher can use it. The need is surely great. From the standpoint of the actual value of the human material involved, nothing is of greater importance than efforts to conserve rather than stifle the most precious asset of the nation—the talent and genius of its bright children.

THE CLEARING HOUSE

A MARKET PROJECT

BY FIRST GRADE PUPILS

I. Description of how the project arose, and how it fitted into the general plan of work.

A formal request to begin a farm project was stimulated through a nature walk during which a farm was visited. This walk was taken on Friday, November 5. Cornstalks were gathered. Later they were broken into eight-inch pieces and tied into shocks. An outline of the various things seen at the farm was made on the board by the teacher, from information given her by the children. The farm was made on the floor. The school yard furnished dirt and stones and soon a cornfield appeared. Pumpkins were made of cheesecloth dyed with soap dye and stuffed, and placed among the corn shocks. (Clay would have been a more æsthetic medium to have used in making the pumpkins, but because it breaks so easily it discourages the children in the beginning.) An apple orchard made of twigs in composite clay with red and green apples next appeared. Celery made of paper and lettuce made of thin paper colored green soon formed a realistic garden. The house, chicken yard, pig pen, and brook all appeared in the course of time.

Soon the question arose as to what the farmer did with his surplus crops. The fact that he sold them, either taking them himself or sending by boat or train, brought out the necessity for a market. The teacher had the idea of the market in her inner consciousness all of the time, not to thrust it upon the children, but if possible to draw it out—in her rôle as the ever-wise guide. The questions asked were printed and posted in the room to stimulate reading. (See "Reading" for a list of these questions.)

A trip was taken to the Municipal Wharf, Union Street Market, and Washington Market. The boats that bring in the produce from Philadelphia to the big wholesale market at the Municipal Wharf were seen. Union Street was full of live chickens, ducks, turkeys, and geese, as this is a Jewish neighborhood. It was the day before Thanksgiving, and Washington Market was a beautiful sight and very stimulating.

When we came back to school the children decided to make a real market. Wood in our section is very scarce, so ordinary work tables were used for counters. Sawdust on the floor made the meat market more realistic. If wood had been plentiful it would have been more educational to have had the children build stalls, etc. Having set up the market, naturally we had to make things to sell. The farm furnished pumpkins, apples, lettuce, and celery. However, just as many of our vegetables come from a distance and not all from nearby farms, so we too had to help the farmer and make more articles. Cheesecloth, cotton batting, and soap dye made suitable materials from which to fashion the following articles: apples, pumpkins, oranges, bananas, frankfurters, turkey, beets, carrots, and ham. Clay, paint, and shellac made the following articles: grapes, chops, tomatoes, and cranberries. Paper bags were made from wrapping paper. An apron was made from black chintz. Money was made from paper, as were also signs and price tags. The articles made were cut out by the teacher because it cost too much to allow experimenting with cheesecloth. We shall always have to sacrifice children until the masses realize the importance of an abundance of material. The children did all of the dyeing, sewing, and stuffing.

A FARM PROJECT

Before the Market Project had progressed very far, the necessity for advertising arose. The result was the making of a number of illustrated charts. The teacher furnished the pictures, which were taken from various magazines. These were shown to the children and the sentences given by them. For instance, a picture of children eating lunch brought forth the sentence:

EVERYTHING FOR LUNCH
PARKER MARKET, UNION STREET

A picture of bacon, tomatoes, and onions *en casserole* had the following statement printed alongside of it:

ONIONS
TOMATOES
BACON
MAKE A GOOD SUPPER.

The picture of the little boy with the market basket, from the *Pictorial Review*, brought forth this idea:

THIS LITTLE BOY BOUGHT HIS CHRISTMAS DINNER AT THE PARKER MARKET.

A number of charts were made, which stimulated reading; then at the end of the week the children were tested to see how many new words they had learned.

As the products accumulated they decided to ask the Mott School First Grade to come and buy their dolls' Christmas dinner. One of the boys printed the circular on the following page with the printing press.

Each succeeding day a new circular was printed giving the prices or some interesting fact about the market. The prices were kept in 5's or multiples of 5.

A MARKET PROJECT

OPENING

PARKER   MARKET

UNION ST.

PHONE   1112-J

FRIDAY, DEC. 17, 1920

MEAT   VEGETABLES   FRUIT

Finally the opening day came and two first grades from the Mott School came to buy, bringing their dolls with them. They had a wonderful time and bought a complete dinner from the turkey down.

Market books.were made by the children in which they drew and in which there were a few rhymes printed by the teacher, as: "To market, to market, to buy a fat pig" and "Higgeldy, Piggledy," etc. They decorated their own covers and printed the name with the printing press.

II. The direct knowledge, skills, etc. which the project yielded were:

1. *Reading:*

The charts stimulated reading and the children were 103 words wiser when they finished the Market Project. Not all of these words were new, but they had been learned in a new relationship which tended to strengthen the old words. A list of the one hundred and twenty-five words follow:

2. *Word list:*

*a	*above
*away	*around
*and	*at
*all	*apple

[The starred words are found in Thorndike's list of words from 1 to 500, in *The Teachers' Word Book.*]

*big
*before
*by
*buy
began

*can
*cut
*care
*corn
*city
cock-a-doodle-doo
cauliflower
cost
cheaper
*country .

*does
*do
*did

*every
*eat

food
fan
farm
*from
*for
*friend
farmer
fat
*father

*great
grapes
*go
grocer

heaven
ham
*how
*home
*his
*he

*it
*is
*into
*if
*I
*in

*love
loving
lemons
lettuce
*little

*me
*more
market
*make

*not
November

oranges
*of
*our
*or
opening
*one

pie
phone
peppers
potatoes

ran

*send
sells
*see
single
spends

*stay
*should
*said
*shall

*talk
*to
*thank
*tell
Thanksgiving
turkey
*train
*them
*the
*then
*this
*think
Union St.

*we
*went
whom

*which
*what
*when

3. *Charts:*

A pumpkin ran away
Before Thanksgiving Day.
"They would make," said he,
"A pie of me, if I should stay."

(Song — Tune, *Chimes of Dunkirk*.)
Illustrated—Crepe paper pumpkin.

Father of all, in Heaven above,
We thank Thee for Thy love.
Our food, our home, and all we wear
Tell of Thy loving care.

Illustrated—Jessie Wilcox Smith picture.

I went into the country
The farmer's friends to see,
And every single one of them
Began to talk to me.

This chart would have made good silent reading if the project had come later in the term:

What does the farmer do with the pumpkins, apples, and corn he cannot use?
The farmer sells them.
How does he send them to the city?
The farmer takes them to the market or sends by train.
Which costs more?
It costs more to send by train.
Then from whom is it cheaper to buy, the farmer or the grocer?
It is cheaper to buy from the farmer at the market.

When I go to market I shall see:

Lettuce	Potatoes
Cauliflower	Tomatoes

This chart was illustrated with a picture of each kind of vegetable, poultry, or meat which the children were likely to see at the market. It tended to make the child see the worthwhile things at the market.

The posters announcing the market and those advertising it were used as reading material.

4. *Arithmetic:*

Counting by 5's was firmly implanted and some idea of buying, selling, and making change was acquired. If this project were used later in the year, or in the second grade, more number work could be brought in.

5. *Industrial Arts:*

Making all of the vegetables, poultry, and other articles needed for the market as previously described.

6. *Fine Arts:*

Drawing in market books.

7. *English:*

Daily discussion about the farm and market. The children came from foreign homes and heard very little English. These discussions as well as the actual buying and selling strengthened their English. It really was in this subject that the greatest amount of power, skill, and growth was seen.

8. *Civics:*

The market products were made during the occupation period in the morning and the supervised industrial art period in the afternoon. While one division of the class worked, the other had a reading lesson. Naturally self-control developed, for it was necessary to be quiet and to go quietly to the closet for material so the other group could read — respect for the rights of others as well as self-control being developed. Self-initiative and self-direction also were developed. Ideas of city markets and co-operation between farmer and city people were gained. Ideas of cleanliness and thrift were instilled.

9. *Music:*

Several songs were taught, among them being "I went into the country"; "A pumpkin ran away"; "There's a big fat turkey"; "Father of all in Heaven above."

Many of these were used in connection with the Thanksgiving preparation, which dovetailed nicely with both the farm and market projects.

10. *Penmanship:*

Very little — but a great deal of printing.

III. *Results.* 1. Leads to new projects:

The Farm Project led to the Market Project and it in turn led to Transportation.

2. By-products of feeling attitudes which affect behavior from social standpoint:

Courtesy habits were fostered, as well as self-initiative, self-direction, and self-control; for example, a choice of the articles made was given, choice of materials, and passing whenever necessary to the cabinet to get the materials. These habits, plus satisfactions and happiness in doing and using one's powers and possibilities were substituted for the old traditional school habits which do not function in life.

IV. *Principles Involved:*

Let us see how the Market Project measures from the various standards applied to it. Dr. Kilpatrick says the child should learn to

> purpose wisely,
> plan intelligently,
> execute with nicety the plans which
>   he has formulated.

I feel that through this project there was opportunity for the above.

Meredith Smith, in an article on "Experimental Studies in Kindergarten Education" edited by Patty Hill, brings out the following points:

1. "The problem must represent the maximum amount of thinking because the ends or purposes are real purposes in the sense that they originate from the children themselves and appear as needs in a social situation."

2. "There must be an evident means for testing the result when it is attained." (Doe

the basket hold the potatoes? Does the boy hold the cranberries?)

3. "The problem should develop problems of suspended judgments." Does the Market Project measure up to these standards?

Opportunity for the only kind of moral training at all worth while presents itself in this project, for the children are freely playing and working together, sharing, coöperating, and assisting each other. Dr. Bonser in *The Elementary School Curriculum* says:

"Life is a succession of activities in meeting needs. From earliest childhood to old age there is an urge within us that expresses itself in the form of needs and attempts to satisfy these needs. Because the purposeful activities of children and adults are so much the same in kind, every experience of the child in meeting some need in a new and better way is a preparation for meeting the same kind of need in the future. Whatever contributes to the solution of any problem in child life is almost sure to be of value in adult life. In this sense the future of the children is really present to them — the adult life all about them represents the kind of needs and activities which they will experience in the future and also the source of a large proportion of their present needs and interests.

"Children are not asked to take an interest in a problem because it will appear as their own at some future time, but because it is a real problem to them now."

Does the Market Project measure up to Dr. Bonser's standards?

If a Project is teaching, using the interests of the children, thinking first of child development, giving the child life more abundantly, treating him as a social being with the human element present, then does the Market Project answer these requirements?

DOROTHY KAY CADWALLADER,
Trenton, N. J.

AS REPORTED

The second annual meeting of the National Conference on Educational Method was gratifyingly successful with regard to the character of the programs as well as the attendance. The failure of the Department of Superintendence to announce the meeting of the Conference in the general program resulted in the inability on the part of some of the friends of the Conference to attend the sessions. Nevertheless, the rooms assigned were well filled on both occasions, particularly on Wednesday morning, when Fullerton Hall of the Art Institute — although it seats some five hundred — proved inadequate.

In the absence of Superintendent C. L. Wright, Miss Margaret Madden, principal of the Doolittle Elementary School in Chicago, a member of the executive committee, presided over the opening session.

In speaking of the present status of educational method, Professor Hosic of Teachers College declared that good progress is being made toward the development of a fundamental concept and corresponding healthful practices. It is true that professors of education on the one hand seem determined to confuse the issue by insisting each in his own way upon popular definitions of the Project, most of them partial rather than complete. We may trust to time, however, to remove this difficulty. One will neutralize another. As for vagaries and overemphasis, these are to be expected and can hardly make matters worse. A little overemphasis on constructiveness is a welcome relief from too much abstraction and formality. When in doubt about the Project Method, use common sense.

The second speaker, Superintendent Gosling of Madison, Wisconsin, outlined the plan by which he succeeds in securing supervision for his schools without the help of a special supervisor. His plan in brief is to call his principals together from time to time and engage with them in a study of the problem of supervision. They are asked to bring forward plans and suggestions. These are discussed and a practical policy developed.

Principal Hotchkiss of the Teacher Training School in Kansas City, Missouri, after giving a brief sketch of project activities in his school, described at some length a project in the study of Africa. One of the striking features of this report was the account of a series of problems, fifteen in number, growing out of the main aims of the enterprise. The whole movement concluded with a red letter day in which the results of the work were presented before the Geography Section of the State Teachers' Association.

The final speaker of the first session was Miss Bessie B. Goodrich, Director of Elementary Education in Des Moines, Iowa, who outlined a series of criteria of project teaching which she had worked out in her schools with the assistance of Mr. R. H. Franzen, Director of the Department of Research. She explained that these criteria were in part the result of suggestions originally made by Dr. John Herring in an article in the *Teachers College Record*. Helpful criteria, she remarked, are not easy to formulate, and she has attempted as yet no extended use of these, but has contented herself with working them out with individual teachers.

The general discussion which followed these papers was conducted by Miss Margaret Noonan of New York University, Vice-President of the Conference. One of the principal questions considered was the possibility of project work in high school and college. Miss Noonan made the point that where the necessary orientation for project work is already present, no elaborate development of the social situation is necessary. She contended that for this reason projects in college might move forward with very definite assignments, inasmuch as the students are fully acquainted with the purposes and plans of the work.

The order of the papers at the second session of the Conference was changed to accommodate Miss Elizabeth Hall, who was presiding over a breakfast of women in administration. The first speaker was Superintendent Fred M. Hunter of Oakland, California, who presented in a most engaging manner an account of project work carried on in some of the classrooms of his city. He began by making clear that the term "ordinary classroom" means in our day a considerable variety of situations such as those where the pupils have been segregated into rapid and slow moving groups, junior high school classes interested in technical subjects, and the like. He stated that in Oakland the policy is to maintain a general course of study committee called the Superintendent's Council, which acts as a clearing house in gathering, organizing, and disseminating ideas concerning the curriculum. In this way the courses of study are constantly being revised. A great variety of projects were described and in many cases illustrated by means of portfolios, charts, and the like prepared by the pupils. The whole presented a most attractive picture of the possibilities of new methods in a progressive school organization.

Professor William H. Kilpatrick of Teachers College followed with a notable address on "Method and Curriculum." He first cleared the ground by explaining in what ways the older ideas of method have proved ineffectual. He then built up a conception of the new point of view of method and what this will mean in terms of the curriculum. The main considerations are, first, the complex character of learning or the simultaneous learnings which inevitably go on, and second, the situation which leads to learning — a situation far more inclusive than has generally been realized. In developing a sound theory of method and curriculum the multiform character of the process of learning and of the stimulations which bring it about must both be fully taken into account. This will render obsolete the outlines of primary knowledges and skills which have so long served us.

The third speaker of the morning, Mr. S. A. Courtis, Director of Instruction, Teacher Training, and Research in Detroit, Michigan, presented in a most concrete way a new view of teacher rating. He gave to the audience a printed account of certain lessons and a rating card and asked that these lessons be ranked in order of merit. When this had been done he gave out a second pamphlet containing analyses of four types of teaching, named respectively Compulsion, Teacher Preparation, Motivation, and Purposing, and called for a second rating of the sample lessons in accordance with this scale. The higher degree of uniformity of rating attained by the use of the rating scale was marked.

The closing address by Miss Hall was necessarily abbreviated because of the lateness of the hour. The speaker rose to the occasion, however, and in a few words made an eloquent plea for the higher type of cooperation between teachers and supervisors in developing more effective schools.

BUSINESS OF THE CONFERENCE

In accordance with the constitution, the Conference at its first meeting adopted a report of the nominating committee appointed to suggest the names of candidates for places on the Board of Directors to succeed the five whose terms expired. The retiring members were as follows: Superintendent J. M. Gwinn of New Orleans, Superintendent Fred M. Hunter of Oakland, California, Miss Bessie B. Goodrich of Des Moines, Iowa, Dean John W. Withers of New York University, and Superintendent C. L. Wright of Huntington, West Virginia. The persons elected to the Board of Directors for a term of three years each are as follows: Miss Goodrich, Superintendent Hunter, and Superintendent Gwinn to succeed themselves; Miss Rose Carrigan, principal of the Shurtleff School, Boston, and Mr. S. A. Courtis, Director of Instruction, Teacher Training, and Research in Detroit.

The new Board of Directors at a meeting held at the close of the Wednesday forenoon program elected officers for the ensuing year as follows: President, Professor Margaret E. Noonan, of the School of Education, New York University; Vice-President, Mr. W. F. Tidyman, Director of the Training School, State Normal School, Farmville, Virginia; member of the executive committee to succeed Mr. C. C. Certain, Mr. J. A. Starkweather, Assistant Superintendent of Schools, Duluth, Minnesota.

The Board voted to hold special meetings in Boston in connection with the National Education Association and directed the Secretary-Treasurer to make application for affiliated membership in that society. It was agreed that overtures should be made to the Department of Elementary Education and also to the Department of Elementary School Principals looking to joint sessions.

Keen regret was also expressed on account of the loss which the Conference sustains through the withdrawal of Superintendent C. L. Wright, the first President, who has resigned his position as Superintendent of Schools in Huntington, West Virginia, to go into business. It is recognized that his enthusiasm and wise advice had much to do with the formation of the Conference and the outlining of its policy.

DESERVED APPRECIATION

The following clipping from the *Brockton* (Mass.) *Daily Enterprise* shows that teachers are not always unhonored and unsung even in their own communities. The teacher referred to had undertaken a Thanksgiving project after a discussion with another teacher who had been studying the subject. As the editor remarks, the following note from an appreciative mother tells its own story:

"You print so many little human happenings that I thought you would find space for this little letter. I have three children in the grade schools. One is in the third grade of the Packard School and for one week before Thanksgiving was inquiring the prices of all good things to eat for the dinner, interested in answering an invitation to the old farm, and finding a picture to represent it; looking up railroad routes and boat fares and marking out maps to the places to which they were going. They even had the table correctly set with paper knives and plates, forks and spoons, and the children impersonated the different characters entertaining. The whole entertainment amounted to so much more than the large dinner at home on the holiday. Two-thirds of the kiddies would get an understanding of the old-fashioned way of spending the day that they would never get in any other way.

"My little boy in the fourth grade of the Perkins School loves to go to school, and he is a lively one, too. His teacher has the rows of the school divided into streets. There is Honesty avenue, Trustworthy place, Pleasant street, etc., each child sitting in the most appropriate place. I think it is a fine thing to send three children to school every day through the year, with the exception of Saturday and Sunday, with kindness and fair treatment handed out all the time. Here's gratitude to some very fine teachers. Money cannot repay them for the work they are doing daily."

THE READER'S GUIDE

THE NEW CIVICS

Two recent volumes by Mr. Arthur W. Dunn illustrate to a remarkable degree the change in point of view which has taken place in civics instruction and to some extent in the whole field of common school education. Formerly school work was aimed at giving to children the results of adult experience, in order that they might be prepared for adult responsibilities when they arrived. Today we seek rather to help the children to interpret their own experience and thus enrich their lives and increase their usefulness here and now, holding that the best preparation for the future is perfect control of the present.

With such purposes as these Mr. Dunn has been led to supplement his earlier *Community and the Citizen* with two books[1] adapted respectively to rural and to urban life. Not that they are or should be wholly different, — the author distinctly holds to the contrary, — but that emphasis must be placed upon reaching civic ideals through the interpretation of the civic situations in which the pupil normally finds himself. Hence, while the general principles are common, their embodiment and illustrations are largely differentiated.

What he means by "community civics" and what he would teach by it Mr. Dunn makes perfectly clear. Beginning with the local community, he would lead on to a conception of the state, the nation, and even of the world as a community. He would train the youthful citizen for active and useful participation in the common life. To do this he would instill these ideas: (1) the common purposes in community life; (2) our interdependence in attaining these purposes; (3) the consequent necessity for

coöperation; and (4) government as a means of securing coöperation (team-work) for the common good.

Both books open not, of course, with a discussion of government, but with studies of community life intended to show our need of some effective means of coöperation. Next come pictures of different types of communities and of the problems, such as those of earning a living, communication, health, recreation, and education, which government helps us to solve. Last of all come chapters explaining how we do actually govern ourselves.

One of the notable features of these books is their wealth of illustrations. Having been for some years a resident of Washington and connected with one of the departments of the government, Mr. Dunn was able to secure from various bureaus a great many pictures and charts which he has used to good advantage. It is to be hoped that many boys and girls will have the opportunity to see both volumes for the sake of the broader impression of their country which they might thus acquire. There are also numerous references to books and pamphlets, many of which the pupils themselves might well help to secure.

SIGNIFICANT ARTICLES

INTELLIGENCE TESTS IN ACTUAL SCHOOL PRACTICE

The *Educational Times* (London) is running a series of supplementary articles on recent educational developments. That for March is by Professor John Adams, of the University of London, who writes on "The Place of Intelligence Tests in Actual School Practice." With that breadth of grasp and easy intimacy of style which characterize

[1] *Community Civics and Rural Life; Community Civics for City Schools.* By Arthur W. Dunn. Boston: D. C. Heath & Co.

everything that Professor Adams writes, this article surveys the present status of these tests and arrives at a definite conclusion as to the policy which classroom teachers will do well to adopt. It is true that there is as yet no general agreement as to what is meant by intelligence, or as to whether it is capable of improvement beyond the age of sixteen. Teachers, nevertheless, are not justified in taking the attitude of distrust which many of them now assume. These tests are not merely an abbreviated and somewhat more reliable form of examination. They go much further in measuring actual capacity as distinguished from attainment. Besides, the psychologists themselves admit that they cannot claim to measure innate capacity entirely apart from the influences of educational training, certainly not by means of a single test. They do claim, however, and justly, that a series of tests will give a good idea of the general average level of intelligence ability of an individual. Professor Adams warns against the fallacy of basing the classification of school children entirely upon mental age. He would take into account also both attainment and character. An example of a proper course for teachers to follow is found in the case of Miss Hughes of Cambridge, who made a study of group tests such as those used in the American army and in the two days granted her by the authorities tested 300 pupils in actual school practice. Testing has two quite distinct spheres: testing of normal children and testing of defectives. With regard to the first, all teachers are concerned. They must expect sooner or later to have to deal with the specialists as well as with the inspector who employs standard tests. They should prepare themselves by the mastery of such books as Ballard's *Mental Tests* and Terman's *The Measurement of Intelligence*.

"We must master," says Professor Adams, "the principles of intelligence testing be-

cause it is an essential part of our equipment as self-respecting craftsmen."

THE PLACE OF THE KINDERGARTEN

Those who look confidently for the extension of the kindergarten so as to provide for all children in all communities will find much food for thought in a discussion of the place of the kindergarten by Professor David Snedden of Teachers College. Writing in *School and Society* of March 4, Professor Snedden sets up a distinction between the natural development on the one hand and training on the other. He doubts whether anyone who is well informed would wish the kindergarten to become primarily a training agency in any narrow sense of the word, such as training to read, spell, or write numbers. The function of the kindergarten is rather to assist natural development. What is needed, therefore, is further information as to how this can best be done. He proposes a definite method of sociological inquiry as to how a constructive policy for the kindergarten can be developed, and offers for critical discussion the following propositions:

"1. For fairly normal children from four to six years of age schools are not greatly needed in the more normal rural, village, and suburban environments.

"2. Nor are they needed in the more prosperous urban environments where mothers regularly devote their available 'working' time to the care of their children.

"3. Wherever schools for normal children from four to six are needed to compensate for specific deficiencies in environment, it is almost certain that similar schools for children from two to four are still more urgently needed.

"4. If practicable, special schools should probably be provided for abnormal children in any environment, their functions to be determined, of course, by the kind and degree of abnormality found.

"5. Some schools for children between ages two and six designed to compensate for deficiencies of environment should probably be in session 300 days each year. Under some conditions they should probably be in session eight or ten hours each day. Other schools might well be in session only one month in each year.

"6. The objectives of each type of school must be determined by local conditions and the discovered needs of specific groups of children. Some of these schools, probably, would not require any rooms — park space would suffice. Some could probably get along very well with sympathetic custodians rather than trained teachers."

THE NEW BOOKS

Training for Effective Study. By Frank W. Thomas. Boston: Houghton Mifflin Co., 1922. Pp. xviii+251. Price, $1.90.

Intended for normal school classes and teachers' reading circles.

Silent and Oral Reading. By Clarence R. Stone. Boston: Houghton Mifflin Co. 1922. Pp. xviii+306.

Reflects recent scientific studies and contains much illustrative material.

English Grammar Drills on Minimum Essentials. By Carl Holliday and Sophia Camenisch. Chicago: Laird & Lee, 1922. Pp. 150.

Claims to include only information needful for correct speaking and writing.

Fundamentals of Education. By Boyd H. Bode. New York: Macmillan Co., 1921. Pp. xiv+245.

An elementary treatment of the philosophy of education.

The Language of America. Book One. Lessons in Elementary English and Citizenship for Adults. By Caroline E. Myers and Garry C. Myers. New York: Newson

& Co., 1921. Pp. 128, illus. Teachers' Manual. Pp. 100.

Both print and script.

Measuring Minds. An Examiner's Manual to Accompany the *Myers Mental Measure.* By Caroline E. Myers and Garry C. Myers. New York: Newson & Co., 1921. Pp. 55.

The *Myers Measure* is intended for use with persons of widely varying ages.

How to Study: Illustrated Through Physics. By Fernando Sanford. New York: Macmillan Co., 1922. Pp. vi+56.

Developing Mental Power. By George Malcolm Stratton. Boston: Houghton Mifflin Co., 1922. Pp. x+72. Price, 80 cents.

Not a plea for formal discipline but for developing coöperation of all the powers.

Hand Craft Projects. For School and Home Shops. By Frank I. Solar. Milwaukee: Bruce Publishing Co., 1921. Book I, pp. 158. Illus.

Drawings and specifications make each "project" clear.

Where We Live — A Home Geography. By Emilie V. Jacobs. Philadelphia: Christopher Sower Co., 1921. Pp. 192. Illus. and maps.

Suggestive of what to teach concerning the geography of other home cities.

A Treasury of Plays for Children. Edited by Montrose J. Moses, with illustrations by Tony Sarg. Boston: Little, Brown & Co., 1921. Pp. xiv+550.

A volume like this has been much needed. It should be in every school library.

The Anderson Arithmetic. By Robert F. Anderson. Boston: Silver, Burdett & Co., 1921. Book One, pp. xiv+274; Book Two, pp. vi+282; Book Three, pp. vi+312.

Fewer topics and better distributed practice are two prominent features.

IN PAPER COVERS

Scientific Determination of the Content of the Elementary School Course in Reading. By Willis Lemon Uhl. University of Wisconsin Studies in the Social Sciences and History, No. 4, 1921.

The Effect of the Physical Make-up of a Book Upon Children's Selection. By Florence E. Bamberger. Baltimore: Johns Hopkins Studies in Education, No. 4, 1922. Price, $2.00.

Studies in the Geography of Europe. Oxford, Ohio: Miami University Bulletin, Series XIX, No. 2.

Projects for Virginia Schools. I. The "Vahispa" Project in the Schools. II. Debating. By James M. Grainger. Bulletin of State Normal School for Women, Farmville, Va., Vol. VIII, No. 1, January, 1922.

Seventy-Second Annual Report of the School Committee of the Town of Winchester, Massachusetts, for the Year Ending December 31, 1921.

The Fruita Survey. An Educational Survey of the Fruita, Colorado, Union High School District. By Samuel Quigley and others. Fruita, Colorado, 1921.

The Schools of Your City. I. — The General Situation. II. — School Buildings and Equipment. Washington, D. C.: Chamber of Commerce of U. S., Civic Development Publications.

Humanism in the Continuation School. Educational Pamphlets, No. 43. London, 1921.

City and Country School. Record of Group VI, 1921. By Leila V. Stott. New York, 165 West 12th St., 1920–21.

Bucyrus City Schools. Survey Bulletin, Vol. III, Nos. 1 and 2. Bucyrus, Ohio, 1922.

Department of the Interior, Bureau of Education, 1921: *Organization for Visual Instruction*, by W. H. Dudley, Bulletin No. 7. *Foreign Criticism of American Education*, by W. J. Osburn, Bulletin No. 8. *Salaries of Administrative Officers and Their Assistants*, by Walter S. Deffenbaugh, Bulletin No. 30. *Music Departments of Libraries*, Bulletin No. 33. *Educational Reconstruction in Belgium*, by Walter A. Montgomery, Bulletin No. 39. *Agricultural Education*, by C. D. Jarvis, Bulletin No. 40. *Teacher Placement by Public Agencies*, by J. F. Abel, Bulletin No. 42. *School Grounds and Play*, by Henry S. Curtis, Bulletin No. 45. *Proceedings of Fifth and Sixth Annual Meetings of the National Council of Primary Education*, Bulletin No. 47. *Method and Content of French Course in Accredited High Schools of the South*, by J. A. Capps, Secondary School Circular No. 10.

Standard Tests recently published: *Gunnison Primary Test A* (Test blanks and Manual of Directions), by Herschel T. Manuel, Colorado State Normal School, Gunnison, Colo. *Witham's Standard Geography Tests, English Vocabulary Tests, and Silent Reading* (including directions for giving and scoring tests, together with standard scores and keys), J. L. Hammett Co., Brooklyn, N. Y. *Army Group Examination Alpha* (with Manual of Instruction); *Group Intelligence Test for School Entrance* (with Class Record Sheet and instructions), by L. W. Cole and Leona E. Vincent, Kansas State Normal School, Bureau of Educational Measurements and Standards. *Otis Self-Administering Tests of Mental Ability: Higher Examination* (Form A and Form B, with Directions, Key, and Record Sheet); *Stenquist Mechanical Aptitude Tests I and II* (with Key, Record Sheet and Manual of Directions); *Detroit First-Grade Intelligence Test*, by Anna M. Engel (Form A, examiner's Guide, Record Sheet); *Miller Mental Ability Test* (with Key, Manual of Directions, Age-Grade Score Sheet, and Percentile Graph); *The Will-Temperament Test* (with Record Card and Manual of Directions), by June E. Downey, World Book Company, Yonkers, N. Y.

THE JOURNAL OF EDUCATIONAL METHOD

Edited by JAMES F. HOSIC

Volume I MAY, 1922 Number 9

PUBLISHED BY THE WORLD BOOK COMPANY FOR
THE NATIONAL CONFERENCE ON EDUCATIONAL METHOD
$3.00 a year   Monthly except July and August   35 cents a copy

THE NATIONAL CONFERENCE ON EDUCATIONAL METHOD

An Association of Persons Interested in Supervision and Teaching

THE JOURNAL OF EDUCATIONAL METHOD is published monthly, from September to June, at Concord, N. H., for the officers, directors, and members of the National Conference on Educational Method by the World Book Company of Yonkers-on-the-Hudson, N. Y. The subscription price is $3.00 a year; the price of single copies is 35 cents.

Postage is prepaid by the publishers on all orders from the United States, Mexico, Cuba, Porto Rico, Panama Canal Zone, Republic of Panama, Bolivia, Colombia, Honduras, Nicaragua, Peru, Hawaiian Islands, Philippine Islands, Guam, and the Samoan Islands. Postage is charged extra as follows: For Canada, 25c on annual subscriptions; other foreign countries not named, 50 cents. All communications regarding subscriptions or advertising should be addressed to World Book Company, Concord, N. H., or Yonkers-on-Hudson, New York.

Address applications for membership to the Secretary of the Conference, 525 West One Hundred and Twentieth Street, New York City. The fee for active members is $3.00, for associate members, $2.00; $2.00 in each case is applied to the support of the journal, for which each member receives a year's subscription.
The editorial office is at 525 West One Hundred and Twentieth Street, New York City.

Entered as second-class matter at the post office at Concord, N. H. under the Act of March 3, 1879.

The Journal of Educational Method

VOLUME I   MAY, 1922   NUMBER 9

EDITORIALLY SPEAKING

SUPERVISION AS A PROFESSION

In his address on Trades and Professions at Albany when the new education building was dedicated, Professor George Herbert Palmer of Harvard defined a profession as an occupation which is entered upon only after a long period of rigorous preparation, maintains definite standards, and gives an unmeasured service. He thought teaching deserves to some extent to be classed as a profession in accordance with these criteria.

Supervision might well be judged by the same tests. If teaching requires a long period of rigorous preparation, surely the work of supervision should be entered upon no less lightly. As matters stand, however, the majority of those engaged in the supervision of teaching have had little or no systematic preparation for it. They have risen from the ranks and have never even for a single year devoted themselves to anything approaching a scientific study of such data as might be examined with a view to the formulation of principles and a working policy, to say nothing of first-hand observation and participation in criticism under direction.

True the body of data bearing on the problems of supervision is neither large nor informing. Nevertheless there is a body of data too valuable to be wholly overlooked. Much of the outcome of educational experience must needs be stated in qualitative terms and may be none the less valuable on that account. Experimentation in the field is, moreover, possible and should receive more attention than it now does.

Educators may well take a leaf out of the book of engineers, whose recently published report on *Waste in Industry* represents a far more exhaustive attempt to weigh the merits of management than teachers have as yet thought of attempting. Perhaps when our turn does come, we shall find likewise that the largest single cause of waste in education is poor leadership and direction, not incompetency on the part of the rank and file of the workers.

Meanwhile, through every possible agency we shall do well to publish the fact that supervision is a distinct occupation in itself, worthy of life-long devotion, and demanding peculiar training and fitness. In this connection membership in the National Conference on Educational Method is no mean help.

VISION AND SUPERVISION

ROWENA KEITH KEYES

Head of English Department, Haaren High School, New York, N. Y.

"Where there is no vision the people perish." Applicable in many post-war connections, these prophetic words might well have been the text of Caroline F. E. Spurgeon in her review of the Report on English in "The Refashioning of English Education" (*Atlantic Monthly*, January).

"The 'indispensable qualification of the teacher of literature,'" she quotes from the report, "'is not learning but passion and a power to communicate it.'"

To one who has hailed with hope the wider recognition of the importance of education, since the war, it appears that here is the note most needed — though least often heard — among the voices raised by theorists on education. True, education for citizenship, development of individual ability, practical preparation for life, the "project method" are among the slogans of today; but most of those who write and speak on such phases of the subject dwell on syllabi, curricula, devices in supervised study, scales and measurements of attainment, systems of training for teachers — a hundred applications of modern intellect and ingenuity to educational problems — and do not emphasize the value of "passion," of sympathy, of inspiration, — a far more difficult and elusive but also a vastly more important matter.

For, great results in character, great movements in life, are never effected through systems elaborated by reason and judgment alone. The will must be roused through feeling. If the essence of mob-violence and of vulgarity is uncontrolled emotion, quite as truly the fires of aspiration and of inspiration can be kindled only by emotion nobly directed. Yet, admitting all this, one questions, "What can be said or done with regard to an aim so spiritual? Granted that inspired teaching is desirable, that 'passion' is the rarest and most precious of teaching assets, is it not true that such passion is communicated from soul to soul, defying analysis or cultivation?"

The answer, I believe, is in a new conception, or at least a new emphasis in our conception, of the function of supervision, a new appreciation of it as not merely a stereotyped *looking-on* or even *looking-over* the things within its immediate scope, but a clear, open-eyed vision from the higher places; not merely planning plus criticism, pruning here, cutting there to bring the supervised into harmony with the supervisor's preconceived notion, but great-minded breadth and depth of observation which sees in order to inspire.

Have we not erred too often, all we of the supervising tribe — heads of departments, principals, superintendents, — in conceiving our function, apart from its administrative side, as consisting mainly in observing to evaluate, in criticising to correct; whereas, far above and beyond all other opportunities, ours is the opportunity of spiritual leadership?

348

I would not be understood to write with the purpose of indiscriminate arraignment. There are diversities of gifts and of operations in supervision as in all human affairs. Men and women of real vision are among us. But I submit that with our American delight in the concrete, the obvious, we have cried up the excellence of plan, of method, of device and have said and thought too little of the power that is exerted through magnanimous supervision.

To illustrate: The principal of the head of department in a high school is charged with the duty of estimating the teaching power of the staff, perhaps with "marking" them. In how many cases the classroom visits become, accordingly, mere opportunities for finding "what is the matter" with this one's method, or showing dissatisfaction because that one has not ridden the supervisor's hobby! And this, not because we intend to be captious or ill-natured, but because in our crowded, hurrying lives the narrow view is the easier to take, or — alas! — because we lack the greatness of heart to be truly human.

In no subject is this type of supervision more lamentable than in English, of which Miss Spurgeon writes: "Great literature, as those who care for it well know, is not only close to life but is a means of life," and (from the report) "We must treat literature not as language merely, but as the self expression of great natures, the record and rekindling of spiritual experiences in daily life, for every one of us the means by which we may, if we will, realize our own impressions and communicate them to our fellows."

No one of us probably but would subscribe to the ideal. Yet how do we carry its spirit into practice?

Here are a few examples from my own observation:

One of us has become impressed with the value of reading aloud as training in and test of appreciation. He visits classes in English and views them with a subconscious eagerness for reading aloud. Criticism, courteous but firm, is meted out to those who do not chance to be having that type of recitation. Another, alive to the tremendous need of improved oral English, finds in a single period devoted to a brief lecture with instruction in how to take notes, "pure waste of time," having no faith in the teacher's perception of special need.

A teacher devoted to history, aware of its civic value, is promoted to a supervisory position and longs to see all English teachers using the labor problem, the tariff, etc. for composition topics. She has awakened enthusiasm herself by the use of such subjects. She assumes that *all* should do it in *all* high school classes. She fails to realize that not all can through this means rouse in pupils of thirteen or fourteen years the "passion" that leads to spontaneous self-expression — the real objective; that indeed to do so is a rare thing, her own peculiar gift, perhaps. She says impatiently, "Why choose for these youngsters such a philosophical subject as 'The Happiest Day of My Life'?" For her that is all the subject presents — a philosophical abstraction. But there are about her dozens of teachers less "civic-minded," but with sympathetic and understanding hearts, who can obtain from their young charges after a discussion of the topic, charmingly genuine, unaffected narratives of the joys of Graduation Day, or of the jolliest Christmas in memory.

I once knew a teacher who devised a scheme for teaching pupils to describe with some degree of vividness. She invented a story which she narrated in serial form, pausing each day at a point where an illustration or description was needed. Eagerly the class supplied from their imaginations the requisite details. She had attained her end, stimulation of imagination through pleasure in the story, followed by free, natural expression. Some other teachers laid hold of the plan and adapted it to their needs, but as its freshness wore off she found herself never again so successful in its use. Some of her own "passion" had vanished. Suppose that as head of department she had gone into all the classes of the grade, so full of that device that all others seemed futile, and had adversely criticised the teachers because they did not adopt this or a similar method. Obviously no inspiration would follow her visits.

Now there is no question that many special devices, many sides of every subject need attention; that all teachers need to have them brought to their notice. The pity is that the supervisor is frequently more alive to the omission of a few of his favorite methods than to the possibilities in the particular teacher before him. In reality the advantage of a fairly large school is in the fact that the pupils are subjected to the influence of a group or a series of varied personalities, each having a special strength as well as the unavoidable human weakness. The head of department must, it is true, stand for a certain steadiness of development, must prevent any teacher from running altogether to a fad, but above and beyond this he should cultivate by hearty encouragement and approval the power of the individual teacher, in which his or her enthusiasm displays itself. Every class is different from every other; every teacher is different from every other. This fact is unalterable as human nature is variable. The big thing, the human thing, then, for us as supervisors is to maintain a breadth of mind, a range of imagination, a depth of heart which seizes upon the talent and enthusiasm of each teacher as the one great means of inspirational teaching.

An elementary school principal once said to me, "I am so fortunate in my staff of teachers; each one seems to have some special quality that I need in the school. Particularly in the special classes — those for subnormal, anæmic, or backward children — I seem to have found just the right ones."

A few visits with her to the classes in question left no doubt in my mind that most of her "good fortune" was due to the quality of her supervision. No suggestions or desires of the teachers were slighted; no one was "snapped up." Each one was encouraged in what seemed to be nearest her heart. Yet I felt the steady undercurrent of wisdom and common sense — the stimulation of comparison and balancing of opinions. There was no "mushy sentimentality," no over-sensitiveness; there was free interchange of ideas. No one could fail to see that for pupils, teacher, and principal the classroom visit was a pleasure.

A high school principal found an English teacher drawing forth the ideas of little ninth-year girls on the old English ballads that they had been reading. He asked permission to take her place for his own pleasure, sat down among the queer foreign little girls and throwing his own delightful personality into the teacher's own method, roused the pupils to ecstatic delight and inspired the teacher to new appreciation of her opportunities.

Compare with his vision that of a principal who freely declares that all the subjects in his school but one, that which was formerly his own, are poorly taught.

If at least a few principals make of their supervision a leading and directing of enthusiasm, what may not superintendents, with their wider influence, effect? I have heard of one superintendent, honest, energetic, a "driver" for work, with much of "Prussian" efficiency in organizing, who, when he leaves all the teachers in a school discouraged and depressed by his destructive criticism, declares that this is the only way to get them out of ruts and make them think. His frequent remark is that this or that subject is "generally very poorly taught." I wonder if he would approve of the teacher's method who should turn toward the pupils such a closed mind as he has turned toward her.

Teachers are not angels nor geniuses, they are "just folks"; but my own experience as department head and administrative assistant, as well as my general observation, leads me to believe them to be rather more in earnest, more idealistic, more ready to "do extras" for a good cause than the common run of other workers. I have found that when my own vision was clear, my heart open for their anxieties, my temper steady, my enthusiasm strong, most of them rose to remarkable heights of unselfishness and to real power in their teaching. When I failed in any or all of these particulars, they weakened, grew petty to meet my pettiness, and showed the effects in their work. The supervisor, high or low, who crowds his days with the mechanics of his work and neglects to cultivate human sympathy is, I verily believe, not only endangering his own soul but those of teachers and pupils.

This is a time when world-wide problems and responsibilities prompt men as never before to prayer. May not we who bear the responsibility for guiding some part — small or great — of the educational forces of the nation make this our prayer:

God give us vision, give us sympathy, give us a divine passion that shall burn away our prejudices and shall make us fit to lead.

CRITERIA FOR JUDGING THE VALUE OF PROJECTS [1]

BESSIE BACON GOODRICH

Director of Elementary Education, Des Moines, Iowa

AND

RAYMOND H. FRANZEN

Director of Department of Research, Des Moines, Iowa

In the *Teachers College Record* of September, 1921, there appeared an article by Dr. John Herring which listed criteria for judging the value of a project. The list is collectively exhaustive, but the items are not intended to be mutually exclusive. In order to provide a basis for formation of curricula, we have rearranged the order and classification that we may better parallel the mental processes of teachers with the vital considerations proposed by Dr. Herring.

Fundamental laws of learning such as may be observed in animal behavior are the *skeletal schema* of the acquisition of the most involved human conduct. Consider the dog that learns to "sit up." Meat or other desirable food is held over his head and he attempts to gain possession of this food by going through all the various forms of behavior in his repertoire. Finally his hind legs tire as he stands and prances on them, trying to reach the food. He falls back on his haunches, his eyes still on the object of his actions. It is then given to him. Next time he falls back on his haunches earlier. He learns to respond in this way through doing it and being satisfied with the consequence of that act. Practice and resultant satisfaction form habits.

Children also face situations that need solutions, and the rewards may be made as important to them as the food is to the dog. These habits may be as simple as saying or writing "4" when confronted with the situation "2 plus 2," or they may combine to form a complex trait such as initiative; but education is not the development of general powers or faculties, it is the process of habit formation. The habits which we want children to form are those that deal with the world as it is, that they may more easily meet life situations. There should be no chasm between school and experience. *Habits are formed by practice when the children are interested in the results of that practice.*

Therefore, children should be stimulated to initiate schemes and enterprises, helped to develop them, and encouraged to evaluate the results. If the activity is *their* activity they will develop habits; if the activity is such as *real life* offers, these habits will be useful acquisitions; if the result is *satisfactory* to them, the habits will be firmly cemented. Education is the *successful and satisfactory use* of movements and thoughts which are necessary to later life.

Table manners cannot be taught by lectures or by pictures but by stimulating their exercise with interest in the

[1] The authors wish to acknowledge the assistance of Miss Kate Kelly in preparing the criteria listed in this article.

results. Sportsmanship, habits of fair play, are learned by the actual playing in which justice to all and sportsmanlike conduct adds to the zest of the game. Habits of justice are developed by exercise of justice where the results are apparent and satisfactory. Justice is not taught by lectures nor by emphasis on good actions in the reading of the children. The worst rogue in the world might be able to draw subtle distinctions between what is good and what is bad.

Children will not learn division nearly as quickly when that itself. is the only goal in view as they will when some enterprise in which they are involved demands the use of such skill. They then have an interest in the results of their practice; the habits of division are cemented by the anticipation of their use in that activity, and later by the satisfaction resulting from their successful application. Children who learn division in order to divide their garden as they want, will establish and fix the habits of division more firmly in less time than children who begin to learn division because it is the next lesson in the book. Often a hypothetical pie is the only material used in a division lesson. What child is interested in a *hypothetical* pie? Professor Thorndike shows very clearly in his late books, *New Methods in Arithmetic* and *The Psychology of Arithmetic*, how little use and consequently how little interest there is in many arithmetic problems.

Children in the seventh grade often answer the questions of problems given in a book or by a teacher by adding, multiplying, dividing, doing anything they can do with the figures. They do everything in *their* repertoire of response

to numbers just as the dog did with the meat held over his head. Still in everyday life they choose the correct arithmetical operation to perform with their marbles. This is because the problems they have met in their arithmetic lessons have been put to no practical use. Their responses to an arithmetic problem from the book are the mental operations basic to guessing rather than those basic to solution of a difficulty.

The criteria submitted are classified under the following main headings:

I. Objectives of Activity.

Obviously the habits developed must be worth while. They must form a portion of the training that tends to make the world a better place in which to live. They must provide an equipment which aids us to gain a better total economy of expression of desire.

II. Springs to Activity.

The springs of behavior in school should be such as are aroused by the world we live in. Mental discipline is no longer a serious possibility. The habits taught must be defined in terms of connections between situations and responses. We cannot train "concentration," "will power," or "memory" any more than we can raise "tree-ness." We can connect the muscular and glandular responses which mean attention to a *certain* situation, just as we can grow a *certain* kind of tree. If we wish to train "memory," we must decide what specific memory of what,—just as we must decide which kind of a tree to plant. "Memory" and such terms are abstractions and may aid descriptive thought but are not profitable considerations for pedagogy.

We must also be sure that each individual's activities are appropriate to his needs. Individual differences are a fact which officers of instruction must reckon with. We cannot in wholesale fashion prescribe texts or methods for Grade VI. The extreme children in Grade VI differ as much in ability as the average of Grade III differs from the average of Grade VIII. Projects must provide springs to activity for all the children of the group, varied as they are in abilities and interests.

III. Economy of Activity.

The abilities and traits which are formed should eventually be integrated into one purposive economy of expression—a vocation. We must avoid a scrap heap of equipment and tendency. Education should weave the myriad desires of man into a tapestry of expression and the patterns of the weaving should be our virtues.

We must then consider each project in relation to the total present activities of the child in the home and in the school as well as the probabilities of future occupation.

IV. Relation of the Child to His Activities.

As was emphasized above, the degree of strength of a connection is related in an important way to the degree of satisfaction in the result. The child must be able to comment favorably on the outcome of the enterprise. It must be *his* value to *his* work.

We believe that these four criteria, which are subdivided and illustrated below, provide a satisfactory basis for analysis of the value of a project. They parallel the psychological processes of learning and can thus be easily applied

to any enterprise. It is, of course, desirable to have some objective tool which will yield quantities in these four qualities, but at the present stage of educational psychology of tendency and trait, it seems impossible to arrive at an acceptable test. We wish to emphasize the fact that the value of having criteria is the value of analysis. To know these rules will not mean that the teaching of projects will be any better, any more than knowing rules of grammar improves oral or written expression, but it will aid in the analysis of the virtue of a project and the diagnosis of its shortcomings, just as a knowledge of grammar will aid in proof reading.

PROJECTS USED FOR ILLUSTRATIVE PURPOSES

1. Geography Project.

The children in one of the sixth grade geography classes, while studying the subject of lumbering, decided to build a model of a modern lumber camp. There were no materials at hand with which to work, but as the various needs developed the children in some way managed to supply the necessary material. The first thing needed was a sand box. Two of the boys made at home a very crude box and brought it to school. Since sand was difficult to secure and heavy to handle, they filled the bottom of the box with straw and sprinkled soil over the top. They then planted their forest, made the lumberman's cabin, and all of the tools which he needed for his work—the handsaws, sawhorses, etc. They also provided some of the machinery found in modern camps and mills. There was a crane for carrying logs, built from an erector, and a circular saw which they themselves had fashioned. Both were run by electric motors which members of the class had furnished.

The study of the industry was not left at this point, but through this activity the children were led to study in some detail the following topics: (1) the principal lumber areas of the United States; (2) the kind of wood produced in each area; (3) the main transportation routes over which these products are shipped; and (4) the most important conservation measures which have been passed.

After they had completed their study, they organized their material and invited two of the supervisors to come to their room to see and to hear the results of their work. Later a forester was invited to speak to them and to answer questions which had arisen in class discussions and for which they had been able to find no answer.

2. Letter Writing Project.

Children in a fifth grade at Burlington, Vermont, wrote letters asking that Des Moines children tell them something of their city and their state. The children in one of the Des Moines fifth grades undertook to answer these letters and to give the information asked for. A large number of pictures and post cards were collected from various sources and each child wrote upon a different phase of life in Iowa. An unusually interesting series of letters resulted, each fully illustrated. These were sent to Vermont and copies will later be made into book form to be read by others.

3. Health Posters in Grade I.

The health work in primary grades concerns itself principally with the food children eat, the care of teeth, bathing, and sleeping with fresh air. An effort is made in the lowest grades to establish these habits and to get the children so interested in the habits themselves that no extraneous incentives are needed.

The children of a 1-B class formulated for themselves certain health standards and made posters illustrating these. Pictures were cut from magazines and mounted on tag board. Each member of the class offered suggestions for the sentence to accompany the picture. The relative merits of the various suggestions were discussed to find which sentence best stated the principle in question. After this was decided, the teacher printed the sentence on the poster. These are some of the statements:

1. Bread makes us strong.
2. Milk makes me fat.
3. How often do you take a bath?
4. I brush my teeth twice a day.

4. A Puppet Theater.

A 5-A class in literature was one day entertained during a recitation period by one of its members showing to them a cardboard theater in which the story of Aladdin was staged. This experience brought from some of the members of the class the request that they be given an opportunity to dramatize a play in this way. The matter was fully discussed, with the result that the class decided to embark upon the undertaking. Since they were at the time reading Pyle's *King Arthur Stories*, they selected some of these for presentation upon their puppet stage.

First a cardboard stage and paper dolls were made, but these proved unsatisfactory to the children. A paper tournament didn't go and paper dolls didn't appear very well in costumes of knights and ladies. After much discussion, cloth dolls were decided upon, patterns were cut, and the play immediately began to take on the semblance of real life. One of the boys made a stage at home and brought it to school. Arthur, Merlin, Sir Kay, Sir Gawain, knights, pages, lords, ladies, the king and queen—·thirty-six dolls in all—were produced. · Twelve horses and many pieces of armor were needed for the tournament. Stage settings in keeping with each part of the story were called for. The teachers of art and sewing were asked to help, as were other teachers, who suggested ways and means of getting materials, color effects, etc. Because costume materials were hard to get, each grade was invited to contribute and all enthusiastically responded. Silks, satins, laces, leather, furs, and feathers were brought in. Books were consulted to find correct style in costumes and armor. Much of the work was done after school, at home, and, at the children's request, they worked at school on Saturday mornings.

At intervals the principal or one of the supervisors was asked to witness the progress of the play and to help with some point. The chosen scenes had to be put in dramatic form. This furnished language work for weeks. Finally a group of supervisors were invited to see the play in its finished form. Their appreciation of it led the class to present it before the Parent-Teachers' Association of their school and before representative groups of children from other schools. Later this group had the privilege of seeing one of the charming performances given by Tony Sarg with his puppet players. There was a very marked and sincere appreciation of this artistic production by the entire group. For four months the puppet theater was the center of interest in this school, and the joy and pride of the children in the undertaking convinced the teachers of the value of this kind of work.

5. Christmas Carol Program.

Each room from the first through the eighth grade in one of the schools had learned a carol to contribute to the Christmas program. This had been done during the music period. This school has no community room so there was no opportunity of getting the classes together as a group. It was finally decided that each class should come out into the hall or on the stairs to sing in order that all might enjoy the music. The program lasted forty minutes and every song was listened to with the greatest appreciation by the rest of the school. The following carols were sung:

1. *O Come, All Ye Faithful* (hummed, with phonograph accompaniment, by 1-B class).
2. *Away in the Manger.*
   The Wind Through the Olive Trees — Grades 1 and 2.
3. *Sleep, Darling, Sleep*—Grade 3.
4. *It Came Upon the Midnight Clear*—Grade 4.
5. *There's a Song in the Air*—Grade 5.
6. *Silent Night, Holy Night* (German)—Grades 6, 7 and 8.
7. *Noël* (French)—Grades 6, 7 and 8.

THE CRITERIA AND THEIR APPLICATION TO THE ABOVE AND OTHER SCHOOLROOM SITUATIONS

I. *Objectives of Activity.*

A. The content and outcome should be or should become important portions of the social heritage.

  1. The material used should be of social value.

    (a) Geography project.

      (1) Facts concerning industry, areas of production, transportation routes, and conservation laws are of social value.

    (b) Letter-writing project.

      (1) Facts concerning Iowa are of social value.

    (c) Christmas carol program.

      (1) Carols represented best type of that material available.

    (d) Health poster project.

      (1) This material contributed to knowledge of health facts concerning food, sleep, care of teeth and skin.

    (e) Puppet theater project.

      (1) Material dramatized, valuable as a piece of literature.

      (2) Material dramatized, valuable as a period in history.

      (3) Art principles established, valuable.

    (f) Songs given to children should have musical merit, literary content, and should be suited to the interests of the children singing them.

  2. The result of the classroom activity should be of social value.

    (a) Geography project.

      (1) Free classroom discussion.

      (2) Class pride and satisfaction in the finished sand table.

      (3) Giving of information to others interested.

    (b) Letter-writing project.

      (1) Letters and booklet were of social value.

    (c) Christmas carol program.

      (1) The same carols were sung in homes and churches, hence the children were able to participate there.

    (d) Health poster project.

      (1) Valuable habits of right living were established for individuals and the group.

    (e) Puppet theater project.

      (1) Coöperation, recognition of individual ability, school spirit, self expression of individuals and class as a whole, desire to share their enterprise with parents and with children of other schools were developed through this enterprise.

    (f) To a large degree the product of students in each typewriting and stenography exercise should actually be used.

B. The knowledges, skills, and attitudes developing through the undertaking should become such that they increase the child's ability to control situations.

  1. Geography project.

    (a) Knowledges.

      (1) Lumber industry.

      (2) Areas of production.

      (3) Transportation routes.

      (4) Conservation laws.

      (5) Organization of material.

      (6) Oral expression.

    (b) Skills.

      (1) Motor skills used in building.

      (2) Using reference material.

      (3) Running a motor.

      (4) Organizing material.

      (5) Expression.

    (c) Attitudes.

      (1) Coöperative spirit.

      (2) Responsibility toward public property.

  2. Letter-writing project.

    (a) Knowledges.

      (1) Facts about Iowa.

      (2) Facts about Vermont.

      (3) Correct letter form.

      (4) Organization of material.

    (b) Skills.

      (1) Writing English.

      (2) Collecting and organizing material.

(3) Improved penmanship.
(c) Attitudes.
    (1) Closer sympathy with children of another state.
    (2) Keener appreciation of resources of two states.
    (3) Pride in each other's work.
3. Christmas carol program.
  (a) Knowledges.
    (1) Carols themselves became part of child's literary equipment.
    (2) Source of carols—English, French, German, etc.
    (3) Organization of a program.
  (b) Skills.
    (1) Using voices so they could be heard upstairs or down.
    (2) Clear enunciation in order to carry meaning and spirit of song.
    (3) The pleasure other children were to receive from the singing made work on tone quality necessary.
  (c) Attitudes.
    (1) Responsibility for the success of the program, appreciation of the meaning and spirit of Christmas, and joy in contributing were very apparent.
4. Health poster project.
  (a) Knowledges.
    (1) Kinds of food of greatest value to children.
    (2) Necessity of fresh air both day and night.
    (3) What happens when teeth are neglected.
    (4) The beauty of clean teeth.
  (b) Skills.
    (1) Brushing teeth correctly.
  (c) Attitudes.
    (1) Desire to be strong, clean, attractive.
    (2) Coöperation, personal responsibility.
5. Puppet theater project.
  (a) Knowledges.
    (1) Stories themselves in their historical setting.
    (2) Many facts about changing narrative material into dramatic form.
    (3) Facts related to the making of a play.
    (4) Historical periods as shown in costume materials and kinds of armor.
    (5) Organization of material.
  (b) Skills.
    (1) Using reference material.
    (2) Manipulation of puppets.
    (3) Stage management.
    (4) Producing pleasing lighting and color effects on stage.
  (c) Attitudes.
    (1) Responsibility.
    (2) Sympathy.
    (3) Coöperation.
    (4) Appreciation of drama and its possibilities for children.
    (5) Pride in their school.
6. Any worth-while dramatization.
  (a) Knowledges.
    (1) Literary material.
    (2) Historical material.
    (3) Setting of drama.
    (4) Structure of drama.
  (b) Skills.
    (1) Planning.
    (2) Impersonation.
    (3) Imagination.
    (4) Execution.
    (5) Judging results.
  (c) Attitudes.
    (1) New interest in material dramatized.
    (2) Keener interest in dramatic art.
    (3) Coöperation.
    (4) Leadership.
    (5) Appreciation of individual ability.
    (6) New confidence, poise, self-respect.
7. Any student council undertaking.
  (a) Knowledges.
    (1) Organization.
    (2) Parliamentary law.
  (b) Skills.
    (1) Conducting a meeting.
  (c) Attitudes.
    (1) A keener appreciation of the need of law.

(2) Coöperation.

(3) Tolerance.

(4) Justice.

8. Spelling should be given when *needed* for written expression.

9. Is the handwriting developed in schools carried over in life?

10. Is handwriting developed in penmanship period used in composition period?

C. The outcome should result in purposes which lead to further activity.

1. Geography project.

(a) Led on to other industrial projects. Children were through this interested to carry out a similar enterprise in the study of coal.

2. Puppet theater project.

(a) Cardboard stage and paper dolls led to more finished production with cloth dolls and horses. Children are planning another play.

3. Does study of home economics lead the child to cook and to sew outside of school?

4. Does the study of music in school lead the child to express himself through good music for pleasure outside of school? Does he choose to listen to good music?

5. Does the study of poetry in school lead to reading of good poetry outside of school?

6. Does study of art lead to use of art principles in dress, in selection of pictures, in house decoration?

7. How many children go of their own volition to visit exhibitions?

II. *Springs to Activity.*

A. The needs and difficulties which give rise to activity should frequently be such as arise in the actual processes of living.

1. Spelling should be given when needed for written language.

(a) Puppet theatre project.

(1) Class needed to know how to spell many new words in putting the story into dramatic form.

2. Arithmetic facts and drill should be given, if possible, when needed to carry out child's undertaking.

(a) Measuring when needed for building.

(b) Addition facts when needed for keeping scores.

(c) Keeping accounts, percentage, simple banking principles when needed in school bank.

3. Stenography drill should be emphasized at points where there has been failure in taking dictation.

4. Music.

(a) Technical points should be stressed when the children feel their limitations in the singing of a particular song; for example:

(1) Key name, rests, note value and time (how adapted to the meaning of the song).

(2) Chorus singing for an audience brings the need for pleasing tone, good ensemble, and careful observance of time.

(3) Need of music for pageants, for seasonal expression (spring, summer, winter, Christmas, Thanksgiving), and for program purposes give rich opportunity for work where there is a "felt need and difficulty" on the part of the children.

5. Art.

(a) Principles of perspective should be given when children are dissatisfied with the results of their effort.

(b) Design should be given when needed for decoration of a particular article which the children want.

(c) Color values should be studied when needed to produce certain desired results.

(1) Example: In planning their stage settings for the puppet theater, lighting, costumes, and equipment for puppet theater, children found they needed to study color and composition in order to get the best arrangement and most pleasing effect.

B. Due consideration should be given to individual differences in:

1. Purposes.

   (a) Industrial training—child should make an article of worth to him or his group.

   (b) Sewing—child should make an article of worth to him or his group.

2. Needs for knowledge and skill.

   (a) Spelling—words needed by the individual should be studied.

   (b) Language—correct forms needed by individual should be drilled upon.

   (c) Physical education—corrective exercises needed by individual should be given.

   (d) Penmanship—individual needs should be considered. Does the child want speed or does he want quality?

3. Inherited capacity.

   (a) Standards of attainment for individual children should be based upon individual ability.

      (1) Example: The best horse in puppet show was made by a girl who stood very low in any abstract part of the work of her class.

C. The mechanical features involved in the plan (nailing shingles, computing, learning number combination) should be so related that when possible no extraneous or artificial incentives are necessary.

1. Examples of such extraneous incentives.

   (a) Stars for spelling or conduct.

   (b) Buttons for health chores.

   (c) Mothers' Club treats (giving special treat to grade which has most mothers present at meetings).

   (d) Prizes for exhibits of school work.

   (e) Devices in phonics, arithmetic, etc.

   (f) Any sugar-coated material.

III. *Economy of Activity.*

A. The purpose should be carried through to an outcome.

1. This has been accomplished when a project is completed and has been judged by the children.

   (a) See Christmas carol program.

   (b) See puppet theater project.

B. All irrelevant facts and attitudes should be excluded or effectively subordinated.

1. In music, literature, art, establish the mood which will tend toward a sympathetic appreciation of the selection studied.

2. Lead children to rule out intelligently all facts which do not bear upon point under consideration.

C. The purpose and outcome (whether satisfying or annoying) should be shared justly by all the members of the group undertaking the enterprise.

1. If a school bank has been started, its success brings honor to the group and its failure brings defeat which must be borne by group.

2. Recognized failure of a dramatization because beyond power of group giving it, or because of insufficient preparation, or because of lack of team work must be shared by group.

D. The purposes involved should be free from conflict with the outside activities of the child.

1. Coming into schoolroom should not mean a break in children's interests. While the outside interests may not be the most worthy interests, the school must recognize these and build upon them, modifying them if that is desirable. Unless it does this, the existing conflict will mean that the school training is likely to break down, since that is the least persistent. The manner of work and conditions under which it is done should as nearly as possible resemble what the child finds outside of school, so that two conflicting sets of habits may not be set up.

IV. *Relation of the Child to His Activities.*

A. The success of the enterprise and the judgment of the values of the outcome are the last steps of the activity. The judgment should be the answer to the question, "Is the original purpose satisfied?"

1. Art—did the design suit the article for which it was planned?

2. Penmanship—where does my writing come on scale?

3. Individual and group graphs showing accomplishment in arithmetic and spelling.
4. Dramatization—are we ready to give it?
5. Have we answered the questions with which we started?
6. Older children should ask, "What have I learned through this undertaking? What mistakes have I made? How may I do better next time?"

(Teacher ought to ask, "Are these pupils growing in their ideals of work? In their standards of accomplishment?")

B. The process and outcome should be satisfying to the individual and to the group or, although in themselves annoying, should be employed as means of satisfaction.

1. Satisfying.
   (a) Geography exercise.
   (b) Letter writing.
   (c) Christmas carol program.
   (d) Puppet theater.

2. Annoying, but employed as means of satisfaction.
   (a) A school bank in the middle of its second year seemed to be failing. Enthusiasm had waned and deposits had fallen off. The members of the class finally called a meeting in which they faced the situation and decided they must either do some very hard work to reëstablish it or give up the project altogether. They decided to do the work although it meant persistent effort in advertising and much after-school work. The bank soon resumed its former place in the school life.

THE PROJECT METHOD IN NORMAL SCHOOLS

I. "How can student teachers be trained to use the project method?"

This topic was chosen for discussion by the normal school group in Education s214B at Columbia University, Summer Session, 1921. The group consisted of representatives from the normal schools of a number of states and Canada. At the close of the session, the following report was made by the Chairman, Dr. H. E. Amoss.[1]

II. Teachers cannot be classed among the pessimistic and faint-hearted. But, as the eye of a careful driver is quick to see rough passages upon a strange road before it becomes aware of smooth stretches, so the first glance of a cautious inquirer is likely to detect dangers, rather than advantages, in any new undertaking. Thus it happened that the attention of the group was first directed to certain obstacles which, under present conditions, appear to block the path of progress.

A. Various difficulties, arising from our present normal school organization, were pointed out:

1. Many teachers connected with training institutions are not familiar with the project method, or, what amounts to the same thing, are not interested in it.

2. Specialization in any academic department tends to overemphasize the teaching of subject matter and to underemphasize the teaching of children, while long-continued schoolroom practice exaggerates the importance of routine detail. Project learning, based as it is upon child purposing, is a reversal of the usual pedagogic perspective since it attempts to look upon life

[1] Dr. Amoss is a member of the faculty of the Normal School in Hamilton, Ontario, Canada.

from the child's point of view rather than from the teacher's. There is a grave danger lest the specialist teacher, concerned with the academic values of her department, and the critic teacher, intent upon the detail of schoolroom management, fail to coöperate in such a way as to make the normal school course itself a project.

3. It takes a man four years to so acquaint himself with the structure and care of thirty-two teeth that he may be in a position to practice dentistry. Is a tooth more difficult to understand than a child? Or should the present two-year normal course be extended?

B. Difficulties arising from the status of students who enter teacher training institutions were also mentioned.

1. These students have had little or no experience with the project method. On the contrary, during their own school careers they have become habituated to other learning processes. They bring no constructive ideas of methods which might be used in the interpretation of school life and in the building up of concepts and skills in the science and art of education; but they do bring an accumulation of false notions which the normal school must clear away in order to obtain a secure foundation for method study.

2. Usually the mental content of these students is in an attic-like state of confusion. Everything is there, but —. This disorganization is the result of teachers having used injective instead of projective methods of instruction. Knowledge has been stowed away, rather than grown in the mind. It is like the street-car tickets in a woman's hand bag; and until this knowledge has been reordered into a handy, *get-at-able* form, the student-teacher cannot use it in her classroom work. The "vicious circle" argument, that these students are the product of normal school trained teachers, might here be advanced. Defense is not offered. No stronger evidence for the necessity of a change in normal methods could be brought forward.

3. A lack of executive ability among the girls entering our training institutions is quite apparent. Their previous school education has been a passive process; and the spirit of enterprise that a system of purposing, planning, executing, and judging should have developed is not present. The fact that, as a result of an out-of-school education in the field of sports, in church or other social organizations, some of these students display an ability to handle situations, goes to show what might have been accomplished under other school conditions and points out the course which must be pursued in the normal school, if these students are to be fitted for the responsibilities of the teaching profession.

4. Girls entering normal school at the age of eighteen or nineteen have a mental set away from the things of childhood. A natural desire to appear mature in action, speech, thought, dress, etc. — however much that wish may be reversed in later years — puts them in an unsympathetic attitude toward the workings of the child mind. No age is so remote from youth as the age just beyond. But since project method is a view of education from the child's standpoint, the student-teacher must be trained to reappreciate her recently abandoned outlook.

III. The above mentioned difficulties were discussed in the light of actual happenings and conditions experienced by the various members of the group; and the following recommendations *re* normal school organization were made:

1. Supporters of the project method must do evangelical work among their fellow teachers.

2. But propaganda in itself is not sufficient. Interest and enthusiasm may thus be aroused, but to become effective that interest must be directed along proper channels. The project method is a scientific process, founded upon scientific bases, and requiring scientific study. One of the greatest obstacles to the spread of this new idea is the practice of certain pseudo project methods which, founded upon a misconception, or a lack of conception, of the true nature of the process inevitably end in failure and cast discredit upon that which has been imitated.

Possibly the most practical way of harnessing the interest created by propaganda would be through the establishment of night schools, in which both normal and city teachers would associate for the purpose of increasing their professional efficiency. The good teacher is always a student, and little difficulty should be encountered in securing the coöperation of the best teachers in any community. The teacher who is not interested in the improvement of her professional status will never be able to handle the project method anyway, since only she who has the student's mind can look upon education from the learner's point of view. To increase the effectiveness of the course, and to hold out material benefits as an additional incentive to enrollment, these night schools should be associated with the extramural courses conducted by Teachers College, New York, and other institutions in which university credits may be obtained.

3. Only by making the normal school course itself a project, in which specialist teacher, critic teacher, and student alike participate, can the closest coöperation of all concerned be secured. As long as the science specialist is chiefly concerned with methods of teaching science, the English specialist with methods of teaching language, and the mathematical specialist with methods of teaching arithmetic, no one is going to be much concerned with methods of teaching children. But when the study of child training becomes the project purpose of the normal course, the efforts of the various method teachers can coördinate toward one end.

Indeed, the problem of the overcrowded curriculum, which is such a source of worry to many teachers, may in this way be largely overcome before it is confronted. No one ever heard of a fisherman's kicking because he had too much tackle; or of a golfer's objecting to an extra supply of sticks and balls; or of a carpenter's growling because he owned too many saws and chisels and bits. And when the graduates of our normal schools shall have been taught to look upon subject matter as an equipment of tools to be used in the training of children, no sensible teacher will be found objecting to the number and variety of instruments placed at her disposal.

4. The present two-year normal course should be extended another year.

As teaching becomes more and more a matter of child training, and less and less a matter of giving instruction, the need for increased professional education arises. So long as the "schoolmarm" taught arithmetic, grammar, geography, etc., an academic knowledge of these subjects, together with a birch rod, was her chief stock-in-trade. But when it becomes her business to teach children, she requires, in addition to this academic knowledge, a comprehension of child psychology, a wide and cultured acquaintance with life, and a thorough grasp of those pedagogical methods whereby the growing child is adjusted to life. In place of a birch rod she must have a familiar sympathy with youthful reactions, and this cannot be picked up in the woods, after a minute's search.

IV. The group next considered the best way of introducing the student-teacher to the project method. Four possible means — practice-teaching, observation, the study of theory, and actual participation — were discussed.

1. Practice-teaching as a first step is out of the question. One cannot practice the unknown. Besides, the welfare of the model-school children must receive consideration.

2. Observation is valueless without a body of interpretative experience to direct attention and enable judgment of results. We get out of an observation only what we see into it. The majority of students entering the normal school are not familiar with the project method of learning, and cannot profit from demonstration lessons during the opening weeks of the term.

3. Theory is an abstract study. An abstract idea can only be gained by a process of induction from a number of particular experiences. A general truth cannot be taught or learned as a thing in itself, apart from the concrete elements out of which it was derived. As the teacher can neither vicariously think nor experience for her students, a study of the theory of project method, before actual experience with the workings of the method, would resolve itself into a study of words.

4. By a process of elimination, it would appear that students entering the normal school must become acquainted with the project method by means of actual participation.

5. Until this method shall have become the recognized and standard mode of learning in our grade and high schools, the first term of the present two-year course — or a longer period in the proposed three-year course — should be devoted to a reorganization of the senior work of the grade school, by means of project study. Such a course should result in:

(a) A richer, better ordered, and more efficient mental content.

(b) The formation of a body of project-method experiences which may function in the interpretation of subsequent observation lessons, and which may form the concrete bases for the future study of abstract theory.

(c) An increased executive control.

V. A sketch, suggesting the possibilities of conducting the normal course by this method upon a project basis, was outlined by the group:

1. The study of theory could begin during the last few weeks of the first

term by an analysis of the students' own project work as mentioned in section IV.

2. After the students had thus secured a fund of interpretative ideas, observation classes could commence at the beginning of the second term of the junior year. These classes would serve a three-fold purpose:

(a) They might be used as laboratories in which data for theory work could be collected, or in which hypotheses arrived at in the theory classes could be tried out. It will be noticed that the first use supposes:

(1) A prediscussion in which some problem has been evolved and clearly stated, and the data to be collected has been ascertained.

(2) A post discussion, during which the data obtained will be used in the solution of the problem under consideration.

The second use recognizes the fact that theory must not only be derived from experience, but that it must also be applicable to experience. Frequently teachers in training and even teachers in practice have difficulty in seeing how theoretical conclusions can be used under actual schoolroom conditions. The horse refuses to back between the shafts of the vehicle. It is the duty of the normal school to acquaint the girls with Mr. Theory in his overalls as well as in his dress suit. The observation period affords an excellent opportunity of again meeting the refined gentleman to whom they were introduced in the lecture hall. This time, however, they will see him in everyday working attire. By using the observation classes in this fashion, the chief aspects of child psychology, laws of learning, school man-

agement, and other phases of the theory course can be analyzed, developed, and tested.

(b) Observation lessons may also be used to synthesize the various elements which have been separately studied into a complete project unit. The machine having been taken apart and examined in detail, the next step is to put it together and see how it runs. This phase of work might begin with the study of simple projects, preferably those completed during one lesson period. More complex and lengthy projects could then be studied in different grades by sets of observation series in which the purpose of each project could be followed from its inception throughout a number of lessons. A score or question card, such as the one submitted, would now aid the student in getting a general grasp of technique.

OBSERVATION SCORE CARD

A. *For Junior and Senior Students.*

1. What was the purpose of the class?
2. How was this purpose made clear to every pupil?
3. How was the undertaking planned?
4. Describe the progressive stages of its execution.
5. What judgments were made by pupils and how were these supported?
6. How was the lesson content organized and each important thing emphasized?
7. What social ideals and habits were being developed?
8. What new "leads" for project work arose? How were these utilized?

B. *For Senior Students Only.*

1. How was the class purpose initiated?
2. What were the purposes of the teacher?
3. What material evidence of preparation on the part of the teacher did you notice?
4. What assistance did the teacher render by question or suggestion?

5. How was participation distributed among the pupils?
6. What evidences of interest and satisfaction did you observe?
7. How were problems of discipline handled?
8. How was the physical welfare of the pupils looked after?

During the second term of the junior year a limited amount of "free teaching," in which the student would act as an assistant to the critic teacher, or take charge of small groups, would help to acclimatize her to the teaching atmosphere. Regular practice teaching would commence at the beginning of the senior year, after the student has acquired a fair working of the principles and technique of the project method. Simple projects should first be undertaken, these to be followed by several series of practice lessons, in each of which a more complex project would be initiated and developed. And here the third use of observation lessons comes in. Each practice series should be preceded by observation in the room where the student is to teach, in order that she may become acquainted with the children and the conditions under which she is to work. The student cannot be saved from making blunders. Even if that were possible, she should not. Blunders are instructive. But frequent conferences with method and critic teacher, during the progress of her practice, will prevent the student from habituating herself to certain blundering methods, and will assist her in putting into practice the principles of education which she has been studying.

During the first half of the second-year term, wherever arrangements can be made, there should be cadet teaching for a period of from five to eight weeks, under the partial supervision of the normal instructors, in other schools where good project work is being done. This is to give the young teacher a sense of power and responsibility — teaching her to swim in deep water, as it were. Then the last ten weeks of the normal course, following this period of cadet experience, should be devoted to a discussion of the difficulties encountered, and to a general rounding up of the teaching idea.

1pm-5p

Thur
Mon.

24 Hour
1pm-5t

Vac 24 Hol
1pm-5, 34
1pm-5t
Thur
Mon

8am-3
8am (ss
8am
8am

review and
mmary

METHOD AND CURRICULUM

(*Concluded*) [1]

WILLIAM HEARD KILPATRICK

Professor of Education, Teachers College, Columbia University

In the first half of the article appearg a month ago three questions were proposed for discussion: What is the problem of method? What is the ‘oblem of the curriculum? What is the _ _lation of method to the curriculum? It was there brought out that tradition, assuming a certain attitude in the matter, has reduced these questions to two, putting them in a form better suited to its ideas: What do we wish these children to learn? How shall we make them learn what we decide is desirable? And tradition has gone on to answer its questions substantially as follows: List the learning needed by the adult and organize this logically into subjects; require the children to learn this subject matter, having arranged it for learning in the order of logical simplicity. Originally, tradition identified learning practically with rote memorizing, and relied chiefly on fear to secure it. For a good many years both rote memorizing and the motivation of fear have been receding into the background; but latterly more radical objections have appeared to this traditional answer. Learning, it now appears, does not go on best with bare, logically simple elements. Again, learning never appears singly, but a host of learnings simultaneously attend any activity in which the child is engaged. Assigning things to be learned becomes thus at all times complex and often self-contradictory. Moreover, many valuable traits cannot be assigned at all for coercive learning, as for example we cannot require the child to acquire an appreciation of a poem. And finally, to teach only adult-needed traits both degrades the child's present life and violates the best conditions of learning.

Having seen thus the breakdown of the traditional answer to our three original questions, we then took up for closer analysis the first of these: What is the problem of method? A distinction of two problems was evident. First, the abstracted problem of method, — how the child best learns spelling, for example. Second, the wider problem of method, — how shall we manage our pupils, seeing that willy-nilly a multitude of learnings are going on at once? This variety of learnings was on examination seen to be the result of multitudinous respondings to the manifold stimulations of the environment. In this James's distinction of focal and marginal attention was found useful, attitudes and ideals being mainly built on marginal responses. Finally, the marginal responses (to their correlative stimuli) were for closer study divided into three groups according to the nearness of their stimuli to the focal stimulus. Most immediate were the

[1] The concluding half of an address made before the National Conference on Educational Method in Chicago, March 1, 1922. All rights reserved by the author.

tone and manner of teacher and fellow pupils and the like. These were found to work potently, affecting at times seriously the focal interest, and helping besides to build attitudes, good or bad, toward subject, teacher, school, and the like. Less immediate but not less important was the stimulation of the general school management as it did or did not satisfy the "natural" cravings of childhood. This we thought went to make a "set" or attitude which determined, for the adolescent at any rate, almost everything else about the school.

This marks the close of last month's discussion.

The still remoter stimulation process is hard to analyze out of the total situation. The most signifi-**Remoter marginal stimulation** cant factor that I can find seems to pertain to a general feeling or attitude that there is or is not a way open ahead for certain kinds of expression. The slave held from infancy in the hopeless and helpless grasp of the master-slave **Master and slave** situation builds gradually an attitude of no stimulus-response activity along the lines of certain independent choice and self-reliant experiences which you and I take as matters of course in our present American democracy. Certain avenues of expression being consistently and effectually denied him, the slave thus comes by the laws of learning to feel practically no stimulation toward them. This no-outlook, no-thoroughfare attitude to be effective needs, of course, to be well built, and to this end great care was exercised in the days of American slavery to keep out any suggestion of a possible change of status.

As cruel as such a denial of hope may seem to us of today, we need not attribute cruelty to the immediate personal treatment involved. In fact the contrary was better psychology; a happy animal contentment — with the lash in the background only as a last resort — was as a rule the most successful procedure for building the unquestioning acceptance necessary to the perpetuation of the institution. Certainty and consistency of satisfaction and annoyance here as elsewhere mark the high road to completest learning.

If a certain situation made the slave, its obverse formed the master. As there were certain directions in **Forming the master** which the slave might not look forward, so contrariwise in exactly these directions the prospective master might and should look ahead. The same régime that built servility and subservience on the one hand, built *pari passu* a spirit of dominance and assured importance on the other. For building two such contrasted outlooks the evident and abiding difference of color was in this particular instance an indubitable asset. Note again the focal and marginal psychology of the situation. While master and slave did, true enough, apply themselves focally to different objects of endeavor and these differences did, to be sure, play their respective parts, still it was the attendant marginal responses that most made the different attitudes. To labor in a cotton field is not inherently degrading, but to labor there consciously as a slave with a servile acceptance of imposed labor is in time to degrade one to the status of a mental and moral slave.

We cannot here too much emphasize the operations of the laws of learning on original tendencies. In the instance just under consideration, each human is born with both mastery and submission potentialities. How these will find outlook depends on the action of the environment, which will encourage mastery here and submission there, fixing each as an almost irresistible habit if consistency of satisfaction and annoyance attend. Such a consistency for the young is most surely attained where uniformity of custom controls the elders. In this sense and manner custom comes easily to be self-perpetuating. If this is to be, custom must begin its selective and fixating work from earliest infancy, and this is exactly what any customary régime will do. The power of a consistently closed outlook ahead to register itself indelibly in the character is all but incredible. The pike which learned from consistent failure that they could not catch the minnows sheltered behind the glass partition well illustrate the point. Once the lesson was thoroughly learned, the minnows were safe even though the partition was removed and the minnows swam freely among the pike. We may by an Æsopian stretch imagine the amazement of a differently trained pike at the self-denying conduct of his minnow-shunning fellows, so different would his tendencies be from theirs. So with any who would judge the products of another régime. Understanding is all but impossible. The slave was largely happy and largely content. Custom fixed his marginal responses in prearranged grooves.

How custom builds attitude

The effect of custom in moulding the respective characters of master and slave is but one of many analogous instances, this being clearer cut perhaps than most, but psychologically one with what is going on everywhere all the time. Always we have had the rich and the poor, with their different outlooks on life. But in a country of abounding opportunities, there are doors open ahead. To be born poor in America is not necessarily final. Hope is not so ruthlessly denied and cast down when it first lifts its head. Eventually, however, for many who find themselves hopelessly enmeshed, poverty gets in its work in appropriate attitudes. A recent writer says in protest that "the worst of poverty is the docility it creates." That our long-standing labor and capital controversy has built relatively permanent attitudes of antagonism out of contrasting marginal responses is but too true. In like manner certain abiding church and national antagonisms illustrate the same point. Wherever any relatively self-contained groups say "our" in any inclusive and exclusive sense, the same thing will appear. The general custom will build that attitude in their young. Any widespread factor that produces a widespread general feeling will inevitably build its correlative attitudes. The threat of Germany has undoubtedly affected the French character, as has for centuries the island situation of Great Britain affected its inhabitants. A common cause of pride will build a correlative common character. Europeans have no difficulty in believing that the size, abundant resources, and material

Further instances of custom-built attitudes

success of this country have registered themselves in the characters of American tourists. Some Americans think the consciousness of the size of Texas has built itself into the character of Texans.

The purpose of all this study of marginal responses is to throw light on the effect of "method." Perhaps not all marginal stimulations are to be included under the head of method. Certainly, however, many such stimulations do belong there. We can practically count that method is the determinant of the open or closed outlet ahead. The character-building effect of method along this line was clearly seen in the case of master and slave. But we need not go so far away. Every woman in this audience can testify to an analogous effect in the contrasted avenues even yet open to boys and girls. The "well-brought-up" girl has, in the past at least, been made to feel almost from her earliest recollection that certain courses open to boys are not open to her. This method of treatment has had profound effect. If the girl acquiesced inwardly as well as outwardly she built one type of character as concerns herself in those matters and their ramifications. If she inwardly rebelled — outwardly conforming as she must — she built a different character. In either event she built a different character from her brother's. I am not now weighing either to praise or to blame. I am but illustrating my point. That this difference of treatment is in some respects passing presents this generation with one of its serious problems. The method effect is correlatively changing. Passing along the street I

Method of treatment the significant factor

heard a young woman say, "If my brother can go to such places I don't see why I cannot, and I am going." Whatever else we may think, we seem bound to conclude that the marginal responses attending this decision were building for this young woman a type of character not hitherto acceptable.

The general character effect of the open or closed outlook upon life is illustrated to me by my own experiences as a boy growing up in the South during and after the devastating days of Reconstruction. Everywhere was decay. Plenty and happiness seemed alike to lie in the irrevocable past. The future promised but little. A leading statesman said in stated words, "The sun sets each day on a poorer South." What to do, what to try to do were baffling questions. Hopelessness lay like a pall over everything. The depressing character effects were but too evident.

Character effect of a general outlook

That the historic régimes have builded their requisite character attitudes on this basis of selecting and fixing marginal responses seems beyond · question. So Sparta built the character of her own sons and the correlative characters of Helots and Periœci. What contrasted marginal responses must have attended those murderous expeditions in which the youthful Spartans practiced war on the Periœci in order to reduce their numbers to a more comfortable basis! What, too, must have been the effect on Spartan maidens as they applauded the youth who could bear scourging even to death at the altar of the goddess! In our own

Historic régimes have so built attitudes

country the "old time darkey" out-lived by some decades his "haughty" master, but at length followed him into the grave whither the fashioning "system" had already gone. In Europe the remains of feudalism are still evident in surviving character attitudes, though the Great War seems to have shaken the moulding customs. In our modern industrialism contending tendencies struggle for mastery. There are those who would still use the marginal responses to ensure subserviency. One of my students acting last year as a foreman at a coal mine was told, "Don't explain to the men what they are about, they will get the attitude of asking why."

Often in the past method has done its work with a minimum of conscious devising. It leads itself, however, to conscious construction in order to fashion the youth to the needs of society. An acute student of contemporary China[1] has reached the conclusion that modernization for his country can best come by building attitudes in the youth correlative with endeavor and open avenues ahead. He gets his educational clue from frontier life in America and its daring resourcefulness, and seeks to introduce self-relying endeavor and enterprise as the principal element in his educative procedure, relying thus mainly on the attendant marginal responses to build the needed modern character. In like manner we who believe in democracy must ask ourselves what attitudes are needed, and must see consciously that our educational régime supplies the needed

Method in the service of society

stimulation on the one hand and opportunities on the other. This problem of method is then exactly the correlative of the problem of civilization with all its needs and all its complexities. Knowing all such, we who guide the youth of our land must study and guide discerningly. Everything that by its stimulation enters through experience into character must receive its due consideration. The wider problem of method is exactly the problem of what these stimuli are and how they act. In these now, as in all historic times, have characters been built. What citizenship we are to have will depend on the manifold stimulation our youth receive.

It thus appears that we confront a far subtler study of both curriculum and method than most have hitherto conceived. The counting of geographical allusions and the psychology of spelling are good and desirable, but in themselves and apart from their promise as methods of attack they are in comparison but the tithing of mint and cumin. The weightier matters are, to be sure, far more difficult to control, but difficult though they be, they must be undertaken. And I for one must find these weightier matters on the one hand in the desired character of our civilization and, on the other, in the characteristics needed to bring such a state of society. Among these needed characteristics are information and skill, yes; but of far greater importance are knowledge and habits and ideals and attitudes. Many if not most of these will come to our youth only as we utilize more adequately the resources of a wider

A new study of method and curriculum

[1] P. C. Chang, of Nankai College, Tientsin, China.

conception of method. And chiefest in this conception I am inclined now to place the marginal responses that attend our more explicit efforts.

As an illustration of desired multiform outcomes I should like to present an analysis I have made **A list of simultaneous outcomes** from a consideration of Mr. Hatch's junior high school class studying the Irish question. His plan contemplated that the pupils should investigate faithfully and weigh carefully the important alternative policies confronting England (in 1920) in the matter of Ireland. The pupils themselves had selected this as their project. What outcomes could he reasonably wish in and from this activity? To save time I shall merely list a number of these in order: (1) a considerable knowledge of the history and politics of England and Ireland; (2) a better knowledge and skill of how to investigate such a problem, how to analyze it, how to use sources, etc.; (3) increased ability to think in this field, individually and collectively to weigh argument and evidence; (4) growth in such traits as open-mindedness, tolerance, the belief that opinions should be based on evidence; (5) progress in gaining certain useful social *concepts* as absentee landlordism, in such social *ideals* as the orderly processes of settling national disputes, in such social *attitudes* as an appreciation of the worth of institutions; (6) the building more or less definitely of certain positive intellectual interests in history and politics, an interest in the Irish question, in English and Irish history, in European history, in history in general; (7) building an attitude of respect for such intellectual

concerns. These are but the more outstanding of the possible outcomes.

To comment adequately on this list would unduly extend this paper, but some things I must point **Valuation of these outcomes** out. Conventional history teaching seems content to seek consciously only the first item of this list, a knowledge — often only information — of the history and politics involved. Whether the conventional chapter assignment and recitation method can give a real knowledge of even this much is to my mind most questionable. Learning properly means a different kind of appropriation. Mr. Hatch got — as tested by a conventional examination — not only what others get, but he got much more, namely, more or less of what I have above outlined. That such attendant learnings, if got, are of great worth is beyond question. That such learning comes from the attendant marginal responses seems almost equally certain. Back of the needed responses and consequently back of this desirable attendant learning is the wise use of method. Mr. Hatch knew *how* to elicit and direct real activity on the part of his pupils. He had faced and solved in gratifying degree the wider problem of method.

But little time is left to discuss the two remaining questions. The ideas regarding the curriculum to **The curriculum** which I now invite your attention stand in my own mind on a somewhat different footing from those presented above regarding method. The main positions taken above in the matter of method seem to me unassailable. What I have to say, however, about the curriculum is rather a sketch made for consideration, plausible perhaps in some respects and desirable from some points of view, but not yet in the state where it can demand acceptance.

The basis on which I would found the curriculum and curriculum making is growing, on the part of the child and of the teacher. I should like to admit into the curriculum no deferred values, and to have subject matter viewed and valued primarily as means for growing. To these ends I propose this criterion for testing the curriculum: Do I see that this child is this week living a richer life because of what I taught him last week? Do I believe that I am this week so guiding the child's education that he will on that account grow best into richer living next week? Such a week by week criterion might for younger children be a day by day affair and for older children might well contemplate a longer stretch; but the test would still be whether my teaching results in positive continuous enrichment. Such an enrichment demands closer analysis: I seem to see in it continually increasing sensitivities to the possibilities of the several situations as they confront the growing children, and continually increasing control by the children over the resulting experiences. In order that there may be such continuous growing from early infancy to the end of life, the teacher will during school days have to know the valuable things that the race has found out in order to guide the process in most fruitful fashion. As the child grows toward what we call adulthood, he must increasingly take over his own guidance, but the need for subject matter will still remain to furnish both a basis for guidance and the means whereby each present experience may as such proceed and may at the same time undergo, under guidance, reconstruction into something higher.

To accomplish such would require, as I now see it, a printed course of study arranged perhaps in some **The course of study** such fashion as this: first, a clear and emphatic statement calling attention to growing as the end and demanding the strict subordination of all subject matter thereto; second, a suggestive list of traits found by competent judges to have been useful in the past for growing, primarily concerned with better ways of behaving, and emphatically not to be "taught" except in such manner and at such time as promise to meet the criterion laid down in the preceding paragraph; third, a detailed description of typical activities that in the judgment of competent critics had under other conditions resulted in desired growing, significant factors being so pointed out as to promise suggestions for teachers; fourth, a list of many more activities that might be used, with appropriate reference materials in the way of books, pictures, etc.; fifth, some typical results that have been achieved so presented as to afford a basis for testing progress, keeping always in mind that it is signs of future growth that most concern us.

How such a course of study would be used leads us, then, to the last question as to the relation of **Method and curriculum** method to the curriculum, and again I speak tentatively, rather to stimulate enquiry than to present a matured judgment. The conception of method applies differently to child and to teacher. The child's method is how best to dispose himself, his resources, the means at hand, to attaining his end in view. As he grows older the further question of how to choose ends to pursue should receive increasing attention. These two aspects of child method are in my rather firm judgment best cared for under the conception of purposeful activity, which I need not here discuss. The teacher's method is strictly correlative with the child's: how to stimulate and guide the child's activity that growing may best ensue. The actual process seems to involve some such steps as these:

First, the teacher being (along with the child) the ultimate curriculum maker and keeping in mind the principles of the course of study as sketched above, will stimulate the children to activity. The degree of definiteness with which the teacher will select in advance the desired activity will vary with many circumstances. Second, the children will respond and variously. Some proffered responses may lie beyond the bounds of acceptability; these will be rejected. Among all, some one or more will be accepted as promising growth. These will be watched and guided as may be necessary, particular attention being given to the marginal responses. This activity, if successful, will mean that the children are living here and now actually and vigorously, that they are using subject matter in the pursuit of the ends in view, that they are accordingly getting a firmer grasp on this subject matter (as skills, ideas, knowledge, etc.), that they have made progress in forming healthy and useful ideals and attitudes, and that they are by reason of all this better disposed and equipped for further fruitful activities. Third, after the activity the teacher will check up in some fashion the progress made by the children. In this will be rated the significant factors that brought or impeded the children's growth, with suggestions for improvements next time.

The final word is the conclusion that the conventional conceptions of both subject matter (curriculum) and method are pitiably inadequate. Subject matter seems best conceived as the basis of and means to successful activities and is to be strictly subordinated to actual growing. In different terms, subject matter consists of better ways of behaving here and now with reference, however, always to still better and more adequate ways further ahead. And method, the teacher's method, is at bottom a matter of so caring for the manifold stimulations that come to the child as to secure from him the best total of responses, focal and marginal. Anything less is a pitiable and tragic blunder; if persisted in, worse than a blunder — a crime.

Conclusion

AN EXPERIMENT IN COÖPERATION
IX. Spelling

JAMES F. HOSIC

Associate Professor of Education, Teachers College, Columbia University

As has been explained in the section on the mechanics of writing, the English centers organized special committees for the attack on spelling. We sought, however, to avoid the inference that spelling is a separate study, to be pursued for its own sake, and talked of it always as merely one aspect of written work. We assumed that spelling must be taught and not left to incidental treatment, and we believed that it might be handled with far more satisfactory results than have commonly been obtained.

DEFINING THE AIMS

Spelling has suffered in company with the other elementary school subjects from indefiniteness of aim. Tradition dictates that children shall learn to spell all the words they meet or are likely to meet. It even goes so far as to declare that the main object of the work in spelling lessons is to increase the vocabulary of the pupils. Numbered in our own ranks were some who held to this view. Many a year elapses before the discoveries of the leaders in the van of educational progress are reported to the rank and file of the army and are accepted as displacing settled beliefs and practices. If some of the scientific investigators were to find out how little impression the publication of their new ideas has actually made on the great mass of the teachers of the country, their enthusiasm would be considerably dampened. For the good of the cause it is probably best that they should never know.

Our first step, then, was to debate the question, "What do we teach spelling for?" The answer took form somewhat as follows: "The work in this field should be so directed that the pupils shall always spell correctly the words they write." We have, it was pointed out, no less than four vocabularies: the words we understand when we hear them spoken, the words we ourselves speak, the words we can read, and the words we write. Many words are, of course, common to the four, but there is much variation, and a sound policy demands that practice in spelling be aimed at mastery of the graphic form of the words to be written rather than those merely to be heard or read. That most of the oral vocabulary should be available for writing is obvious.

That perfect spelling requires more than knowledge and skill should be equally evident. Carelessness and inattention are in large measure responsible for bad spelling and hence the learner must develop a "spelling conscience," he must *aspire* to spell correctly. And what is more, he must be able to realize his aspirations. He must know how to master new words and have the habit of doing so and not of taking chances. Our aims, therefore, were made to include the setting up of ideals of methods and of mastery as well as the specific skills required from grade to grade. It will be seen that these aims were at once broader and more immediate than those which have for a long time been cherished.

STANDARDS OF THE COURSE

The schools had a spelling book, compiled by a committee, and supplemented by certain drill lists. They had a so-called course also, which directed that a certain number of words be taught in each grade. As usual the course and the book did not agree — though both were made in the city by members of the same system. The course left the choice of words to the teacher, prescribing only that they be those "used in the grade." It left to inference the fact that other words might be necessary. The book contained more than 6,000 words, many obviously taken from textbooks in use and including terms which curiously enough were not supposed to be stressed in the subjects concerned. Formal grammar, for example, had been largely eliminated, but its terms might still be seen in the spelling museum. A new list of words had been provided, but its exact status was uncertain, and in any case its derivation was unknown.

The total situation lent itself admirably to a new deal. Accordingly each teacher was asked to contribute as much as she could to our knowledge of what words the children of each grade must needs learn to spell. If she had kept lists, these should now be checked up and a new inventory made. She would also learn what she could as to the relative difficulty of words and how far her teaching of spelling must be an individual matter. Presently she would be asked to report her findings to a committee in charge of the spelling problem of her school. Thus we started with the individual teacher, working with individual children, in an individual school, and were resolved to choose as common material and set up as common standards only what we found by our investigation to be common. What is more, we assumed that spelling will be largely an individual matter for each child, each class, and each school to the end of the chapter. Human nature, we thought, had settled that matter once for all and in advance.

How, then, would the teacher know when her pupils were doing well or ill in spelling? By their deeds! If at least seventy-five per cent of the children spelled correctly all the words they wrote, wherever and whenever they wrote them, she could say that she had scored. But she must find a way to avoid the learner's restricting his choice of words to those he could surely spell. She must anticipate his needs and encourage him to new conquests, not foster in him a timid avoidance of new words.

As a means of comparison and checking up she would do well to consult the various lists of common words available, especially any which were scaled by grades; she would remember that the spelling "demons" are found for the most part among the earliest acquired speaking vocabulary; and she would regard technical terms as "subject words," to be learned, if at all, in the connection in which they were used. Especially were the teachers of the early grades, up to and including the fifth, made to realize that a child's spelling vocabulary is mainly acquired in those years. Nearly all of the "demons" are freely used there.

THE QUESTION OF METHOD

The rank and file of a teaching corps find it difficult to keep up with the published results of educational experience. We were not surprised when it appeared that most of our helpers required guidance in working out new methods in spelling. As Thorndike aided us in reading and Sheridan and Mahoney in composition, so Tidyman, supported by Suzzallo, Horn, Pryor and others, aided us in spelling. Each teacher was asked to read Tidyman's *The Teaching of Spelling*, ponder, and inwardly digest, then try out his ideas as best she might. Meanwhile, each spelling committee was encouraged to undertake to compile a body of suggestions on method for the school which it represented. As in the matter of mechanics, no effort was made to dictate the policy of any committee and variations were welcomed. What proved to be common to all could afterward be commended to the city.

The presentation of these reports, first to the teachers of a school and then to the principals of the district, proved to be a very salutary and impressive experience. All met on a common ground of professional interest and the discussions were hearty, direct, and stimulating. No better example of genuine democratization of the school group could be wished. A gratifying tendency to give teachers throughout the city a larger share in developing educational policies was, moreover, clearly evident.

A sample report, prepared by teachers in the Doolittle School, is as follows:

REPORT OF THE COMMITTEE ON SPELLING

The Committee on Spelling collected the words contained in the recommended list as follows:

The teachers in each grade collected from the written compositions of their pupils the words commonly misspelled. A word was said to be commonly misspelled if 25% of the children wrote it incorrectly. Each teacher sent her list to the grade chairman. The chairman eliminated duplicates, starring them as "demons" if they appeared on each list. The chairmen of the various grades met and, beginning with the first grade, read their lists in turn, the grades above the reader drawing a line through any word which appeared on their respective lists. The result was that the word repeated in various grades was placed in the grade in which it first appeared as a difficulty. A separate list has been made of these "demons" since they must be attacked by every grade at present until a more systematic study of spelling shall have conquered them where they should be conquered — below the fifth grade.

The committee has not included words peculiar to the various subjects of the Course of Study, but recommends that each room make subject lists of words persistently misspelled and that these be mastered in connection with the subject.

The committee checked the lists for common words omitted by using the "Report of the Committee on Economy of Time." It was found that very few words had to be inserted.

Obviously a list prepared in this experimental way is not a finished list but will be added to constantly. The committee believes, however, that the list submitted for each grade may be reasonably required as a minimum to be achieved with perfection by 75% of the pupils in each grade. It is expected that the "demons" will be mastered in every grade in which they first appear.

TEACHING OF SPELLING

The committee recommends the following method of procedure: The class

> Sees the word.
> Hears the word.

Pronounces the word.
Examines the word.
Spells the word.
Writes the word.

1. The teacher writes the word on the board, pronounces it, spells it, and uses it in a sentence.

2. The class pronounces and spells the word. Individuals pronounce, spell, and use it in sentences.

3. The class examines the word for familiar parts, if there are any. The teacher calls attention to peculiarities of the word, e.g., silent letters, the letter frequently omitted, the syllable carelessly pronounced, the root, prefix, etc.

4. The class spells the word; individuals spell it. The word is erased. 4 is repeated.

5. After each word has been treated as above, the teacher dictates the words studied.

The committee recommends the following device for discovering which words need special stress, and for recording the progress of the class. The plan is taken from Tidyman's *The Teaching of Spelling.*

Each Friday a list of words equal to the number which will be taught during the following week is dictated without preparation by the pupils, and the number of errors recorded. The words are then taught two, three, or five words a day, according to the grade, and the result of each day's lesson is recorded. On Friday there is a general review. One week from that time the same words are dictated without special preparation, to see how many of the words need further emphasis. The following second grade record sheet may be taken as a typical example of how the plan works out.

Points of Advice in the Teaching of Spelling:

1. Teach first; test last.

2. Teach a limited number of new words daily — in no grade more than five. (Suggestion: 1st grade, one word; 2nd grade, two words; 3rd grade, three words; 4th, 5th, 6th, 7th, and 8th, five words.)

3. Review frequently.

4. Insist on careful enunciation of words. *February, especially, recognize, surprised* and *would have* are generally misspelled because they are pronounced *Febuary, expecially, reconized, suprised* and *would of.*

5. See that every word is used in a sentence; written in a sentence from third grade up, besides being given orally.

6. Go through the class compositions occasionally to replenish the room list. If a word is missed by 25% of the pupils, it should be on the room list.

7. Conquer the "demons."

8. Encourage the children to use, independently as far as possible, in their study time the methods used by the teacher, in order to master their individual lists.

9. Make sure that each child knows how to form his letters properly. *Note.* — Many children misspell because they have not mastered the mechanics of joining letters properly. Typical errors: *loy* for *boy, cone* for *come, bisiness* for *business, usial* for *usual.*

10. Teach *two* and *too* with other words but not in the same lesson, e.g. too much, two boys.

What to Avoid in the Teaching of Spelling.

1. Teaching homonyms in the same lesson. *Piece* and *peace* are best taught as independent facts.

GRADE 2B	Preliminary test, Friday March 19	Mon.,	Tues.,	Wed.,	Thur.,	Fri.,	Review test Fri., April 2
Number present	23	24	25	23	26	26	26
1. late	19	2	..	..	..	..	2
2. sing	9	0	..	..	..	..	1
3. name	16	..	⌃	..	..	..	⌃
4. school	1	..	⌄	..	..	..	⌄
5. today	3	..	..	2	..	..	⌄
6. little	2	..	..	0	..	..	⌃
7. sky	11	..	..	..	0	..	2
8. pretty	17	..	..	..	2	..	3
9. take	7	.	..	..	..	0	3
10. best	10	..	..	..	..	0	1

2. Teaching words not used by children of the grade.

3. Teaching words already known by 90% of the children.

4. Teaching too many words in a lesson.

5. Writing wrong form on the board.

6. Mechanical repetition without attention. Hence, giving a list to be written over and over again for "busy" work or for punishment is to be avoided.

Suggested Devices to Improve Spelling.

1. Spelling matches. Friendly emulation between rooms.

2. Class lists (words missed by 25% of the pupils).

3. Individual or "Never Again" lists.

4. Find words within words.

5. Notice that there is not a single word in which *q* is not followed by *u*.

6. Learn — *I* before *E* except after *C*,
      or when sounded as *A*
      As in *neighbor* or *weigh*.

7. Give children practice in arranging words beginning with the same letter, in strict alphabetical order (a short list for each assignment).

List of "Demons"

about	built
afraid	buried
again	business
allow	busy
all right	buy
almost	
already	catch
always	caught
among	choose
another	chose
answer	coming
any	could
around	cried
asked	
	does
because	dollar
before	done
beginning	
believe	early
blew	easy
breakfast	easily
brought	eight
build	either

enough	quiet
evening	quite
every	receive
except	
'	should
father	shining
February	stopped
first	straight
fourth	such
forty	sure
friend	surprise
frighten	
	than
girl	their
goes	then
great	there
	these
have	themselves
heard	thought
here	to
	together
its	two
	toward
just	truly
	too
kept	
knew	until
know	used to
lose	very
	was
making	weather
many	were
minute	where
much	whether
	which
off	while
often	whole
once	women
only	would
one	write
	wrong
paid	wrote
piece	
please	yesterday
	your

Words Frequently Misspelled in Grades 5–8
(In addition to the "demons")

buried — 6	foreign — 6
character — 6	governor — 6
disappoint — 5	government — 5

groceries — 5
interesting — 4
judgment — 6
kerosene — 6
· library — 4
necessary — 6
occurred — 7
perhaps — 4
principal — 6

really — 6
separate — 5
sincerely — 5
truly — 5
useful — 4
usual — 5
vegetable — 4
visitor — 4
wrapped — 5

(The number indicates the grade in which the word has been placed for teaching.)

THE CONSUMMATION

In the final assembling and editing of material for the course in English for the city, all of the lists of words and suggestions on method gathered by the various centers were placed in the hands of Mr. D. J. Beeby, principal of the Oglesby School. Mr. Beeby had been at work for some years collecting facts as a basis for a course in spelling. He now added to his data the evidence collected in the course of our experiment and selected from a total of 15,000 words included in the findings of Ayres, Jones, Cook, O'Shea, Tidyman, Pryor, Ashbaugh, and others a list of 1920. No word was chosen unless named at least three times by competent investigators. The placing of the words was determined, not by their difficulty but by their use. Each word appeared as soon as a given grade was found to have need of it.[1] The superiority for actual teaching purposes of a list so arranged over a list graded according to difficulty will be at once apparent. Our goal was a course in spelling scientifically and at the same time psychologically determined. Such results as were obtained by objective measures indicated that we had attained a gratifying measure of success.

THE SELF-TESTING OF THE TEACHER OF COMPOSITION

GENEVIEVE APGAR

Head of the Department of English, Harris Teachers College, St. Louis, Missouri

Nothing brings us so definitely face to face with a situation as the need for giving an answer to a question. All decisions are answers to questions, explicit or implicit. Any inventory is the result of taking an account of stock on hand, whether the stock be material accumulation, intellectual or moral attainment, or service rendered.

To measure attainments in education, we are coming, and wisely so, to rely more and more upon educational tests. But no test will reveal everything about any one phase of achievement. Many schoolroom situations can best be judged by the teacher's own insight, if she be skilled, discriminating, and unbiased. Her relation to composition work and to the individuals under her instruction in composition, and the reaction of the children to that instruction can well be tested by the teacher through answers she gives when she asks of herself questions pertinent to her own procedure and to the results obtained by that procedure. These answers, aided by the use of such composition scales as we have, will be very

[1] The list as arranged by Mr. Beeby will be found in Bulletin No. 21 of the Chicago Board of Education. This may be obtained of the Business Manager of the Board at a cost of twenty-five cents.

valuable to the teacher in planning the work that lies immediately ahead. This is not scientific testing, of course. It may result only in an "I think so" conclusion; it may lead to scientific testing to verify the judgment. In any case, facing the question squarely and searching for a truthful answer will be enlightening as to the real condition, suggestive for future procedure, and stimulating for higher achievement.

Questions for self-testing are particularly needed by the elementary teacher of language, or composition. That work is very complex. It involves habit-building, which necessitates drill in both oral and written language. It involves accumulation of ideas, gained from observation of the world and people, and from books. It involves organization of those ideas. It involves training of the imagination. It involves vocabulary-building and the development of a keen sentence-sense. It involves training in the correct use of the voice, and in the proper bearing before an audience. So complex is it with its manifold ends to be sought that unless the teacher keeps before her very clearly the details of its complexities, much work and much time can easily be spent with little achievement.

The following list of questions may prove helpful. They were compiled with the needs chiefly of the elementary teacher in mind, but many are applicable to secondary schoolroom conditions.

QUESTIONS FOR THE SELF-TESTING
OF THE TEACHER OF ELEMEN-
TARY COMPOSITION

A. *Questions that consider the procedure of the teacher.*

1. Have I a definite aim for each lesson hour?
2. Do I make clear to the children the particular purpose of any one exercise?

3. Are my assignments sufficiently narrow in scope to admit of unified, connected expression?
4. Am I acquainted with the interests of my class?
5. Am I alert to catch hints from the conversations and activities of the children as to their interests?
6. Am I suiting my assignments to the interests of the children?
7. Do I appreciate the children's view of the subject given?
8. Do the lessons follow in an order to produce the desired development in the children's power?
9. Am I using well-chosen models?
10. Do I plan my lessons so carefully that the children are impressed by the importance I attach to them?
11. Am I encouraging the use of the imagination too much? Sufficiently?
12. Am I training in clear thinking?
13. Am I training in organization of thought?
14. How many difficulties do I attack at once?
15. Do I give the children sufficient encouragement?
16. Do I succeed in arousing the timid children?
17. Do I assist the slow children as much as I should?
18. Do I stimulate the more capable children as much as I should?
19. Do I expect too much of the children?
20. Do I expect enough of the children?
21. How can I save time and accomplish more work in the class hour?
22. Does each child get, in his turn, my personal help, criticism, and correction?
23. Do I have as many personal conferences with the children as my time permits?
24. Am I furnishing the proper incentive to bring out the best effort of each individual child?
25. Should I talk less during the composition hour?
26. Am I suppressing spontaneity and social development by placing myself in the foreground too much?
27. Do I hold the children responsible for what they have already been taught?
28. Are my corrections of children's compositions based upon an able judgment?

29. Am I able to separate content from form in judging the worth of a composition?
30. Am I giving the right amount of time to the different phases of the language work: spelling, enunciation drill, vocabulary-building, oral composition, written composition, correct usage drill, grammar?
31. Would the work of my class bear comparison with that of any other class of the same grade and quarter and of the same social environment?
32. What are the weakest things about my teaching of composition?
33. Can I do with more than a fair degree of success the thing I am asking the children to do?
34. Can I stand before an audience and address it in a self-possessed manner?
35. Do I exercise at all times the same care in my own language, spoken and written, as I demand of the children?

B. *Questions that consider the achievement of the children.*

36. Do the children enjoy the composition period?
37. Do the children give their oral themes in a interested and interesting manner?
38. Are the children getting out of their work what is most useful for their future development?
39. In what particulars do I see improvement in the children's work?
40. Do I observe a steady, though slow, improvement in (a) willingness to compose, (b) subject matter, (c) variety of expression, (d) enlargement of vocabulary?
41. Does the effort made by the children during the English period to talk connectedly carry over into the geography, history, and nature recitations?
42. Are the children realizing a need for oral and written composition?
43. Are the children gaining courage and perseverance in their efforts to express themselves more effectively?
44. Are the children becoming more accurate observers?

45. Do the children stick to the point they are making?
46. Are the children developing a critical attitude toward their own work?
47. Are the children growing in power of constructive criticism?
48. Are the criticisms of the class made in the spirit of mutual helpfulness?
49. Are the children gaining in ability to sense mistakes rapidly?
50. Is the "and" type of sentence disappearing from the talks given by the children?
51. Is the "and" type of sentence disappearing from the paragraphs written by the children?
52. Are the children aware of the need of increasing their vocabulary?
53. Are the children as alert to good expressions as to bad?
54. Are the children acquiring a regard for the apt word or phrase and an enthusiasm in the quest of such word or phrase?
55. Is there evidence that the children's appreciation of word values is growing?
56. Are the children using the dictionary intelligently?
57. Are the children learning to be attentive listeners?
58. Is the progress made by the slow children as great in proportion as that made by the bright children?

C. *Questions that consider habit-building in English.*

59. Am I arousing in the children a desire to improve their habits of speech?
60. Am I arousing a class pride in the use of correct forms?
61. What common errors of speech have been eliminated (or partly so) by the children?
62. Are the children making progress in the use of correct verb forms?
63. What common errors of speech are the children now striving to eliminate?
64. What drill on correct forms am I giving?
65. What specific language habits am I inculcating in the children?
66. What am I doing toward building habits of clear articulation and enunciation?

THE CLEARING HOUSE

BECOMING ACQUAINTED WITH FRANCE
AND THE FRENCH THROUGH CORRE-
SPONDENCE WITH PUPILS IN FRENCH
SECONDARY SCHOOLS

A delightful talk given to our high-school pupils by Mademoiselle Clément of France was the source, the following day, of the most lively discussion in all of the classes in French. The pupils were enthusiastic in their appreciation of the charm of the lecturer's personality, and were delighted with such things as her admiration of their school building and her praise of their manner of rendering *La Marseillaise*, sung upon this occasion in her honor. Several of her statements, however, they strongly resented. For example, they took exception to her assertion that the scholarship in French secondary schools was far superior to that prevailing in the American high school. They doubted her claim that the French pupil had far more highly developed powers of concentration, application, etc., and made a wholly unsuccessful appeal to their teacher to refute these and similar criticisms.

The teacher, conscious of their dissatisfaction, suggested that they consult, in search of satisfying information, all possible sources, and asked for their opinions and suggestions in regard to the matter. Finally a committee of five — one member elected from each of the sections in French — took the matter under consideration and, after three days, submitted to the assembled pupils of our French department a report which informed them that there was no material of value available in either school or town library, and that the members of the committee strongly recommended correspondence between pupils of America and France, "not only for the purpose of settling the matters under discussion, but also

with the idea of learning, first hand, more about the country and the people whose language we are studying."

The pupils, after receiving from the teacher a favorable answer to a question raised as to the possibility of such a correspondence, voted unanimously for the carrying into execution of the committee's plan.

A newly elected committee took charge of writing to an Educational Correspondence Bureau, the address of which was furnished, at their request, by the teacher. They filled out the application blanks sent in return, collected the enrollment fees, and distributed the names and addresses forwarded by the Bureau. The members of this committee — a representative from each section — cautioned the pupils in regard to postal rates between the United States and France (information obtained from employees at the local post office), and explained briefly abbreviations and other puzzling details in the addresses (information sought and received from the teacher).

The teacher, questioned by pupils in all sections as to the real significance of the term "département" so prominent in the French addresses, supplied the information to classes sufficiently far advanced in the form of a dictation lesson in French. This dictated lesson resulted in many intelligent questions asked by pupils in regard to the French Government, all of which were answered by further dictation work.

The majority of the pupils decided to write the initial letter in English, and these letters were submitted to the members of a committee elected for exceptional ability in English composition work. The replies were most impatiently awaited. During the interval, many pupils of their own accord consulted atlases and geographies in an attempt to become acquainted with the location and chief physical features of the section of France in which their individual correspondents were living.

Finally the letters began to arrive from France and, as they came, each was brought to the teacher to be shared with her and with the other pupils. The letters proved to be informational not only to the point of convincing the students that the school day in France was longer, that the number of subjects studied during the school year by a pupil in a French secondary school was greater, that the pupil graduated from the French school at an earlier age, but were instructive in regard to such points as the physical features, natural products, and industries of various sections of France. Photographs and post cards from various cities, towns, and villages gave a clearer idea of the country, and photographs of the writers themselves made the correspondents and their land seem nearer and more real.

Many points of contact were established. Music pupils in our school found that their French correspondents were playing, on piano or violin, selections studied and executed by themselves. Boys enthusiastic over sports gained interesting information in regard to the varieties in which their French friends indulged. Girls exchanged ideas and patterns in embroidery. A commercial pupil received from her French correspondent a diagram of the keyboard of a French typewriter. The pupils exchanged Christmas gifts and New Year cards, and in a few months strong friendships were formed; the consciousness of distance between the countries lessened; and the original feeling of antagonism was almost wholly destroyed.

In class there were many mature, thoughtful discussions of relations — points of difference and of resemblance — between the two peoples and, in addition to these important considerations, there was noticeable a marked improvement in the grade of work done in French. The pupils had a new incentive for learning how to express their thoughts in French words and in the French idiom. Faults in the English idiom as employed by the French pupil writing in English not only made much more clear the real significance of the term idiom, but also suggested or impressed the French idiom which had been literally translated into English. Numerals, dates, age idioms, and other kindred phases of the subject, including the relative value of franc and centime and the chief features of the metric system, were learned naturally by beginning pupils through inquiries in connection with their correspondence.

The letters brought to the teacher were dictated in French to the other pupils by one chosen for ability in the reading of the language, or were translated into English by a member of the class especially proficient along that line, such an arrangement creating a wholesome spirit of rivalry which resulted in marked improvement in these two phases of the subject.

The project has been of general and of specific value, both social and educational.

MILDRED P. NEAL,
Amesbury, Mass.

A CHILD'S PROJECT PROBLEM

Just north of our school were some great billboards in two vacant lots. I did not wish to suggest the removal of these boards to the children, but wished them to suggest their removal.

Preparatory to our crusade against the billboard, also preparatory to the chapter in Civics on "Beauty in a Community," children were asked to bring to school lists of places in the school vicinity that they thought added to the beauty of our city. They were also asked to bring a list of things that detracted from beauty.

This was my way of approach. I hoped through this plan to have some pupil suggest the removal of the boards.

Our school district is in one of the best residential parts of the city. There are few things to offend the eye and many things to please.

When the children were asked to make out this list one girl said: "Last week I took a picture of a telephone pole on the corner of our street that is covered with woodbine." With no further suggestion the pupils decided to take their kodaks as they made this tour of inspection. One boy, whose father is a photographer, offered to develop films for those who could not develop their own.

The next day the pupils brought their lists to class. They had noted where a sidewalk had been curved to give room for the growth of a large tree; they spoke of broken places in the sidewalk, of shrubbery in yards, of well kept yards, of unclean alleys, of an ornamental seat where passengers could rest while waiting for the street car. Among the things listed in the "beauty" column was the Fall Creek Boulevard. This is a part of our park system and is made for pleasure vehicles, not for heavy traffic.

When the boulevard was mentioned, one boy said, "Father says he thinks the Park Board are not consistent. They make an expensive boulevard for us and just across the Creek they let a long row of ugly billboards stay."

Another pupil said: "We don't need to go to Fall Creek to find billboards. We can look right out of our room and see them."

This brought the question from the teacher as to the purpose of the boards. "Why are they there?"

The pupils decided that we had near us something that took away from the beauty of our school neighborhood. They discovered that there was something for them to do. A discussion followed as to the best plan of procedure. They decided to find the name of the owner of the lot. A committee was appointed to go to the City Hall, interview the City Engineer, and get all needful information. One of the pupils said: "At the Court House we can get this information, too."

The teacher proposed for the next day an informal debate in which pupils were to favor or oppose the billboard. She also suggested that they consult their parents at home and find material or pictures that would bear out the argument they were going to make.

The next day pupils brought notebooks to school. In these they had listed short sentences to be used as guides in their debate. The sides were nearly balanced. The committee made its report first. It was to the effect that the owner of the lot lived in Brooklyn and the committee had not been able to find the name of his rental agent. An informal debate followed this report. These are some of the arguments as I remember them:

"Billboards are crude in color. They detract from beauty. The lettering is large and you can't help see it."

"I should think Mr. Cochrane's family would get tired of looking at those boards every day when they sit on the porch. I don't think it's fair or right for the boards to interfere with their view."

"I believe it would detract somewhat from his property if he wished to sell it."

"The billboard is not sanitary."

Another pupil said,—"I should like you to prove that." The reply was:

"I went behind them last night and saw lots of leaves, brush, old tin cans, baskets, and bottles piled up there. There was water in the cans, and flies and mosquitoes breed there."

Arguments on the other side were:

"The man who owns these lots doesn't live here. He has to pay the city taxes. The lots are an expense to him and he can get money from the Billboard Company by letting them use his lots."

"Taxes are so heavy now because of the new boulevard. He has no house on his lot, so I think he has a right to get money in this way."

"Companies have a right to call attention to their wares. People are sure to see the billboard. They might not read advertisements in the paper."

"We know what the theater programs are, because the plays are always advertised on them."

As the lesson went on it developed that the billboard had some champions. All agreed that it was not good to have them near our school grounds or near Mr. Cochrane's home.

Pupils in their talks distinguished between the little boards used by rental agents for sale of lots and those that were near us.

When they reached the conclusion that the boards did not add to our school surroundings, the teacher's question came, "What shall we do about it?" One pupil said: "Write the owner and tell him what we think. Ask him to break his contract with the company." On second thought pupils said he could not do that because the billboard companies had rights. It was then thought best to ask him not to enter into a new contract the following year.

This prepared the way for a letter the next day — a letter to a real person, with a real motive in writing it. The letters submitted were read and pupils expressed their preferences. Here they had to use some choice and judgment. The letters that were chosen were submitted to the principal of the building so that she might make the final choice.

The next week a letter was received from the owner. He said he was pleased with the civic spirit entertained by the class. He referred them to his rental agent for further consultation. No further steps were taken by the class as the School Board bought the two lots for an extension of our playground. The billboards went down. The children felt that they had not accomplished as much as they had hoped to do.

In June, when the children graduated, one member of the class gave as her part of the program the experience we had had, so the neighborhood knew we had tried to do some real civic work.

I felt that the pupils had accomplished a great deal. There was spontaneity and joy in this work because *they* were doing it. They had made some useful observations and investigations leading to a real outcome. They had collected their own material. They had learned that there are two sides to a question. They had learned that this school experience of their's touched other phases — the law regulated heights of billboards. They had learned that other questions aside from beauty came in — sanitation, fairness to neighbors. They made distinctions based on values. They took this school work into their homes and talked it over with their parents. The subject matter was the life about them. They were sharing in it. The plan was formulated by the teacher but no suggestion of her purpose was given to the children. Interest led them to take part in the debate, to write the letters to the owner of the lots. There was real motivation. Pupils organized their own work. I believe good habits were inculcated. Children gladly followed this work with something similar — the investigation of the alleys near our school. Reports were made to the principal and to the City Board of Health following these investigations. Reports were also made to the Fire Department.

I believe the billboard could be listed as a problem. There was a situation. The problem could be stated. There was an objective to be reached. There was activity on the part of the children. The interest in the outcome led them to collect material, to write letters and to think toward an end. There was helpfulness and unity in the work. It connected itself with the Course of Study.

FLORA SWAN.

AS REPORTED

SUMMER MEETING OF THE N. E. A.

The sixtieth annual meeting of the National Education Association will be held in Boston, July 2 to 8. Besides the principal association there will be numerous meetings of departments and allied organizations. The National Conference on Educational Method will unite with the Department of Elementary Education in a joint meeting on Wednesday, at which a number of important papers will be presented. On Thursday the National Conference, meeting by itself, will consider the Practical Problems of Supervision as presented by Miss Mary A. S. Mugan, Assistant Superintendent of Schools in Fall River, Massachusetts; Scientific Reorganization of the Curriculum, by Professor Harold Rugg of the Lincoln School of Teachers College, New York; The Practical Workings of the Project Method, by Miss Rose Carrigan, principal of the Shurtleff School, Boston, and others.

The general theme of the program of the main association is *The Democratic Awakening*. This will be presented in its relation to a new world outlook, the importance of professional training for teachers, the shaping of educational policies for the future, a higher type of patriotism, and progress toward the realization of early American ideals. Among the prominent speakers announced are Sir Arthur Currie, President of McGill University, Toronto, Canada, Ex-Commissioner P. P. Claxton, now Provost of the University of Alabama, Thomas E. Finegan, State Commissioner of Education for Pennsylvania, Honorable Calvin Coolidge, Vice-President of the United States, General John J. Pershing, Chief of Staff of the United States Army, Honorable William E. Borah, Senator from Idaho.

A number of important commissions will make reports, including the Legislative Committee, by George D. Strayer, the Committee on Foreign Relations, by Augustus O. Thomas, the Commission on Research Agencies, by Jesse H. Newlon, the Illiteracy Commission, by Cora Wilson Stewart, the Committee on Sources of Revenue, by William B. Owen, and the Committee on Health Problems, by Thomas D. Wood.

The advance announcements of the meeting give promise of a session of great value, and the attendance will no doubt be large.

THE GEDDES REPORT

All who are interested in the progress of education in Great Britain will acknowledge an obligation to Dr. Kandel of Teachers College, who reports briefly in the *Educational Review* for April the present status of English education and the Geddes Report. It appears that the committee advocates a reduction of £18,000,000 in the budget for education. This is to be made to go around by such backward steps as raising the school admission age to six, closing small schools, putting more pupils under one teacher and paying the teacher less, limiting free-place pupils to 25%, raising fees, granting scholarships only to students of unusual ability and industry, postponing the development of technical education, reducing contributions by the State to teachers' pensions, and in general putting all the local authorities on definite "rations."

Quotations from the *Manchester Guardian* and the *Spectator* indicate that the Report does not represent public opinion in England. There is no reason, therefore, why it should be quoted in support of reactionary policies in America.

THE READER'S GUIDE

THINKING AND STUDY

The interest in popular discussions of the problems of teaching is perennial. Every year witnesses the accession to our shelves of numerous volumes which, while for the most part made up of a new arrangement and a new statement of well-known facts and principles, doubtless find many readers among the multitude of teachers new to the profession. Fashions in pedagogy change like other fashions and almost as soon. One must have a new book on teaching just as he must have a new hat or a new car, and often there are improvements.

The two books[1] here reviewed have much in common though intended to serve somewhat different purposes. Both are intended for teachers in training and both would bring about more emphasis on intelligent self-direction as a chief aim of education. The treatment in both is simple and it includes to a large degree a reworking of numerous other treatments usually of a nontechnical character. The two books belong to the class popular in teachers' reading circles and ought to prove of considerable use there. Taken by itself, however, either might throw the matters of which it treats a little out of perspective.

This is more largely true of Mr. Boraas's *Teaching to Think*. Since, as he says, thinking may be considered, if we like, a form of behavior, there is a natural tendency to review all the laws and processes of behavior from this single point of view. The outcome is a work which the novice may easily mistake for a fairly complete view of the whole process of learning and teaching. In the normal school the class should have in hand as a text a more fully rounded view of

their task, or should at least give as much attention to Rowe's *Habit Formation and the Science of Teaching* as to this volume. Both together will leave large portions of the ground covered in Thorndike's *Principles of Teaching* untouched.

As compared with Dewey's *How We Think*, this more recent book is distinctly discursive. It roams over a larger field but with less incisiveness in dealing with its theme. It does, however, reflect the writer's familiarity with the daily working of the common school and it presents a variety of practical expedients of recent popularity, such as the score card, the making of questions by pupils, and sentence-completion and other similar tests. The teacher himself is provided in a closing chapter with special methods of increasing his efficiency in thinking. A difference obvious at a glance is the addition of "Thought Exercises" to the various chapters. These would lend themselves very well to general discussion, but in some cases the students would probably lack sufficient data.

Mr. Thomas aims directly at developing a better school procedure. He would put the recitation hour to new uses, training the pupils to do a much larger proportion of their work independently. In order to accomplish this he would put the students in the normal school through a course of preparation for such a procedure.

The writer recognizes the fact that others before him have analyzed the principles of study, but he contends that they have not anticipated changed uses for the class hour. If further justification be needed it may be found, he thinks, in the fact that the project method, now coming into vogue, requires

[1] *Teaching to Think*, by Julius Boraas. The Macmillan Company; and *Training for Effective Study*, by Frank W. Thomas, Houghton Mifflin Company.

a much greater degree of independent work than the older systems of class work have done.

In fact Mr. Thomas has added very little to our knowledge of the art of study. He makes no claim indeed to originality in that regard. McMurry, whom he quotes from time to time, is still the better authority and has the more exhaustive treatment. The justification for a new book must be found in the author's attempt to present and illustrate an organized school procedure. If the book does something to help break up the formal hearing of lessons conned from books, which, as he affirms, is still too common, it will justify itself. At the least the numerous illustrations from actual school work which the writer has scattered through his pages will help students to see what the movement for better study habits means.

There is nothing novel about the method of appeal which either of these two writers has used. The reviewer wonders why it might not have been possible to make each of the books more directly an instrument for doing for its readers the thing which they in turn are expected to pass on to others. Perhaps the time is not ripe for teachers of education to practice as well as to preach.

SIGNIFICANT ARTICLES

CAN WE DEPEND UPON GROUP TESTS OF INTELLIGENCE?

The most comprehensive survey of what has been done in the way of determining the validity of intelligence tests has been made by Mr. Denton L. Geyer, of the Chicago Normal College, who publishes his results in the *Chicago Schools Journal* for March. He distinguishes between the reliability of a test and its validity, that is, its value as an actual measure of what it purports to measure, namely, intelligence. He then proceeds to compare intelligence scores with (a) officers' estimates of the efficiency of

soldiers tested by the Army Scale; (b) teachers' estimates of the intelligence of school children; (c) teachers' marks or grades; (d) standardized educational tests of pupil attainment; (e) success in life measured by such factors as salary, professional reputation, etc.; (f) experiments in putting test scores to practical use for purposes such as classifying of school children.

These comparisons prove on the whole to be distinctly favorable to intelligence tests when all factors are taken into consideration. The lowest correlation is between intelligence scores and school marks. This is accounted for by the fact that school marks are given primarily for achievement and indicate many things besides, such as approval of effort even when the effort does not bring results, disapproval as a means of breaking up habits of indolence, and the like.

When compared with achievement, correlations are found to be high with the results of reasoning tests in arithmetic and low when compared with results of writing scales. This Mr. Geyer thinks is what is to be expected. If intelligence may be defined as ability to learn, particularly to learn in school, then undoubtedly we may accept intelligence tests as of real value in classifying and advising pupils. As to their validity in general, the words of Thorndike are quoted with approval:

"The sound practical argument for the use of objective tests of intellect is not the infallibility of such tests, but the extreme fallibility of the estimates which they replace or amend. Our tests suffer from the constant error of emphasizing what can be done with a pen on paper, but parents' judgments suffer from constant errors far worse. Our tests have taken too narrow a view of intellect, but the school teachers' view is still narrower. Our tests have too large probable errors and too low correlations, but many of the judgments of intelligence, currently made, approach zero correlation."

THE NEW BOOKS

Gardening. An Elementary School Text Treating of the Science and Art of Vegetable Growing. By A. B. Stout. In *New-World Science Series*, edited by John W. Ritchie. World Book Co., 1922. Pp. xvi+354. Illus. Price, $1.60.

Primarily for junior high school grades.

Methods and Material for Composition in Intermediate and Grammar Grades. By Alhambra G. Deming. Chicago: Beckley-Cardy Co., 1921. Pp. 232.

A teacher's desk book.

The Dalton Laboratory Plan. By Evelyn Dewey. New York: E. P. Dutton & Co., 1922. Pp. 173.

An account of individual instruction as a substitute for the usual recitation.

Self-help English Lessons. By Julia H. Wohlfarth and John J. Mahoney. Yonkers, N. Y.: World Book Co., 1922.

For the fifth and sixth grades, being the second of a three-book series.

Graded Outlines in Hygiene. Book One. By Walter Frank Cobb. Yonkers, N. Y.: World Book Co., 1922. Pp. x+214. Price, $1.50.

For the kindergarten and the first three grades of the elementary school. Modern and highly suggestive in method.

The Technique of Teaching. By Sheldon E. Davis. New York: Macmillan Co., 1922. Pp. x+346.

All of the chapters except the first are devoted to methods of teaching various school subjects.

The Art of Thinking. By T. Sharper Knowlson. New York: T. Y. Crowell Co., 1921. Pp. x+165.

A general rather than a pedagogical discussion.

Selected Stories from O. Henry. Edited by C. Alphonso Smith. Garden City, N. Y.: Doubleday, Page & Co., 1922. Pp. xvi+255. Price, $1.25.

A representative collection which all admirers of O. Henry will be glad to see.

American Chemistry. A Record of Achievement — the Basis for Future Progress. By Harrison Hale. New York: D. Van Nostrand Co., 1921. Pp. viii+215. Illus.

A very informing account of the more significant developments in this field—not a high-school manual.

Homework and Hobby Horses. New Poems by Boys of the Perse School, Cambridge, England. Edited by H. Caldwell Cook. New York: E. P. Dutton & Co., 1922. Pp. xii+58. Price, $1.25.

More examples of the "play way" which the author expounded in the book of that name.

IN PAPER COVERS

A Manual for Teachers of English in the Central High School. Springfield, Massachusetts, 1921.

An Analysis of the 1922–1923 Budget Requests of the Board of Education, City of Detroit. By Arthur B. Moehlman, J. F. Thomas, and H. W. Anderson. Detroit Educational Bulletin, No. 8, 1922.

Experiments in French Primary Schools. By M. Roger Cousinet. Progressive Education Association, Washington, D. C., Bulletin No. 12, March, 1922.

A Guide for Grown-Ups to Books of Prose and Poetry. By Marian E. Tobey. Public Schools, Ithaca, N. Y.

Department of the Interior, Bureau of Education Bulletins, 1921: *English Grammar in American Schools Before 1850*, by Rollo LaVerne Lyman. No. 12. *The Reorganization of Mathematics in Secondary Education.* No. 32. *School Grounds and Play*, by Henry S. Curtis. No. 45. *Statistics of Nurse Training Schools*, 1919–1920. No. 51. *Record of Current Educational Publications.* No. 52. *What Libraries Learned From the War*, by Carl H. Milan. Library Leaflet No. 14, 1922.

Report of the Bureau of Research. Public Schools of Akron, Ohio, 1920–21.

THE JOURNAL OF EDUCATIONAL METHOD

Edited by JAMES F. HOSIC

Volume I JUNE, 1922 Number 10

PUBLISHED BY THE WORLD BOOK COMPANY FOR
THE NATIONAL CONFERENCE ON EDUCATIONAL METHOD

$3.00 a year   Monthly except July and August   35 cents a copy

THE NATIONAL CONFERENCE ON EDUCATIONAL METHOD

An Association of Persons Interested in Supervision and Teaching

---

Officers of the Conference

President, MARGARET NOONAN, School of Education, New York University, Washington Square, New York City.
Vice-President, W. F. TIDYMAN, State Normal School, Farmville, Va.
Secretary-Treasurer, JAMES F. HOSIC, Teachers College, New York City.

Executive Committee

THE PRESIDENT AND THE SECRETARY-TREASURER, *ex officio*.
MARGARET MADDEN, Doolittle Elementary School, Chicago, Ill.
MARY E. PENNELL, Assistant Superintendent of Schools, Kansas City, Mo.
J. A. STARKWEATHER, Assistant Superintendent of Schools, Duluth, Minn.

Board of Directors

C. C. CERTAIN, Assistant Principal and Head of Department of English, Northwestern High School, Detroit, Mich.
BESSIE B. GOODRICH, Assistant Superintendent of Schools, Des Moines, Ia.
J. M. GWINN, Superintendent of Schools, New Orleans, La.
KATHARINE HAMILTON, Assistant Superintendent of Schools, St. Paul, Minn.
JAMES F. HOSIC, Associate Professor of Education in Charge of Extramural Courses, Teachers College, Columbia University.
FRED M. HUNTER, Superintendent of Schools, Oakland, Calif.
WILLIAM H. KILPATRICK, Professor of Philosophy of Education, Teachers College, Columbia University.
MARGARET MADDEN, Principal, Doolittle Elementary School, Chicago, Ill.
F. M. McMURRY, Professor of Elementary Education, Teachers College, Columbia University.
MARGARET NOONAN, School of Education, New York University, New York City.
MARY E. PENNELL, Assistant Superintendent of Schools, Kansas City, Mo.
J. A. STARKWEATHER, Assistant Superintendent of Schools, Duluth, Minn.
W. F. TIDYMAN, Director of the Training School, State Normal School, Farmville, Va.
ROSE A. CARRIGAN, Supervising Principal, Shurtleff School, Boston, Mass.
STUART A. COURTIS, Director of Instruction, Teacher Training, and Research, Detroit, Mich.

THE JOURNAL OF EDUCATIONAL METHOD is published monthly, from September to June, at Concord, N. H., for the officers, directors, and members of the National Conference on Educational Method by the World Book Company of Yonkers-on-the-Hudson, N. Y. The subscription price is $3.00 a year; the price of single copies is 35 cents.

Postage is prepaid by the publishers on all orders from the United States, Mexico, Cuba, Porto Rico, Panama Canal Zone, Republic of Panama, Bolivia, Colombia, Honduras, Nicaragua, Peru, Hawaiian Islands, Philippine Islands, Guam, and the Samoan Islands.

Postage is charged extra as follows: For Canada, 25c on annual subscriptions; other foreign countries not named, 50 cents. All communications regarding subscriptions or advertising should be addressed to World Book Company, Concord, N. H., or Yonkers-on-Hudson, New York.

Address applications for membership to the Secretary of the Conference, 525 West One Hundred and Twentieth Street, New York City. The fee for active members is $3.00, for associate members, $2.00; $2.00 in each case is applied to the support of the journal, for which each member receives a year's subscription.

The editorial office is at 525 West One Hundred and Twentieth Street, New York City.

Entered as second-class matter at the post office at Concord, N. H. under the Act of March 3, 1879.

The Journal of Educational Method

VOLUME I   JUNE, 1922   NUMBER 10

EDITORIALLY SPEAKING

CHOOSE BOTH

Two school reports on the editor's table suggest certain reflections as to contrasting tendencies. The first is a circumstantial record of the doings of Group VI in the City and Country School of New York City, made in coöperation with the Bureau of Educational Experiments. The other is Survey Bulletin, Volume III, Number 2, issued by the superintendent of schools in Bucyrus, Ohio.

This mid-year issue of the survey is the second part of a three-part cycle which has been carried out during two preceding years and is being continued. The testing is done by the supervisory staff and the rating is made at the central office. Then through a series of conferences the teachers are acquainted with the scores and are assisted in shaping their programs in the light of them.

During the present year tests are being administered in spelling, arithmetic, English composition, silent reading, and handwriting. The results of these tests are set forth in modern statistical and graphic fashion, with comparisons of schools in terms of fall, mid-year, and standard scores. Accompanying the reports in each subject are succinct accounts of the steps which were instituted to bring about the improvement that was seen to be possible and desirable.

The record from the City and Country School is not less orderly. It consists of an itemized account arranged by months of all that Group VI did. Instead, however, of the customary subjects, we find the headings, Play Experiences, Practical Experiences, Special Training, and Organization of Information, with sub-heads, some of which are familiar, like spelling, and others not, such as Blocks and Store.

From the preface we learn that the object of the notes was to construct a curriculum for six-year-olds by writing it as it was made by the teacher and the pupils. The teachers made rough notes from day to day and then summarized these by months. Stories were taken down verbatim as told by the children. The work of individual pupils is often referred to, the pupils being designated by their initials.

The account marks a considerable departure from conventional practices and is valuable as suggesting the possibility of new emphases in teaching.

Particularly it shows how teachers may follow more closely than is common the work of individual children. Taken by itself, it is inconclusive and merely paves the way for studies and generalizations which may be aided by it. Some would refuse to call it scientific. There are no graphs or tables of statistics, it is true, but it does represent an effort at systematic gathering of facts. It tells not what pupils might do or ought to do, but what they actually did. It does not take the place of quantitative studies of the kind so well presented in the Bucyrus report; but then neither do reports of that type render such as this of Group VI useless. Both are needed.

The point is that progress in education depends upon a happy combination of both qualitative and quantitative studies, of the carrying out of new aims as well as the economical realization of old ones. Measurements will help to dispel illusions; free experimentation will tend to keep us out of ruts. The greatest good will come from the harmonious and well-coördinated working of the two. Instead of pinning our faith to either alone, let us rather be eclectic and choose both.

A LARGE-GROUP CIVIC SUPERVISORY PROJECT

JENNY LIND GREEN

Supervisor of Grammar Grades, San Antonio, Texas

Classified on one basis, supervisory projects are of two kinds: one involves the work of one school, the other necessitates the coöperative activity of a group of schools. Classified on another basis, again, roughly speaking, they are of two kinds: one deals with the outer community indirectly, the other deals with it directly as a plan to meet a specific need. The project to be described is a large-group civic project. It involved the coöperation of twenty-eight grammar schools and was undertaken because of a community civic situation it hoped to remedy by direct action.

I. Origin and Purpose of the Project.

The project had its origin in work done by the children immediately following the flood in this city (San Antonio) last September. At that time, following the lead of press, home, and school, they were busy emptying standing water, sprinkling lime on damp ground, cleaning clothes, furniture, walls, yards, etc. The work made them eager to do something more for their city and led directly to the wish to make others see a "Greater San Antonio." They therefore undertook what they called the "Greater San Antonio Campaign." Its specific purpose was to make others interested in and appreciative of their city and its prospects for development.

II. General Plan of Campaign.

The campaign consisted of investigating their city and giving publicity to the results. The investigations were largely first-hand investigations and were made public first by talks given during Good English Week and, second, by a magazine. The talks were given by children to members of their own classes, to other grades in the school, and in addition to other schools, so that the aspect of the campaign was both a school and inter-school publicity campaign. The magazine was published by the grammar schools as a whole and contained such results of their investigations as the various schools wished to make public and felt would be appreciated by the greatest number. The magazine was to be sold to pay expenses, and one-seventh of the total number of copies was to be distributed free in various parts of the country.

III. Content of Investigations.

This is illustrated by material in the magazine. The general nature of it is hinted at in the "Word of Explanation," which states: "It is an attempt to make children love their city as a greater city. It is an attempt to tell what is not in books, yet what makes us more interested in books. It is an attempt to make people curious about the things around them. It is an attempt to tell not what we already know but what we have wanted to find out. It is not an attempt to tell everything about anything, but is an attempt to tell just enough to make others wish to find out more for themselves."

Each school investigated what it believed it needed most. While each school worked to a large extent with local neighborhood problems, each also worked on problems of general importance. Consequently material ranged all the way from, "Why Government Hill Is a Good Place to Build a Home," to "How Our Banks Help Us." It

included material which, when organized by the organization committee of teachers, fell into the following groups: "A Bit of Interesting History," "A City of Homes," "Health," "Recreation," "Industry and Business," "Public Service," etc.

IV. Specific Content.

The opening contribution indicates the tone of the magazine. It is a letter to the reader, and is as follows:

Mother, Father, Friend, Stranger:
This little book is for you. We want to give you something we love. We love our city. And so we have written in this little book some of the things we have been thinking about it.
THE CHILDREN.

The first department is headed, "A Bit of Interesting History." It includes the following articles: first, a report by a group of children describing their visit to our local missions, stating the history of the missions as the guide told it to them, together with their own personal comments; second, an *invitation* to tourists living in states bordering on the Old Spanish Trail which connects the Atlantic and Pacific seaboards and passes through San Antonio. The opening sentence indicates the nature of the invitation:

"To you whose homes border the Old Spanish Trail and to you who live within close range of this ocean-to-ocean highway, we, the young citizens of San Antonio, extend to you a hearty welcome to visit the historic city at the heart of the trail. We acknowledge your attractions and invite you to see ours."

Then follows an acknowledgment of the attractions of each city along the trail, together with the offering of our own city. A third article in this department is intended to serve as a guide-book to tourists along the Trail. The information was collected by the children by means of letters written to the various centers, from railroad guides, etc. A cut of the stagecoach trail to the Pacific as it was in 1840 and the present Spanish Trail, a poem, "The O. S. T.," a child's map of all trails to San Antonio, and an article on the Pastores, complete this section. The Pastores Christmas celebration, peculiar to this part of the country, is interwoven with our romantic history.

The department having to do with homes opens with the statement: "One of the most beautiful things in the world is a city of *people*. The next most beautiful thing in all the world is a city of *homes*." This is followed by a creed for the home-builder and a creed for the renter. Another article sets forth the nature of our city as a home city, reasons for it, how our homes are adapted to our climate, where the materials for building them come from, costs, and practical advice to home-makers.

An article headed, "Home-Makers Are Law-Makers and Inspectors of Food," is intended to make people feel that no matter how much the state and city do to make pure food and cleanliness possible, it is after all finally in the hands of the home-maker to carry on the good work or drop it. A letter from a seventh grade class of one of the schools, written to the Real Estate Board of the city, details their plans for the year to win the loving cup for having the most attractive school home in the city. A market calendar helps the housewife know what fruits and vegeta-

bles are available each month of the year. It is made up of a study of grocery stores, fruit markets, market reports, and returns from letters of inquiry. A comparison of San Antonio market prices with prices in the East accompanies the market calendar. This department closes with recipes for preparing delectable dishes from products that are typically San Antonian.

The department called "Industry and Business" opens with general editorials. One describes San Antonio as a center, picturing graphically her relation to sections producing raw materials. "If I drew lines leading from the sections having truck gardens to San Antonio, our city would look like a hub with many spokes, leading in every direction. If I wrote on that map the names of all the vegetables produced in these truck gardens, the map would have to be very large indeed, for the list would need to include the following." The article proceeds to build up the map until the city is seen as a center of territory producing raw stuffs for more than one hundred and sixty San Antonio manufactures. Articles having to do with San Antonio as a gateway to Mexico, a summary of our foreign trade relations, our irrigation projects and their promise, and descriptions of manufacturing processes as the children saw them on their tours of personal inspection, constitute a large part of the department. Two stories grouped with the foregoing are human interest stories connected with our industries. One is, "What I Saw in a Bowl of Chili on a Cold Night." The other is the result of a personal interview with a vender of Mexican candies. The latter begins,

"'Dulces, dulces para vender! Cinco centavos,' was the greeting I received from an old Mexican man each morning on my way to school. One morning as I was buying some candy, I asked him his history and this is what he told me." There follows the story of his life as told by the vender. These venders, found on nearly every street corner, though conducting trade independently are an industrial asset to the city.

"The Sweetest Thing in Town and The Next Sweetest Thing in Town," introduce the reader to our candy manufactures and the great Uvalde honey-producing section. Articles concerning meat-packing, drug manufactures, iron and steel, mattresses, macaroni, Fuller's earth, and others are included. A lengthy article, the result of considerable research and experiment, gives detailed advice to the prospective investor in pecan orchards. It advises kinds to select and why, selection and care of graft twigs, how to graft, care of orchards, a discussion of pecan-tree pests, how to handle the crop without injuring the trees, what market conditions for pecans are at present, and how to grade the nuts and pack them for shipment.

"Banks Help Us" is a lengthy article written from a personal standpoint, and undertakes to tell why and how banks guard money to the advantage of the depositors. It includes a simple story of why money is precious, how we have developed our present money, why it sometimes depreciates, some advice to would-be depositors, and closes with a bit of interesting history concerning the effect of the Federal Reserve Bank system on San Antonio banks. A graph shows increase in banking deposits here over a twenty-year period.

Other graphs show building permits, increase in telephones, population, etc. A reporter writes a description of his impression of our market square in the early morning. The section closes with an article describing San Antonio as a city of conventions and undertakes to account for it.

The department called "Health" opens with a black and white graphic presentation of Sanitary San Antonio as the center to which all health roads converge. The roads are named: Fresh Air, Garbage Department, etc. "What Makes a City Sanitary," a description of San Antonio's department of sanitation and its work, an editorial on "Health in San Antonio," and articles on "The People Who Handle Your Food Guard Your Health" and "Our Water Supply" complete the department.

The section on "Recreation" includes reports of visits made to the parks of the city, our drives, etc. "A Day of Sports in Our Favorite Parks," "Outdoor Sports," "The Alpine Drive," "Good Roads and Scenery," "Our Army Camps," indicate the nature of the articles. A description of a bird most characteristic of this section and articles on "Foreign Lands at Home," "Curios for the Curious," and "Little Mexico," make up the remainder of the section.

Our climate as an attraction is discussed in a letter to Mr. Tourist, also in a prose poem by a Mexican boy in which he describes our autumn, thus:

"Today is a beautiful autumn day. It is in the middle of October. The weather is just fine. But there comes a cold wind that makes the leaves go away from the trees to sleep on the ground. Birds are singing on the corona vines, but most of them have gone South.

"On such a day as this I would like to be in a cotton field where all the cotton has been picked and the cows are eating the stalks up. Or I wish to be on the edge of a river where tall trees with long branches are sending down their nuts. How good it would be if I could only be in a place like that."

A climate calendar in poetry is written for tourists. It tells climate both for San Antonio and for "As North You Go" by describing what is to be seen and done during the various months.

An article on our fire department, what constitutes it and its service, together with a picture taken by the children showing them drilling, an article about San Antonio as a music center, and a San Antonio girl's creed, closed the magazine.

The magazine consisted of forty-six pages, ten and a half inches by fourteen inches, with three-quarter inch margins, and twelve-point type. This size of type made it very readable for children.

V. General Method of Work.

Briefly, each school, each group in each school, and to a large extent each child in each group selected what seemed to fit the special need. Sometimes a report was the work of a single child, but checked or assisted by others; sometimes it was the work of several grades.

No meeting or *organized* effort of any sort directed or discussed the progress of the work until twenty-two schools had become involved in it in some way. The work spread informally from school to school. Then when time seemed ripe for it, a teachers' committee was organized. It consisted of one teacher from each school, selected by the supervisor. The principals were also invited to send an additional teacher if they wished. In some cases English teachers were selected, in some cases teachers of geography, history, mathematics, or hygiene, depending upon what that special school needed to work on, was working on, and also on the peculiar readiness of the individual for that work. Readiness in this sense did not always mean that the teacher knew just what she was going to do. There was some informal discussion by the teachers of work done, plans, etc. The large committee selected smaller committees — one to organize material for the magazine when it should be presented, another to receive from each school its tentative program for Good English Week talks on the campaign, another to help share the responsibility for selecting from the cover designs submitted by the children the cover to be used for the magazine, another to make advertising, financial, and distributing arrangements for the magazine.

Direction, a systematic outline as to what each school should do, was deliberately avoided — the aim being development, not direction. Consequently, teachers and schools as a whole varied considerably in the time at which they entered the campaign. Presumably they entered when interest and ability enabled them to care to ask and help themselves. Some did not enter at all. The conclusion probably is that the supervisor failed to get all her teachers to the point at which of their own free will they would investigate the matter. It would seem, however, that individual variation would account for the fact that some teachers did not work on that particular project. There may also have been other reasons.

VI. Extra Supervisory Helps.

An *extra* supervisory measure was the inclusion of questions relating to the content of the articles in the magazine. No questions were included which were not being raised and discussed by some group of children, though there is probably no good reason why others might not have been included also. These questions were placed following the articles to which they related. They were included to help children who read articles they themselves did not help prepare, and to suggest what some other children had thought about in following up their research for the magazine. They were also intended to help teachers to a more solid footing in appreciating the questions which arise from an enjoyable inspection of what is around us, and a feeling of their relation to the course of study. The questions appeared after not more than fifty per cent of the articles, thus leaving something to the initiative of teachers who read the articles their classes did not prepare. An effort was made also to omit questions where there might be a tendency on the part of the average home reader to lay down the magazine. The children's effort was directed toward a type of information that would be

read, and the policy was to see that nothing else in the magazine interfered with this.

The questions cover a fair range of interests and while some are very simple others are more complex, the effort being to catch as many readers as possible by means of some questions, for home readers as well as the children have inquisitive natures. The nature of the questions may be illustrated by the following extracts:

An article described a visit to curio stores, particularly the Japanese and Chinese. Questions following it are: How much does a visit to these stores make you know about the way these people live and work? How do the goods in the Japanese and Chinese stores differ? How do you account for it? What are our trade relations with these countries? Why? How do you account for the increase in the last ten years? A cartoon appeared recently in our magazine, showing a picture of a foreigner. Below the picture was the line, "All dressed up and nowhere to go." To what country did that foreigner belong? Why were those words below the picture?

Following a description of iron manufactures in our city are these questions: Where does the iron for that steel come from? Why do we buy it from that section of the country? Look at a big building in process of construction, such as the building on —— Street. What uses for iron and steel products will they meet before it is completed? What inventions have been made possible because of iron and steel manufactures? What is the outlook for the expansion of such manufactures in San Antonio?

Following an article on cotton cloth: Some things I can't help thinking. We raise much cotton in this section and have for years. Why have we just begun to open cotton factories? Who has been doing our cotton manufacturing? Why? What is the outlook here for more cotton factories?

An article beginning: "Some is thick and some is thin; some is long and some is short; some is red and some is green, and I've even seen it striped. Guess!" — continues, "I'll tell you this much about it. They get most of the material for it from Sugar Land, Texas," and then proceeds to describe processes in candy making. The article is followed by these comments and questions: "I'm so glad there is a Sugar Land. I wonder where it is. Are there any besides the one in Texas? Where? How do they differ? I wonder how sugars are made. Perhaps you would like to make some. For what are the different sugars used? Mother can tell you about this. What other countries help supply sugar for 'The Sweetest Thing?'"

Other extra supervisory helps were the personal letters sent to principals and teachers early in the year following the clean-up work. These asked for suggestions as to the best way in which to meet the children's demands for something else they could do to help their city, and asked if they cared to take the matter up with the children and see what *they* wished to do. No special attempt has been made to describe the general work of supervision in such a project. It is too lengthy a process.

Another supervisory help was the personal letter of Dr. Rhodes, the city superintendent of schools. This personal letter to the children was included in the magazine. It was a message concerning their work on the campaign and was written from the standpoint of a fellow campaigner.

VII. General Results.

These are discussed under the following headings: Leads into other activity, data on extent of campaign, and general results in teaching ability. The three are not, however, so entirely separate as the headings would seem to indicate.

A. Leads into other activity.

1. Hygiene clubs have been organized for active work to make homes which keep us healthy.

2. Home clubs have been organized to help us enjoy our home hours. Some of the sub-projects involved are: research to compile dinner jokes, games to be played on rainy days and after dinner. Home helps, such as caring for pets, caring for room, beautifying, repairing, are a part of the work.

3. The Old Spanish Trail Association, after reading the magazine, sent a letter asking if we would be interested in competing for a picture of some historical spot by doing some research work which would interest people in the Old Spanish Trail. This may develop into some valuable projects.

4. Some schools are using local natural and industrial features as art studies.

5. The research resulting in articles led to worth-while problems in hygiene, history, mathematics, geography, and English.

The results have come to me without effort to ascertain them.

VIII. Data on Extent of Campaign as a Measure of Results.

Twenty-eight schools cooperated in the Good English publicity campaign. Twenty-eight schools cooperated to produce the magazine. All of the 32 grammar schools cooperated in teachers' committees, but only 28 contributed by active teaching. Between seven and eight thousand children worked on the campaign.

Classes were selected at random to obtain general data on the thoroughness of the campaign. We wished to know if they were interested in their city as a result, were more wide-awake, and if what they found out went to their people and constituted to any extent a home campaign for their city. Eight hundred and twenty grammar grade children responded as follows:

Discussed the campaign at home.......	98%
Discussed their own work and what they found out......................	94%
Learned what they had not known before.........................	98%
Learned since the campaign something about their city which they were ready to tell, and believed they might not have noticed but for the campaign	94%

Two hundred and twelve children who did not work in the campaign were selected from the same schools as the 820 workers. Of these groups, no children recalled discussing at home any matters pertaining to their city during the three months' campaign. Less than fifteen per cent recalled having found out anything they remembered about it during those months.

This very incomplete data seemed to indicate that children working on the magazine became interested in their city more than those who did not, that they discussed it at home, and that they noticed matters pertaining to it more than' children who did not do that work. Further testing was not planned because any cooperative project should leave those involved more cooperative than before, and since this was one of the first of the sort, we had the feeling that further testing might well be done when teachers and children wished to do it themselves, even if it meant less definiteness of knowledge about detailed results. For the same reason, results of increased teaching efficiency will be noted as teachers themselves seem ready and anxious to take up the matter.

The problems developed by the teachers in the course of this work were made the basis of discussion during teachers' meetings. This request came from a number of the teachers and those who presented their plans likewise took the initiative in organizing their material so it could be presented briefly, and in collecting tangible results of it — papers, graphs, charts, collections, etc. — to show the other teachers. Some of this material had to do with English, — the work of getting results from an interview, organizing an article, writing a beginning that would make the reader wish to read the article through to the end, and writing interesting headlines, together with the problems of choice of word, sentence structure, paragraphing, etc. Some of it had to do with hygiene, some related to Texas history, some to commercial geography, and so on.

The project, therefore, was not an end in itself, but a *beginning*.

A VOCABULARY AND PHRASE STUDY FOR THE FIRST GRADE

Myrtle L. Kaufmann

Elementary Supervisor, Logansport, Indiana

I. The Need of Definite Requirements in First Grade.

In any department of teaching, efficiency depends first of all upon the direction of emphasis, and second, upon the method of procedure. It is therefore of great importance that well-considered specific requirements be determined upon. Perhaps the first grade reading has suffered more than any other portion of the elementary field for want of such direction, and this despite the fact that for years beginning reading has received much emphasis upon method, both professional and commercial.

Now that every department of study looks to the results of standardized tests for guidance in the direction of teaching effort, we might expect beginning reading to get some help from this quarter. But again, we find the first grade reading almost entirely neglected. Those tests which may be used before the end of the first year are based largely upon vocabulary, and this without consideration of the particular vocabulary which has been acquired by the pupils. In those schools which consider a very early application of phonics detrimental to the formation of good reading habits, the primer class child does not have fair advantage in any test except one based upon the vocabulary studied. Hence from the standpoint of efficient teaching and also from the standpoint of satisfactory testing, it is necessary to determine what the teacher should teach to the point of mastery.

Since the teacher of first-year reading faces the entire field of the subject, it is very important that she be wisely selective as to what should be mastered first. Certainly it should be that vocabulary of which the child can make the greatest immediate use, viz., the words most recurrent in his reading from the very beginning. Granted that the pupils are to be given content material to read, that emphasis is to be focused upon thought, and that some silent reading is to be taught from the outset, it still remains necessary to devote some time each day to the mastery of the mechanics. This brings us to a study of words, even though we keep them in their phrase settings so far as possible.

II. A Vocabulary Study of a Series of Basal Readers.

It is commonly known that no word is taught once for all time. Before a word is really known, it must be met in context a sufficient number of times to become fixed. Hence time spent in drill upon many words which are not frequently recurring is largely wasted. For the purpose of directing the drill efforts of the primary teachers, and also for the purpose of ascertaining the classes in which these words may be drilled upon most economically, a vocabulary study was made of the Winston Primer and the Winston First

400

Reader,[1] these being the books in use in the school system with which we are concerned. Besides noting the frequency with which a word is used in each of these books, account was taken of whether or not the word occurs in more than one story in the book in which it is used. Next, a comparison was made between these findings and the frequency recorded for each of these words in the study which Mr. J. L. Packer made of ten first readers.[2]

Let us consider a few illustrative words. *After* occurs eleven times in the Winston Primer, nine times in the First Reader, and in Mr. Packer's study is reported as occurring a total of forty times in seven of the ten first readers on which he based his study. Surely, then, if a primer class is taught the word *after* there is some assurance that the word will be met sufficiently often in the primer and in the books following to justify the effort put upon it. The word, *all* occurs three times in the Winston Primer, fifteen times in the Winston First Reader, and is found in all ten of the first readers on which Mr. Packer reports, with a total frequency of 380. This word, then, may be more appropriately taught in the first reader class than in the primer class, and this despite the fact that it is a shorter word than *after*, apparently an easy word, and a word to which a number of other words bear phonetic similarity. Carrying illustrations a bit further, we find the word *at* but once in the primer and hence will not select it for mastery at that time. The word *bear* is used twenty-three times in the primer, and is limited in its use to only one of the stories; it is not found in the first reader, and occurs in but three of the first readers in Mr. Packer's study. Hence, it is sufficient for the pupils to know it as they meet it in the one story, and it is not necessary that they learn it to the point of absolute mastery at this time.

Clearly, if we are to proceed on the basis of need rather than on the basis of opinion, we should depend upon such a study, with the result that there should be an elimination of waste and an assurance that children will retain more of what is taught.

We would not be understood as desiring to organize reading or reading material about a vocabulary. Rather the former determines the latter. Consequently, we expect a content primer or reader to contain some words occurring but a few times. Many such words are easily absorbed in phrases or recognized from context. Hence, the fact that a word appears but once is no indication that it necessarily offers difficulty when it is met. Then, too, some words are so easily recognized that though peculiar to a story they offer less difficulty than others more commonly used. For example, the word *gingerbread* occurs thirty times in the Winston Primer, and in only the one story. Yet it offers no difficulty to children.

After making a tabulation of frequencies, it was necessary to determine what frequency justifies the selection of a word for mastery. As an arbitrary basis it was decided to select approximately a hundred words from each list. With this in mind, it was found that a word

[1] The vocabulary study was made by the writer with the assistance of Miss Marguerite DeLano, of Springfield, Illinois.
[2] Twentieth Year Book, N. S. S. E., Part II, Chapter IX.

appearing as many as four times in the primer, not limited to use in one story and met again in the first reader, might be marked for mastery in the primer class. The first reader words selected are those which appear as often as three times in the first reader and which are also reported as occurring in five or more of the first readers used in the study made by Mr. Packer.

A few words were selected because a closely related word is selected. To take an example from the primer list, while teaching *jump* it seems justifiable to teach *jumped*, though the latter appears but three times. Likewise, in the first reader, while teaching *Oh* it is a simple thing to teach the form *O*, though the latter occurs but twice in that book.

An illustrative portion of the vocabulary study is given and will probably furnish some unexpected findings in regard to the relative importance of some of the words listed. The number in the first column indicates the frequency with which a word occurs in the primer. The number in the second column indicates the frequency with which a word occurs in the first reader. The numbers in the third column are taken from the study by Packer. The first number indicates the number of times the word occurs in all of the ten first readers on which his report was made; the second number indicates the number of those readers in which he finds the words occurring.

The check mark x placed before a word indicates that it is selected for mastery in the primer class if the check is in the primer column, or in the first reader class if the check is in the first

	WINSTON PRIMER	WINSTON FIRST READER	TEN FIRST READERS
O			
of	x 5	17	707 — 10
off	1	2 *	55 — 7
Oh	2	x 13	170 — 8
old	x 37	33	231 — 9
on	x 30	34	561 — 10
once	3	x 12	56 — 7
one	x 9	19	375 — 10
opened	1	x 9	11 — 6
or	1		83 — 9
Ouf	3 *		
out	x 10	25	251 — 9
over	x 11	10	149 — 9
ox	10 *		14 — 1
O		x 2 *	42 — 5
only		1	53 — 7
onions		1	
open		x 10	37 — 6
other		1	45 — 6
our	/	x 5	161 — 9

reader column. The sign * after a figure indicates that the word occurs in only one story in the book indicated at the head of the column.

III. A Phrase Study.

But our study can not close here, lest we leave it with an emphasis upon words as such. Since we hold that for the sake of good reading habits it is necessary to emphasize the phrase from the outset, this vocabulary study became the basis of a phrase study.

A thorough search of the two textbooks with constant reference to the vocabulary study gave us a knowledge of those phrases on which drill should be focused. All phrases which contained only such words as had been selected for mastery were listed. Hence in the

WINSTON PRIMER

PAGE	CARD NUMBER	
2	P. 1	She called
3	P. 2	Who will help me
	P. 3	Not I
	P. 4	Said the cat
	P. 5	Said the pig
	P. 6	Then I will
	P. 7	And she did
4	P. 8	Then I will cut
8	P. 9	The cat said
	·P. 10	I will
	P. 11	The pig said
9	P. 12	You would not
	P. 13	You shall not
	P. 14	Shall eat
	P. 15	And they did

WINSTON FIRST READER

PAGE	CARD NUMBER	
2	1	One day
	2	was going
	3	On the way
	4	into a bag
3	5	rapped on the door
	6	opened the door
4	7	I am going
	8	leave my bag
	9	Yes, you may
	10	Do not open
5	11	the fox had gone
	12	what is
	13	in this bag
	14	I will see
	15	So she opened

WINSTON FIRST READER — REVIEW

(Words mastered in connection with the primer and reviewed in new phrase settings when they occur in the first reader.)

PAGE	CARD NUMBER	
2	R. 1	he caught
	R. 2	He put
	R. 3	Then he went on
3	R. 4	came to a house
	R. 5	A woman came
4	R. 6	May I
	R. 7	The woman said
5	R. 8	out flew
6	R. 9	flew out
7	R. 10	Then give me
	R. 11	and put him
8	R. 12	Soon the fox
12	R. 13	Soon he saw
	R. 14	A little boy
	R. 15	got away

primer group we list the phrases "said the cat" and "said the pig," but not "said the goose," since the word *goose* is not met sufficiently often to justify thorough drill upon it at this time.

Following the same plan, in the first reader we listed phrases containing new words to be mastered. Also we made a separate list of words mastered in the primer class but appearing in new phrase arrangement when met in the first reader.

As an outcome of this phrase study we have a list of 159 phrases to be learned in connection with the primer work; 98 phrases make their initial appearance in the first reader, but offer no new vocabulary; each of 241 first reader phrases contains one or more words selected for mastery in connection with the first reader work. This complete group of 499 phrases, comprising a vocabulary of 111 words from the primer and 124 words from the first reader, offers minimum requirements as a working basis in teaching and gives a practical vocabulary on which to test pupils for promotion and for grouping.

Illustrative phrases here given indicate the type of phrases which are selected for intensive drill. All have been printed on cards and numbered for the convenience of the teacher.

Such definite requirements make it possible for each teacher to do individual work, keeping a record of the cards recognized by each pupil. The report also indicates which phrases offer greatest difficulty. This definite record can be handed to the teacher receiving a child at promotion time or upon transfer. Thus the individual can be taught what he has not yet learned and no time need be wasted in "trying out" a class. This is especially important in the case of young pupils whose reticence in the presence of a new teacher may place them at a disadvantage for some time.

THE TEACHING OF SILENT READING

W. F. TIDYMAN

Head of Department of Education and Director of Training School, Farmville, Virginia

I. Values in Reading.

Like other school activities the value of reading is judged by the extent to which it contributes to living—not living in the narrow vocational sense, but living in its fullness, richness, completeness. The life of the child in and out of school, as well as adult life, should be considered. We may well ask, "What are the demands of life upon reading?" Or more specifically, "What attitudes, what habits, what knowledge, and what skill should the well-trained reader possess?"

The best readers love to read and show good taste in the selection of reading material; they read silently, rapidly, and accurately, and they are oblivious of the printed page.

Are children dragged to the reading lesson, or led? Does the teacher spend the time in urging children, or in guiding them? Do children lay the book aside with regret or disgust? Have they learned to love reading or to hate it? Have they formed the "reading habit," or the habit of avoiding reading? This is the ultimate test of the work of the school. Unless children learn to enjoy reading and, by choice, go to books for pleasure and information, the primary purpose of the reading work has not been accomplished.

The second value is complementary to the first. It is not enough that a child should learn to love to read. He must learn what to read as well. With love for reading may go a perverted taste for the cheap, sensational literature of the street. The object of the school is to cultivate a taste for better things. Stevenson, Scott, Cooper, Alcott, Dana, and a host of other authors provide a mine of material which, if given a chance, will enthrall the minds and fire the imaginations of boys and girls without leaving unwholesome images and ideas. Good taste is shown in the breadth as well as in the depth of reading; therefore, children should come to know and appreciate history, biography, and poetry, as well as fiction.

Since the invention of printing and the widespread circulation of reading material, the practical need for oral reading has greatly diminished. Yet the oral reading methods fixed in school practice centuries ago still dominate school practice to a large extent. Probably 98 per cent of the reading that adults do in life is reading to oneself, or silent reading. As compared with the silent reading of the daily paper, business correspondence, books, etc., which is an important part of the life of every educated adult, there are a few isolated instances of oral reading, as in the case of a friendly letter or a paragraph from the newspaper. Outside the work of teachers, preachers, and lawyers, oral reading is an art that is little needed and little used. Yet the school still spends a very large proportion of its time in teaching the technique of oral reading. The development of good silent reading habits is frequently left to chance or to incidental instruction in connection with other subjects, with the apparent assumption that the child who learns to read well orally will of necessity learn how to read well silently. The truth is that children have to be taught how to read silently as well as orally, and that overemphasis or untimely emphasis upon oral reading may seriously interfere with the development of proper silent reading habits. Much practice in oral reading must be justified largely by the training it gives in the elements of oral expression, such as pronunciation, enunciation, inflection, phrasing, and quality of voice. It seems reasonable that this training should be gained chiefly in situations in which oral language is naturally used, namely, oral composition.

In addition to the principles of ready and accurate thought-getting common to all kinds of reading, instruction may distinguish the peculiarities of the process as applied to the story, history text, arithmetic problem, poem, encyclopedia, dictionary, and newspaper. The details of the process will vary also with the purpose of the reader. Such purposes as getting the gist of the selection, finding a particular fact, fixing a series of facts in mind, and picking out main thoughts will call for special variations in procedure.

Finally, the good reader is unmindful of the printed page. Words are merely windows to thought, and he thinks best who is least conscious of the reading process.

The importance of reading in school and in life outside the school is taken for granted. Reading is an indispensable tool in acquiring knowledge, and it is probably unequalled as a source of harmless enjoyment. The development of good reading habits adds immeasurably to one's practical equipment and possibilities for pleasure.

As a school problem, the teaching of reading depends upon the selection of good reading material and presenting this in such a way as to arouse the child's interest and to develop economical and effective reading habits. The experience of teachers and the scientific studies of the complex problems involved will in time show us how to do this. At present there are many gaps in our knowledge; we must proceed cautiously and haltingly, but withal courageously.

The primary purpose of this article is to stimulate thought and experimentation with the teaching of silent reading by presenting concrete and workable suggestions for conducting the work.

These, we believe, are consistent with established facts, and practically all of them have been used in the classroom. The teacher should accept these suggestions tentatively, and changes should be made as experimentation throws further light upon the many problems involved, and as classroom experience dictates.

II. Kinds of Reading.

The reading of children and adults may be divided roughly into three classes: studious or purposeful reading, consultative reading, and cursory reading or reading for pleasure. Reading of the first class is such as is done by the physician in looking up a medical case, a merchant in studying market reports, a teacher in consulting Bagley's *Classroom Management*, a pupil in reading history, geography, or Washington's *Farewell Address*. Reading of this sort is usually directed toward getting useful information; it is seldom an end in itself. It is often called "study."

Consultative reading is similar in purpose to studious reading, but is directed primarily toward finding a particular fact in a mass of related material; for example, consulting a dictionary or encyclopedia. The habits to be formed are those of rapidly sifting a large amount of matter, and isolating the desired fact.

Cursory reading is the kind of reading that is done by children and adults in their leisure hours. Its primary purpose is pleasure, and it includes much of the reading of books, newspapers, and magazines.

III. Reading Material.

Securing an adequate supply of appropriate material is one of the problems that emphasis upon silent reading raises. It is not unusual for the children to cover as much ground in one grade as they formerly covered throughout the elementary school course when every selection was read aloud. Instead of three sets of readers per grade, the school can easily use twelve sets per grade. The purpose of the common text is for class study, in which study habits are developed; and types of literature, authors, and the like, are introduced. The bulk of the work in reading, as far as quantity is concerned, is done by children independently, in gathering information, fixing interests, and applying habits begun in class study. With limited funds the teacher can reduce the number of class copies and invest a part of her money in single copies of books. A set of miscellaneous texts will give as many books as there are members in the class; and if the school is entirely without funds, the children may buy these instead of or in addition to the common text. In addition, children can bring books from home, grade libraries may be built up, and advantage may be taken of facilities offered by local and state libraries for the loaning of sets of books.

In order to develop breadth of taste and interest it is well to include in the grade lists a variety of selections. Stories, biographies, history, poetry, drama, addresses, editorials, and important news and informational items should find their places in the reading class sooner or later. The approach may be made through the simpler and more appealing types, but the child should not suffer an arrest of development in the story. Following the introduction of a new type through class study, supplementary books should be provided, and the children should be encouraged to read them. The material obviously should be such as appeals, or may be made to appeal to children; and it should not be too difficult. It should be graded one grade lower than for oral reading. The children should not have to labor over unfamiliar words, concepts, grammatical constructions, etc. These difficulties may be removed in part in the assignment. It is desirable also that the selection be a natural unit, a literary whole. The short story is an excellent example.

A number of graded lists of books for silent reading have been prepared. Dr. O'Brien in his book, *Silent Reading*, gives a list prepared by Professor James F. Hosic. Brief lists are found also in Kendall and Minch's *How to Teach the Fundamental Subjects*.

IV. Methods — Types.

The typical methods to be employed correspond to the kinds of reading. They are studious, consultative, and cursory.

A. Studious or Purposeful Reading.

The reading activities of ordinary life are significant not only for determining the purpose and kinds of reading, but also for determining the main steps or stages in the reading process. First, there is a pressing problem, which gives the whole process purpose and form. Second, pertinent ideas or thoughts are selected from the printed page and organized. Third, the ideas or thoughts are fixed in mind or applied in meeting a concrete situation.

Apparently, the main steps in serious reading are: finding a purpose or problem, getting the thought, and applying the thought or fixing it in mind.

1. *Purpose or problem.* In out-of-school life reading is called into play in meeting pressing situations. The physician has a wave of influenza to meet. The lawyer is concerned with a point of law. The farmer is preparing plans for the construction of a concrete platform. The teacher has a troublesome case of discipline. In each case, previous experience or present need provides the problem or purpose for reading. The occasion which calls forth reading may be an emergency or a temporary situation, or reading may follow a habitual bent. The former is illustrated above. The latter is illustrated by the baseball fan who follows from day to day the performances of his favorite teams. The interest may be general or highly specialized, as interest in all charitable work, and interest in reading the account of the activities of a particular organization.

The practical question is, "Can the teacher produce in the schoolroom a semblance of these conditions? Can the work of the school be made as real and vital to children as the work of life is to adults?" The answer of experience seems to be that this can be accomplished to a certain extent.

The child world, like the adult world, is full of interests, activities, problems. They are part and parcel of child life. On the other hand, books are full of information, ideas and incidents that can help the child meet his problems, and that draw the child to them when they are given a chance. Having selected books that have a possible significance and value for children, the teacher's next concern is to present the selection in such a way as to show its relation to the child's problems. The child's problem may represent an emergency situation, such as learning how to play a new game, or it may be a relatively permanent interest, as in boy scout life and activities. The need may be actual, that is, conscious; or it may be potential, that is, something to be brought out by the teacher. There is practically no limit to the ingenuity of the teacher in discovering children's actual and potential needs, and practically no limit to skill in presenting reading material in a vital and appealing manner. Some of the child's needs are practical — doing something, such as making a wagon, learning to make a kite, and dramatizing an historical event. Other needs are intellectual or emotional in character — to understand, and to be entertained. The latter class of needs has received greater recognition in the classroom.

In teaching reading, problems may be found in (1) recalling a similar experience, as in *The Fish I Didn't Catch;* (2) reproducing the historical setting, as in the *Star Spangled Banner,* and *Washington's Farewell Address;* (3) raising a question of historical fact, as "Was the South justified in withdrawing from the Union?" "What were Washington's ideas on disarmament, preparedness and foreign alliances?"; (4) tracing historical origins and growth, as, "Trace the development and spread of the idea of democracy"; (5) making comparisons, as, "Compare Spartan and modern ideas and practices in physical education";

(6) explaining striking statements of facts and observed phenomena, as, "Why is Africa called 'the dark continent?'" and "Why do we have four seasons in the year?"; (7) explaining physical principles, as, "Why is the wheel of a passenger train taller than the wheel of a freight train?" and "What is the effect of winds upon climate?"; (8) raising live social and economic problems, as, "How can Farmville keep its sidewalks free from snow and ice?" Problems such as these are developed through a study of pictures, preliminary reading or glancing through the selection, reading the selection to the children, presenting facts and figures, and recalling related experiences.

The value of this preliminary step in reading is that it arouses the interest of the child, and serves as a guide to the selection and organization of ideas. It gives the child a cue in regard to what is to follow. It directs the procedure. Care should be taken in this step to clear away serious difficulties such as uncommon words, involved thought, involved figures of speech, unusual grammatical constructions, and the like.

2. *Thought-getting.* The second step suggested by the observation of ordinary reading is "thought-getting." By this is meant getting a series of incidents, a number of miscellaneous facts, relationships existing between facts or events, answers to single pointed questions, and the like. These processes involve the comprehension, selection, evaluation, and organization of ideas, one or more of which may be prominent in a particular selection. The activities of the class will be guided by the im-

mediate purpose or problem. If the immediate purpose is to gain a comprehension of the whole selection, attention will be directed to this end. On the other hand, if the component parts are to be emphasized, then the efforts of the children are directed to this work.

Training in thought-getting should be begun with sentences and paragraphs. As facility and power are gained, advance may be made to the larger units and, finally, to the whole selection. The ability of children to get thought will vary naturally with the difficulty of the selection. It will be relatively high in simple narrative, and low in such reading as history, geography, and arithmetic. The purpose of this training is largely to give children skill in thought-getting. It usually takes the form of class study with the teacher. Care must be taken not to delay the progress of the class on a low level by unduly protracted drill. Waste of time, and loss of interest and power result. Attention should be given to speed as well as thoroughness and accuracy. Most of the training in reading, beyond the mastery of elementary skills involved in getting the thought accurately and readily from sentence and paragraph, should take the form of ordinary supervised study, or independent study followed by class discussion.

The direction of the class study by the teacher will take the form of detailed questions followed by discussion, such as, "What things does the paragraph tell? Which is the most important — contains the largest thought? What things are included in, or said about, or are illustrations of the main thought?" In this work, the idea of

the topic sentence and its place in the paragraph are developed. Underlining the chief sentence and word, and writing out the main thought are helpful exercises. Let the children criticize their statements, and prove their own answers by the text. Don't *waste* time in class discussion. It is a reading lesson, not an oral language lesson. To keep children together in reading the selection, books may be closed when the answer is gotten, with the finger marking the place. Keep up the speed, occasionally timing and testing their rate of reading.

The study of larger units of work usually takes the form of independent study, directed through careful assignments by the teacher. The assignment is detailed or general depending upon the skill and maturity of the class, and the nature of the selection. The assignment takes the form of questions or exercises. Having the children prepare questions, outlines, synopses, paragraph headings, summaries, and the like are helpful exercises. Supervision is very close in the early stages of the work, and in the reading of difficult material. It becomes less close as children gain power to work independently and when the reading is easy.

The main principles of habit formation apply to developing power in thought-getting. Let the children take up one set of habits at a time. Make the procedure clear. Practice. As facility is gained on the power levels, advance to the next level in the hierarchy of reading habits.

3. *Memorization.* When the information is gathered, the problem solved, the question answered, the series of

incidents made clear, the conclusion reached, it is usually desirable in studious or purposeful reading to take the further step of fixing the thoughts in mind while they are fresh. This is designated as the third step. Such devices as the following may be used: recall and pass in review mentally the chief points of the selection; repeat the conclusion or principle; recall the main steps in development; look through the selection, recalling problems or topics and the main sub-topics; review sectional and paragraph headings, or printed summaries; glance through the index and look up unfamiliar references; prepare written outlines or synopses; apply conclusions to new cases; compare with similar experiences or facts.

B. Consultative Reading.

Consultative reading aims at securing as directly and quickly as possible a useful fact or bit of information. It is commonly used in consulting dictionaries, encyclopedias, and reference books. It is similar in purpose and method to studious or purposeful reading, except in certain important particulars. Thoroughness means getting just the desired facts and no others; therefore, much emphasis is placed upon omissions. In order to omit intelligently and readily, it is necessary that pupils know definitely what they are looking for, that they maintain a certain mental alertness, and that they use wisely contextual heading for getting thought. That is, they should recognize at once through the headings broad divisions and sections that contain irrelevant matter. Having located the section in which the desired information will be

found, the next step is to pick out and pass over rapidly the unnecessary paragraphs until the right paragraph is reached. This will mean moderating the speed of reading and noting paragraph headings or topic sentences for thought. The class drill upon paragraph study suggested above should aid the pupils here in locating readily the key sentences and words.

The development of these principles in close study, and application by the pupils with less and less supervision by the teacher, will serve to fix in mind the essential features of this type of reading. Follow-up work by the teacher will prove effective in fixing the best study habits.

C. Cursory Reading.

The third type of reading which we have distinguished is cursory reading or reading for pleasure. This is the kind of reading most universally and frequently used, and the kind most poorly taught. It is the reading which is done voluntarily, for its own sake, such as the reading of stories, histories, biographies, poems, editorials, current events, and the like. It is impossible to draw a clear line of demarcation between reading of this sort and studious reading. There will of necessity be much overlapping, and at times the distinction will be found in the attitude of the learner rather than in the subject matter or even method of procedure. The chief variations in method of procedure from the first type will be noted here.

1. *Problem.* In studious reading a clear, definite problem is necessary as a guide to thought. In cursory reading the well defined thought problem is less

necessary. A problem may or may not be definitely worded. The purpose of the preparatory step is chiefly to put children in the right mental attitude to enjoy the piece. The desired attitude is one of anticipation and interest. The preparation period has the additional function of clearing away difficulties of thought and form.

The general suggestions and devices mentioned for studious reading will be useful in this phase of reading, such as giving the historical setting, as in *Paul Revere's Ride*, relating similar experiences, and asking questions to recall similar experiences and to indicate the trend of thought. The attention of the children should be directed to the particular value of the selection.

2. *Thought or feeling.* In the second step, the emphasis is frequently placed upon the emotional response of the child. The results are measured primarily in terms of attitudes and feelings and only secondarily in terms of facts and principles.

The question to be asked in each selection is, "What is there here to be enjoyed?" This will vary naturally according to the selection. Among the things to be enjoyed will be found the story or plot, as in *Pinnochio;* the character, as in biography and hero stories; rhythm, as in *The Bells;* pictures; beauties of form — sentences, as in the *Beatitudes;* figures of speech, as in Byron's *To the Ocean;* wit, as in first scene of *Julius Cæsar;* humor; pathos; sublimity of thought, as in the *Psalm of Life.*

The method, whether oral reading by the teacher, silent reading by the class, or oral reading by the class, will be adapted to bringing out vividly the thing to be enjoyed. The questions set by the teacher will bring out the special values of the selection, and usually they will be less detailed. Avoid the tendency to emphasize matters of technique, to overanalyze, and to rehash a piece. Ask no more questions than are necessary for complete thought or feeling. Let the children feel and know the piece directly, by hearing it and reading as a whole. Occasionally let them try to express the same thought in their own words. Several repetitions of the piece from different points of view are helpful.

3. *Memorization.* In regard to the third step we may say that the emphasis in cursory reading is upon appreciation, not use. Nevertheless it is frequently worth while in reading a book of literary merit to take time to fix in mind some of the main characters of the story, the principal points, and our reaction to the story while it is fresh in mind. Such bits of knowledge and attitudes distinguish in part the cultured from the uncultured, the systematic from the careless reader, the well-read from the assiduous reader.

The use of the newspaper and popular magazine, because of their universality, are forms of cursory reading which should be given particular attention. The special aims of the work should be to elevate taste and teach how to get thought quickly from a long printed report or discussion. Children may be taught to distinguish between the sensational and trivial, the common gossip of the press and the more important items having to do with political and economic questions of local and national importance; to prefer the moderate, thoughtful editorials to the front page attractions; to consider the political affiliations and interests of the paper in weighing its statements and stand on public questions; to give preference to Associated Press items and signed articles; to gather the gist of articles from main and sub-headings; and to limit thorough reading to a few of the most important ones, such as presidential messages.

V. Provision for Increasing Vocabulary.

What is to be our attitude toward word drills which have had such a prominent place in traditional methods? Placing emphasis upon extensive, silent reading will undoubtedly lessen the need of formal drill upon isolated words. The teacher will rely upon the frequent contact with words in varying contexts, rather than upon intensive drill as the primary means of increasing the vocabulary.

In the preparatory step and in the class discussions the crucial and vital words will naturally receive special attention as a means to thought-getting. Words of less importance may be passed over with slight attention. As in the case of adult reading, it is not necessary that the child know the exact meaning of every word in order to get the meaning of the selection. In practice some distinction should be made here in the various kinds of reading. More exact knowledge of words is needed obviously in the studious and systematic types.

Some word drill will be unavoidable. However, this should be made incidental and as unobtrusive as possible. Meanings should grow out of the context,

and if necessary should be given outright until children gain power to use the dictionary effectively.

VI. Speed.

Rate of reading, that is, rate of comprehending thought, is not an unmodifiable trait, fixed by heredity. It is extremely modifiable, and determined in large part by the following factors: methods of beginning reading, the attitude of the learner, innate capacity, and habits. In a great majority of individuals speed is subject to vast improvement. O'Brien shows that speed may be developed in a remarkably short time, without loss in comprehension. The direction of improvement lies in (1) making direct associations between words and ideas (reducing vocalization), (2) increasing the perception span to take in larger units at a single glance, such as phrases instead of words, (3) increasing familiarity with words, (4) broadening and deepening child's knowledge-apperception, (5) skill in locating thought, (6) habits of alertness and attention, and (7) practice. Dr. O'Brien gives an excellent discussion of this phase of the work in his *Silent Reading*.

VII. Incentives.

The child's interest may be aroused by tying up reading with things that the child wants to do; stimulating his love for stories, curiosity, desire for attainment; offering immediate rewards and suggesting more remote values and utilities. Motive will vary with the kinds of reading and with children. Means to be employed are: good selections, not too difficult; problems;

dramatizations; games; enthusiasm of the teacher.

VIII. Class Work.

Probably the most apparent difficulty confronting teachers beginning this work is what to do in class. By way of reviewing and amplifying the suggestions already made, we may note the following activities: (1) class study, in which a selection is taken up for the first time; children receive instruction as to methods of study, principles already developed are practised; children are made acquainted with new types of literature and new values in literature; new words, phrases, and figures are studied. (2) Class discussions of work prepared outside of class. In this work ideas are compared, difficulties of thought and phrasing are cleared up, and particular parts of selections are discussed or re-read for enjoyment. (3) Assignments. This may take the form of an introduction to a selection, suggesting problems, setting definite tasks including questions. (4) Individual reports on outside reading. (5) Oral reading to the class.

IX. Independent Study-Assignments.

A large amount of the work in reading will be carried on by children independently. In fact, the efforts of the teacher are largely directed toward extending independent, spontaneous reading, and giving the children the power to carry it on intelligently. The study-reproduction methods of class work will give way largely to independent study of whole selections as soon as the children have gained the skill requisite to carrying on the work independently. This will naturally vary with the character and difficulty of the material. Children will apply principles previously learned.

The direction of independent study is through assignments, largely. The assignment should be definite and graduated to the child's maturity and skill. It will be detailed at first. It may guide the child in any of the activities previously described as a part of studious or cursory reading, and will take the form of questions, written or verbal. By the time the children leave the elementary school, they should be able to perform intelligently all the steps of the process independently, following a simple statement of the problem. In addition to directing study, the assignment will frequently include an introduction to a selection, the purpose of which is to get an attitude of interest and anticipation, and to clear up difficulties of thought and form.

X. Correlation.

The principles controlling thought-getting through silent reading should be applied in all subjects in which reading is a tool, such as history, geography, arithmetic, and science. Consistency in the application of sound principles will add greatly to the efficiency of all reading work.

XI. Hygiene.

In silent reading the chief matters of hygiene concern the use of the eyes. The factors affecting them are position of book, print, paper, arrangement of page, leading, and length of line. These questions are discussed thoroughly by Huey in the reference cited.

XII. Standards and Tests.

For the school as a whole we may say that it has accomplished its purpose when children habitually go to worthy books for instruction and pleasure, and comprehend the thought readily and accurately. The standard for each grade is relative to this. A rough measure of the standing of a class may be found in the use of such tests as the *Kansas Silent Reading Test* and *Starch's Test*. These tests should weigh both speed and comprehension. Other tests designed to measure specific growth in rate and comprehension, and to diagnose particular reading difficulties, should supplement these.

XIII. Oral Reading.

Is oral reading to be neglected entirely, then? Clearly not. It always will have at least two important functions — thought-getting, or studying aloud, and the expression of thought. The first function is important in the lower grades, and in the upper grades where subject matter is difficult or unfamiliar. It is useful also in getting full value from such types as poetry, drama, orations, and addresses. The amount of oral reading needed for the expression of ideas is very limited, and it is a question just how much emphasis it should receive in the school. Kendall and Mirick suggest a division of time in which oral reading receives 90 to 95 per cent of the time in Grade I, and decreases gradually to 5 to 10 per cent in Grade VIII. When oral reading is taught, it should be with definite ends in view and not simply *heard*.

References

Kendall and Mirick. *How to Teach the Fundamental Subjects*, pp. 8–68. One of the best practical presentations of methods of teaching silent reading for all grades.

Reorganization of English in Secondary Schools, pp. 31–33, 45–54, 63–84. United States Bureau of Education, Bulletin, 1917, No. 2. A splendid recent discussion of aims, organization, and methods.

Klapper, Paul. *Teaching Children to Read*. General discussion of the problems and methods of oral reading.

Briggs and Coffman. *Reading in the Public Schools*. Contains helpful suggestions but, in the main, devotes itself to oral reading problems.

Arnold, Sarah L. *Reading — How to Teach It*. Contains many helpful suggestions. Note Chapter IV especially.

Lowth, E. J. "Advanced Reading — Ten Definite Assignments." *Normal Instructor and Primary Plans*, November, 1919, p. 46. Gives typical assignments for upper grades.

Jenkins, Frances. *Reading in the Primary Grades*. Has many practical suggestions for primary work, but related in the main to oral reading.

Huey, E. B. *The Psychology and Pedagogy of Reading*, pp. 387–418.

J. B. O'Brien. *Silent Reading*. Excellent discussion based upon scientific data, with special emphasis upon speed.

Emma M. Bolenius. *Silent and Oral Reading in the Elementary School.*

DISCIPLINING CHILDREN[1]

William Heard Kilpatrick

Professor of Education, Teachers College, Columbia University

Not so long ago while on a sleeping car I heard a man tell his seven-year-old daughter, "It is time to go to bed. The conductor has just told me that little girls on a sleeping car must go to bed by nine o'clock." The child hesitated, but finally said she didn't believe it. Now how can that child grow up truthful? Since then I have thought a good deal about parents and the way some of them manage their children, and the characters that necessarily result. Some of these thoughts I am going to discuss with you today.

How some parents act

First, let us ask whether in the management of our children we seek character or conduct. Many will say at once, "It is character we seek." Whether or not they say this because character has such a good name among men, I do not know; but if we ask whether they in fact so act as to build character, the reply wouldn't come so quickly. Aside from pious wishes, what do parents really seek? Is it character or is it conduct? When the long-suffering mother says, "Children, stop making so much noise," or "John, I have told you once to stop teasing your sister," it is safe to say that it is the present peace and comfort of the family that is mostly sought. Possibly the tired father's attitude is more striking. The children annoy him by their noise. "Can't you make those

Do we seek character or conduct?

children keep quiet?" he will ask impatiently. The mother tells the children that father has been working for them hard all day and is tired tonight and they must consider his feelings and keep quiet. They mind for a while; then, as they forget, the father will often rail out, "If I have to speak to you again, you'll go to bed at once. Do you hear me?" Now I ask again, is it character or is it conduct he is seeking? We'll discuss later what he is getting; but let us now try to answer the question asked.

Is it character or is it conduct? We wish character, because without it we have no sure basis for expecting conduct. It seems then that we wish both, good conduct as the rule of life and character because it furnishes the basis and hope for such conduct. But this is not all. While we thus set up character as our educational aim, we are forced back on good conduct as the only means for building good character. Good conduct—immediate conduct—is the means to good character just as this good character is the means to later and further good conduct. Going back to the angry parent, he is so much concerned over the effects of the immediate conduct on his own peace and happiness that he forgets to ask the effect of his speech and tone on the children. He forgets for the time the character they are building. In point of fact, they are most likely as a result of his

[1] The substance of a talk delivered before various parents' associations. All rights reserved by the author.

threat to learn prudence, "not to make a noise when father is tired," rather than to acquire consideration for a tired and unselfish father. Which do our children acquire, prudence or consideration? Can we manage it so that the one (or both) and not merely the other is built into the child's character?

How, then, is any trait built into character? The word trait as here used means the same thing as habit, only habit is often (but wrongly) thought of as being bad, like the drink habit. Habit properly means any acquired trait, any learned way of thinking or feeling or acting. Everyone knows the force of habit, how it will try to act itself out, how in fact it will, if strong enough, act itself out in face of resolutions to the contrary and in spite of the tears and pleadings of dear ones injured by the evil practice. Now good habits can be just as strong as bad habits. Building character is exactly building up strong good habits, habits of consideration of others, habits of dealing honestly, habits of thinking before we act, habits of preferring the happiness of wife or children to our own. How to build such habits is a matter for psychology to tell us, and fortunately modern psychology has some very definite and helpful advice to give us.

Character means habits

The first point in building habit is to practice the desired habit, the trait to be acquired. This, you say, is old, old advice. So it is and none the worse for that, but we must be very sure what trait is being practiced. When the tired father, angry over the continued noise, railed out with his

Specific practice, specific habit

shut-up-or-go-to-bed threat, the children responded by practicing along several lines. One might be as suggested above, "He's mad, we'd better look out." Another might be, "I wish he'd stay away all the time or anyhow let us alone." On the other hand it might be, "I'm awfully sorry we worried father, he is so tired. I'd like to tell him so, but I am afraid." So the parent or teacher must ask himself or herself, "What traits am I having my children practice? Is it prudent restraint or fear or angry resentment, or consideration of others or regret at thoughtlessness?" Is it not clear that the angry threat might make the child outwardly quiet with any one of these respondings going on inside? Practice builds habit, yes, we cannot too often say it to ourselves; but everything turns on what is being practiced. Here is where our responsibility as parents or teachers call for closer thought than many of us have given.

But practice is not all. The attitude of the learner plays a very important part. Practice with satisfaction builds, but practice with annoyance tears down. Modern psychology has made no discovery more important in its practical bearings. To build a habit we must not only practice it, but must feel that our practice works and be in some measure glad that it works. If I practice something with continued failure and annoyance, I shall find myself less and less inclined to do it. If this long enough continues so, I build in the end an aversion. Continued satisfaction will build a positive habit; continued annoyance will build

Satisfaction builds; annoyance tears down

an aversion. If my child practices prudential restraint in my presence and it works to his satisfaction, he will build the habit of prudential restraint when he is with me. If he practices making me his confidant and I abuse his confidence or make him feel ridiculous, he will cease to make me his confidant or even worse he may build an aversion to talking with me about anything vital to him. The annoyance will get in its work. Whether practice builds a strong positive habit or builds an aversion depends, then, on the attitude of the learner. Satisfaction builds, annoyance tears down.

It is at once evident that the principle just laid down greatly limits our part in building the characters of our children. We can require some sort of (outward) practice, but we are often helpless as to the resultant satisfaction or annoyance. For this reason many of you will begin to say to yourselves that you are not going to accept any such limiting and hindering principle. If so, I can only point out that your very rejection but illustrates the very principle you would reject. You find it annoying and you therefore reject it. I am sorry if you do reject it, because your children will none the less build their characters on it, and you will be but throwing away the guidance and insight you might otherwise have.

Our problem today is that of discipline. As commonly understood, punishment and coercion are

Punishment and coercion the central features of discipline. I shall wish to take exception to so negative a view of discipline, but this side we must understand. Punishment in the light of the preceding paragraph seems best conceived as an artificially induced annoyance; while coercion may be thought of as the effort to induce action by the threat of punishment or other disagreeable experience.[1] It will be at once evident that coercion and punishment are better adapted to securing immediate and outward conformity than they are to securing the practice of those inward attitudes which constitute so large a part of the good character. Indeed punishment may do harm. The child who is caught in some wrongdoing and punished will be annoyed, and will accordingly be less inclined to the same thing next time. But at what is he annoyed? At his wrongdoing or at getting caught? If he does indeed truly regret his wrongdoing, he will be less likely to engage in it next time. But if he regrets, not his wrongdoing, but only that he was caught, he will in that case be less likely to get caught next time. Whether we build character or teach slyness in wrongdoing or resentment at our interference is thus at stake and in doubt every time we punish. Punishment, as Thorndike has pointed out,[2] may prove useful where there is only one thing to learn and that is *not* to do something,—not to pull dishes off the dinner table; but where there are many possibilities it may well do more harm than good.

Perhaps we had better pause to notice an idea frequently found among the most conscientious of parents, that wrongdoing by its very nature demands

[1] For a further discussion of coercion, see articles by the author in the January and February numbers of this magazine.
[2] E. L. Thorndike, *Education* (N. Y., 1912), p. 201-202

punishment, that the parent is then morally bound to punish wrongdoing, that the results must be good. This is not the place for lengthy discussions of theories of punishment, and we must particularly avoid theological complications. I wish, however, to deny that the parent is under such an obligation to punish. In my own judgment incalculable harm has been done both to children and to criminals by following this vindictive theory of punishment. If we are going to punish, let us punish only as we can see that it promises to do positive good. Almost the only good that can come to the older child who has done wrong is by way of seeing and feeling and regretting that he has done wrong. To punish in blind faith that good must somehow come, regardless of evident consequences, is to practice a fatuous cruelty on our children.

No vindictive punishment

But some of you will say, "We cannot do without coercion; our children must learn to face disagreeable things; life is not made up wholly of the agreeable." Others will say, "We cannot consent to spoil our children." And I should wish to agree emphatically with both as to what you wish. But I am not sure about the means. Our children must indeed learn to face unflinchingly the disagreeable things of life, and they are many. And spoiling is a real danger. What do we mean by a "spoiled" child? I take it to mean a child who acts on the principle that his wish is sufficient reason why he should have anything he wishes and that if he makes himself sufficiently disagreeable he'll get it in the end. Before we take

up these points let us look at learning from a further point of view.

Learning implies typically, if not necessarily, three steps—variation, selection, fixing. So stated these are merely cryptic. What do they mean? By variation, I mean learning faces always several possibilities, more ways of doing than can be selected. The baby learning to say "ma ma" has in fact at the time been using many other syllables, any one of which might have been chosen. By selection I mean that something or some one chose a certain one from among the many in preference to the others. At first any little crowing sound of the baby delighted the mother's heart, but after a while amid the many syllables some one sounded at least faintly like "ma ma." This the mother seized upon, selected, for fixing. By fixing I refer to the habit building discussed above. From among the many sounds (*variation*) the baby uses, the mother *selects* one that is dear to her and proceeds to *fix* it in the baby as an accomplishment. This she does by applauding and approving the baby when he says, "ma ma." And where is the baby old enough to say "ma ma" that fails to get satisfaction from the approval his mother gives? After he can say "ma ma," the mother notices that he will say "ma ma" to father, to nurse, to mother, to sister, to almost anybody. Here again is variation; and again the mother selects by approving only when he says "ma ma" to mother. This only will bring satisfaction. And the new accomplishment is fixed. I once chanced into a household where there were twins just at this stage; one

Variation, selection, fixing

was "mother's boy" and one was "father's boy." And strange but true, one could say "ma ma," but not "da da," and the other could say "da da," but not "ma ma." A partial selection had done its work.

The same holds of spoiling, of obedience, of facing disagreeable things.

Spoiling Take James's instance. The mother thinks her child now old enough to say "please." She holds out an apple and says, "say please." Instead he follows the more natural course and snatches at it. The mother says, "No, you can't have it unless you say 'please.'" The child then does the next most natural thing, he cries for it. Now suppose the mother relents and lets him have it. From among the three possibilities (variation) of snatching, crying, and saying please, crying has then been selected. Further, the crying thus brings satisfaction, while snatching didn't. Next time he will be somewhat less likely to snatch, but more likely to try crying. The mother is fixing this habit in him. If this is repeated in other instances, the child will eventually build in himself the trait, "I want what I want when I want it," and "if I cry loud enough I'll get it." He is spoiled and the mother did it. Firmness and consistency would have built "say please" as the only feasible way to get the apple. The mother might have hastened the process by a not-too-great slapping the hand that snatched. This would increase the annoyance attached to snatching otherwise only by failure.

If this process is begun early enough and adhered to consistently enough, there need be no fear of a spoiled child.

Now the case of facing the disagreeable things of life is a little more complicated. Suppose my

Facing the disagreeable child flinches before a disagreeable duty. What can I do? Suppose I use coercion and make him do it. Many of you would approve and say, "Yes, he must learn it. You are doing right to teach him." But is he learning it? Am I teaching it? To learn he must practice, practice exactly what he is to learn, and practice it with satisfaction to himself (or negatively, failure must bring annoyance). If I force him to do the disagreeable, is it satisfaction or annoyance that attends? I fear it will be a double annoyance; the thing itself is annoying, being made to do it is even more so. So by the plain teaching of psychology, if this is the whole case, the child will next time be still less likely to do the disagreeable thing. More exactly, it is probable that what he mainly practiced was obeying me under coercion. If the task at hand does prove as disagreeable as he expected, he will at most learn to obey me when I speak (because it does give him some satisfaction to avoid the pain that he thinks disobedience would bring).

But learning to obey me and learning to face disagreeable things when away from me are two quite different affairs. I am not so sure of his obeying me always—if I make it sufficiently disagreeable he will cease in time to do that; he will rebel, he will run away. I am reasonably sure that this method of coercion is not the way in which you or I really learned to do disagreeable things.

Let us be honest with ourselves. Do we do disagreeable things? Yes, often. Why? Think of some case.

Learning to face the disagreeable

Some of the ladies present will say, "washing dishes." If it is disagreeable, why do you do it? "Because no one else will." Why not let the dishes go unwashed? "Because I am not willing to eat from unwashed dishes or to let my family do it, or even to have unwashed dishes about. Besides, I'd be ashamed; my self-respect wouldn't let me. I don't know what people would say if they heard I didn't wash my dishes. I'd even be afraid of disease. Why, it would never do, no decent person would think of letting the dishes go unwashed." Exactly so. This sort of answer tells us in the case of this one disagreeable thing why it is done. It is all of these attendant ways in which we think and feel that make us do disagreeable things. In other words, we learn only indirectly to do disagreeable things. No one goes about looking for disagreeable things to do. The disagreeable things come in connection with things we like and we do the disagreeable things in order to get the things we like. The lady who answered above likes to eat from clean dishes. She likes to think of her house as clean and attractive in all respects. She wishes her family to enjoy the home life. She wishes also to keep the good opinion of others. She fears disease for herself and her family. In a less dignified detail, she fears also "Croton bugs" (roaches) and knows how she has to work to keep them away. Out of all these likes and dislikes, many disagreeable things have to be faced.

The latter are faced for the sake of the former.

The way, then, to teach my child to face disagreeable things is twofold: first, help him to build up a network of proper interests that cover the whole range of life; and second, help him to learn to work for these interests in spite of disagreeable hindrances. There is absolutely no other way to learn to face disagreeable things. Your rough-and-ready way of "making the boy do it" may keep him from getting spoiled, but is almost sure to do harm, perhaps great harm. In that it seems to him arbitrary, it may fail to teach what you wish him to learn. It will, moreover, likely alienate him from you.

Time and space suffice now for only one other question, that of obedience.

Teaching obedience

Some of you are perhaps saying, "Well, he means to leave the child free to do as it pleases." No, I do not mean that. There are difficulties, and the opinion I express may be disputed; but I myself believe in obedience—plain, common, everyday obedience. But I do not, however, fool myself. Obedience is a great convenience—to me—but it is far from being the whole of the child's moral character. Indeed it is at most but a small part of it. Still, as a convenience, I believe it is worth having. Two questions arise: How shall we build obedience? And when and how shall we use it? As to the first, begin very early. You can hardly begin too early. Be very consistent. In the earliest years of infancy, you may safely use some corporal punishment to enforce it. The question of how to build it is far easier—difficult as many find it—than the second question of when and how to use it. Remember that the child is to grow—in our country—into a self-directing citizen. Remember too that the very essence of morality is respect for personality. We must then always temper our demands for obedience by a consideration of these two principles. Avoid frequent appeals to obedience. Let the child learn as much as he possibly can from his own experiences. As he gets older, appeal to obedience less and less. Be fair and kind and always above every suspicion of selfishness or arbitrariness.

In conclusion, although the word discipline perhaps directs attention most

Conclusion to the ugly side of character building, let us not make the mistake of thinking that punishment and coercion and obedience are the main bases of this building—far otherwise. The main reliance is by all odds on the positive side of activity, achievement, working to ends, coöperation in common purposes, building interests. Our part is mainly one' of guiding, with but little of correcting. Obedience, coercion, and punishment belong to the occasional emergency, not to the rule of life. They may indicate present zeal but much more do they point to past failure—our failure to direct matters aright. Let obedience, then, be but rarely called into play, coercion less often, and punishment hardly at all. For parents to have to use punishment in the older years is practically a sign of permanent failure. As the child gets older let the parents cherish increasingly—not decreasingly, as too often happens—the child's confidence in their sympathy and fairness. This is often hard for us, for they can try our patience sorely. But it is our insurance against the day of evil. The time will come when coercion is no longer available in any form. Happy is the parent who has long since learned to do without it. The ties of love and sympathy need never grow old.

AN EXPERIMENT IN COÖPERATION
X. Comments by the Way

James F. Hosic

Associate Professor of Education, Teachers College, Columbia University

The limits of the present volume of the *Journal of Educational Method* will not permit my presenting our experience in the field of reading and literature. All should clearly understand, however, that we were aiming at a balanced program. Remembering the man who tried to pull himself over the fence by his bootstraps, and his equally foolish brother who tried to dip water out of a dry well, we sought to avoid leaving our pupils with no resources of vocabulary and ideas except what they brought with them to school. We therefore made a special effort to organize general or home reading. In this we were greatly aided by the public library, which arranged to supply each room in the English centers with a box of fifty books. How these were selected, how they were commended to the pupils and discussed in the reading groups, and how finally a library list for the city was compiled may perhaps be told in a later series of articles.

In similar fashion we undertook to develop and improve the story-telling and the teaching of literature through reading. Important as we thought the composition to be, we at no time felt disposed to underestimate the need of better methods in introducing young people to the joys of literature. Indeed, the tradition of the school has in large measure been opposed to the development of appreciation. So much stress has been laid on the acquisition of knowledge and growth in practical skills that the different attitude which must be assumed in the treatment of the arts proves difficult to many teachers. There is besides too often a lack of adequate background. The account of our experiment in literature must also be postponed until a later day.

THE USE OF TESTS

As has been explained, we did not introduce our experiment by giving a series of standard tests in English. Only a very limited use of such tests had as yet been made in the schools. The tests available, moreover, by no means covered the ground of our proposed experiment. To have attempted to measure the pupils by existing tests, with the idea of judging our progress at the end of one or more years by retesting, would have reacted most unfavorably upon our entire body of workers. What was needed was a better definition of aims and redirection of methods. In a word, we needed to get started in the right direction. Ultimately tests could be used with a proper perspective.

I may add that none of us had overmuch faith in the norms assigned to the various tests, nor the scores obtained in the surveys. To have attempted to compare the results obtained in our schools with those obtained elsewhere would in all probability have been misleading. The matter is not so simple. As Mr. Courtis so well shows in his account of the Gary school system, a great wealth of facts must be taken into account in order to establish just conclusions with regard to the work of a school or a school system. Particularly we felt that tests probably fail in many cases to reveal the true ability of the pupils. They are too much outside the picture. In other words, the tests have not behind them the incentives and orientation which first-class work requires.

Notwithstanding, we resolved to include the giving of tests in our experiment. While refusing to be judged by any particular test or series of tests, we did wish to make our contribution to existing knowledge as to the utility of the tests available. We accordingly asked and obtained from the superintendent of schools the privilege of drawing upon the Bureau of Research for sufficient quantities of typical tests to enable us to make a fair tryout.

The method of selection which we employed was this: a representative committee consisting of superintendents, principals, and teachers was appointed to choose the tests and formulate a plan of procedure. Samples of all the English tests in print were obtained and examined by the members of the committee and a choice of those likely to be most useful made. Certain tests could not be employed for the reason that they had already been made familiar to the pupils. The Ayres Spelling Test, for example, was included in the spelling book furnished by the Board of Education. It was thought, moreover, to distinguish between tests probably worthy of a general trial and those to be used only in a limited way.

Among the tests chosen and used were the Monroe Silent Reading Tests as revised for the Illinois battery, the Ashbaugh Dictation and Column Test in Spelling, the Greene Organization Test, the Haggerty-Noonan Achievement Test in Reading for the first three grades, the Burgess Picture Supplement Test in Reading. None of the tests in language and grammar then available was thought worth while. As for composition scales, while samples of the Thorndike-Hillegas Extension, of the Nassau Supplement, and of the Willing Scale were distributed, no general use was made of them for the reason mentioned earlier in this series of articles — none of these scales distinguishes sufficiently between achievement in composition and achievement in mechanics. Indeed the Willing Scale is the only one in the list which even attempts to do so. Since our experiment in composition had rested in part upon the separation of composition from mechanics, we felt that it would be unfortunate to blur this distinction when we were completing the enterprise. This is not to deny that for purposes of a general survey grading by means of one of the standard scales, providing the readers have been adequately trained, will be more uniform than if done without such aids. It cannot be too clearly understood, however, that ours was not a problem of a general survey but of the improvement of teaching.

Several of the schools reported the scores obtained on the various tests. These scores without exception were creditable as compared with those obtained in other cities. The principal stress, however, in gathering up the results of the testing was laid not upon comparative scores but upon the general merits of the tests themselves. Each group of teachers in conference was asked to formulate standards or criteria by which each test might be judged. These criteria included such points as whether the children readily grasped what was required, whether the abilities tested were those which the teacher cared most to develop, whether the tests were easily scored, and whether in general they were a sufficient addition to the apparatus of teaching to make it worth while to plan for their future use. Among the most satisfactory of the tests employed, as it turned out, were such simple tests of intelligence as the Pressey Primer Scale, the Holley Picture Completion Test, and the Trabue Language Completion Test. In a few cases the Otis Group Intelligence Scale was given and, while somewhat elaborate, proved distinctly worth while as an aid to classification.

IN GENERAL

To sum up briefly the account of our experiment so far as it has been given, we may say that the key to the improvement of the teaching of a school subject such as English, for example, is definite, whole-hearted, and systematic coöperation on the part of all concerned. Regarding the problem to be solved as an opportunity for service, all must feel free to contribute the best they have to give. No matter how humble the offering, it must be considered respectfully, whether it can be accepted or not. The test is that the one offering it shall feel encouraged to come again.

One thing should be attempted at a time. Divide and conquer! The subject of English is many-sided. It involves a variety of abilities distinctly different in character, even highly antagonistic. For example, spelling and reading probably tend to nullify each other. The process involved in learning to spell a word is not the process required for quick and instant recognition in the course of reading. Again, too much theory may actually hinder practice. In other words, teachers may be deeply impressed with the importance of a knowledge of the principles of rhetoric and grammar and as a result may be inclined to devote too many class hours to formal recitations dealing with those subjects instead of conducting vital practice in composition in situations which the pupils feel to be real.

Similarly from the standpoint of method it seems clear that our procedure was wise in avoiding any general scheme of methodology. The project method had been rather widely exploited in the city and it was confidently expected by many that we would announce with some flourish of trumpets that we were about to introduce the project method of English into the city schools. As a matter of fact the word "project" was probably not used once in the course of the conferences with the teachers throughout the first year. The single conception of purpose was pressed to the fore and enthusiasm aroused to discover what would come of it if the subject of reading were taught with this idea prominently in the mind of the teacher. The use of Thorndike's *Reading as Reasoning* supported this concept and showed what its practical application would mean. That a very distinct improvement in the power of the pupils to attack the printed page and get its meaning for themselves took place there seems to be not the slightest doubt. Best of all, this power carried over to the other studies from the class in reading. Pupils were quick to see its application in United States history. For example, a class in the seventh grade which had been apathetic and of which the teacher felt more or less in despair, readily pointed out that the side headings in their text were intended to suggest the gist of the various paragraphs and sections. They discovered that many of the headings were badly written and did not actually suggest the chief thoughts of the passages. They rewrote them and in doing so made a good start on the way to critical and constructive reading and study.

The idea of purpose proved equally effective in oral and written composition. Teachers who had too often permitted their pupils to pick flaws in the pronunciation or grammar of the work of a classmate as their sole contribution readily learned how to consider precisely what purpose the speaker or writer had in mind and whether it had been effectively carried out. Even in such mechanical matters as spelling, the definite attempt to reach a certain standard resulted in redoubling the efforts of the pupils and in a marked improvement in their scores. The spirit which developed is well typified in the remark of a little girl who stopped at the teacher's desk at the close of the hour and said, "Please speak to those two boys. They are spoiling our record."

THE CLEARING HOUSE

A MODEL OFFICE

Project: To try to secure a model office for use by future classes in Senior Commercial English.

Our class had for some time supplied secretaries for the teachers of the school who need help with their correspondence. In class one day these secretaries complained that (a) they could not always secure a typewriter when they needed one; and (b) that they had no suitable place in which to write. One boy asked why we could not have a corner set aside for secretarial purposes and secure a typewriter for our class use. At once we began to discuss ways and means. A committee was chosen to go over the building and see if any room was available. On oral theme day the members of this committee reported on various parts of the building which they had never before visited or known even existed. No room could be discovered suitable for our office. A second committee was elected to interview the manual arts department to see if they would allow one end of their long room and office to be partitioned off for our use. The manual arts department, it was reported, was perfectly willing, but had no authority to build the partition. The question arose then as to the authority to be consulted. One boy, who is also a member of the class in Community Civics, said he thought it was the job of the Public Property Commissioner. He was at once delegated to consult the Commissioner, and gave a very fine talk on his interview with the man. Incidentally, he himself learned and informed the class of the duties of such a Commissioner. He brought, however, the sad news that, though we might build the partition, we must ourselves stand the expense.

The girls now rose to the occasion and said they would give a cake and candy sale to defray the expenses of the partition. The food was to be prepared by the girls taking Household Economics. A discussion arose as to what material to use for the partition. One boy said that, in an emergency, beaver board had been used in Room 303b. A committee inspected this room and found it good, then went to a carpenter, got a list of comparative prices of various materials, and reported to the class. The girls decided that they could make enough at their sale to pay for beaver board, and voted to buy it. Boys in this class, who also study manual arts, volunteered to take the measurements and do the actual work. The engineer and the fireman were consulted as to whether there would be heat and ventilation in the walled-off space. Reports of every step were made and given as "oral themes." Written financial reports were submitted by the girls and audited by members of the class in accounting.

With a room secured, the pupils now chose a delegate to consult the powers about a typewriter. The Headmaster and the head of the Commercial Department were sympathetic, but not encouraging. The typewriters were all in use for classroom purposes. One girl, however, whose father is a shoe manufacturer, thought that her father had an old Oliver machine, but feared that it was out of repair. The boys then said that Roy could repair typewriters, and

one of the boys and the girl accompanied him to the father's office. The father was glad to lend the machine and Roy did actually patch it up under the encouragement of the rest of the class.

The secretaries now had a place in which to write and a machine to use, but no place to put the carbon copies of letters which the teachers desired to have kept. Appeal was made again to the English class and suggestions were given. A vote resulted in the decision to appeal for a filing cabinet. Another group approached the Public Property Commissioner, who said that there was no money for cabinets or any other furniture. But in their explorations the group had seen that the Dean's office had recently been painted and furnished with expensive willow and chintz furniture. The discrepancy struck the group and they besieged the Commissioner with carefully prepared "follow-up" letters, giving the prices of cabinets which they had secured from catalogues of local dealers and through business letters from mail order houses. The cabinet did not come, however, so the boys made an old packing box into compartments and stained it. The girls made folders out of book binding paper, and we all consulted textbooks on Business English in order to decide on the best method of lettering. We voted to use the simple alphabetical system. A progressive committee on filing was chosen and now does all that work.

Several of the teachers now asked us to make copies of tests for classes. In school we already have a multigraph, and suggestions were made by members of the class as to who were the best operators. These operators asked the head of the Commercial Department for the use of the machine in our office at a certain hour every day, and two of the boys volunteered to see that it was carried down from Room 215 to our office at that time. A vaudeville performance by amateurs from our class, with an admission fee of ten cents each, bought a new drum and type for our special use of the multigraph machine.

We now grew ambitious and desired more equipment for our office. I had to assert my authority to prevent two boys from tapping the wire and putting in a private line of telephone with instruments found in the physics laboratory. None of us was quite sure of the machines we needed, so we divided into committees and visited the offices of the large shoe firms in town to see how they were equipped. Some pupils who had relatives in the nearby shoe towns wrote to them to ask about office equipment. We read the answers to these letters, compared notes on the reports of those who had visited offices, and decided just what we must have and what were merely luxuries. We found that we could use the school dictaphone, if we had more records and transmitters. We conducted a daylight party in the gymnasium, with a volunteer orchestra from our class, and got enough money for two sets. The accounts of all our money-making schemes were kept by a volunteer treasurer and audited by a volunteer auditor. We decided that we should have to do without a duplicator and an adding machine, or else borrow the latter from the accounting class. We have a volunteer corps of workers who take turns in keeping our office neat. Much work now comes to us from the school office in connection with the regular routine of the school. Volunteer messengers from our class report to the teachers and the office for work to be done in our office. We write notices also for the school paper stating that we are prepared to do clerical work if desired, and we have sent advertising letters to members of the faculty.

This is as far as we have advanced, but we are scheming for further additions in the near future. We are writing to other high schools in order to find out how much of their clerical work is done by pupils. When we have our statistics, compiled by class members, we shall be prepared to offer our services to take the place of one assistant clerk whose salary, we compute, ought fairly to be applied to the necessities of our office.

Educational Comment. This project accomplished the following things for the pupils: A large number of allied school subjects were introduced in the project. Practical business forms were used instead of mere imaginary book models. A knowledge of the duties of various city officials was gained. Spelling and punctuation were much improved by the necessity of sending perfect business letters. Practical knowledge of business problems was secured. A sense of comparative values was developed by the feeling of unfairness which arose from comparing the Dean's office furniture with our own homemade makeshifts. Co-operation was greatly increased. Responsibility and care for future classes were fostered. The pupils certainly put their whole heart into the project. Accounting and auditing became the real thing. Economy and thrift were outgrowths, as shown by the plan to replace the office clerk. The spirit of real social service was especially prominent in the whole project.

ALICE E. SHERBURNE,
Haverhill, Mass.

AS REPORTED

A MESSAGE TO YOUNG PEOPLE

The Secretary of the N. E. A. has sent out the following plea to those eligible to enter the teaching profession:

Serve Democracy's Greatest Need

America's best talent should be dedicated to the training of the youth for citizenship. The National Education Association appreciates the efforts of its members to enlist in the educational army the strongest men and women in every locality. It is recommended to our best young people that they consider the following advantages of the profession of teaching:

1. Teaching pays. Besides ever-increasing financial compensation, the teaching profession offers the highest social sanctions and rewards.

2. Teaching is a growing profession. The Nation now requires the services of 700,000 teachers. There is a strong demand that teachers be better trained. As training increases, the financial and social rewards likewise increase.

3. Teaching offers a growing career. The well-trained teacher need have no fear of unemployment, but may look forward to increasing opportunities commensurate with added training and growth in personal fitness.

4. Teaching offers mental and moral growth. The soundest mental and moral processes are involved in the making of good citizens.

5. Teaching is building. The teacher shapes the unfolding life of childhood and radiates ideals and purposes that in the citizenship of tomorrow will become the fabric of an improved social structure.

6. Teaching inspires high ideals. There is nothing nobler or more practical than to shape and to guide the ideals and practices of the young citizens who are soon to be the Nation's responsible leaders.

7. Teaching is service. Those who enter this high calling enjoy the spiritual development and true happiness that come from rendering real service to the Republic.

8. Teaching insures big opportunities. With growth and inspiration come multiplied opportunities for self-improvement, for rearing the family in a wholesome atmosphere, and for living and building on life's best side.

9. Teaching is practical patriotism. Inspiring young citizens and directing problems of citizenship practice is a ministry essential to a democracy.

10. Teaching is the profession of professions. Measured by the standards that make life genuinely rich and happy, teaching offers opportunities beyond those of other professions. Teaching is the clearing-house of the past, the guide of the present, and the prophet of the future. It is therefore necessary that the Nation's finest talents should be consecrated to public education upon which the perpetuity of American ideals and the salvation of the Republic depend.

MR. WELLS STIRS THEM UP

If the well-known anecdote of the boys who got astride of the roof of the coal shed because the teacher warned them that was the *one* thing she would not permit may be taken as fairly typical of human nature in general, then the recent publication of the views of historians on Mr. Wells' *Outline of History* will cause a substantial increase in his bank account. The National Civic Federation of New York sent out a questionnaire asking for opinions on four points:

(1) the accuracy and dependability of Mr. Wells' statement of facts and deductions; (2) his qualifications in general as a historian; (3) whether his social and moral philosophy qualify him to be a leader and teacher of youth; and (4) whether the gripping qualities attributed to his presentation are so important as to render his accuracy and philosophy of little moment.

These questions were asked of various professors of history throughout the country. The returns have been gathered into a pamphlet of some forty-five pages, which is sent out accompanied by a statement by Mr. Condé B. Pallen, chairman of the Department on the Study of Revolutionary Movements of the Federation. The consensus of opinion, as Mr. Pallen declares, is undoubtedly against Wells. The objections to him are mainly that his history is inaccurate and that his conclusions are socialistic. An examination of the various answers shows, however, a sufficient lack of unanimity among the professors of history to soften somewhat the adverse judgment which they give. For instance, one finds no "gripping" qualities whatever, while others admit that the book is written with rare appeal to interest.

The fact seems to be that, whatever else Mr. Wells has done, he has departed from the beaten track and must suffer the consequences. If his personal treatment of history is suitable for use in schools, then a number of copyrights fall in value over night. Though only natural and human that those who have written history as they think it ought to be written should turn upon the innovator, the fact remains, as has just been suggested, that a little more unanimity in the briefs which have been prepared against him would be more convincing to the outsider. In any case all who have not read the *Outline of History* will now do so at the earliest opportunity in order to see for themselves whether the views of the historians are to be accepted or not. Whether school authorities or professors will be influenced one way or another in the matter of adopting the book as a text for class use is problematical.

FORT WAYNE RETRACTS

More than ordinary interest attaches to the announcement by Superintendent L. C. Ward of Fort Wayne, Indiana, that the junior high school has been abandoned in his system. He states that most of the teachers in the so-called junior high schools of his city were merely departmental teachers of the upper grades, with no special training for the work. Before the junior high schools were established, he found as a high school principal little to complain of in the work of the children of the ninth grade. With the coming of the junior high school, Latin, typewriting, general science, junior high school mathematics, and various forms of extracurricular activities were introduced into the program of studies. As a result all departments of the high school noted a loss of ability on the part of entering pupils to concentrate on the subject in hand, a looseness of morale, and a hitherto unknown failure in reasonable discipline. Since there were no compensating gains, it seemed best to return to the simpler type of intermediate school.

Mr. Ward says that before a system commits itself to the junior high school movement it should ascertain whether the ninth grade pupil really has more in common with pupils of the seventh and eighth grades than he has with those of the tenth; whether a widely diversified curriculum with many electives is better for the mental growth of the child than the simpler, more compact courses; whether also the drill phase of education can be completed by the end of the sixth grade or even the seventh grade. Finally, he would lay great stress upon the necessity for a fund of common knowledge upon which to rear a national fabric.

THE READER'S GUIDE

RESEARCH VERSUS PROPAGANDA IN VISUAL
EDUCATION

A timely plea for more research and less propaganda in visual education is made by Professor Freeman, of the University of Chicago, in the May number of the *Journal of Educational Psychology*. He points out that new ideas in education generally pass through three stages: initial enthusiasm, reaction and decline, and a return to a moderate view. He thinks the second stage might be avoided if the initial enthusiasm were subjected to proper criticism. Inasmuch as we have now an appropriate scientific technique of investigation, there seems to be no reason why visual education should not escape the reaction which has overtaken so many other new ideas.

Specifically he points out that the current tendency to belittle language as a means of conveying ideas is unfortunate. The real humor and pathos of the movies is largely dependent upon the captions which accompany the pictures. It is true, moreover, that visual presentation in general tends to dispense with the personal influence of the teacher and the social interaction of the members of the group. Experiments should be entered into freely to determine just what the movies can best do and what they cannot do. The times require research rather than propaganda.

GRADING AND PROMOTION IN RELATION TO
INTELLIGENCE TESTING

One of the most valuable features of the Department of Superintendence at Chicago was the evening meeting held jointly with the National Society for the Study of Education. The general theme of the meeting was the use of intelligence tests. The open-ing address by Henry W. Holmes, Dean of the Graduate School of Education, Harvard University, on "The General Philosophy of Grading and Promotion in Relation to Intelligence Testing" has been published in *School and Society* for April 29. The speaker pointed out that there must still be argu-ments as well as scientific work in education. "Determination of facts does not deter-mine aims." . . . "In education it is never out of place to argue about aims."

He then presented a summary of the posi-tions which he assumed in the current Year Book of the society. Among his contentions were: first, that tests of intelligence distin-guish with reasonable accuracy between children of superior intellectual ability and their duller companions; second, segrega-tion of gifted children is to their advantage; third, this does not necessarily result in pushing bright children beyond their perma-nent powers of accomplishment; fourth, segregation is not undemocratic; fifth, but there is nothing in all this which proves the advisability of advancing gifted children more rapidly through the grades; sixth, rapid advancement may be justifiable for individuals, but it is questionable as an ad-ministrative policy.

Dr. Holmes contended that it is possible to enrich the course of study so as to do jus-tice to bright children without pushing them through the grades in a shorter time than that required by others. "We ought not to consider rapid advancement the only possi-bility. To do so argues poverty of resources and ingenuity."

THE PROJECT WORK AND DEMOCRACY

Mr. J. Leroy Stockton, Vice-President of the State Teachers College at Santa Bar-bara, California, contributes to the *Journal*

430

of the *National Education Association* for May an interesting summary of his book on *The Project Method* published some little time ago. He once more distinguishes between the project as method and the project as a subject of instruction. Under the first head he traces the development of the project idea from Rousseau through Pestalozzi and Froebel to Dewey, McMurry, and others of the present time. He agrees with Professor Kilpatrick in settling upon purposeful activity as the essential feature.

From the standpoint of project work as a subject of instruction, Mr. Stockton points out the possibility of developing in the schools work as the central element just as it is in our democracy at large. From this point of view the whole of the school course would be devoted to purposeful activities either in work or in play. A changed attitude of the pupil toward all work would result. He would realize its necessity, its dignity, its benefits, and its variety suited to individual capacities. Such a course might be developed through the expansion of the present course in manual training.

THE NEW BOOKS

The Atlantic Book of Modern Plays. Edited by Sterling Andrus Leonard. Boston: Atlantic Monthly Press, 1921. Pp. xiv+ 324. Price, $1.50.

Fifteen plays in full with admirable helps for the high-school or other student.

The Language of America. Book Two. By Caroline E. Myers and Garry C. Myers. New York: Newson & Co., 1922. Pp. 160.

Material for teaching English to foreigners—largely biographical.

Dramatized Bible Stories for Young People. By Mary M. Russell. New York: Geo. H. Doran Co., 1921. Pp. 92. Price, $1.00.

Everyday Manners for American Boys and Girls. By the Faculty of the South Philadelphia High School for Girls. New York:

Macmillan Co., 1922. Pp. xiv+115. Illus.

The outgrowth of needs of which the young people themselves became aware.

Modern Essays. Selected by Christopher Morley. New York: Harcourt, Brace & Co., 1921. Pp. xii+256.

From both England and America.

Longer Plays by Modern Authors. Edited by Helen Louise Cohen. New York: Harcourt, Brace & Co., 1922. Pp. xxviii +357.

A companion to a similar volume of short plays.

Teaching to Think. By Julius Boraas. New York: Macmillan Co., 1922. Pp. 289.

A manual for teachers, with numerous practical exercises, including practice for the teacher himself.

How to Teach Silent Reading to Beginners. By Emma Watkins. Philadelphia: J. B. Lippincott Co., 1922. Pp. 133.

In the School Project series.

Community Life and Civic Problems. By Howard Copeland Hill. Boston: Ginn & Co., 1922. Pp. xxii+528+xxxiii. Illus.

A text that provides for extensive correlations with English, particularly composition.

Our Little West Indian Cousin. By Emily Goddard Taylor. Boston: Page Co., 1922. Pp. 95. Illus.

Another "cousin" in the already long list presented in this series.

Principles of Teaching High School Pupils. By Hubert Wilbur Nutt. New York: Century Co., 1922. Pp. xiv+359.

The high school subjects are looked upon as means to certain aspects of growth on the part of the pupils.

The Divine Comedy of Dante Alighieri. Translated by Melville Best Anderson. Yonkers, N. Y.: World Book Co., 1922. Pp. 448.

A charming rendering into modern English verse, adapted to the reader of the time, but nevertheless a faithful translation.

Lives of Poor Boys Who Became Famous. New York: T. Y. Crowell, 1922. Pp. 375.

A new edition, well printed, of a standard classic for young people.

Utah, The Land of Blossoming Valleys. By George Wharton James. Boston: Page Co., 1922. Pp. 370. Illus. Price, $5.00.

A new number in the "See America First" series, all of which might well be in a school library.

Assets of the Ideal City. By Charles M. Fassett. New York: T. Y. Crowell, 1922. Pp. 177.

Handbook of Municipal Government. By Charles M. Fassett. New York: T. Y. Crowell, 1922. Pp. 192.

A summary of present practice by a former mayor.

Social Studies in Secondary Schools. By a Commission on Correlation of Secondary and Collegiate Education, with Particular Reference to Business Education. Chicago: University of Chicago Press, 1922. Pp. 117.

A program, with an elaborate bibliography.

Short Stories of America. By Robert L. Ramsay. Boston: Houghton, Mifflin Co., 1921. Pp. xii+348.

Representative stories selected for their regional coloring — both the more and the less familiar.

Loyal Citizenship. By Thomas H. Reed. Yonkers, N. Y.: World Book Co., 1922. Pp. 333.

Government, economics, and sociology simply and concretely presented for pupils in the upper grammar grades or first of high school.

The Teacher's Technique. By Charles Elmer Holley. New York: Century Co., 1922. Pp. x+378.

A simple and comprehensive presentation of current doctrines, with bibliographies and exercises.

IN PAPER COVERS

Silent and Oral Reading in the Elementary School. By Emma M. Bolenius. *The Project Method.* By H. B. Wilson and G. M.

Wilson. *Material for the Teaching of Citizenship in the Elementary School.* By Henry J. Peterson. Boston: Houghton, Mifflin Co., 1922, Educational Progress, Volume I, Nos. 1, 2, and 3.

State Normal School, Salem, Massachusetts. Sixty-eighth Year, 1921–1922. May, 1922.

Arbor Days and Bird Days. Friday, April 14th and Friday, April 21st, 1922. Harrisburg, Pa.: Department of Public Instruction.

Course of Study for Safety Education in Oregon Schools, 1921. State Printing Dept., Salem, Oregon.

The Thorndike College Entrance Tests in the University of California. Compiled by J. V. Breitwieser. Berkeley, Cal.: University of California Press, January, 1922.

Scales for Measuring Results of Physical Teaching. By Harold Laverne Camp. University of Iowa Studies in Education, Vol. II, No. 2.

Girard College. President's Report for the Year 1921. Philadelphia, Pa.

The Home and Moving Pictures. By Minnie E. Kennedy. *Training in Thrift.* By Eleanor R. Larrison. American Home Series. New York: Abingdon Press, 1921.

Department of the Interior, Bureau of Education: *Higher Standards for Teachers of Industrial Subjects; Organisation of Instructional Material in Individual Units; The Contribution of Correspondence—Instruction Methods to Industrial Education; Helping the Shop Teacher Through Supervision,* by William T. Bawden. Industrial Education Circular, 1922, Nos. 8, 9, 10. *Statistics of Nurse Training Schools, 1919–1920,* Bulletin, 1921, No. 51; *Statistics of State Universities and State Colleges,* Bulletin, 1921, No. 53.